Copyright © 2002 A.D.A. EDITA Tokyo Co., Ltd.
3-12-14 Sendagaya, Shibuya-ku, Tokyo 151-0051, Japan
All rights reserved. No part of this publication may be reproduced,
stored in a retrieval system, or transmitted, in any form or by any means,
electronic, mechanical, photocopying, recording, or otherwise,
without permission in writing from the publisher.

The drawings of Frank Lloyd Wright are
Copyright © The Frank Lloyd Wright Foundation 2002
Text Copyright © The Frank Lloyd Wright Foundation 2002
Copyright of photographs © 2002 GA photographers: Yukio Futagawa &
Associated Photographers

The red square with FRANK LLOYD WRIGHT in block letters is a
registered trademark belonging to The Frank Lloyd Wright Foundation.
The Frank Lloyd Wright Foundation grants permission for
A.D.A. EDITA Tokyo to use the mark in its block.

"GA" logotype design: Gan Hosoya

ISBN4-87140-614-8 C1352

Printed and bound in Japan

Frank Lloyd Wright
Prairie Houses

Edited and Photographed by Yukio Futagawa
Text by Bruce Brooks Pfeiffer

004

Frank Lloyd Wright
Prairie

34	**William H. Winslow House and Stables** River Forest, Illinois, 1893
64	**Ward W. Willits House** Highland Park, Illinois, 1902
86	**Frank Thomas House** Oak Park, Illinois, 1901
110	**Susan Lawrence Dana House** Springfield, Illinois, 1902
170	**Arthur Heurtley House** Oak Park, Illinois, 1902
190	**Darwin D. Martin House** Buffalo, New York, 1903
224	**Frederick C. Robie House** Chicago, Illinois, 1908
246	**F. F. Tomek House** Riverside, Illinois, 1907
262	**Avery Coonley House** Riverside, Illinois, 1907
298	**E. E. Boynton House** Rochester, New York, 1907
322	**Meyer May House** Grand Rapids, Michigan, 1909

Cover: Susan Lawrence Dana House

Houses

Prairie Houses   *by Bruce Brooks Pfeiffer*

The terrain of southwestern Wisconsin is one of rolling hills, deep forests, verdant fields, limestone outcroppings, rivers, streams, lakes, and abundant wild flowers. In winter it is a white world of extreme cold while spring brings foliage and blossoms in a rich and varied array. Summers are hot and humid with birch, oak and elm trees in full leaf, midst evergreen firs and pines. Autumn finds a landscape of tawny colors, bittersweet in the forests, wild antimony and sumac across the fields. In every respect it is a lush and pastoral land with startling seasonal changes.

It was into this environment that Frank Lloyd Wright was born on June 8, 1867. His early years were spent in various towns in the Midwest and on the East Coast as his minister father accepted new appointments. In 1878, they returned to Wisconsin where they settled in Madison. Thirty-six miles west, near the town of Spring Green, lay the valley to which his grandfather, Richard Lloyd Jones, with his family, had migrated from Wales in the mid-nineteenth century. There his mother's uncles had established farms and at age eleven, Frank's Uncle James came to Madison, put the boy on a horse driven wagon, and said to him, "Ready now, Frank? .... [We're] Going to make a farmer out of you, my boy."[1]

After a fairly carefree childhood, this experience of hard work day after day was at first difficult and painful for him, yet eventually he gained through it a profound insight into the land on which he was working, and it instilled in him a life long love and respect for the agrarian way of life.

When at the age of twenty he left Wisconsin and went to Chicago to seek work in architecture, he was suddenly exposed to a totally different landscape—the great American prairie. His reaction to this new environment was strong and immediate: "I loved the prairie by instinct as, itself, a great simplicity; the trees, flowers, and sky were thrilling by contrast ... the gently rolling or level prairies of our great Middle West ... every tree towers above the great calm plains of flowered surfaces as the plain lies serene beneath a wonderful unlimited sweep of sky."[2]

After nearly seven years working as a draftsman for the firm of Adler & Sullivan, Wright set up his own architectural practice, with

ウィスコンシン州南西部の大地は、起伏する丘、深い森、青々とした野原、花崗岩の露頭、川、小川、湖、豊かな野生の花々で覆われている。春は葉群や花々が華麗で多彩な衣装をまとい、冬は厳しい寒さの続く白銀の世界となる。夏は高温多湿で、モミやマツの常緑樹のなかにカバやカシやニレの木々が鬱蒼と葉を茂らせる。秋になると、森の緋色、野に広がる野生のアンチモンやウルシの木などで、風景は黄褐色に染まる。それは、あらゆる点で、新鮮な驚きをもたらす季節の変化を伴った、瑞々しく、豪奢で牧歌的な土地である。

フランク・ロイド・ライトは、1867年6月8日、こうした環境のなかに生まれた。幼年時代を中西部や、牧師であった父が新たな招請を受けたのに従って移った東海岸のいくつかの町で過ごし、1878年、ウィスコンシン州に戻り、マディソンの町に落ち着いた。西に36マイル、スプリング・グリーンの町に近いところには、19世紀の半ば、祖父、リチャード・ロイド・ジョーンズが家族と共にウェールズから移住してきた谷間が横たわっている。そこに、母方の叔父たちが農場をつくっており、ライトが11歳のとき、その一人、ジェイムズ叔父さんがマディソンを訪ねてきて、少年を馬車に乗せるとこう言った。「いいかね、フランク……これからおまえを農夫に鍛えあげてやろう。」[1]

かなりのんびりとした子供時代を送った後での、毎日きつい労働の続くこの体験は、最初は厳しくつらいものであったが、結局、その労働を通して、彼は自らがその上で働く大地を深く理解することになった。そしてそれは、農耕生活に対する、生涯に渡る愛と尊敬を彼の心に吹き込んだのである。

20歳のとき、ライトはウィスコンシンを離れ、建築の仕事を求めてシカゴに行き、そこで、今までとは全く異なった風景——アメリカの大草原（グレート・プレイリー）と突然、向き合った。この新しい環境に、彼は即座に強く反応した。「私は、大草原を、その壮大な単純性（シンプリシティ）を、直感的に愛した。その木々や花々や空の対比は感動的であった……我が広大な中西部の、緩やかに起伏しあるいは平坦に広がる草原……木々はみな、花に覆われた静かで広大な草原の上に高く直立し、草原は無限に広がる素晴らしい空の下に穏やかに横たわっている。」[2]

アドラー＆サリヴァンの事務所で、7年近くドラフトマンとして働いたのち、ライトは独立し、建築事務所をシカゴ市内とオーク・パーク郊外にある自宅に開いた。彼はプレイリーとそのあらゆる特徴を知ったために、当時よく見られた古めかしいヴィクトリア朝風住宅はこの地には全く相応しいものではないと実感していた。「私が目にした、プレイリーに建つ住宅の何が問題なのだろうか？……まずはじめに、その住宅はあらゆる点において〈まやかし〉であると言っておこう。そこには一体感もなければ、自由な国の、自由な民衆の一人である自由な人間に所属すべき空間感覚も存在しない……。これらの"家"と称するどの一軒を取り去っても、風景は前より良くなり、空気はさわやかになることだろう……。それゆえ、私が最初に感じたのは、単純性に対する憧れだった。"有機体"としての単純性という新しい感覚である。これは、ウィンズ

offices in the city of Chicago, and at his home in the suburb of Oak Park. As he became aware of the prairie and all its features, he realized that the old Victorian houses of the period were totally inappropriate. "What was the matter with the kind of house I found on the prairie? .... Just for a beginning, let's say that house *lied* about everything. It had no sense of Unity at all nor any such sense of space as should belong to a free man among a free people in a free country .... To take any one of those so-called 'homes' away would have improved the landscape and cleared the atmosphere .... My first feeling therefore had been a yearning for simplicity. A new sense of simplicity as 'organic'. This had barely begun to take shape in my mind when the Winslow house was planned. But now it began in practice."[3]

The William H. Winslow house, in Riverside, Illinois, his first independent commission, was indeed a revolutionary statement. The low pitched roof, projecting over the second floor windows, the placement of the building close to the ground, the honest use of materials, and the mature sense of elegant proportions set this house as a corner stone of modern, residential architecture. Its simplicity is apparent, except for the ornate frieze that covers the second story. Of this he admitted, "In the Winslow house ... you may see Sullivan in the frieze—you see him nowhere else."[4]

From the time his first client came to him in 1893, he had a steady progression of commissions until he closed his Oak Park workshop seventeen years later. It is estimated that over that period of time, with the aid of his draftsmen, his studio produced an average of one set of working drawings every six weeks. Naturally, commissions for larger and more complex work took longer.

The Joseph Husser house, built in Chicago in 1899 and tragically demolished, has frequently been called the first "prairie house". The plan is a "pin-wheel": the living room with its broad, covered porch, faces one direction, the dining room another, with the entrance stairs from the ground level in yet another. The brick wall surfaces of the first two levels are unadorned flat planes, while the third floor articulation of arches and windows is somewhat Sullivanesque in treatment. The living-dining area is raised above the ground floor (which is the basement no longer under ground) to afford views over Lake Michigan; the fireplace-chimney masses are wide; the roofs are gently sloped with projecting eaves to protect windows and porch. If the Winslow house is considered a "transition" work, the Husser house clearly goes much further. Indeed, the concept of a house for the prairie, or what has since been celebrated as "the prairie house", was taking shape.

"I saw that a little height on the prairie was enough to look like much more—every detail as to height becoming intensely significant, breadths all falling short .... I had an idea that the horizontal planes in buildings, those planes parallel to earth, identify themselves with the ground—make the building belong to the ground. I began putting this

ロウ邸の設計が始まったとき,心のなかでかすかに形を取り始めていた。しかし今,それは現実のものになり始めている。」[3]

イリノイ州リヴァーサイドに建つウィリアム・H・ウィンズロウ邸は,ライトが独立して最初の仕事であり,まさに革新的な宣言であった。2階の窓を覆って突き出す低い勾配屋根,地表近くを延びて行く建物の配置,材料の真摯な使い方,優美な均整をつくりあげている成熟した感覚が,この住宅を近代住宅建築の基本に位置づけることになった。2階を覆う装飾的なフリーズを除いて,その単純性は明白である。この点についてライトは認めている。「ウィンズロウ邸では……そのフリーズにサリヴァンを見つけるだろう——そこ以外に彼はどこにも存在しない。」[4]

1893年,最初の顧客が訪ねて来たときから,17年後にオーク・パークの事務所を閉ざすまで,仕事は順調に入ってきた。その全期間に渡り,ドラフトマンの助けを借りて,彼の事務所は平均,6週間に一式の実施図面を仕上げてきたと概算される。当然のことながら,大きく,複雑な建物はそれより長い時間を必要とした。

1899年,シカゴに建てられ,不幸にも取り壊されてしまったジョセフ・ハッサー邸は,最初の"プレイリー・ハウス"としばしば呼ばれてきた。風車型の平面で,広い,屋根付きのポーチのあるリビングが一面を向き,ダイニングルームが別の一面を,1階から入るエントランスの階段がまた別な方向を向いている。下層2階分を覆う煉瓦壁の表面は,装飾のない平らな面である一方,3階のアーチと窓の分節には,幾分,サリヴァン風の扱いがなされている。リビング／ダイニング・エリアは,1階（もはや地面の下にあるのではないかつての地下室）の上に持ち上げられ,ミシガン湖が見晴らせる。暖炉と煙突のマッスは幅が広く,窓やポーチを覆う突きだした軒を持つ屋根はゆるやかに傾斜している。ウィンズロウ邸が"転換点"に立つ作品とするならば,ハッサー邸は明らかに,そこから遙かに前進している。まさに,プレイリーのもの,つまり,以来"プレイリー・ハウス"として世に知られてきた住宅概念が形をとっている。

「プレイリーの上では,少しの高さでも,それ以上の高さを感じるに十分だ——高さが際立つにつれて,ディテールはすべて広がりが不十分なものとなる……。建物の水平面,大地に平行し,地表と結びついた水平な面は——建物を土地に所属させてくれる,という考えが私にはあった。私はこの考えを作品に注ぎ込み始めた。」[5]

この,水平線の感覚を実現するために,ライトはまず,屋根裏部屋を納めた急勾配の屋根をはずした。習慣として,使用人の部屋がそこに置かれていたのだが,屋根裏がなくなったので,それは主階の台所近くに移された。ウィンズロウ邸に見られるように,急勾配の屋根は,幅広の,覆いかぶさるような,緩やかな勾配の屋根に取って代わり,2階の窓を守るように建物壁面を越えて突き出すことになった。ウィンズロウ邸の窓は,当時の窓が皆そうであったように上げ下げ窓であった。しかしライトはすぐに,窓全体を外に開放するために,開き窓を指定し始める。それは戸外を内に招き入れるかのようで,はるかに優美な窓割りの方法

idea to work."[5]

To achieve this sense of the horizontal line, he first eliminated the steeply pitched roof, housing the attic. Customarily the servants were housed there, but with the attic gone, the servants were placed near the kitchen on the main level. The steep roof was replaced, as it was in the Winslow house, by a broad, sheltering, low pitched one, that projected out over the walls of the house to protect the second story windows. The windows in the Winslow house were double hung, as were all windows at that time. But soon Wright began to specify open-swinging casement windows in order to open the entire window space to the outside, as if inviting the outside to come in—a more gracious solution to fenestration. These were so new in that era that he had to have special hardware made to operate them.

He saw the damp basement as a needless hole in the ground, its unseemly walls protruding a few feet above ground, the house perched upon them. "I had an idea that every house in that low region should begin *on* the ground, not *in* it as they then began, with damp cellars. This feeling—become an idea also—eliminated the basement. I devised one at ground level. And the feeling that the house should *look* as though it began there, *at* the ground, put a projecting base course as a visible edge to this foundation, where, as a platform, it was evident preparation for the building itself and welded the structure to the ground."[6]

This elevated the main floor, containing reception room, living room, dining room, library, and kitchen, with its accommodation for servants next to it, to the usual second floor level affording a greater view across the prairie. It also provided greater privacy with the outlook from living and dining rooms higher than the sidewalk and street. It was in this general living area that he introduced "the open plan" by eliminating unnecessary walls, partitions, and doors, allowing the rooms to flow together. Exterior walls he began to treat as screens, rather than walls pierced with holes for windows. Continuous bands of windows placed in the outer surface took the place of former holes in the walls. "My sense of 'wall' was no longer the side of a box. It was enclosure of space affording protection against storm or heat only when needed. But it was also to bring the outside world into the house and let the inside of the house go outside. In this sense I was working away at the wall as a wall and bringing it towards the function of a screen, a means of opening up space which, as control of building-materials improved, would finally permit the free use of the whole space without affecting the soundness of the structure."[7]

"Thus came an end to the cluttered house. Fewer doors; fewer window holes through greater window area; windows and doors lowered to convenient human heights[8].... As these ideals worked away from house to house, finally freedom of floor space and elimination of useless heights worked a miracle in the new dwelling place. A sense of appropriate freedom had changed its whole aspect. The

となった。開き窓は当時としては新しく、ライトはそれらの窓を開け閉めするために特別な金具をつくらねばならなかった。

　彼は湿気のある地下室を、地中にあけられた不必要な穴であるとみていた。その不体裁な壁は数フィート地上に飛び出し、家はその上に腰を据えている。「私は、この低地帯に建つ家はすべて、〈地上〉から始まるべきであり、当時そうであったように、湿った倉庫のある〈地下〉から始まるべきではないと考えていた。この気持——ひとつのアイディアにもなるもの——は地下室を消し去った。私は地下室を地上階に置くという一計を案じた。家は、あたかも、そこから、つまり〈地上〉から始まっているように〈見える〉べきだという気持は、建物基礎の先端を目に見えるものとして突き出させ、そこは、基壇を構成して建物そのものの明らかな出発点となり、建物を地上に結び付けることになった。」[6]

　これによって、レセプション・ルーム、居間、食堂、書斎、台所が置かれる主階は、隣接する使用人室と共に、通常の2階の高さまで持ち上げられ、プレイリーを見渡せる視界が開けた。また、脇道や前の道より高くなった居間や食堂から見える景色と共に、大幅なプライバシーも提供してくれた。この全般的な生活領域に、彼は、不必要な壁や間仕切りやドアを取り去って、"オープン・プラン"を導入し、部屋から部屋へよどみのない流れが生まれるようにしたのである。外壁は、窓で穴の空いた壁というよりもスクリーンとして扱われ始めた。外壁面に配置された窓が構成する連続する帯は、以前の、壁に穿たれた穴に取って代った。「私はもはや、"壁"を箱の側面であると感じていなかった。それは、必要なときにのみ、嵐や暑さを防いでくれる、空間の囲いであった。しかしそれはまた、外の世界を内部に運び込み、住宅の内部を外に向かわせなければならない。この意味で、私は、壁にスクリーンの機能を持たせる方向、つまり空間を開放する方法へと進めることをいろいろ考えていた。建築材料の調整が進むにつれて、最終的には建物の頑丈さを損ねることなく空間全体を自由に使うことができるようになるだろう。」[7]

　「こうして、乱雑な住宅は滅び去った。ドアは少なくなり、穴のように穿たれた窓は減り、窓やドアは人間の背丈にとって手頃な高さにまで低くされた[8]……。これらの理想を、一つの住宅から一つの住宅へと休みなく実践し続けてきた結果、自由なフロアスペースと、無意味な壁高の消去は、ついに新しい住空間のなかに奇跡を起こした。適切な自由の感覚は、住空間の全体像を変えた。全体は、今までとは異なるが、人の住まいにより相応しく、その敷地により自然なものとなった。」[9]

　ライトは、インテリアを、建物の全体的なプランと同じく単純につくりあげた。壁は、木の縁取りをまわしたプラスターの簡素な面として残し、壁紙や塗装はまったく用いられていない。暖炉は今や家の中心的存在となり、たっぷりと幅の広い、人を暖かく迎える石や煉瓦積みのマッスをかたちづくり、そのなかでは火が激しく燃えている。木の縁取りや壁の鏡板はステインがかけられたが、塗装されることはなかった。その結果、クライアントがその新しい家に、前の家から、この新しい背景にはまったく合わない折衷様式や時代様式の家具を持ち込んでくるのを見

whole became different but more fit for human habitation and more natural on its site."[9]

Wright fashioned the interior with the same sense of simplicity that was evident in the general plan of the structure: walls left a plain surface of plaster with wood trim, devoid of any paper or painting; the fireplace now a central feature of the home—a generous, broad, welcoming masonry mass with the fire burning deeply within; wood trim or paneling stained, but never painted. Consequently, he was frequently dismayed to see his clients move into their new homes with the furniture from their previous ones, eclectic and period items totally inappropriate in this new setting. To integrate items of furniture with the interior, he began to design built-in seats, bookcases, dining room buffets for linen and china, grilled screens to give a sense of privacy in certain areas within the general free flowing sense of space—all of these of the same woodwork as the trim along the plaster walls and ceilings. He then designed freestanding furniture: tables, chairs, hassocks, plant stands, and such as required by each client. By this integration of furnishings and structure, he was achieving a sense of *unity* that had rarely been realized in residential designs prior to this work.

He soon found it necessary to include landscaping as part of his architectural services along with furnishings. The homes of the period featured a basement rising out of the ground with the house set down upon it. To conceal this, they arranged the planting of shrubs and bushes up against the house, especially where the house faced the street. Wright's prairie houses, on the other hand, were set upon a stone or concrete water table, really a platform, rising no more than nine or ten inches above the ground. Wright wished to reveal this connection between home and earth, and made landscape plans that would group plantings at certain parts of the structure, but leave the rest clear, the lawn running up to the building. The perspective of the Ward Willits house (Highland Park, Illinois, 1902) is a splendid example of this type of landscaping. A narrow path of garden flowers and shrubs follows the walk from the street to the house, but leaves the rest of the house free of planting, except for another group tangent to the covered porch off the dining room.

Wright used the term "plasticity" to explain what he was achieving in these houses. "Plasticity may be seen in the expressive flesh-covering of the skeleton as contrasted with the articulation of the skeleton itself. If form really 'followed function'… here was the direct means of expression of the more spiritual idea that the form and function are one: the only true means I could see then or can see now to eliminate the separation and complication of cut-and-butt joinery in favor of the expressive flow of continuous surface. Here, by instinct at first—all ideas germinate—a principle entered into building that has since gone on developing. In my work the idea of plasticity may now be seen as the element of continuity."[10]

て，ライトはしばしば落胆させられた。家具をインテリアと調和させるために，彼は造り付けの椅子，書棚，リネンや陶器をしまう食堂の食器棚，全体が自由で流れるような空間のある部分にプライバシーを与える格子スクリーンなどをデザインし始めた。こうしたものすべては，プラスターの壁や天井に沿った縁取りと同様に木工細工でつくられた。次には，テーブル，椅子，低いクッション付きの椅子，植木鉢用の台，そして個々のクライアントの要請によるものなど，個別の家具をデザインした。家具と建物とのこうした統合によって，彼は，それまでの住宅作品では希にしかみられなかった，〈一体感〉をつくりだすことに成功したのである。

　まもなく，家具とともに，景観構成も彼の建築業務のなかに含める必要に気付いた。当時の住宅は地下室に特徴があった。地下室は地盤内から立ち上がり，その上に建物本体が据えられる。それを隠すために，特に通りに面しては，低木を建物に沿って植え込んでいた。一方，ライトのプレイリー・ハウスは，石かコンクリートの水切り石の上に据えられており，それはまさに台座であり，地表から9インチか10インチ以上出ることはなかった。ライトはこの，家と大地との繋がりを見えるようにしたいと思い，建物の特定の部分に沿って植え込みを集め，他の部分はすっきりと残し，芝生が建物の足元まで延びて行く景観構成を計画した。ウォード・ウィリッツ邸（ハイランド・パーク，イリノイ，1902年）の全体像は，この種の景観構成の素晴らしい実例である。庭の草花や茂みが，道路から家まで歩いて行く細い小道に付き従ってくるが，建物の残りの部分は，食堂の外の屋根付きポーチ脇の植栽以外には，植え込みから解放されている。

　ライトは，これらの住宅で自分が達成したいと思っていることを説明するために"可塑性"という言葉を使った。「可塑性というのは，骨格そのものを分節することとは対照的な，骨格を包む表現的な肉の覆いのなかに見られるものかも知れない。もし形態が真に"機能に従う"ものであるならば……形態と機能は一つであることの，より精神的なアイディアを表現する直截な方法がここにあった。可塑性は，連続する面の流れを表現し，分断をなくし，建具類の複雑さを消し去るための唯一正しい方法であると，私は，当時も今もそうみている。まず直感によって——すべての発想が芽生え——原則が建物に入り込み，展開してゆく。私の作品では，可塑性という考え方が，今や，連続性をつくりあげる要素と見なされることになるだろう。」[10]

　「それから，一歩一歩，一般解から特殊解へと進みながら，幅の広い建築手法としての可塑性は，私を捉え，その自らの意志で動き始めた。ハートレイ邸，マーティン邸，ヒース邸，トーマス邸，トメク邸，クーンレイ邸，その他，たくさんの住宅のなかに既に明らかに認められる，可塑性の帰結であるシークェンス，その空間の流れを見守ることに心を奪われたものだった。

　「古い建築は，その文法に関する限り，私にとっては，文字通り消え去り始めた。あたかも魔法によって，新しい建築的効果が生気を帯びは

"Proceeding, then, step by step from generals to particulars, plasticity as a large means in architecture began to grip me and to work its own will. Fascinated I would watch its sequences, seeing other sequences in those consequences already in evidence: as in the Heurtley, Martin, Heath, Thomas, Tomek, Coonley and dozens of other houses.

"The old architecture, so far as its grammar went, for me began, literally, to disappear. As if by magic new architectural effects came to life—effects genuinely knew in the whole cycle of architecture owing simply to the working of this spiritual principle. Vistas of inevitable simplicity and ineffable harmonies would open, so beautiful to me that I was not only delighted, but often startled. Yes, sometimes amazed."[11]

The Warren Hickox and B. Harley Bradley houses (Kankakee, Illinois, 1900) are clear examples of cement stucco as the complete skin of the structures, illustrating Wright's connotation of plasticity, "the expressive flesh-covering of the skeleton", as he phrased it.

In the Willits house another architectural feature, subtle but most important, can be seen in the treatment of the exterior wall of the living room and the bedrooms above. The window mullions of the living room correspond to those of the upper level. Rather than have them as two distinct elements, separated the one from the other, Wright has placed vertical wood bands, embedded in the exterior stucco wall to connect aesthetically the lower mullions with the upper ones. This is another example of what he meant by plasticity.

The house for Susan Lawrence Dana (Springfield, Illinois, 1902) carried open planning even further with a vertical flow of space. A prominent staircase rises from ground level to the third floor, becoming as pronounced a feature of the interior as the horizontal open plan on the level that contains living room, reception, and dining room. Roman brick is used uniformly as the exterior material with a terracotta frieze on the third level, rising from the windowsill level to the roof soffit above. Even though the Dana house is a very large building, it still maintains a sense of human scale throughout. "Taking a human being for my scale, I brought the whole house down in height to fit a normal one .... Believing in no other scale than the human being I broadened the mass out all I possibly could to bring it down into spaciousness."[12]

Leaded glass windows were a common element at that time. Shops and artisans producing stained glass were abundant, and the use of such glass was prevalent.[13] However, Wright's designs for these windows were made by using a T-square and triangle, purely geometrical components as opposed to the freehand glass one associates, for example, with the work of Louis Comfort Tiffany. By this more architectural method, glass could be cut and assembled without the laborious time and cost has handcrafted processes. In the Dana house, his designs for stained glass attained a level of exuberance

じめたかのように——建築の全周期のなかで真に新しい効果であり、それは自然に、この精神的な原則の作用ゆえに生まれているのである。必然ともいえる単純性と、言葉では表現し得ない調和に満ちた光景が広がるだろう。私にとってそれは単に喜ばしいばかりでなく、しばしば息をのむほどの美しさだった。そう、時に、驚嘆の念さえ覚えたものだった。」[11]

ウォーレン・ヒコックス邸とB・ハーレイ・ブラッドレー邸（カンカキー、イリノイ、1900年）は、建物全体の被膜にセメント・スタッコを用いた明解な例であり、それはライトが「骨格の表現的な肉の覆い」と述べる可塑性の意味するものを具体的に示している。

ウィリッツ邸では、微妙でとらえがたくはあるが、最も重要な、もう一つの建築的特徴が、居間と上階の寝室の外壁の扱いに見ることができる。そこでは、居間の窓のマリオンは、2階のマリオンと呼応している。マリオンを2つの別の要素へと分離するのではなく、ライトは、幅の広い垂直の帯板を、スタッコの外壁にはめ込み、上下階のマリオンを美しく繋ぐように配置した。これは、ライトが可塑性によって意図したもののまた別の一例である。

スーザン・ローレンス・ダナ邸（スプリングフィールド、イリノイ、1902年）では、垂直方向への空間の流れによって、オープン・プランをさらに徹底して持ち込んでいる。存在感のある階段が1階から3階まで立ち上がり、居間・レセプション・食堂を納めた1階の、水平に広がるオープン・プランというインテリアの特徴を告示する。ローマ煉瓦が外壁全体に使われ、3階の窓のド枠のところから、屋根のド端までテラコッタ製のフリーズが施されている。ダナ邸は大邸宅ではあるが、全体に人間的なスケール感が保たれている。「私の身体の大きさを人間の代表としてとりあげて、普通の人に適合させるために家全体の高さを低くした……。人間の身体ではなく他の尺度によっては、空間の広がりへとマッスを落とすことは出来ないだろうと信じながら。」[12]

ガラス片を鉛線にはめこんで接合する鉛枠のガラス窓は、当時、一般的に使われていたものである。ステンドグラスを製作する工房や職人の数はありあまるほどで、こうしたガラスの使用は広く行き渡っていた。[13] しかし、これらの窓に対するライトのデザインは、T定規と三角定規を使って制作されており、たとえばルイス・カムフォート・ティファニーの作品から連想されるような、フリーハンドの絵柄で構成されたガラスとは正反対の、純粋に幾何学的な構図のものであった。この、より建築的な方法によって、ガラスは、手工芸による制作プロセスにかかる時間的労力やコストなしに、切断し、組み立てることができた。ダナ邸では、彼のステンド・グラスのデザインは溢れんばかりの豊かさで、彼の全作品のなかでもその素晴らしさは抜きんでている。

プレイリー・ハウスのすべてに見られるもう一つの建築要素は、木製の縁取りであるが、これはライトが"バック・バンド"と呼んでいたもので、プラスターの壁や天井に付けられた細い木の帯である。これらの帯は、実用と美しさ、その両方の目的を果たしていた。プラスター壁は、

that stands out as the finest of any in his career.

Another architectural element that occurs in all the prairie houses is the wood trim, what Wright called, "back band"—the slender wood strips set on the plaster walls and ceilings. These strips served both practical and aesthetic purposes. Wright realized that where plaster walls turned the corner, or met the floor, the plaster was vulnerable to damage. Wood strips at these locations acted as protection. He also used the wood strips where one material met another, such as where a plaster wall butted up against a masonry wall. The application of the wood strips throughout the interior created a sense of continuity—plasticity—throughout interior space and rendering it all into a coherent sense of unity.

"In my day the edges were the bête noir of every building. Because where things come together, that is where the trouble always is. I invented this little back band—if you see those early houses of mine, you will see the casing, you will see the cornices, you will see everything and following it you will see a little flat band running, and the back band would go over where two materials came together, where the plaster met the wood, or where the stone met the plaster or the wood .... That is the machine age use ... when you are using the machine and machine work, using the machine as a tool, you have to devise those things that the machine can do very well."

Along with his respect for wood as a material, he possessed, as was evident in the very beginning of his work in the Winslow house, an inherent feeling about the appropriate nature of materials. At the time he began his work, he found nothing written on the subject.

"So I began, in my fashion, to study the nature of materials .... I began to see brick as brick. I learned to see wood as wood and learned to see concrete or glass or metal each for itself and all as themselves .... Each different material required a different handling, and each different handling ... had new possibilities of use peculiar to the nature of each. Appropriate designs for one material would not be at all appropriate for any other material. In the light of this ideal of building-form as an organic simplicity, most architecture fell to the ground; that is to say, the buildings were obsolete in the light of the idea of space determining form from within, all materials modifying if indeed they did not create, 'form'—when used with understanding according to the limitations of process and purpose. Architecture might begin life anew."[14]

It soon became apparent to Wright that the ideas and concepts underlying his designs for the prairie house were equally applicable in locations other than the Midwest. His residential work soon spread east to Buffalo and Rochester, New York, south to Frankfurt, Kentucky, and west to McCook, Nebraska. In Buffalo for the Darwin D. Martin (1903) and William Heath (1905) houses, he provided full basements for playroom, laundry, and storage. The E. E. Boynton house, in Rochester (1907) also has a full basement. In order to allow

角をまわるところと床と接するところで損傷を受けやすいことにライトは気付いていた。木の縁取りはこれらの箇所で保護の役割を果たしている。彼はまた，一つの材料が他の材料と接する箇所，たとえばプラスター壁が煉瓦積みの壁とぶつかるところに木製の縁取りを使った。インテリア全体に添加された木の帯板は，連続感——可塑性——を内部空間全体につくりだし，すべてを一つにまとめあげる。

「あの頃は，エッジの部分は，どんな建物でもまったく嫌なものだった。物が交差するところ，つまり常に問題が発生するところだからだ。私はこのちょっとしたバック・バンドを思いついた——初期の住宅作品を見ると，ケーシングがあるし，コーニスがあり，すべてがある。そしてそれに続いて，小さな平らな帯が巡らされていることが分かる。そして二種の材料が集まるところでバック・バンドに切り替わってゆく。プラスターが木と出会い，石がプラスターや木と出会うところで……。あれは機械時代の使い方だ……機械や機械製作のものを使っているとき，機械を道具として使うとき，機械が上手く出来るこれらのことを工夫する必要がある。」

材料としての木に対する敬意と共に，ライトは，最初期の作品であるウィンズロウ邸で明らかなように，材料固有の性格についても生来の感覚を身につけていた。自分の仕事を始めた当時，彼は，この問題に関して書かれた資料を見つけることができなかった。

「そこで，私は，私のやり方で材料の本質についての勉強を始めた……。煉瓦は煉瓦として見ることを始めた。木は木として見ることを学び，コンクリートやガラスや金属それぞれをそれら自身として見ることを学んだ……。それぞれに異なる材料は，異なった扱い方を要求し，それぞれ異なった扱い方は……それぞれの本質に固有の使い方について新たな可能性を持っていた。ある材料に相応しいデザインは，他の材料にはまったく適さないかもしれない。有機的な単純性としての建築形態という理想から見ると，ほとんどの建築が失敗している。つまり，内部から形態が規定され，すべての材料が——そのプロセスと目的の限界を理解したうえで使われた時——なるほど"形態"を創り出さないにしても形態に属性を与えている空間という考えから見ると，それらの建物は時代遅れであった。建築は新たに生き始めるだろう。」[11]

プレイリー・ハウスのデザインの根底にある発想やコンセプトは，中西部以外の場所でも同様に適用可能であることが，ライトにはまもなく明らかなものとなった。彼の住宅作品は，東はニューヨーク州のバッファローやロチェスター，南はケンタッキー州フランクフルト，西はネブラスカ州マッコークまですぐに広がった。バッファローのダーウィン・D・マーティン邸（1903年）とウィリアム・ヒース邸（1905年）では，建物の下全面を地下室にして，プレイルーム，ランドリー，収納をそこに配した。ロチェスターのE・E・ボイントン邸（1907年）においてもまた，地下を全面に設けている。こうした地盤面より下のスペースに外光を入れるために，ライトは必要な窓割りを建物そのものの一部として取り込んでいる。これによって，光のために単に"はめ込まれた"エレ

light into these belowground areas, Wright has incorporated the necessary fenestration as a part of the house itself. In this way, a sense of continuity is maintained with the windows incorporated into the general grammar of the architecture rather than elements simply "stuck on" for light.

During the prairie house years 1899-1910, more than 90 residences were constructed, many others planned but not executed. They vary in location, building materials, size, and scope. In his autobiography he especially recollected those of Arthur Heurtley (Oak Park, Illinois, 1902), Darwin D. Martin, William Heath, Frank Thomas (Oak Park, Illinois, 1901), F. F. Tomek (Riverside, Illinois, 1907), and Avery Coonley (Riverside, Illinois, 1907).

The Coonley house stands out as one of his most successful commissions, both from the point of view of the building itself, and from the extensive freedom he had in designing all its interior furnishings, including carpets.

"About this time Mr. and Mrs. Avery Coonley came to the Oak Park workshop to ask me to build a home for them at Riverside, Illinois. They had gone to see nearly everything they could learn that I had done before they came. The day they finally came into the Oak Park workshop Mrs. Coonley said they had come because it seemed to them they saw in my houses 'the countenance of principle'. This was to me a great and sincere compliment. So I put my best into the Coonley house. Looking back upon it, I feel now that that building was the best I could then do in the way of a house."[15]

For the Frederick Robie house (Chicago, Illinois, 1908), Robie, himself, had certain specific requirements and needs in mind even before he came to Frank Lloyd Wright. He wanted a fireproof house, rooms without interruptions, windows without the usual curvatures of the day, all the natural light he could get in the house, but shaded by overhanging eaves to protect windows from the weather, morning light in his living room, a view down the street without any sacrifice of his privacy, no wide trim on doors and windows, but instead narrow trim to give him more light from the windows, a brick house with reinforced concrete floors surfaced with hardwood, a brick wall to safeguard his children from wandering into the street. When he had listed these requirements and more, he began to visit local architects. From them, he invariably received the same advice: "I know what you want, one of those Wright houses." That seemed like sound advise, and so it was that a client who had very concise, definite, and somewhat scientific ideas about the type of house in which he wished to live found the architect who was to interpret those ideas into one of the most extraordinary residences built in the early part of the twentieth century.

Wright's early work, both residential and public, launched a revolution in architecture that had repercussions worldwide. In 1908, his buildings were comprehensively published in the United States.[16]

メントというよりも，建築の全体的な文法のなかに組み込まれた窓による連続感が維持されている。

1899年から1910年にわたるプレイリー・ハウス時代のあいだに，90以上の住宅が建てられ，その他，実施にいたらなかった多くの計画案が生まれた。それらは場所，建築材料，大きさ，広がりなど様々である。ライトは自伝のなかで，特に，アーサー・ハートレイ邸（オーク・パーク，イリノイ，1902年），ダーウィン・D・マーティン邸，ウィリアム・ヒース邸，フランク・トーマス邸（オーク・パーク，イリノイ，1901年），F・F・トメク邸（リヴァーサイド，イリノイ，1907），そしてエイヴリー・クーンレイ邸（リヴァーサイド，イリノイ，1907年）について回想している。

クーンレイ邸は，建物自体の点からも，カーペットを含め内装全体のデザインに至るまで自由に任された点からも，ライトの最も成功した仕事の一つとして傑出したものである。

「その頃，エイヴリー・クーンレイ夫妻が，イリノイ州リヴァーサイドに自分たちの家を建ててほしいと，オーク・パークの仕事場を訪ねてきた。夫妻は，ここに来る前に，私がつくったもので，知ることの出来たほとんどすべての建物を見に行っていた。ついにオーク・パークのスタジオを訪ねて来たその日，クーンレイ夫人は，あなたの住宅には"本質的な落ち着き"があるように思われたので伺いました，と述べた。これは私にとって，素晴らしくまた誠実な賞讃だった。それで，私はクーンレイ邸には最善の努力を注いだ。振り返って見ると，この建物は，住宅として，その当時私に成し得る最善のものだったと，今も感じている。」[15]

フレデリック・ロビー邸（シカゴ，イリノイ，1908年）の場合，ロビー氏自身には，フランク・ロイド・ライトの元を訪れる前に既に，いくつかの特定の要求事項が心にあった。耐火性があり，各部屋は遮るものなく広がり，窓には普通起こる日差しのひずみがなく，住宅内に採り入れ可能な外光はすべて受け入れるが，軒の張り出しが影を落とし，雨風から窓を守り，彼の居室には朝の光が入り，プライバシーを損ねることなく通りが見下ろせ，ドアや窓には幅広の縁取りではなく細い縁取りが巡り窓からさらに豊かな光を採り込む，堅い木材を張ったコンクリート床の煉瓦の家。子供たちが道にさまよい出て行かないように巡らした煉瓦塀。これらの要求やその他を書き出してリストにしたところで，彼は地元の建築家を訪ね始めた。訪ねた建築家たちからは，判で押したように同じ助言を受けた。「あなたが何をお望みか分かりますよ。ライトさんが設計した家ですね。」それは助言であるように響いた。それで，自らが望む住まいについて，ごく簡潔明瞭でいくぶん科学的な抱負を持ったそのクライアントは，これらの考えを，20世紀初期に建てられた最も非凡な住宅の一つへと翻案してくれることになる建築家に出会ったのだった。

ライトの初期作品は，住宅，公共建築の別を問わず，建築に革命を起こし，その波紋は世界に広がった。1908年，彼の建物を広範に納めた本

△ W. R. Heath House, Buffalo, New York, 1905

▽ M. W. Wood House, Decatur, Illinois, 1915

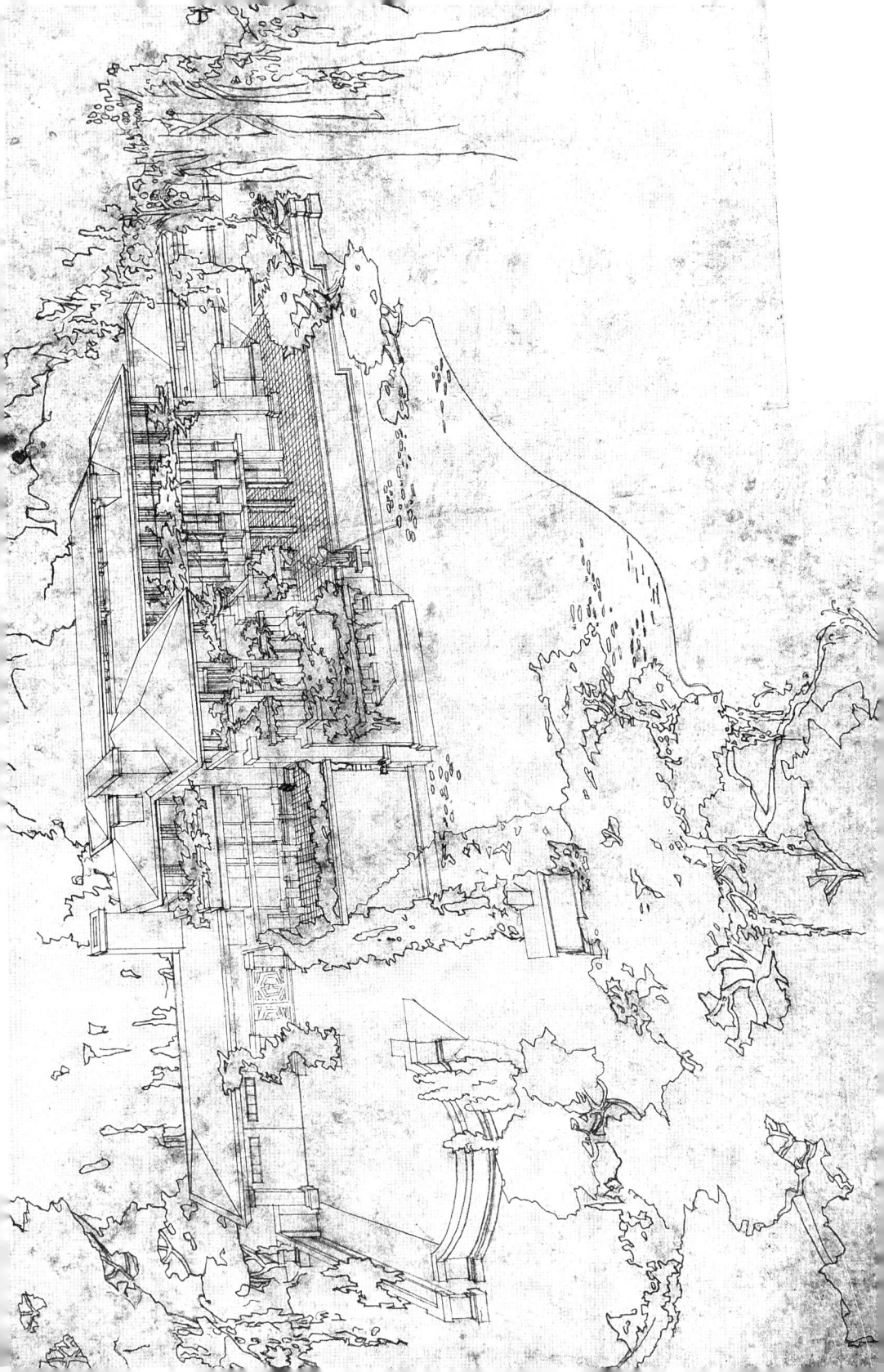

Two years later Wright traveled to Germany to work with Ernst Wasmuth on a two-volume elephant portfolio of his work.[17] Referring to the Berlin monograph, Wright's son Lloyd recalled "Soon after the work was published in Germany, we found they were using the folio and drawings in schools and universities for textbooks. There, men like Gropius and Mies van der Rohe were students of my age and greatly impressed and I heard later Gropius' mother gave him one of the collections he claimed he made his Bible."[18]

Following his sojourn, Frank Lloyd Wright returned to the United States and abandoned Oak Park and all associated with it and moved to his ancestral valley in southwestern Wisconsin. Here, in 1911, on land his mother acquired for him, he built his home, Taliesin.

After Wright had re-established his architectural practice at Taliesin, he received commissions from several new clients who wished to build on locations in the countryside, no longer confined to suburban lots such as in Oak Park, River Forest, and Riverside. The Prairie house, in these works, represented a shift in plan elements that differed considerably from his earlier work. Houses, such as the Sherman Booth house (Glencoe, Illinois, 1911), the Arthur Cutten house (Downer's Grove, Illinois, 1911) and his own home, Taliesin (Spring Green, Wisconsin, 1911) are examples of how his concept of the plan radically changed.

The Booth house is composed of three stories, due to its location on the edge of a ravine. Responding to the landscape and site conditions, it ranks among Wright's most romantic designs in the way in which the house is married to the ravine on one side, and a hill crown on the other. The Cutten house, on the other hand, was designed for a flat site of considerable acreage. The living area is no longer placed on an elevated position above the ground floor that, in the Prairie houses, was reserved for heating, laundry, and storage. The plan is generously spread out, and the living and dining room are flushed with outside stone-paved terraces and adjoining gardens. French doors placed between stone piers give easy access from inside to outside. A long covered pergola connects the house with a summer teahouse, likewise flush with terraces and gardens. The Prairie house here is blended into and around the landscape in a manner that was not seen in the work in Chicago and its suburbs. Perhaps the only Prairie house that had such close association between house and garden might be said to be the Darwin D. Martin house (Buffalo, New York, 1903).

The M. W. Wood house (Decatur, Illinois, 1915) was designed for a gentle, sloping site with a small pond. The pond becomes the feature of the house, all three stories opening out onto it. The lowest level called "basement" on the plan, houses a playroom that gains access to a terrace at pool level. The living room, directly above the playroom, has access, via outside stairs, down to this lower terrace

がアメリカで出版された。[16] 2年後，ライトは，彼の作品を集めた，エレファント判（584×711ミリ）のポートフォリオ全2冊を，エルンスト・ヴァスムートとつくるためにドイツに旅した。[17] このベルリン・モノグラフについて，ライトの息子ロイドはこう回想している。「作品がドイツで出版されるとすぐ，そのフォリオや図面は，学校や大学で，テキストとして使われていることを知りました。当時，グロピウスやミース・ファン・デル・ローエのような人たちは，僕の歳ごろの学生で，非常な感銘を受けたといいます。後に，グロピウスのお母さんが息子に与えたコレクションの1冊は，彼のバイブルになったと断言したと聞いています。」[18]

　ヨーロッパ滞在の後，フランク・ロイド・ライトはアメリカに帰国すると，オーク・パークとそこに関わるすべてを捨て，祖先の地であるウィスコンシン州南西部の谷間に戻った。ここで，1911年，母が手に入れてくれた土地に，彼は自らの家である，タリアセンを建設した。

　タリアセンに，再び設計事務所を開いたライトには，何人かの新しいクライアントから家を建てたいという依頼がきた。田園のなかにある土地で，もはや，オーク・パークやリヴァー・フォレストやリヴァーサイドのような限定された郊外地ではない。これらの住宅には，以前の作品から著しく変貌した平面要素のなかに，プレイリー・ハウスからの転換が示されている。シャーマン・ブース邸（グレンコー，イリノイ，1911年），アーサー・カッテン邸（ダウナーズ・グローヴ，イリノイ，1911年），そして自邸であるタリアセン（スプリング・グリーン，ウィスコンシン，1911年）などの家は，平面に対するコンセプトの本質的な変化を示す好例である。

　ブース邸は敷地が渓谷の縁にあるために，3層で構成されている。風景や敷地条件に応答しているこの住宅は，片側を渓谷に，片側を丘の頂上と固く結ばれているその方法において，ライトの作品のなかで最もロマンティックなデザインの一つとして位置づけられる。一方，カッテン邸はかなりの広さの平坦な土地に設計されている。リビング・エリアは，プレイリー・ハウスでは暖房設備，洗濯，収納スペースにあてられていたグラウンド・フロアの，その上に持ち上げられた位置にもはや置かれることはない。平面は大きく伸び広がり，リビングとダイニング・ルームの床は石を敷き詰めた屋外テラスや隣接する庭と同じ高さである。石の角柱の間にはさまれたフレンチ・ドアから，外へ簡単に出て行ける。長いパーゴラが家と夏の東屋を結んでいるが，ここもまたテラスや庭と高さを揃えている。プレイリー・ハウスはここで，シカゴやその郊外に建てられた住宅には見られなかった方法で，ランドスケープに溶け込んでいる。恐らく，住宅と庭のあいだにこうした密接な関係を持つ唯一のプレイリー・ハウスはダーウィン・D・マーティン邸（バッファロー，ニューヨーク，1903年）であると言ってよいだろう。

　M・W・ウッド邸（ディケーター，イリノイ，1915年）は，小さな池のある，緩やかな斜面に建てられている。池がこの家の特徴となり，3

Sherman M. Booth House, Glencoe, Illinois, 1911

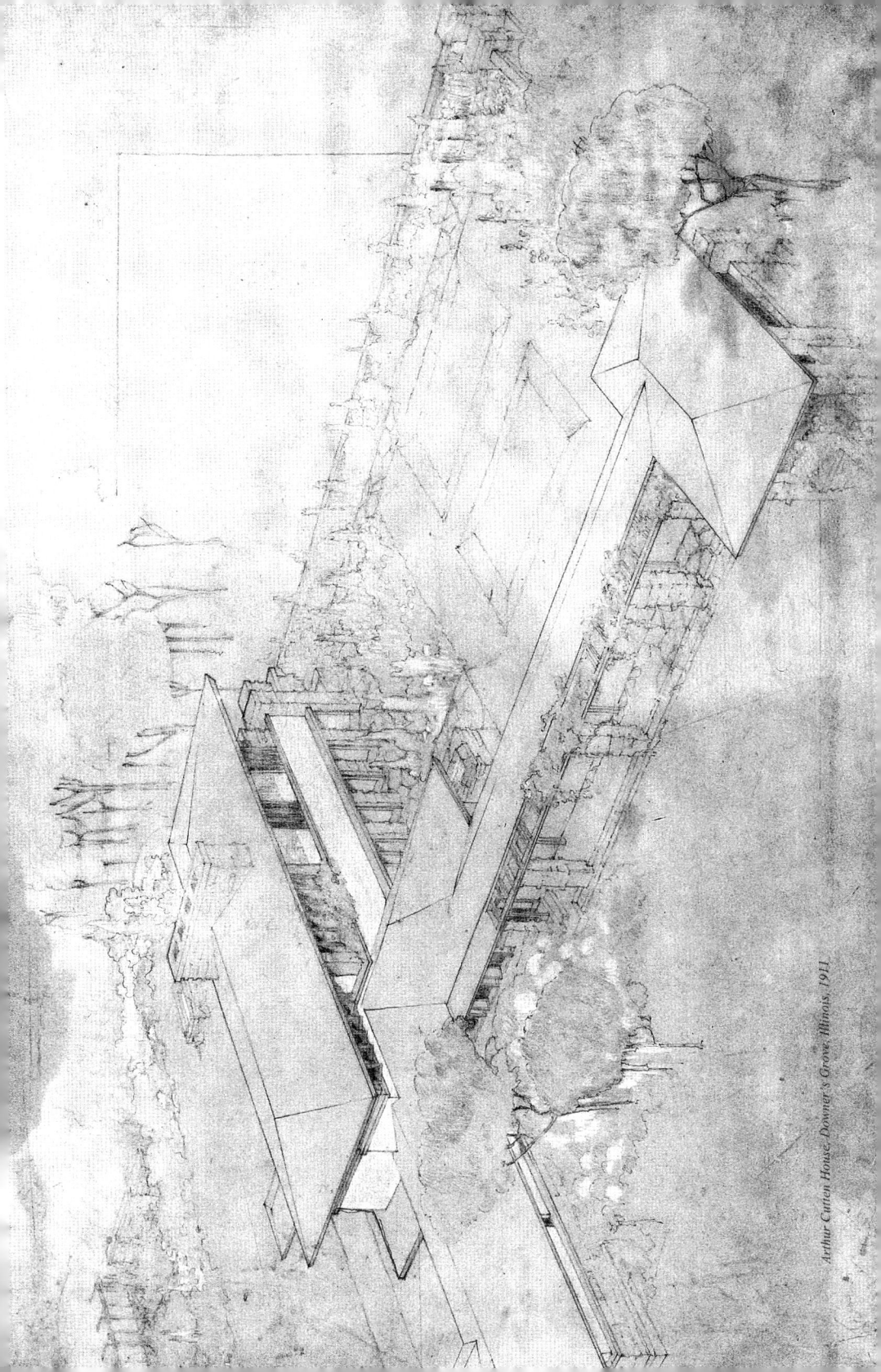

Arthur Cutten House, Downer's Grove, Illinois, 1911

by the pond.

In some respects these later houses cannot really be called Prairie houses, the chief difference seen in plans and elevation that more openly connect them with the landscape. And yet, the grammar of the designs—the gently sloping roofs, wide overhanging eaves, broad masonry fireplace masses, and the honest use of materials—is the same as that seen in such early houses such as Willits, Dana, Hardy, and Coonley, to cite but a few examples.

Taliesin, on the other hand, represents a complete shift in Wright's residential work. Undoubtedly, it is the most personal of all his work. First built in 1911, it closes one era of his life and opens another both personally and professionally. There are certain elements in the building that one finds in all of his residential work from the beginning of the century on: respect for the nature of materials; free flowing interior space; and the integration of interior and exterior spaces, what Wright called "the destruction of the box". But Taliesin was infinitely more than just another Wright residence. Wright was deeply attached to this valley and intimately familiar with every aspect of the landscape here. The site for the residence is a hill, carefully chosen, and Taliesin (a Welsh word meaning, "shining brow") became the brow of that particular hill.

" I knew well that no house should ever be *on* a hill, or *on* anything. It should be *of* the hill. Belonging to it. Hill and house should live together each the happier for the other .... I scanned the hills of the region where the rock came cropping out in strata to suggest buildings .... There must be some kind of house that would belong to that hill, as trees and the ledges of rock did: as Grandfather and Grandmother had belonged to it in their sense of it all .... The stone went down for pavements of terraces and courts. Stone was sent along the slopes into great walls. Stone stepped up like ledges on to the hill, and flung long arms in any direction that brought house to the ground. The ground! My Grandfather's ground. It was lovingly felt as intimate in all this .... Each court had its fountain and the winding stream below had a great dam. A thick stone wall was thrown across it, to make a pond at the very foot of the hill, and raise the water in the Valley to within sight from Taliesin .... Taliesin was to be an abstract combination of stone and wood as they naturally met in the aspect of the hills around about. And the lines of the hills were the lines of the roofs, the slopes of the hills their slopes, the plastered surfaces of the light wood-walls, set back into the shade beneath broad eaves, were like the flat stretches of sand in the river below and the same in color, for that is where the material that covered them came from ....

"Taliesin's order was such that when all was clean and in place its countenance beamed, wore a happy smile of well-being and welcome for all." [19]

In the summer of 1914, the living quarters of Taliesin were de-

層すべてが池に向かって開いている。平面図では"地階"と記されている一番下の階にはプレイルームが置かれ、プール・レベルのテラスへの出入り口となっている。プレイルームの真上にあるリビングルームからは、外部階段を経て池のそばにあるこの低い方のテラスへ出て行ける。

　いくつかの点で、これら、シカゴを離れてからの住宅は、本来のプレイリー・ハウスと呼ぶことは出来ない。その大きな違いは、平面と立面において、ランドスケープとのつながりがより開かれたものになっていることだ。にもかかわらず、デザインの文法——緩やかに傾斜する屋根、広い軒の出、石積みの暖炉の幅広のマッス、そして材料の真摯な使い方——は、少数例ではあるが、ウィリッツ、ダナ、ハーディー、クーンレイなどの初期の住宅に見られるものと同じである。

　一方、タリアセンは、ライトの住宅作品の完全な転換を示している。疑いなく、それは彼の全仕事のなかで最も個人的な作品である。1911年に最初に建てられたタリアセンは、個人的にも職業的にも、彼の生涯の一時代を閉じ、新しい時代を開くものであった。この建物には、20世紀初頭以降のライトの住宅作品のなかに常に見いだされるいくつかの要素がある。自由に流れる空間、ライトが"箱の破壊"と呼んだ、内部空間と外部空間の統合である。しかしタリアセンは単にライトのもう一つの住宅というより遙かに重要なものである。ライトはこの谷間と深いきずなを持ち、その風景のあらゆる様相を知り抜いていた。この住宅の敷地は、注意深く選ばれた丘であり、タリアセン（ウェールズ語で、"輝く額"を意味する）は、その比類ない丘の"額"になった。

　「住宅は、丘の〈上〉や何かの〈上〉にただあるべきではないことを私はよく知っていた。それは丘の〈もの〉であるべきなのだ。そこに所属するもの。丘と家は、お互いをより幸せなものにしながら共に生きるべきなのだ……。私は、建物を示唆するかのように岩が層を描いて顔を出しているこの地方の丘の連なりをゆっくりと眺め渡した……。木々や岩棚がそうしているように、あの丘に所属することになる何らかの住宅があるに違いない。私の祖父母がその気持によってあの丘の全体に所属していたように……。石はテラスやコートの敷石となって広がる。石は斜面に沿って大きな壁をつくりあげる。石は岩棚のように丘の上に向かって段を刻み、長い腕を四方に差し出し、家を大地に運ぶ。大地！　私の祖父の土地。そのすべてが親しみのあるものとして優しく感じられた……。それぞれのコートには泉があり、下の蛇行する流れには大きな貯水池がある。厚い石の壁がそこに架け渡され、丘のちょうど麓に池をつくり、谷間の水を、タリアセンから見えるところまで持ち上げる……。タリアセンは、周囲を取り巻く丘の姿に自然に結びついた、石と木の抽象化された組み合せになるだろう。そして、丘の線は屋根の線であり、丘の傾斜は屋根の傾斜であり、幅の広い軒の下に落ちる影のなかに後退する軽い木の壁のプラスター塗りの表層は、下を流れる川の砂底の平らな広がりに似て、色も同じである。そうした、建物を覆う材料はその場所からもたらされているのだから……。

　「タリアセンのオーダーは、すべてが整い、場所を得たとき、健康で

stroyed by fire. Shortly thereafter, Wright rebuilt, enlarging it considerably. Again, in 1925, the living quarters once more were victim to fire. Again Wright rebuilt, and again he enlarged the house, adding a second story for bedrooms for his two daughters. Not a year went by, until his death in 1959, that he was not modifying, changing, expanding Taliesin, a luxury he could not indulge with the homes of his clients. In this regard it is beyond doubt his most personal work in architecture, and can be compared only to his winter home and studio, Taliesin West, in Scottsdale, Arizona.

"'Wingspread' the Herbert Johnson prairie house," Frank Lloyd Wright wrote in 1938, "is another experiment in the articulation which began with the Coonley House ... in 1909, wherein the Living Room, Dining Room, Kitchen, Family sleeping rooms, Guest rooms were each separate units grouped together and connected by corridor ....

"At the center of the four zones the spacious Living Room stands. A tall chimneystack with five fireplaces divides this vertical space into spaces for the various domestic functions: Entrance Hall, Family Living Room, Library Living Room, and Dining Room. Extending from this lofty central room is four wings ... one with mezzanine floor and galleries is for the master, mistress, and young daughter. Another wing extends from the central space for their several boys; a playroom at the end—another wing for service and utilities—another for guests and five motor cars. Each wing has independent views on two sides ....

"This extended wing plan lies, very much at home, integral with the prairie landscape which is, through it, made more significant and beautiful ....

"This house, while resembling the Coonley house, is much more bold, masculine and direct in form and treatment—executed in more permanent materials ....

"Another prairie house in 1938 here joins the early ones of 1901-1910." [20]

Frank Lloyd Wright had succeeded in introducing an architecture indigenous to the American ideal of Democracy, for free men "among free people living in a free country," as he expressed it.[21] He had liberated architecture from the old containment of the box, and given new meaning to interior space.

"As these ideals worked away from house to house, finally freedom of floor space and elimination of useless heights worked a miracle in the new dwelling place. A sense of appropriate freedom had changed its whole aspect. The whole became different but more fit for human habitation and more natural on its site. It was impossible to imagine a house once built on these principles somewhere else. An entirely new sense of space-values in architecture came home. It now appears these new values came into the architecture of the world.

充足した状態に笑顔を浮かべ，すべての人を歓迎し，その外貌を光輝かせる，そういったものなのだ。」[19]

　1914年夏，タリアセンの住居部分は火災で消失した。その後まもなく，ライトは前よりかなり大きなものとしてそれを再建した。再び，1925年，そこは火災に見舞われた。再び，ライトはそこを再建した。今回も前より大きくし，二人の娘の寝室をつくるために2階を増築した。1959年の死に至るまで，彼がタリアセンの改修，改変，拡張に手をつけずに1年が過ぎることはなかった。それは依頼された仕事では，欲しいままに楽しむことのできなかった贅沢である。この点において，それは疑いなくライトの最も個人的な建築作品であり，それと比肩できるのは，アリゾナ州スコッツデールの冬の家とスタジオの他にない。

　「"ウィングスプレッド" つまりハーバート・ジョンソンのプレイリー・ハウスは」とフランク・ロイド・ライトは1938年に記している。「1909年の……クーンレイ邸で始めたもう一つの建築上の実験である。そこではリビングルーム，ダイニングルーム，厨房，家族の寝室，ゲストルームはそれぞれが一つにまとめられ，廊下で繋がれた別なユニットとなっていた……。

　「4つのゾーンの中心に，広いリビングルームが立ち上がる。5つの暖炉が付いた背の高い煙突がこの垂直に伸びる空間を家の持つ様々な機能空間に分割する。エントランス・ホール，家族のリビングルーム，書斎であるリビングルーム，ダイニングルーム。そびえ立つ中央の部屋から4つの翼が伸びる……中2階とギャラリーが付いた翼は主人，女主人，娘たちのためのものである。中央空間から伸びる別な翼は息子たちのスペースで，終端にプレイルームがある——別な一つにはサービスとユーティリティ——もう一つにはゲストルームと5台収容できるガレージがある。各翼からは，両側にそれぞれの眺望が開けている……。

　「この翼を広げたプランは，環境に非常によく順応し，プレイリーの風景に溶け込んでいるが，それによって，家はさらに魅力的で美しいものになる……。

　「この住宅は，クーンレイ邸に似ているが，形態と扱いの点でさらに大胆で，力強く，直接的なものであり——より恒久的な材料でつくられている……。

　「この，1938年のもう一つのプレイリー・ハウスは，1901年から1910年の初期のプレイリー・ハウスの列に加わる。」[20]

　フランク・ロイド・ライトは，「自由な国に住む自由な国民のなかの」と彼が表現するような自由な人間のための，民主主義というアメリカの理想に固有の建築を導入することを成し遂げた。[21] 彼は箱という古い束縛から建築を解放し，内部空間に新しい意味を与えた。

　「これらの理想は，一つの家から一つの家へとたゆまない努力を続けるなかで，ついに自由な平面と無駄な高さを省くことによって，新しい住空間のなかに奇跡を起こした。それぞれの家に適合した自由の感覚は

New sense of repose in quiet streamline effects had arrived. The streamline and the plain surface seen as the flat plane had then and there found their way into buildings as we see them in steamships, aeroplanes and motorcars, although they were intimately related to building materials, environment and the human being." [22]

Bruce Brooks Pfeiffer

Taliesin West May 2001

1: Frank Lloyd Wright, *An Autobiography* (New York: Barnes & Noble Books, 1998), p.18

2: Frank Lloyd Wright, *An American Architecture*, edited by Edgar Kaufmann (New York: Barnes & Noble Books, 1998), p. 193

3: *An Autobiography*, p.139

4: Frank Lloyd Wright to Lewis Mumford, July 7, 1930

5: *An Autobiography*, pp.139-140

6: Frank Lloyd Wright, *Recollections—United States 1893-1920* (London: Architect's Journal, July 16, 1936), p.77

7: *An Autobiography*, pp.141-142

8: ibid., p.143

9: ibid., p.145

10: ibid., p.146

11: ibid., pp.146-147

12: ibid., p.141

13: Scholar and glass conservator Julie Sloan notes that while not all of Wright's windows used lead, the term "leaded glass" was used to distinguish these windows from "art glass" which was considered cheap and popular and "stained glass" which was associated with ecclesiastical windows or mansions. Wright did use lead before 1905, although he also used zinc and brass. There were no comparable terms for windows made from these metals. See Julie Sloan, *Light Screens: The Complete Leaded-Glass Windows of Frank Lloyd Wright* (New York: Rizzoli, 2001).

14: *Recollections—United States 1893-1920* Part Two (London: Architect's Journal, July 23, 1936), p.112

15: *An Autobiography*, p.161

16: *The Architectural Record*, May, 1908

17: *Ausgeführte Bauten und Entwürfe von Frank Lloyd Wright* (Berlin: Ernst Wasmuth Verlag, 1910)

18: Letter from Lloyd Wright to Linn Cowles, February 3, 1966, used with permission.

19: Frank Lloyd Wright, *An Autobiography* (New York: Barnes & Noble Books, 1998), pp.168-174

20: *The Architectural Forum*, January 1938, p.56

21: *An Autobiography*, p.139

22: ibid., pp.145-146

その全体像を変えた。全体は異なるものになったが、人間の住まいにより相応しく、その敷地にとってさらに自然なものになった。これらの原則に基づいた住宅が、かつてどこかに建てられたことを想像するのは不可能であった。建築の空間的価値に対するまったく新しい感覚が住宅に生まれた。今、建築の世界にもたらされたこれらの新しい価値が表れる。静かな流線形が発する効果のなかに、安息の新しい感覚が表現される。蒸気船や飛行機や自動車のなかに見られる流線形や平坦な面は、すぐさま建物のなかにもその場所を見つけた。材料や環境や人間と密接に関わりながら。」[22]

ブルース・ブルックス・ファイファー
　　　　　　　　　　　タリアセン・ウェストにて　2001年5月

註：
1：Frank Lloyd Wright, "An Autobiography"(New York: Barns & Noble Books, 1998), p.18(樋口清訳『ライト　自伝―ある芸術の形成―』、中央公論美術出版、2000年（再販））
2：Frank Lloyd Wright, "An American Architecture", edited by Edgar Kaufmann (New York: Barnes & Noble Books, 1998), p.193
3："An Autobiography", p.139
4：フランク・ロイド・ライトからルイス・マンフォードへ。1930年7月7日
5："An Autobiography", pp.139-140
6：Frank Lloyd Wright, "Recollections―United States 1893-1920" (London: Architect's Journal, July 16, 1936), p.77
7："An Autobiography", pp.141-142
8：前掲書、p.143
9：前掲書、p.145
10：前掲書、p.146
11：前掲書、pp.146-147
12：前掲書、p.141
13：学者でありガラス作品の保護者であるジュリー・スローンは、ライトの窓のすべてが、鉛を使っているわけではない一方で、"leaded glass"（ガラス片を鉛線にはめこんで接合する鉛枠ガラス）という用語が用いられたのは、安価でポピュラーな"アート・グラス"や、教会の窓やマンションと結びついた"ステンドグラス"とライトの窓を区別するためであった、と指摘する。ライトは鉛を1905年以前から用いていたが、亜鉛や真鍮も使っていた。これらの金属を用いたガラス窓に対応する用語はない。Julie Sloan, "Light Screens: The Complete Leaded-Glass Windows of Frank Lloyd Wright"(New York: Rizzoli, 2001)
14："Recollections―United States 1893-1920" Part Two (London: Architect's Journal, July 23, 1936), p.112
15："An Autobiography", p.161
16："The Architectural Record", May, 1908
17："Ausgeführte Bauten und Entwürfe von Frank Lloyd Wright" (Berlin: Ernst Wasmuth Verlag, 1910)
18：フランク・ロイド・ライトからリン・コウルズへの手紙。1966年2月3日付け。許可を得て掲載。
19：Frank Lloyd Wright, "An Autobiography"(New York: Barnes & Noble Books, 1998), pp.168-174
20："The Architectural Forum", January, 1938, p.56
21："An Autobiography", p.139
22：前掲書、pp.145-146

William H. Winslow House and Stables
River Forest, Illinois, 1893

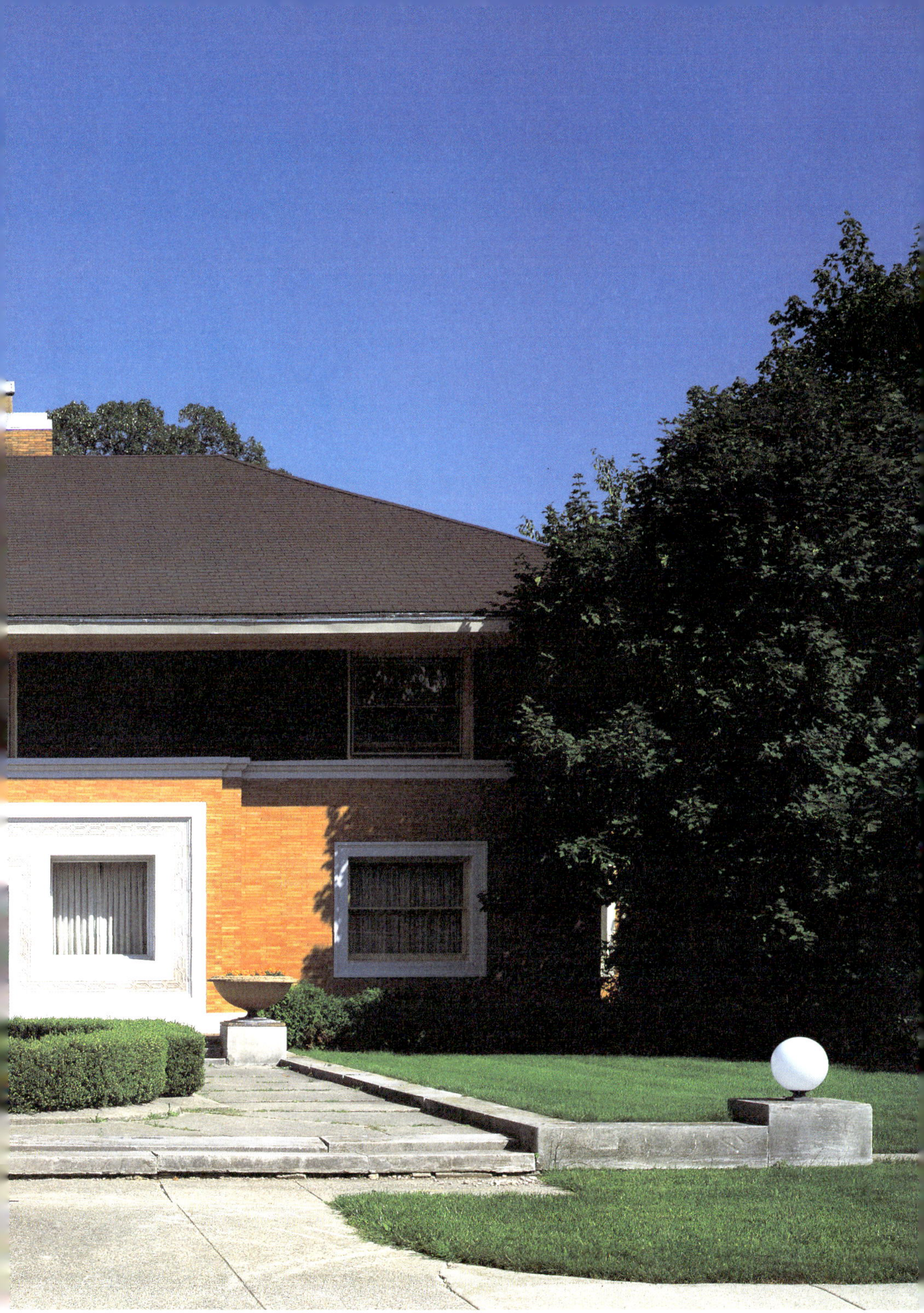

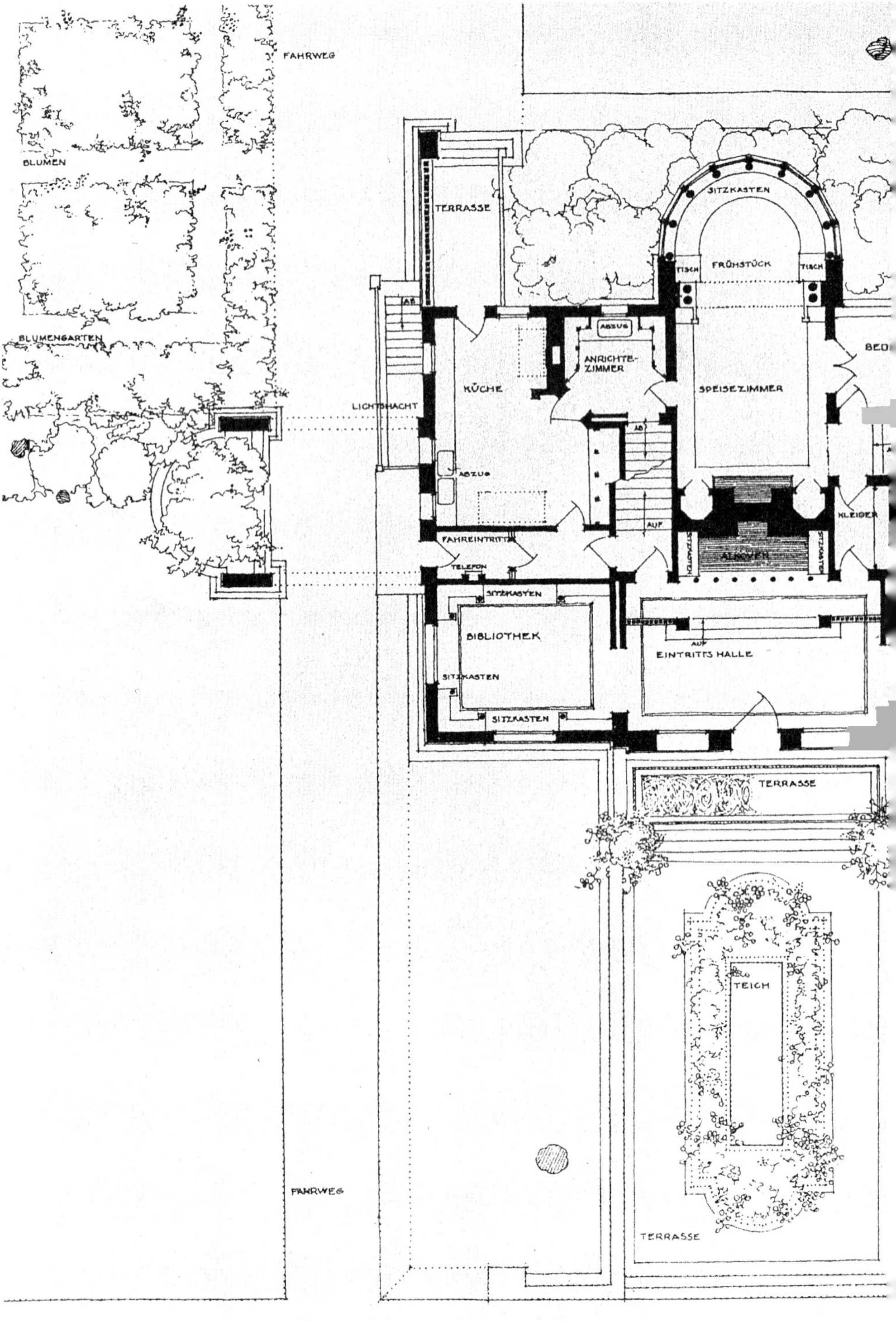
FAHRWEG
BLUMEN
BLUMENGARTEN
TERRASSE
SITZKASTEN
TISCH
FRÜHSTÜCK
TISCH
ABZUG
ANRICHTE-
ZIMMER
KÜCHE
SPEISEZIMMER
LICHTSCHACHT
AB
ABZUG
AUF
KLEIDER
FAHREINTRITT
TELEFON
SITZKASTEN
ALKOVEN
SITZKASTEN
BIBLIOTHEK
AUF
EINTRITTS HALLE
SITZKASTEN
SITZKASTEN
TERRASSE
TEICH
FAHRWEG
TERRASSE

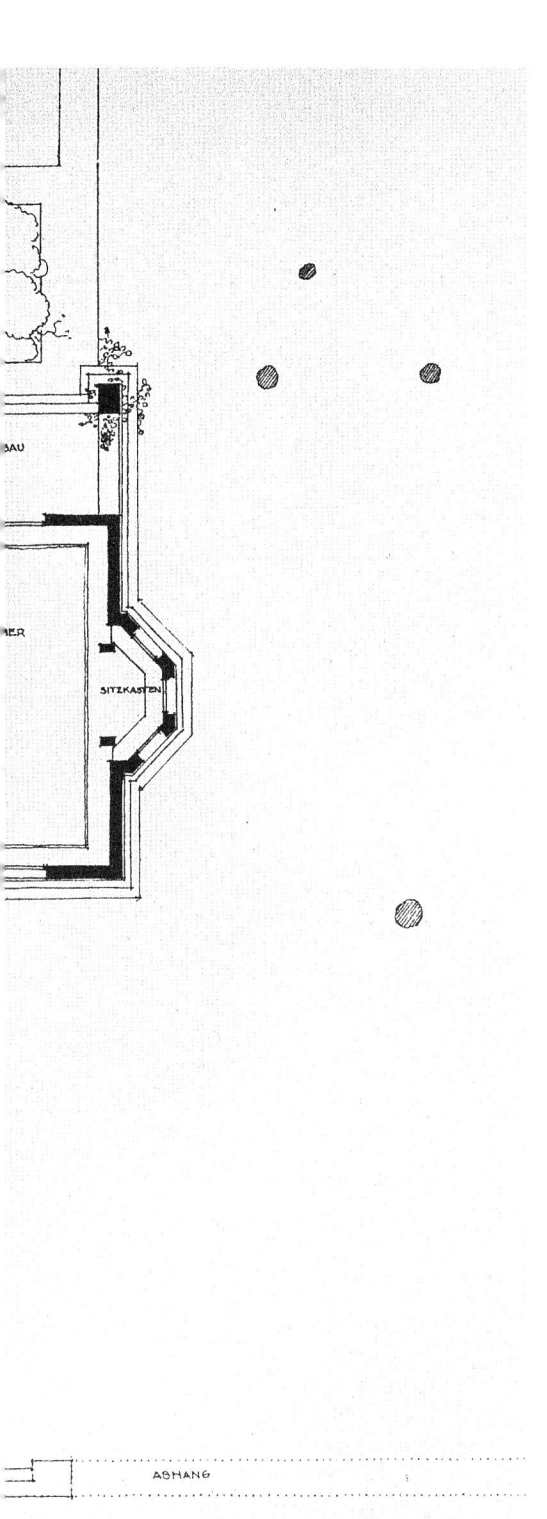

Plan

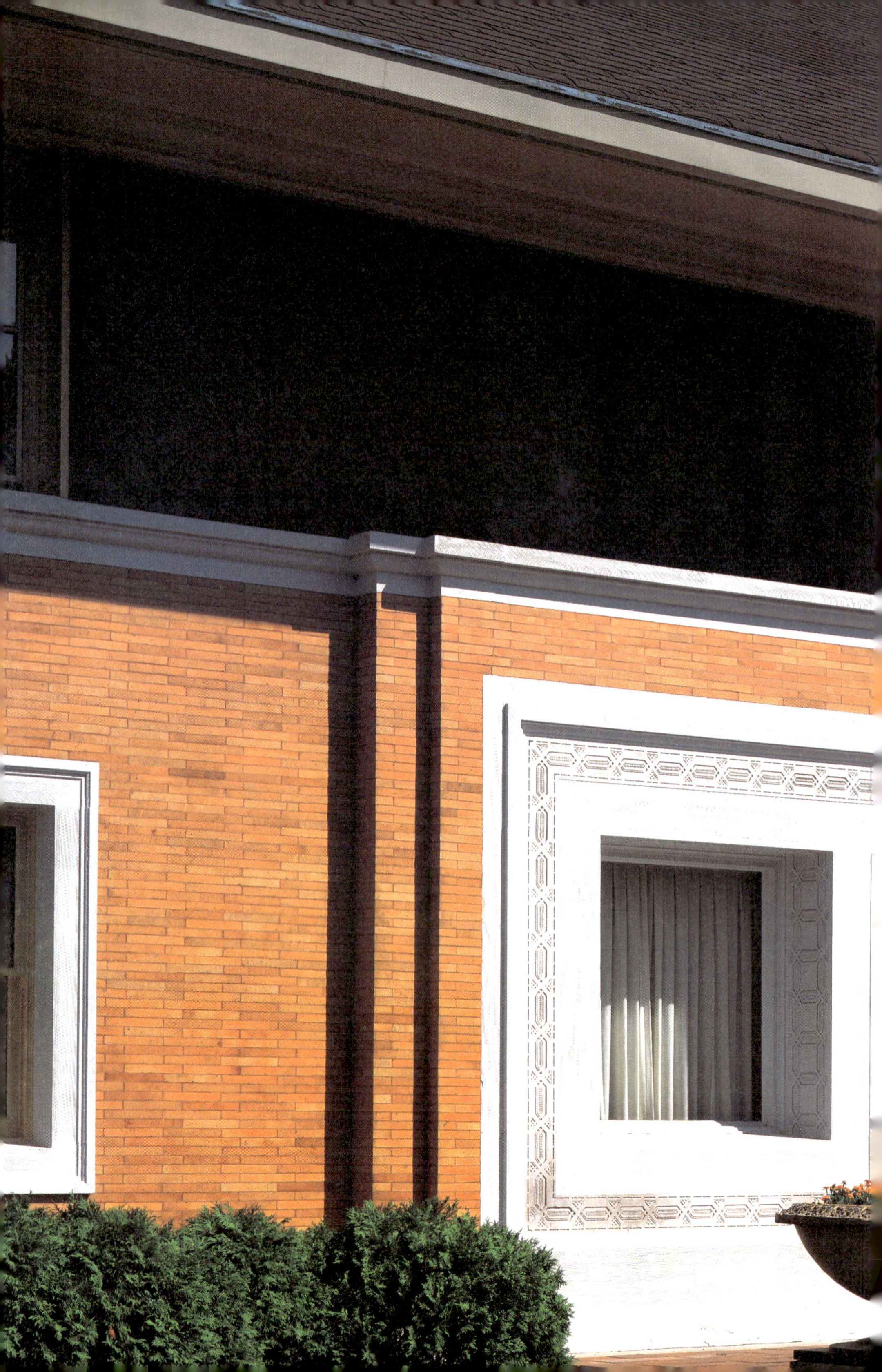

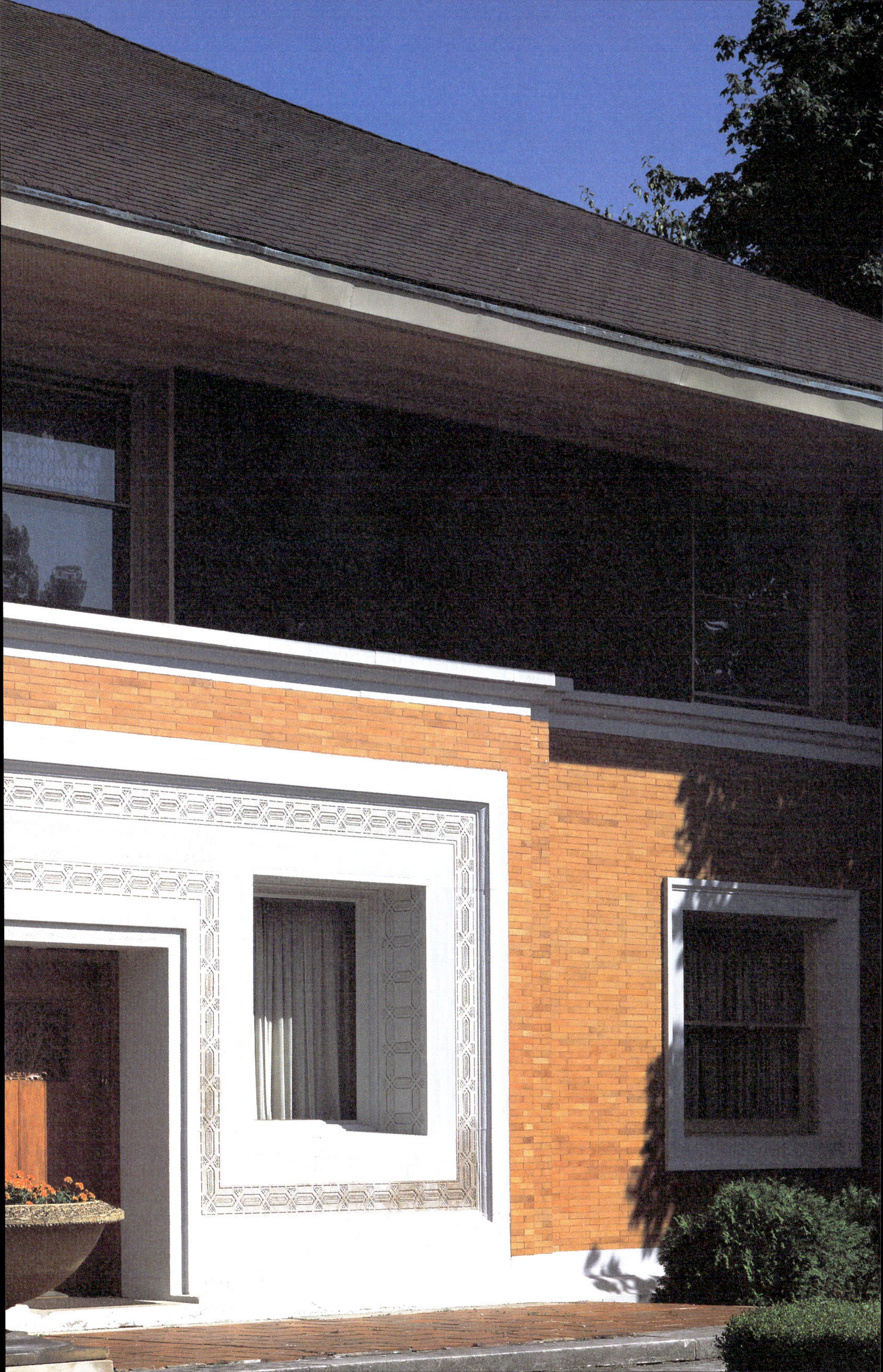

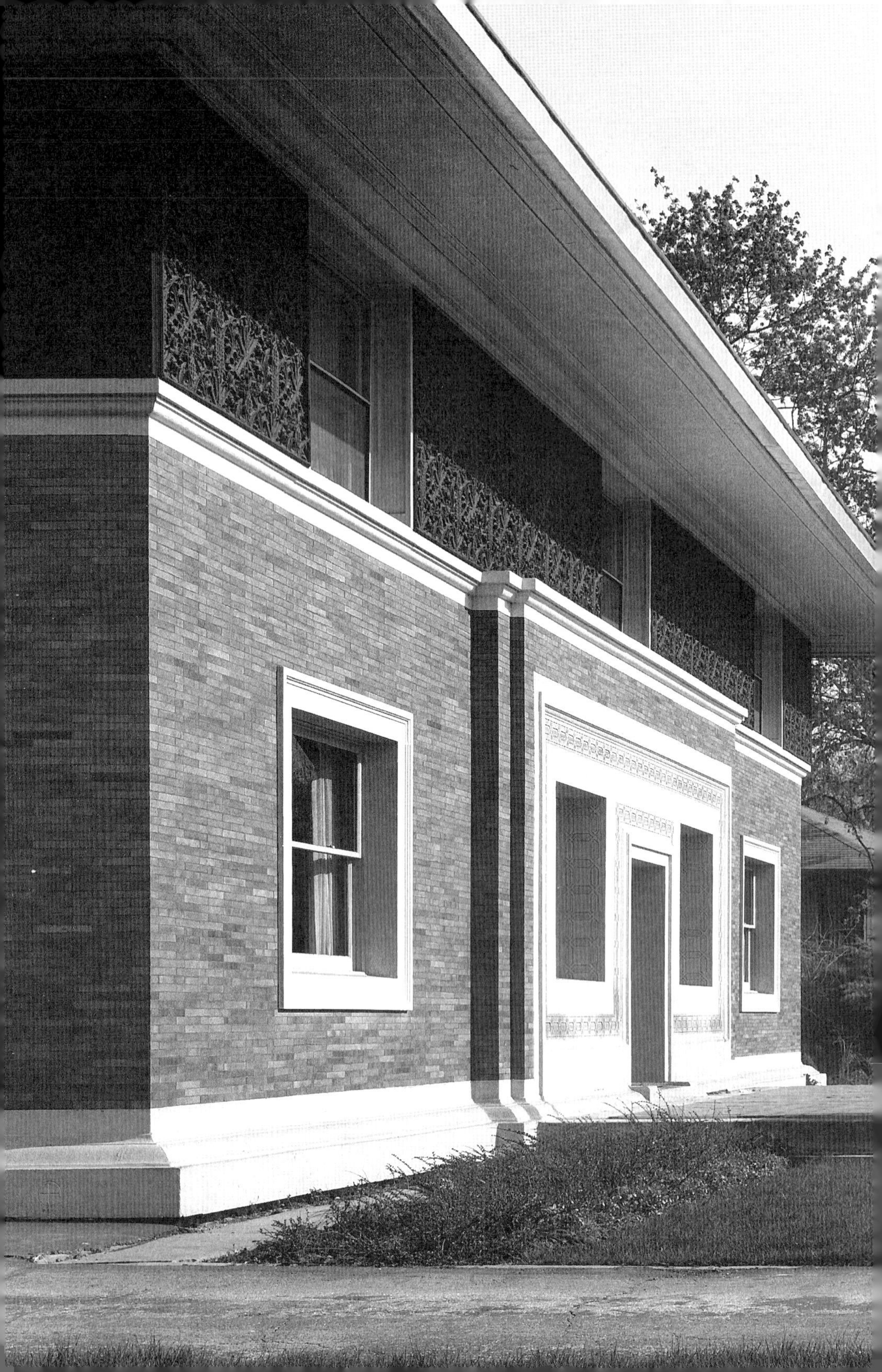

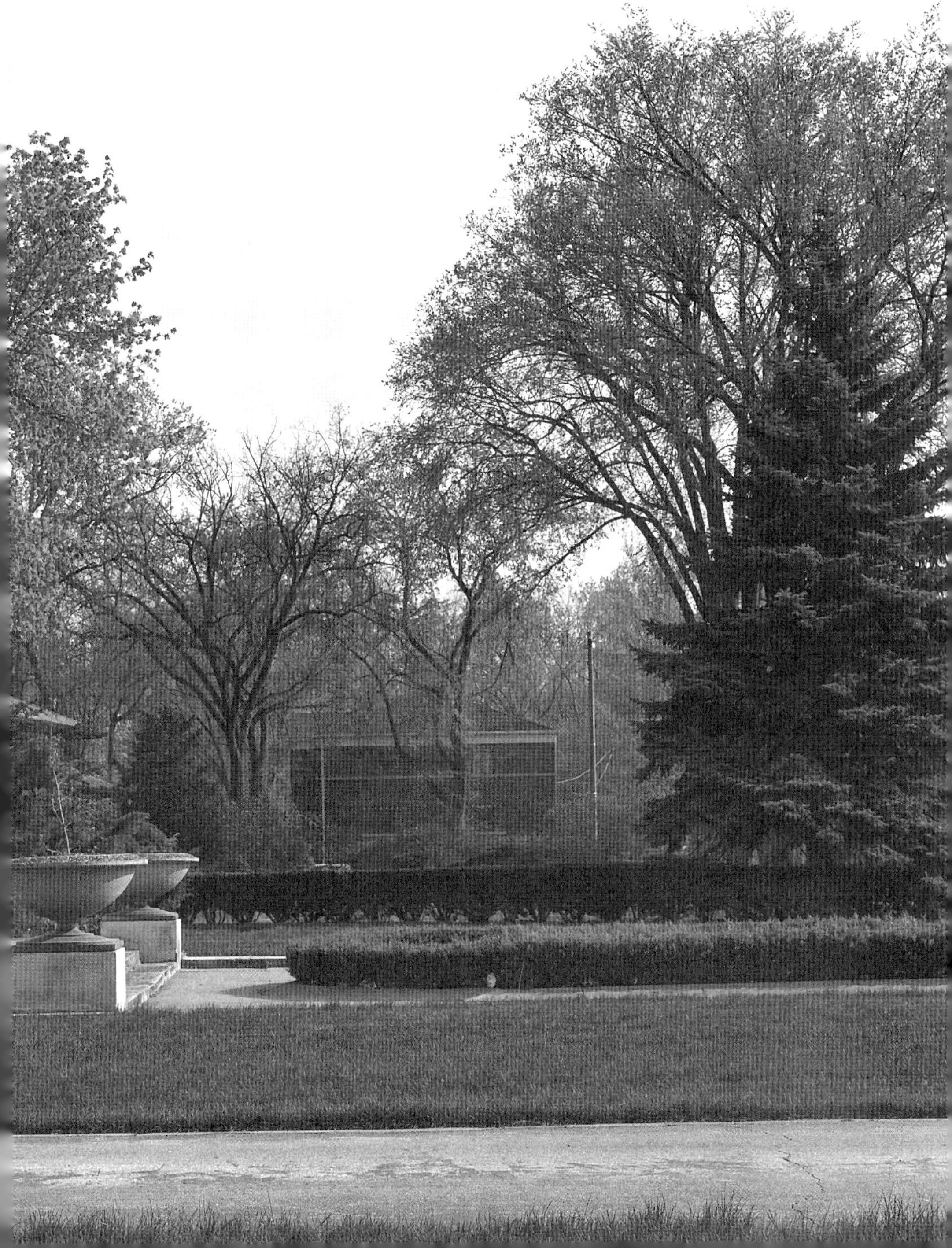

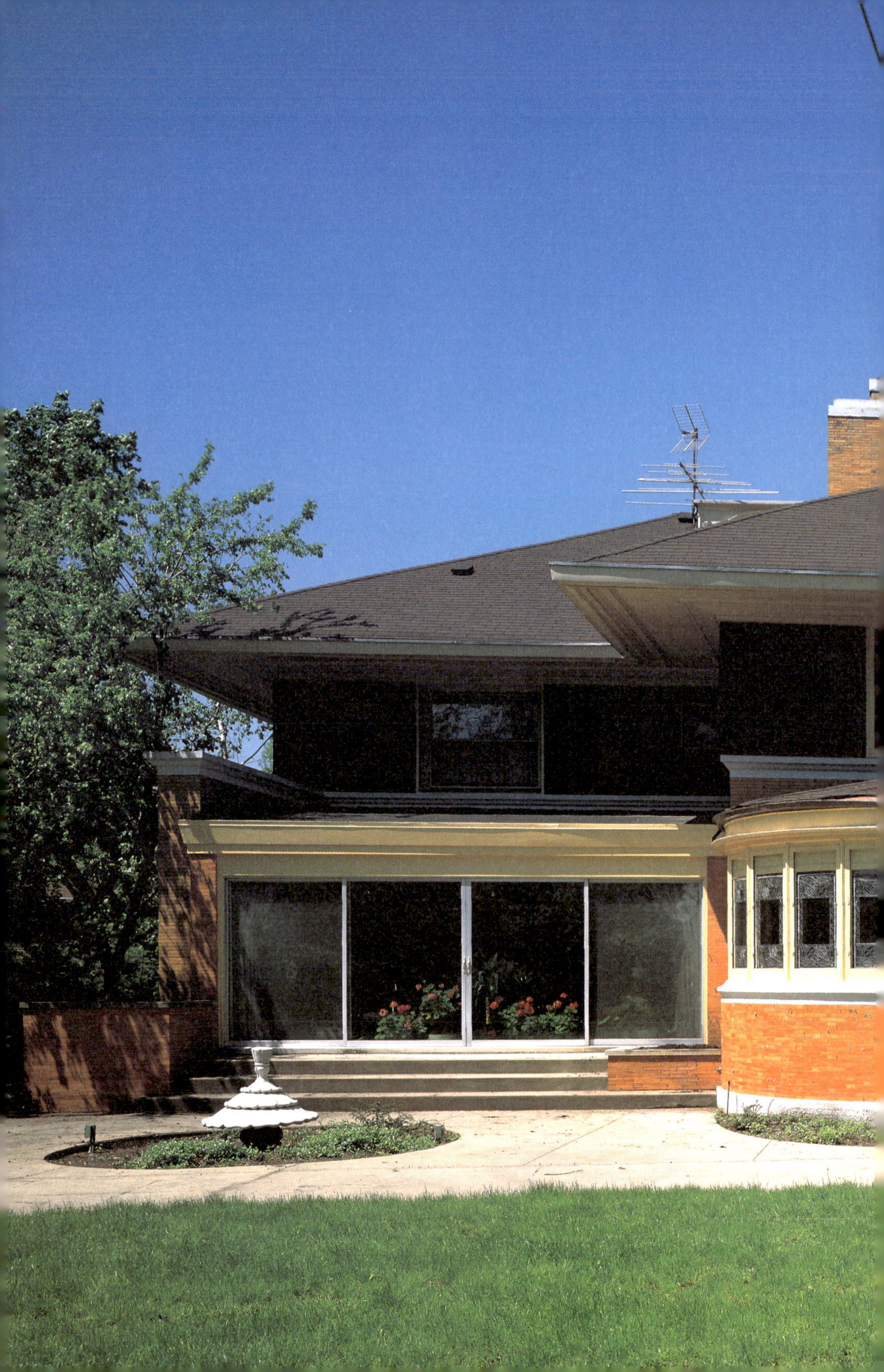

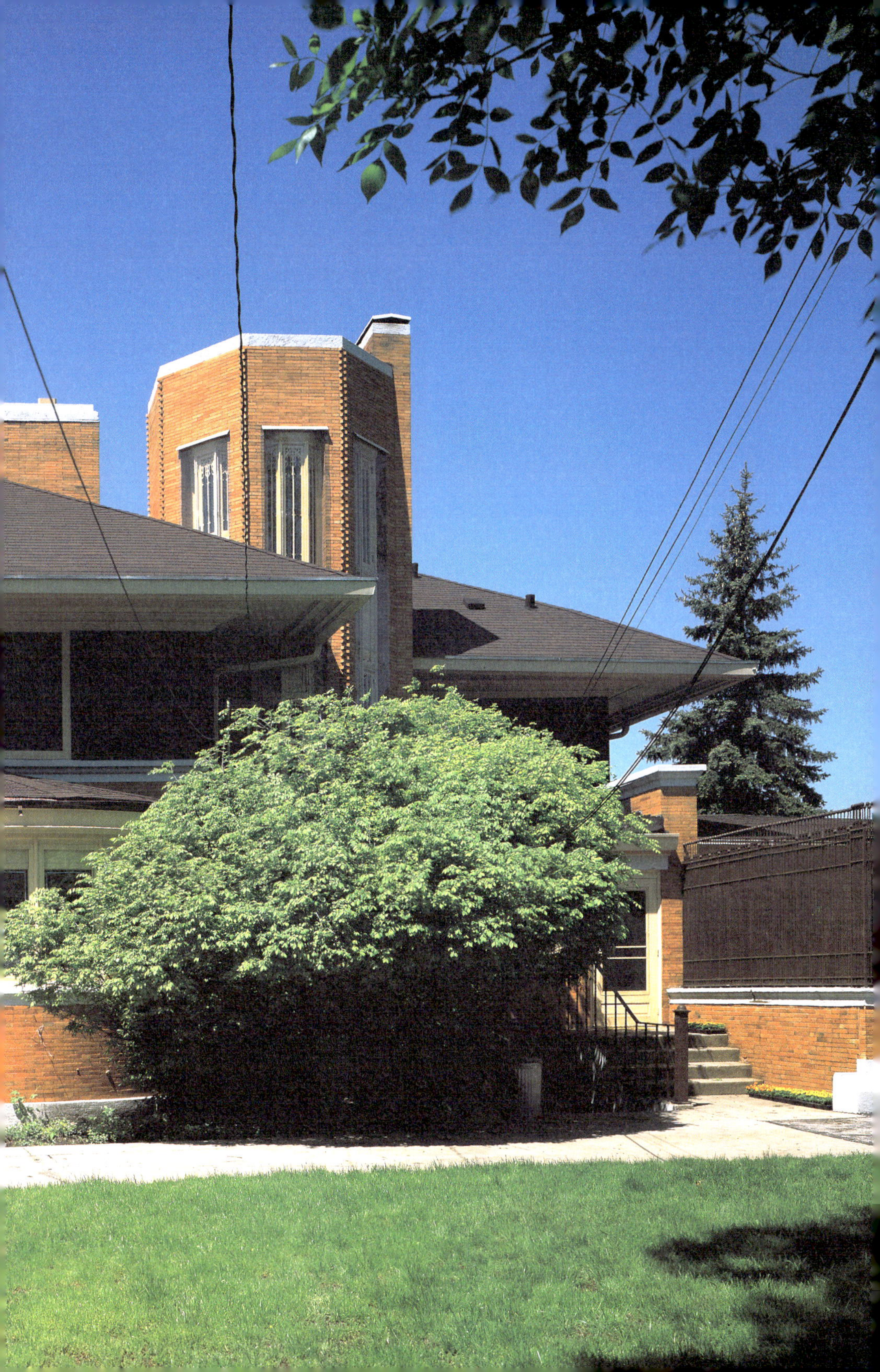

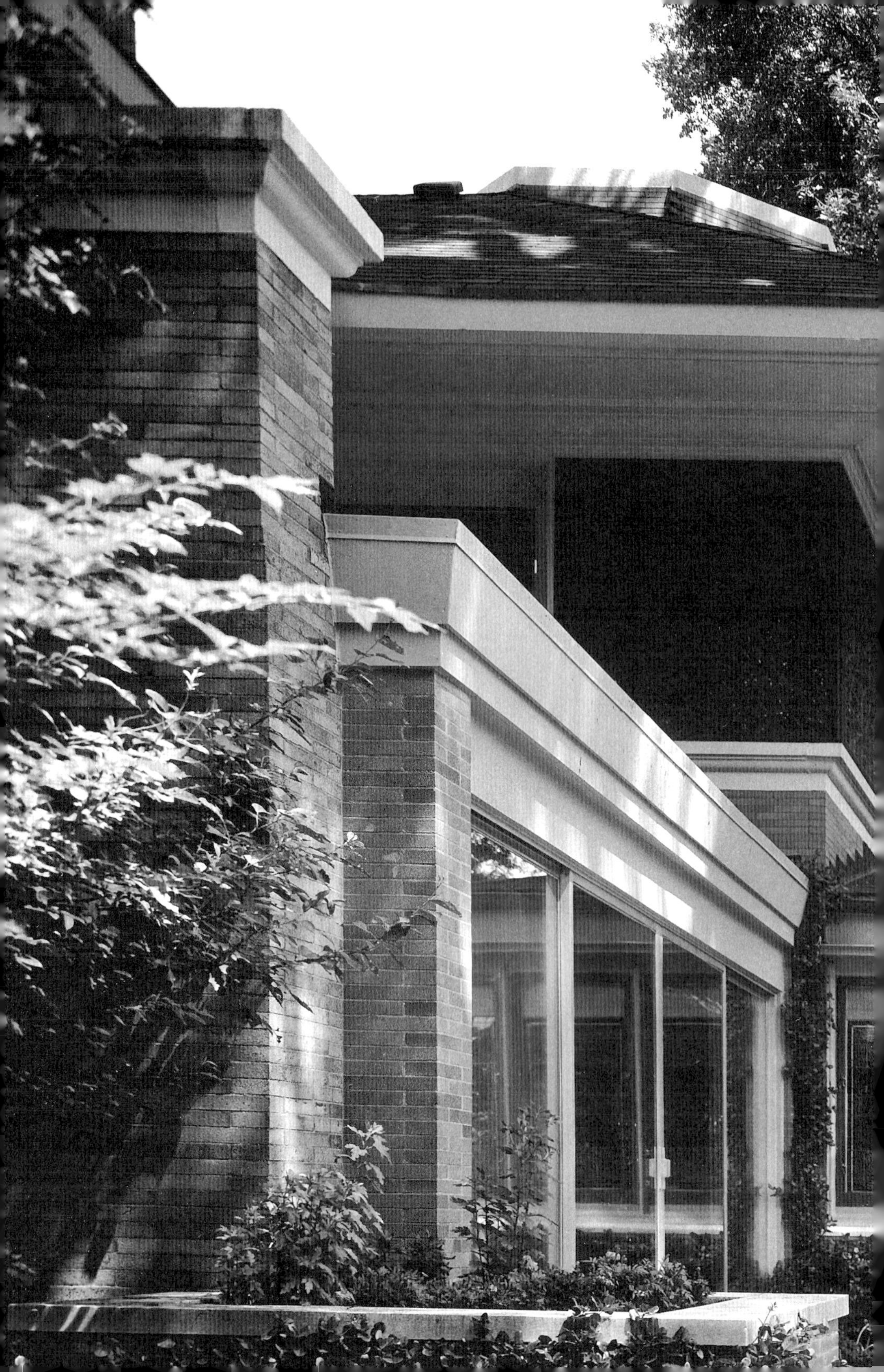

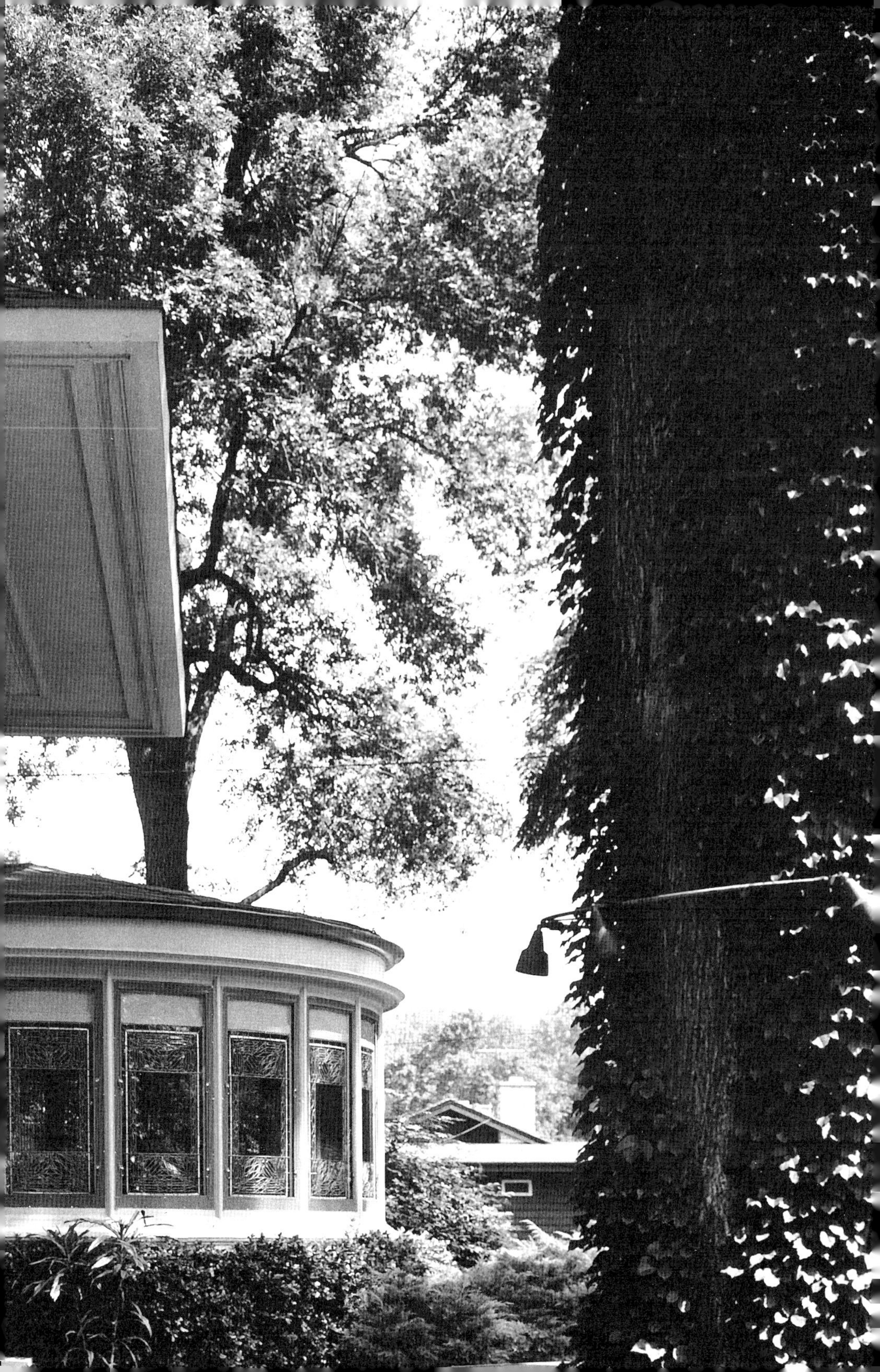

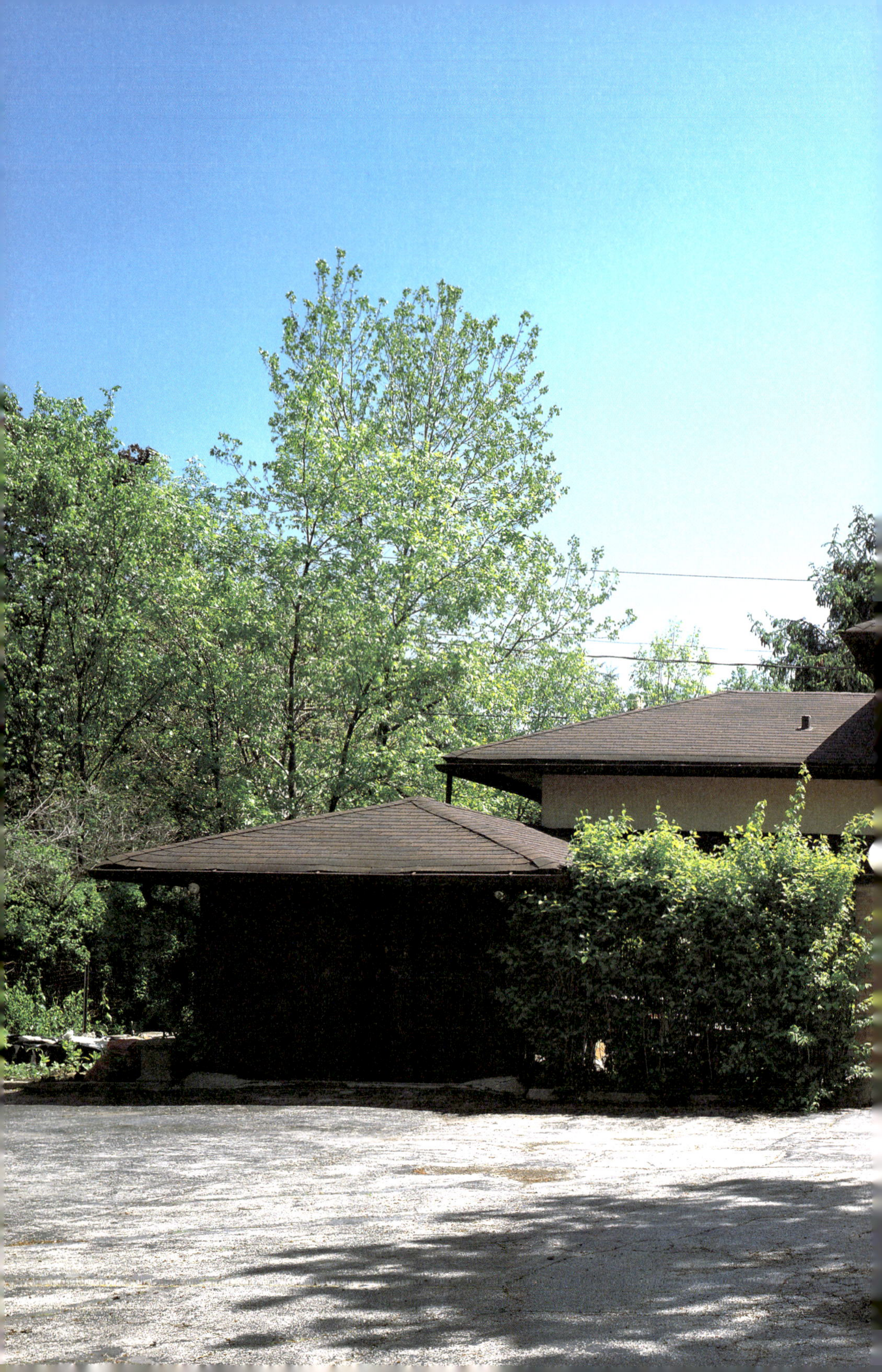

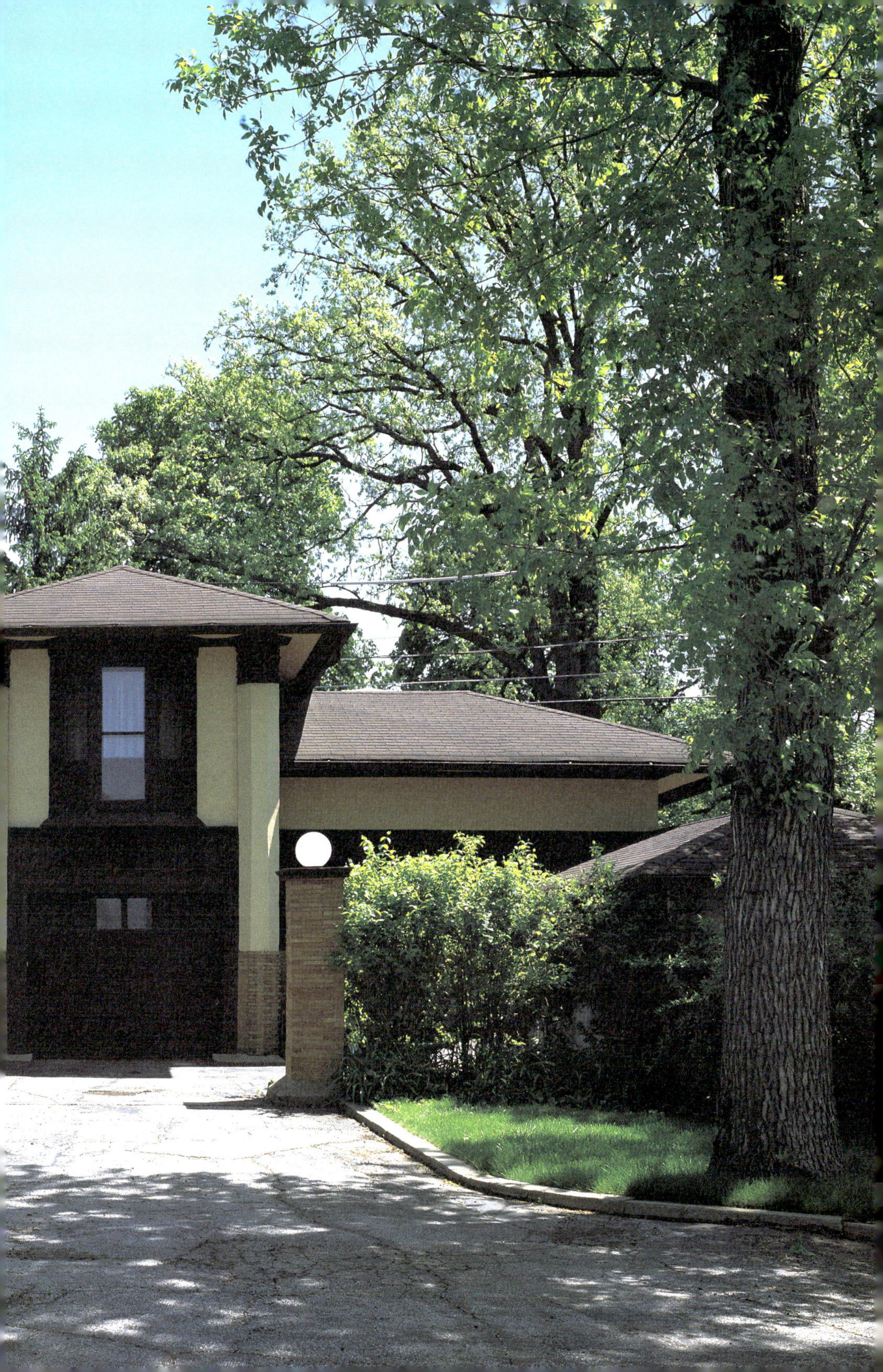

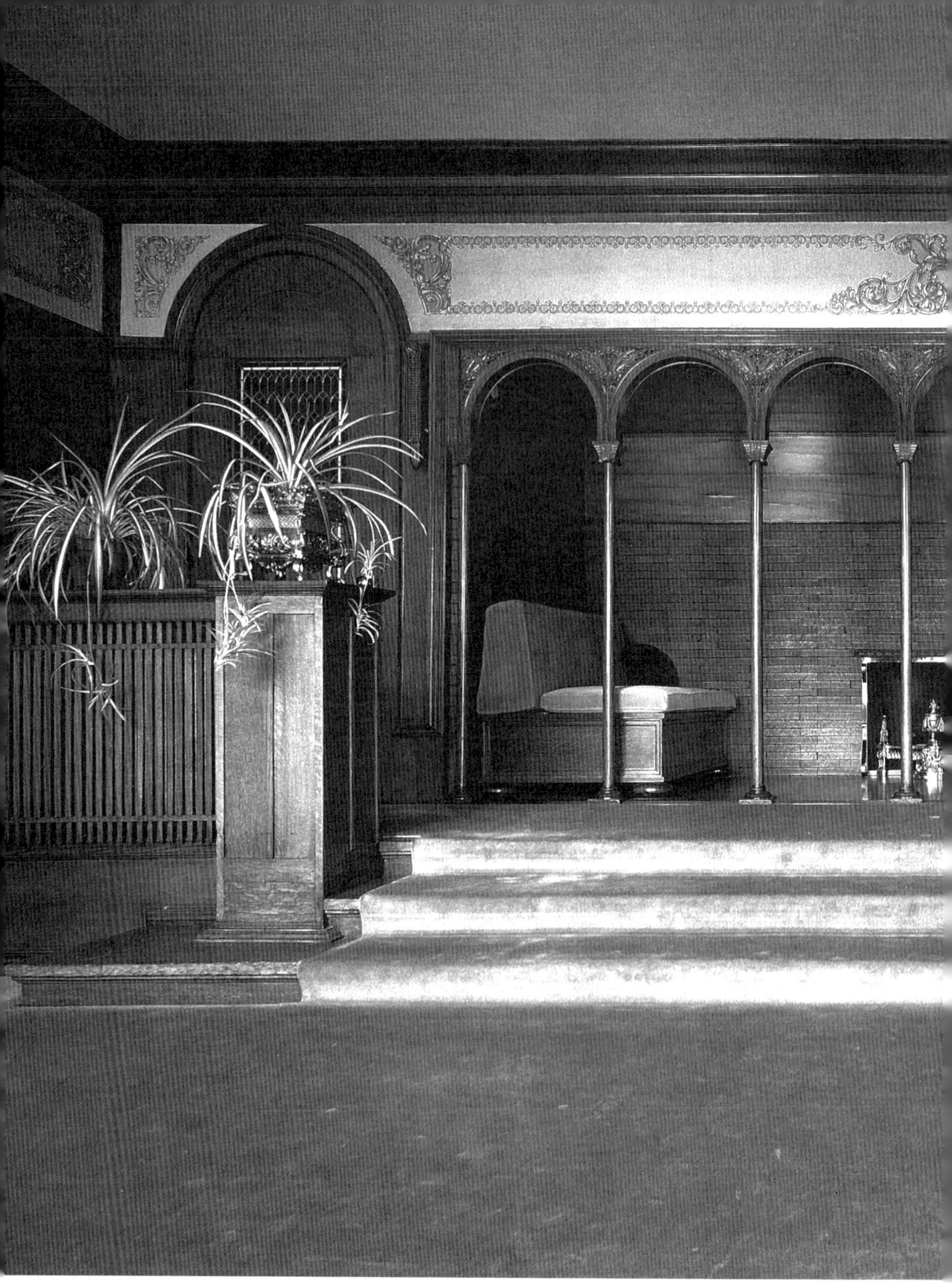

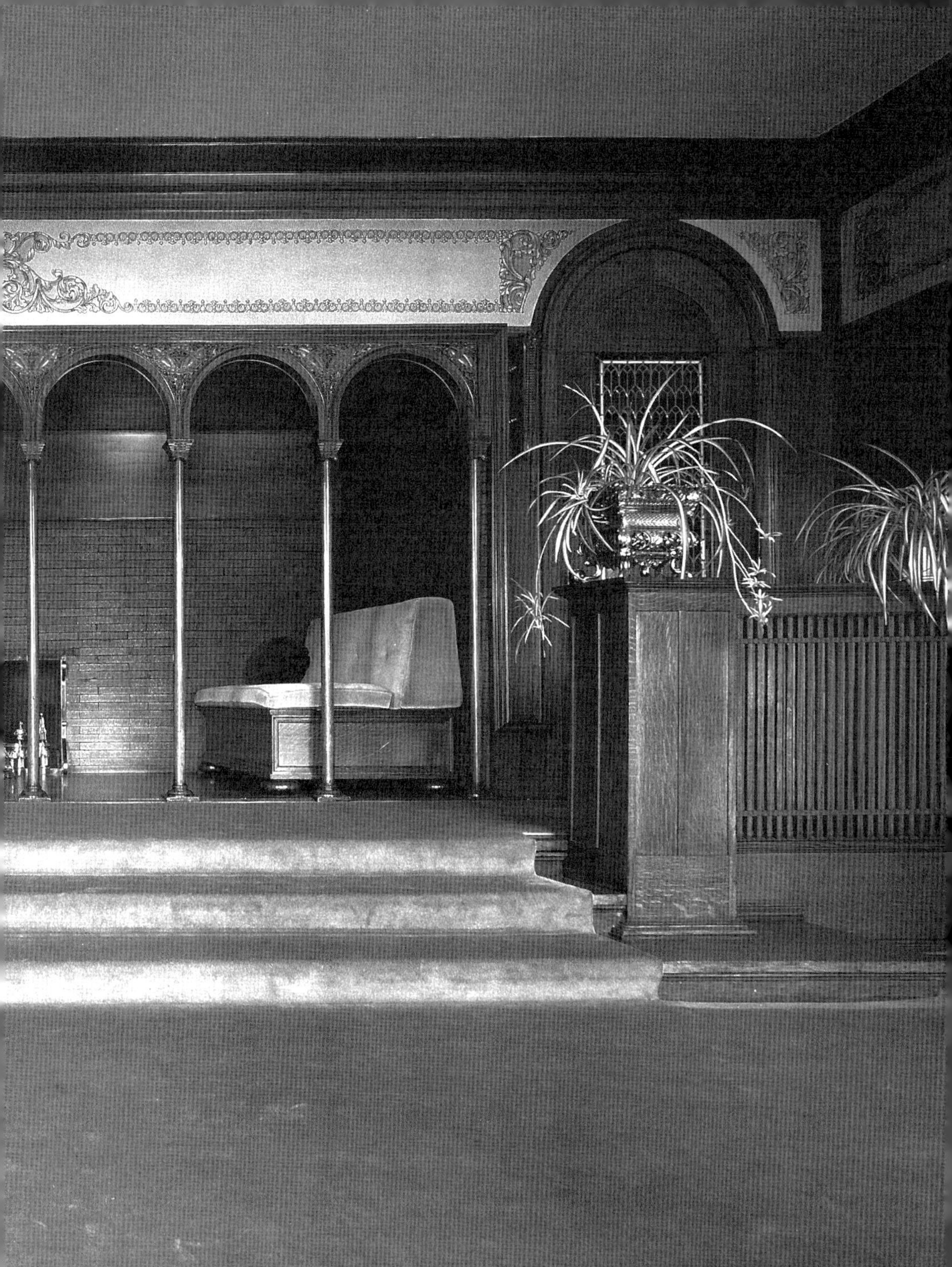

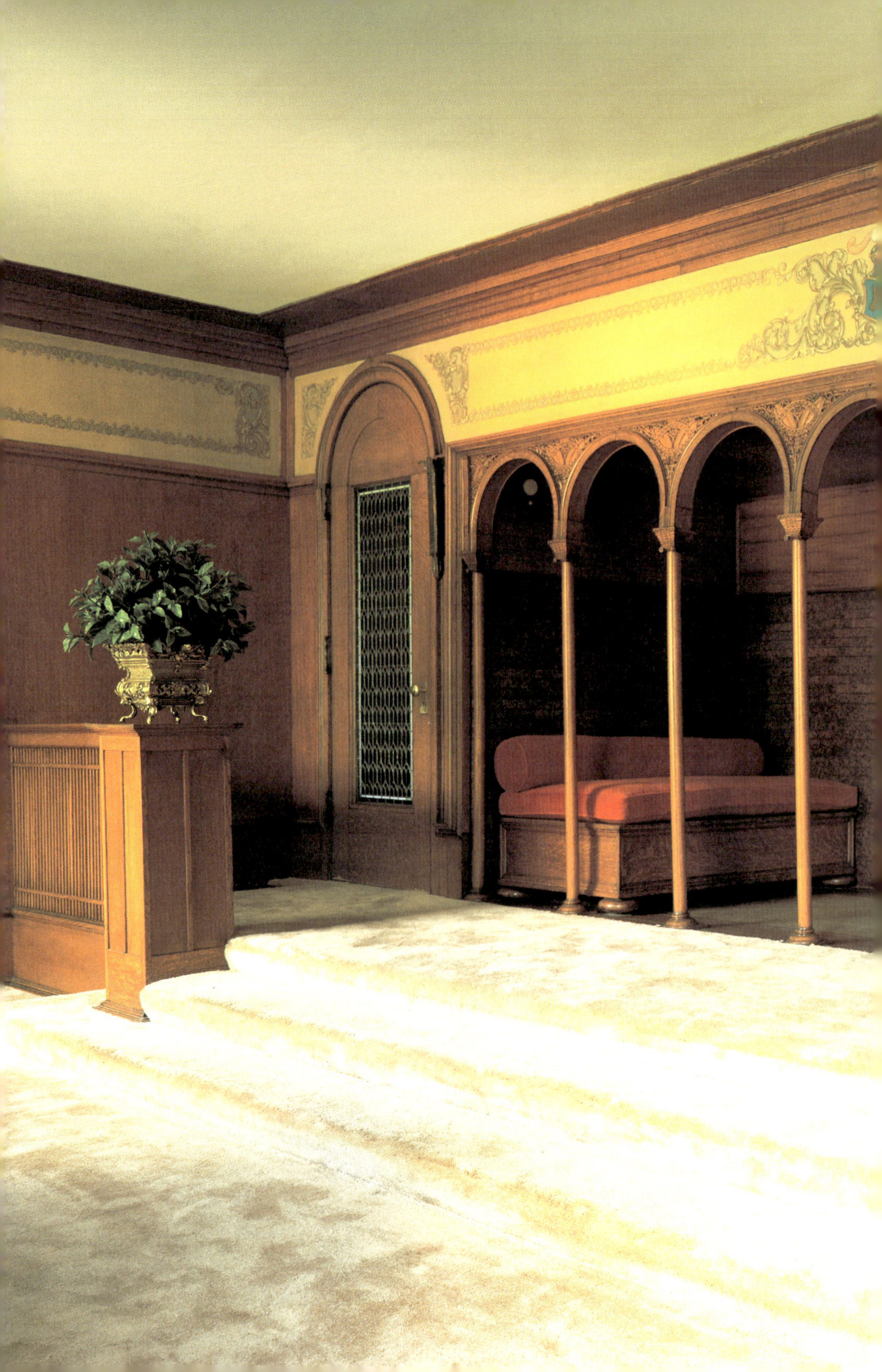

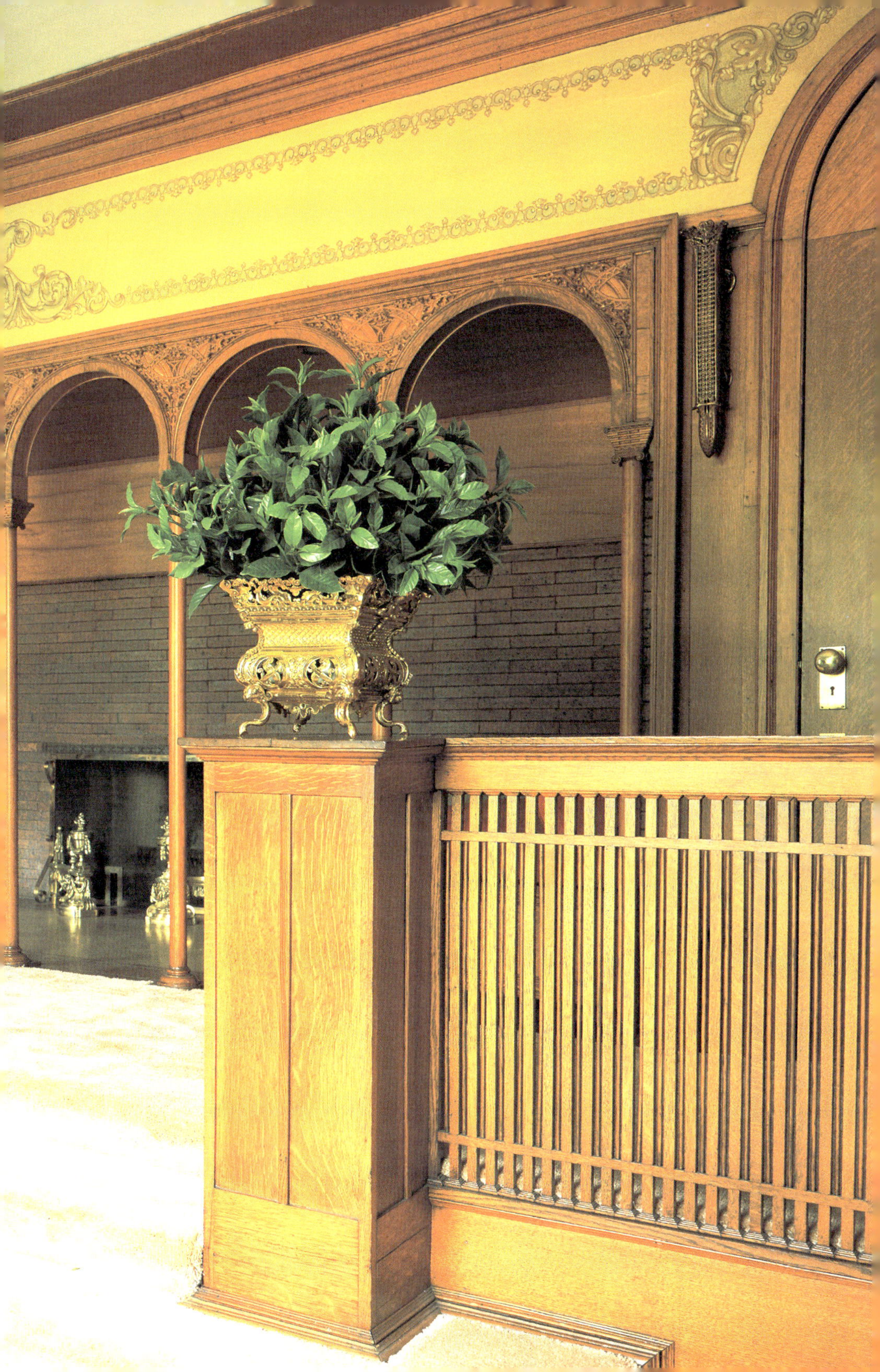

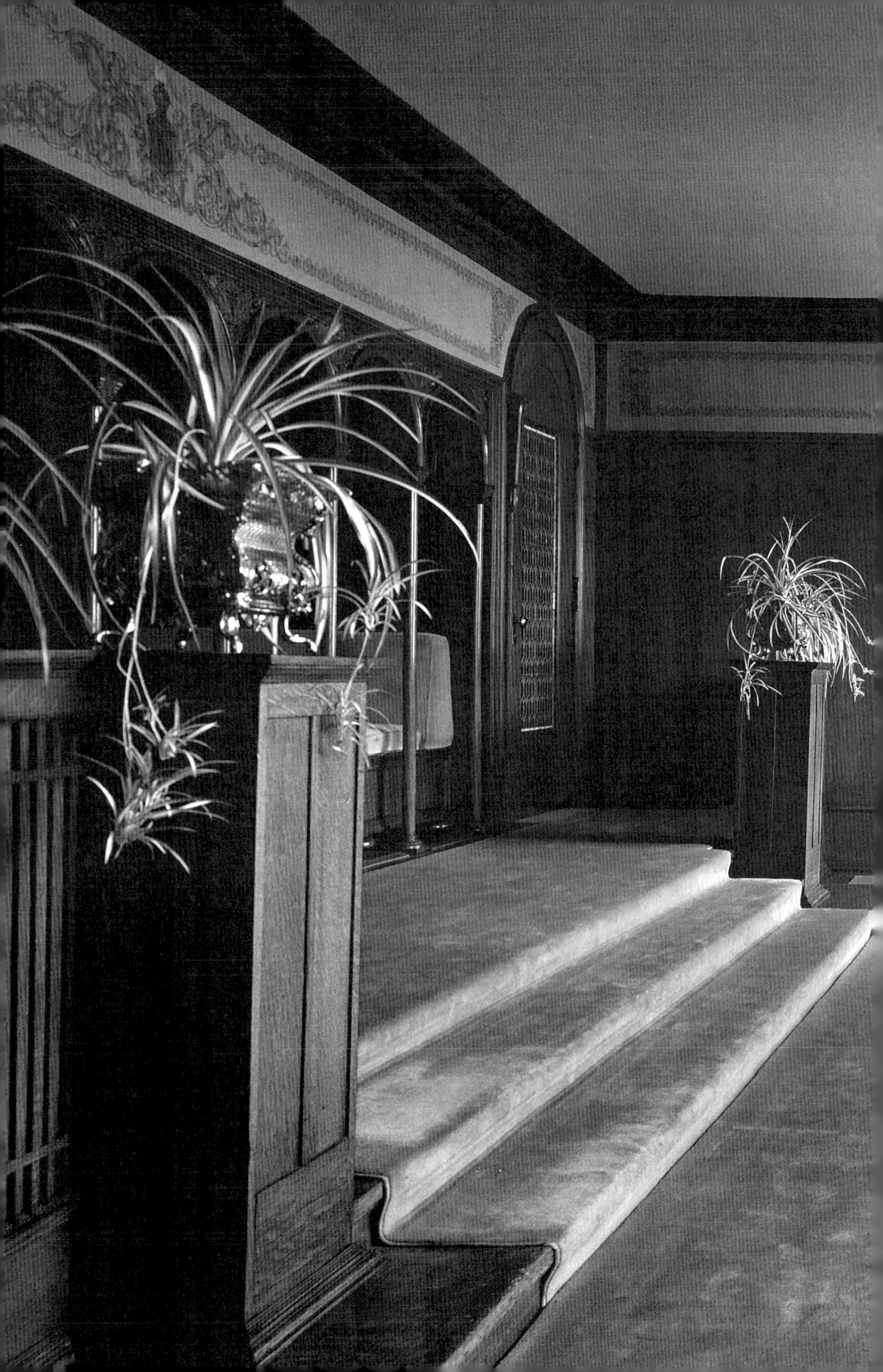

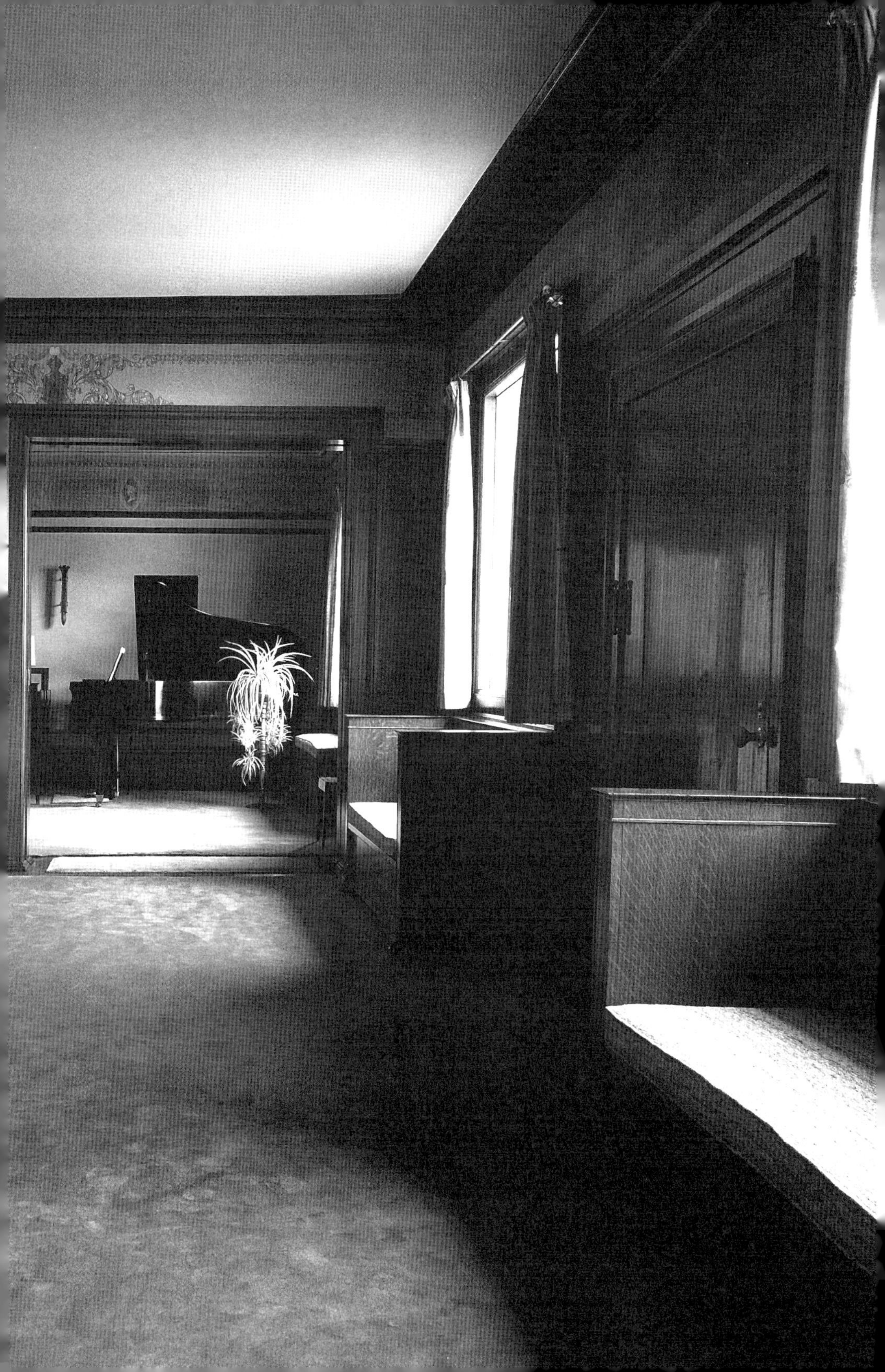

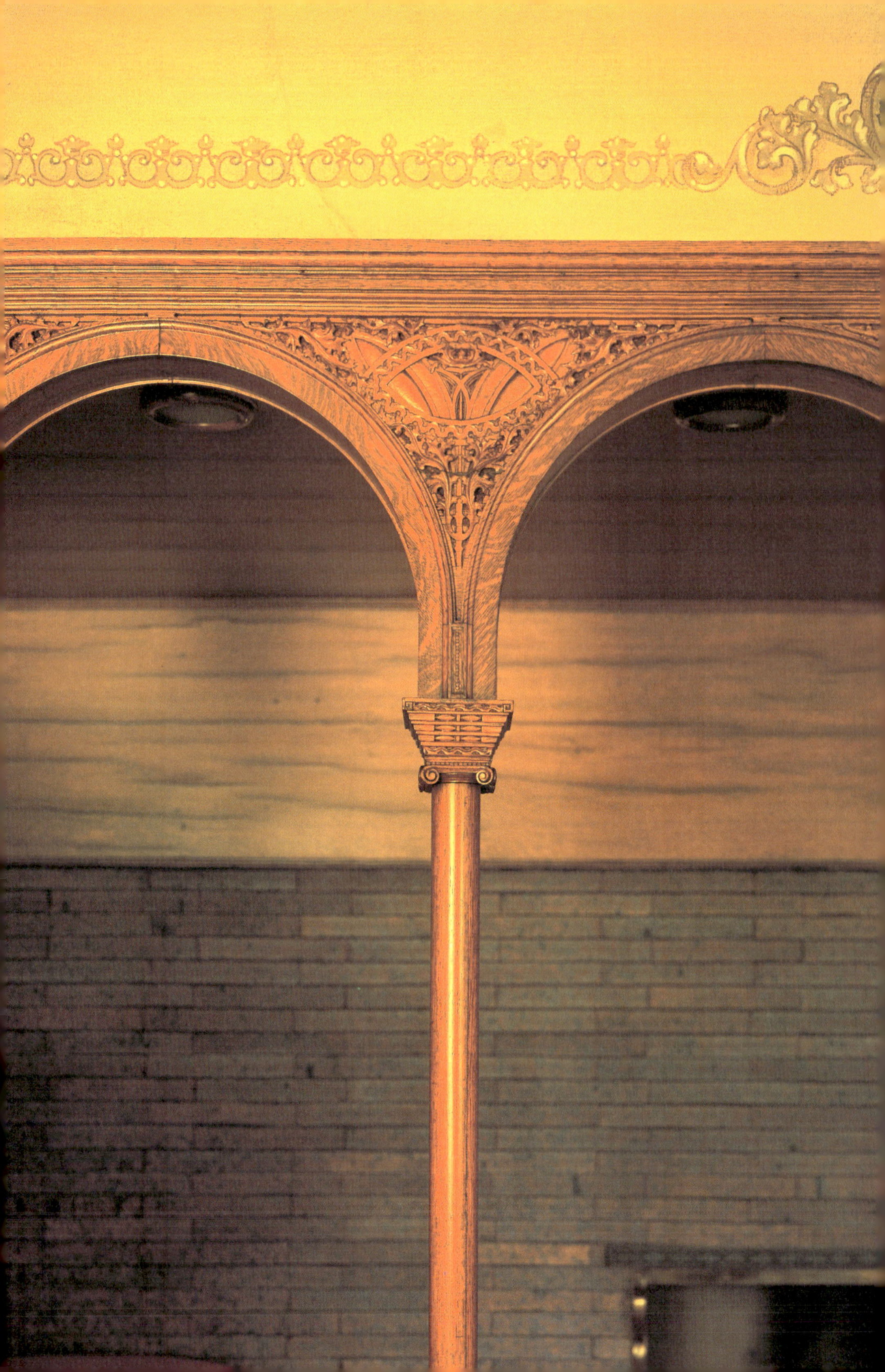

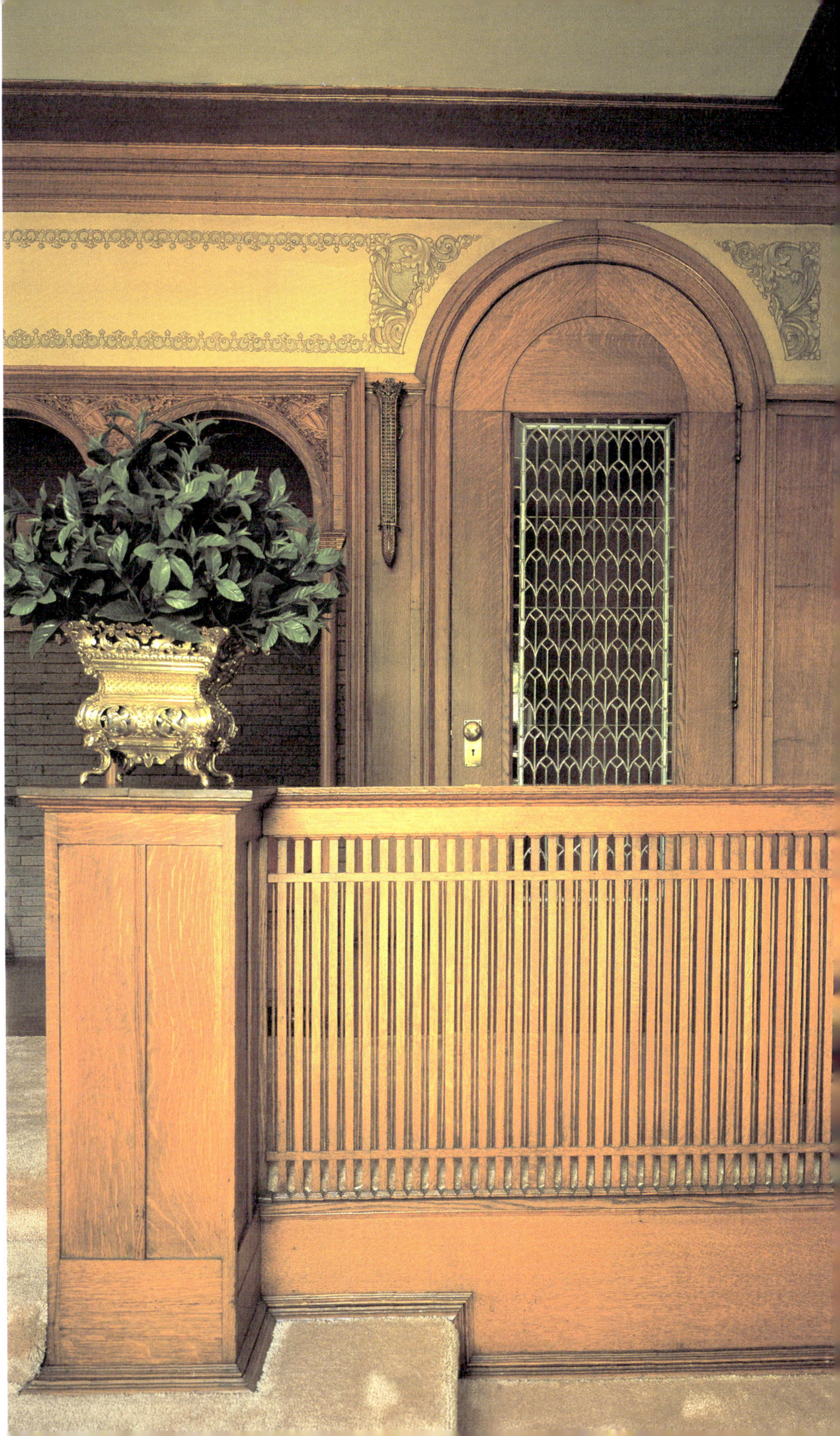

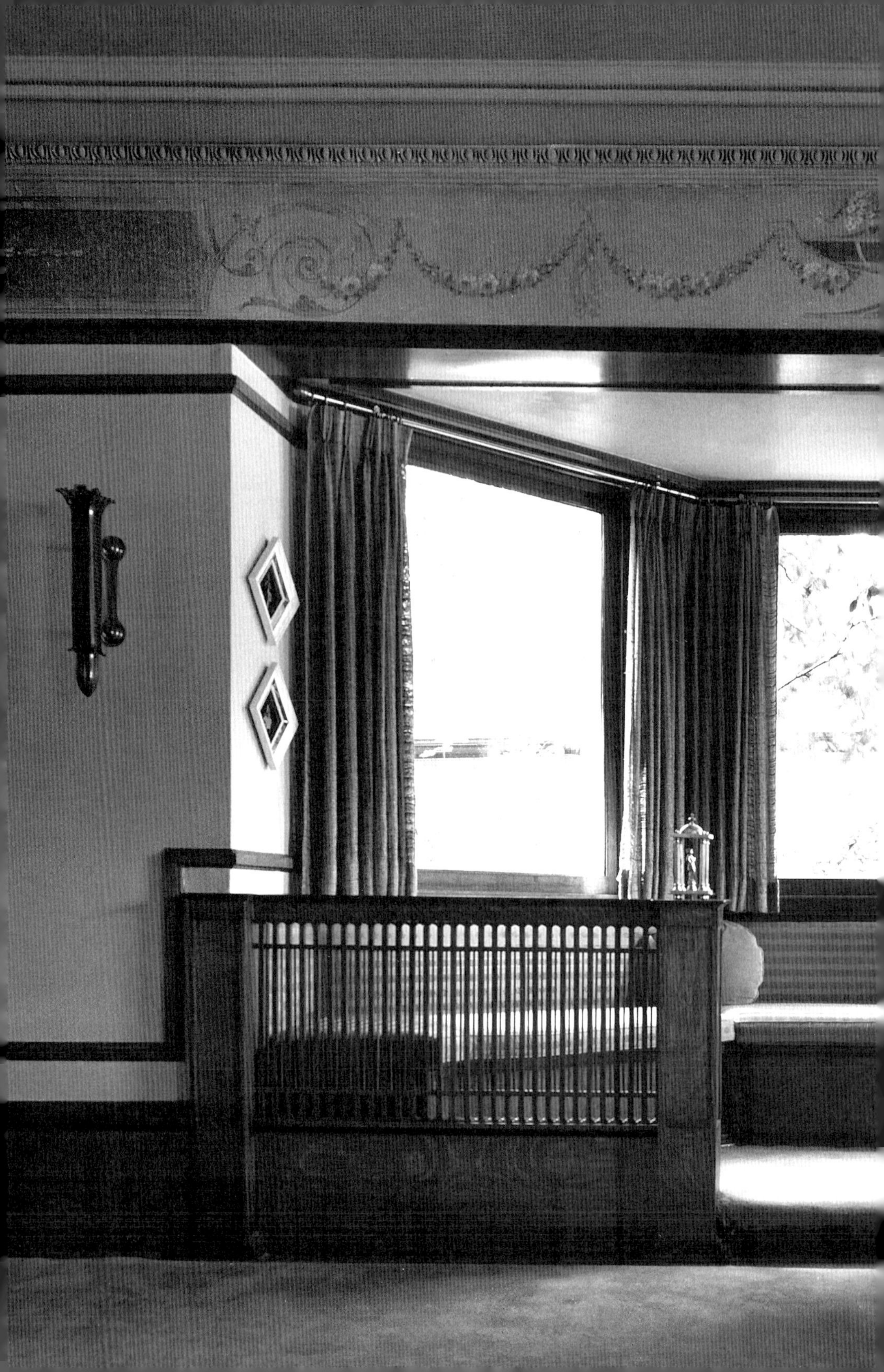

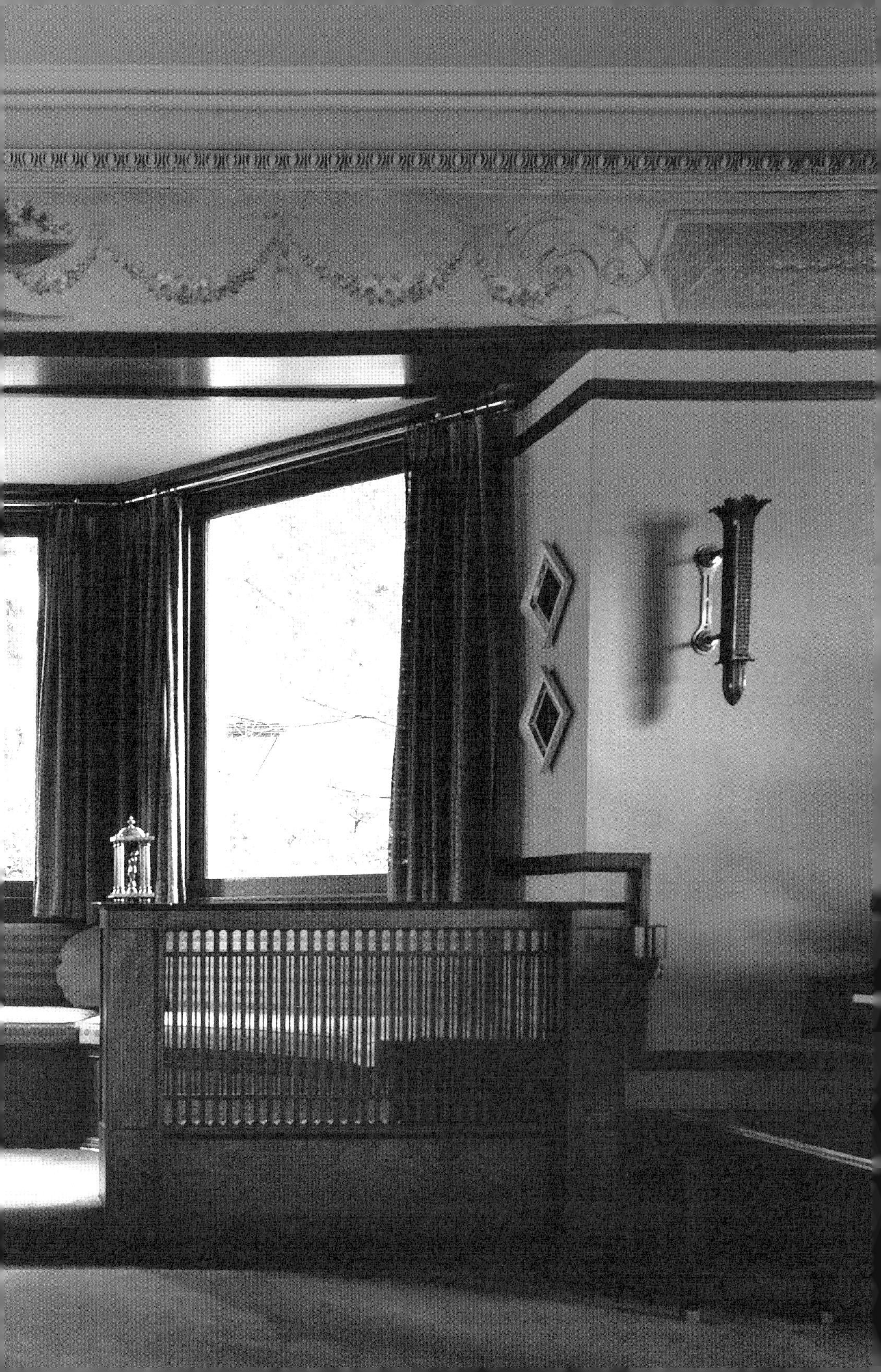

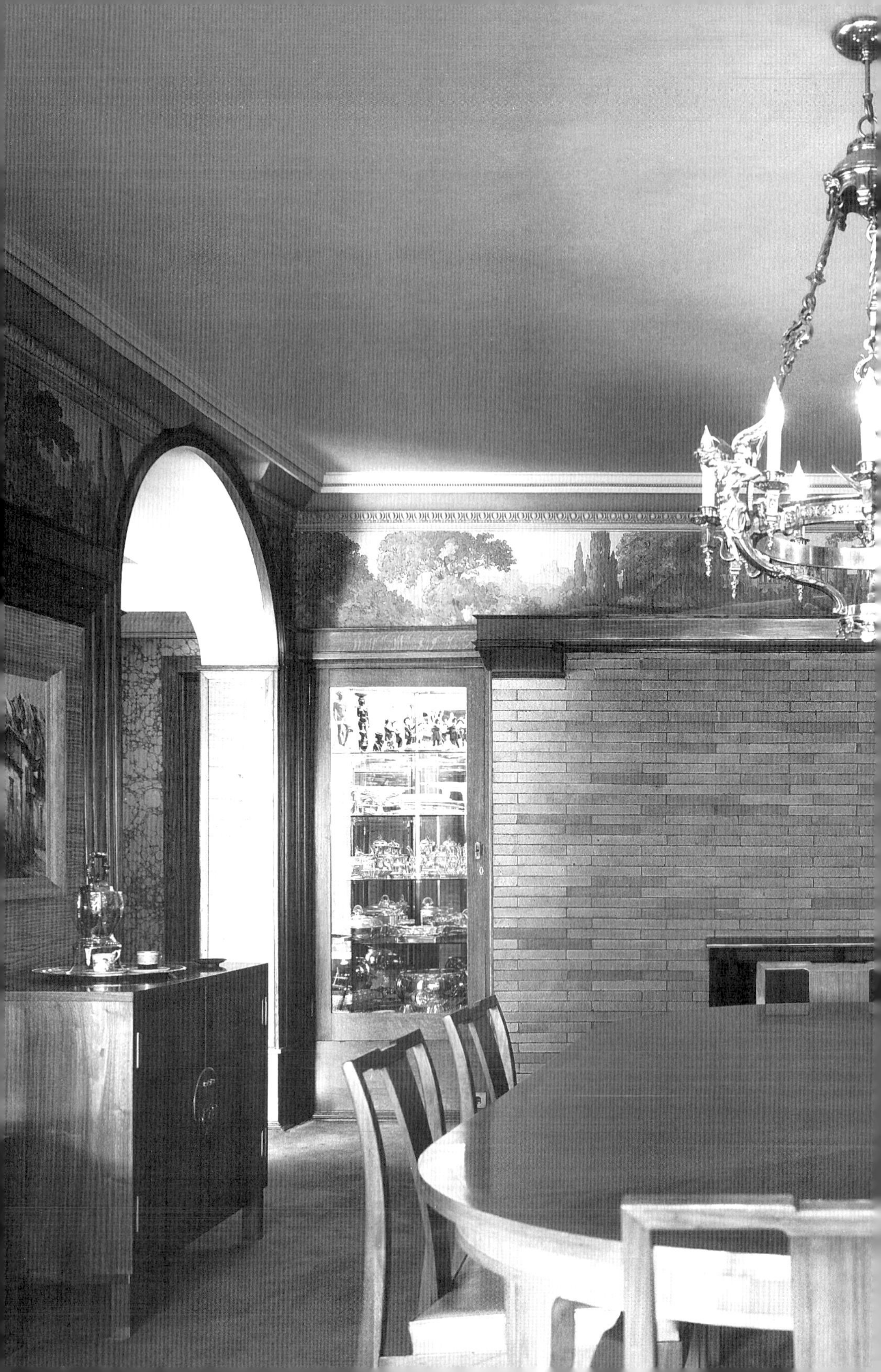

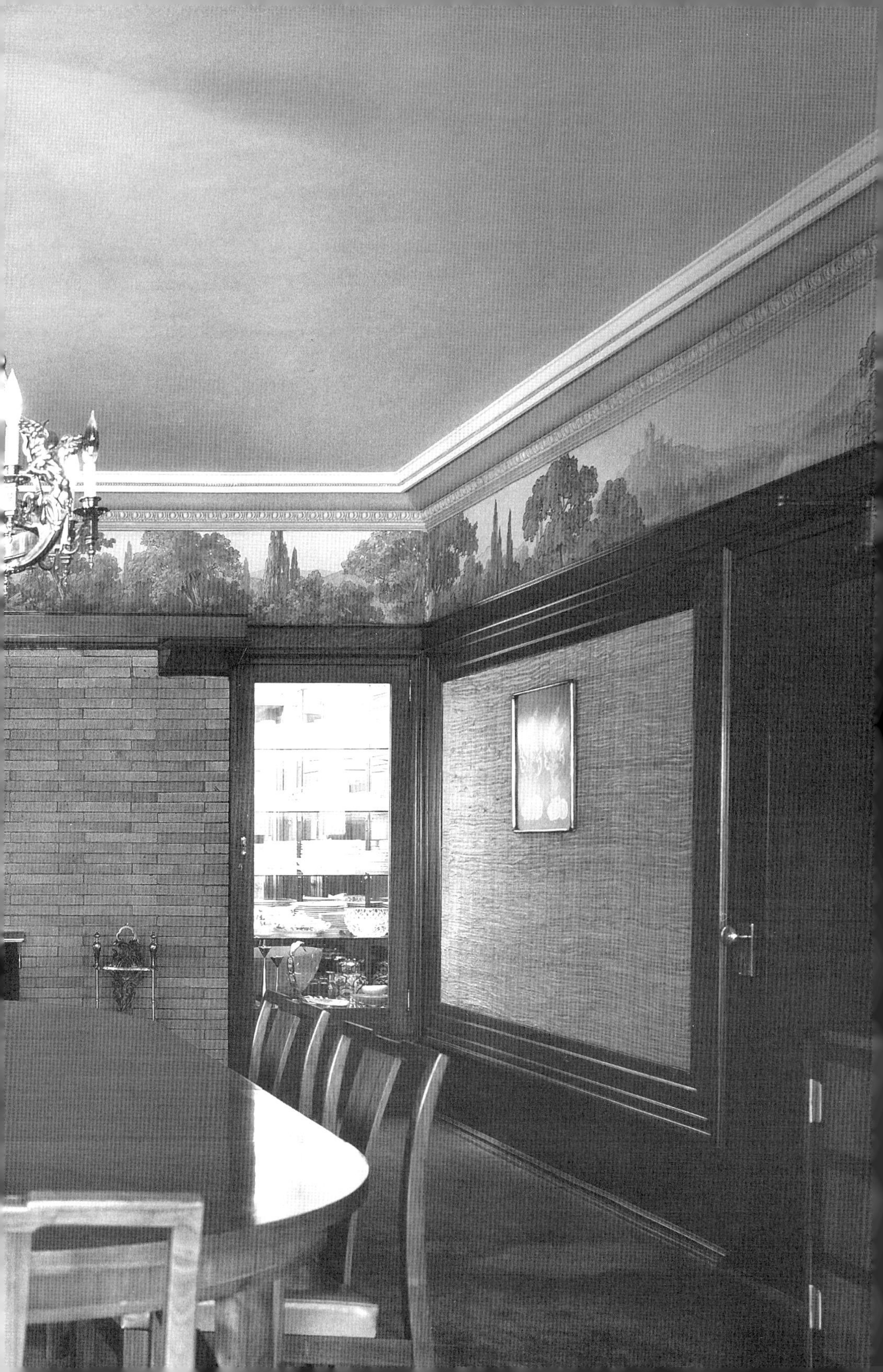

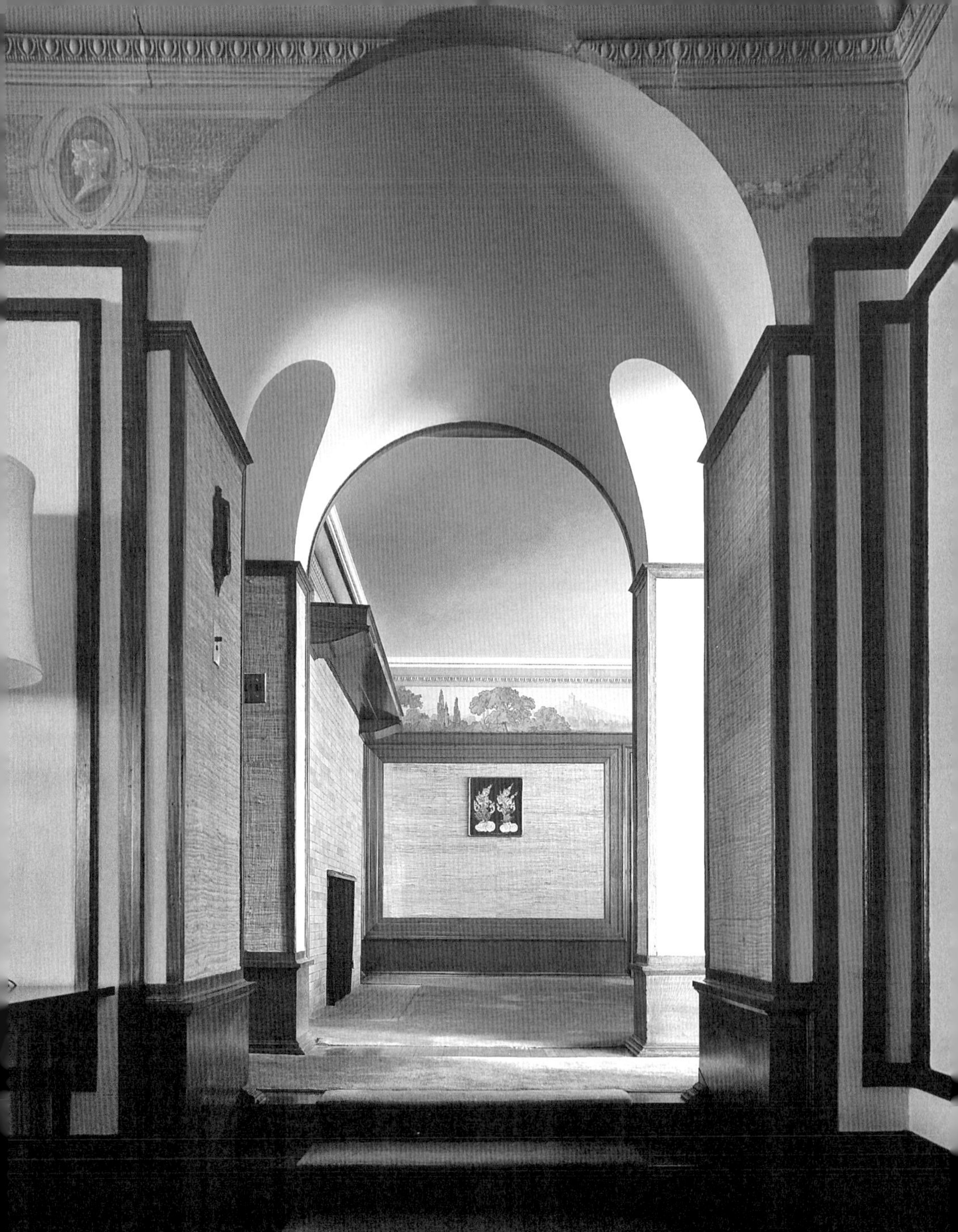

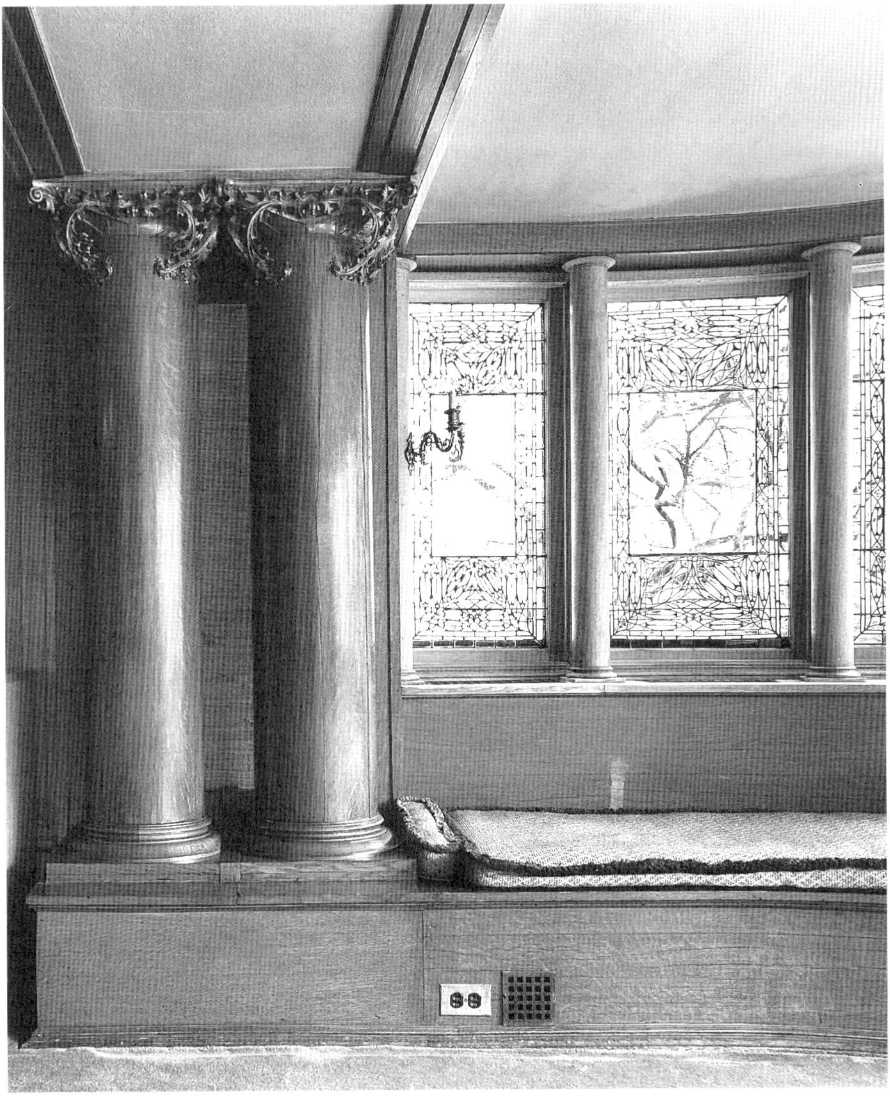

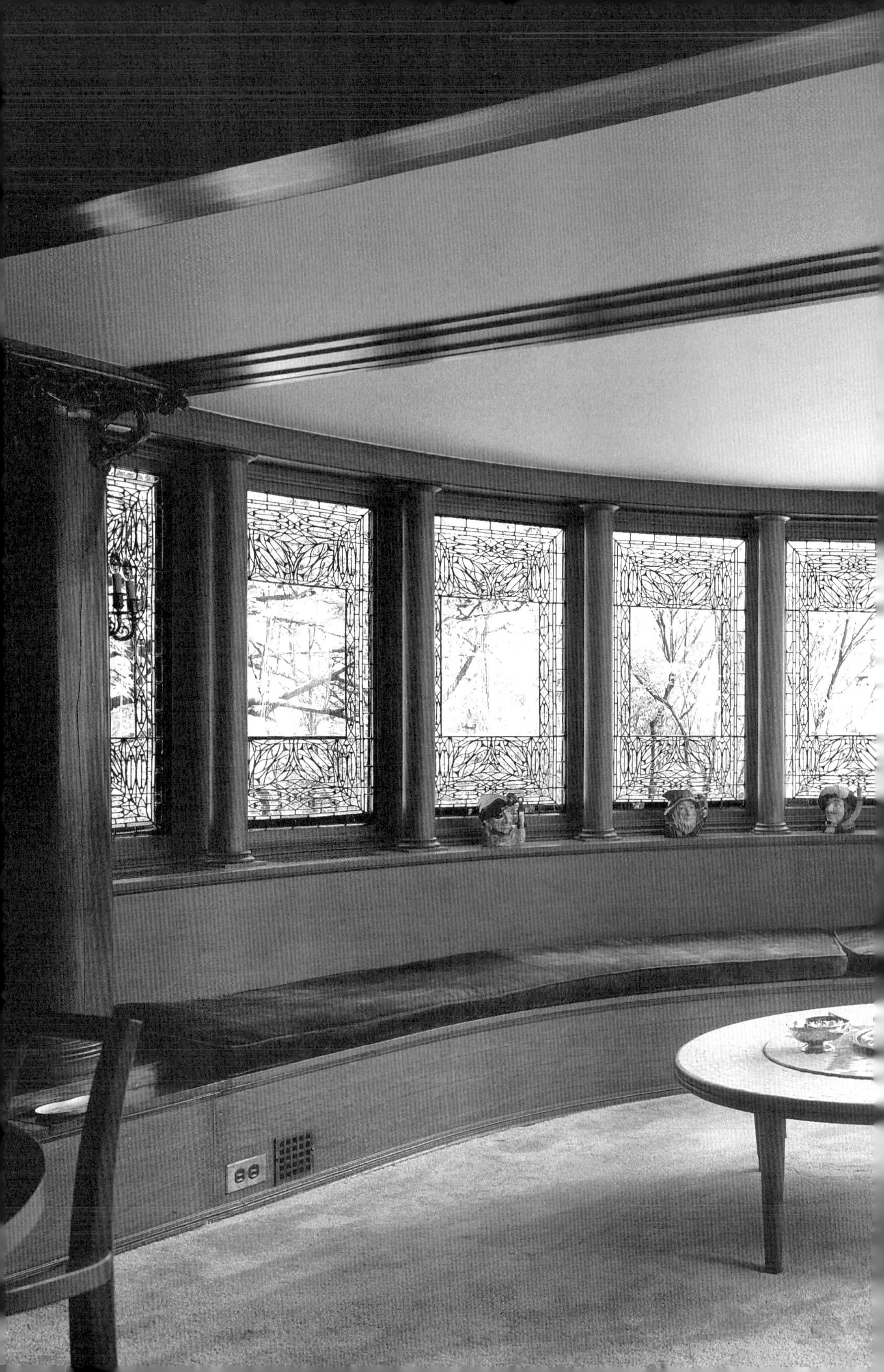

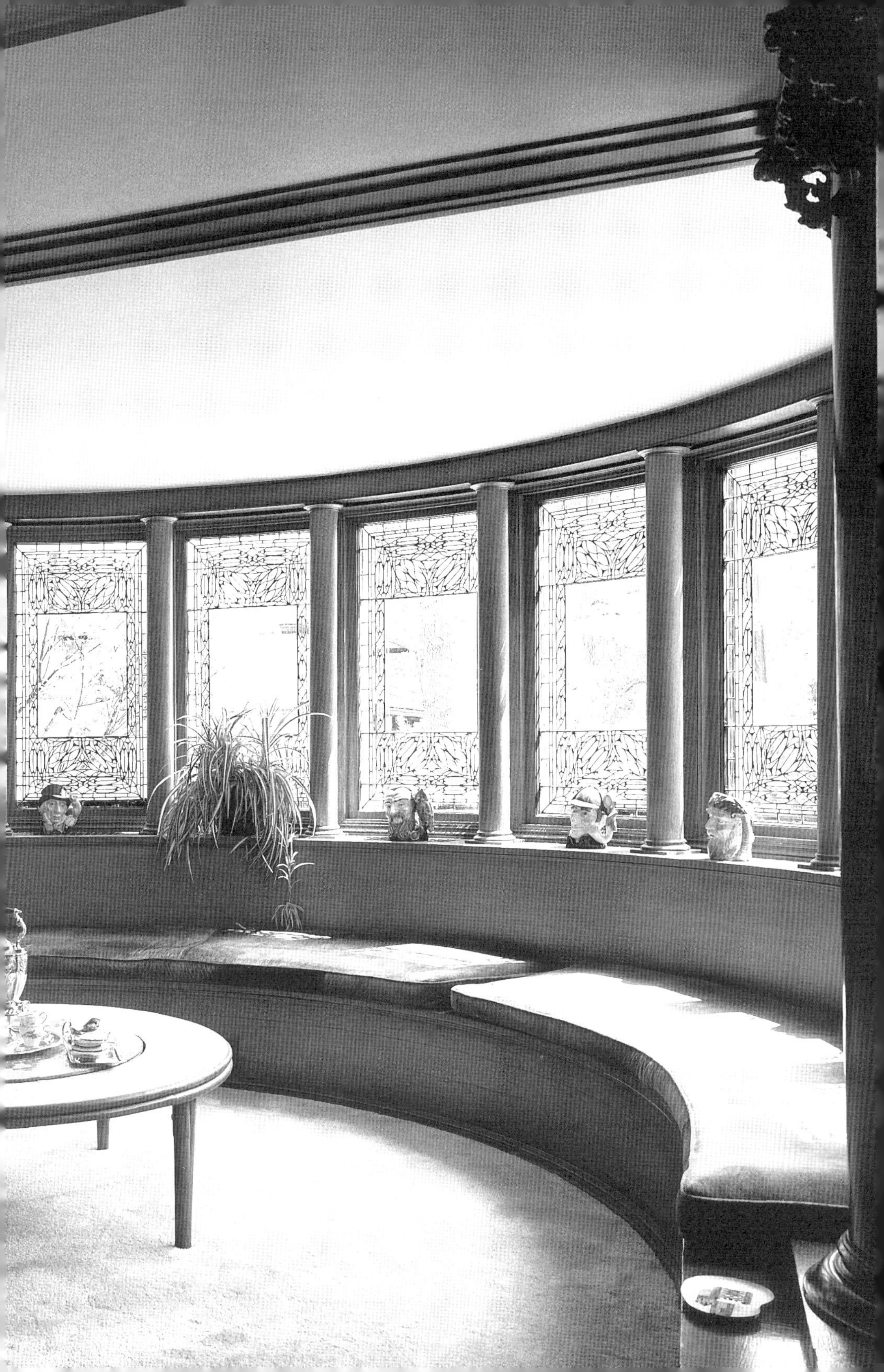

Ward W. Willits House
Highland Park, Illinois, 1902

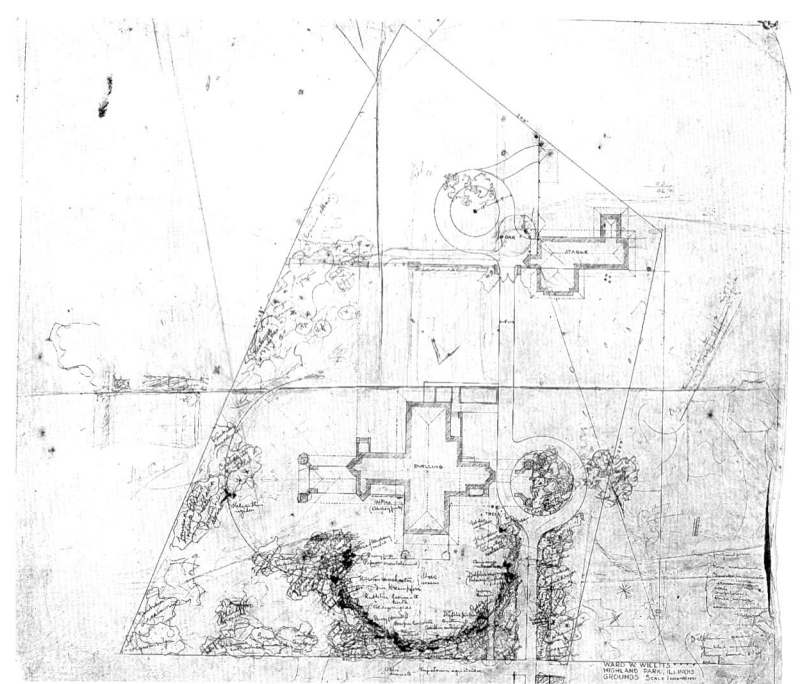

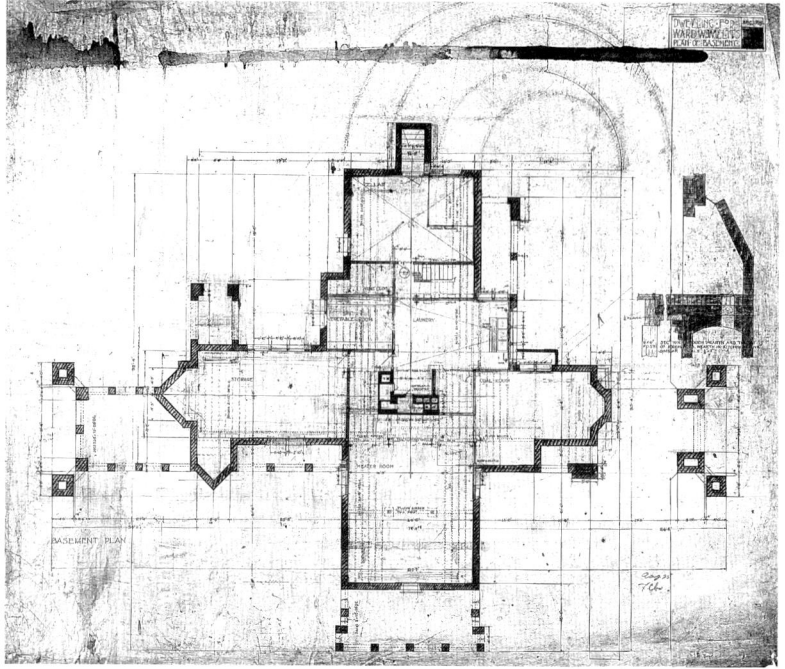

Site plan

Basement

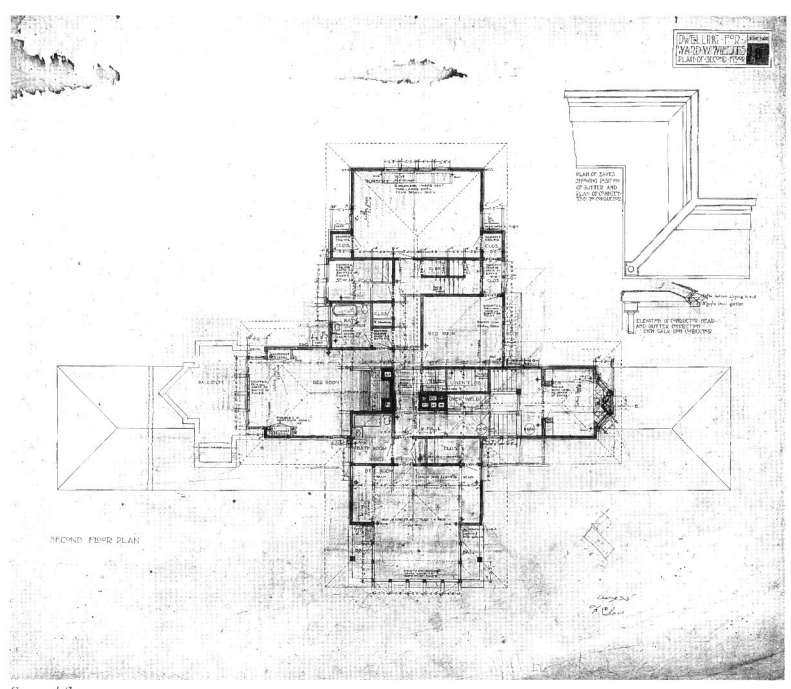

Second floor

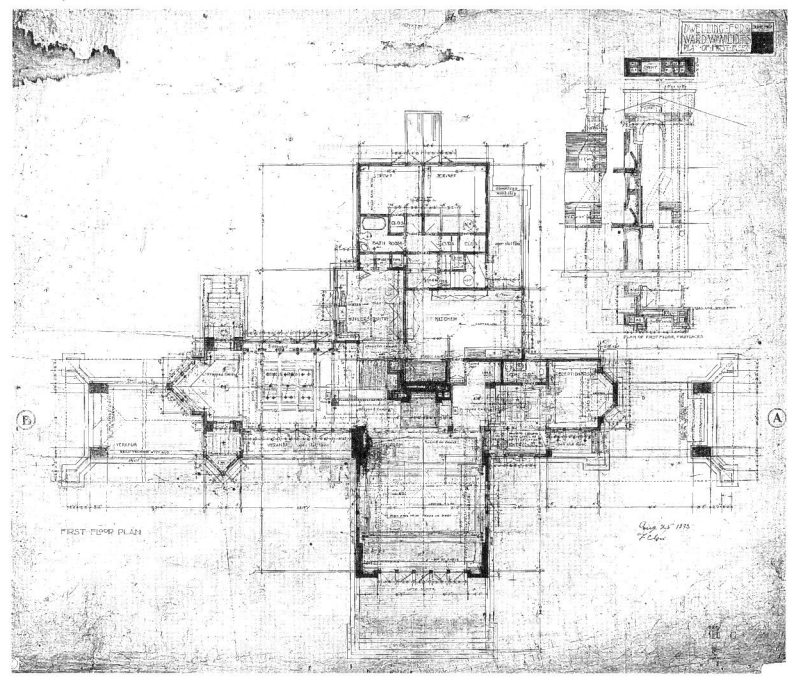

First floor

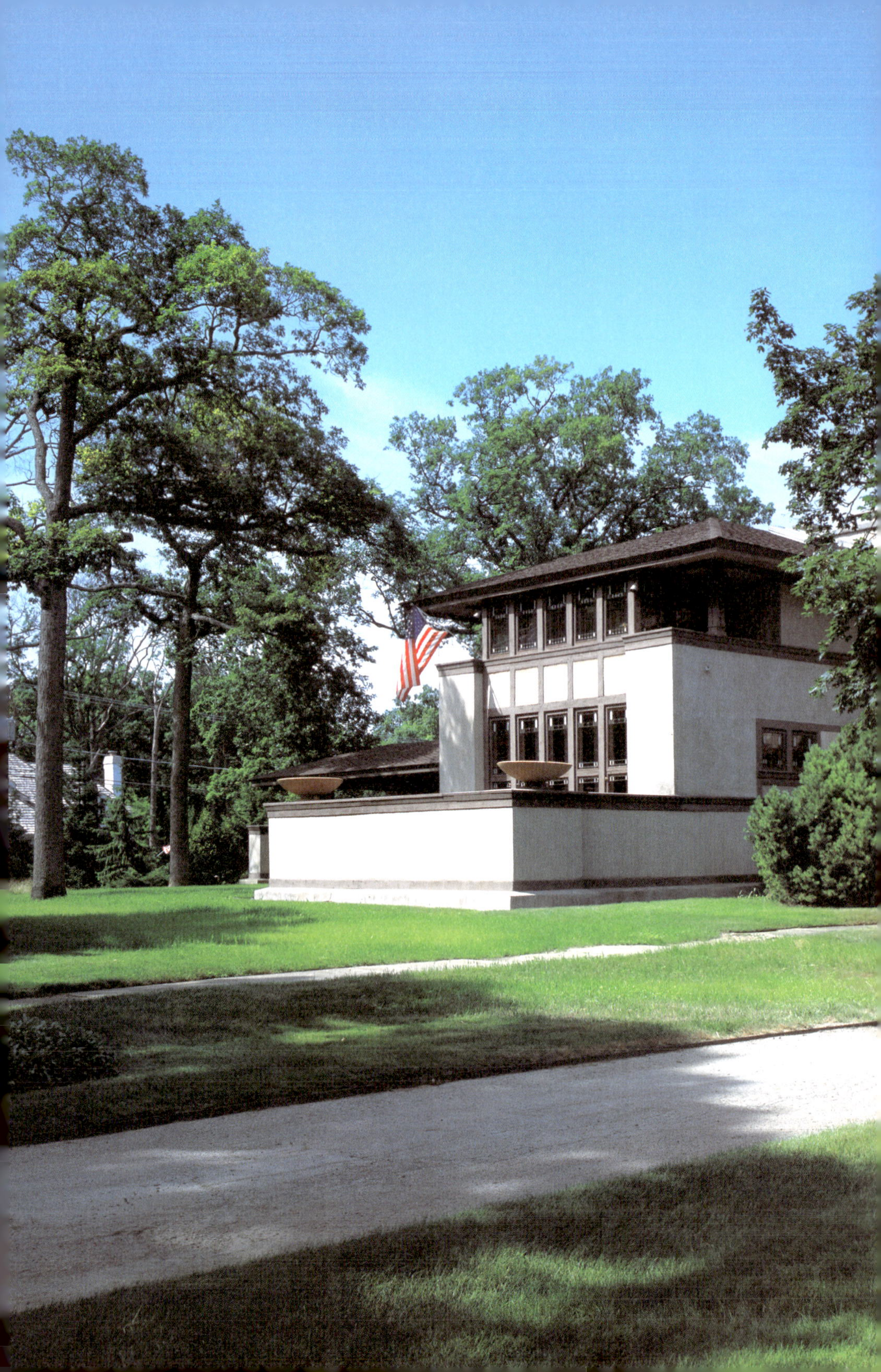

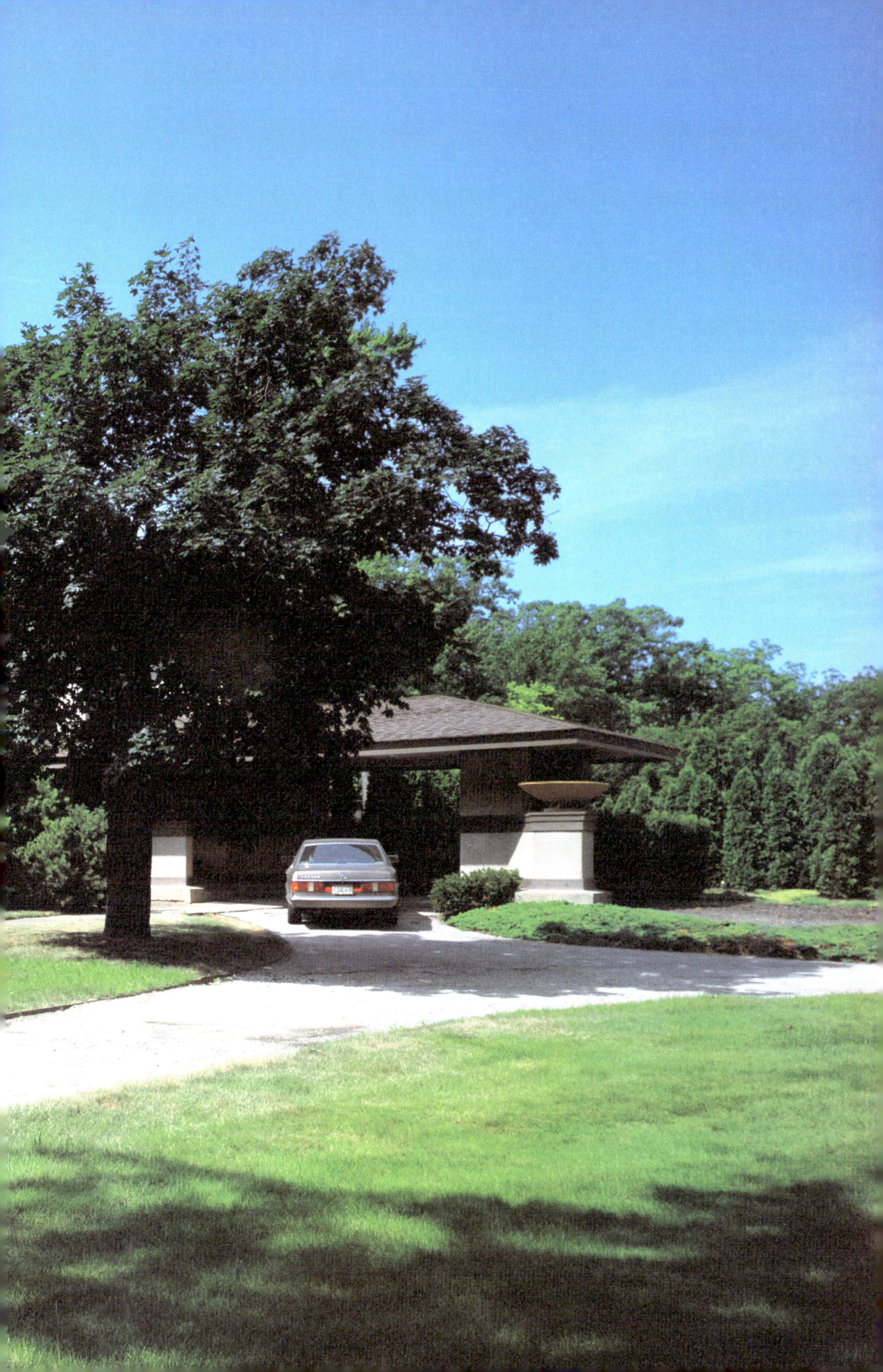

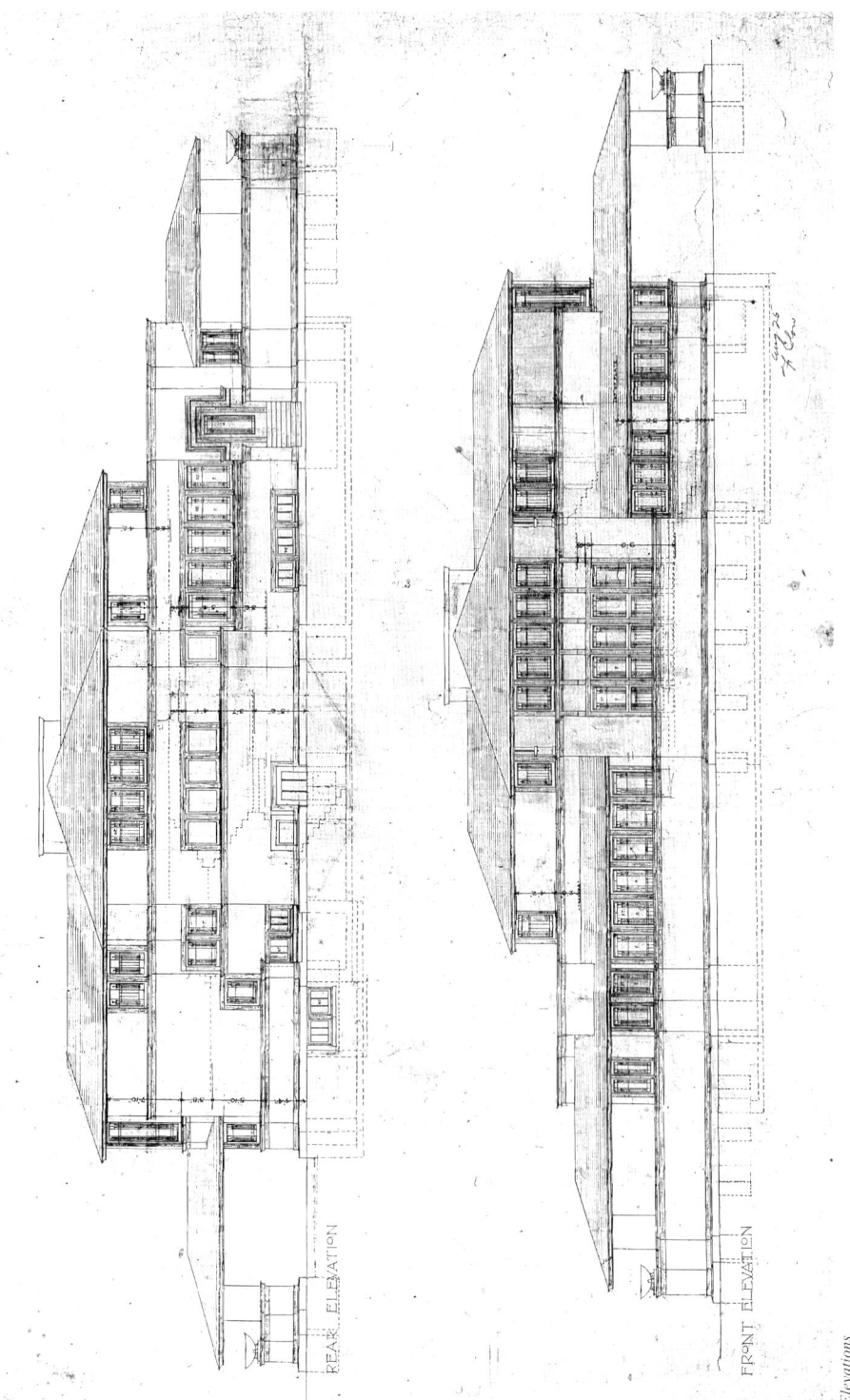

Elevations

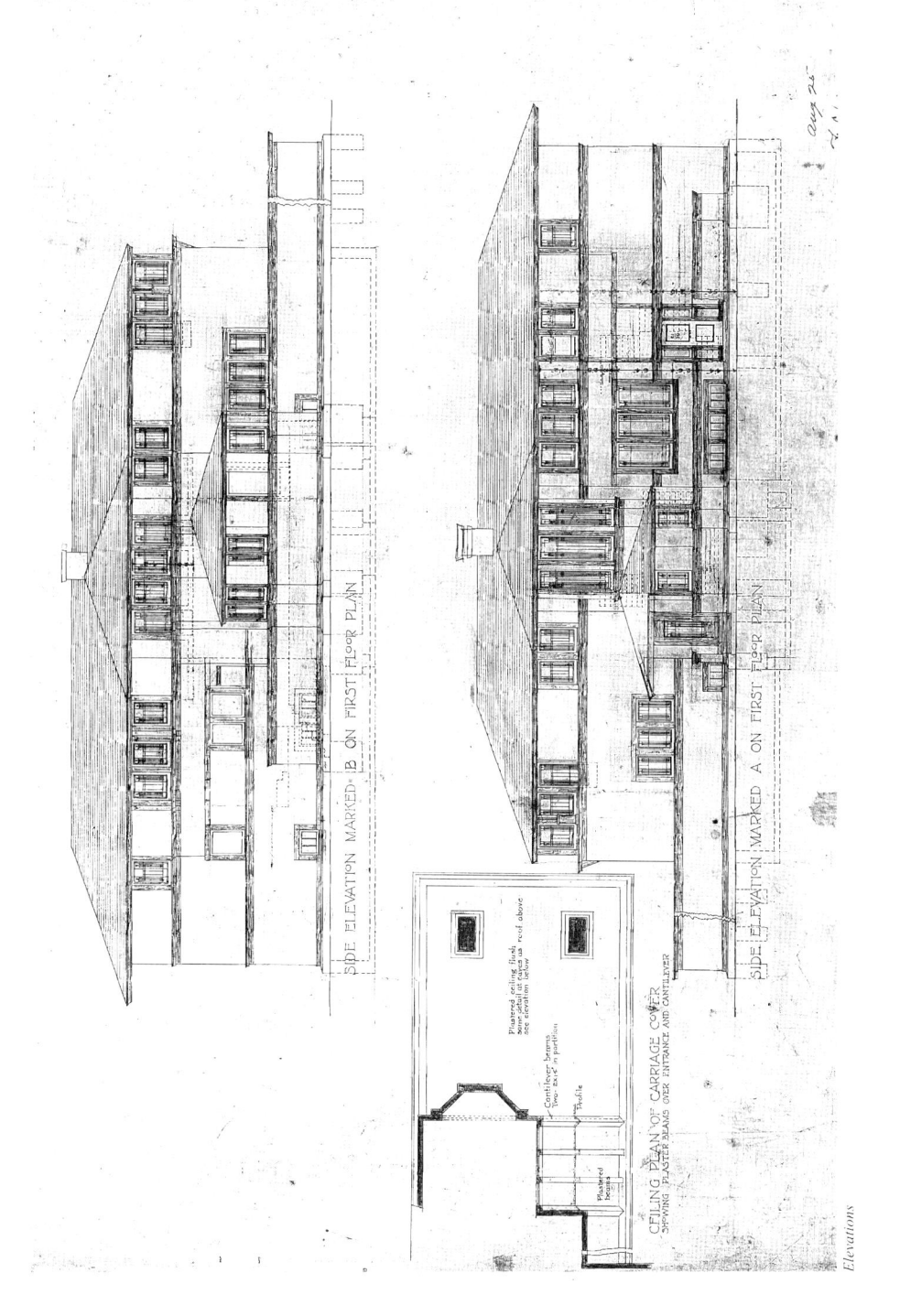

Elevations

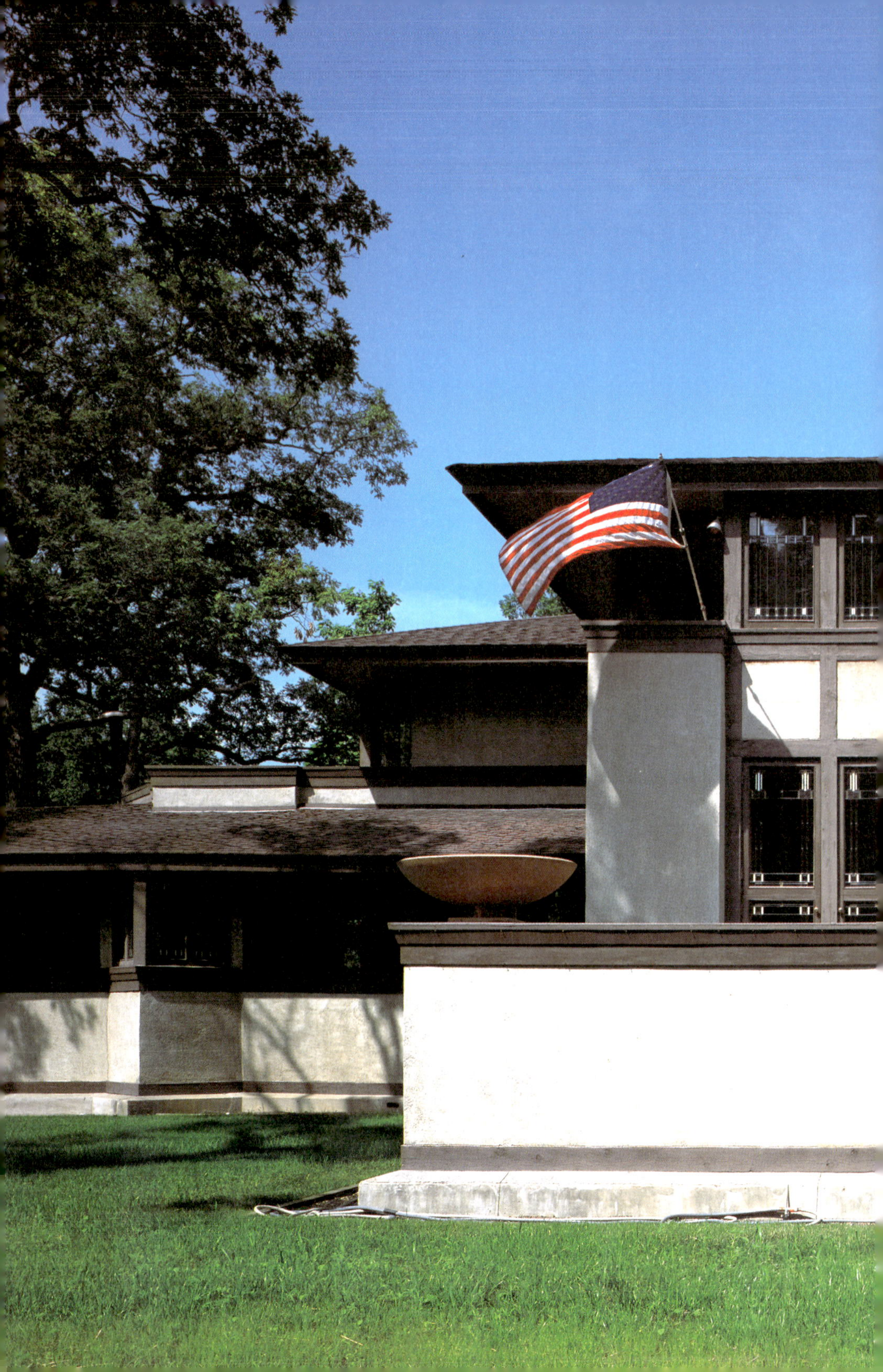

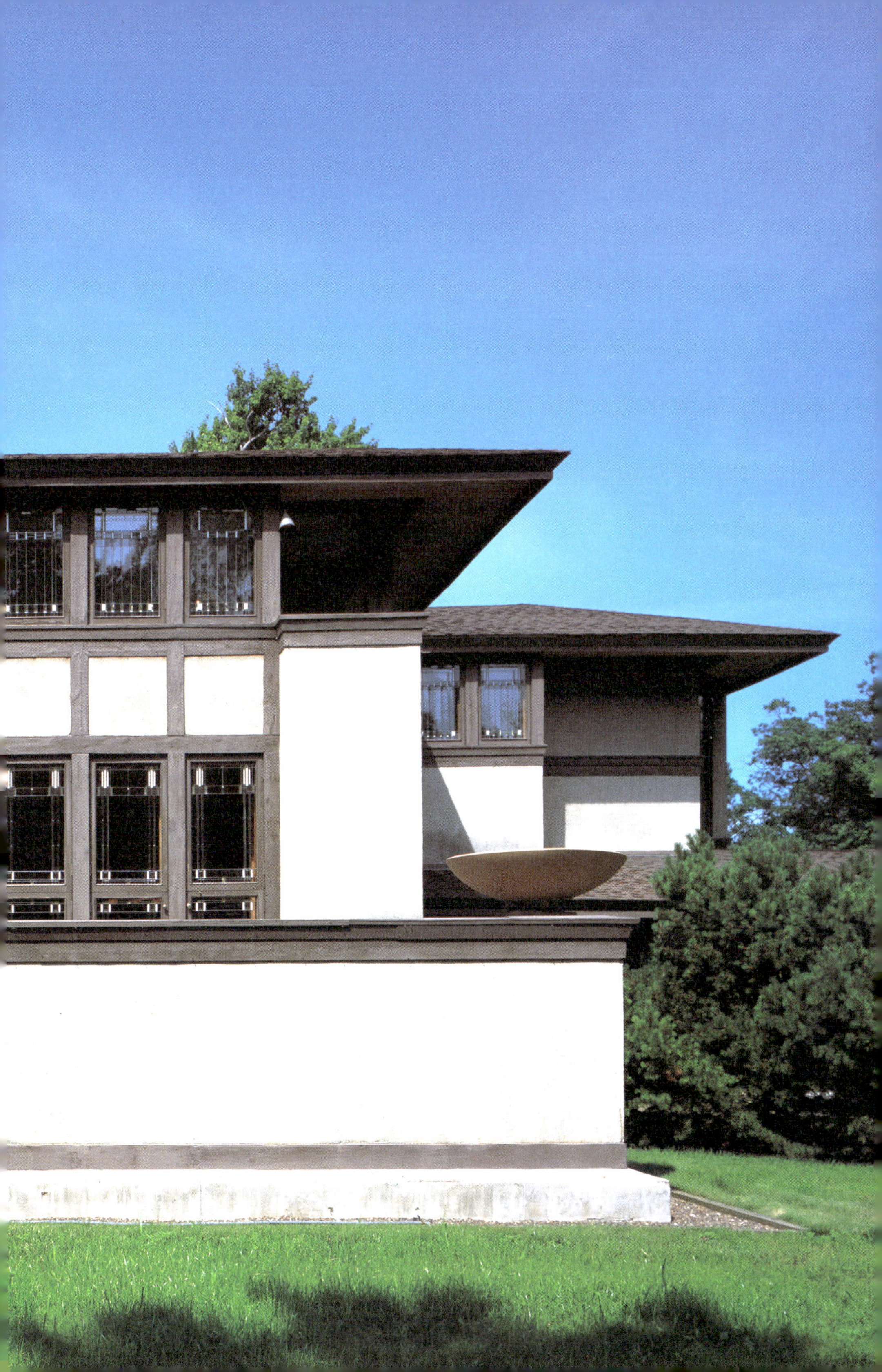

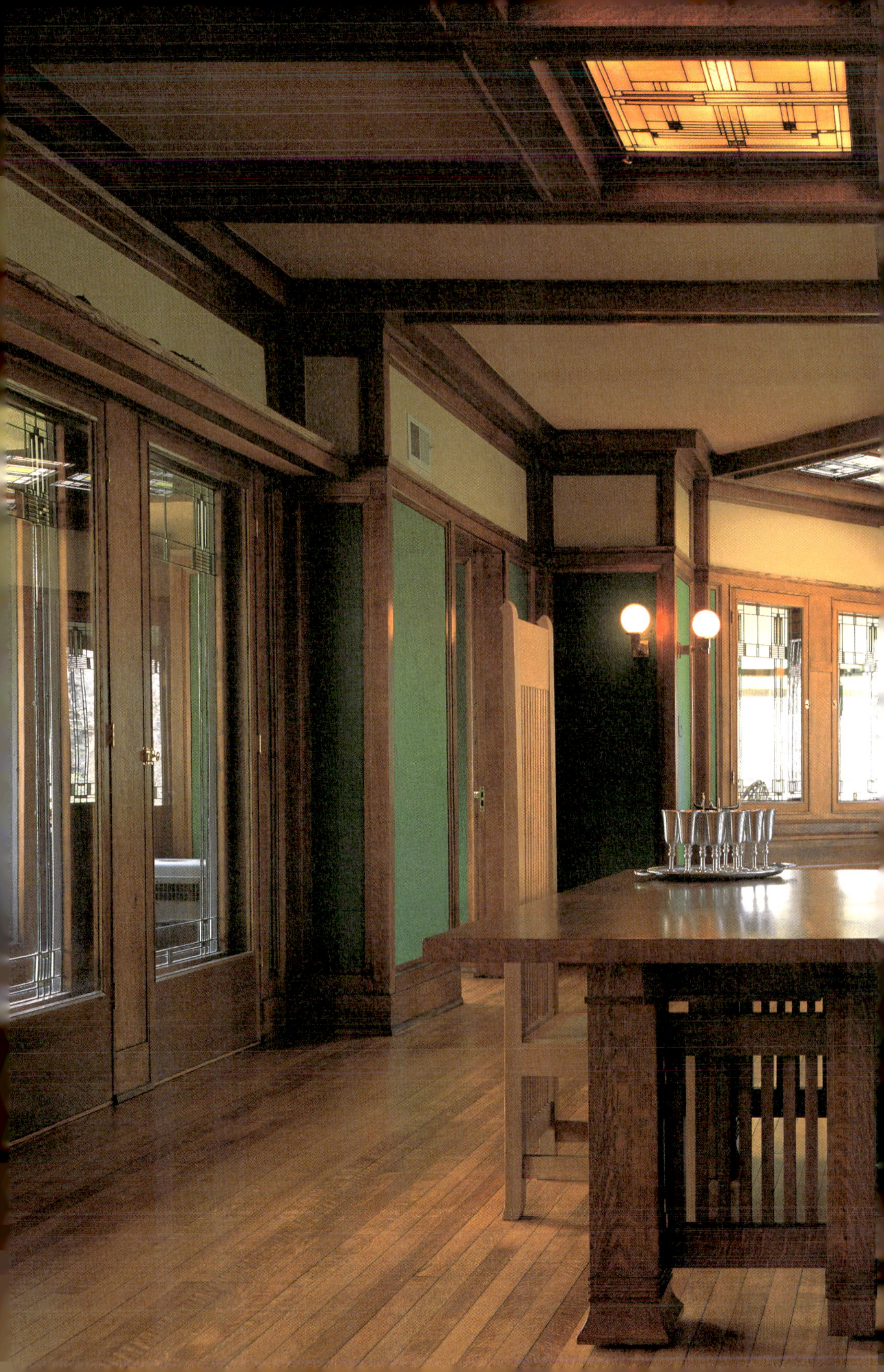

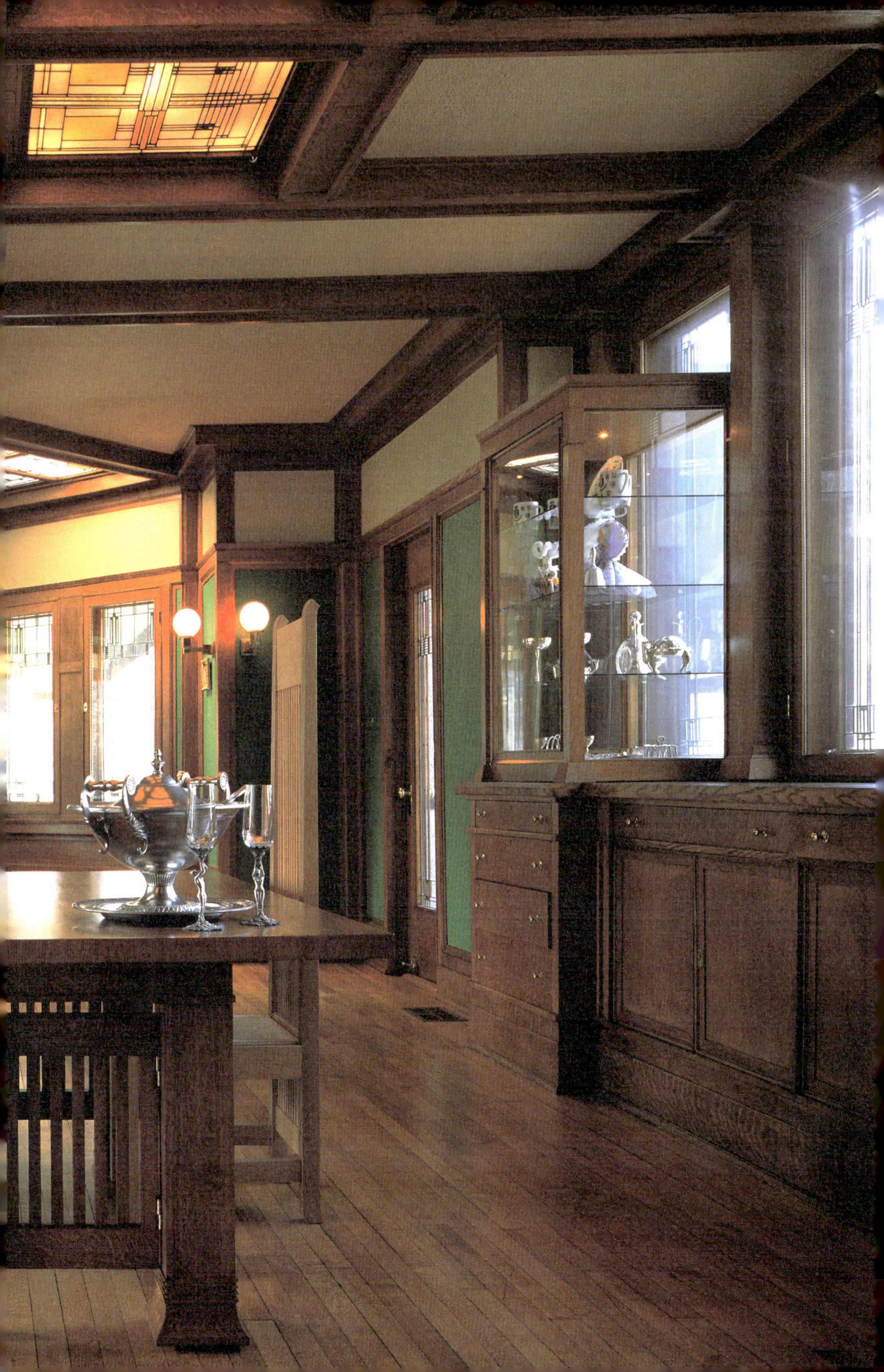

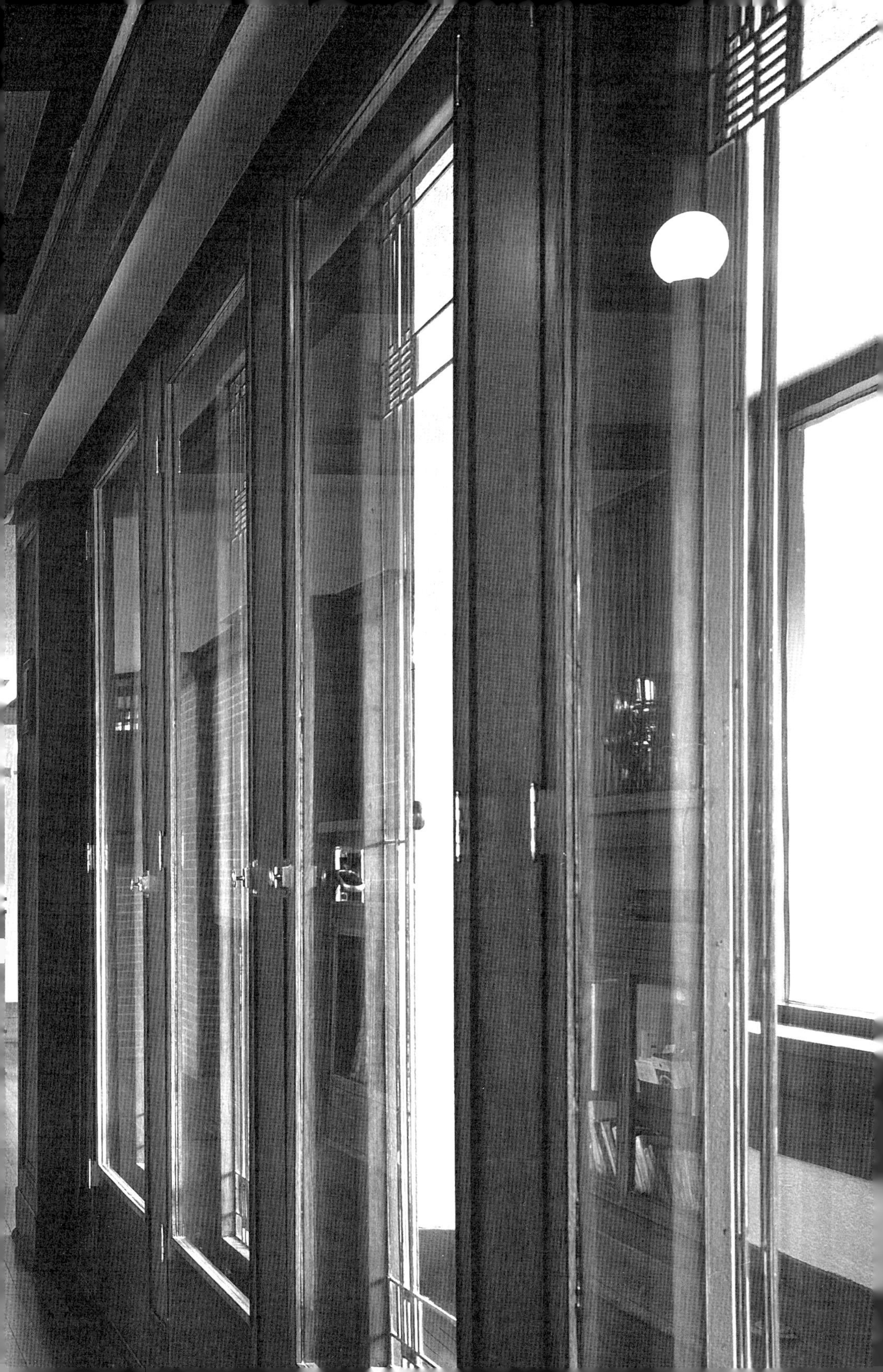

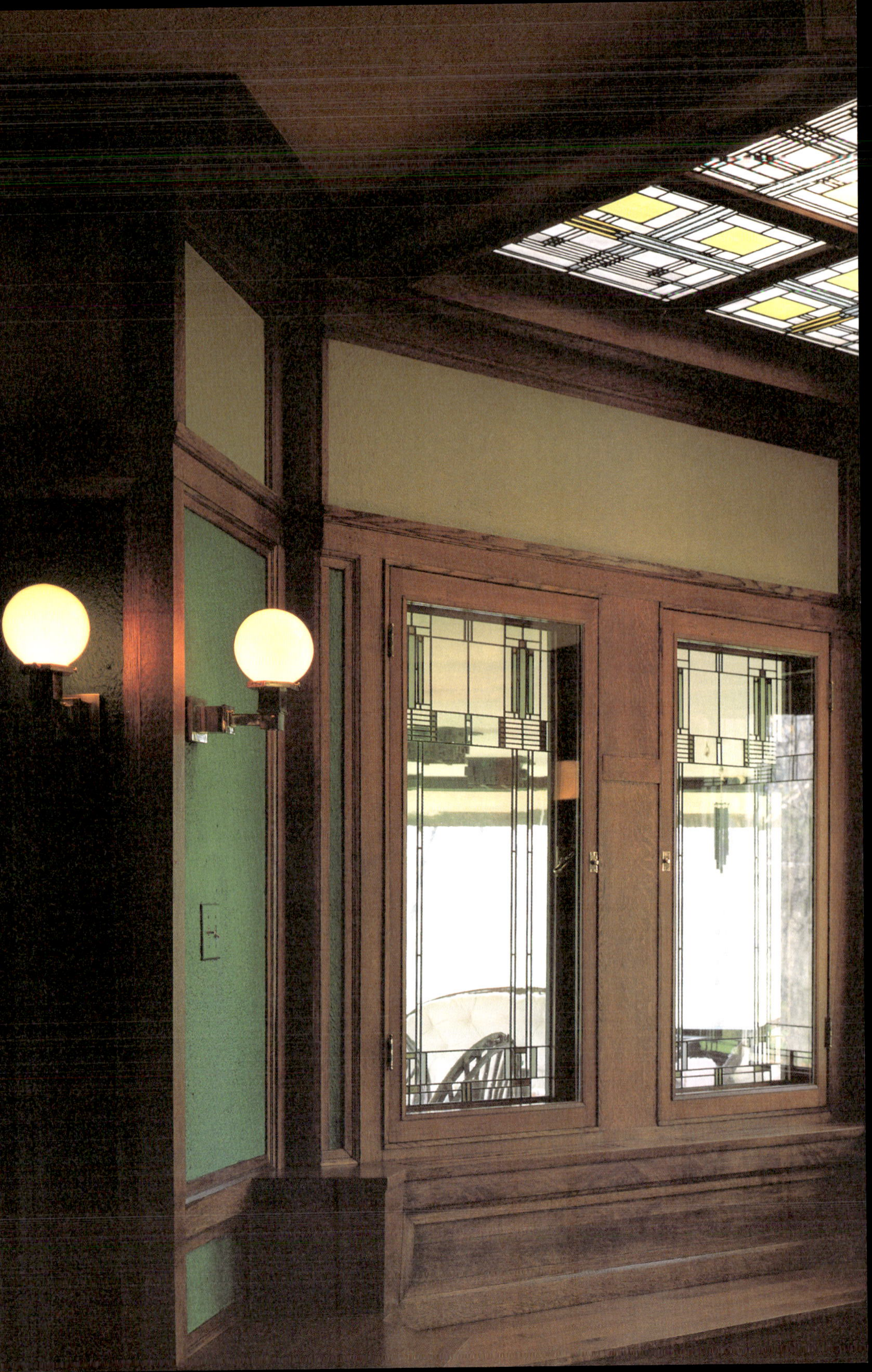

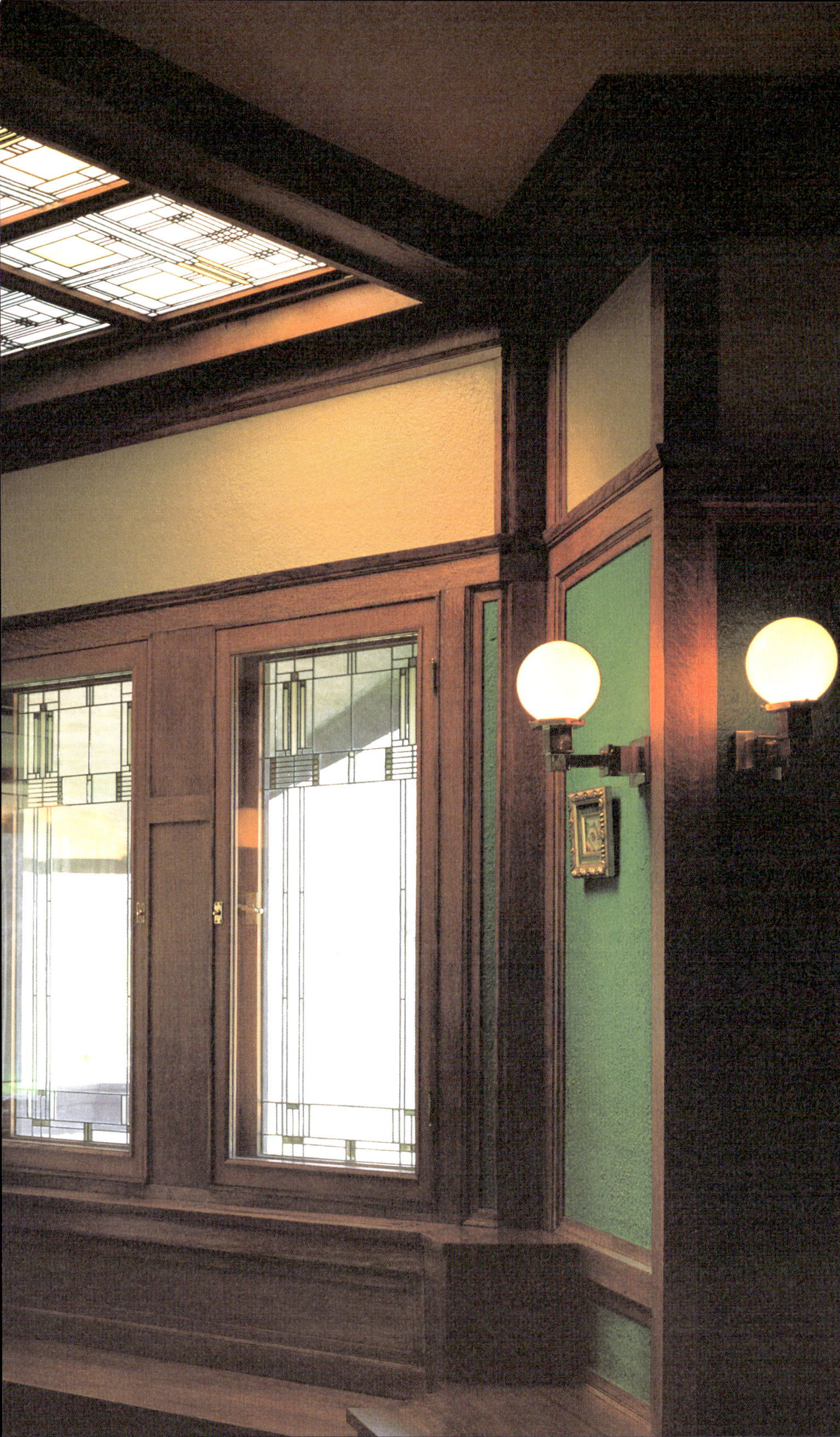

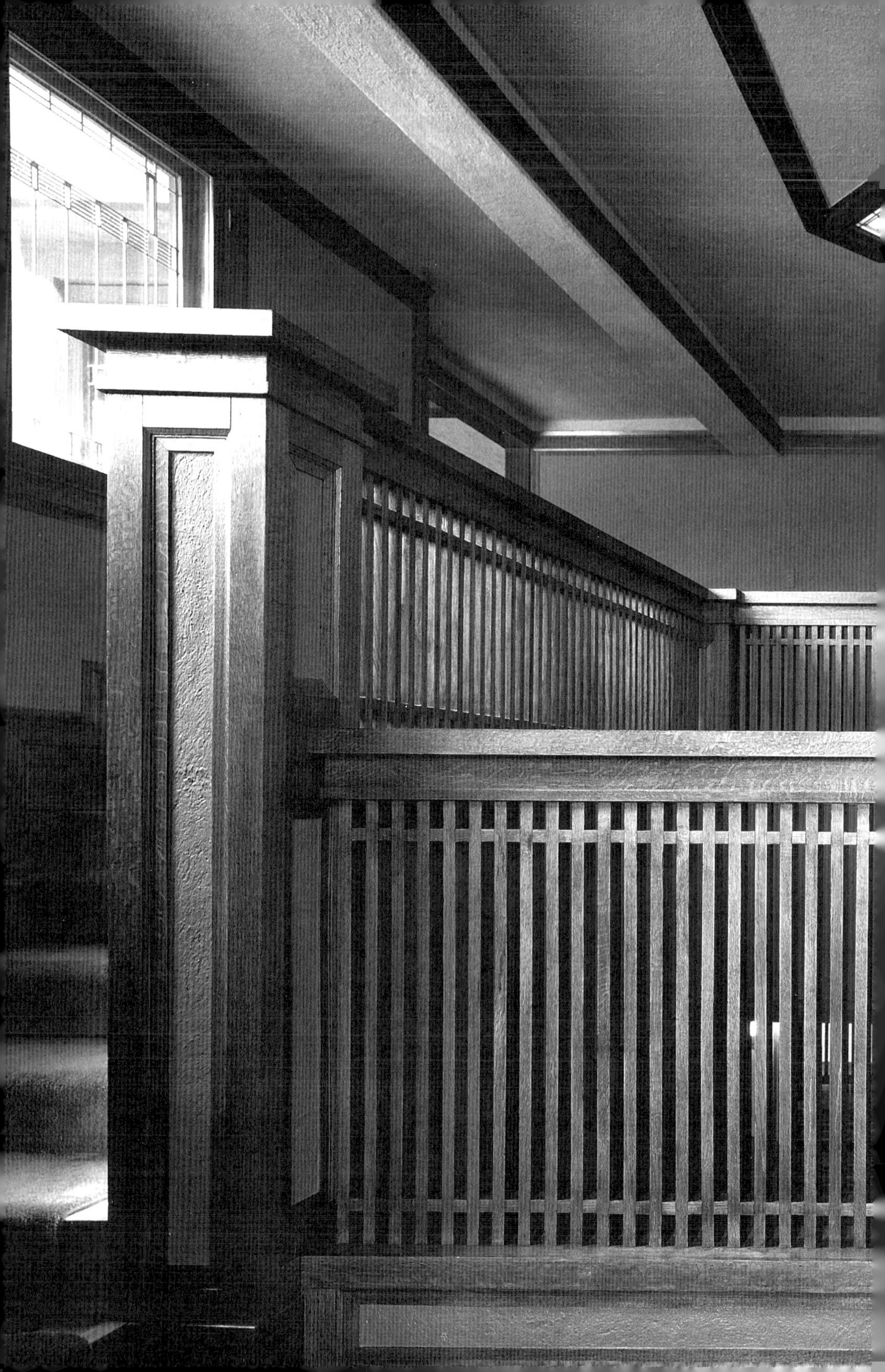

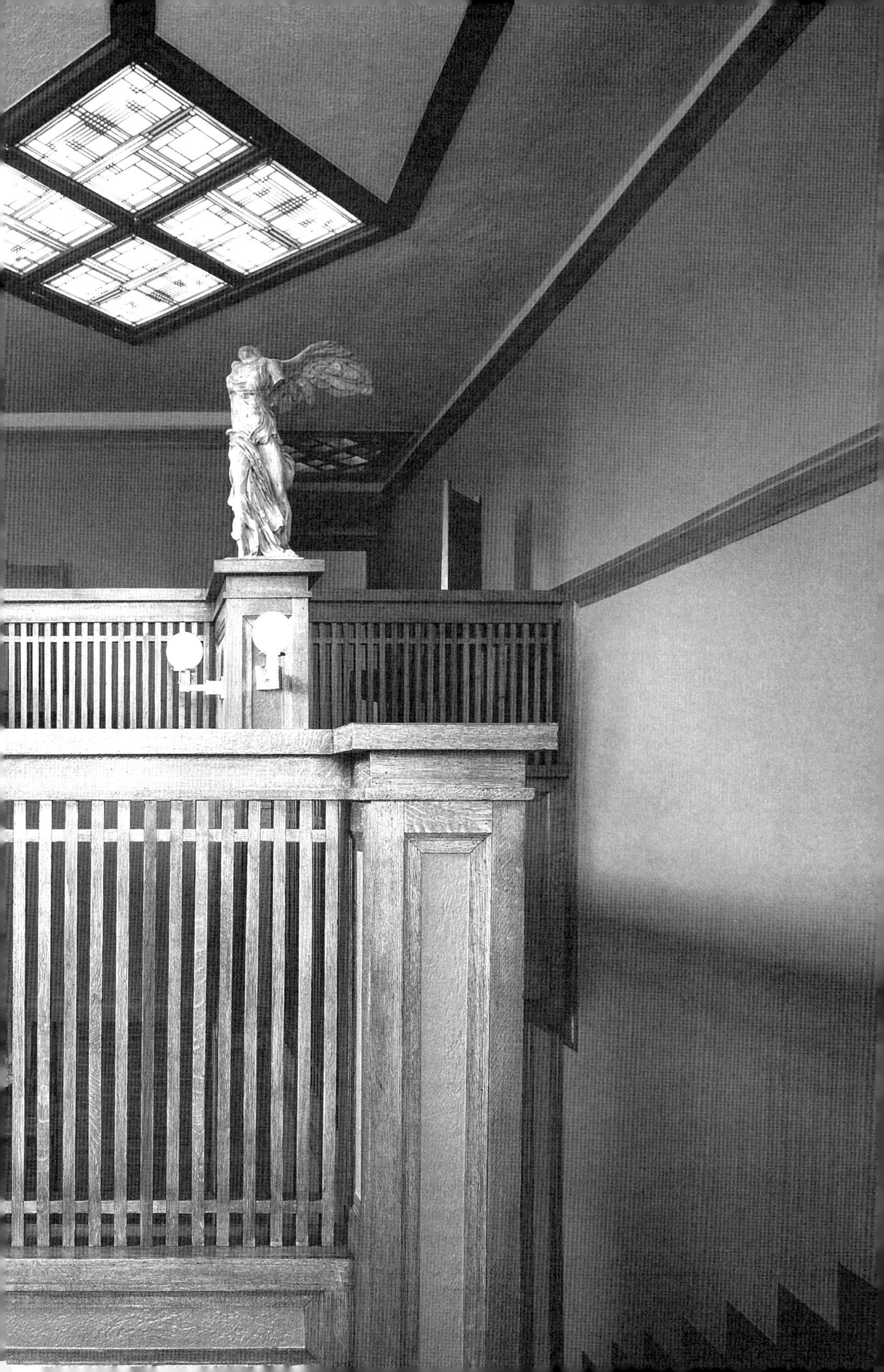

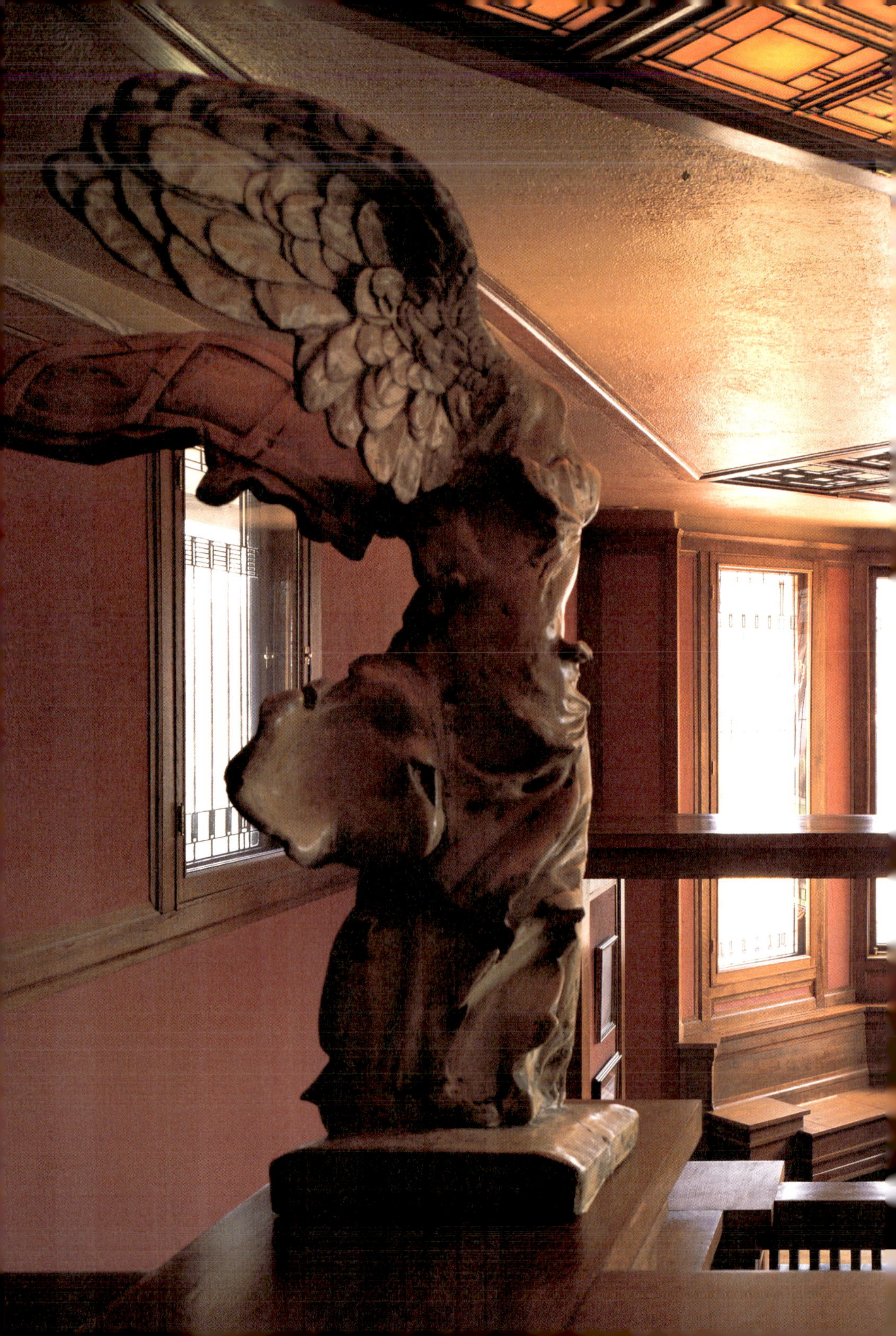

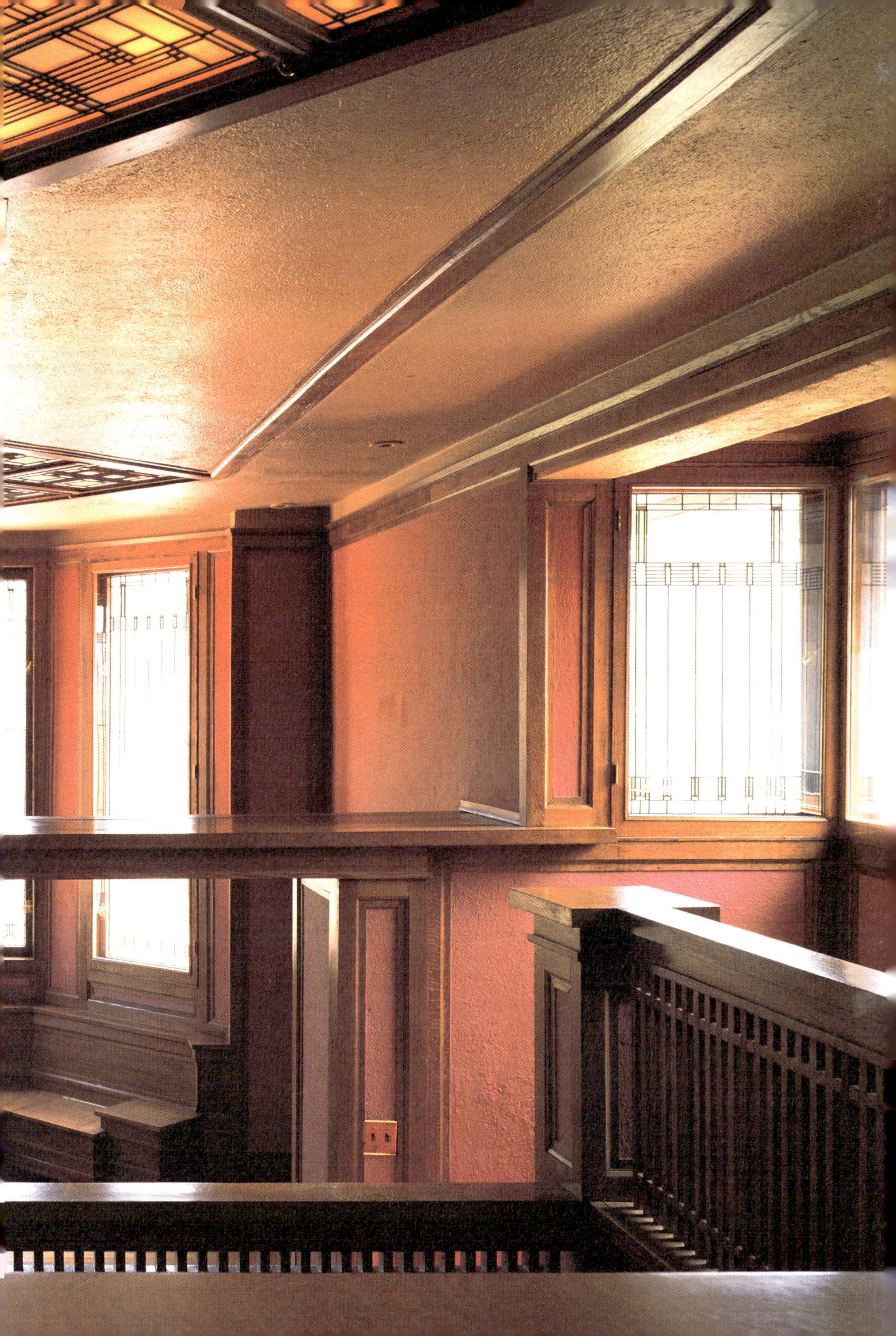

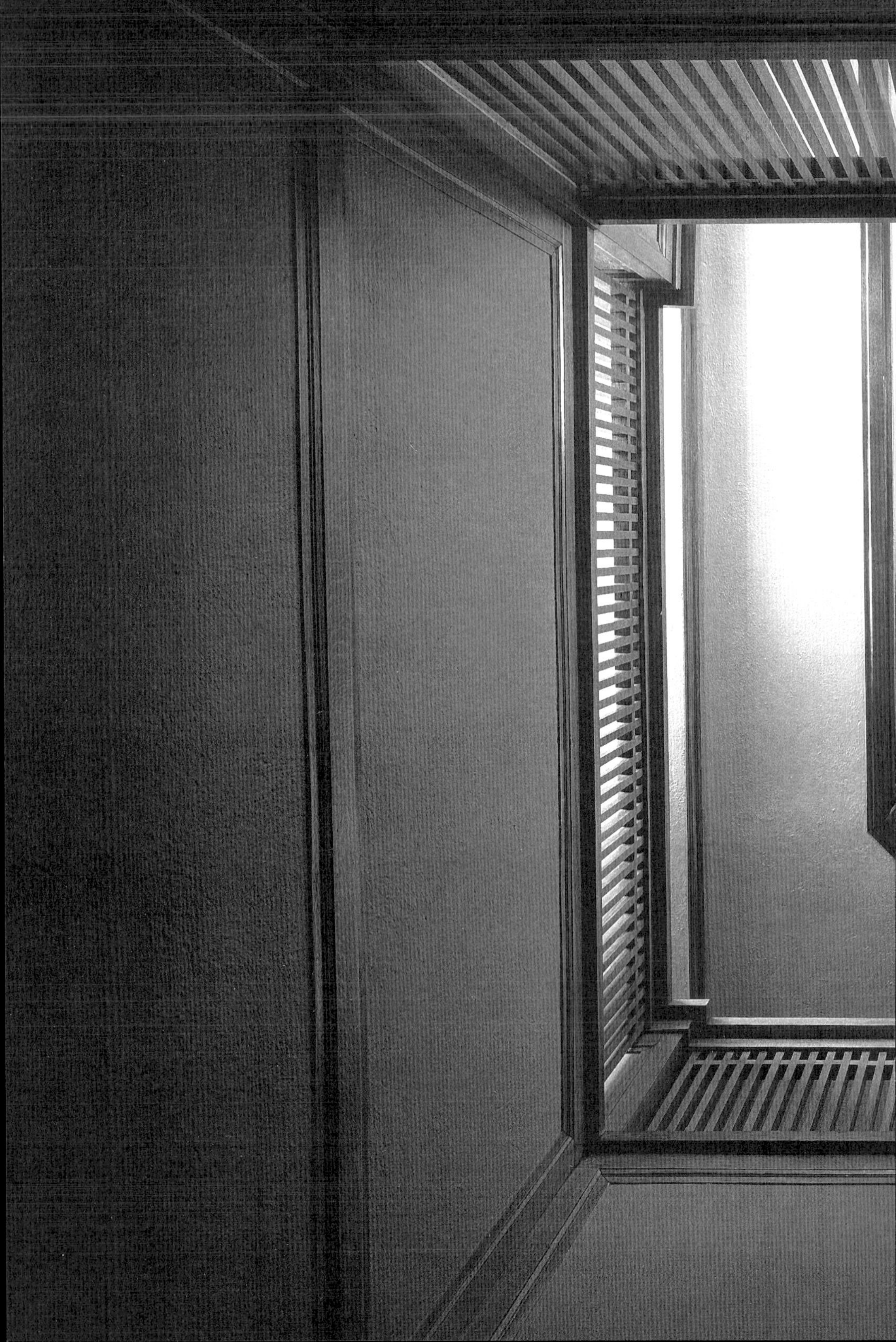

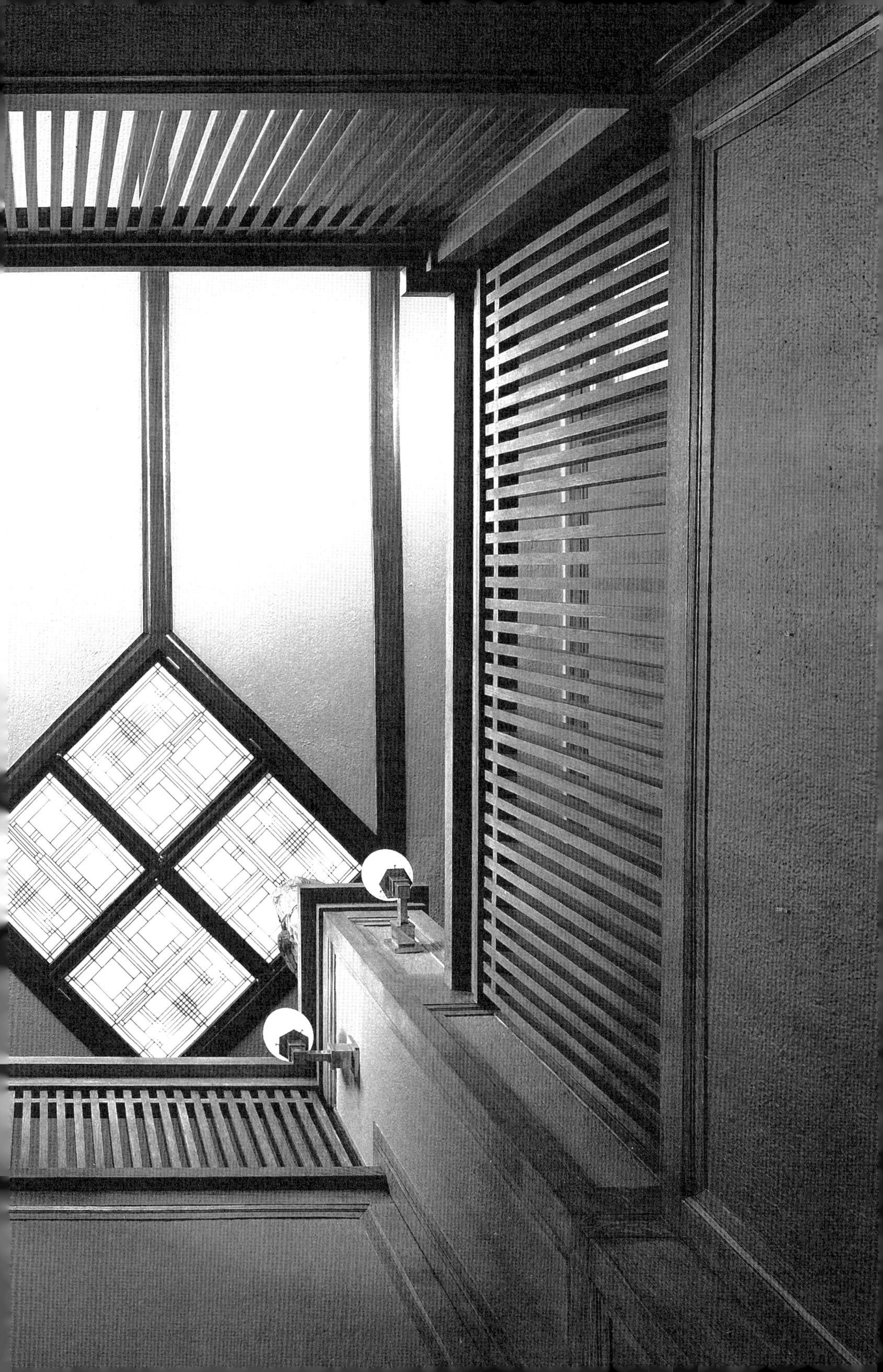

Frank Thomas House
Oak Park, Illinois, 1901

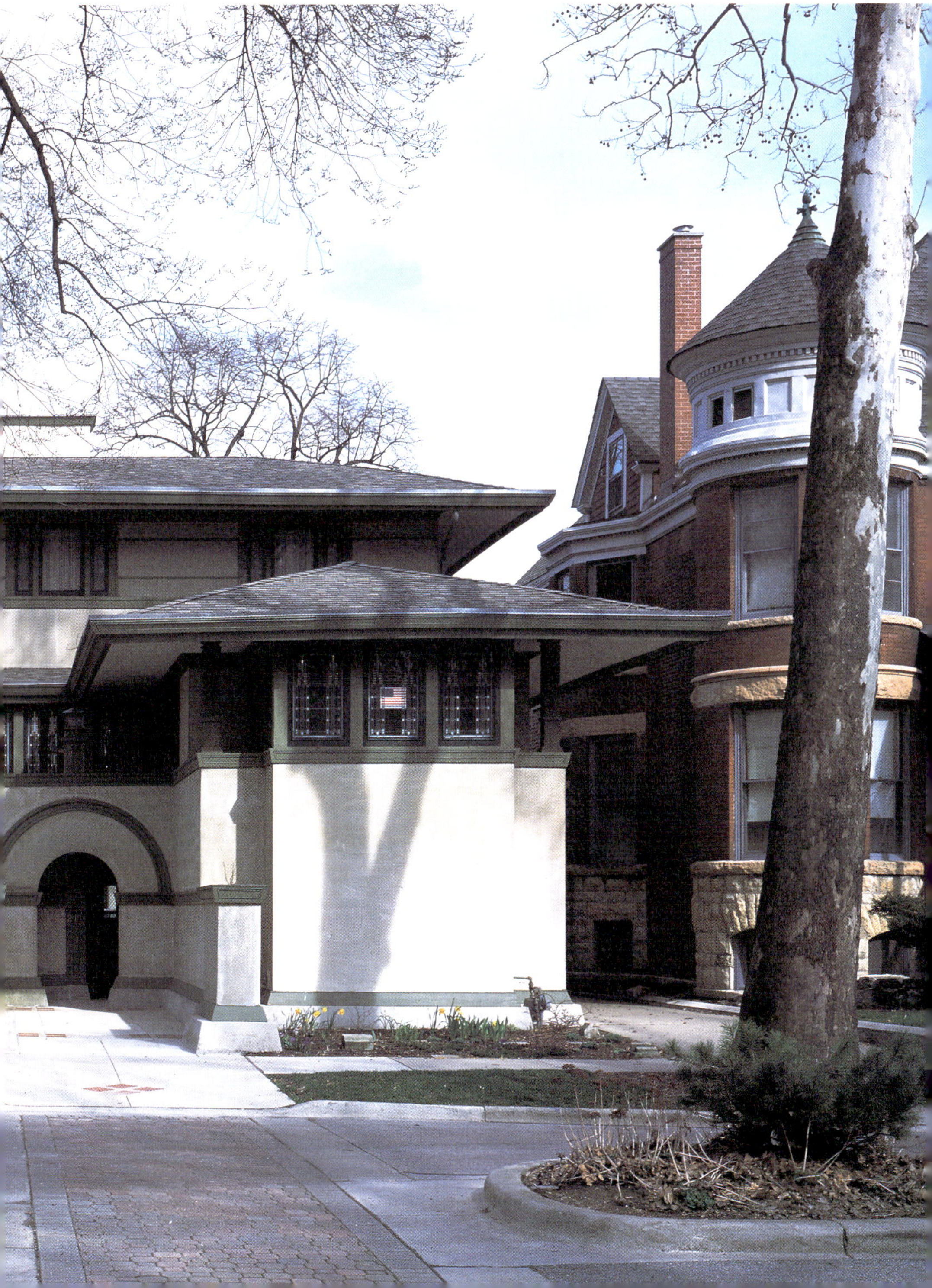

First floor

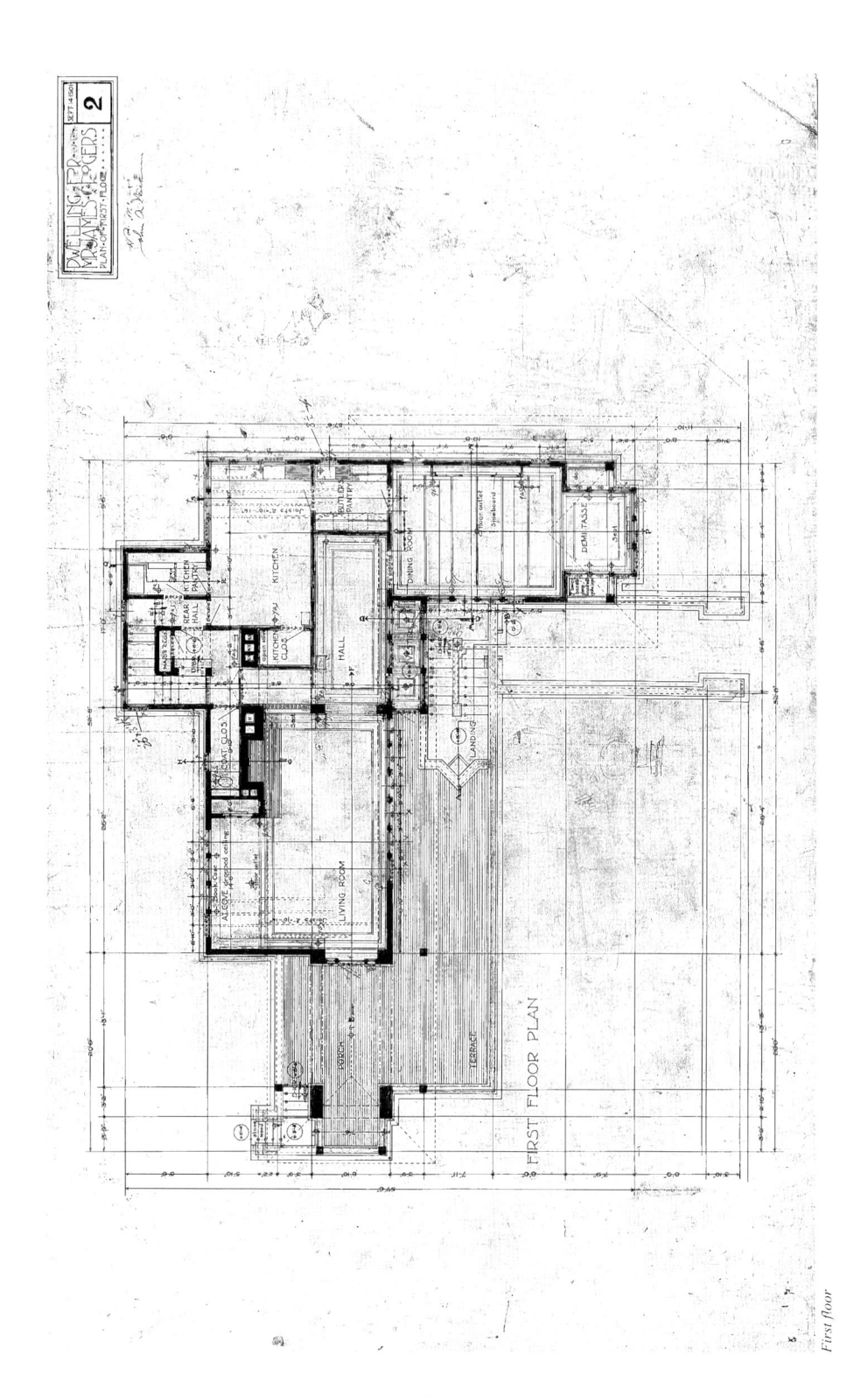

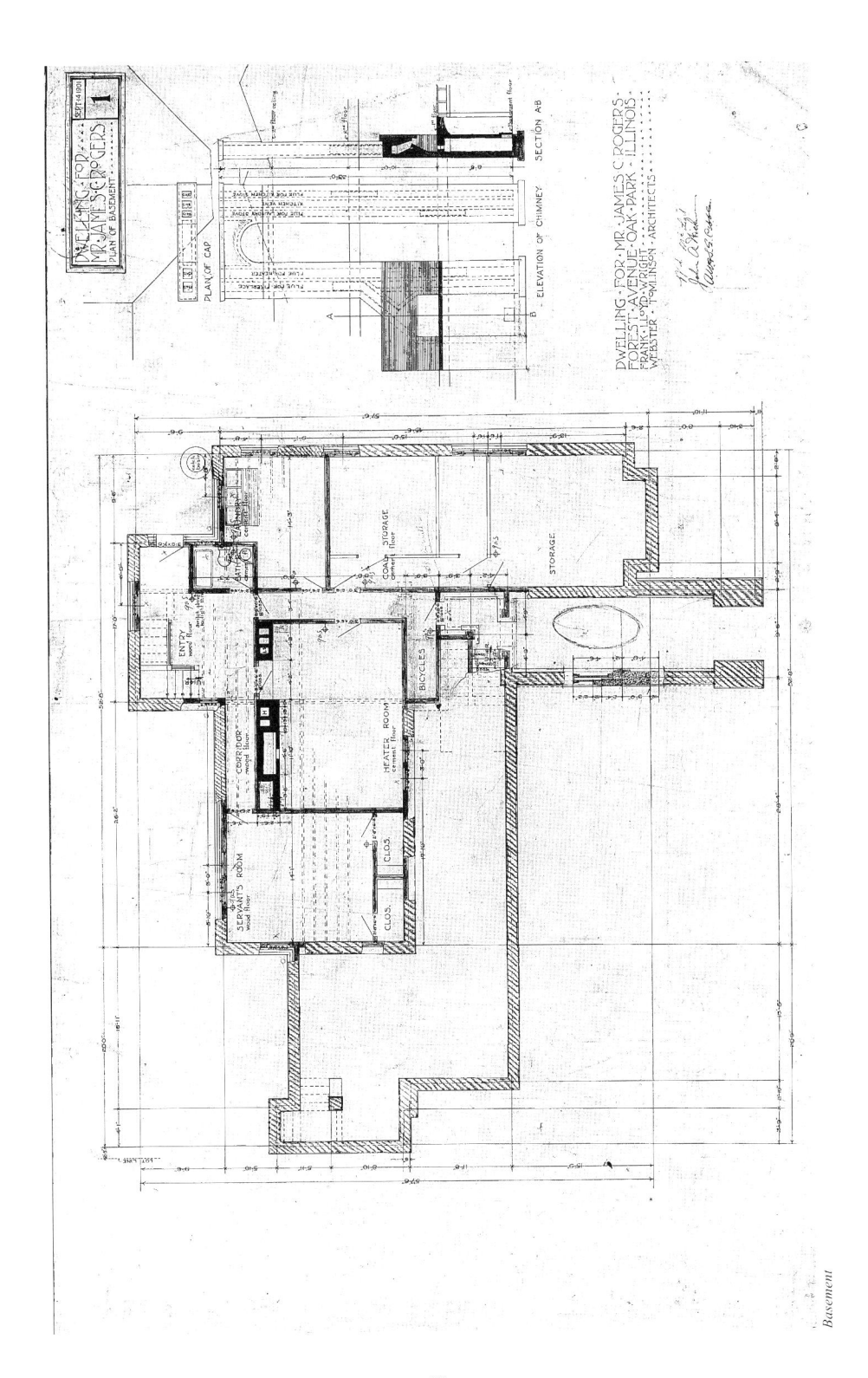

Basement

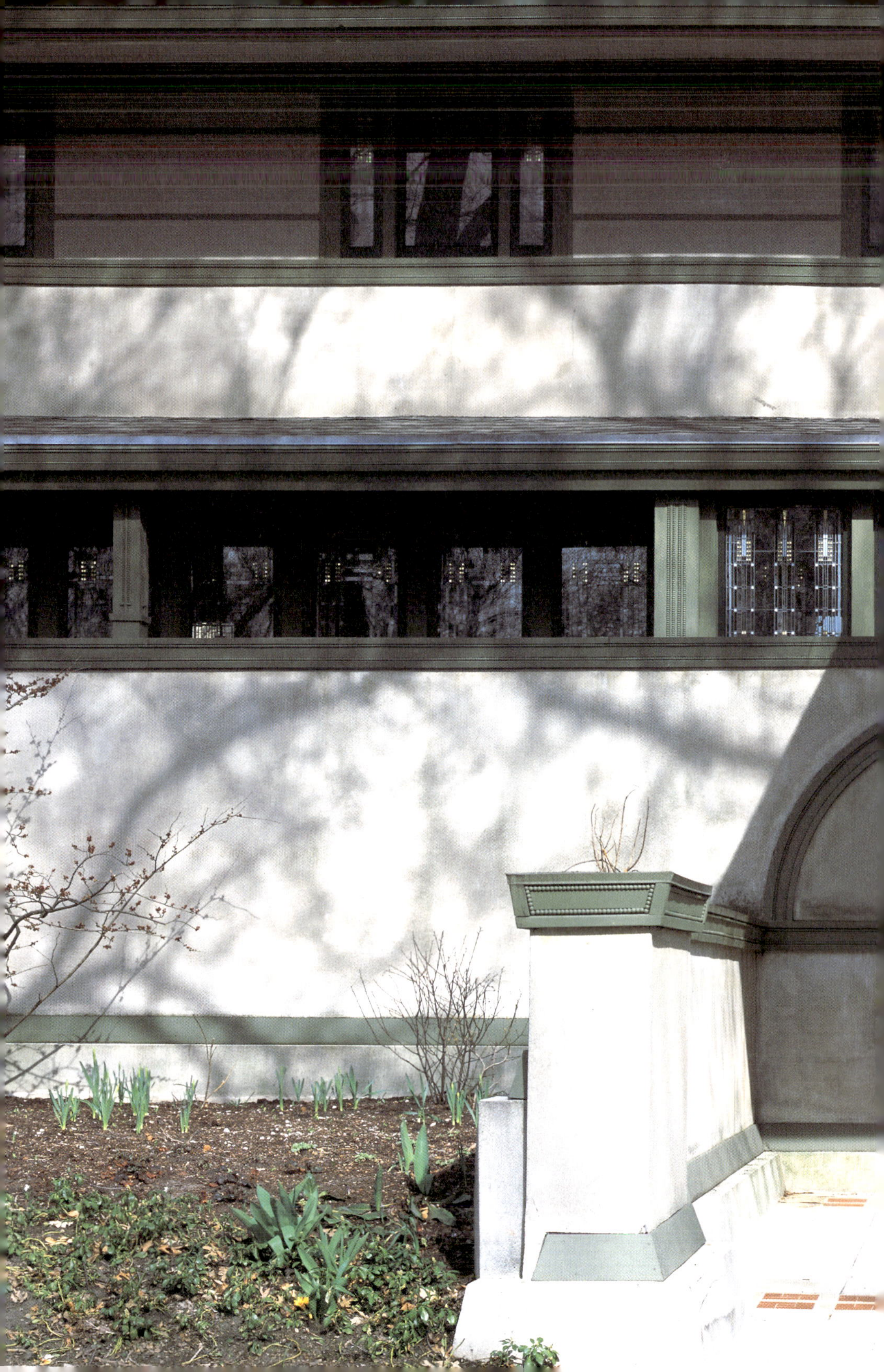

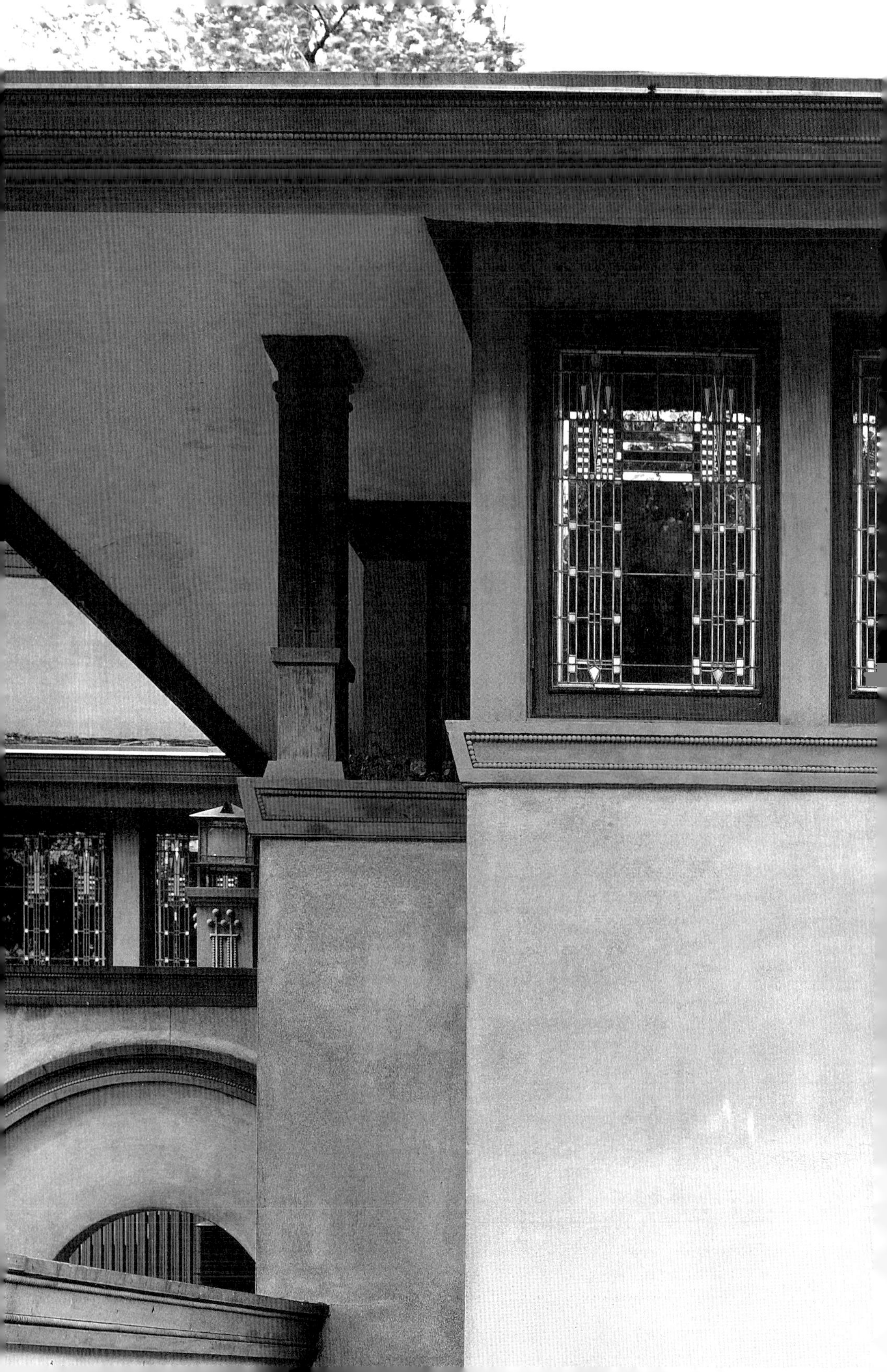

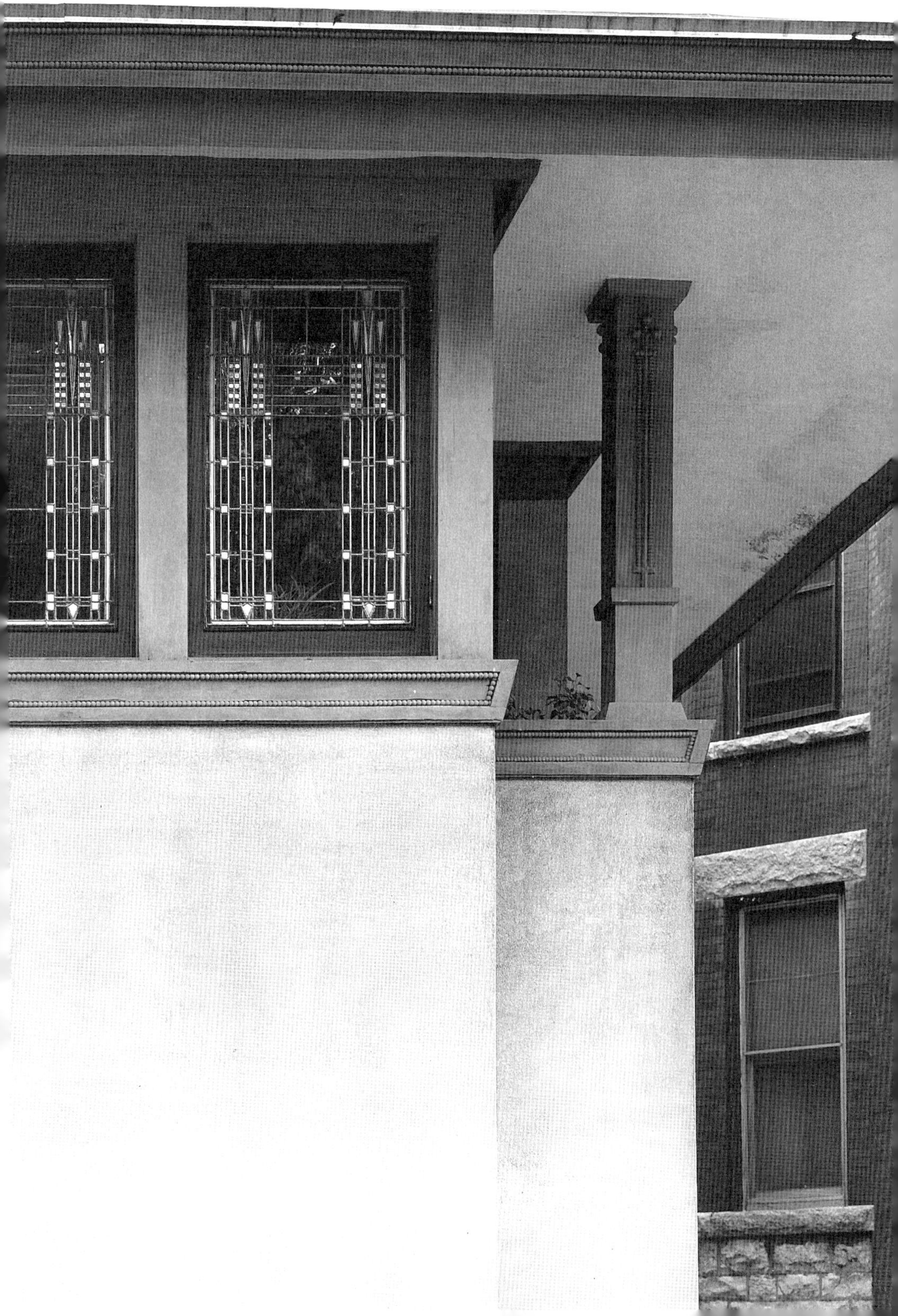

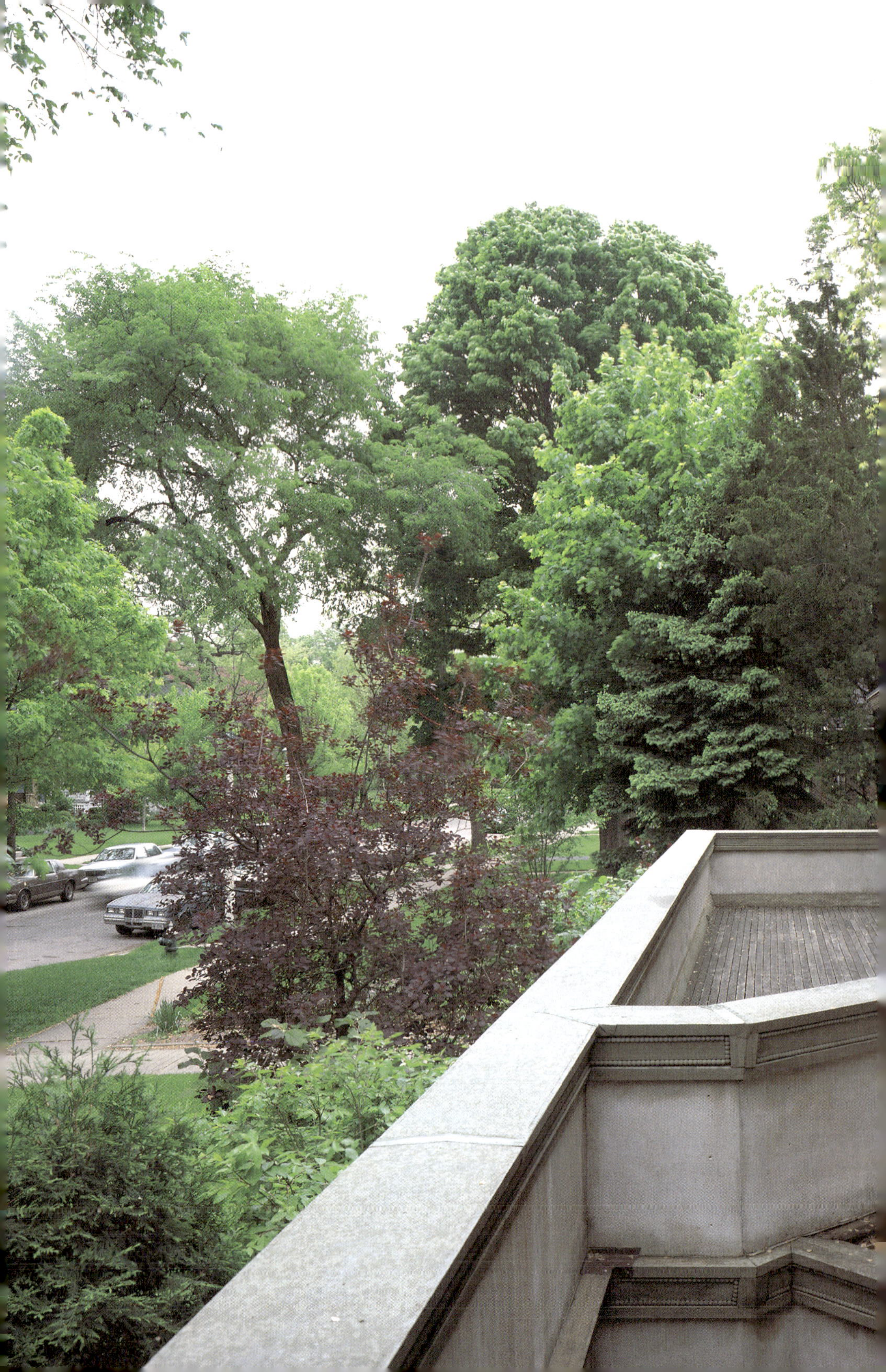

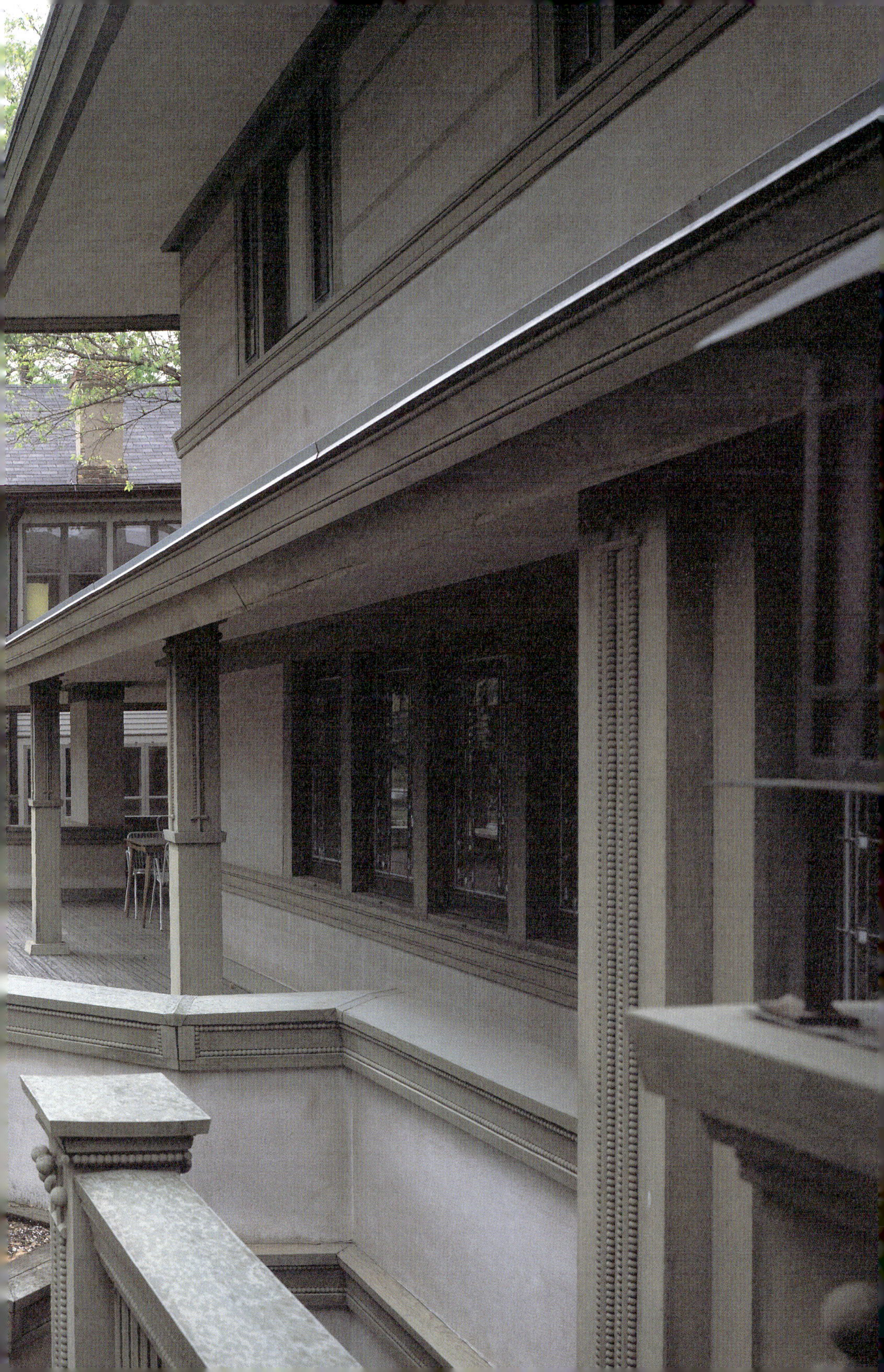

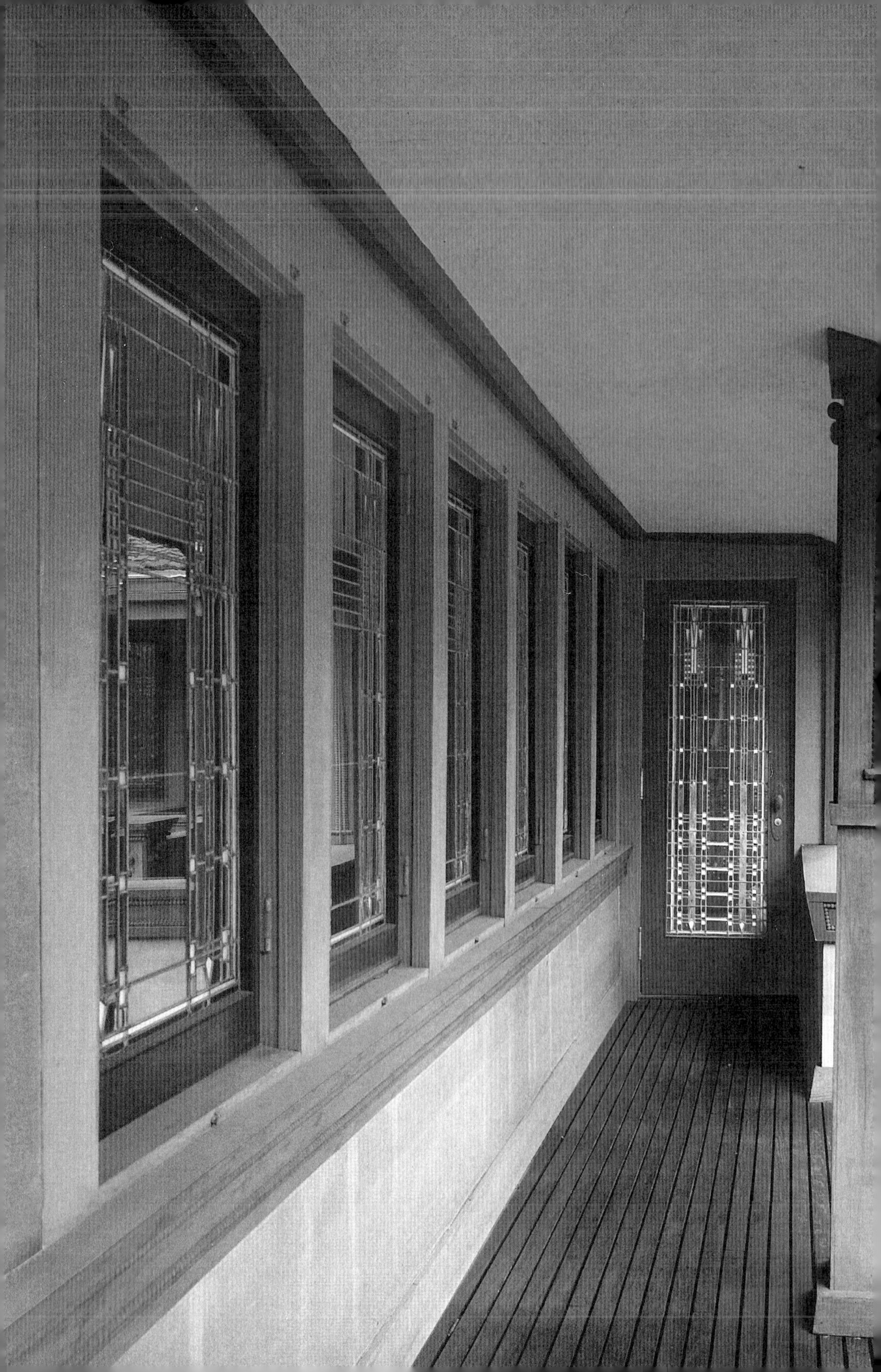

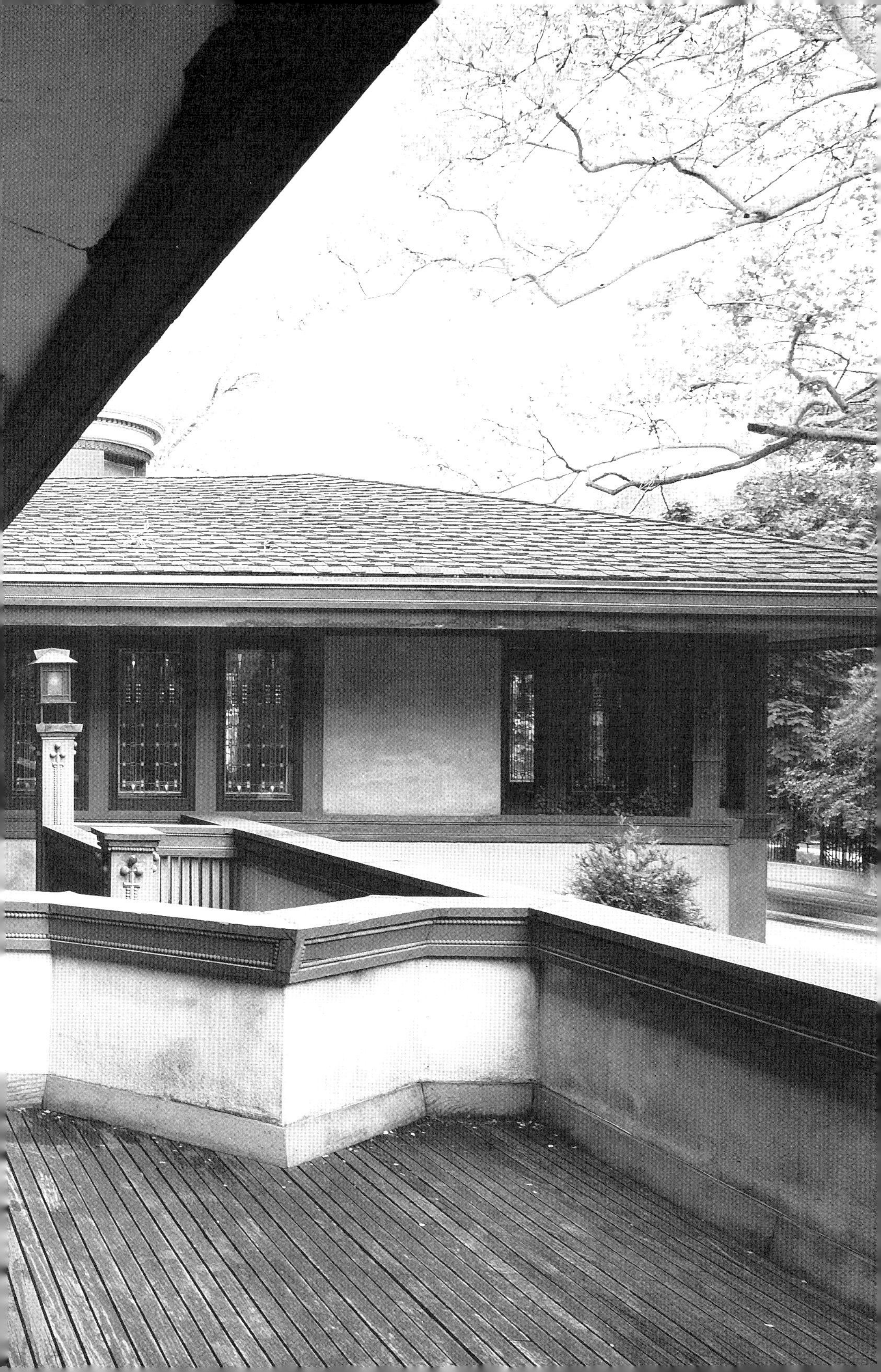

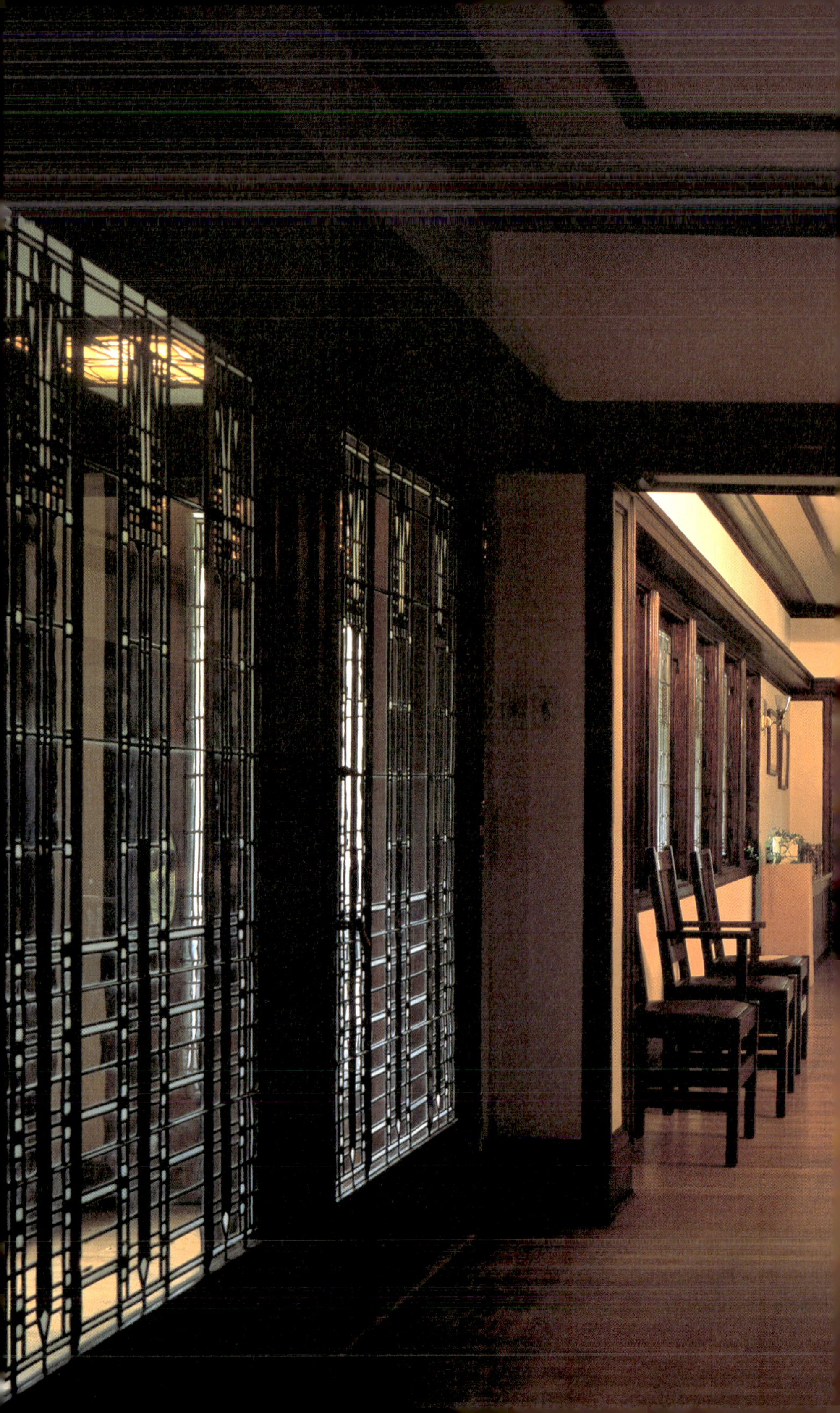

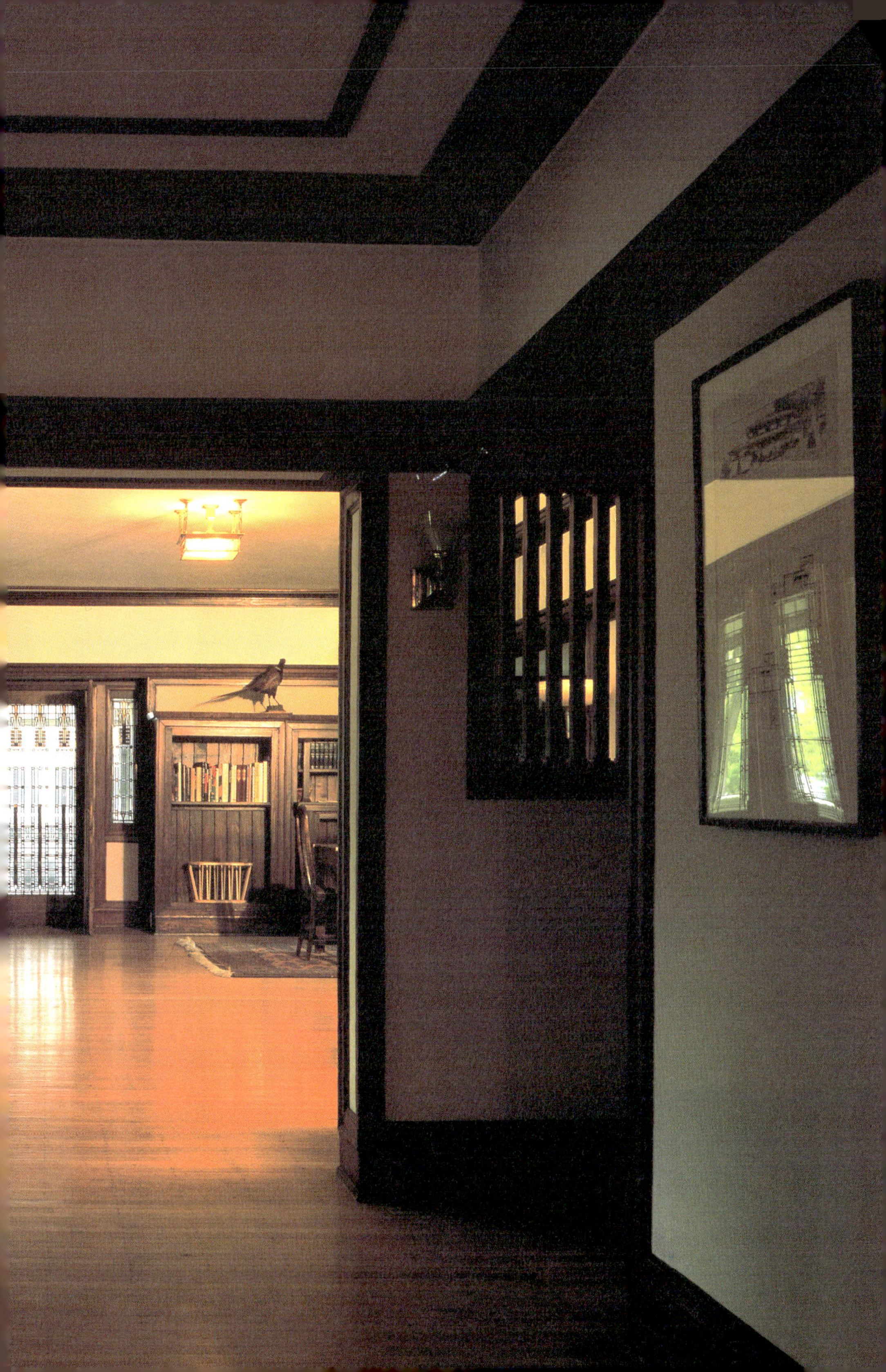

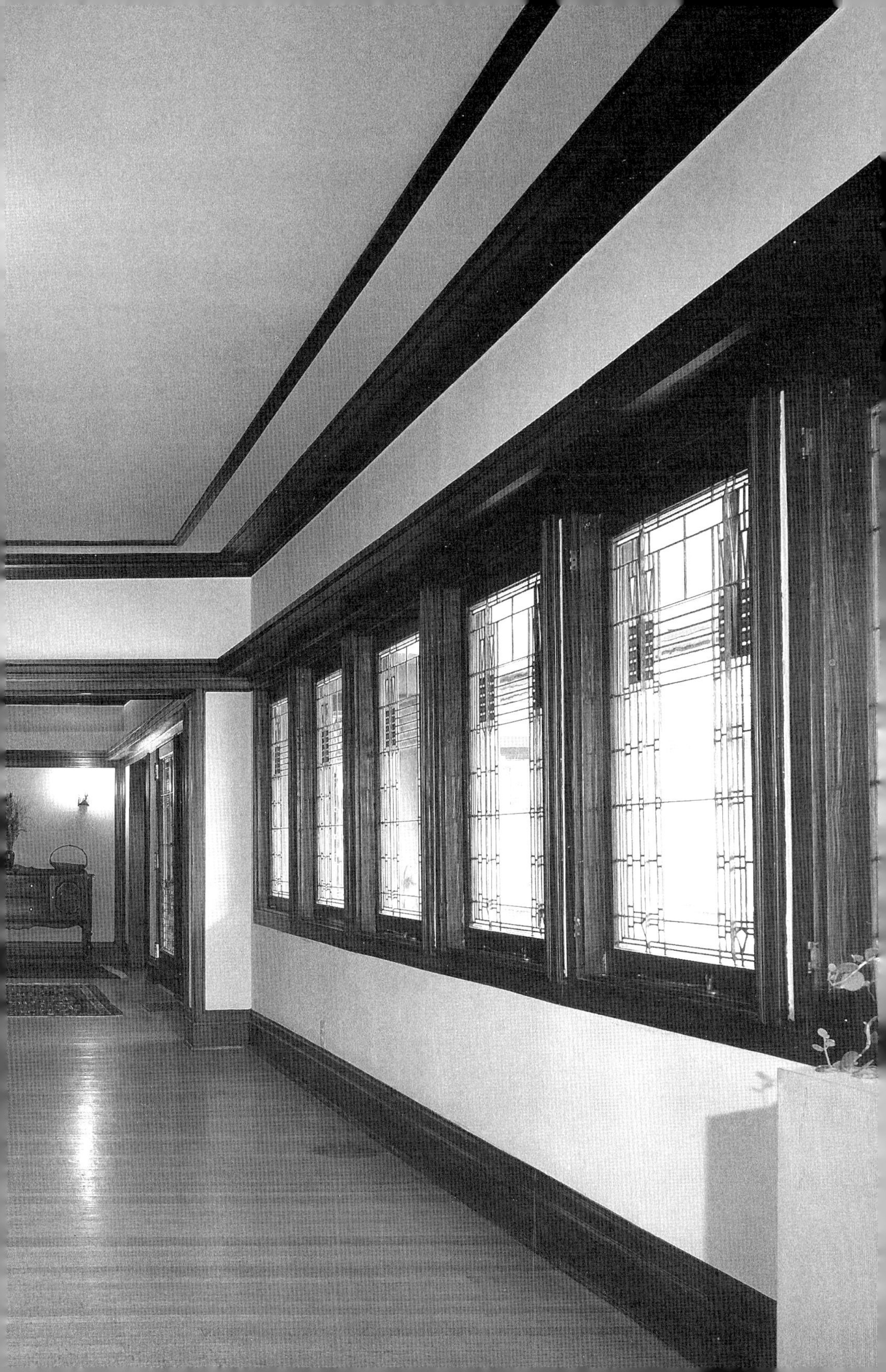

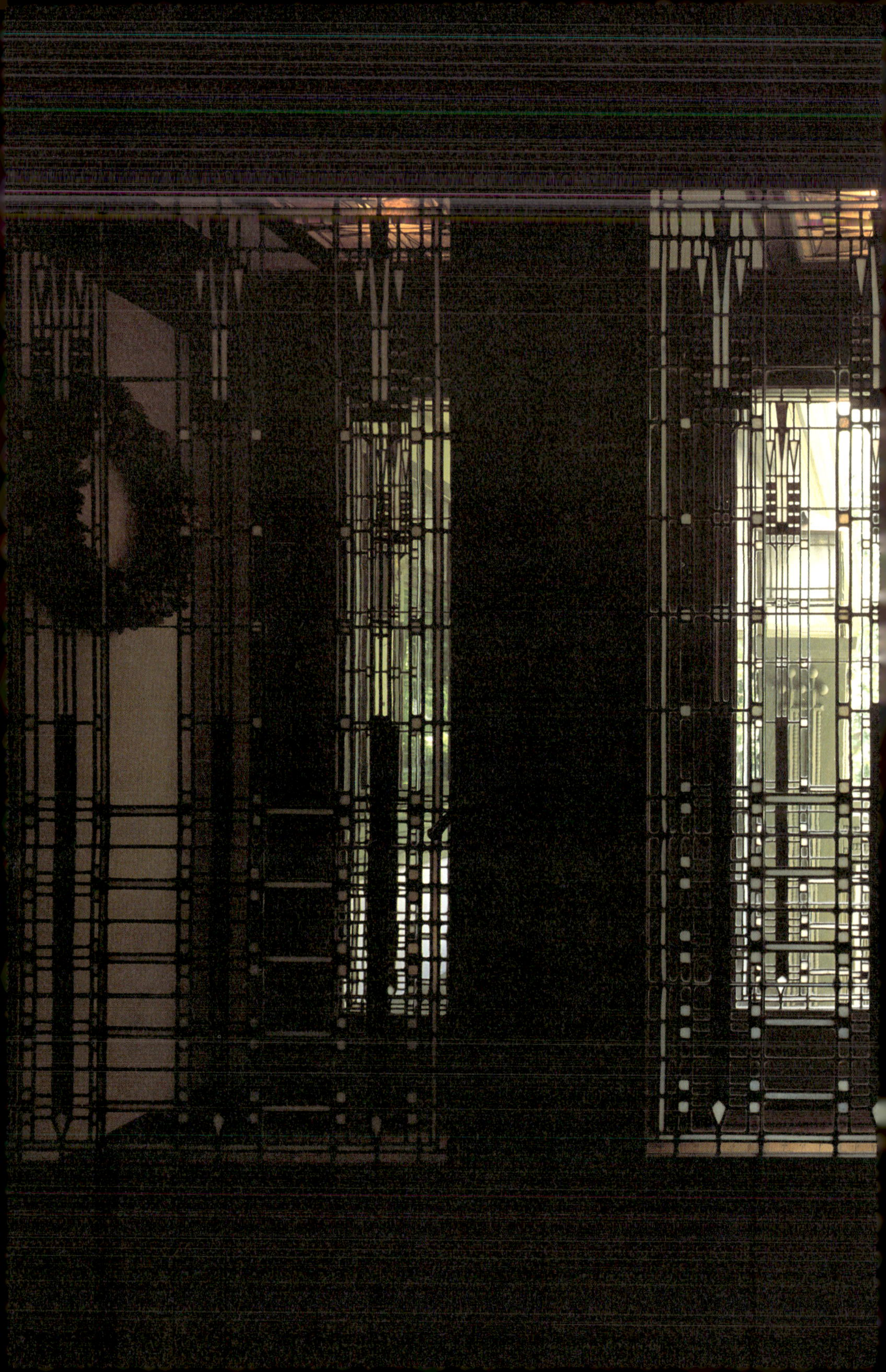

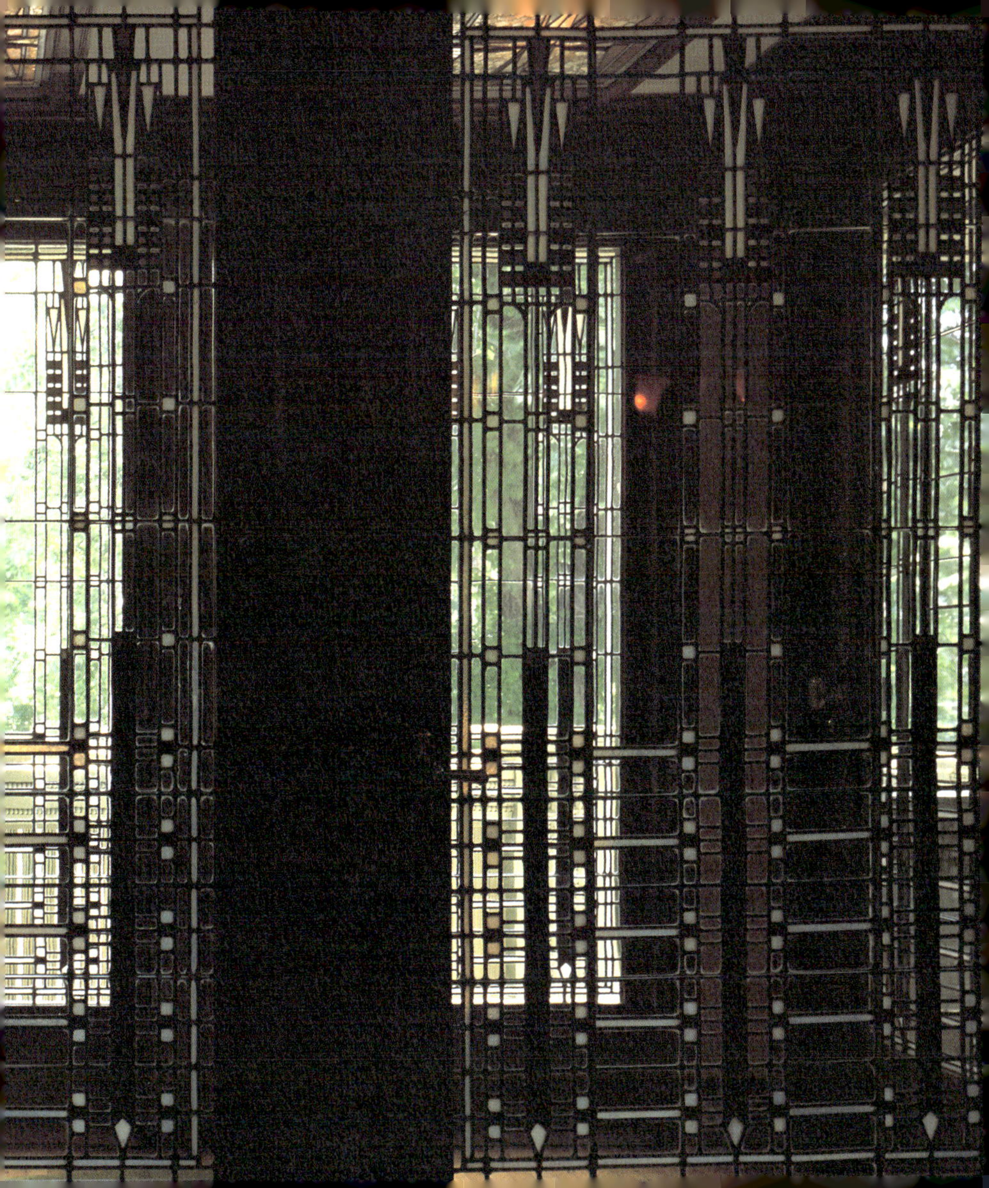

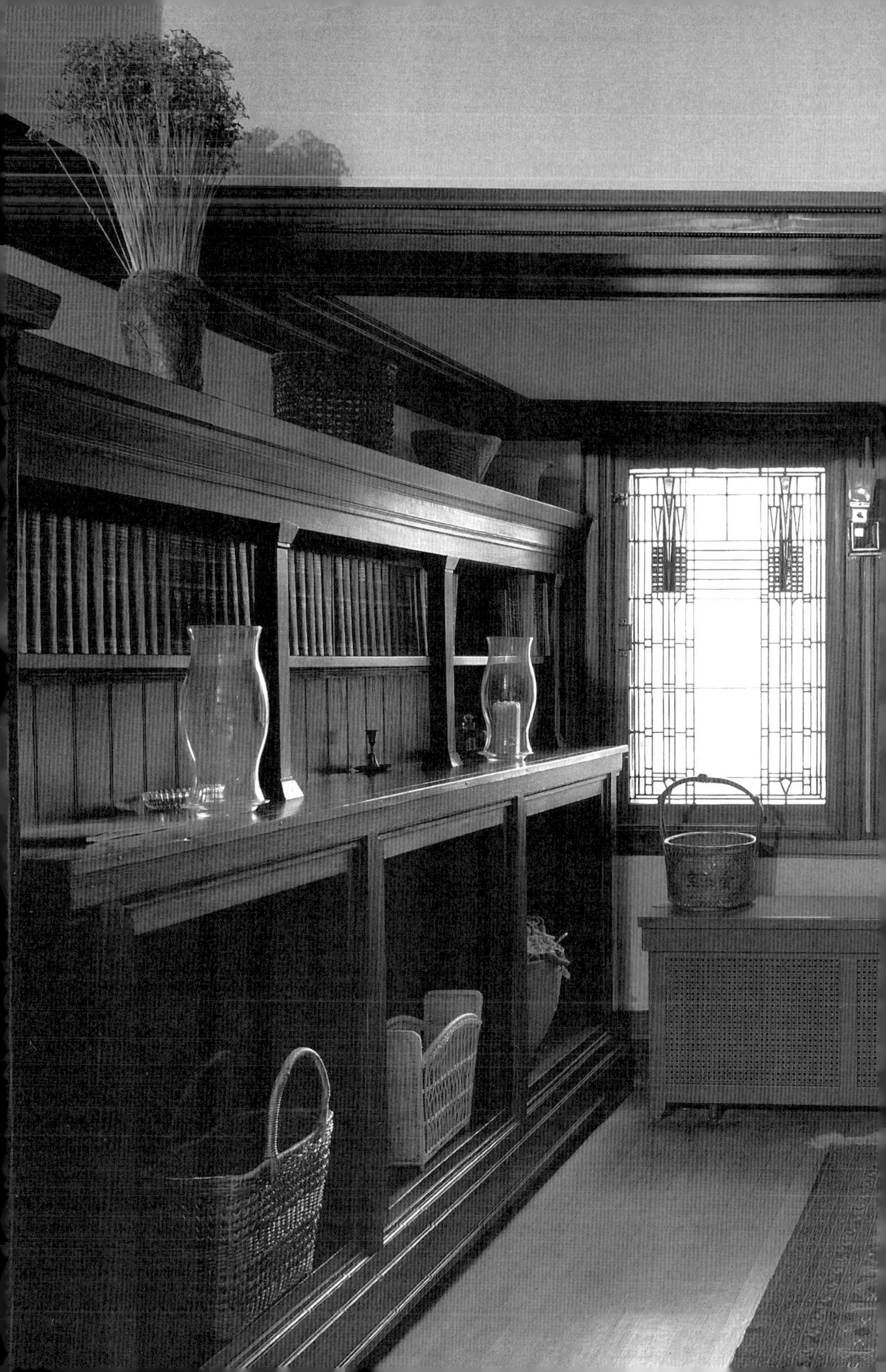

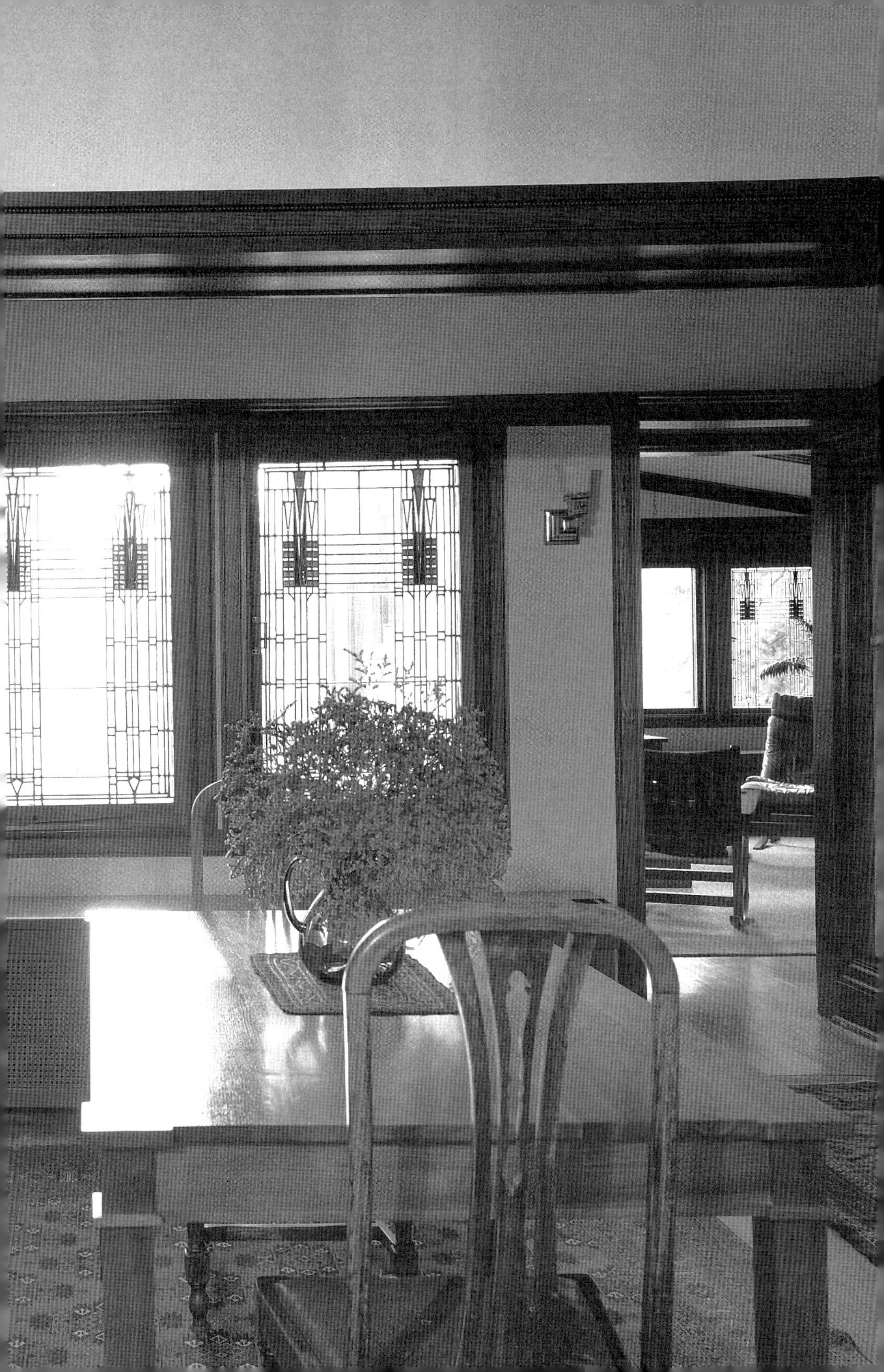

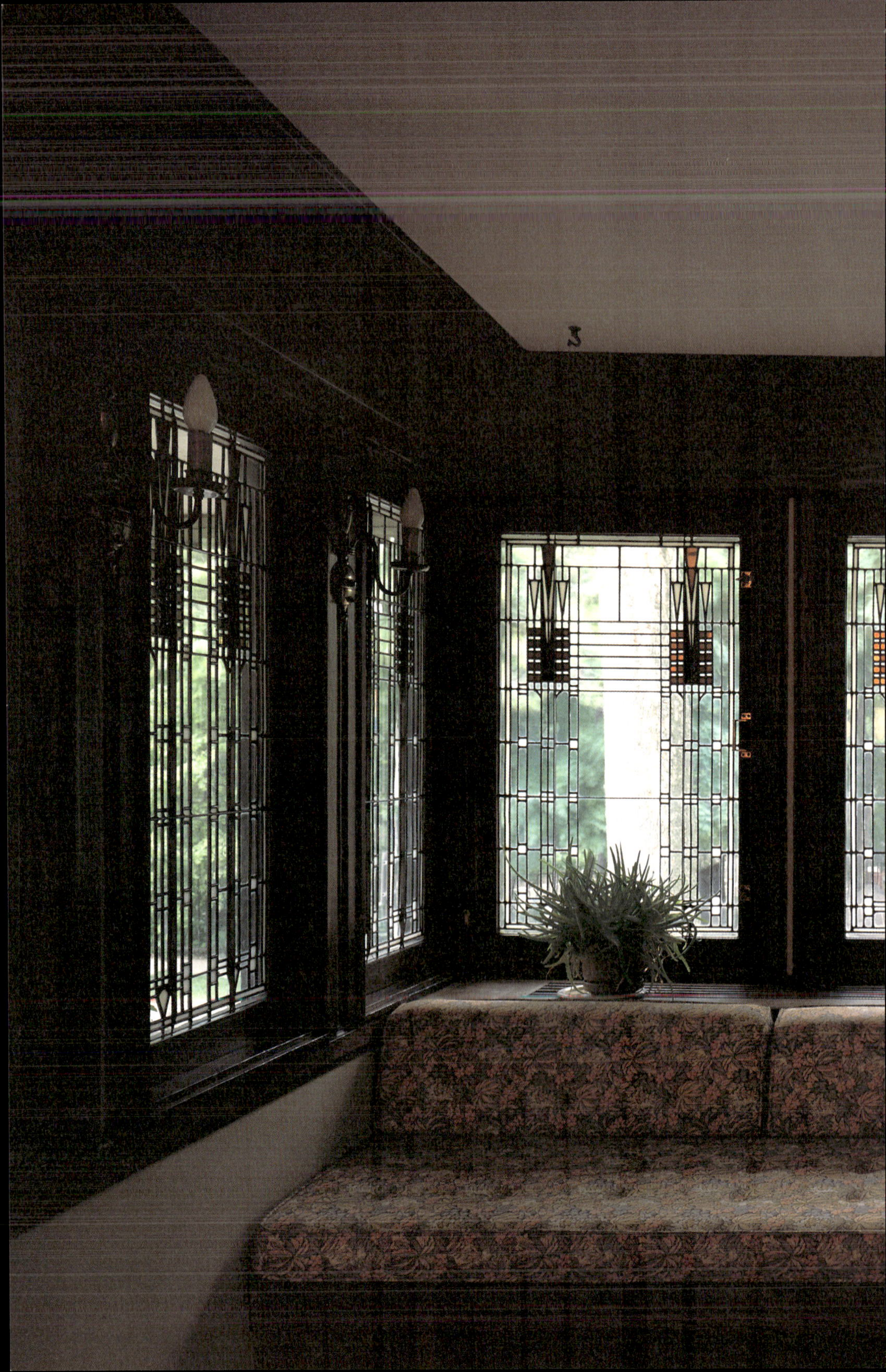

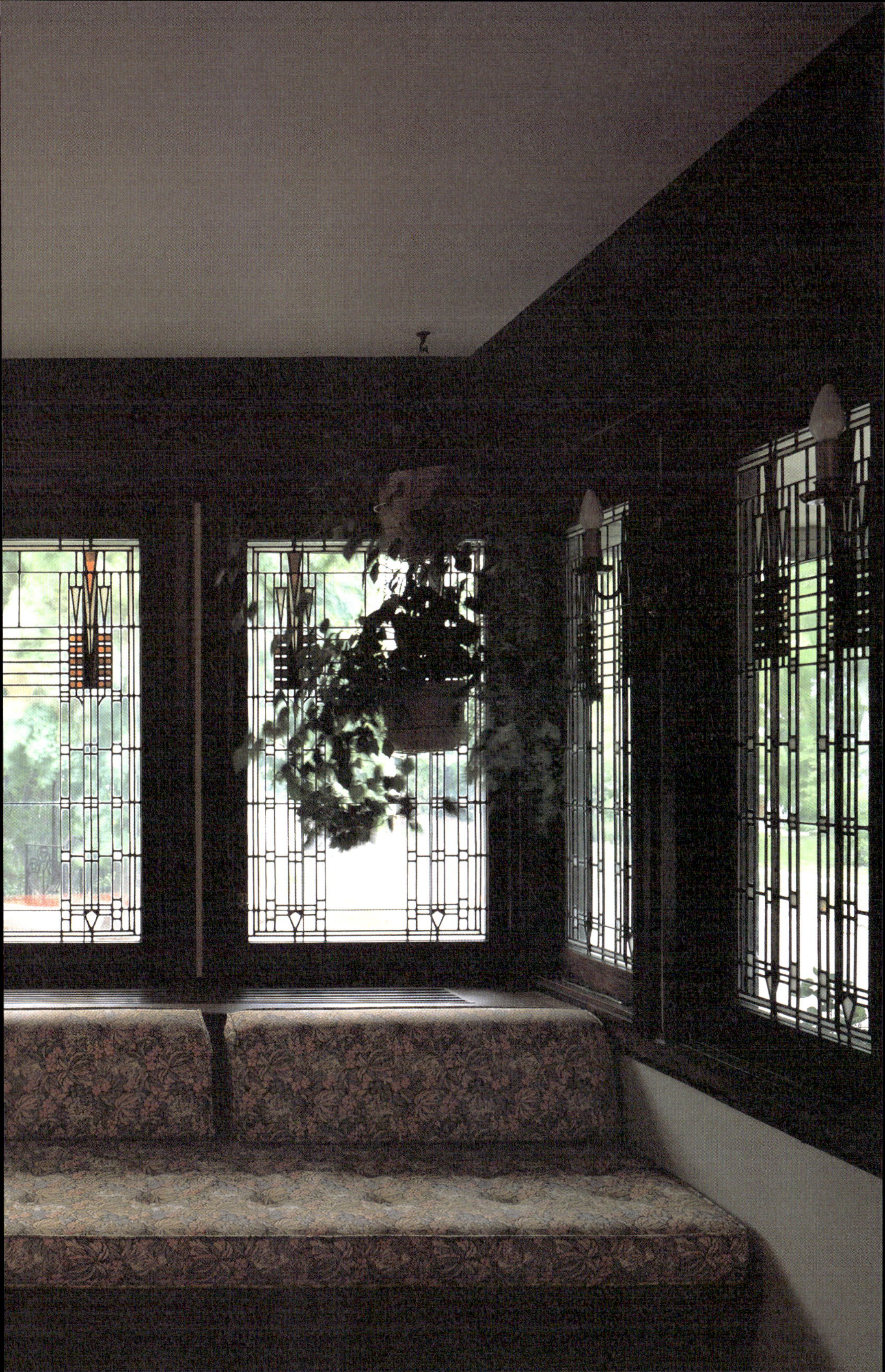

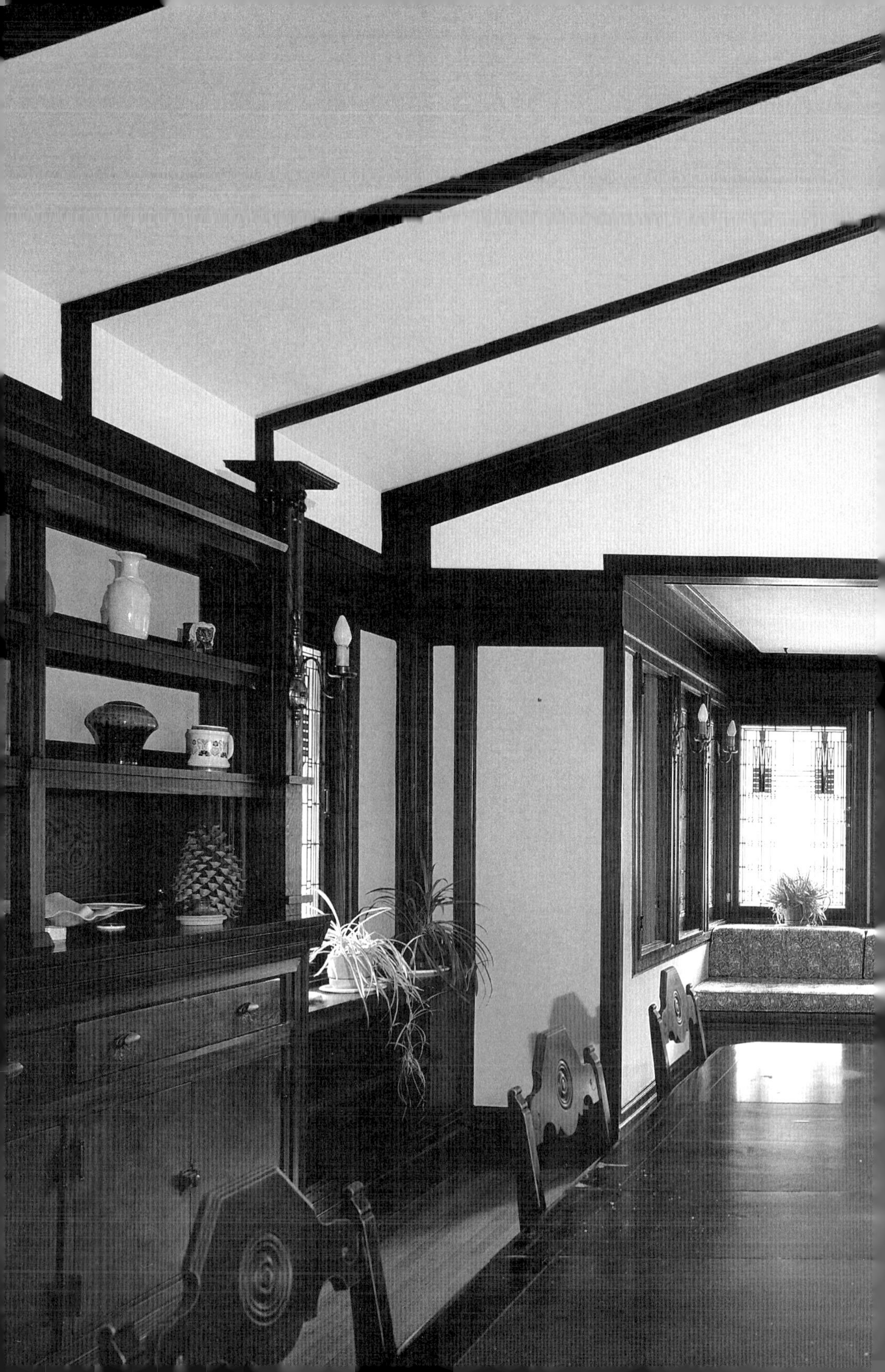

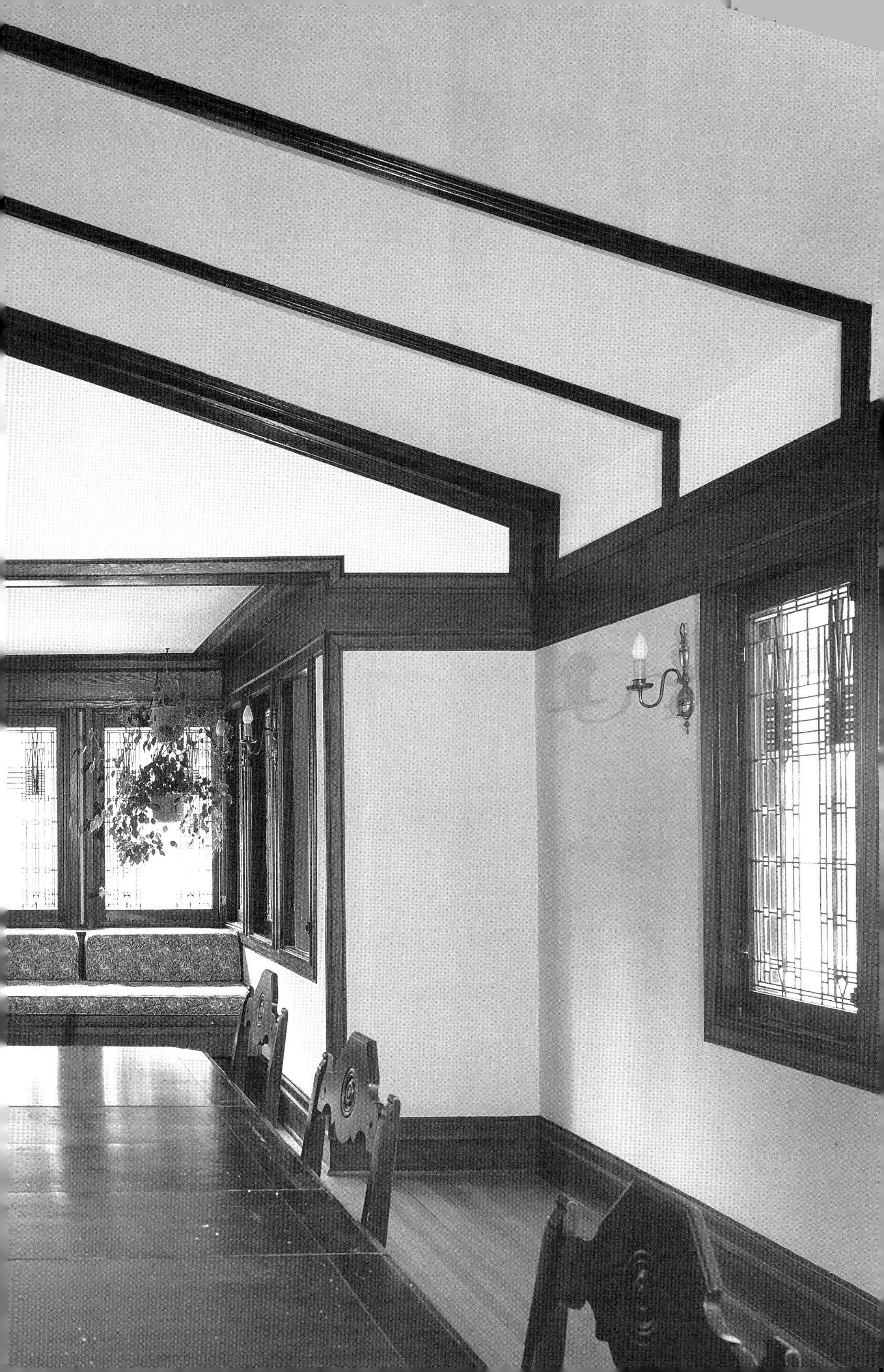

Susan Lawrence Dana House
Springfield, Illinois, 1902

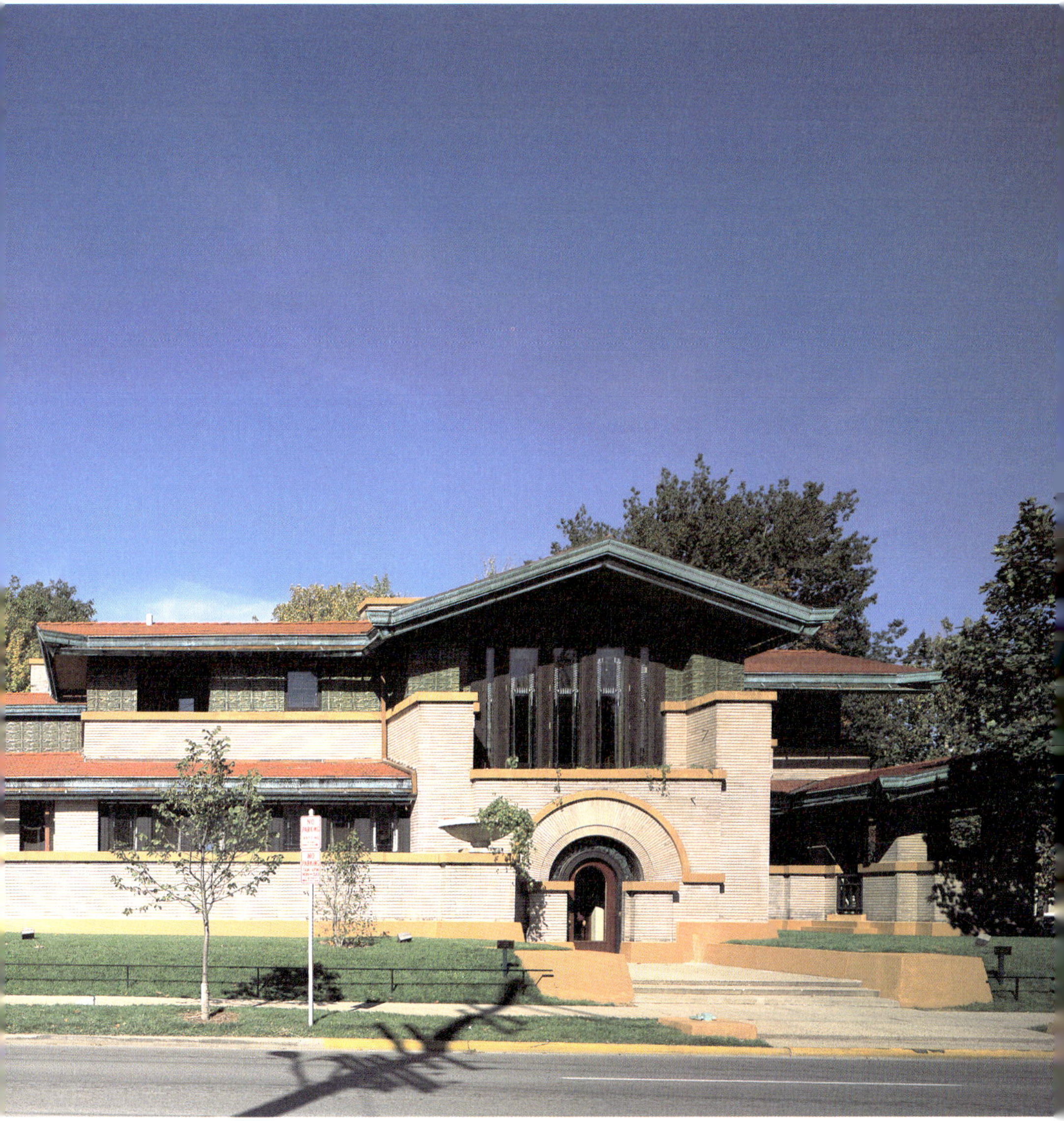

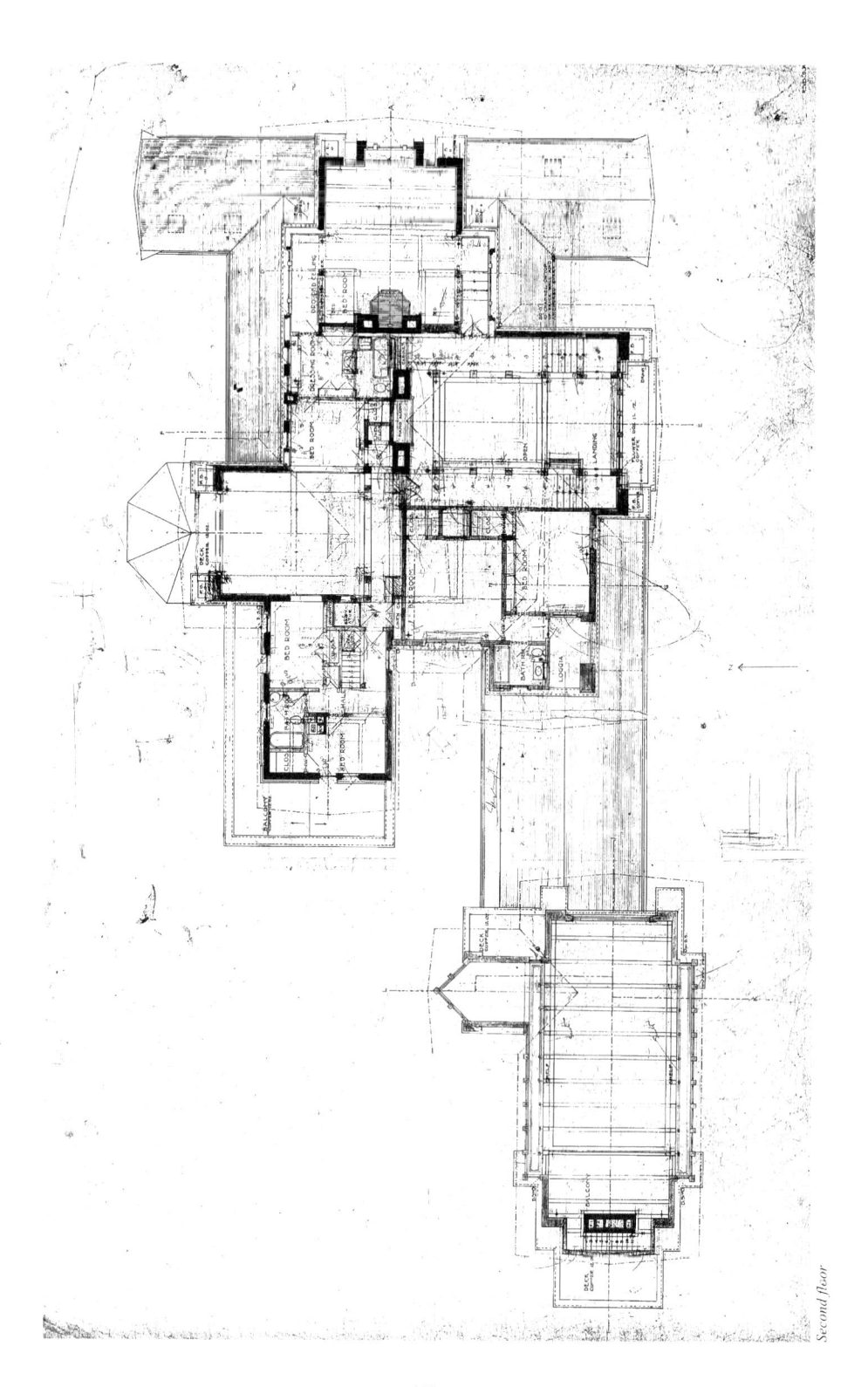

Second floor

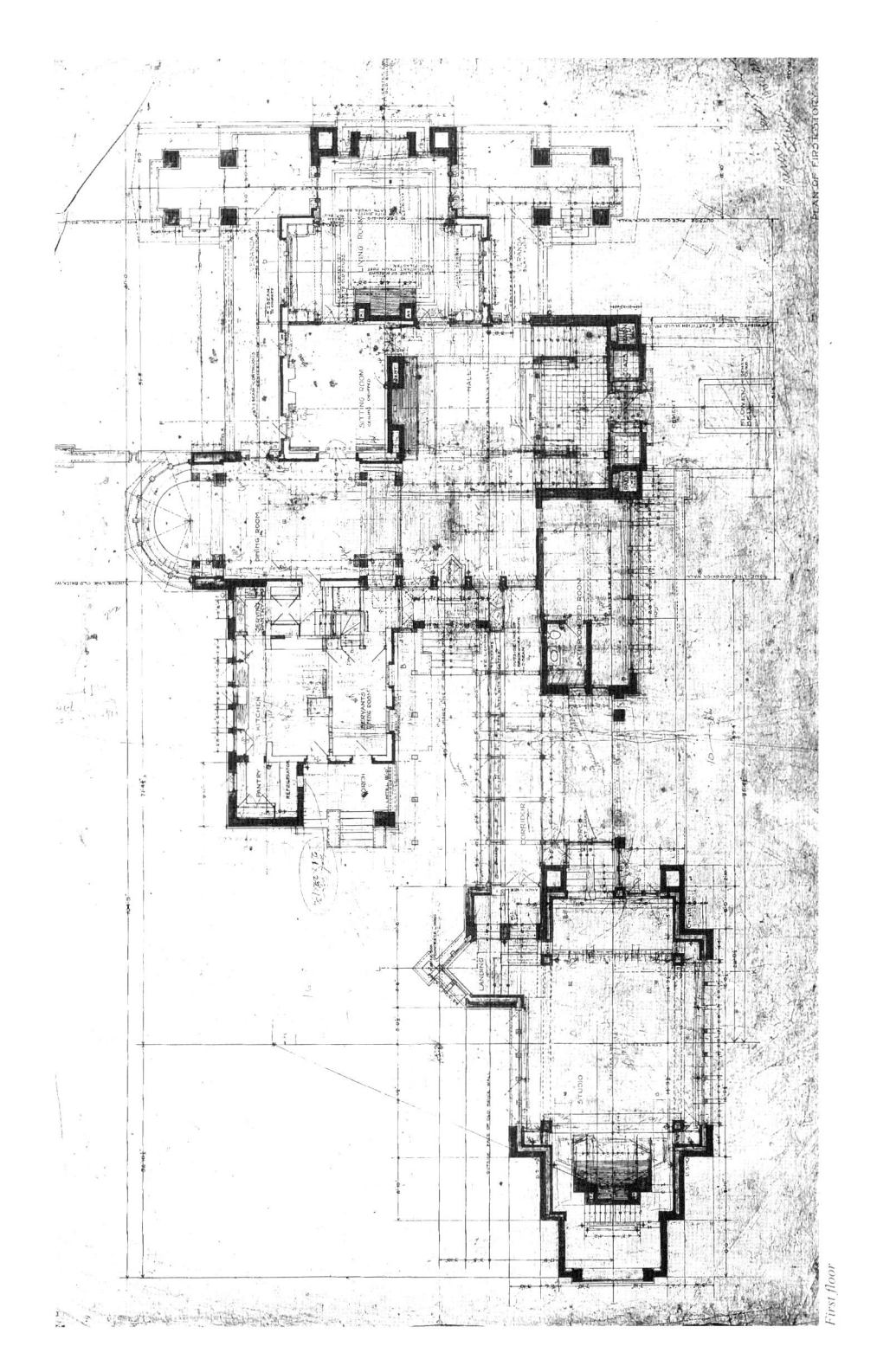

First Floor

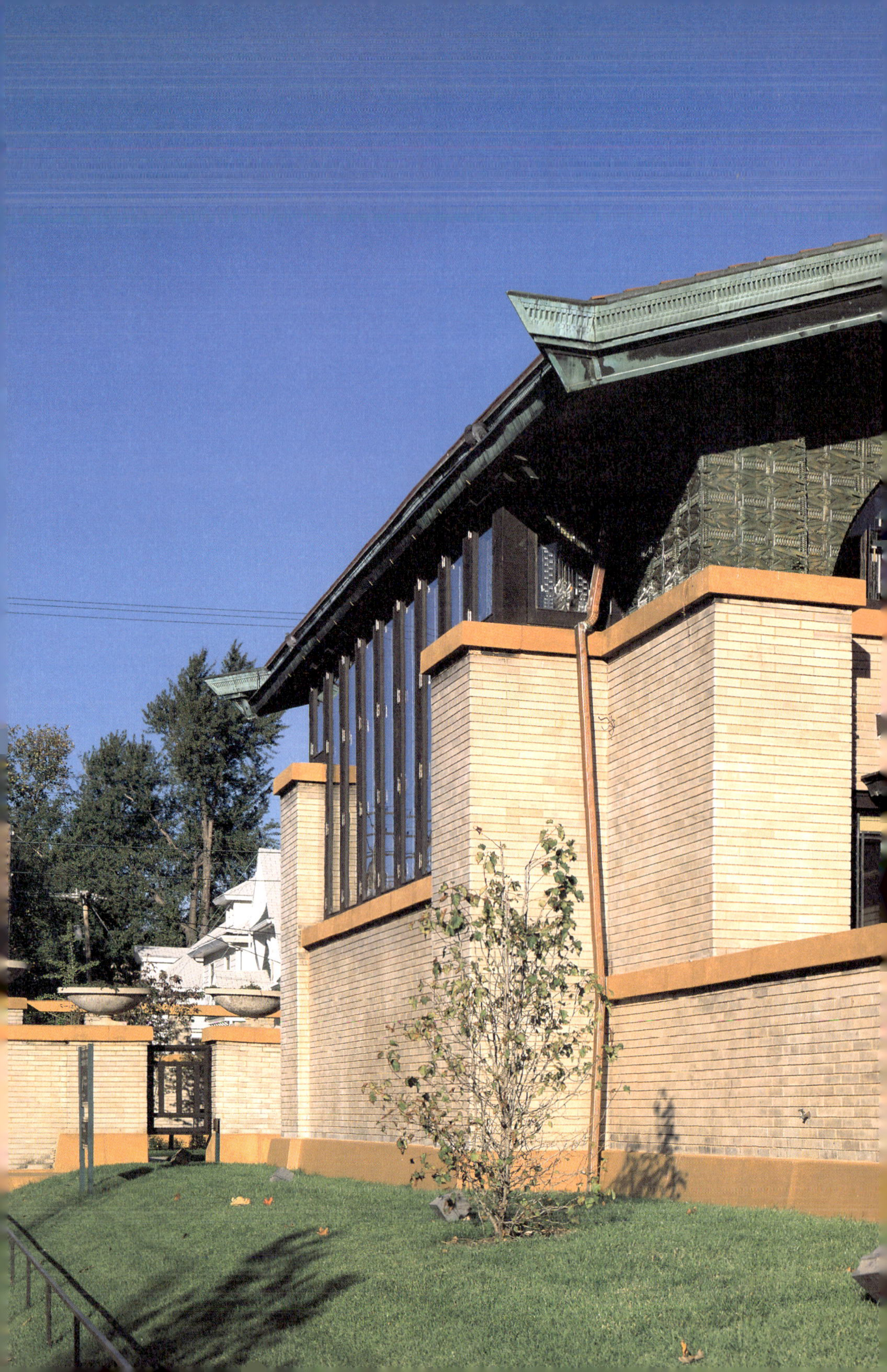

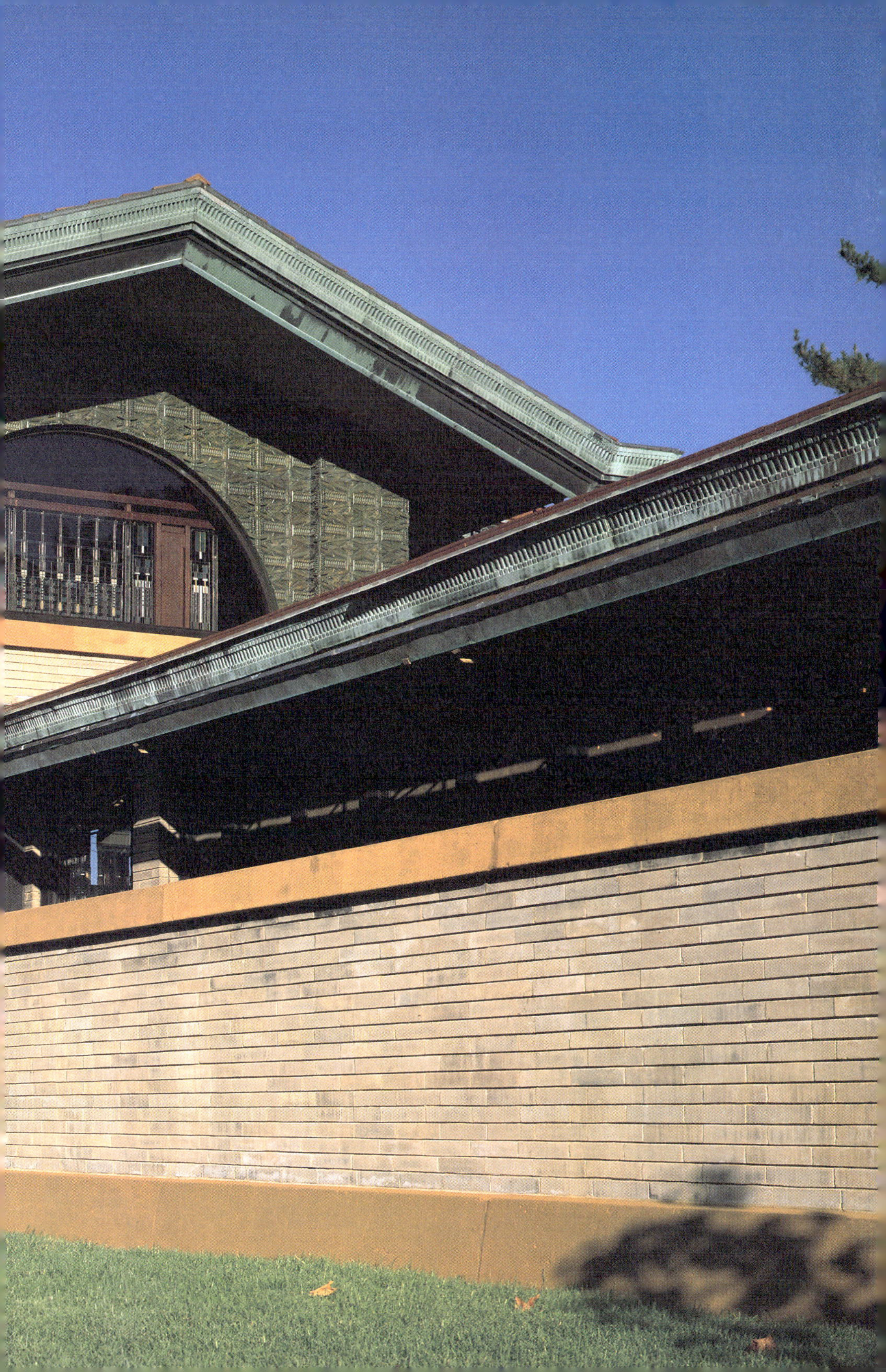

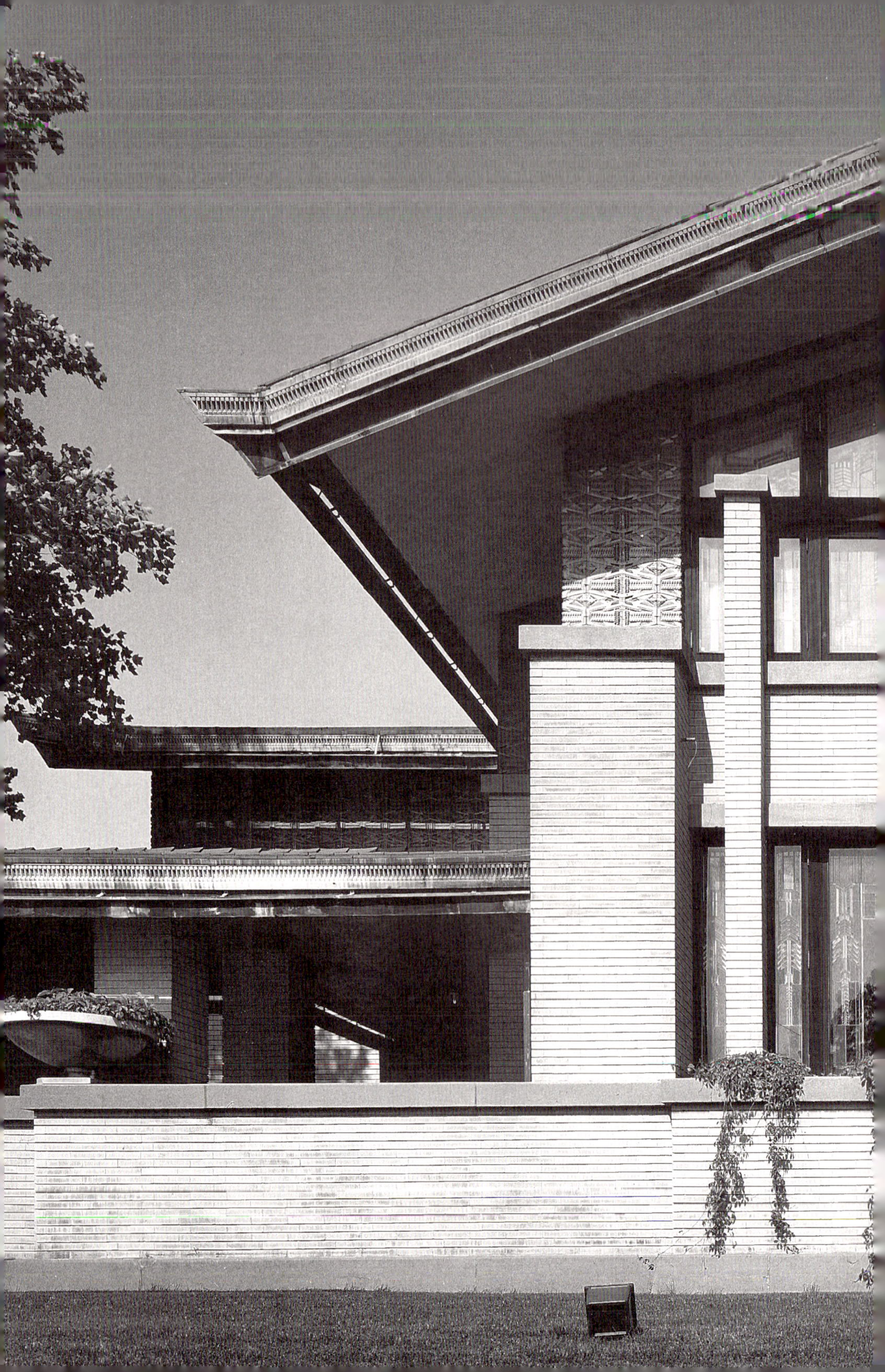

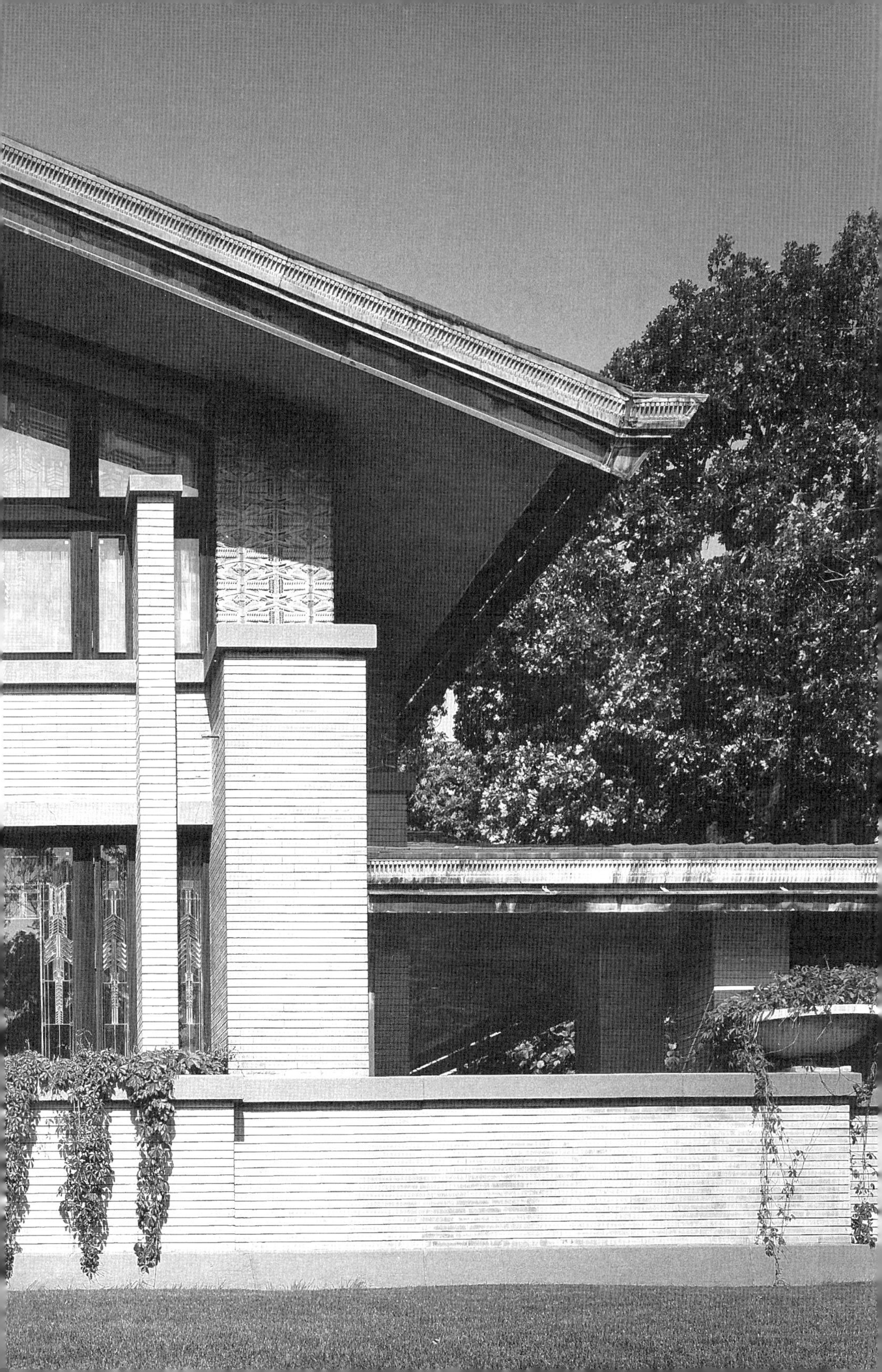

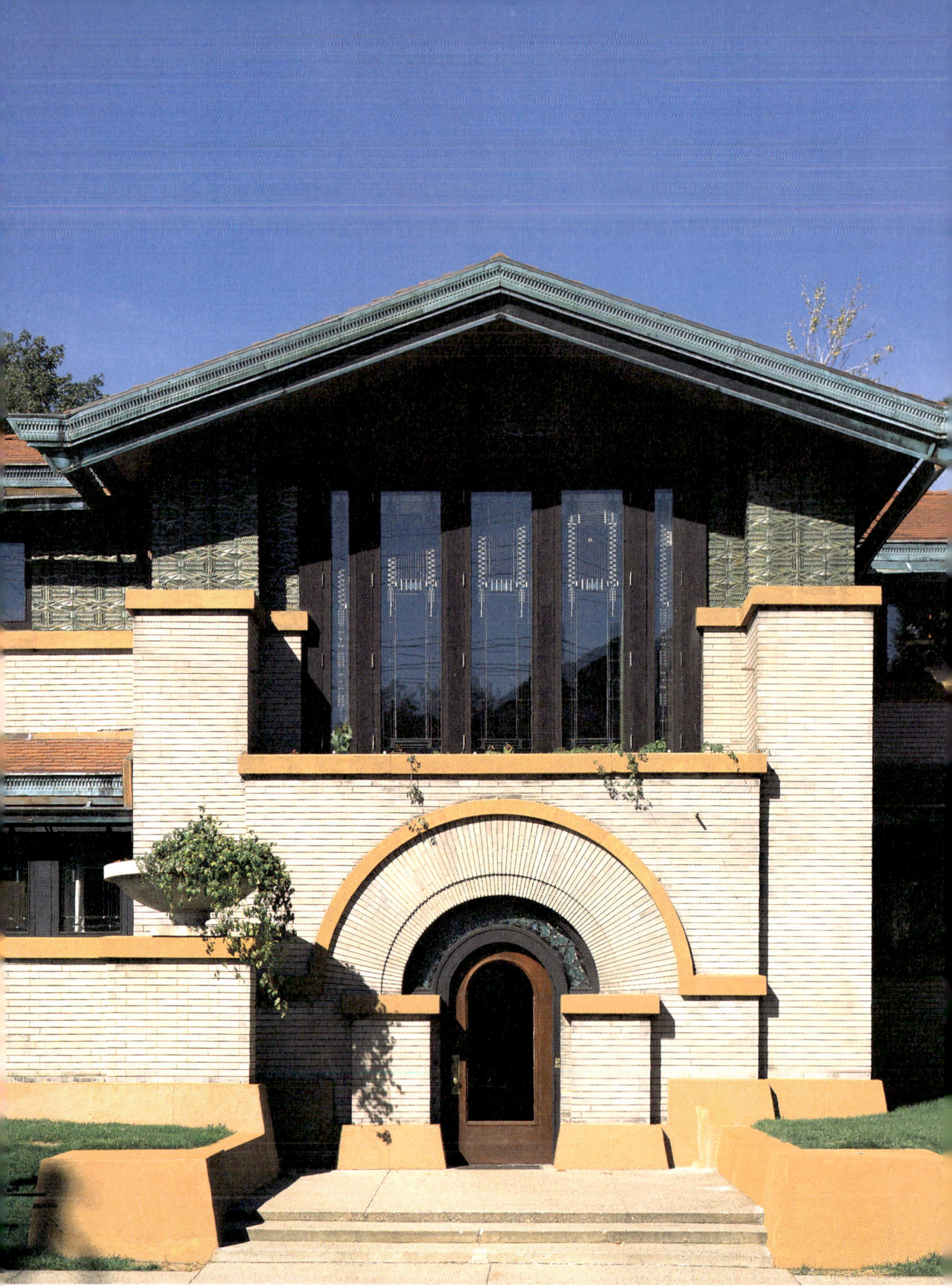

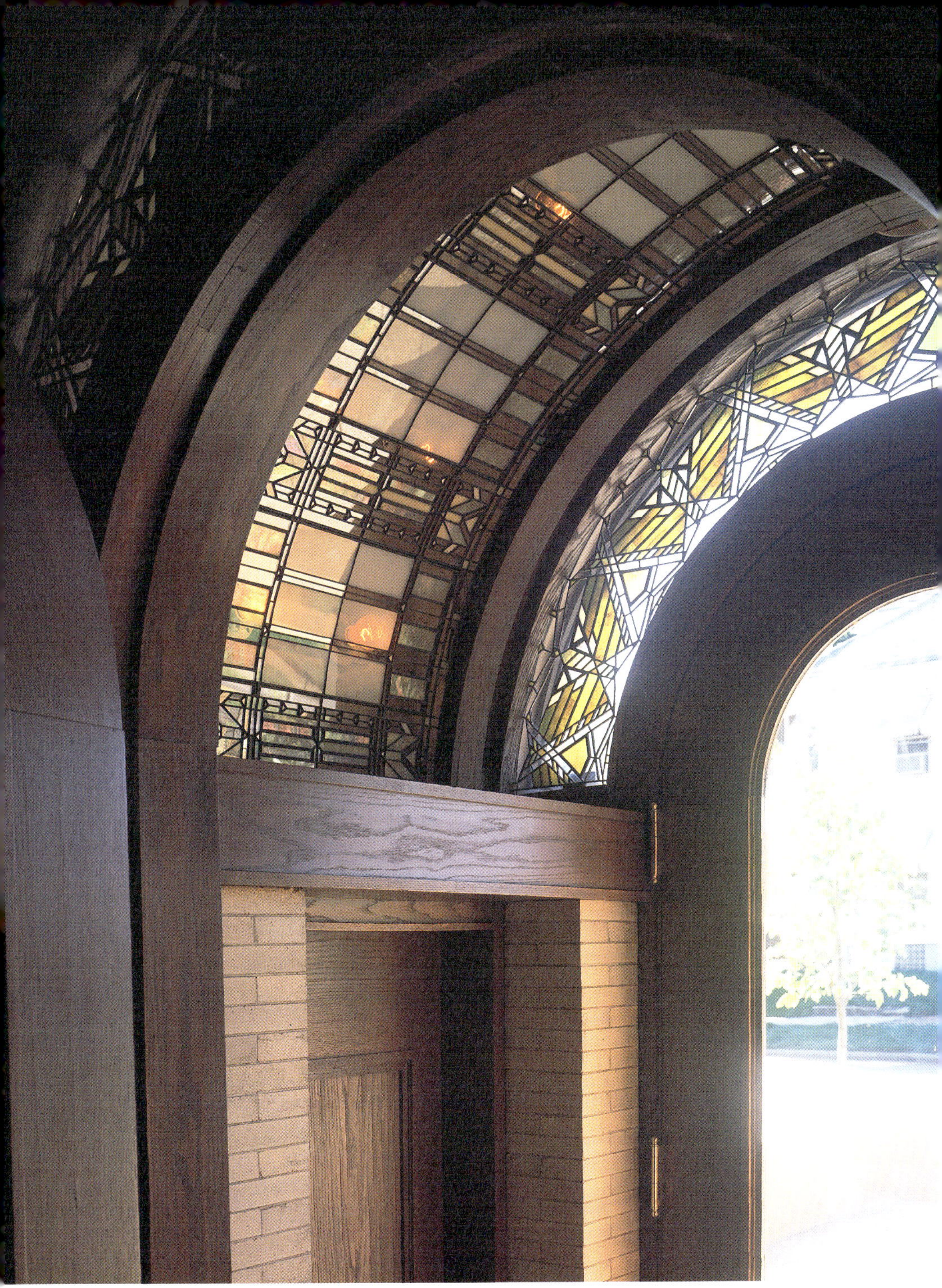

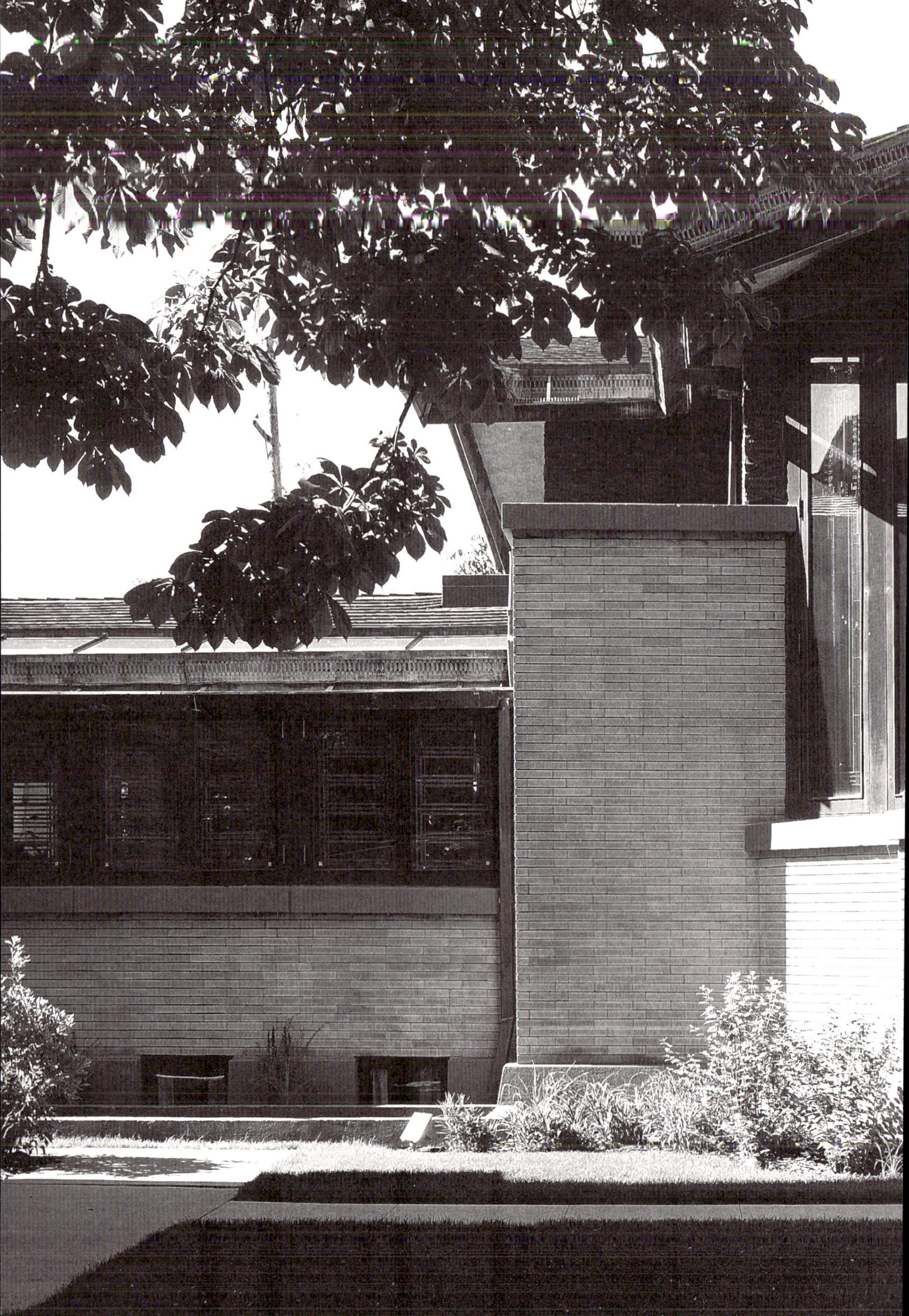

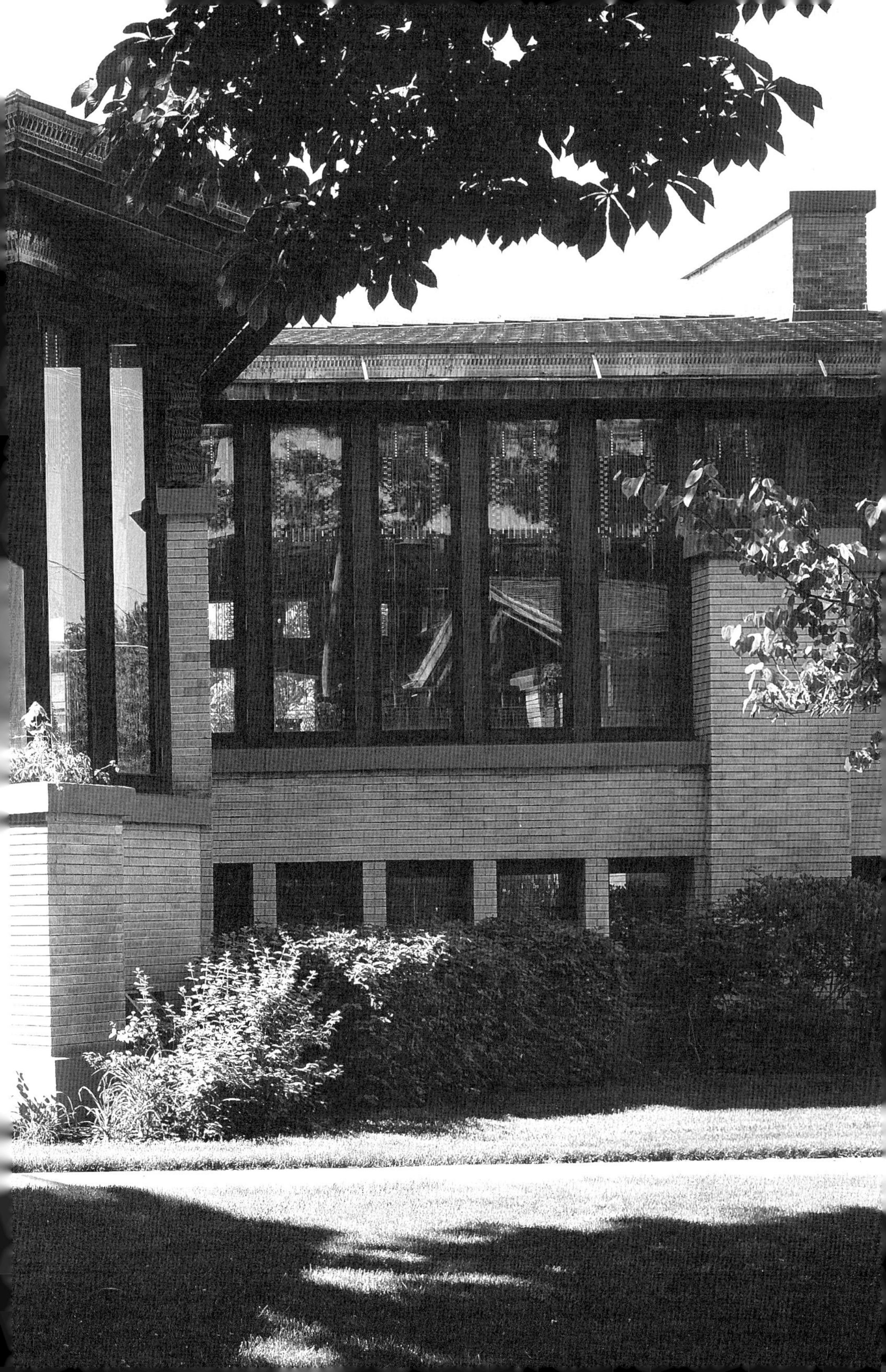

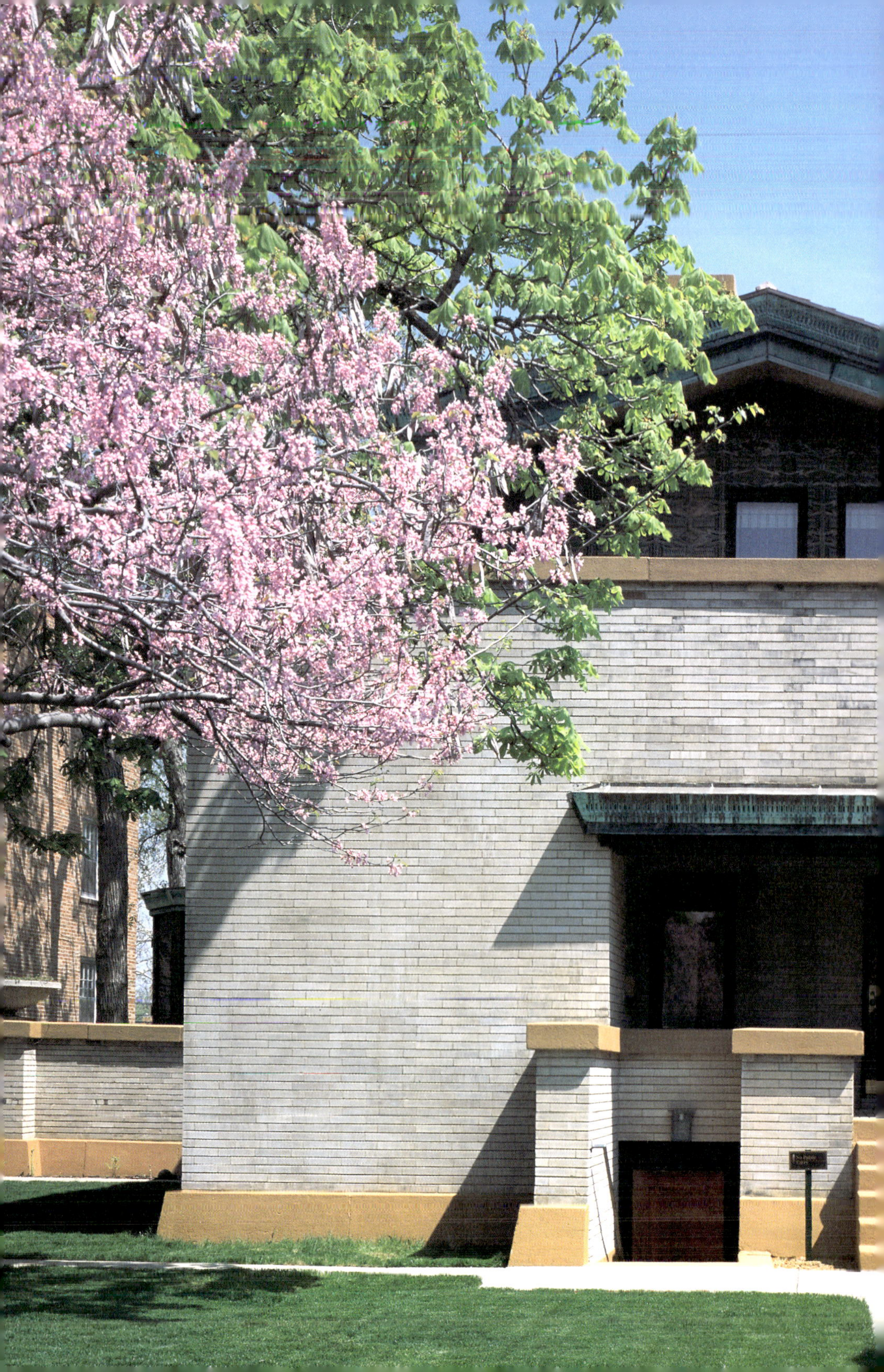

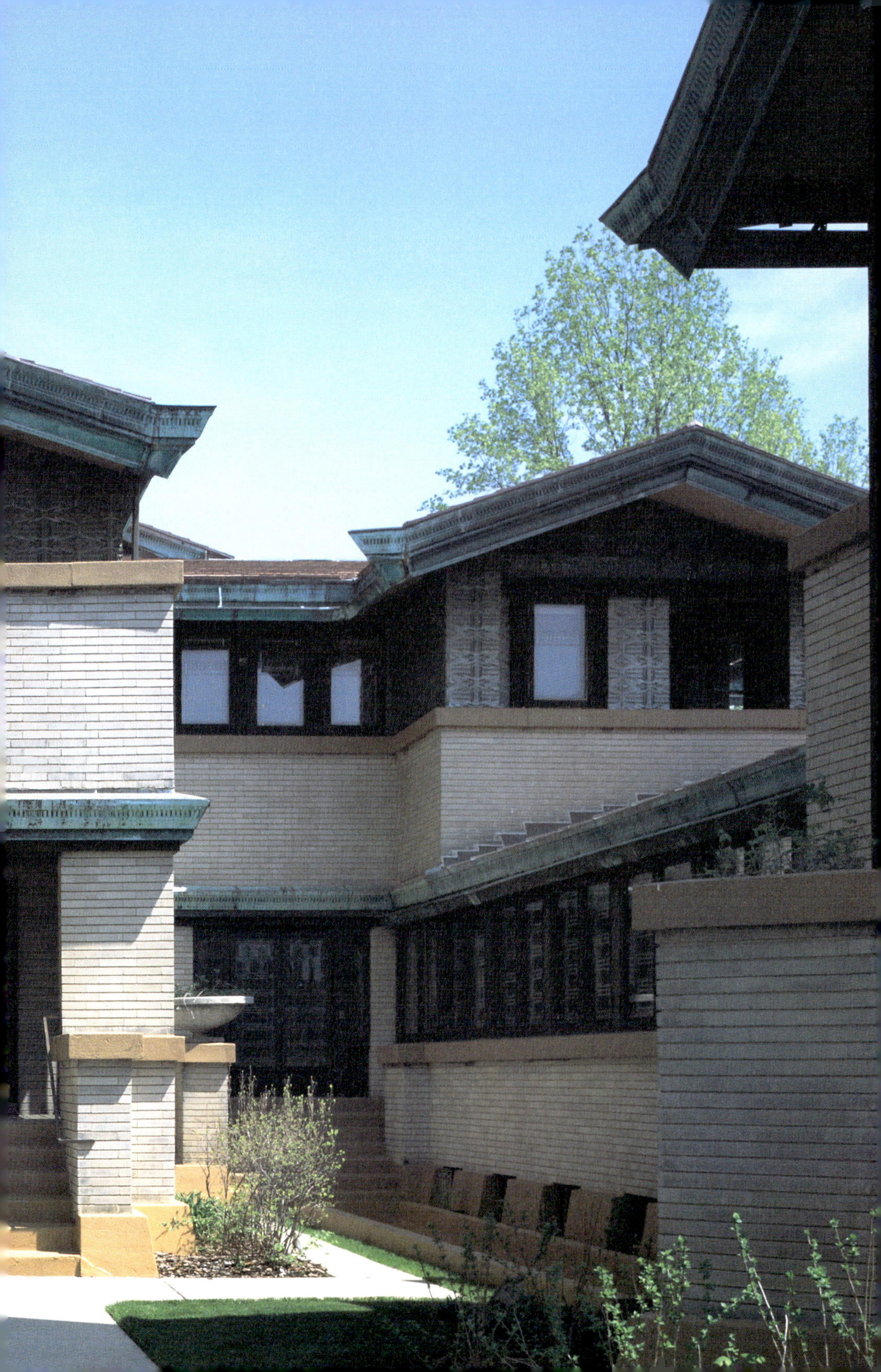

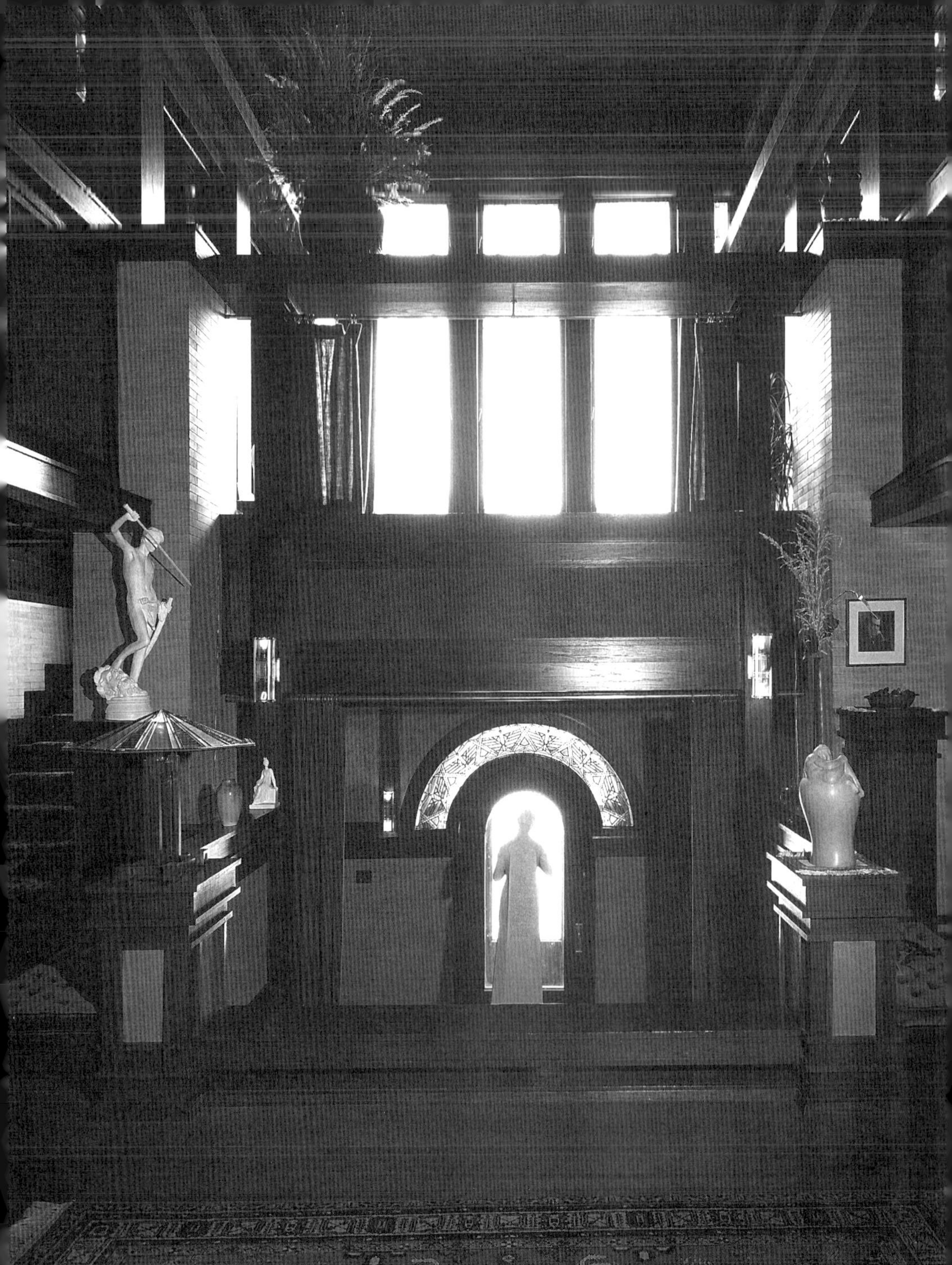

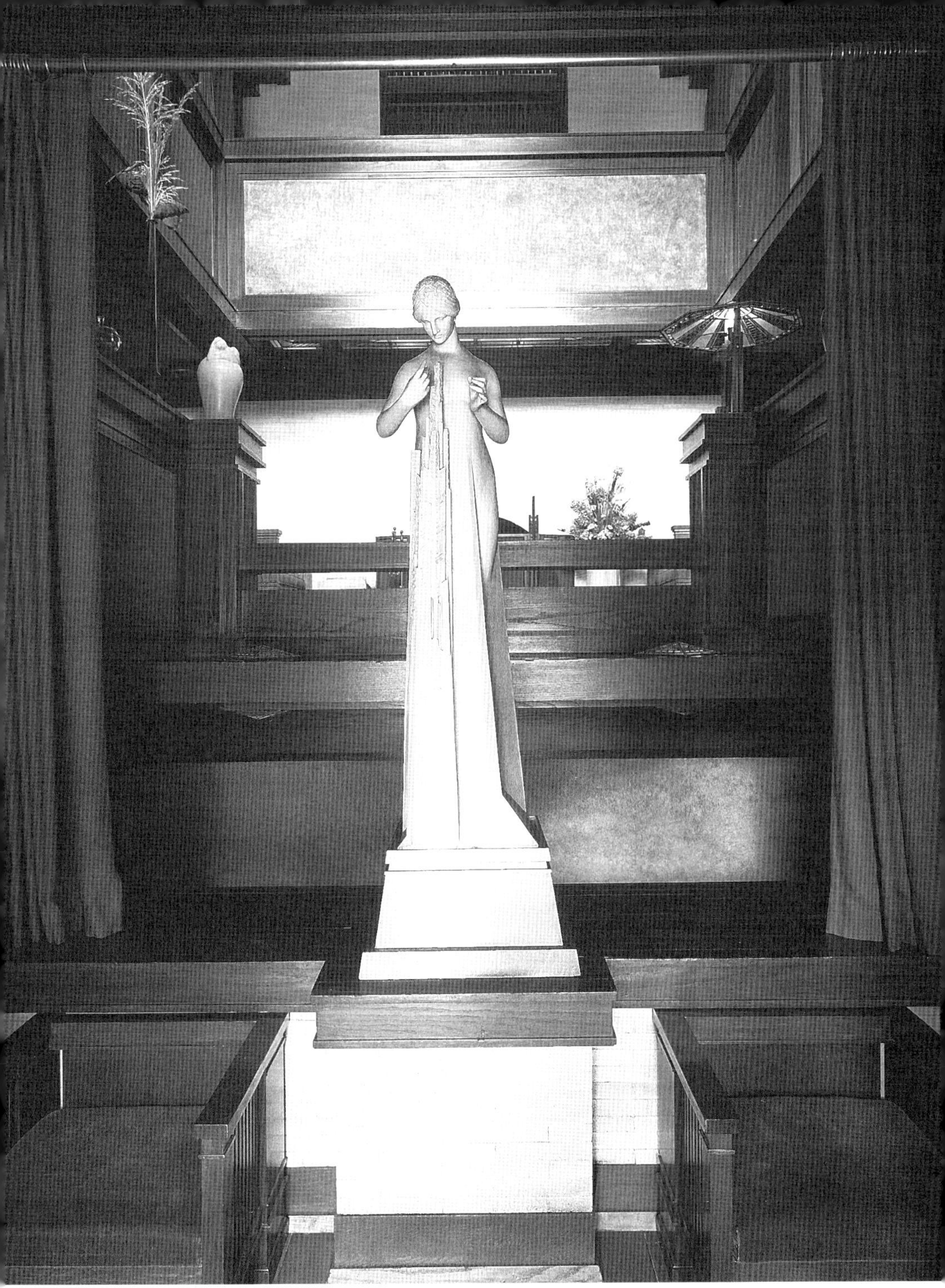

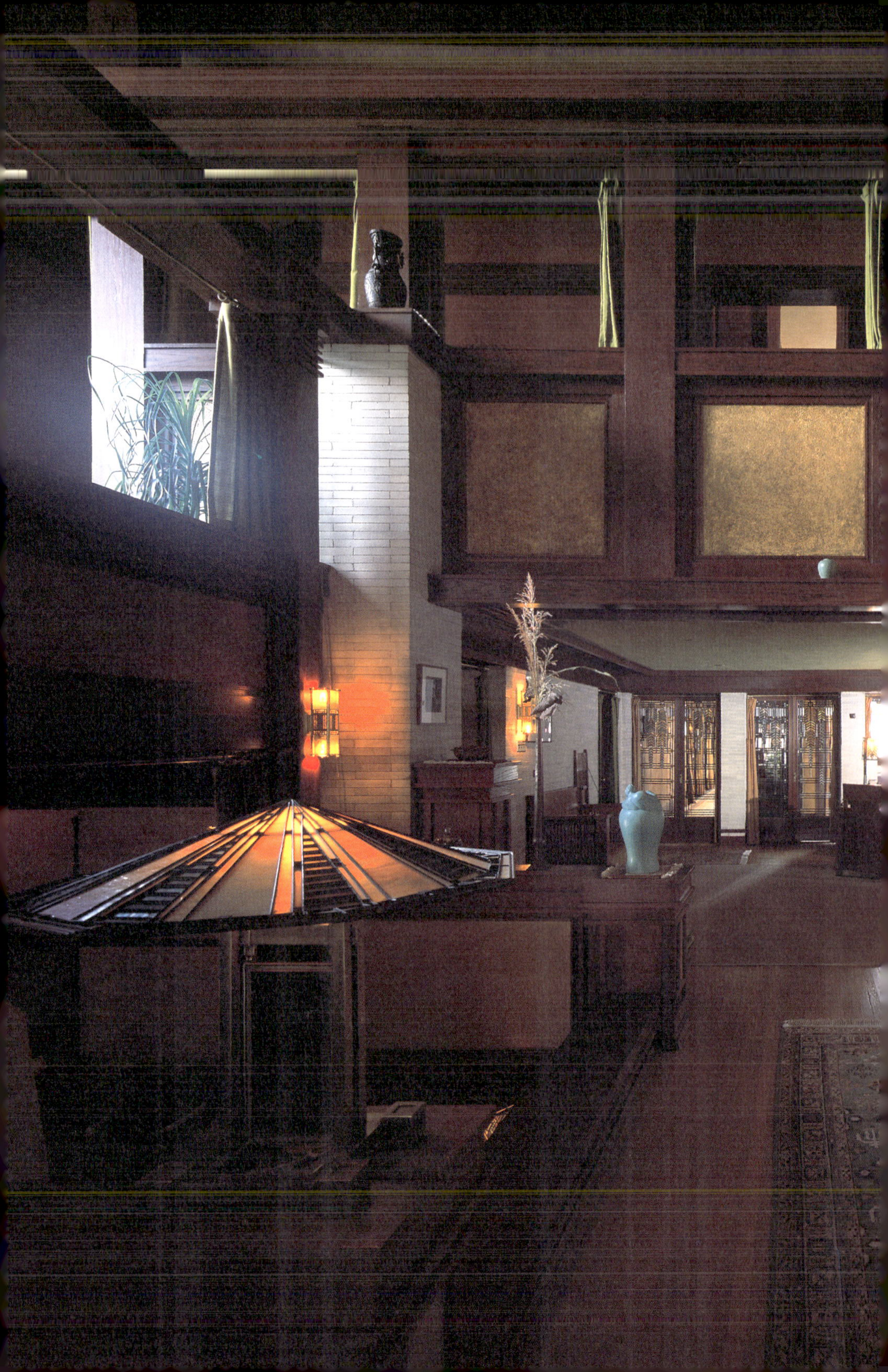

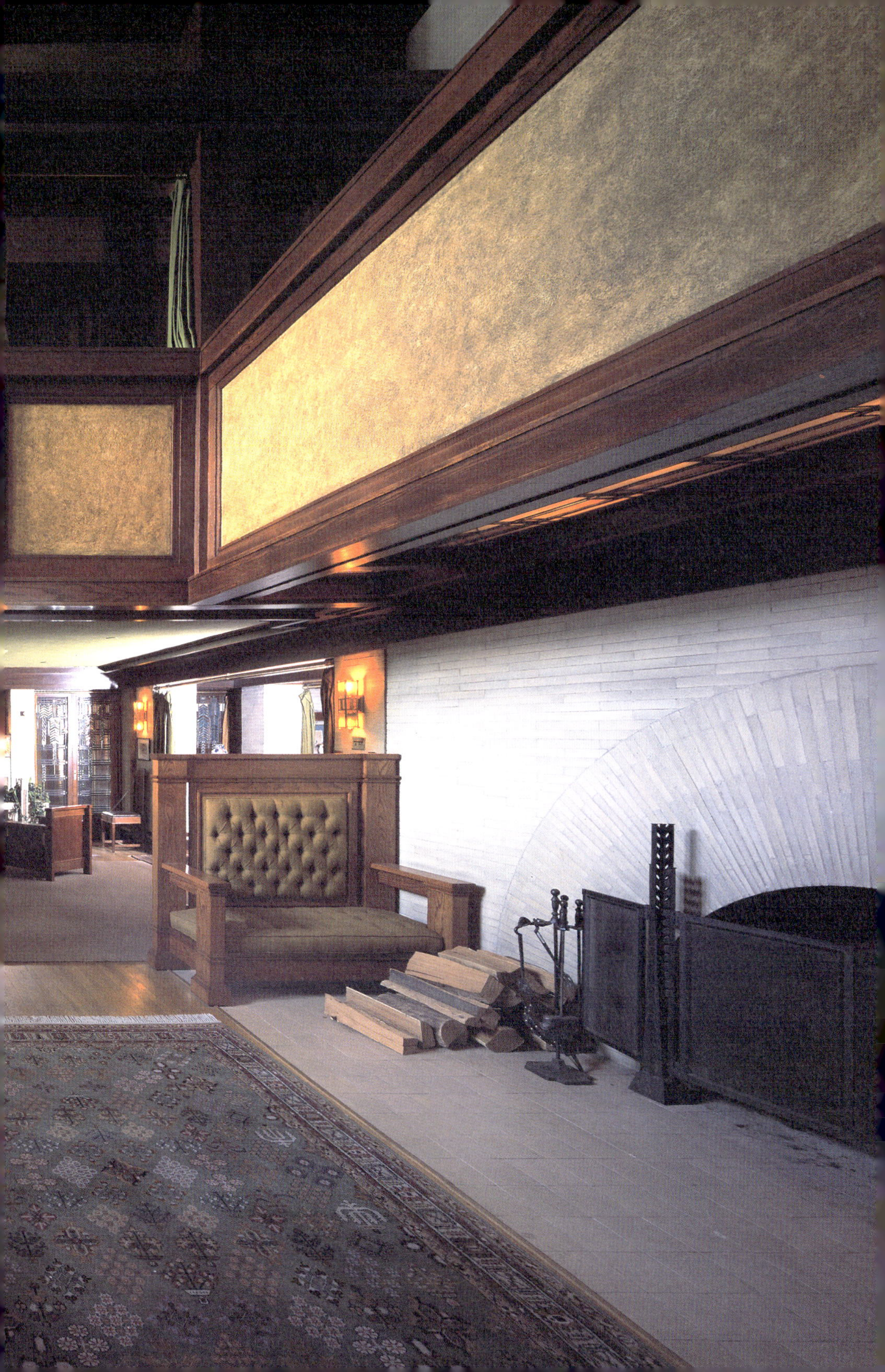

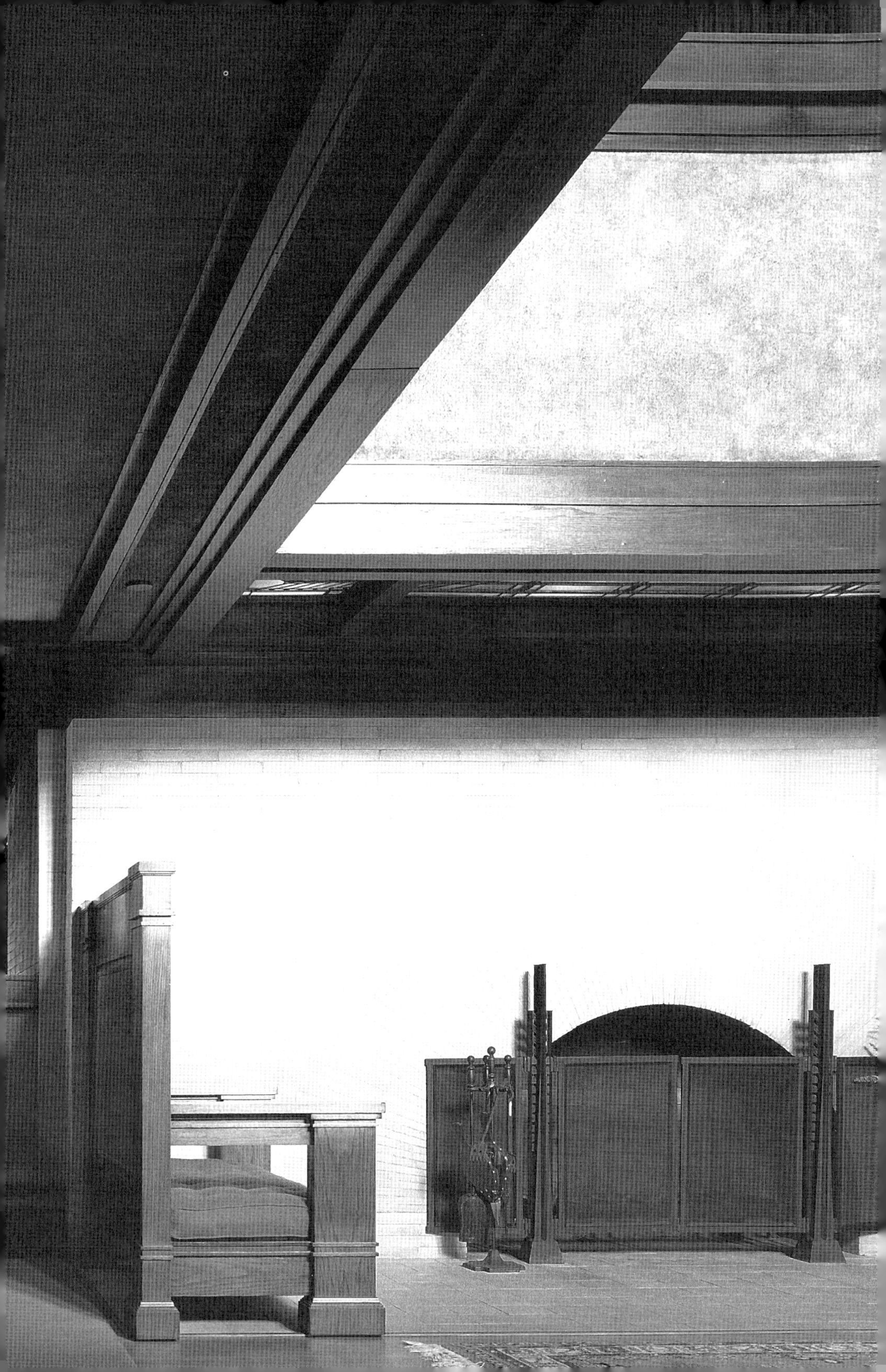

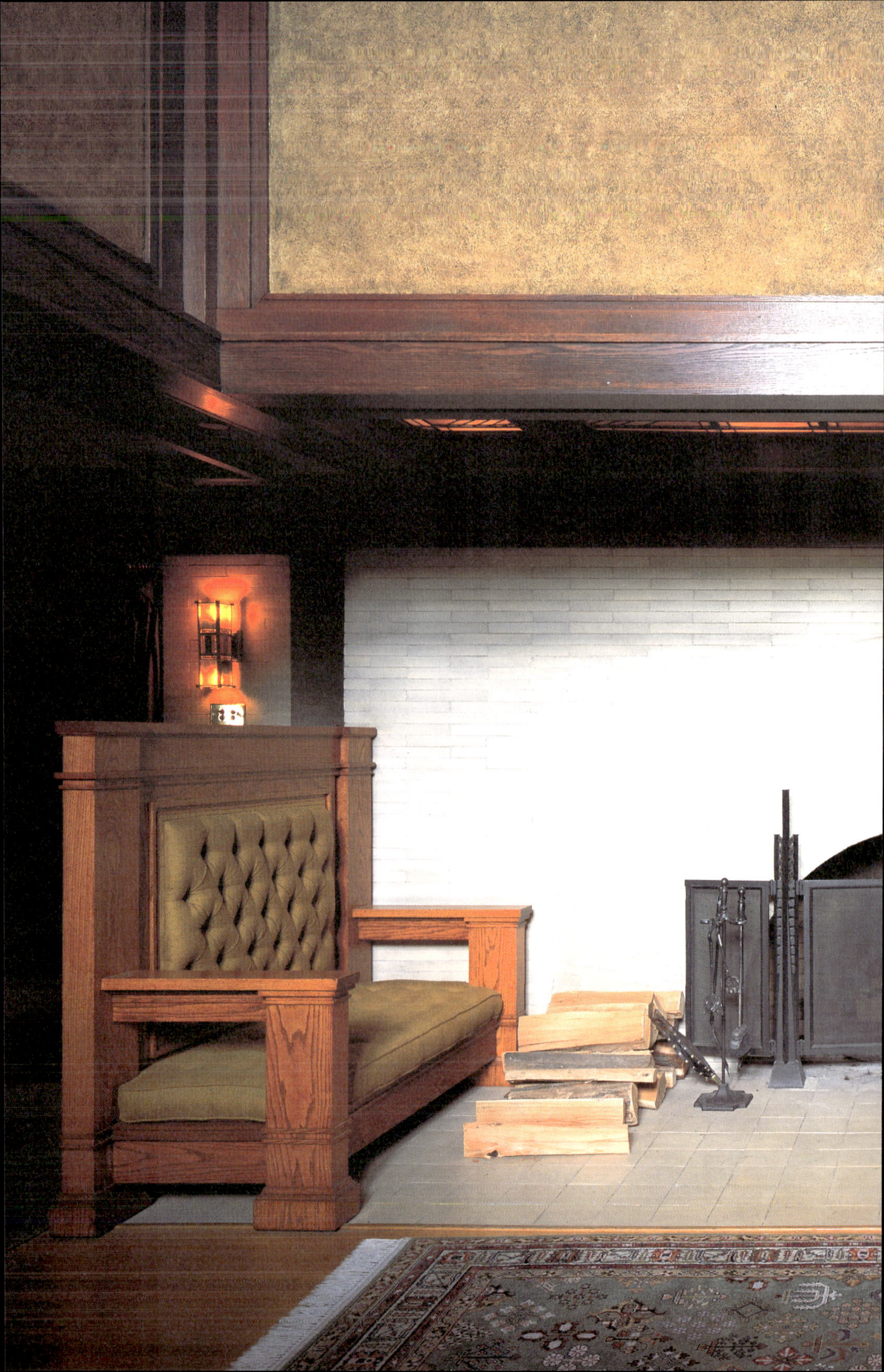

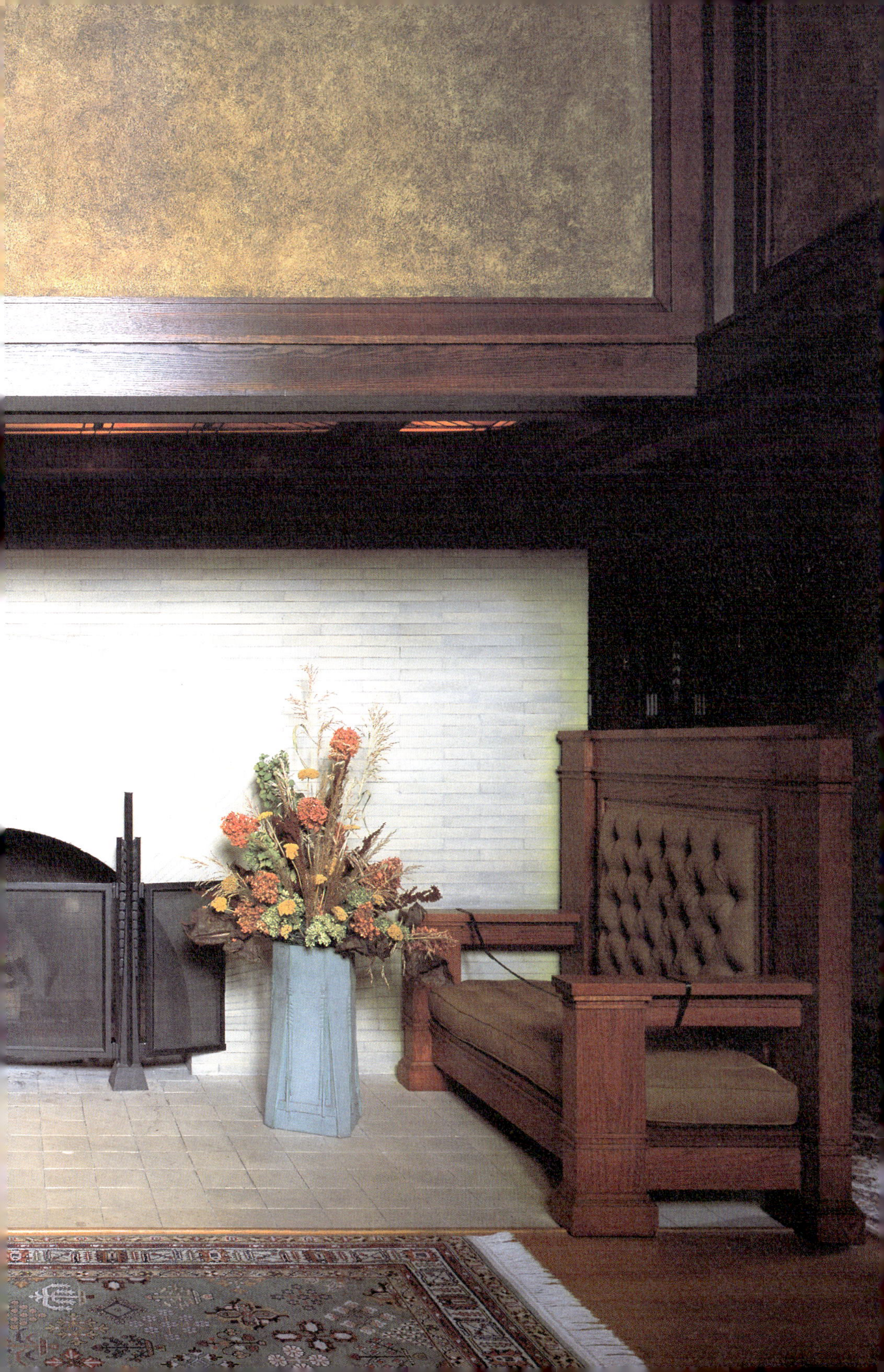

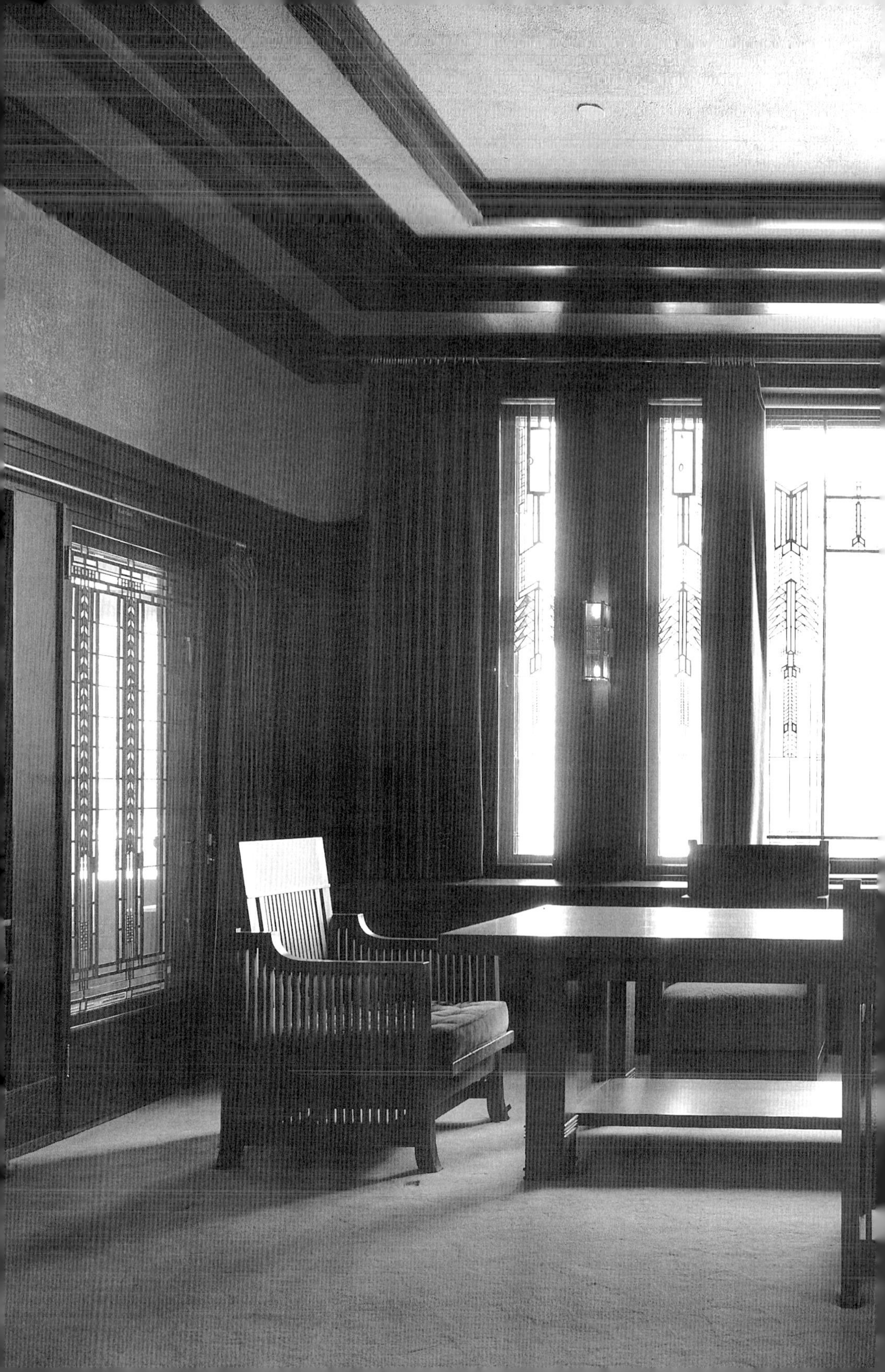

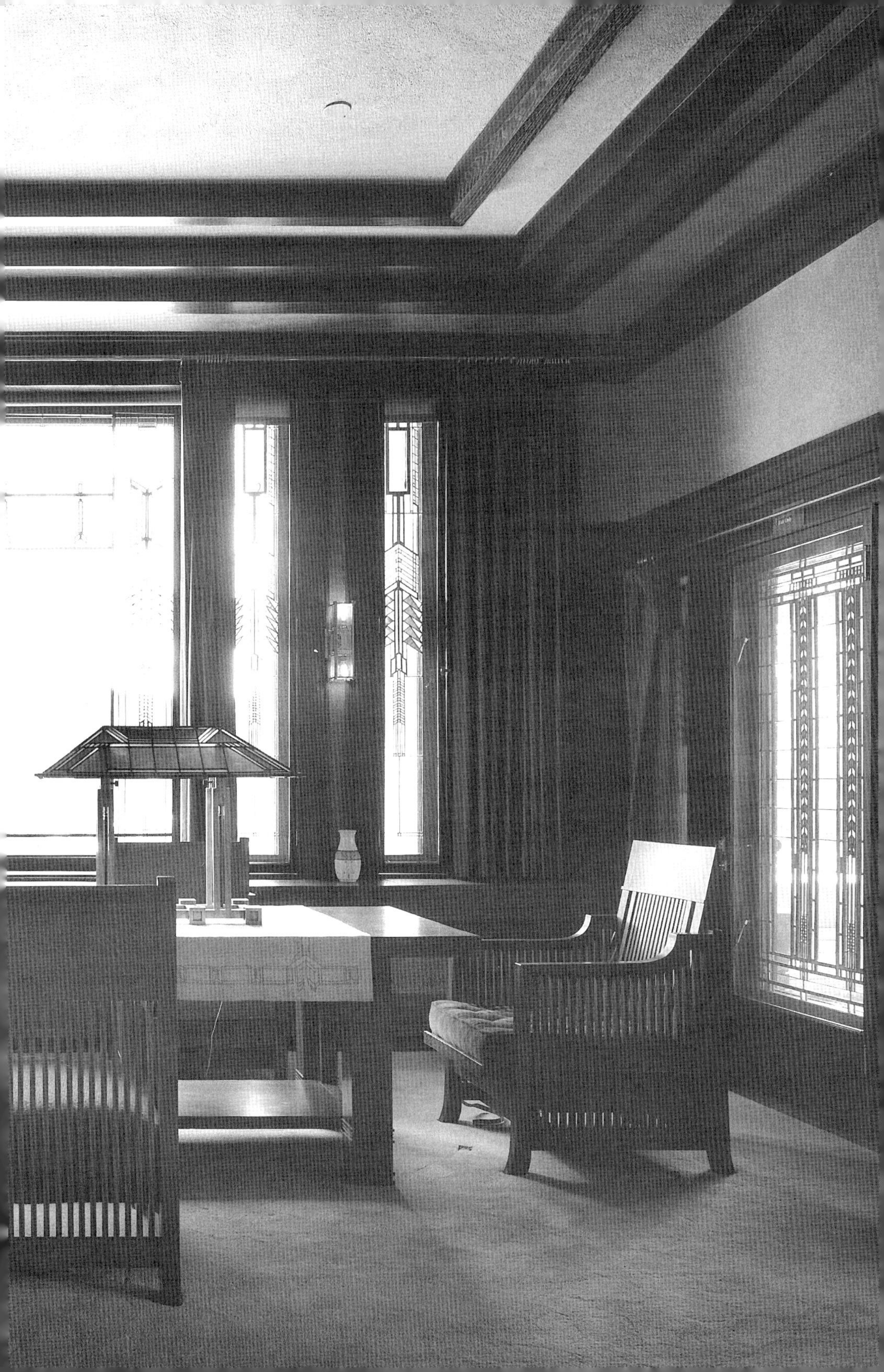

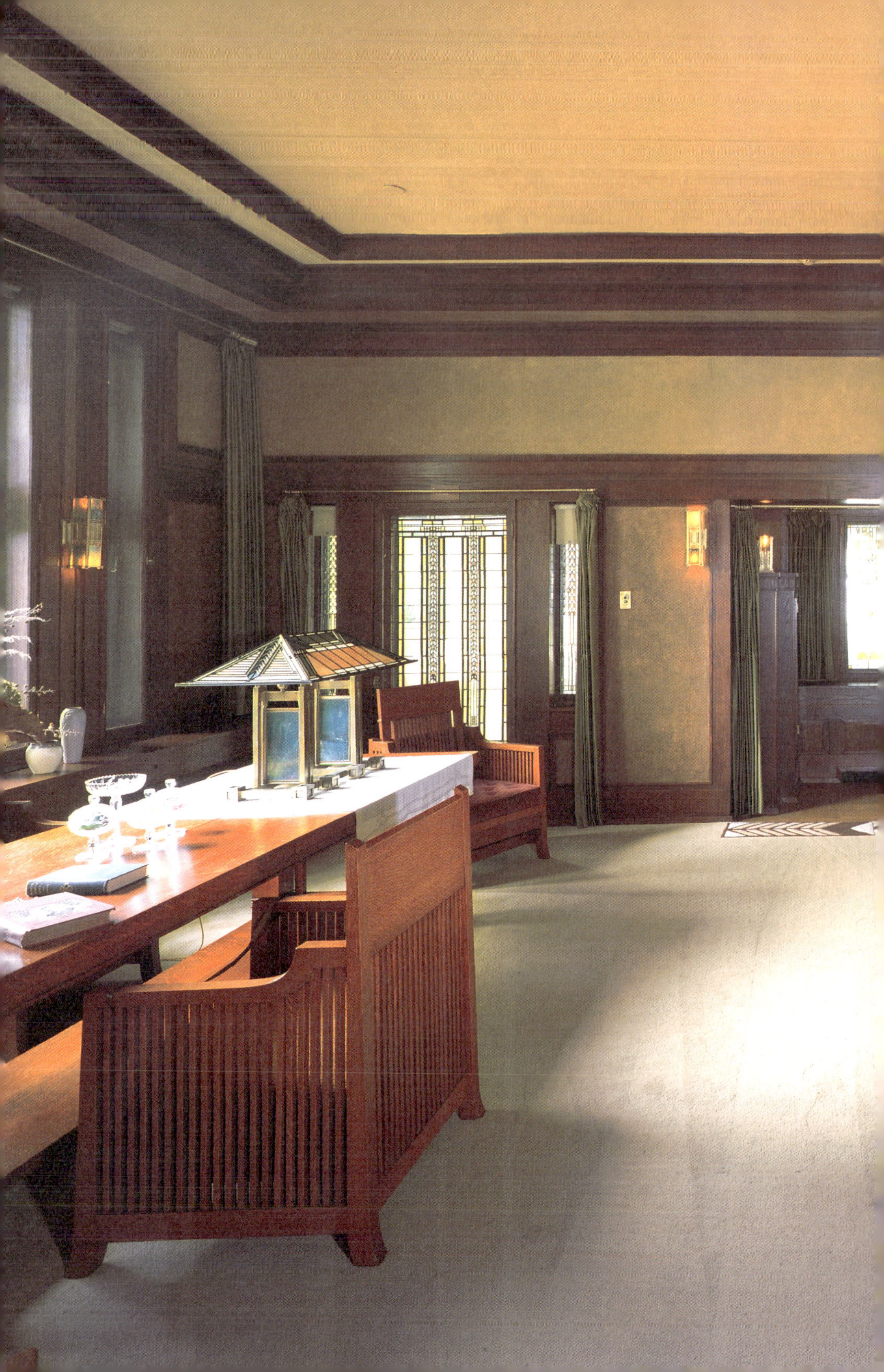

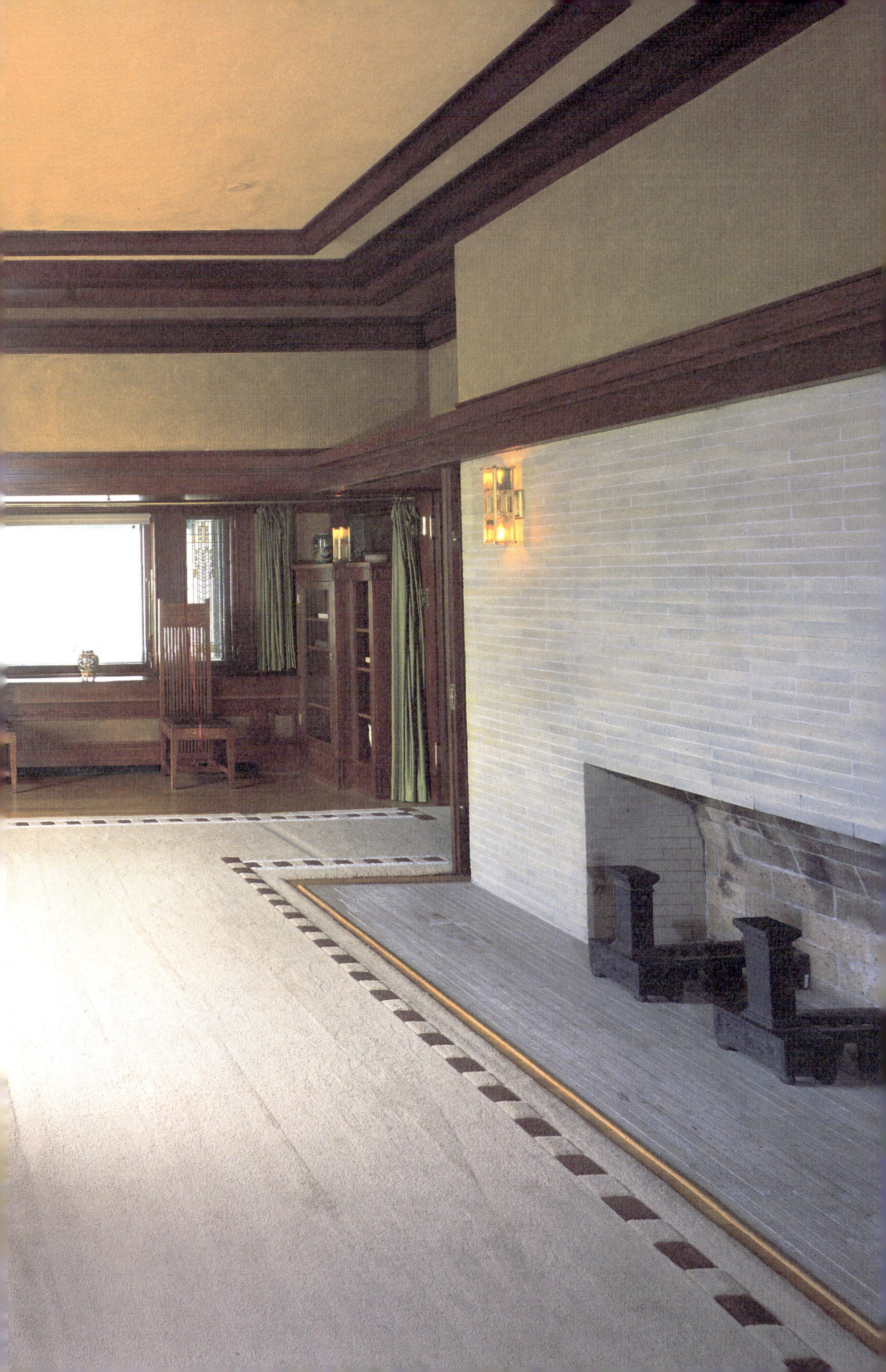

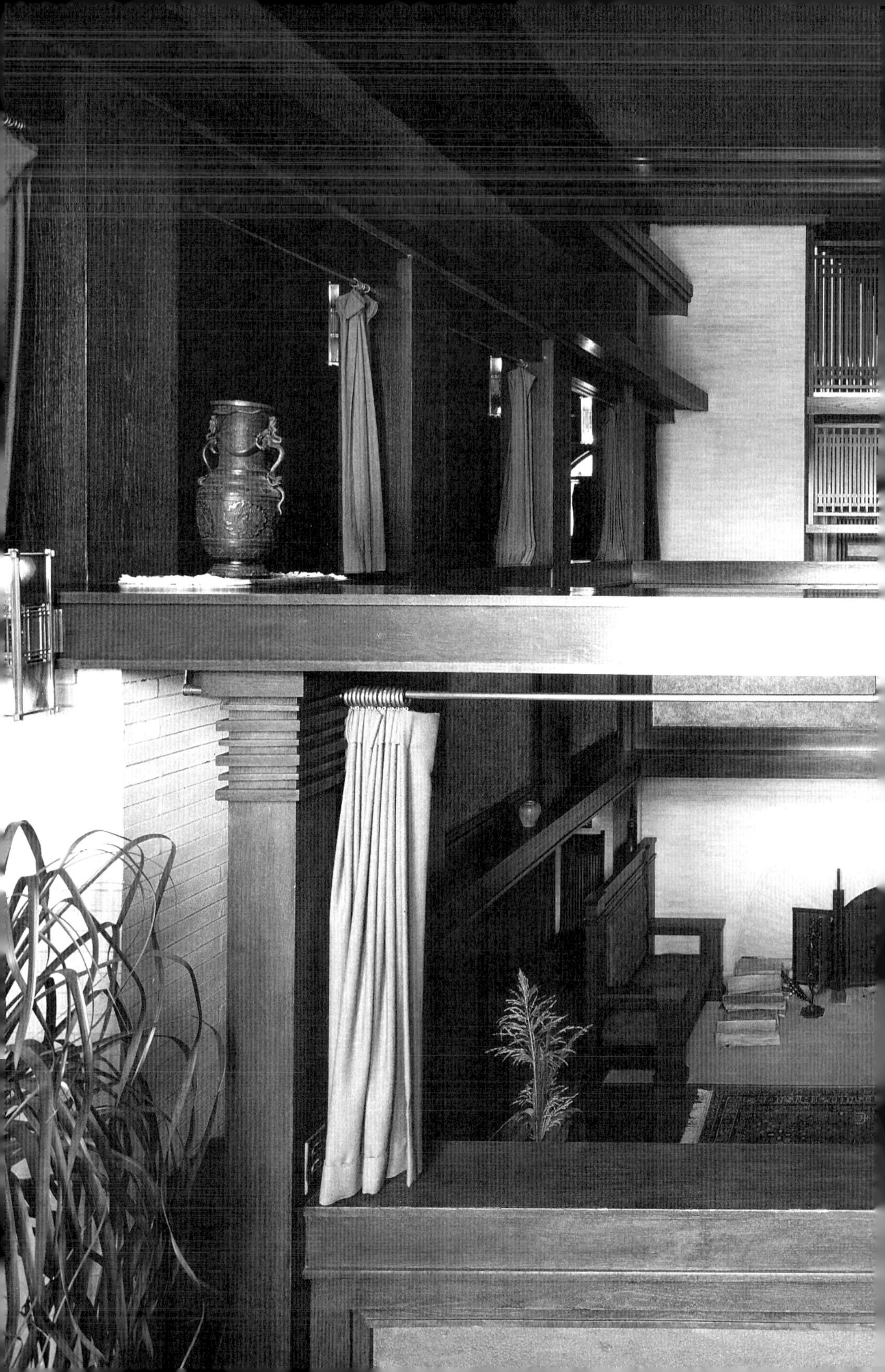

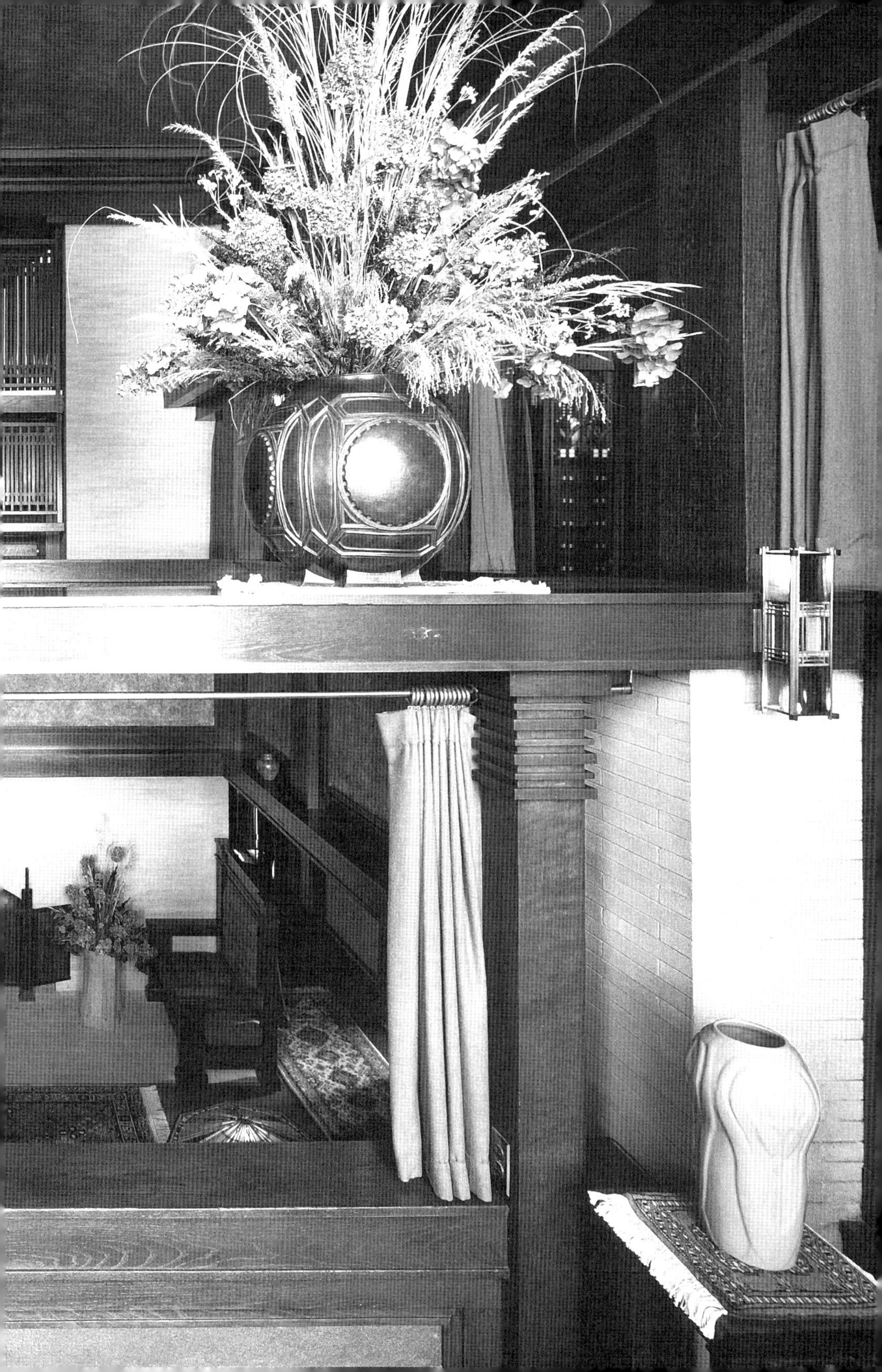

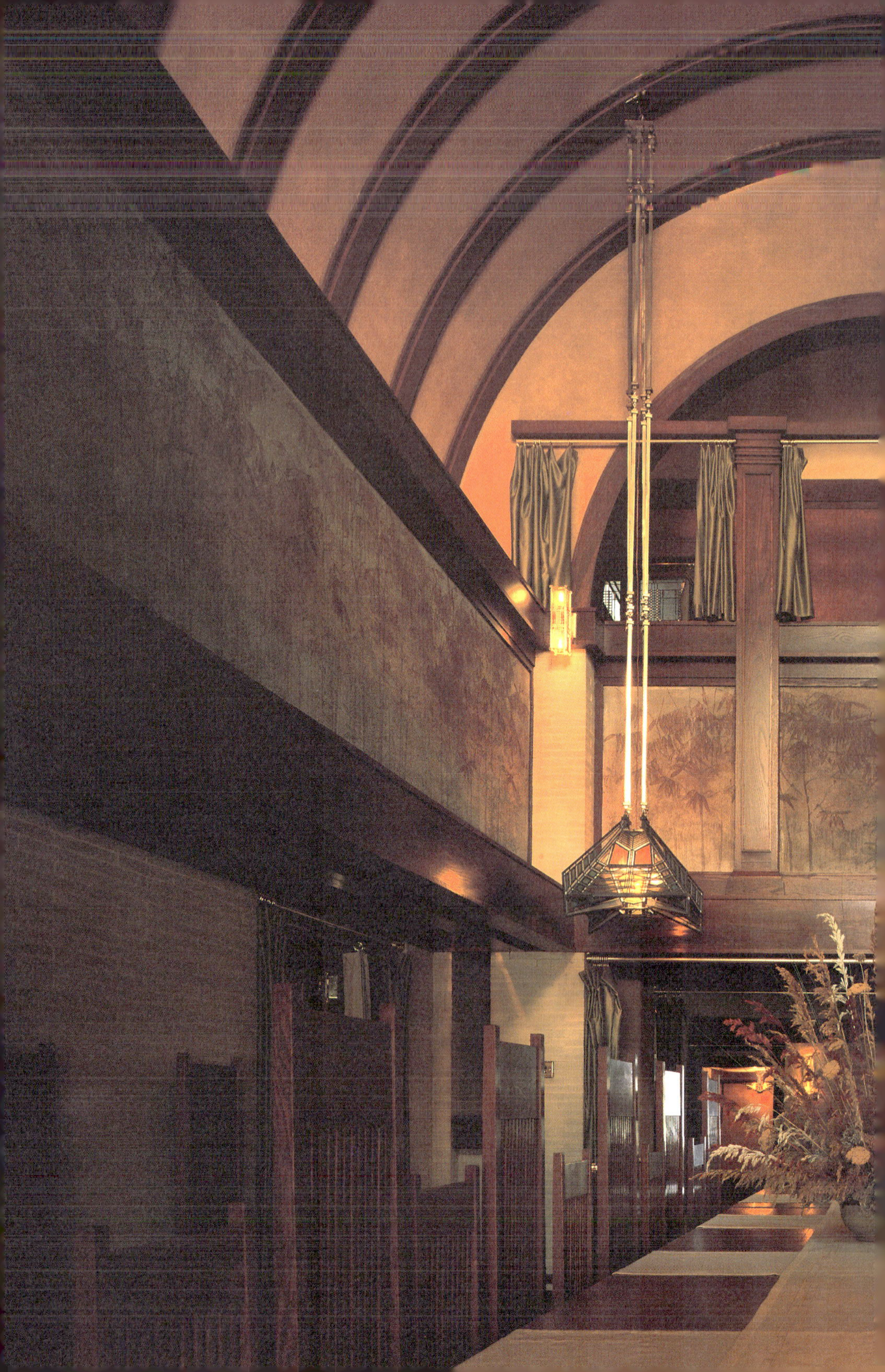

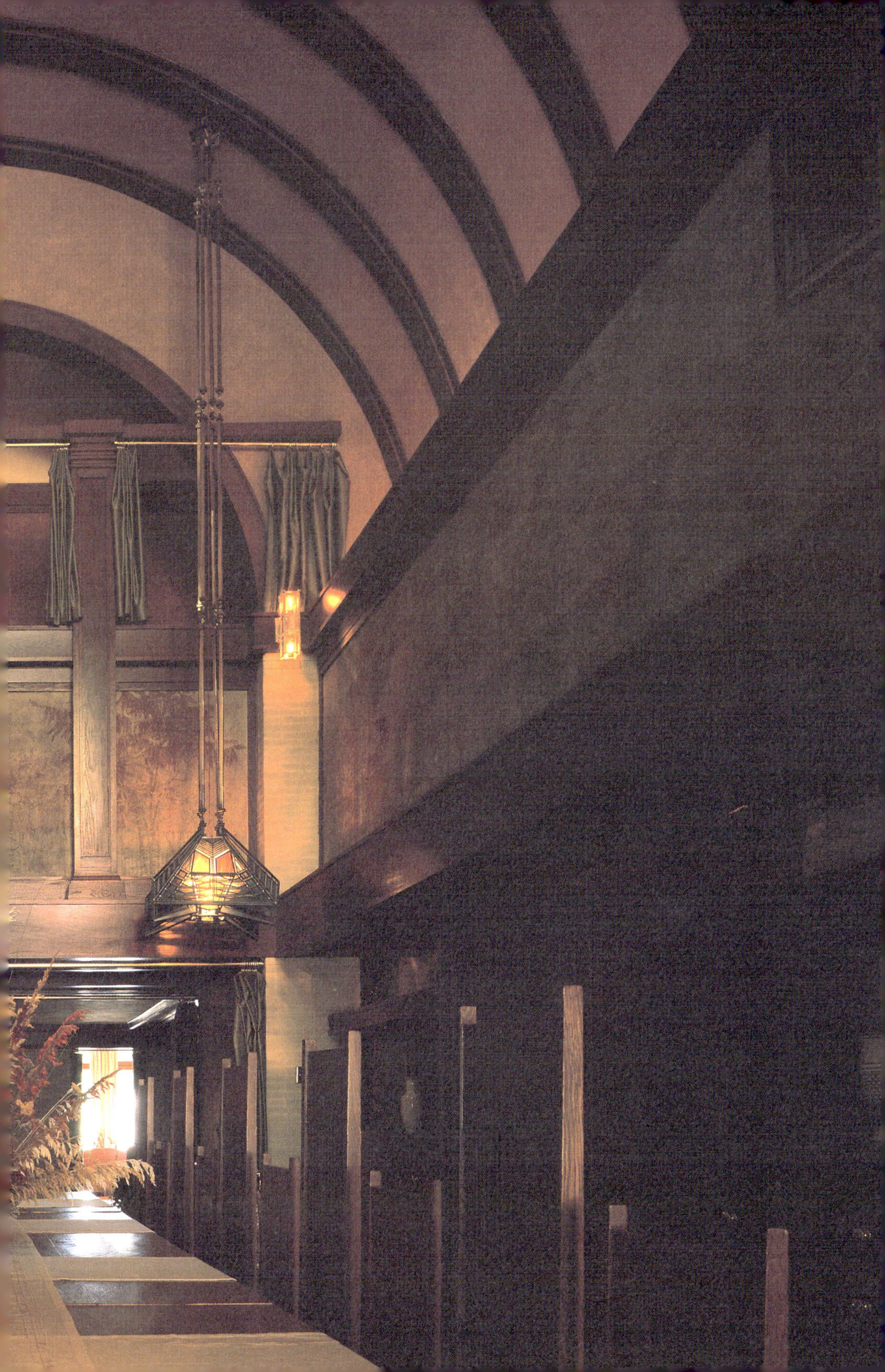

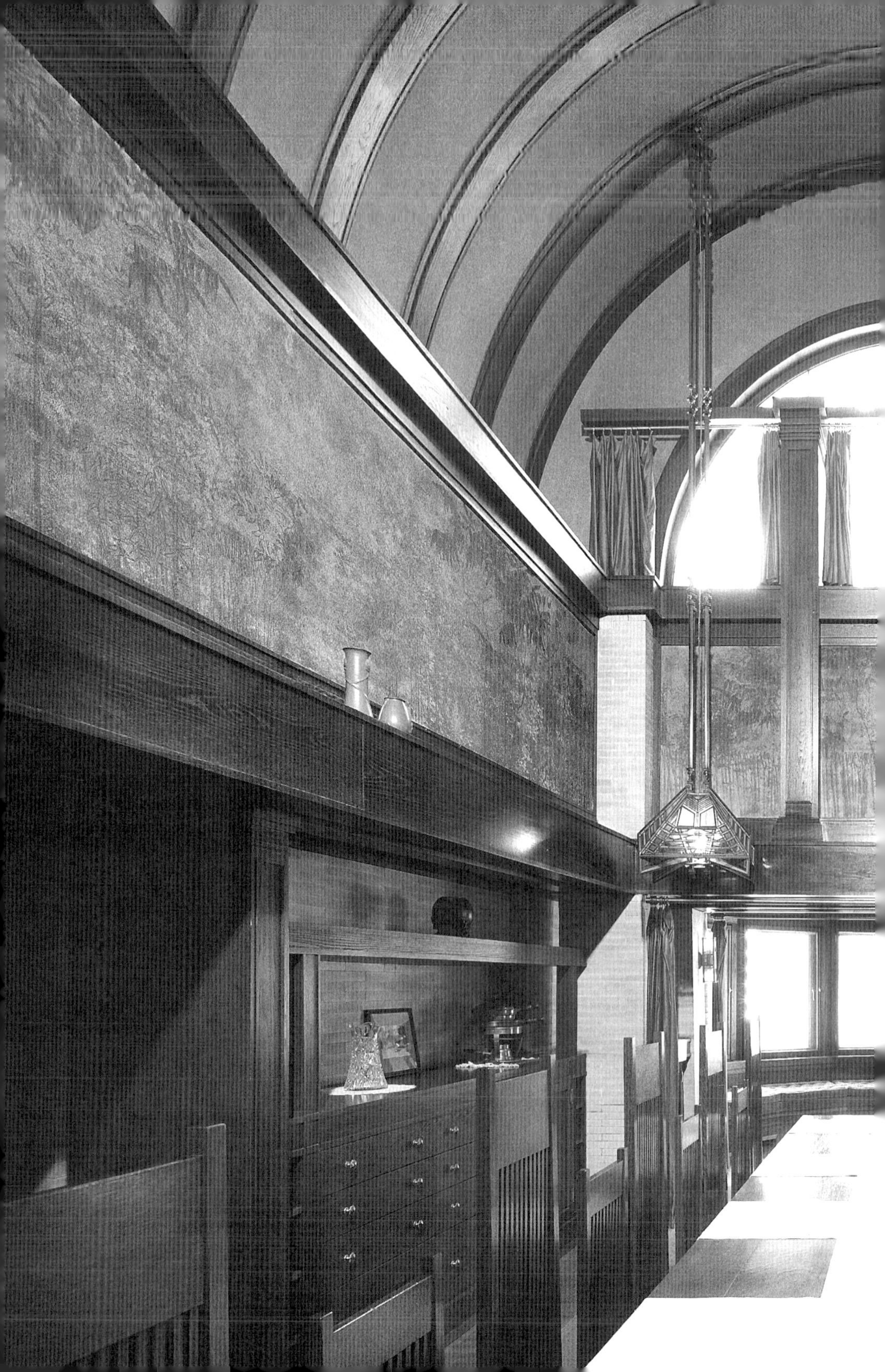

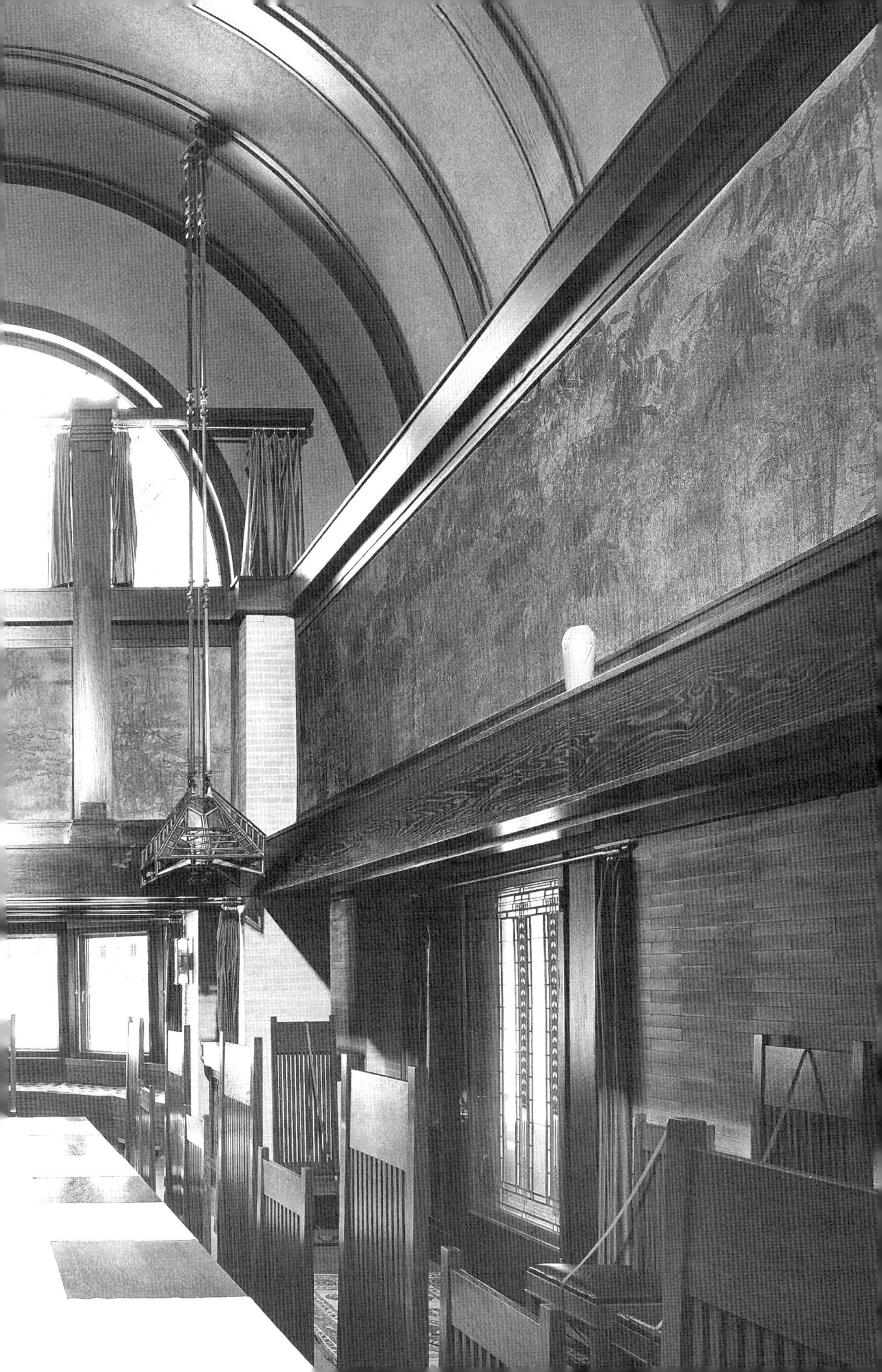

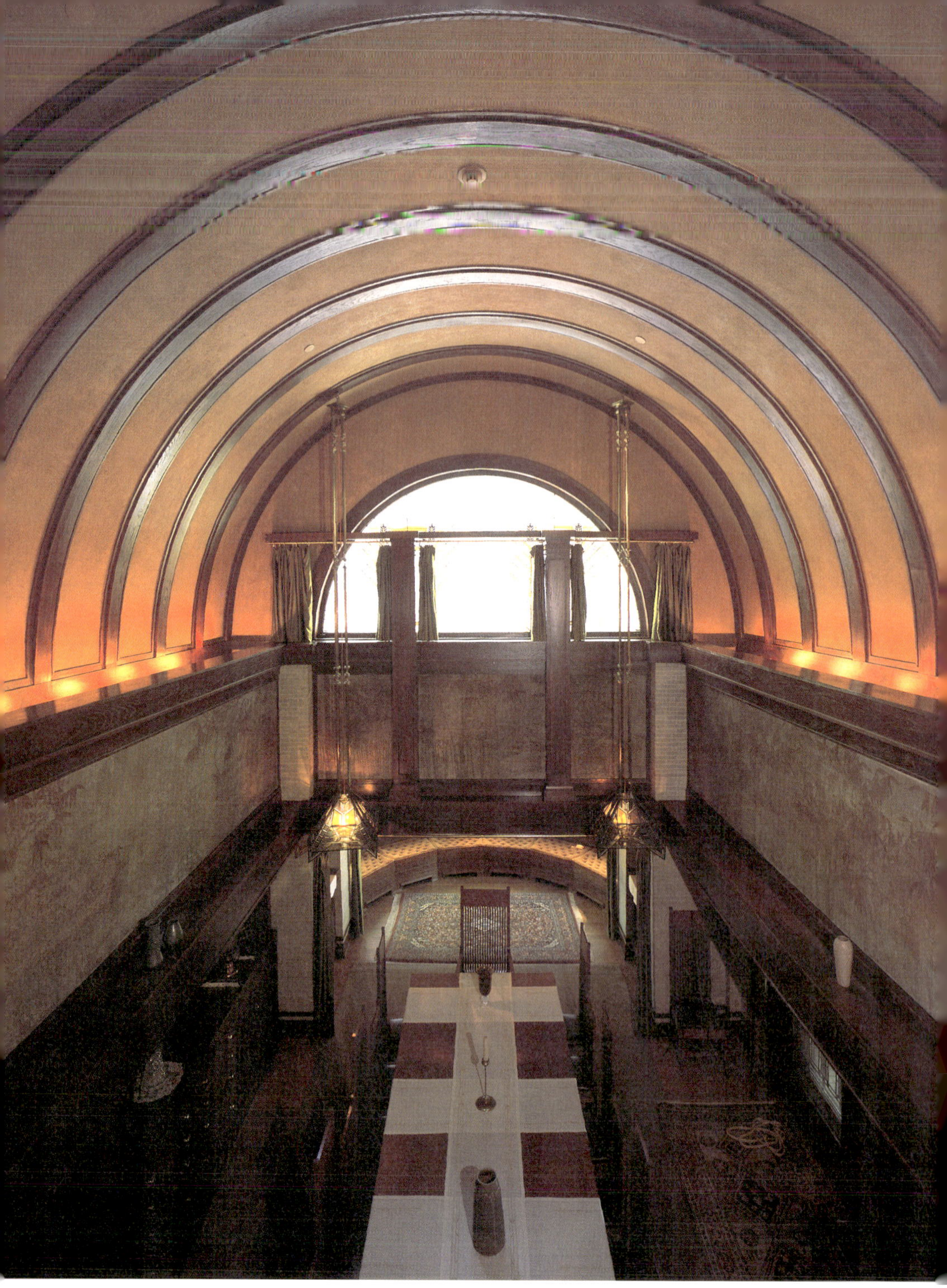

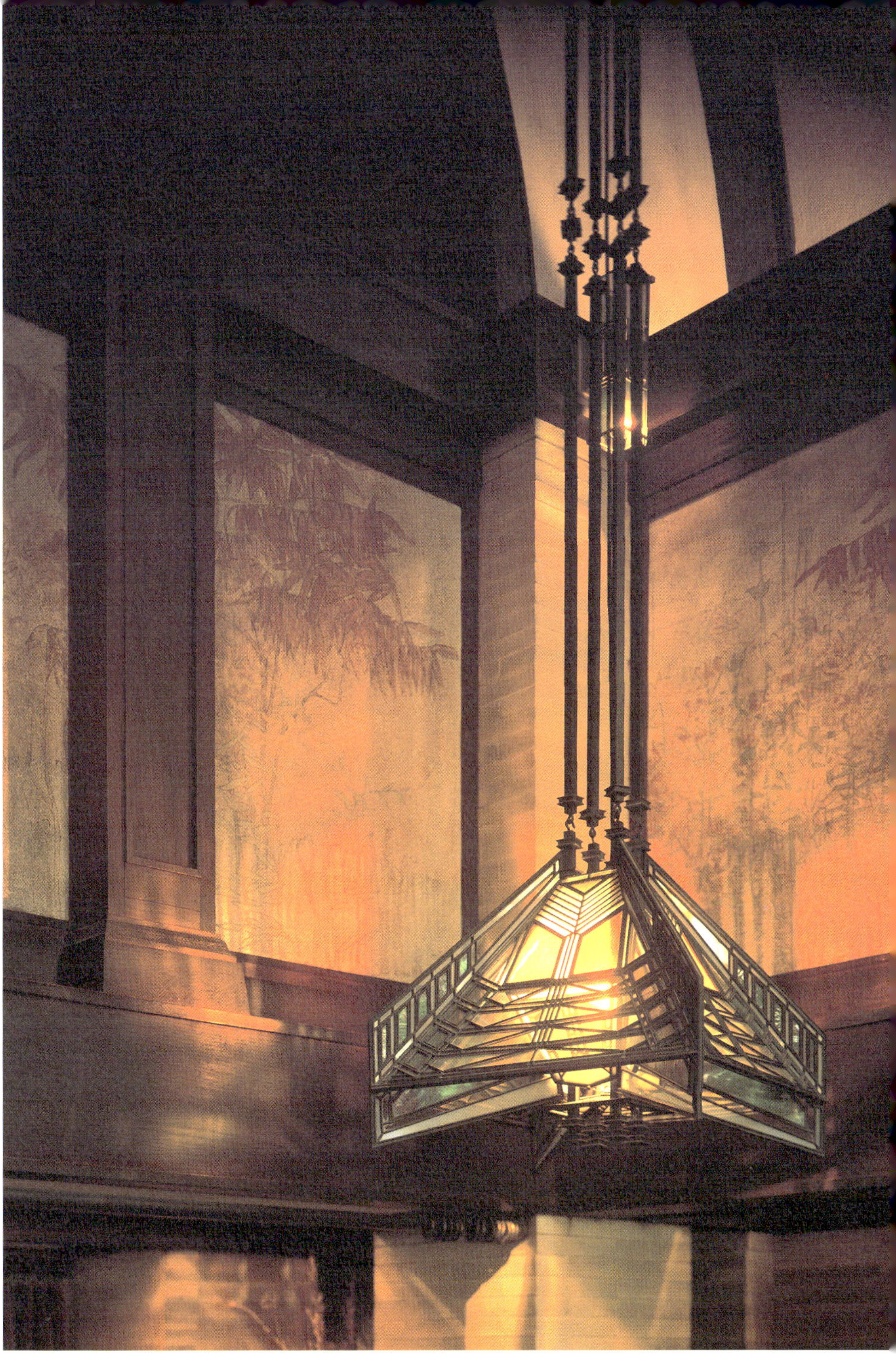

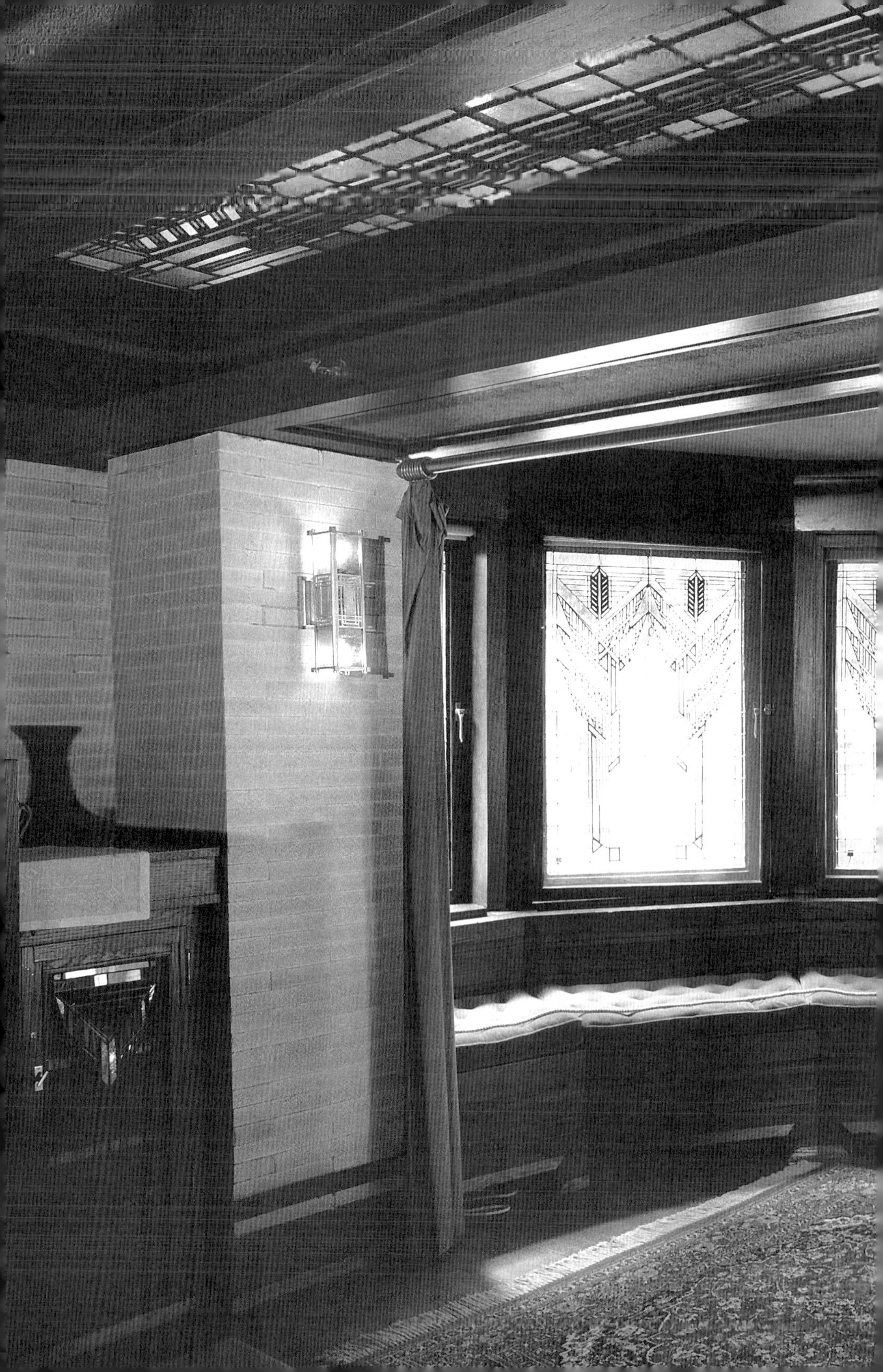

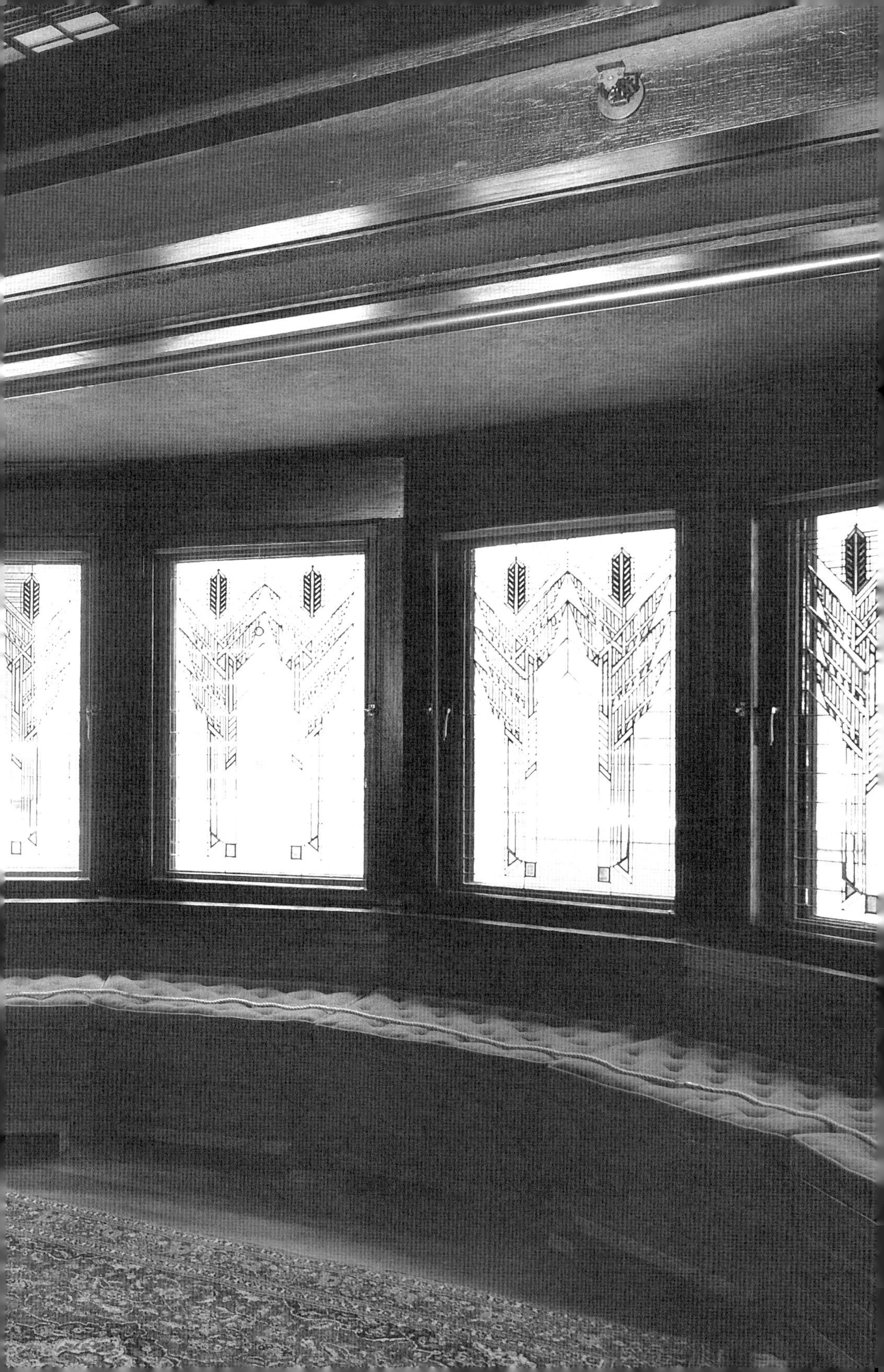

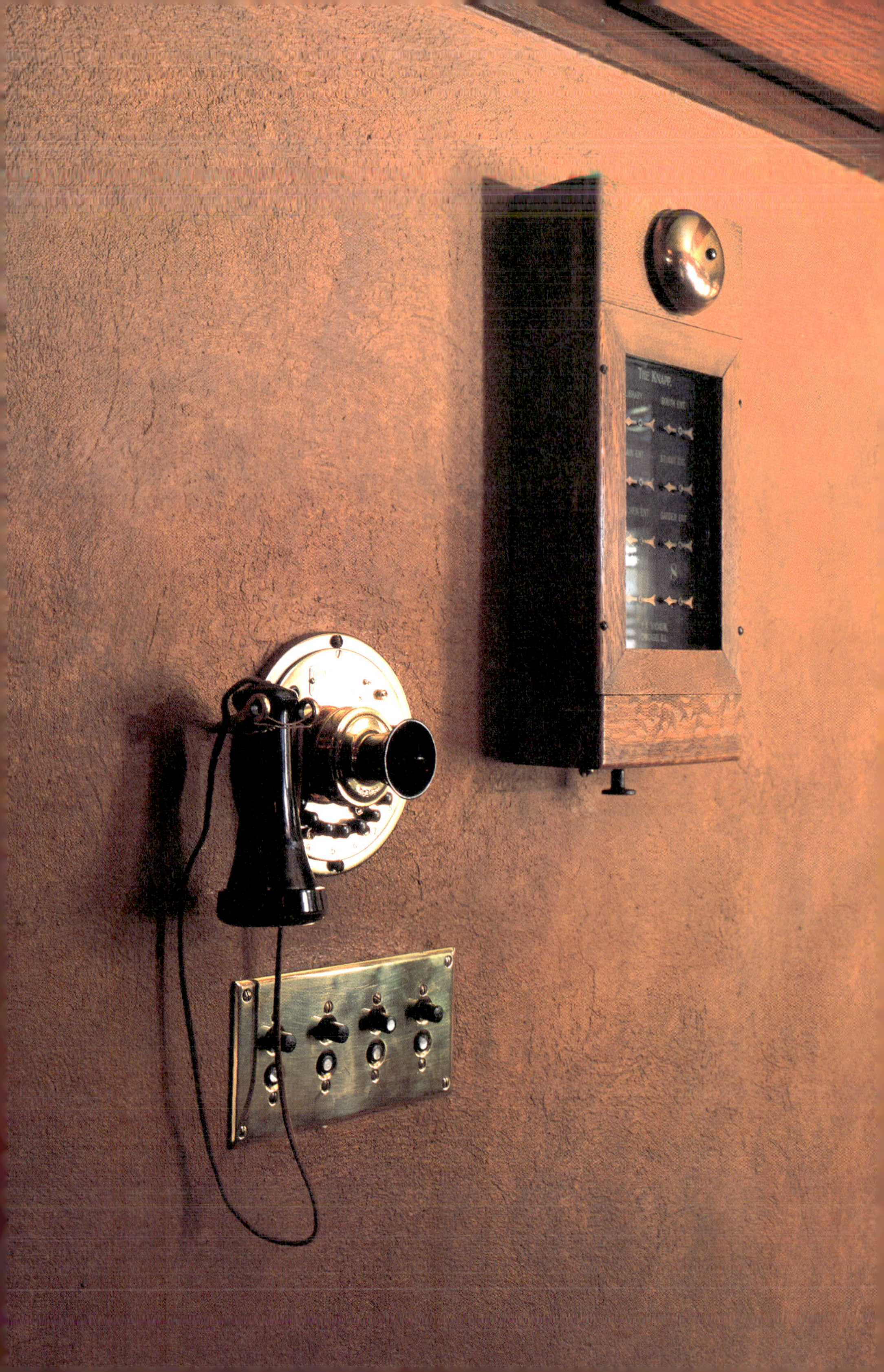

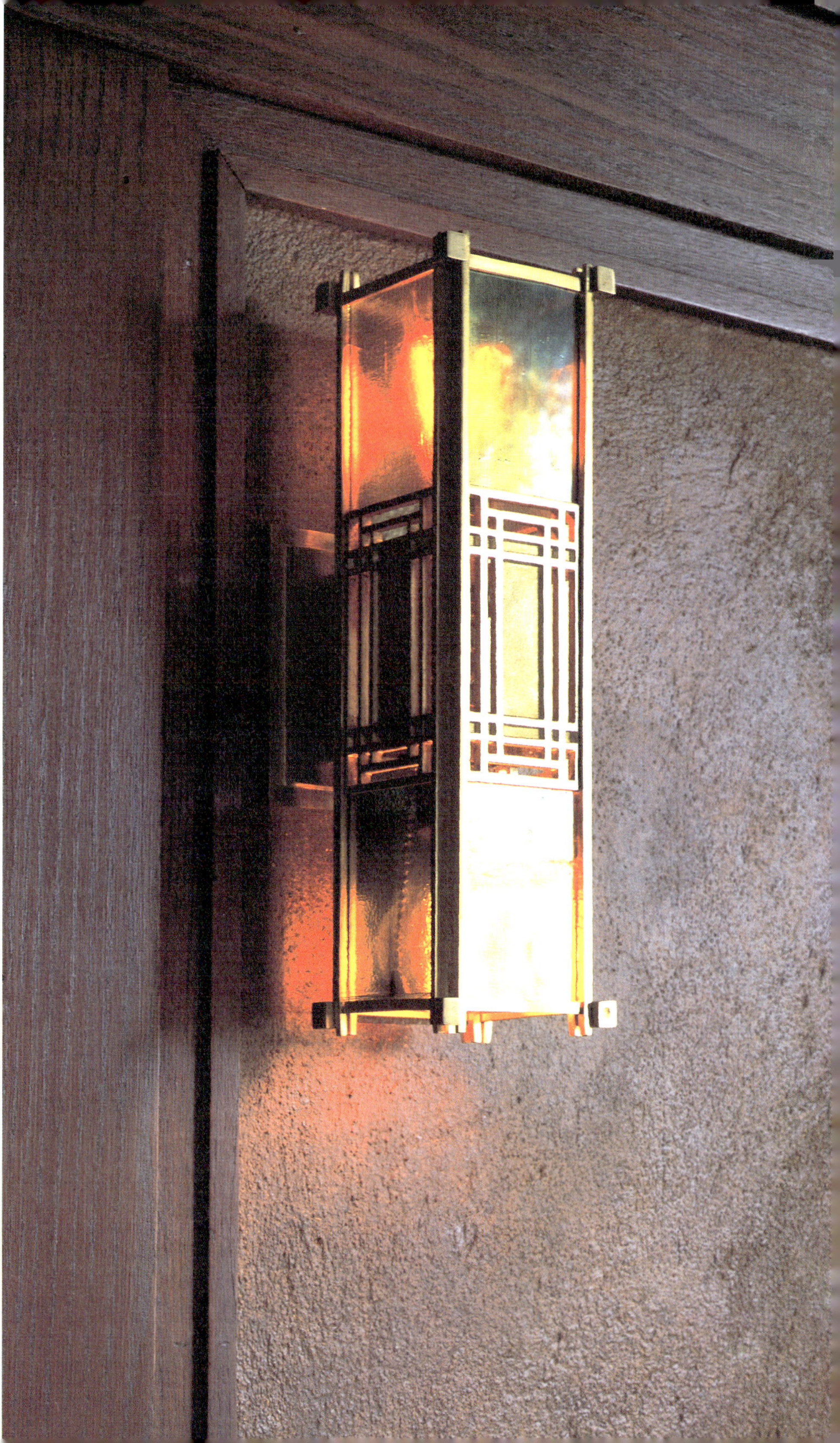

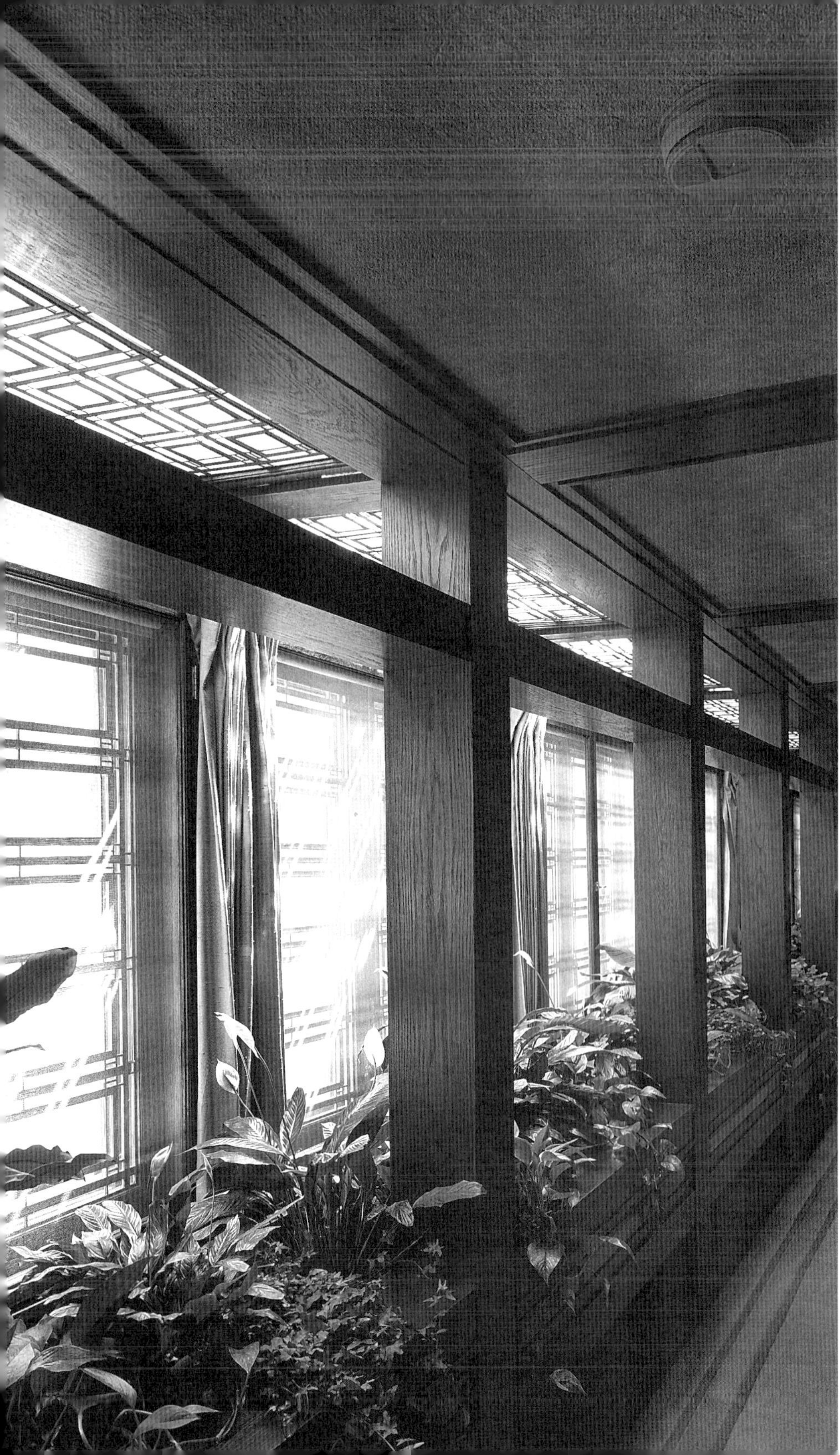

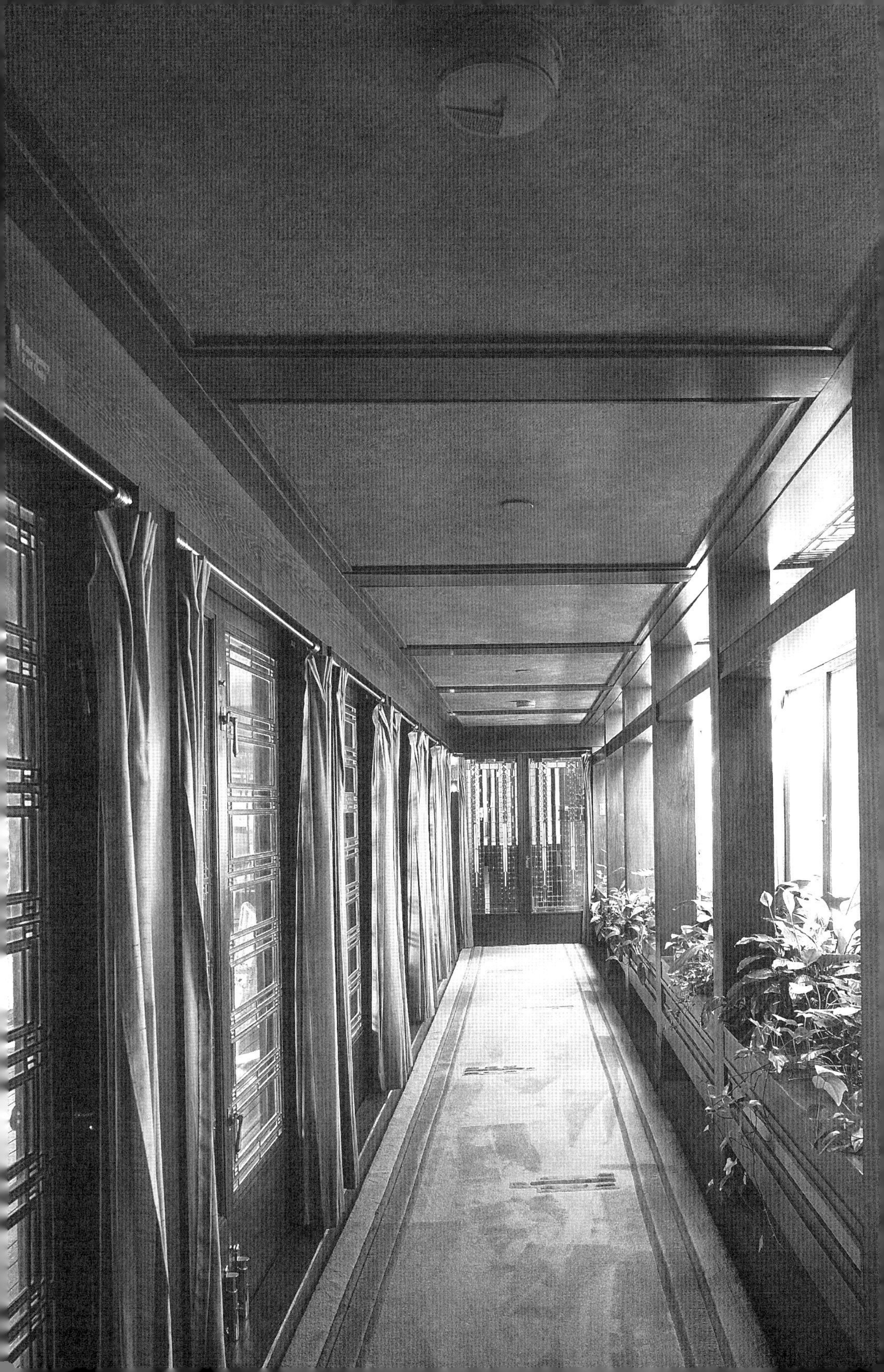

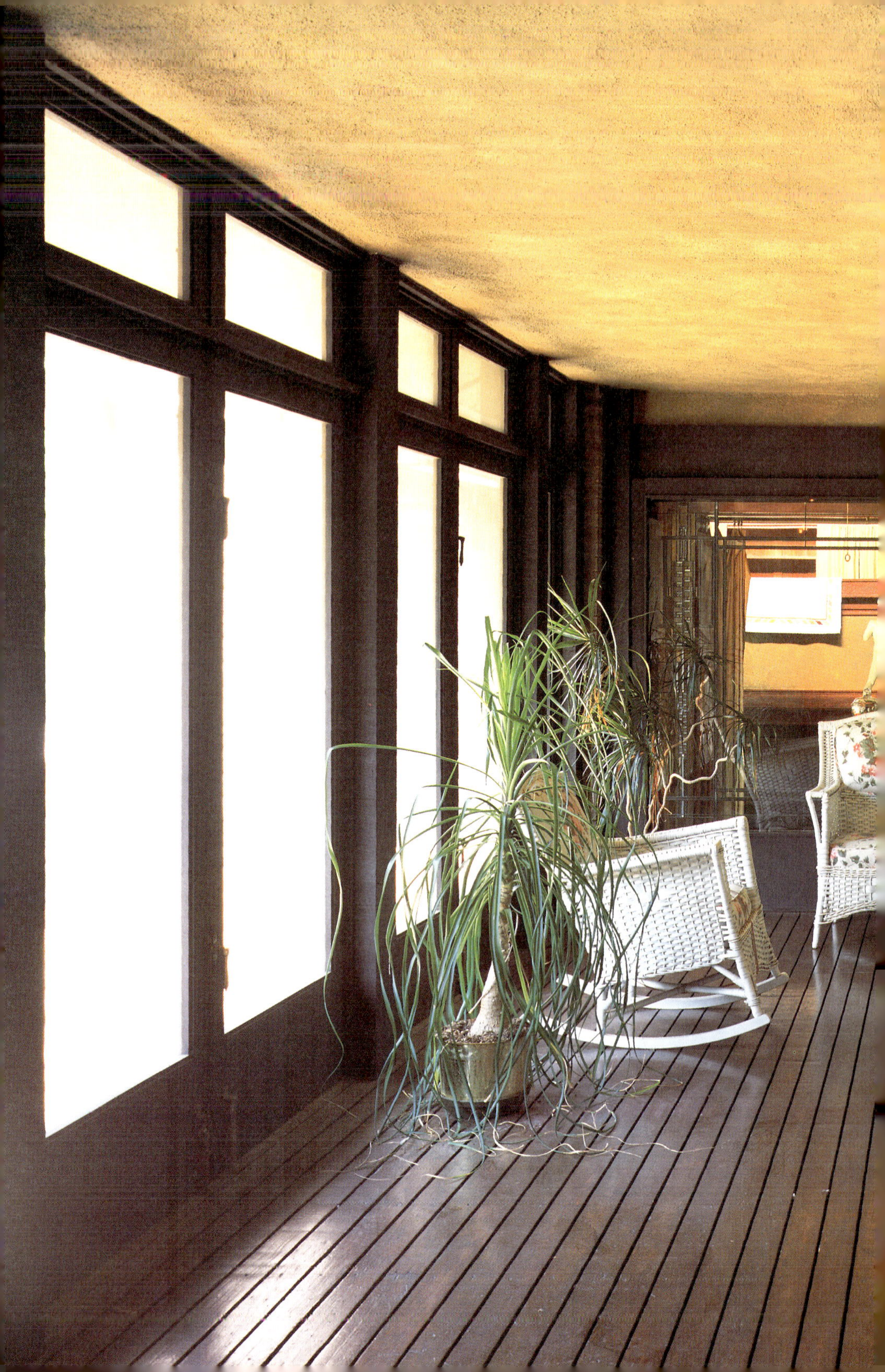

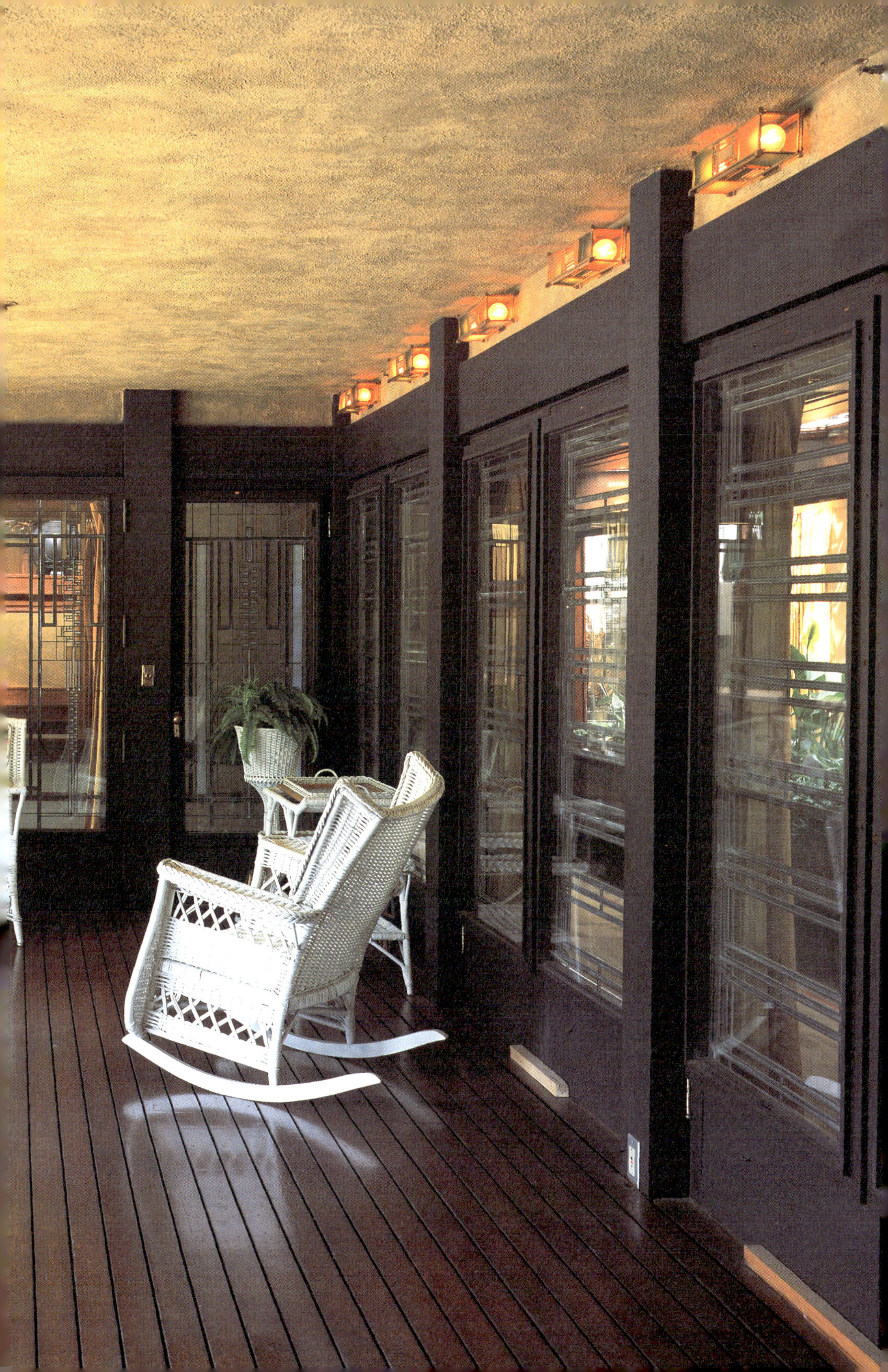

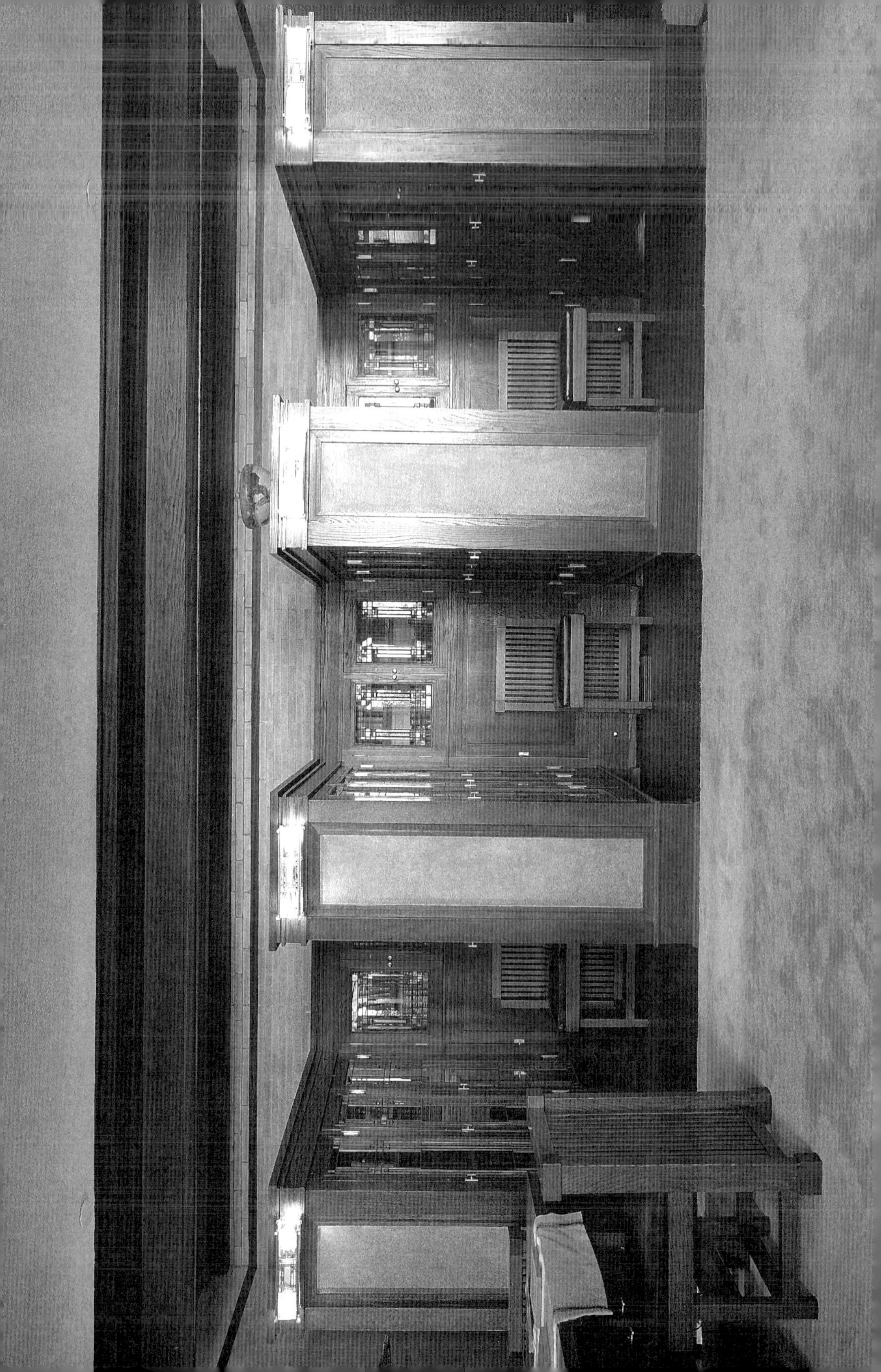

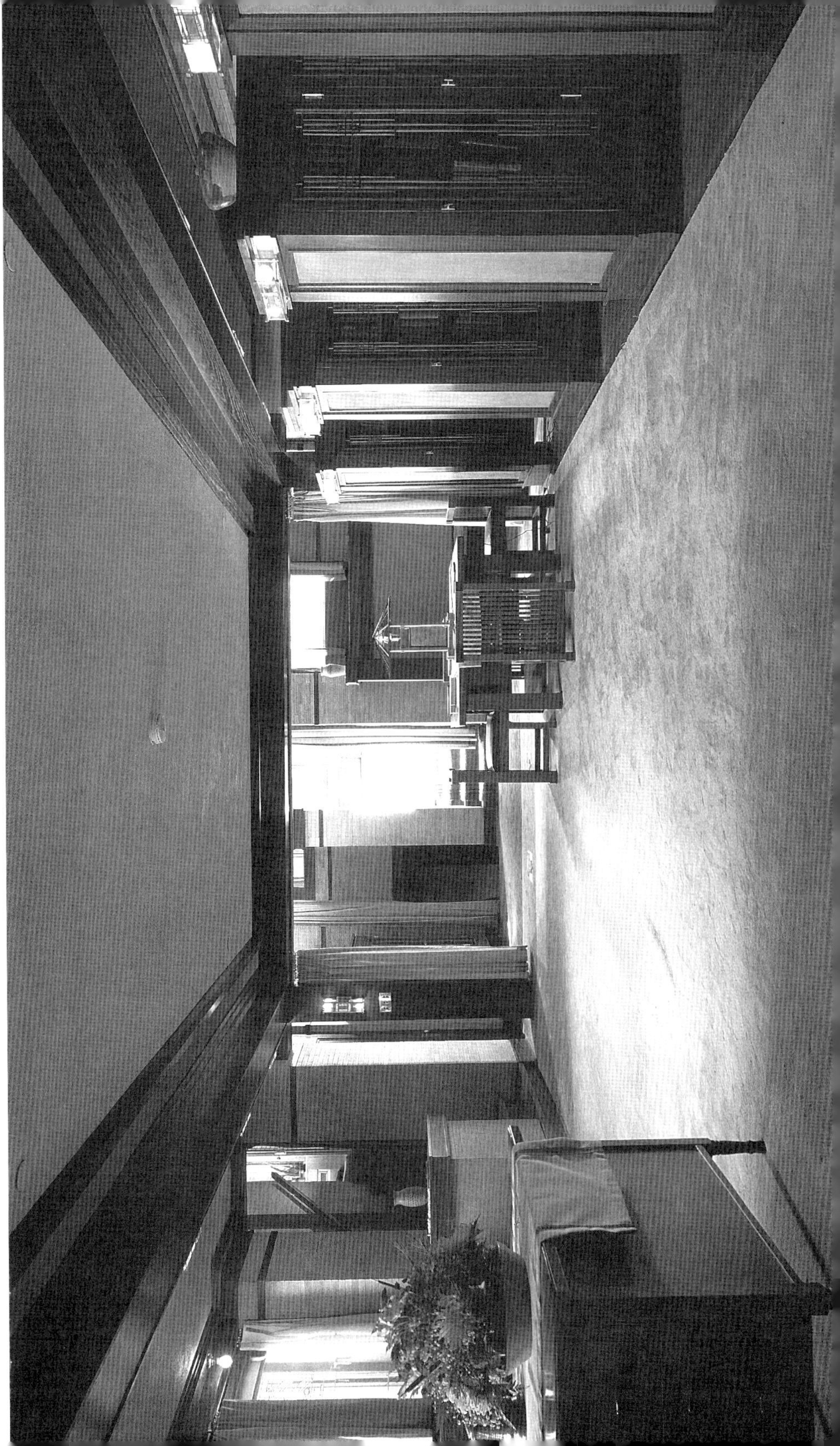

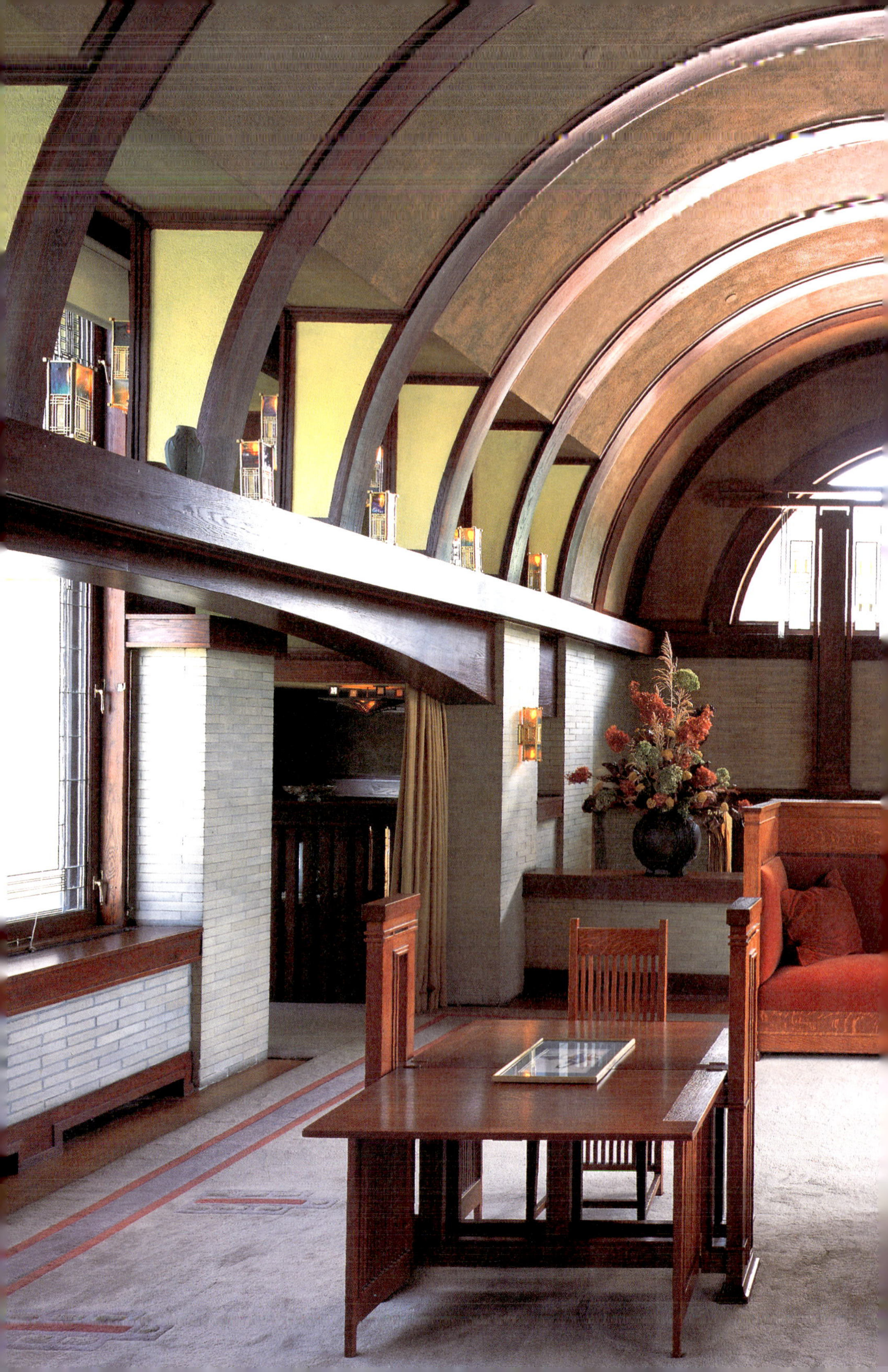

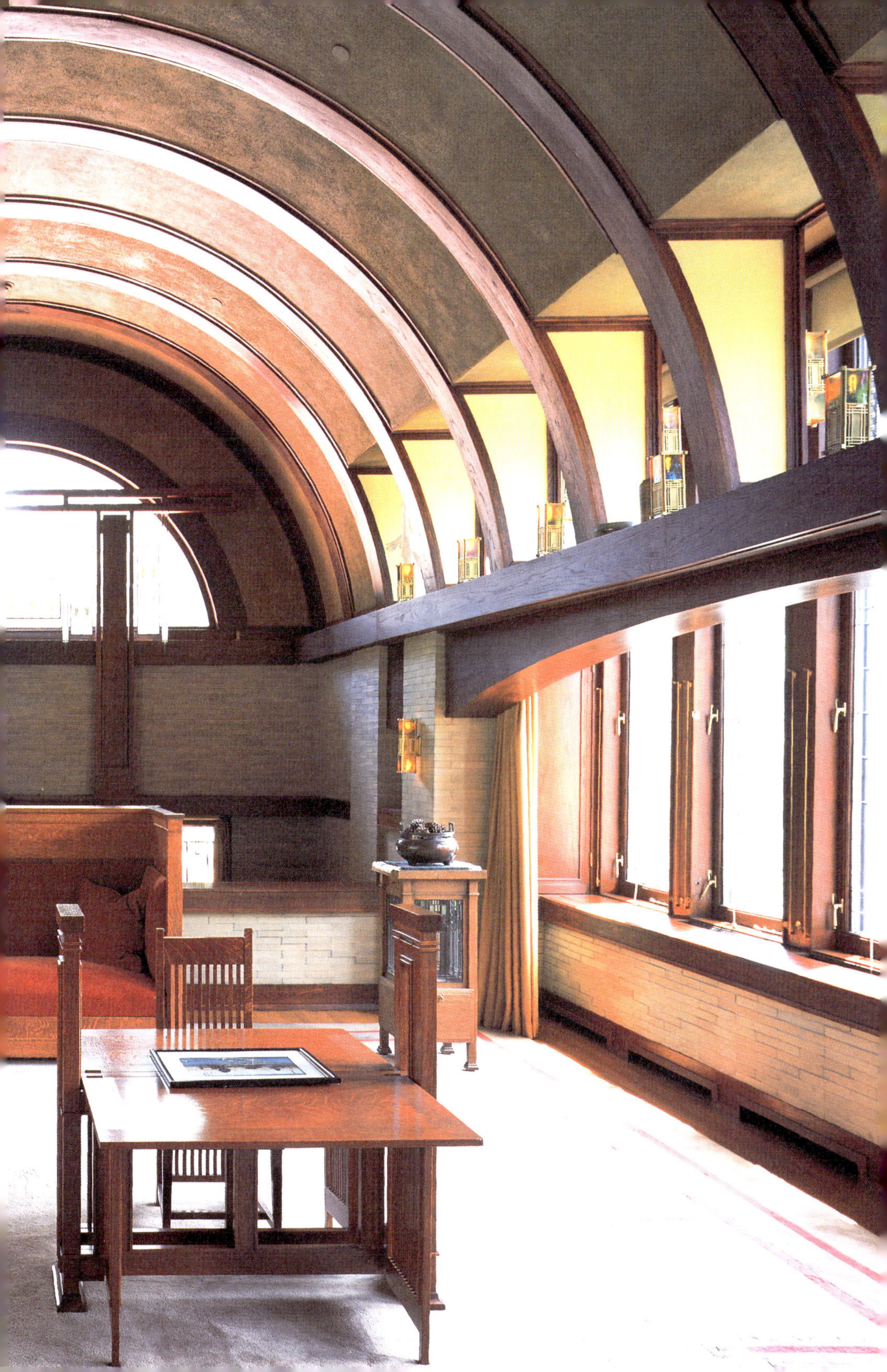

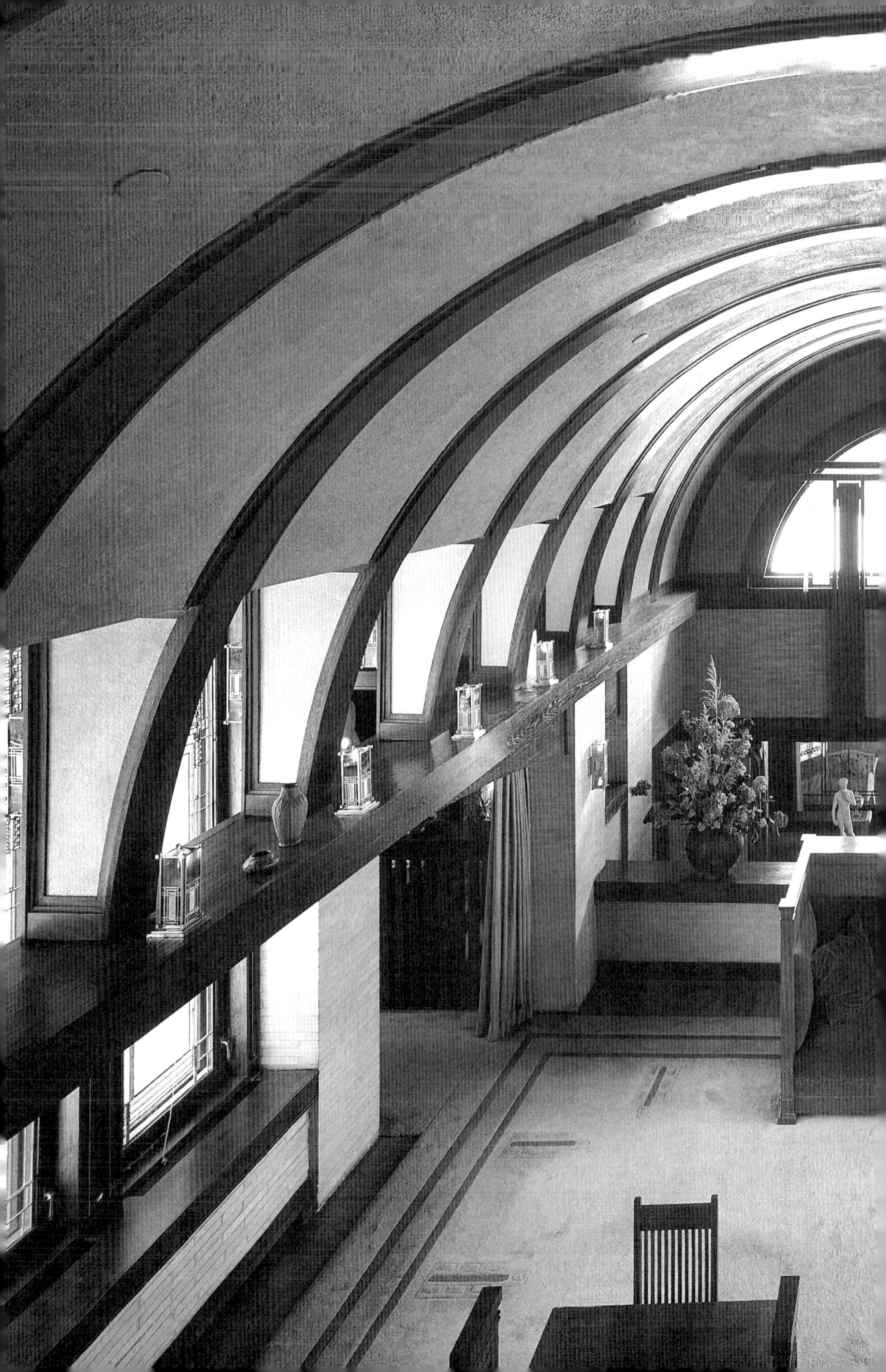

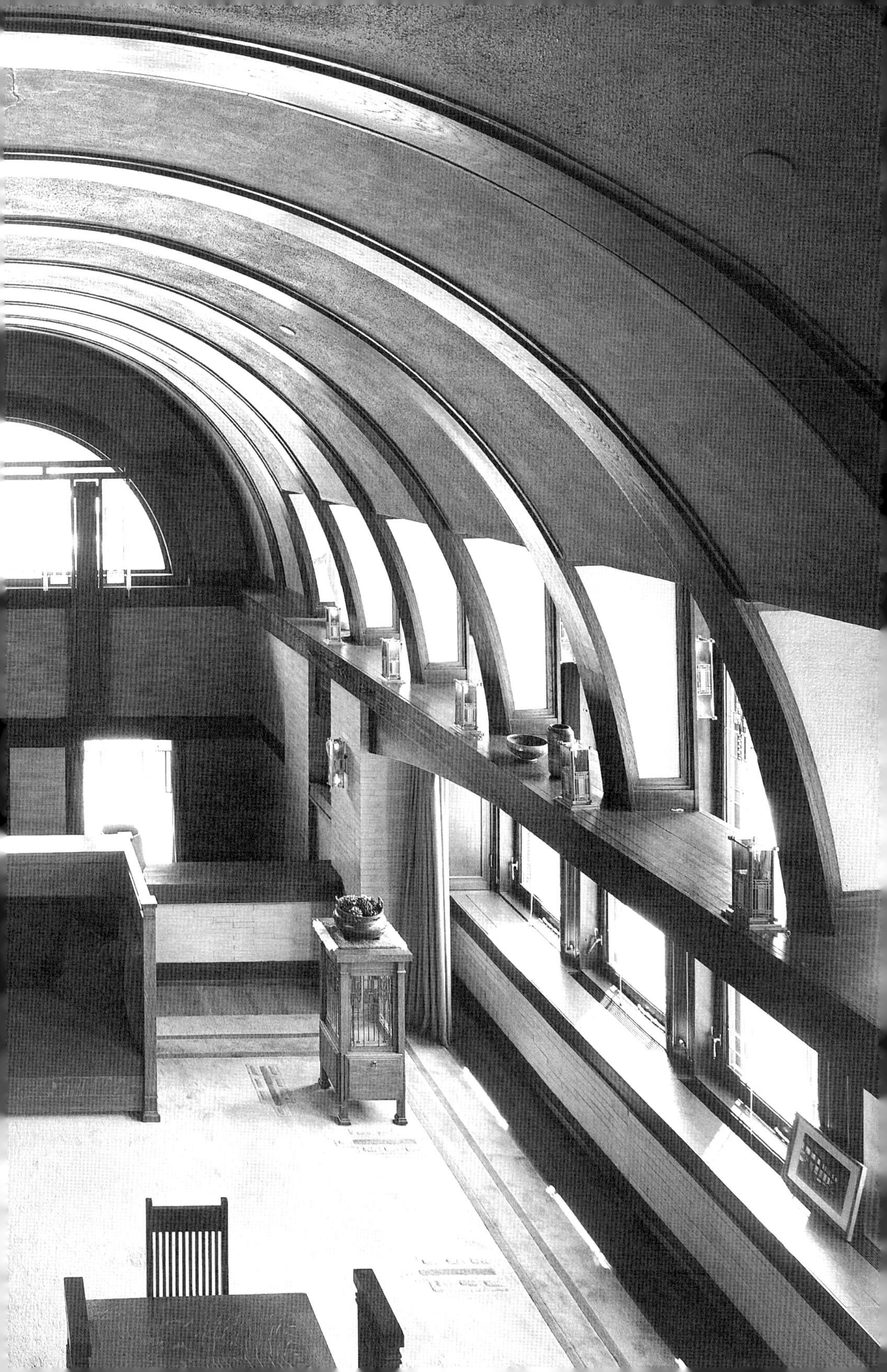

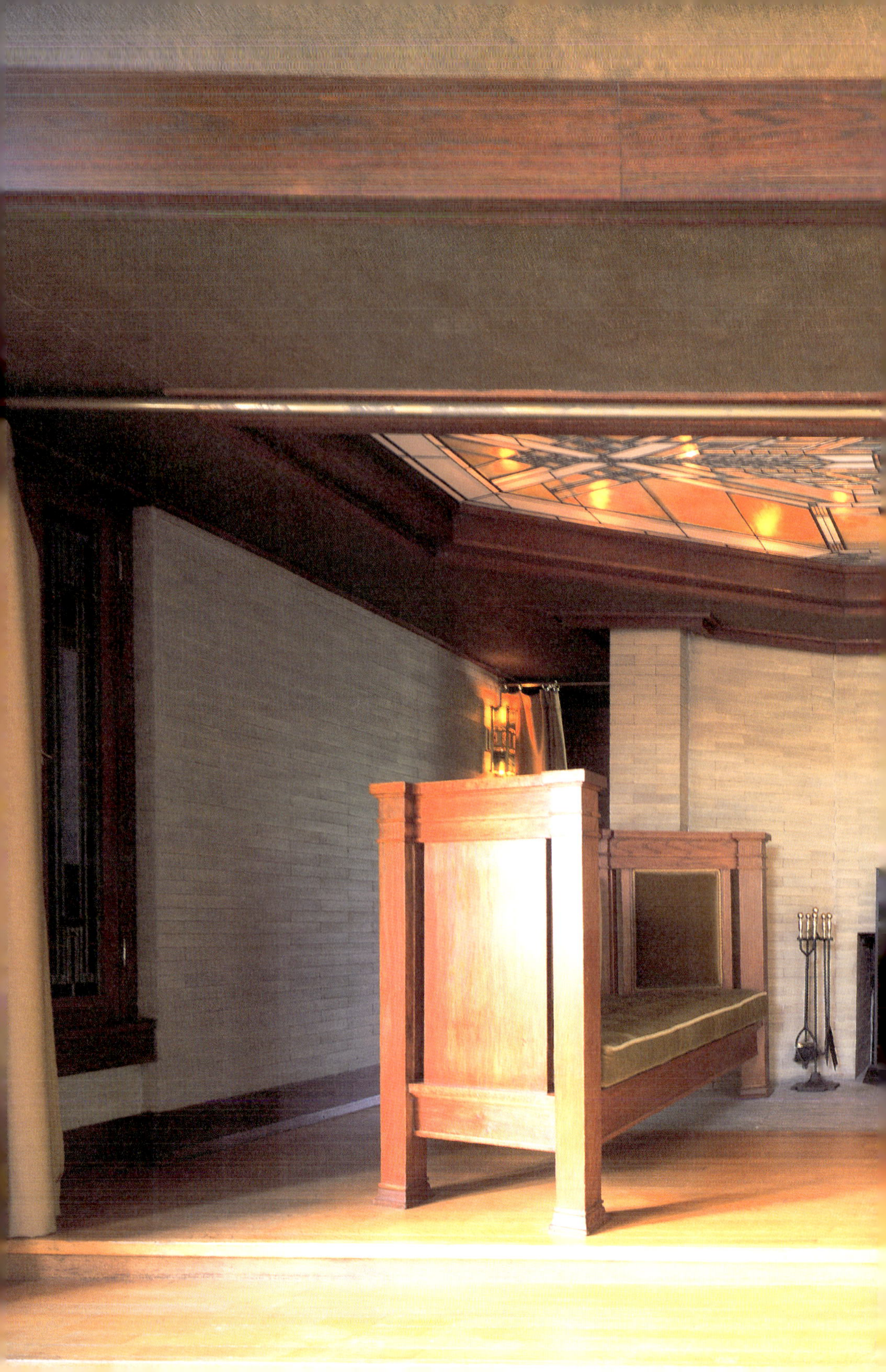

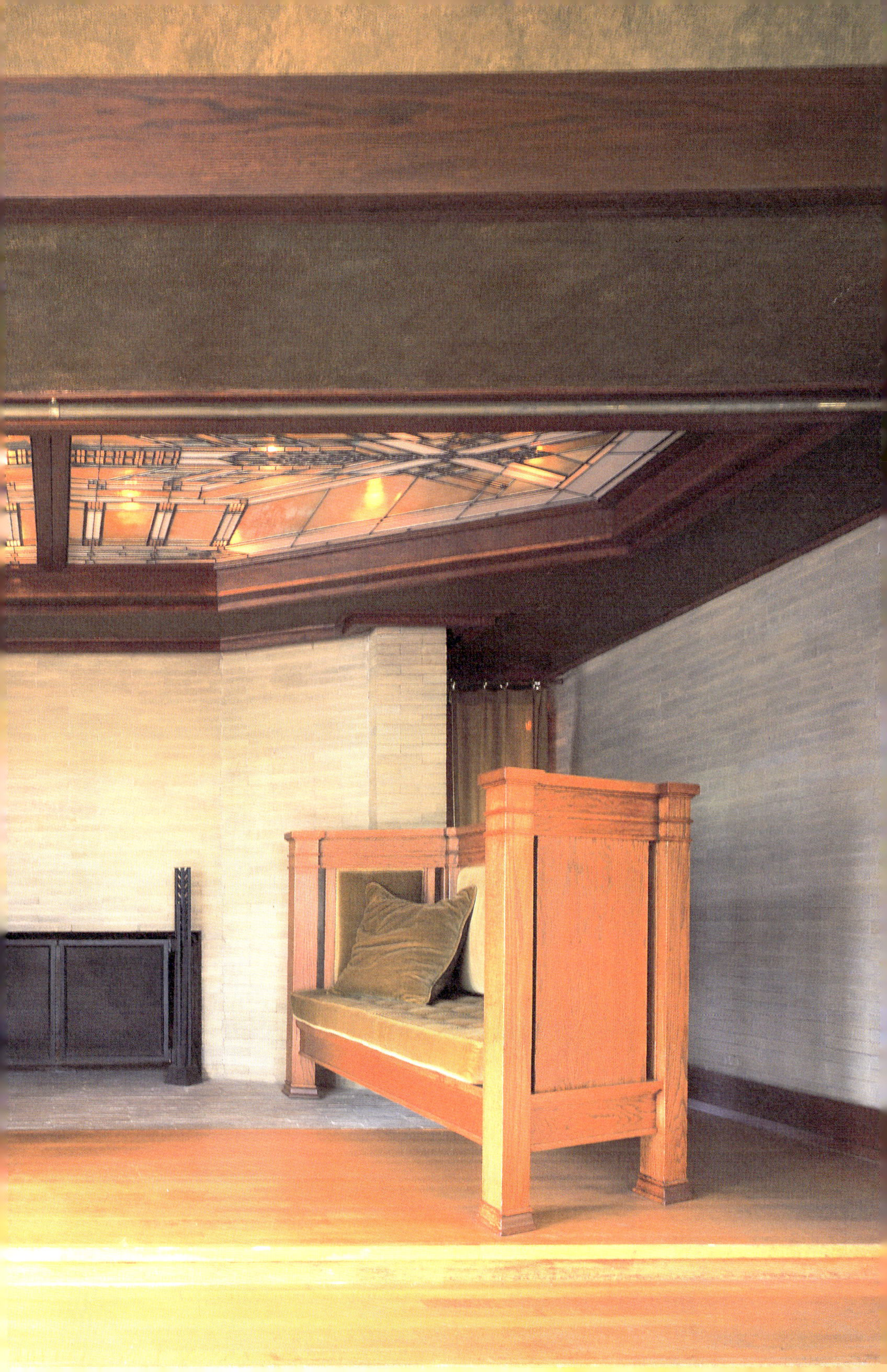

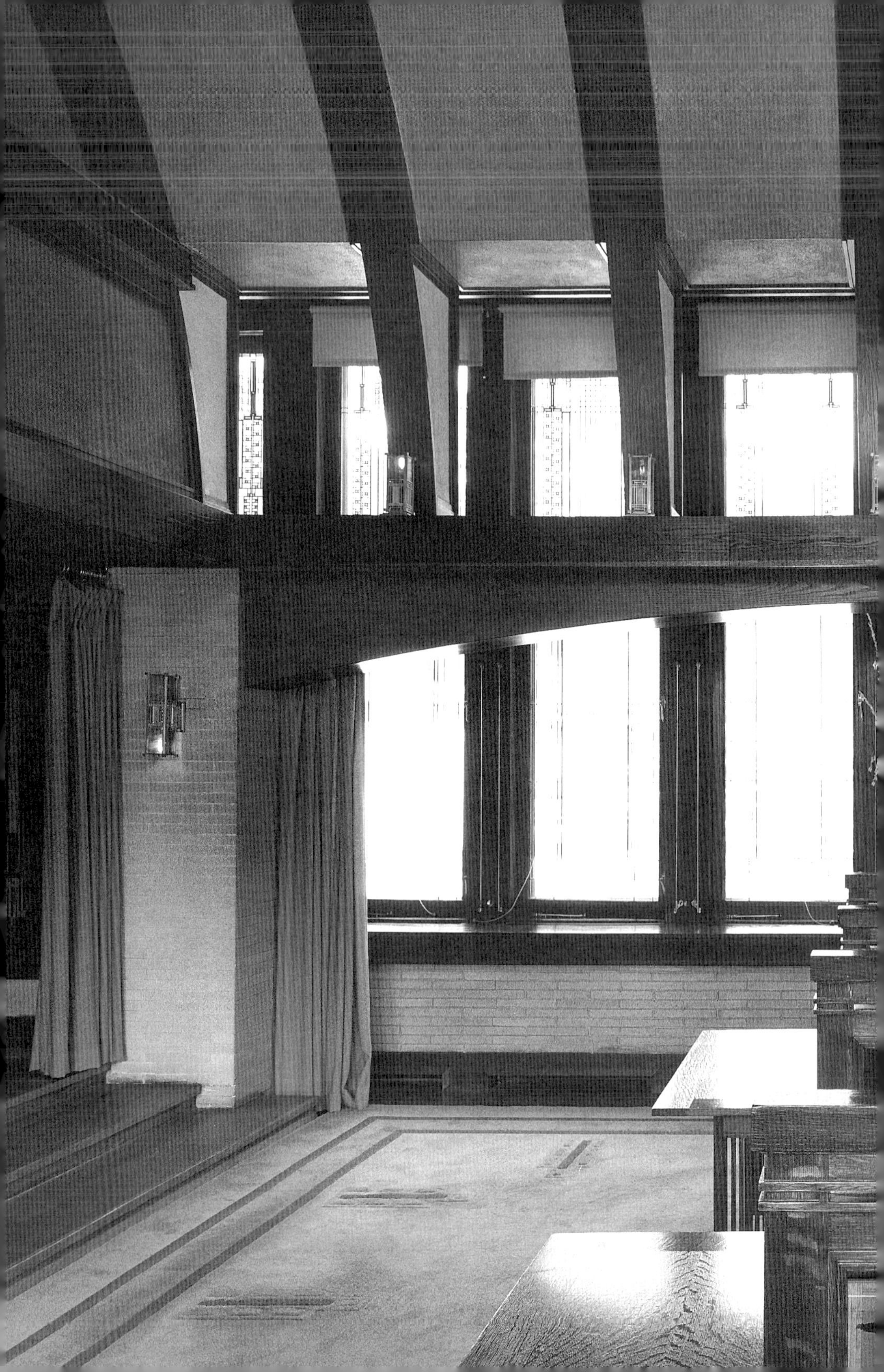

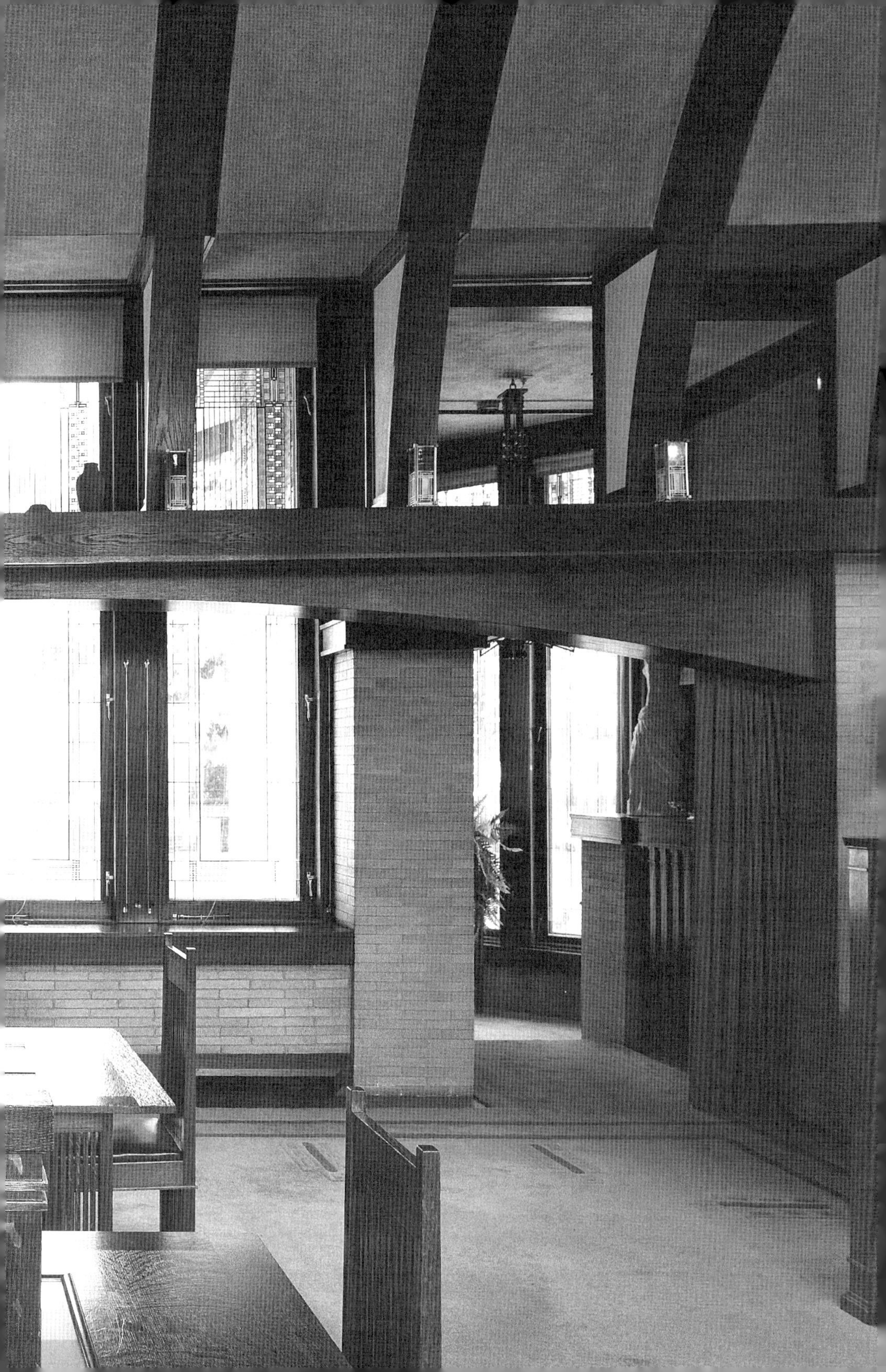

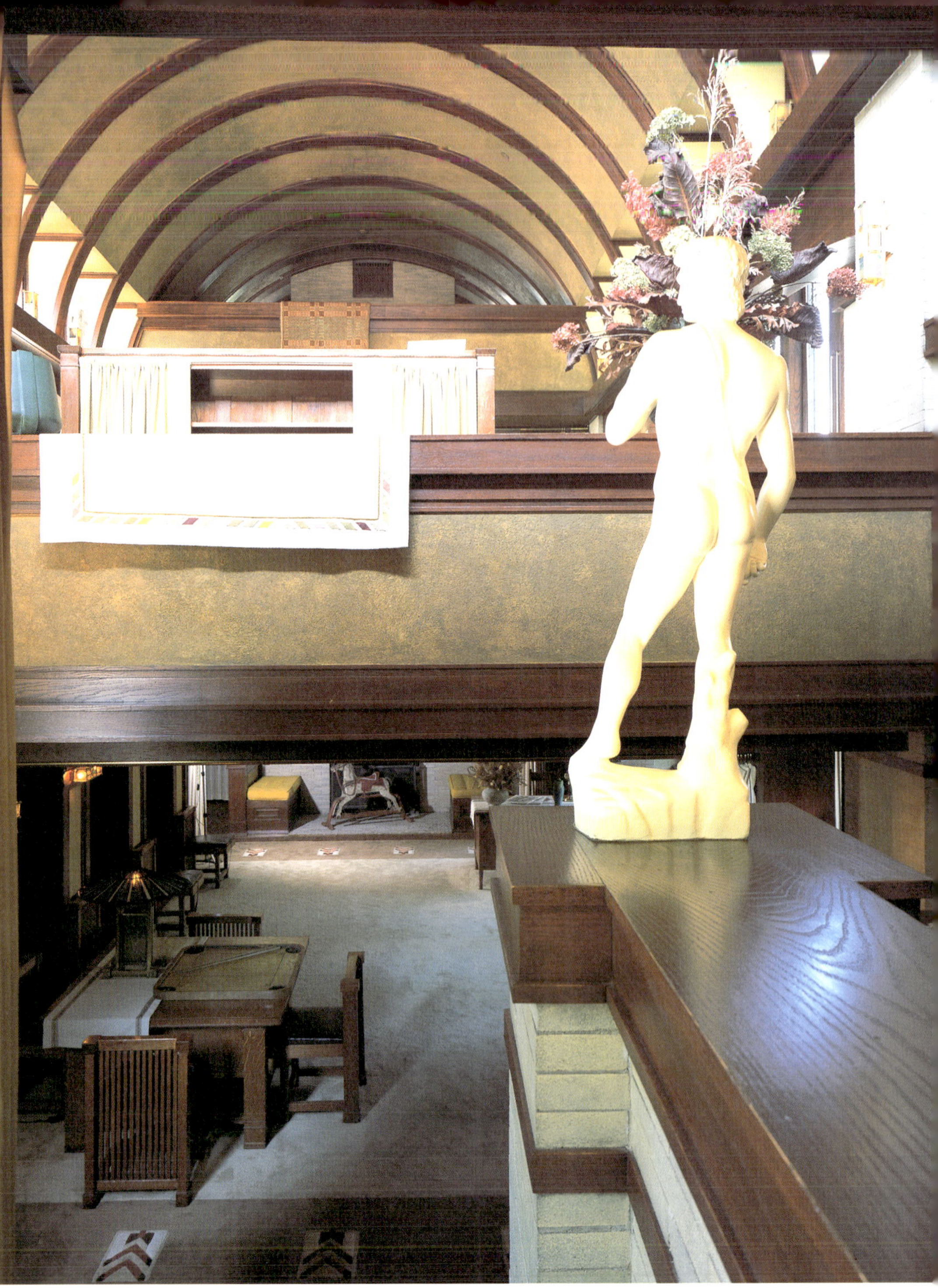

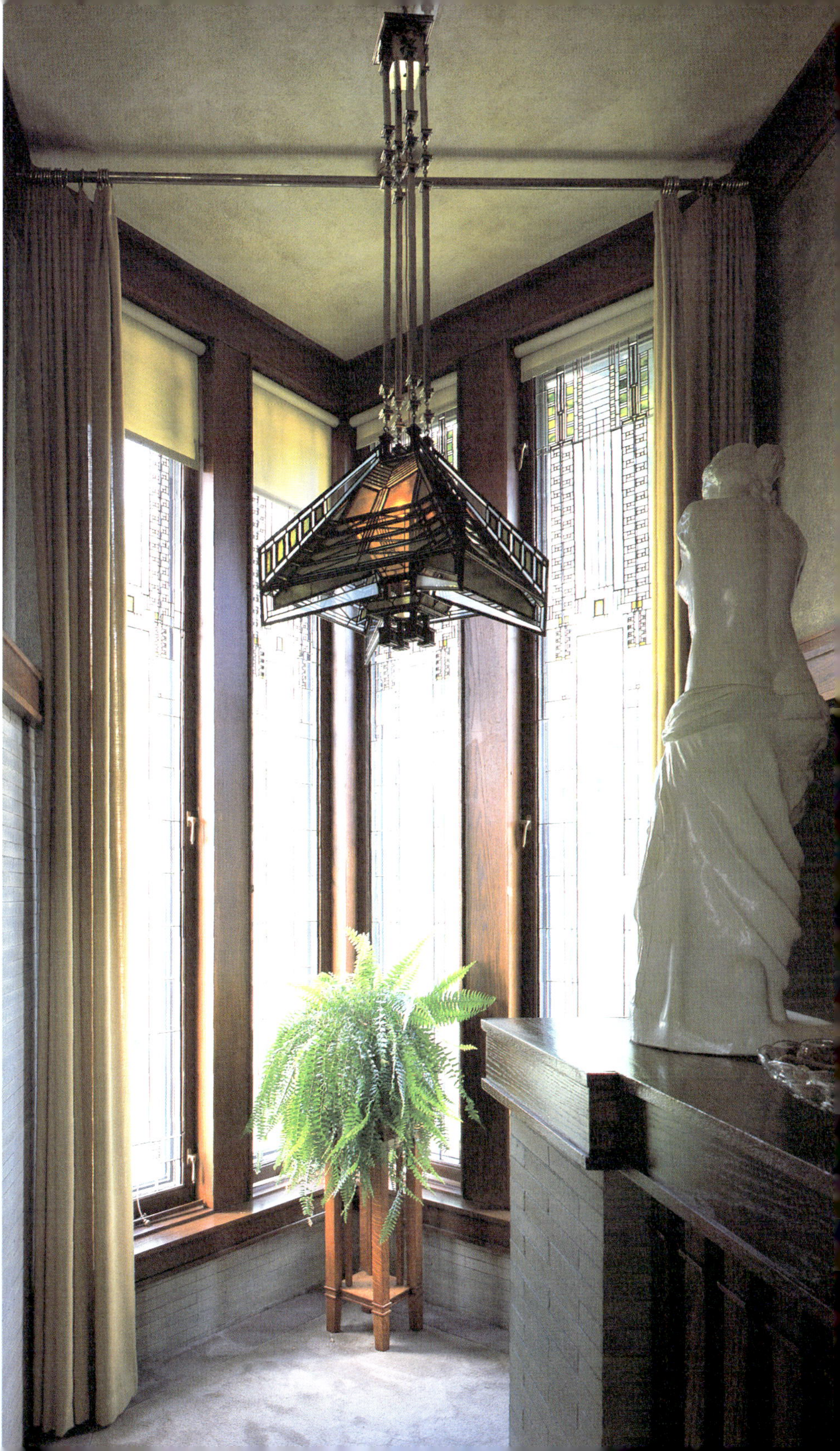

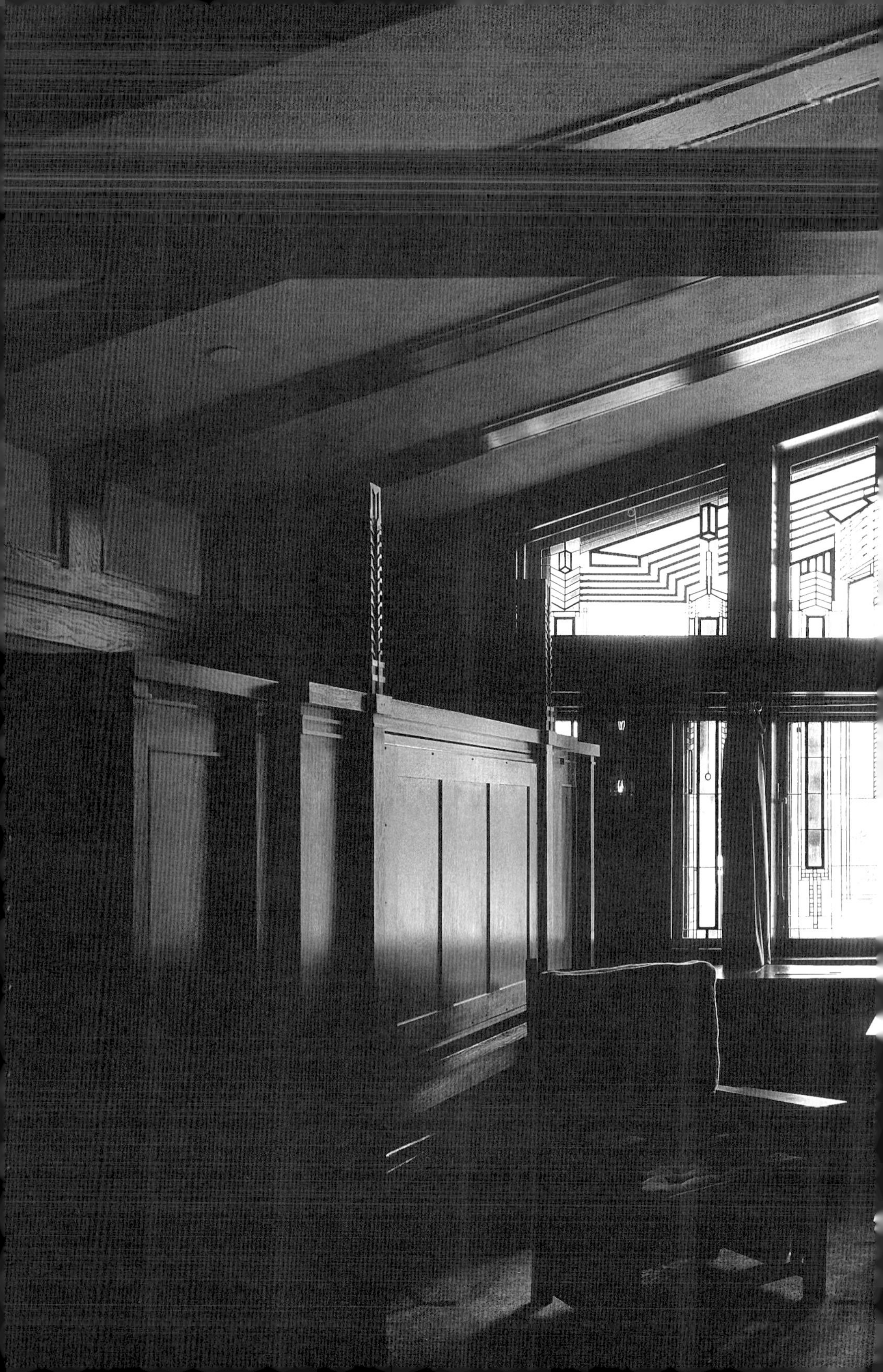

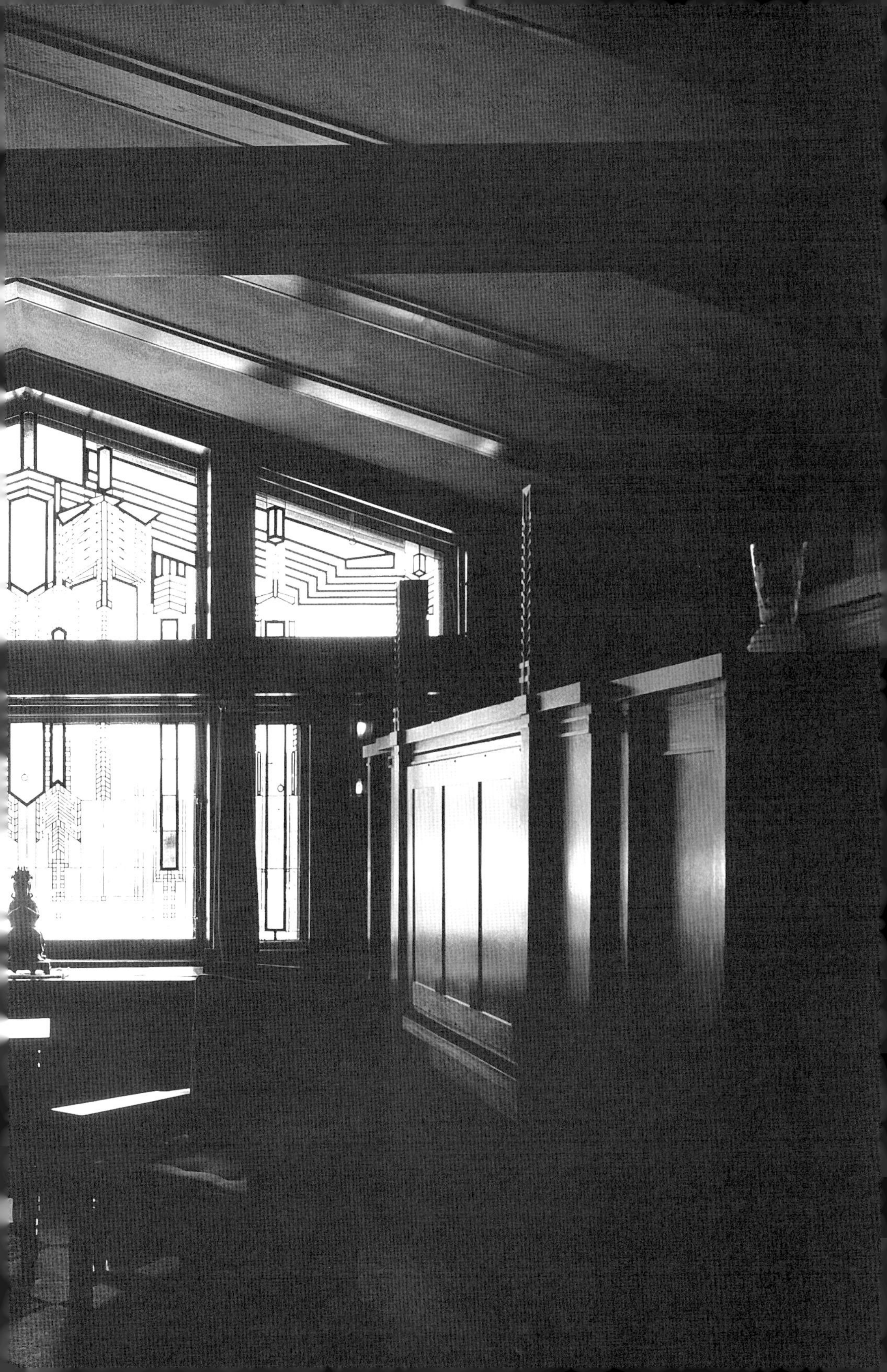

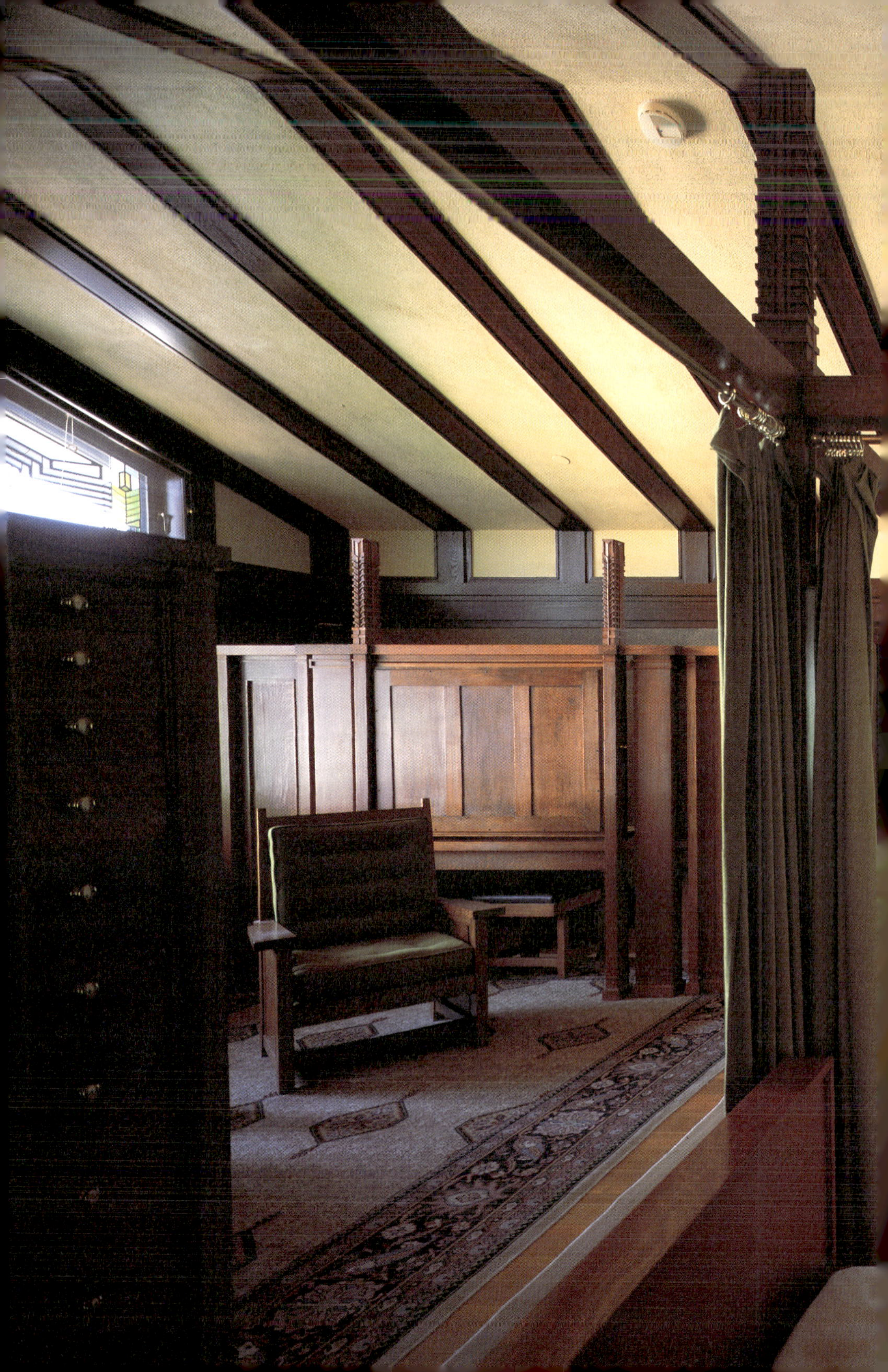

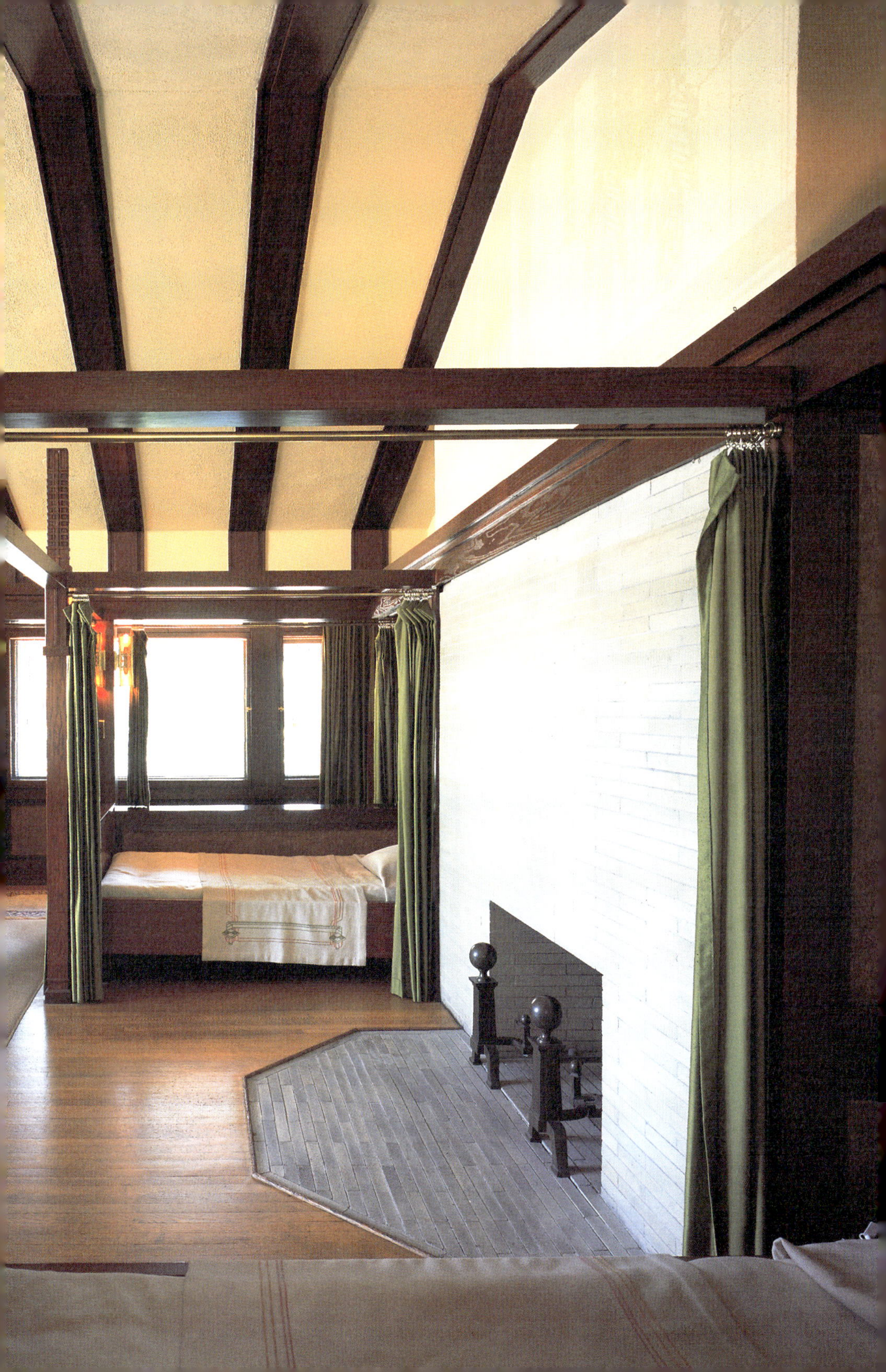

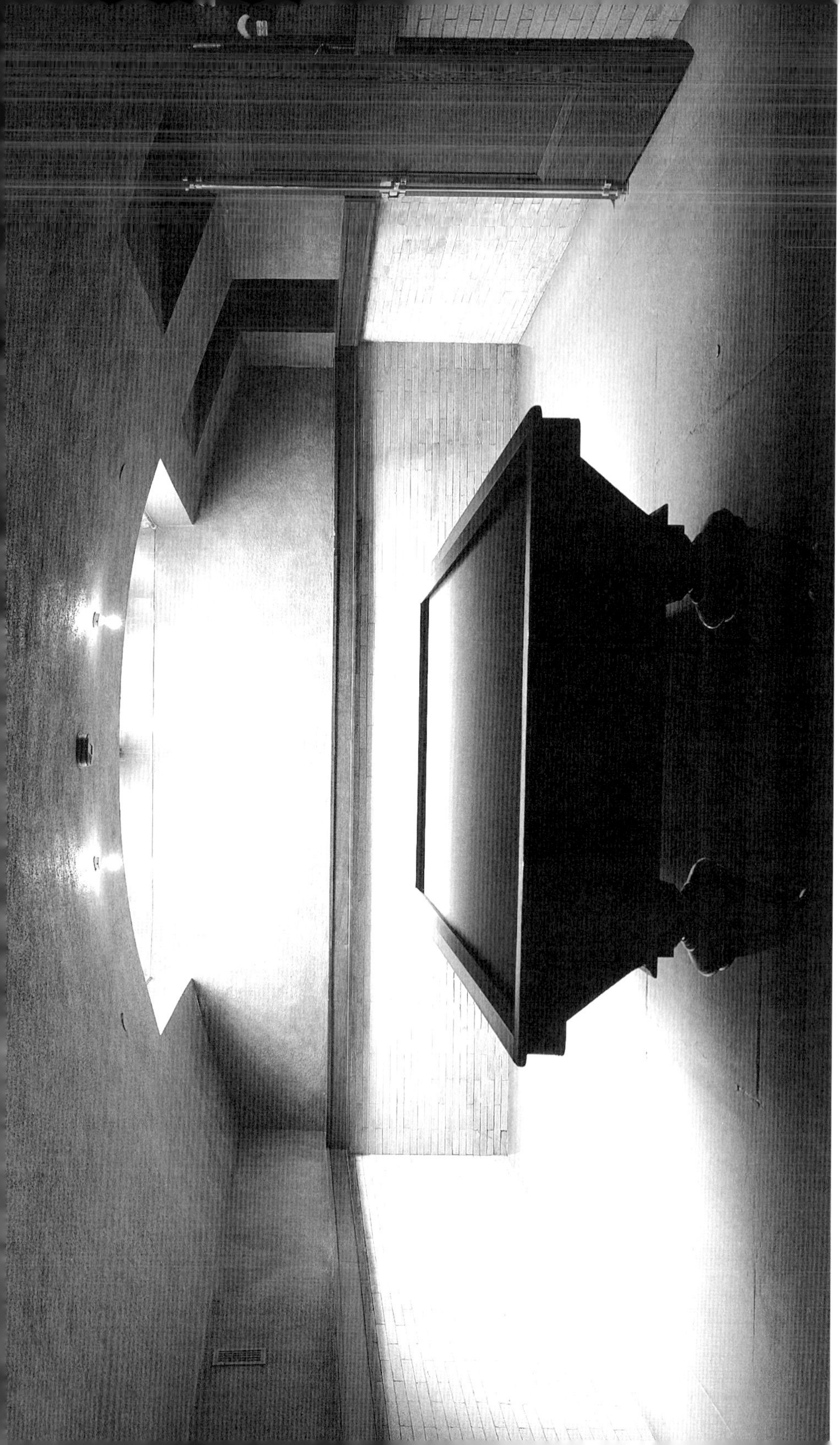

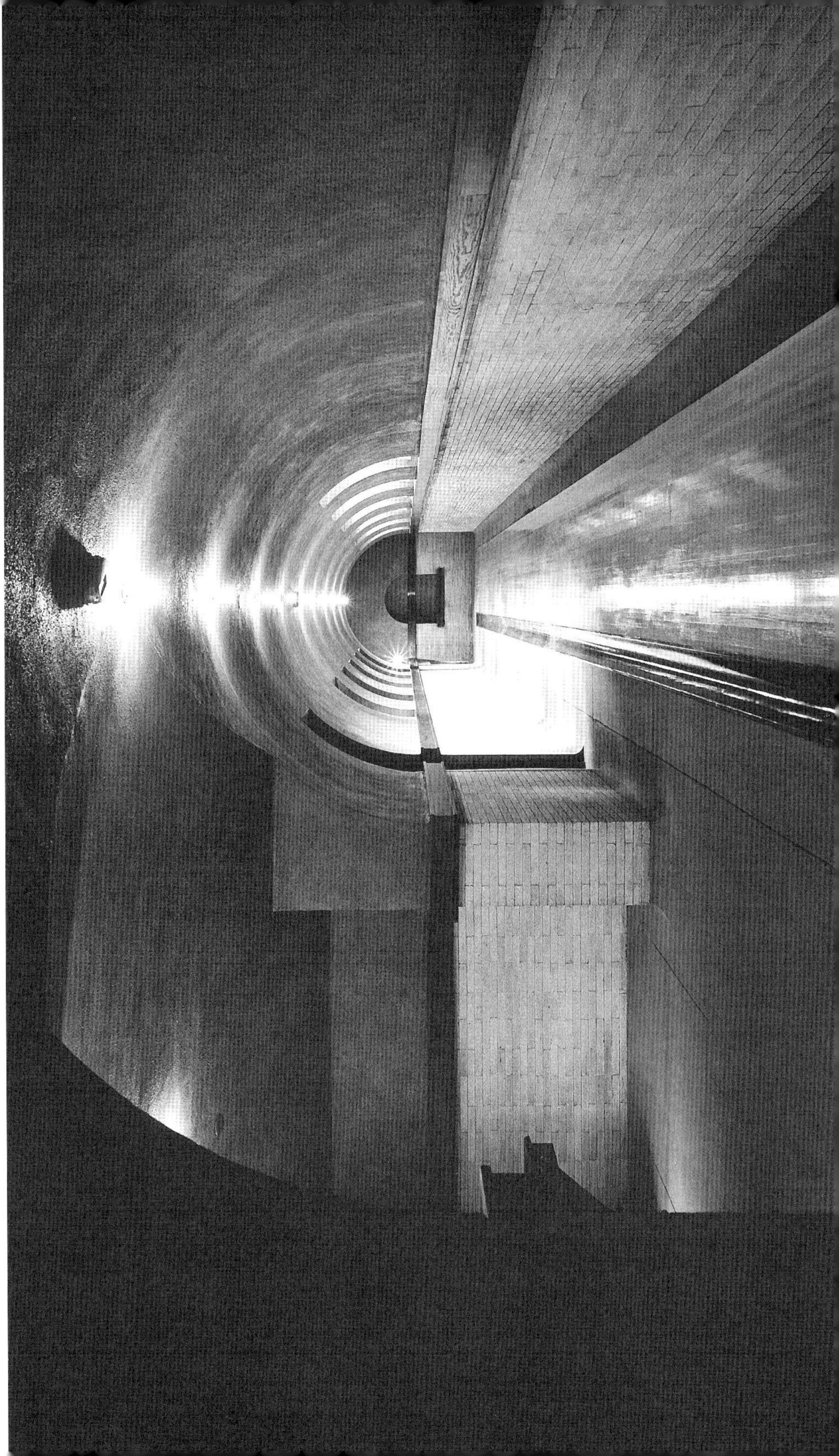

Arthur Heurtley House
Oak Park, Illinois, 1902

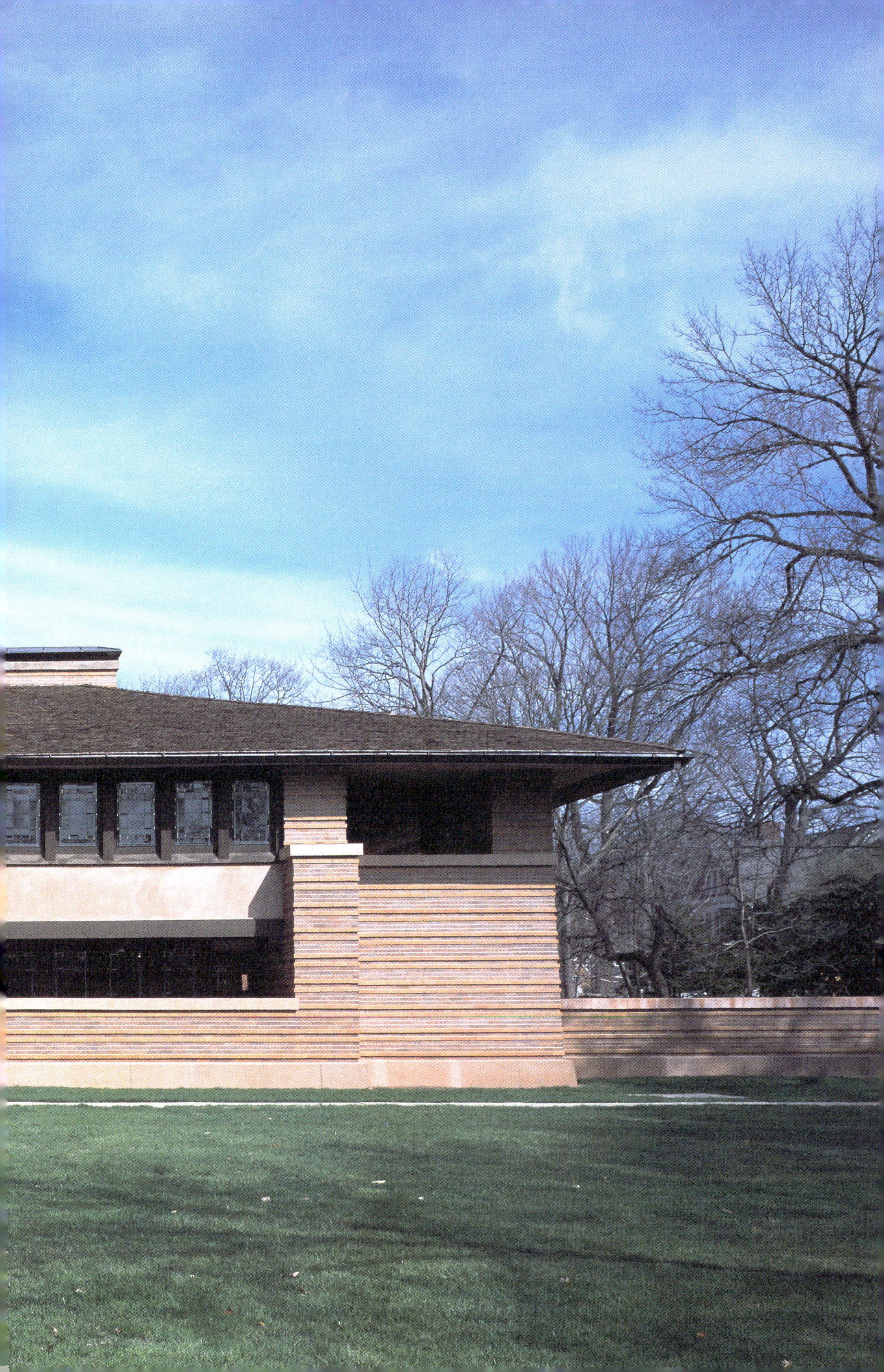

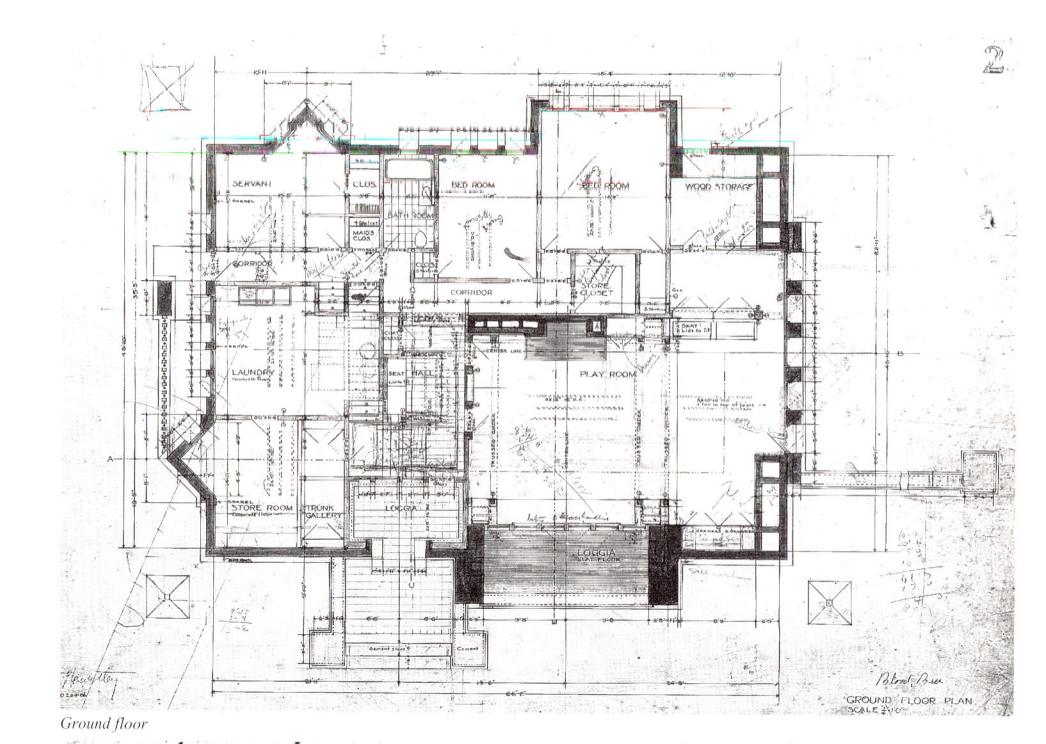

Ground floor

Basement

Main floor

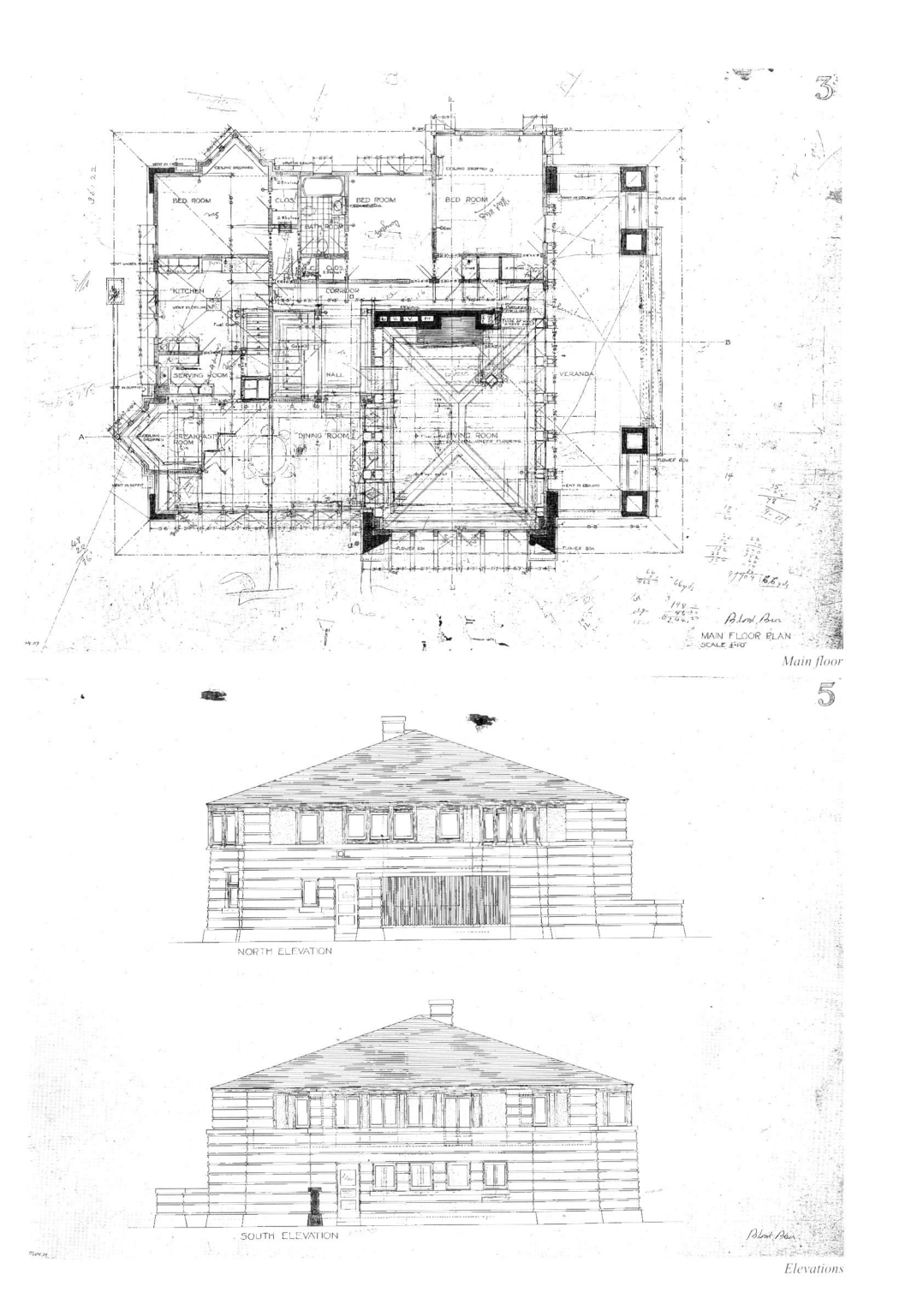

Elevations

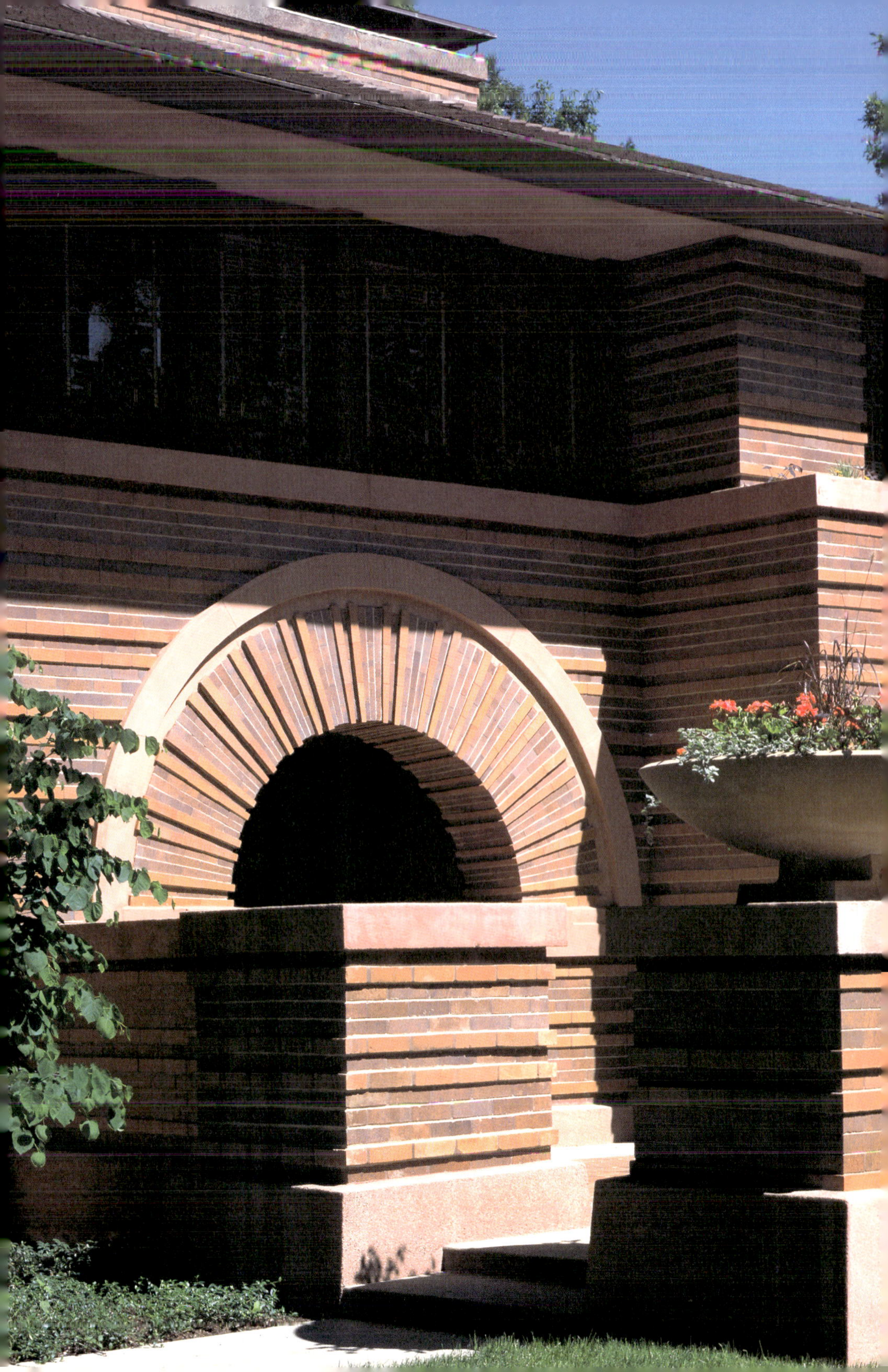

318

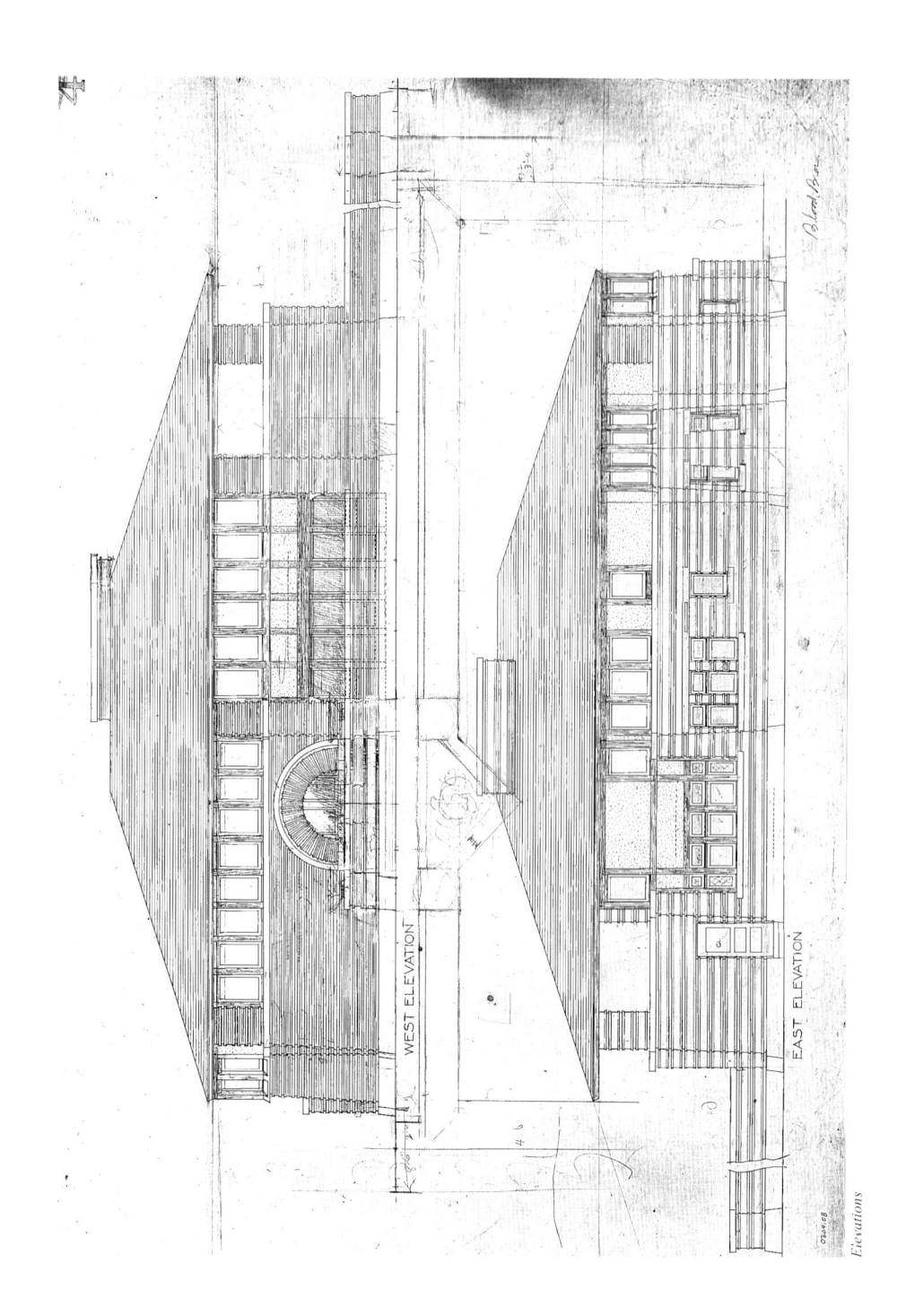

WEST ELEVATION

EAST ELEVATION

Elevations

Sections

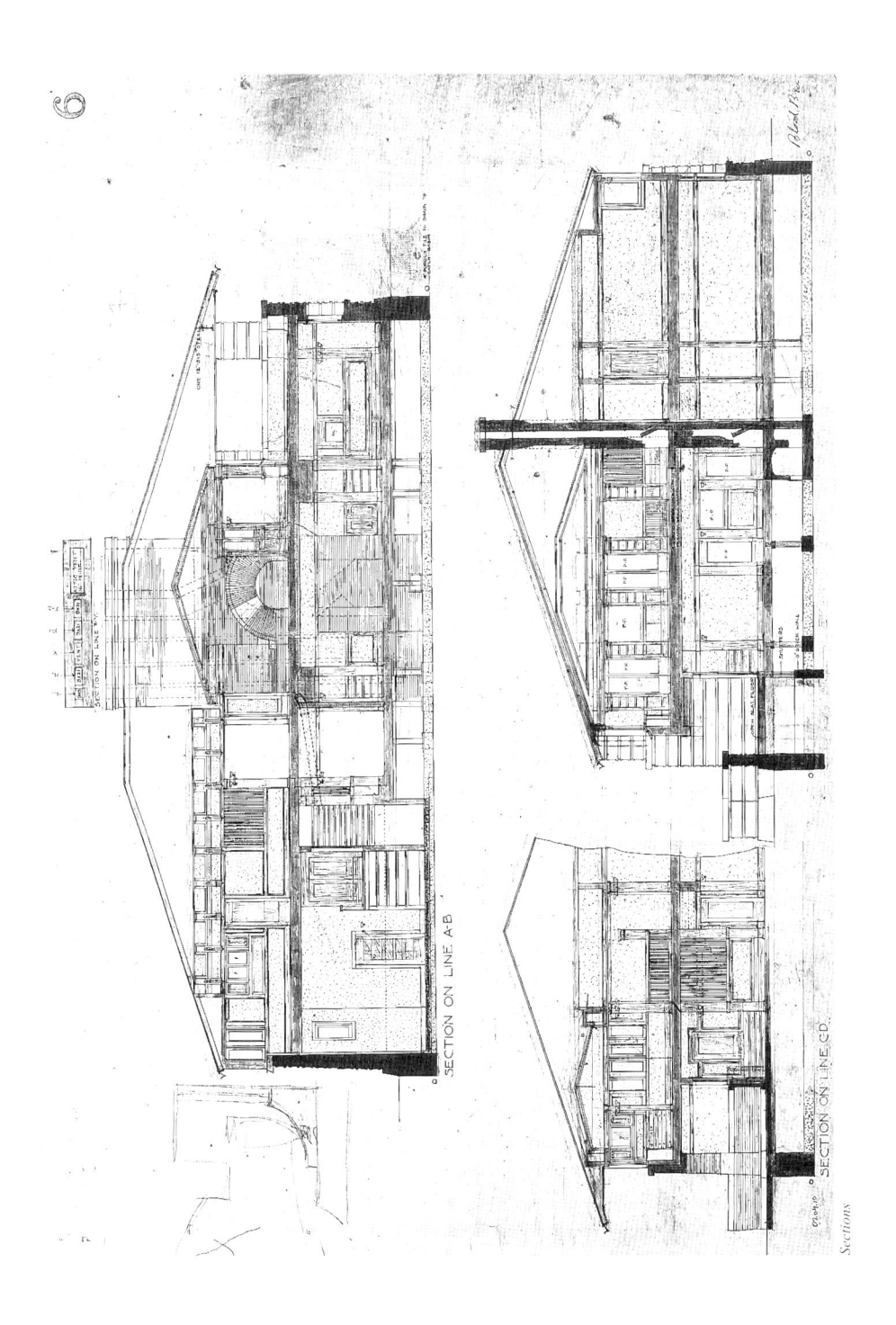

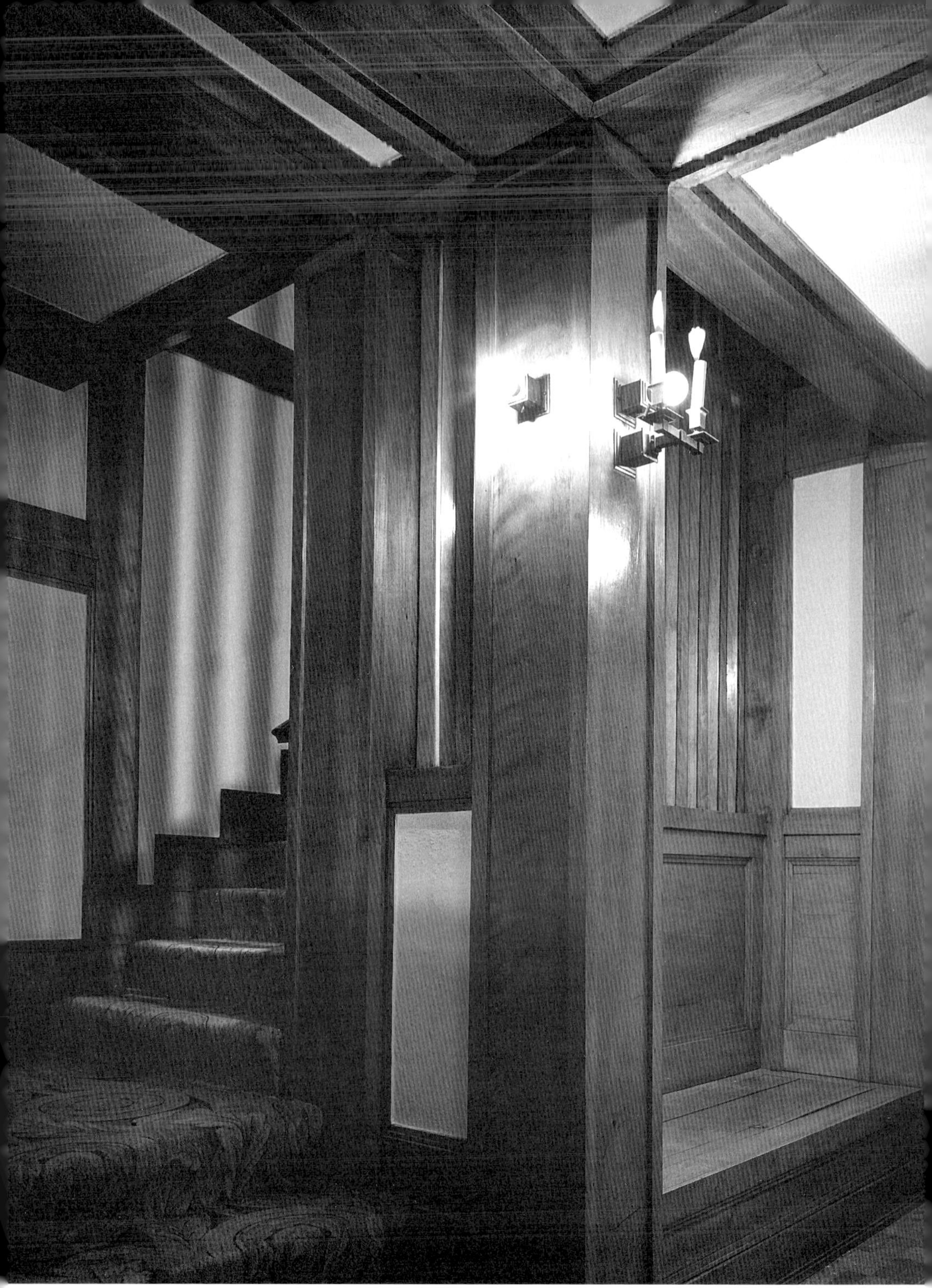

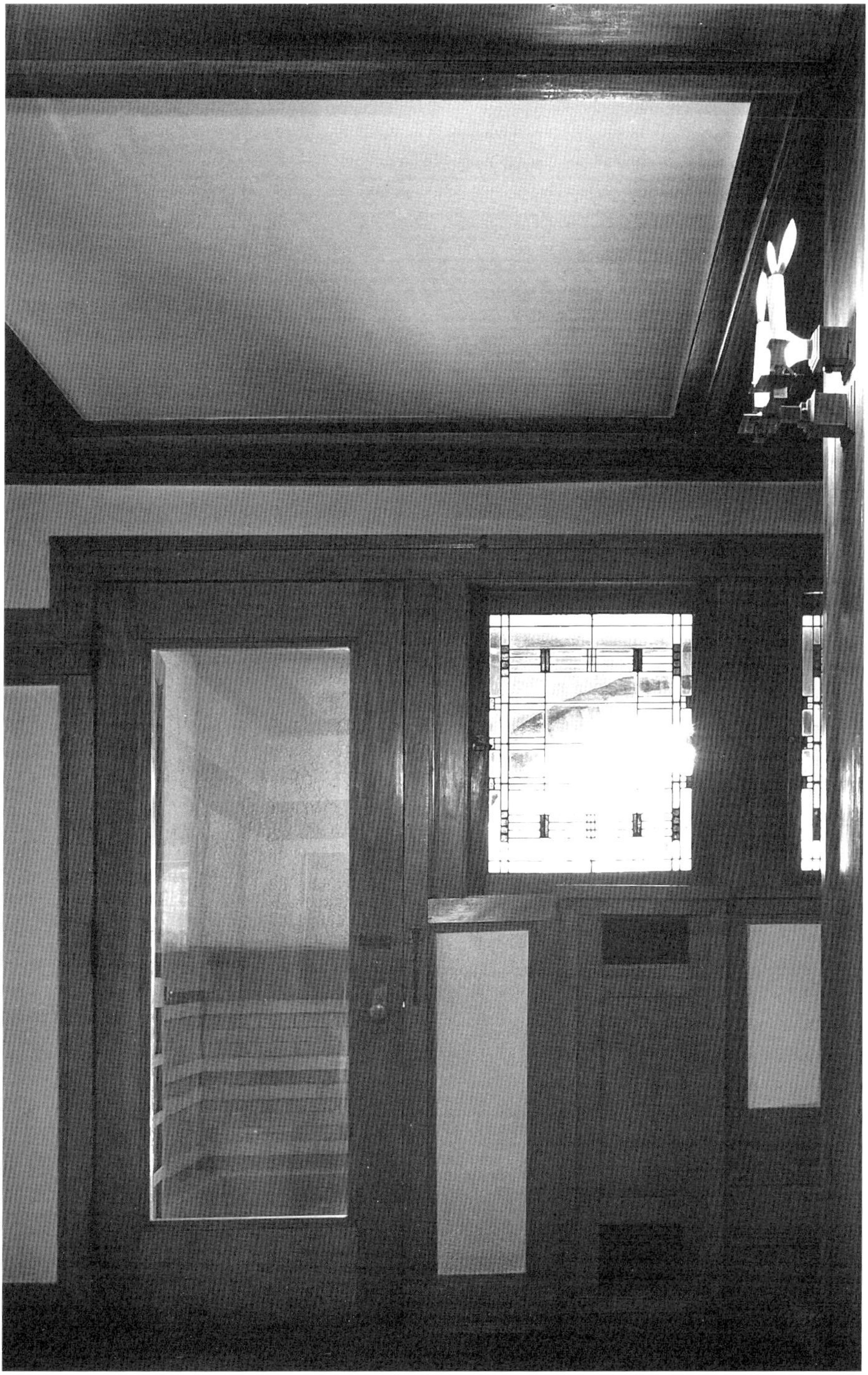

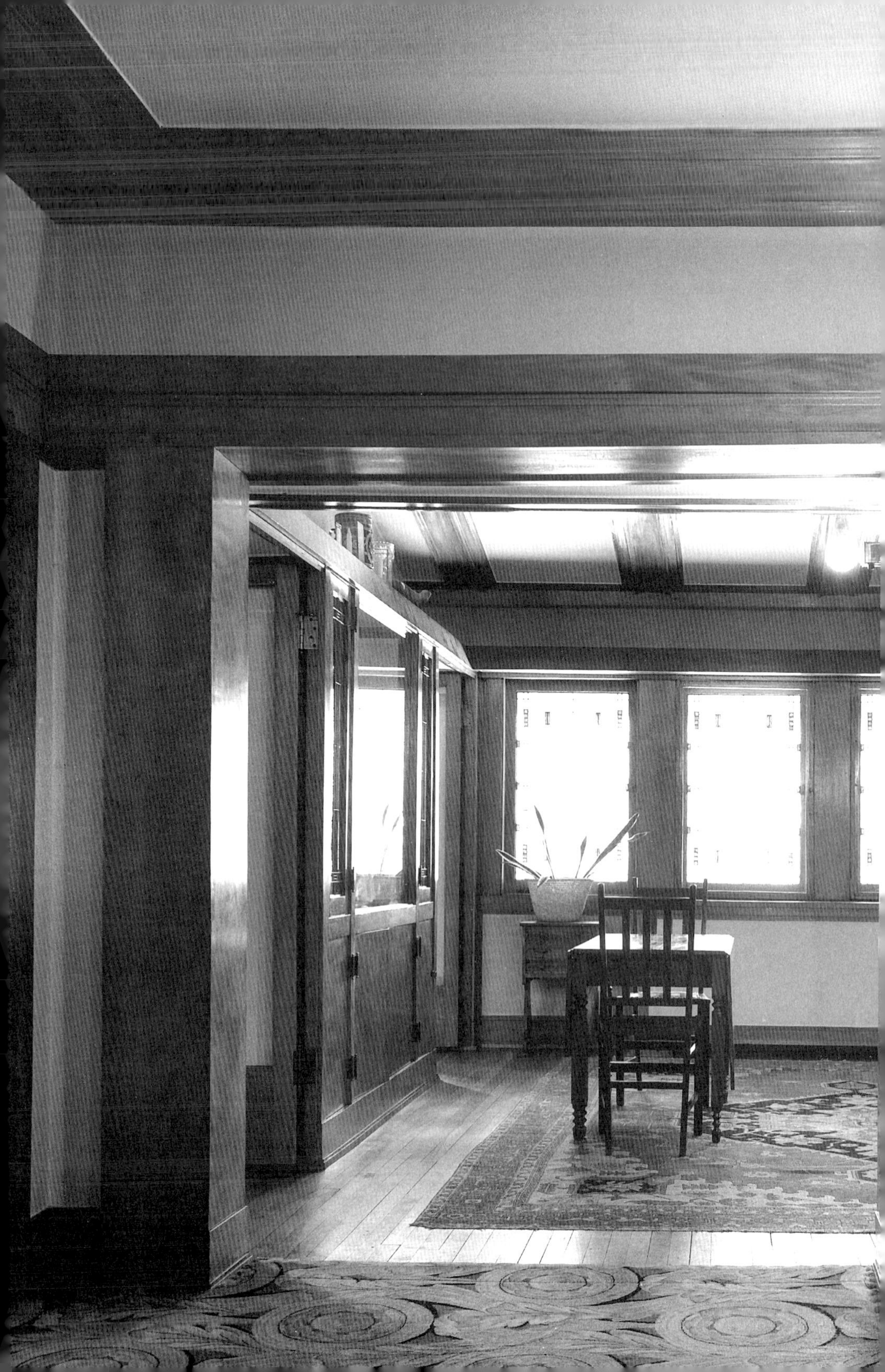

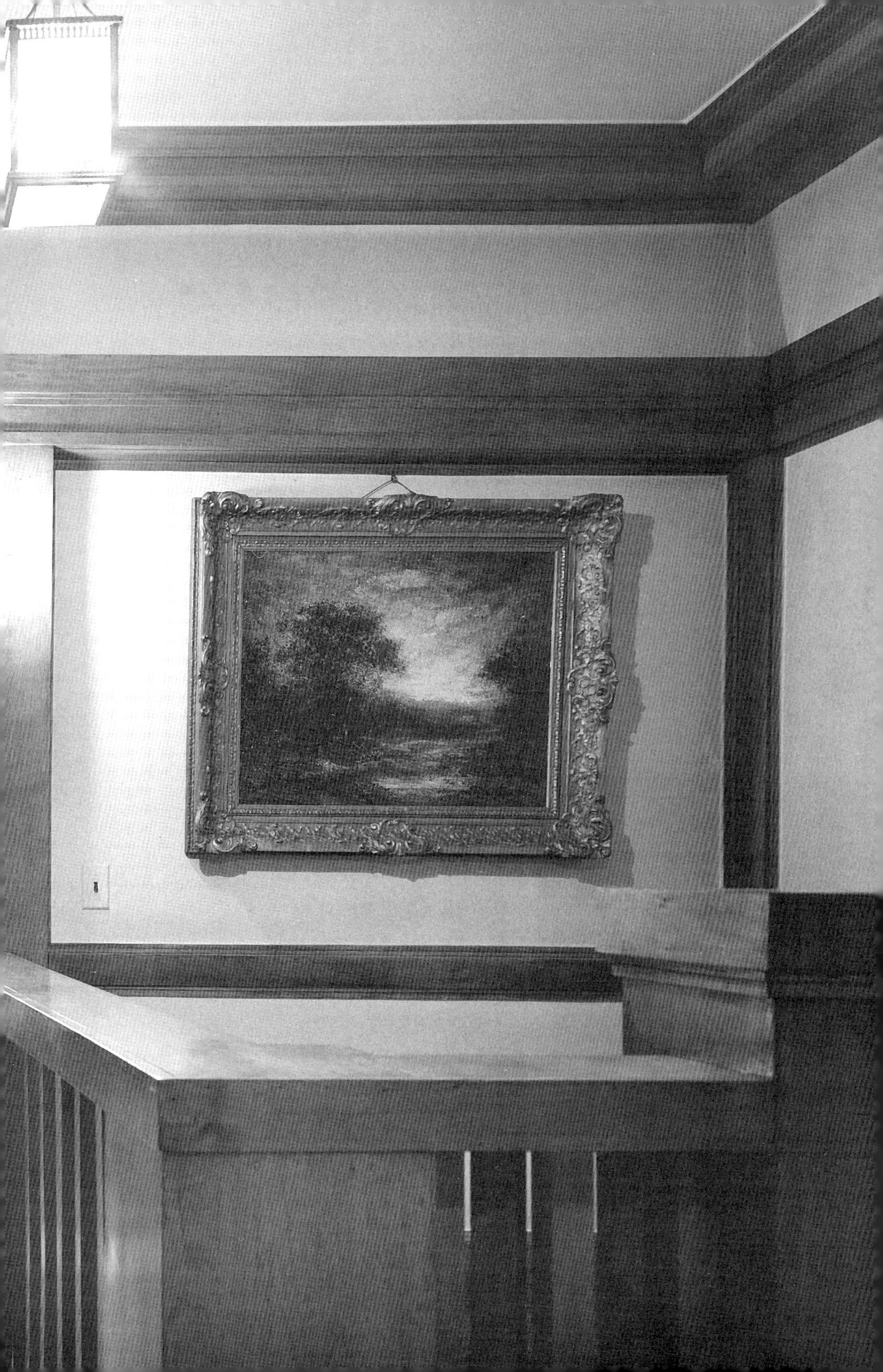

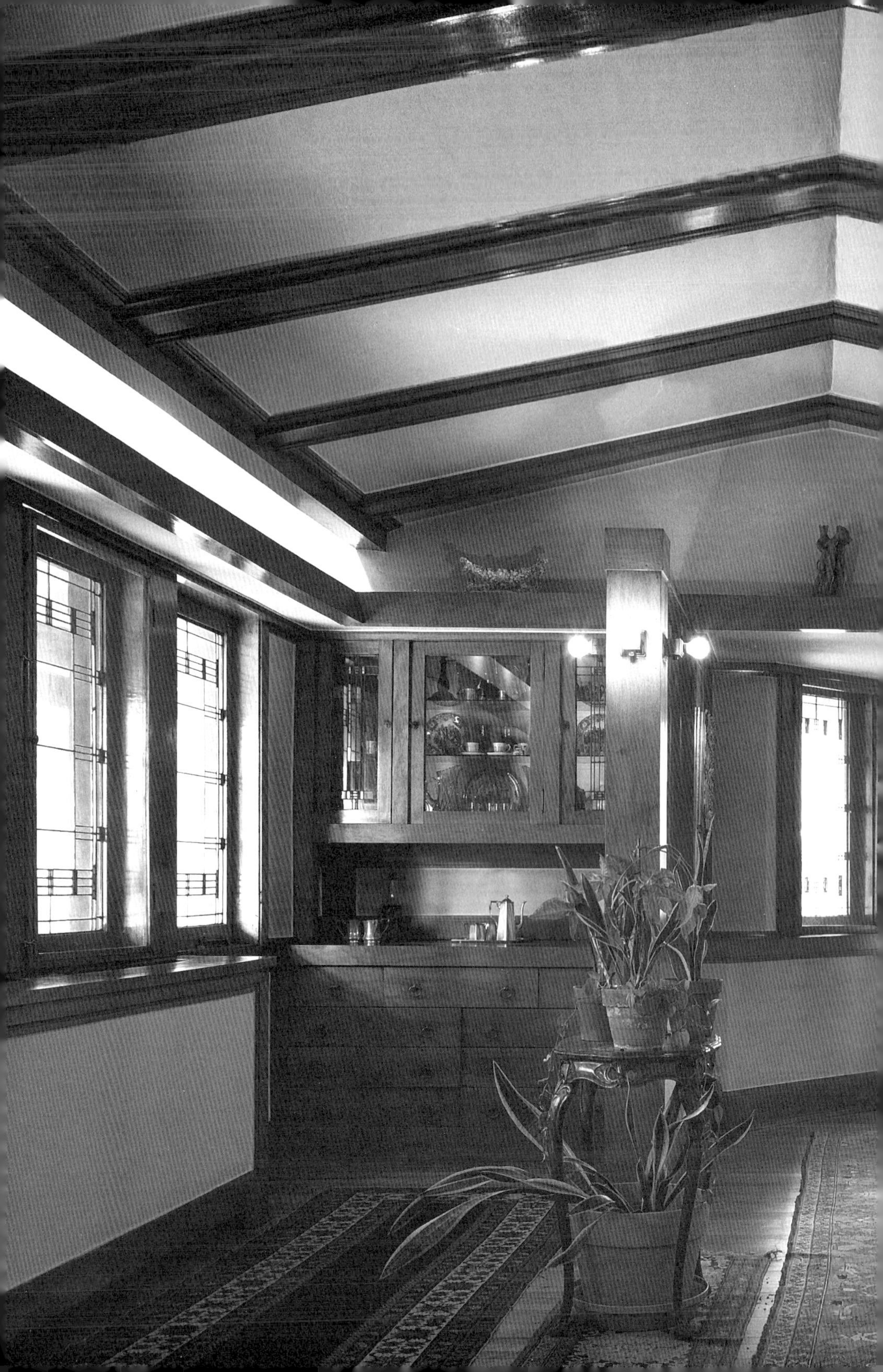

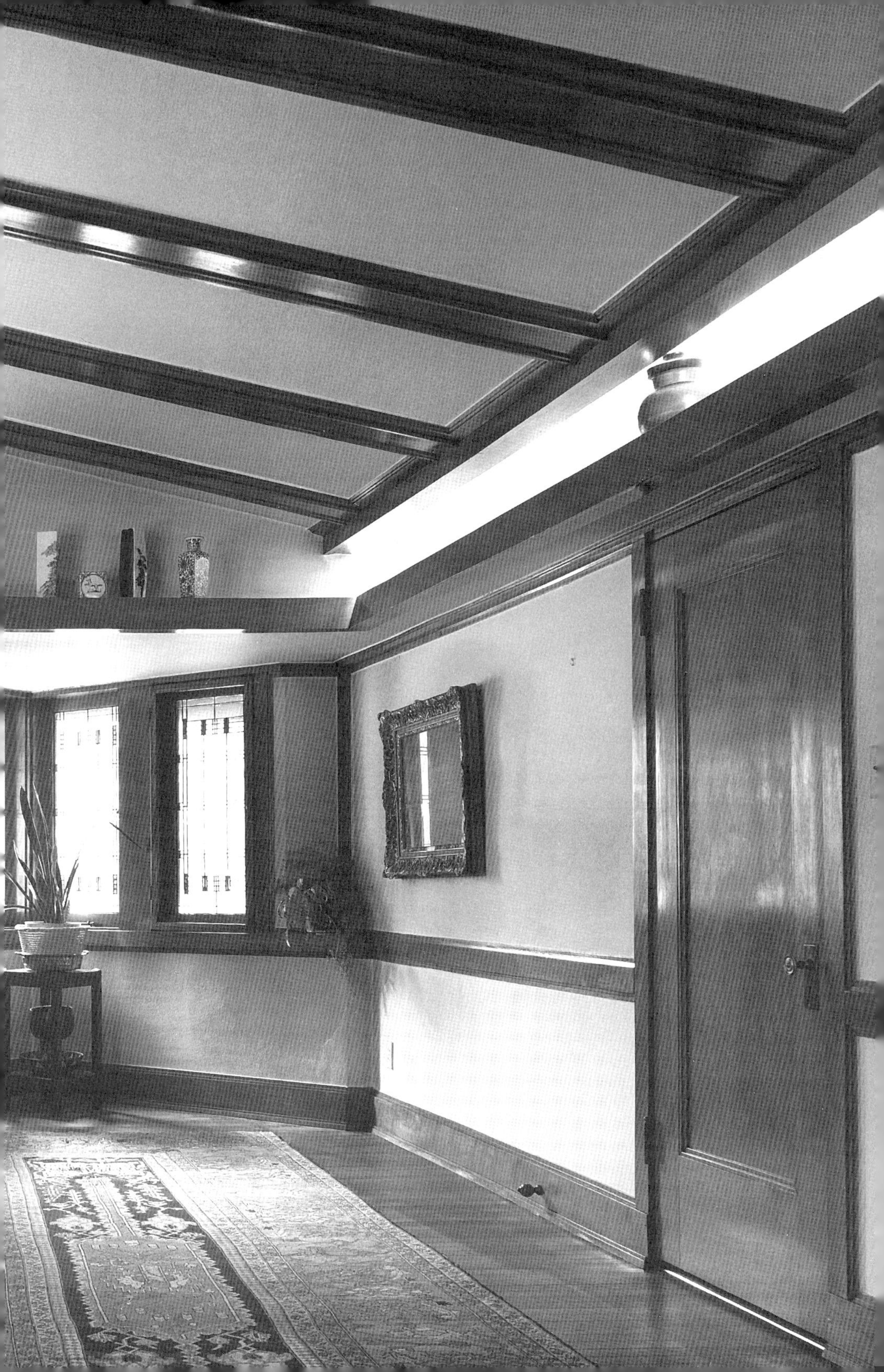

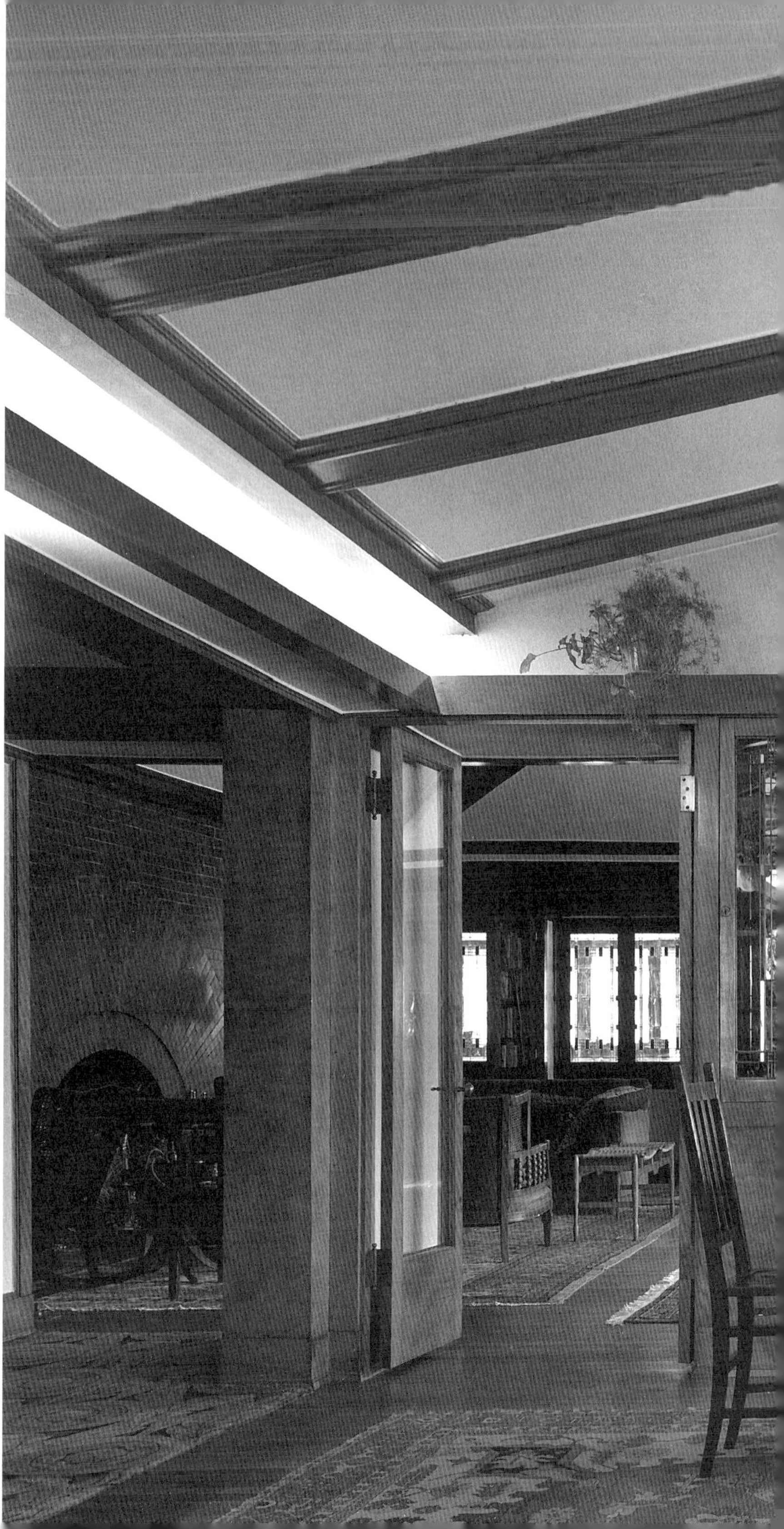

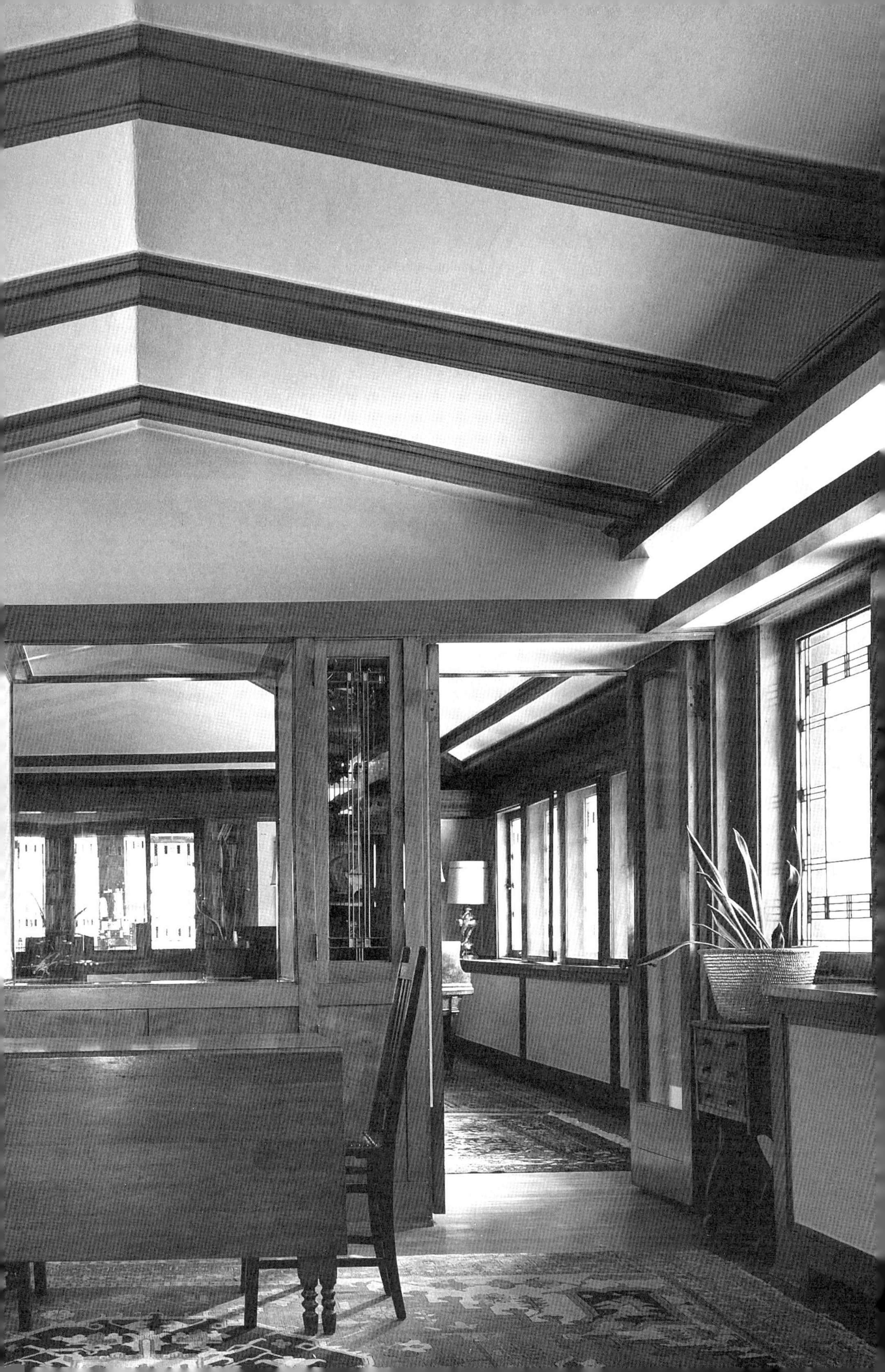

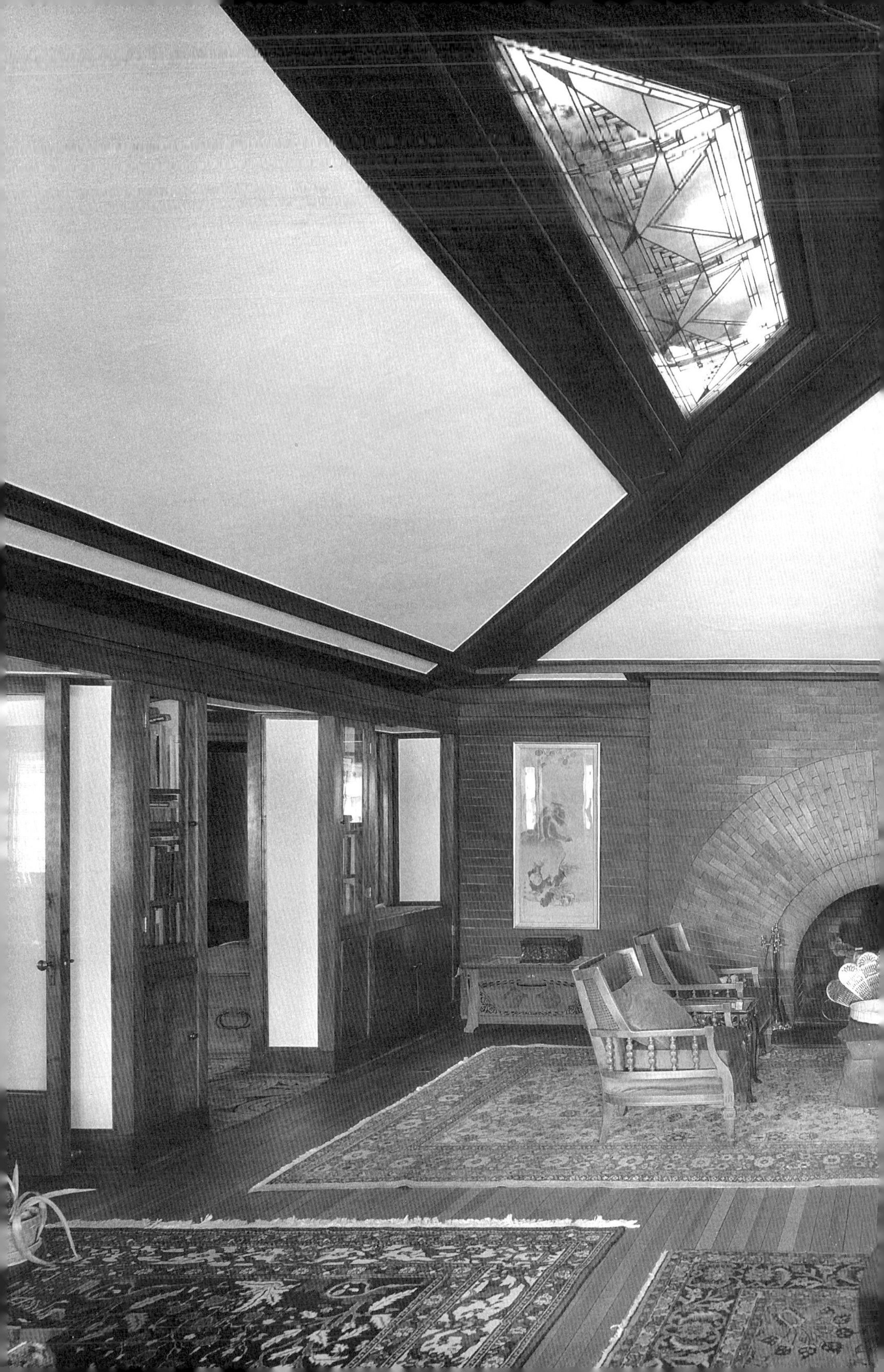

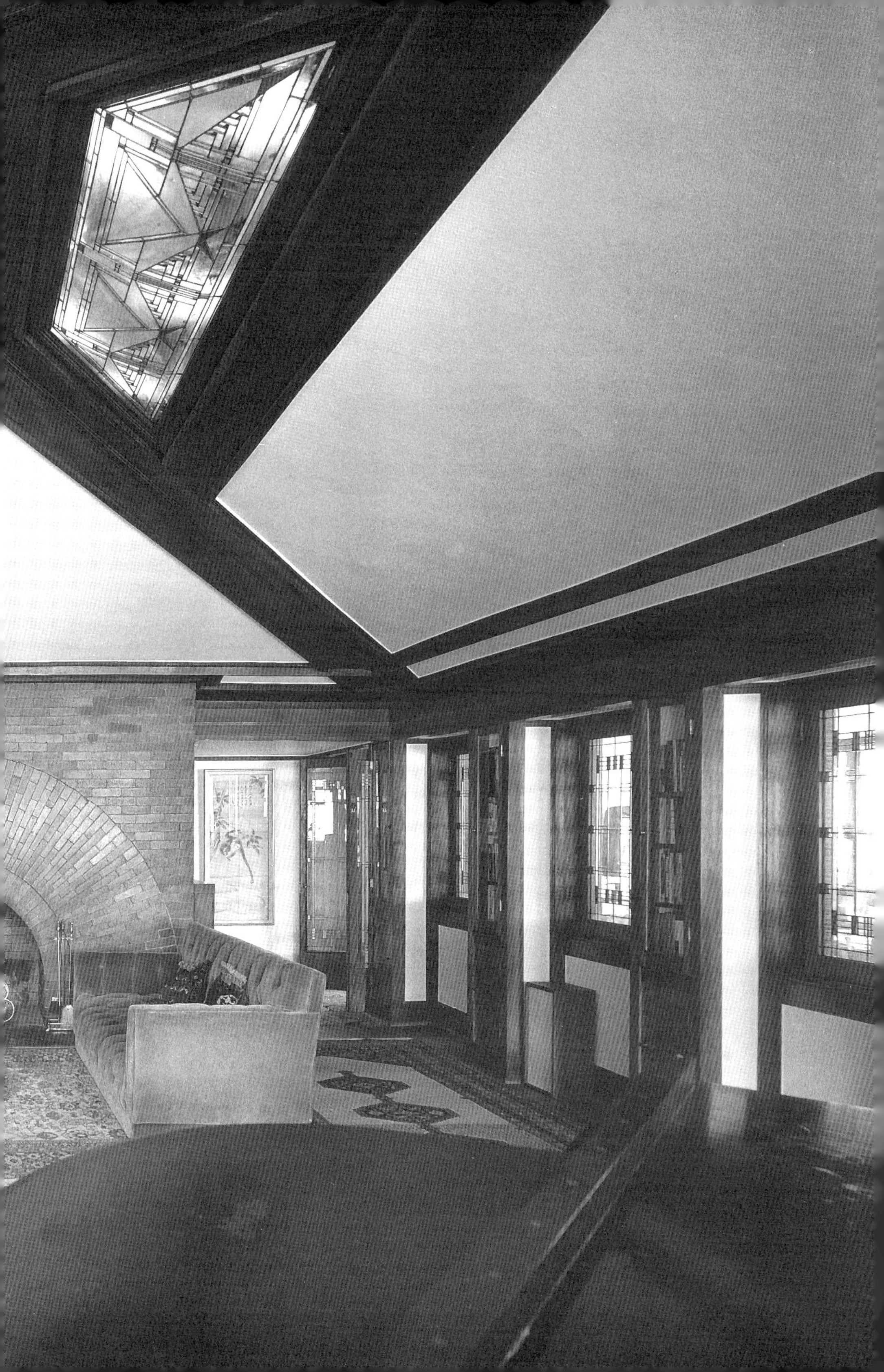

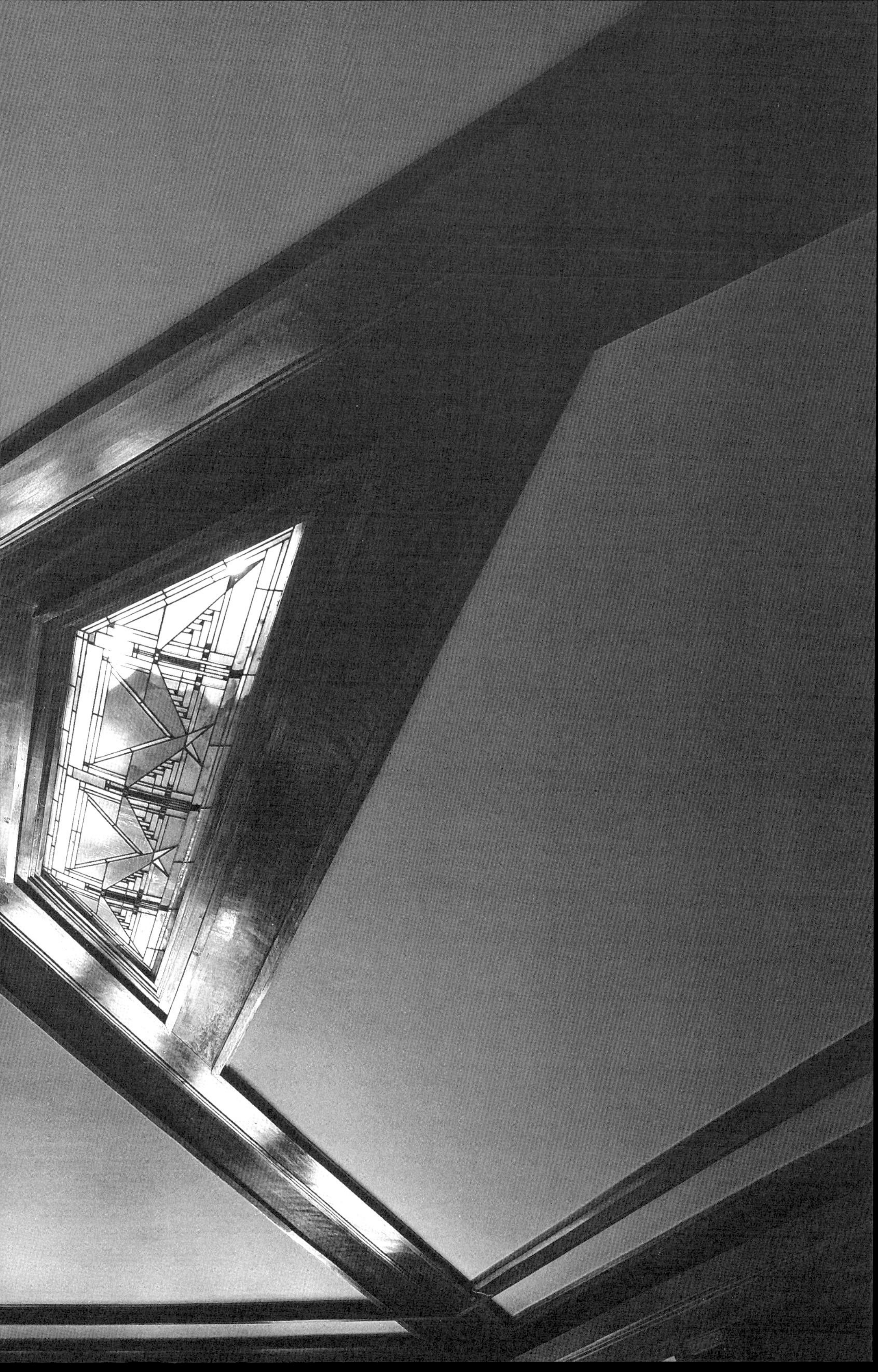

Darwin D. Martin House
Buffalo, New York, 1903

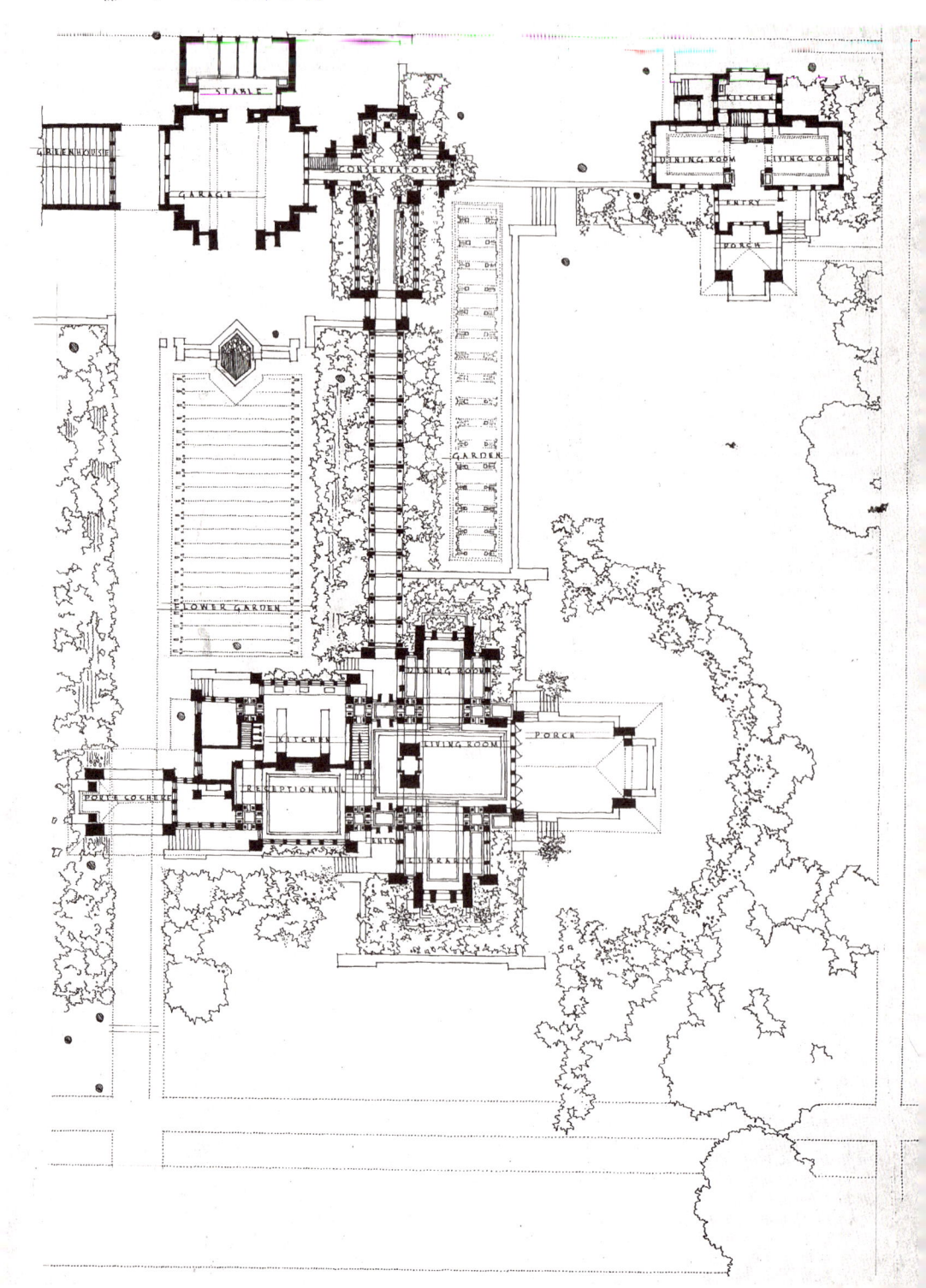

Second floor

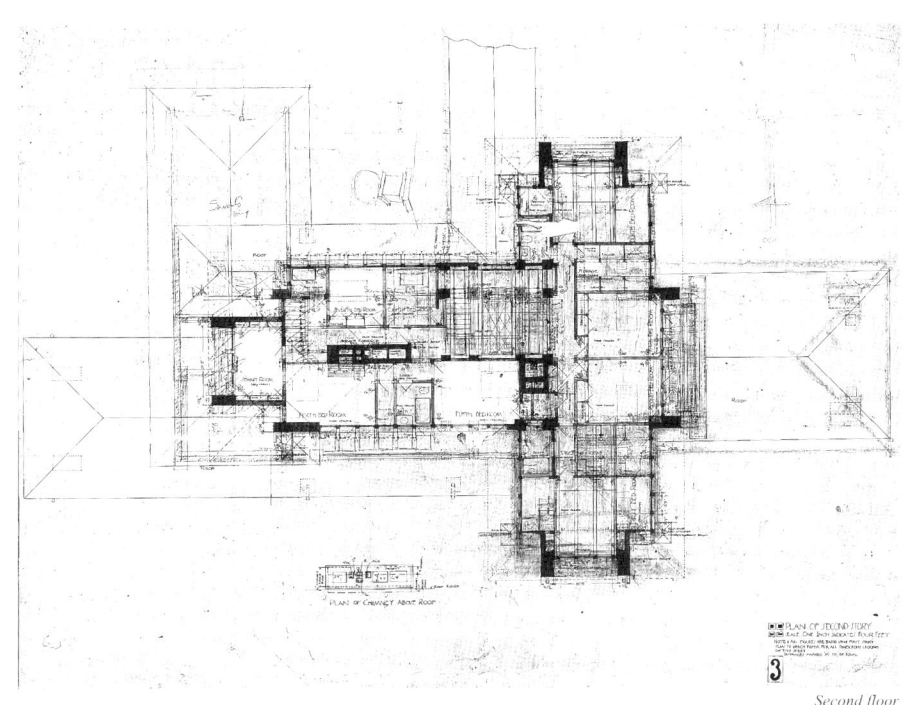

Site plan *First floor*

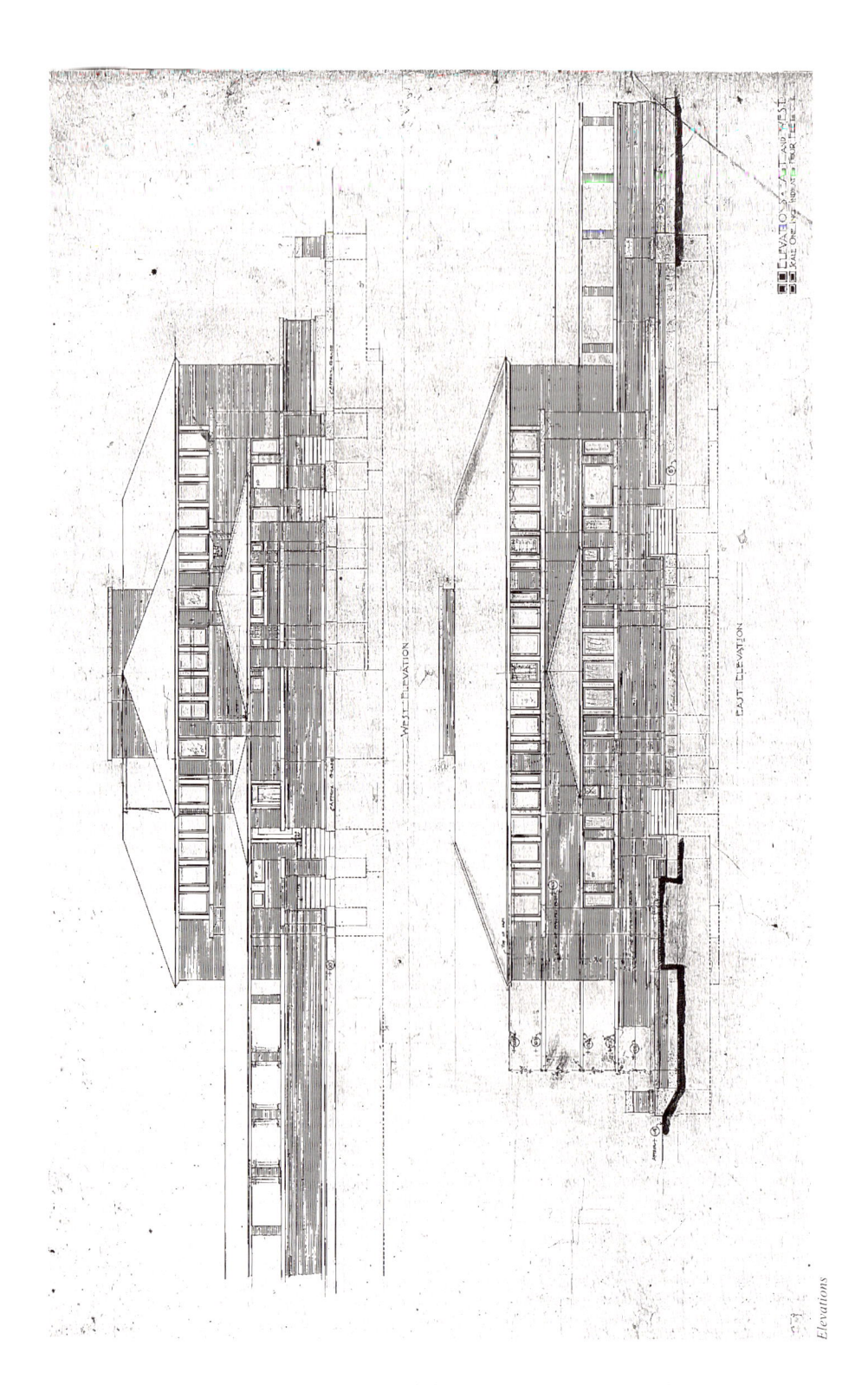

Elevations

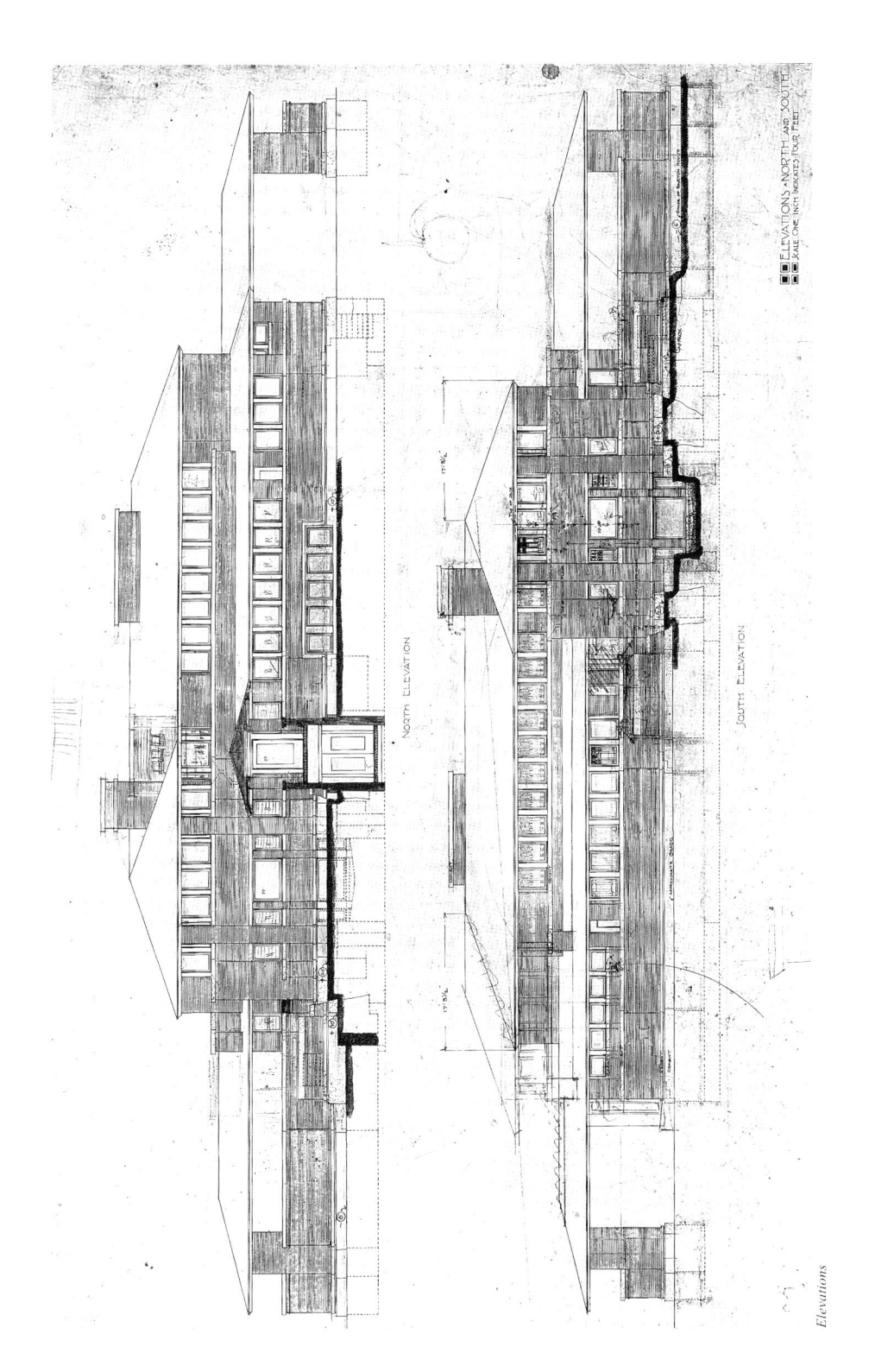

Elevations

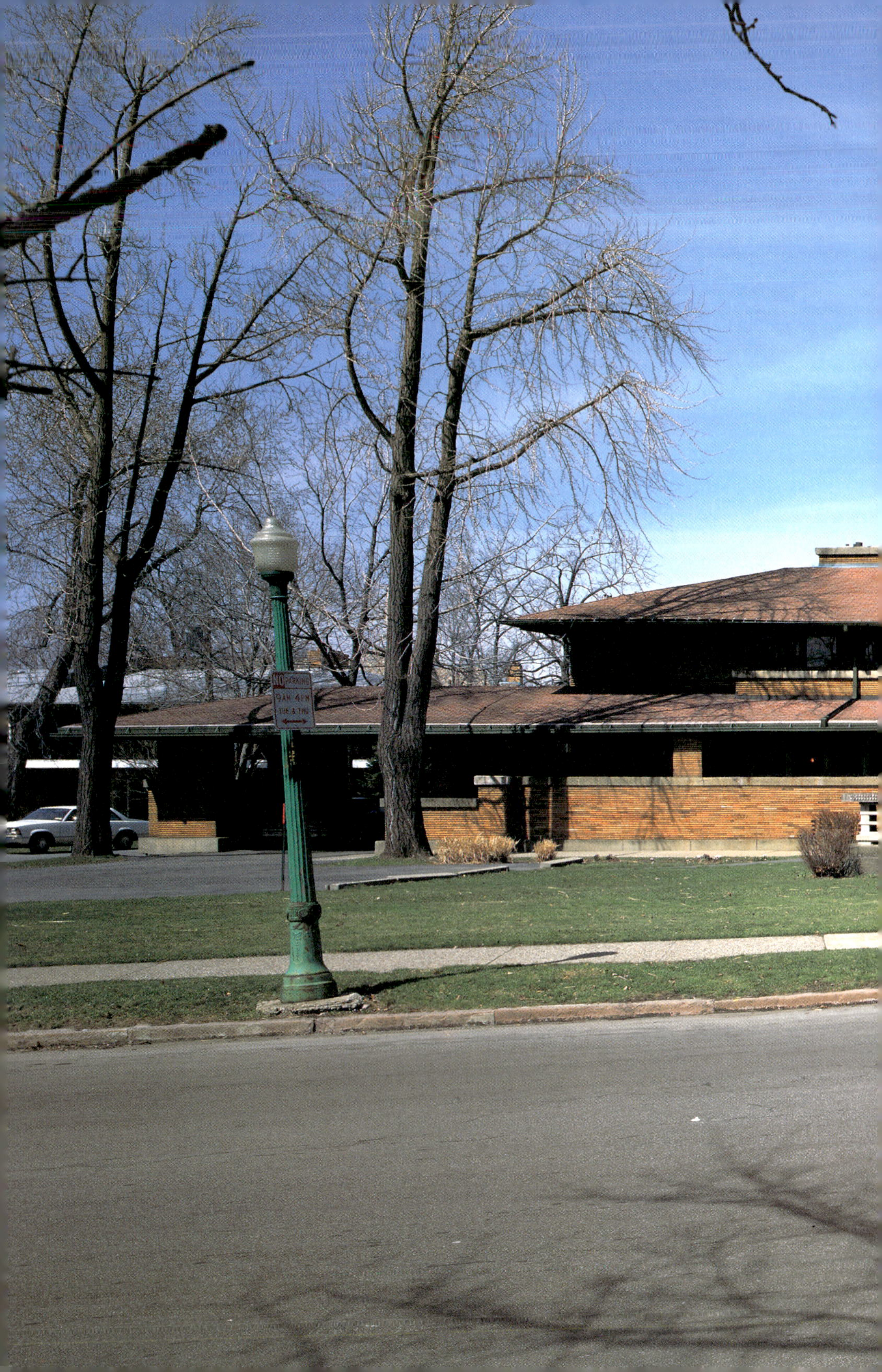
NO PARKING
9AM 4PM
TUE & THU

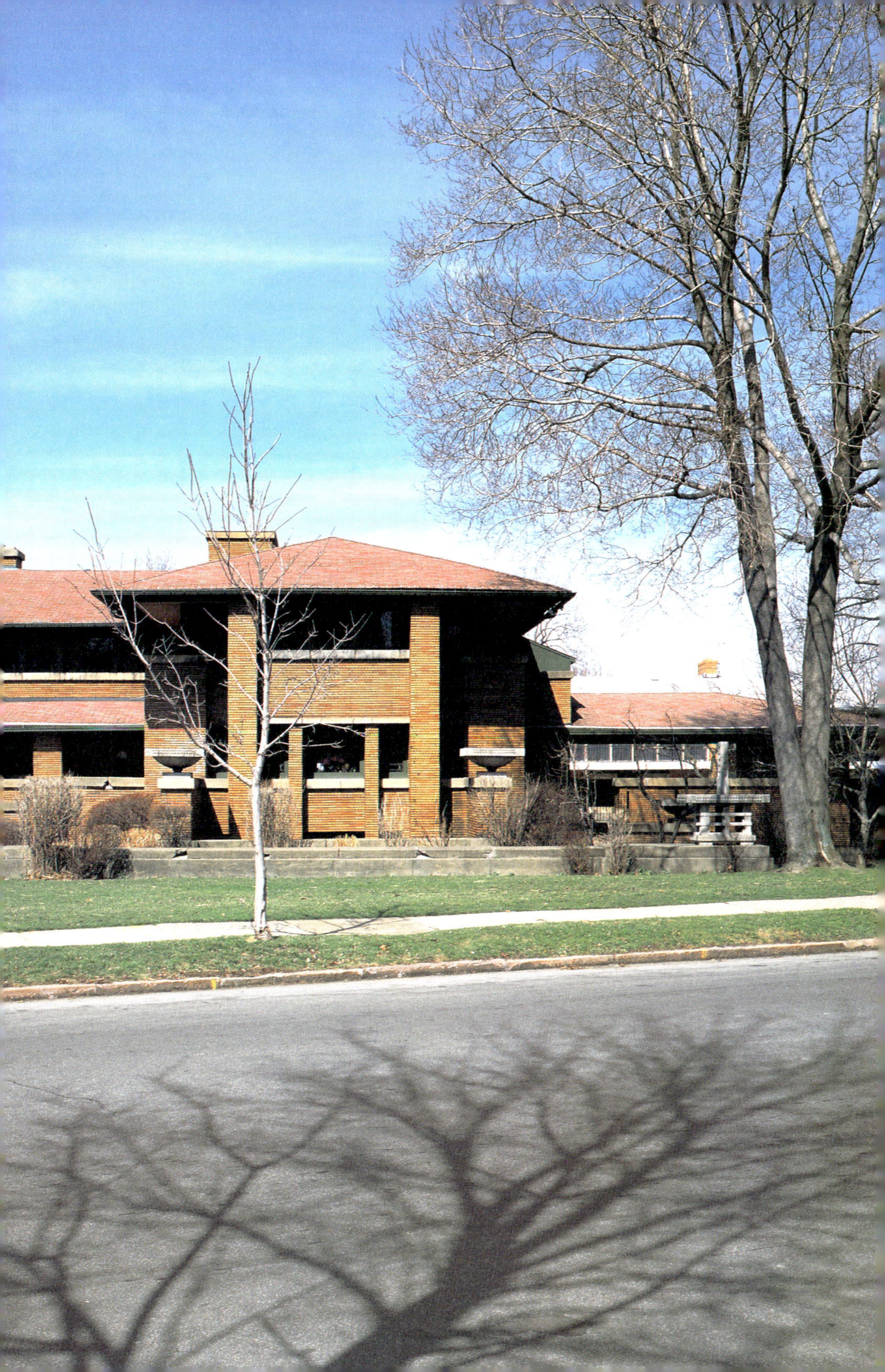

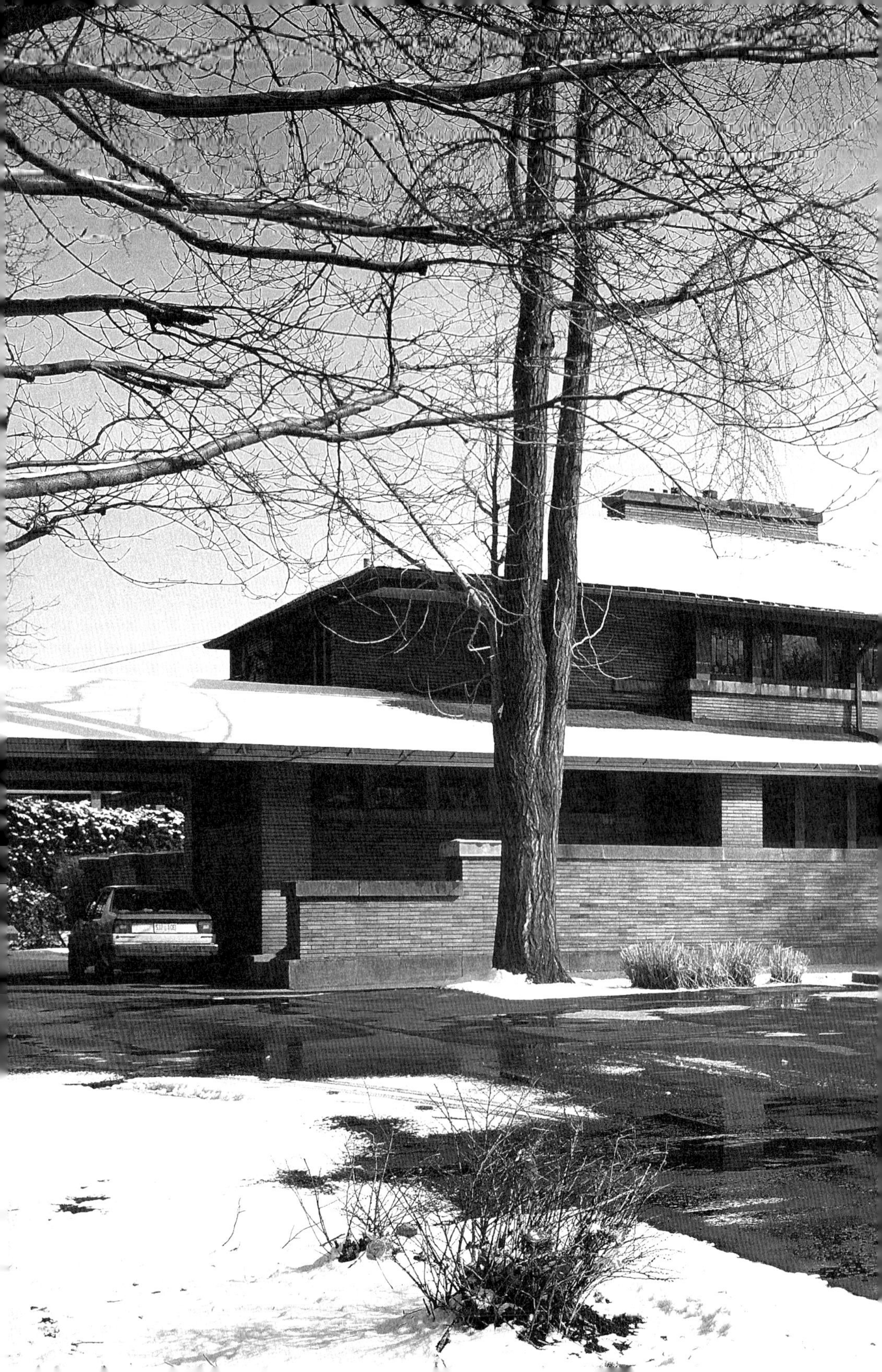

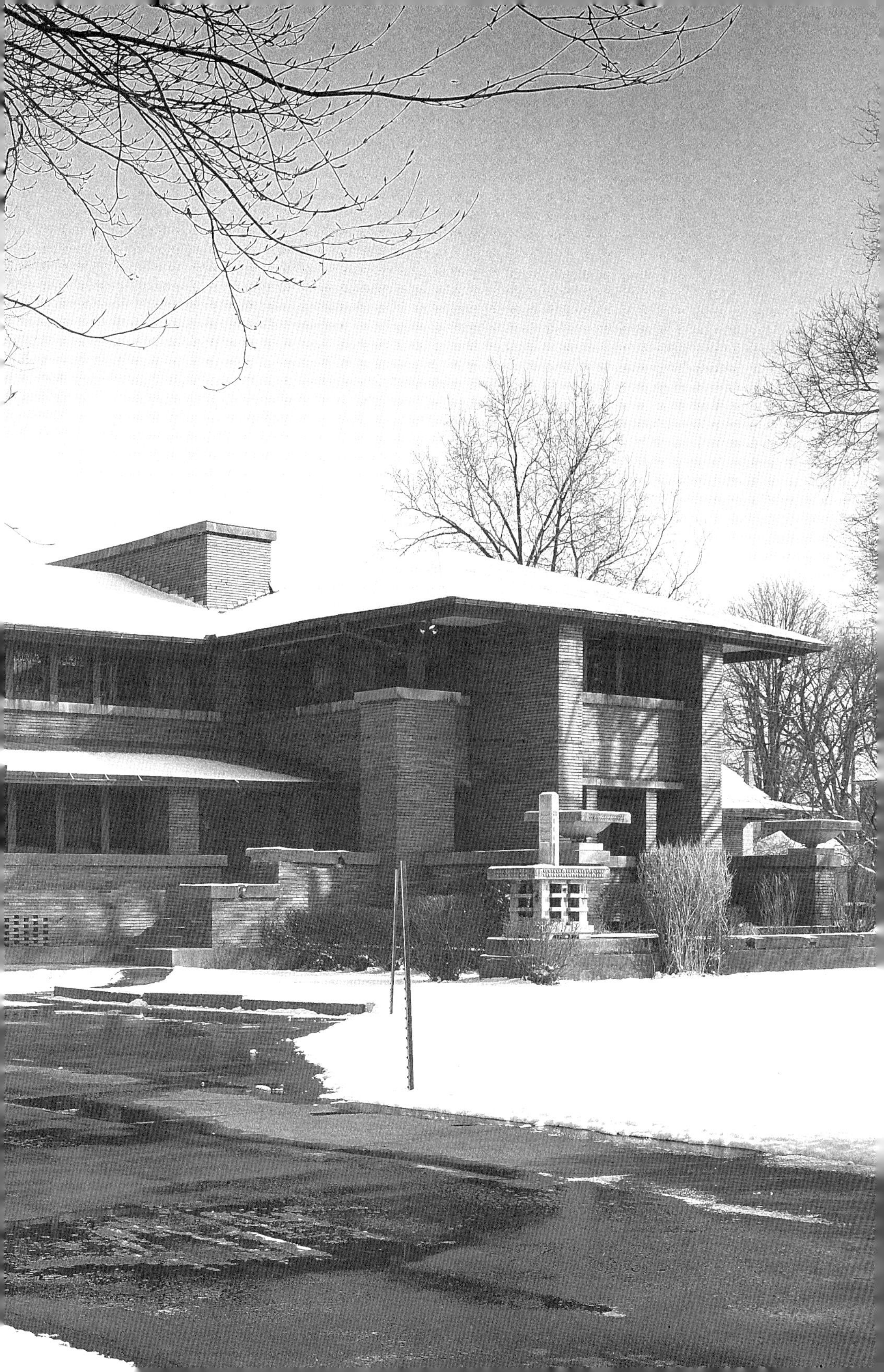

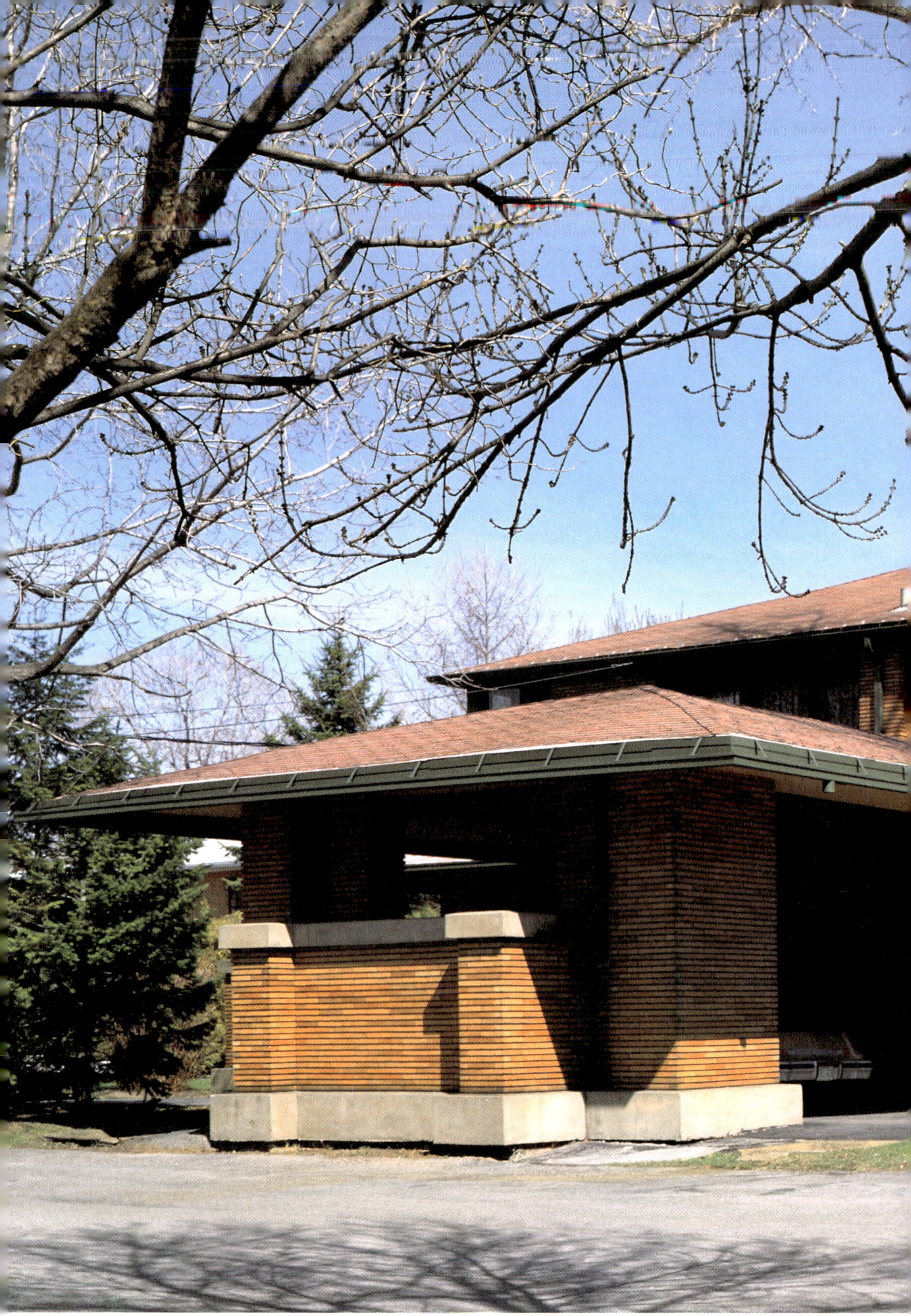

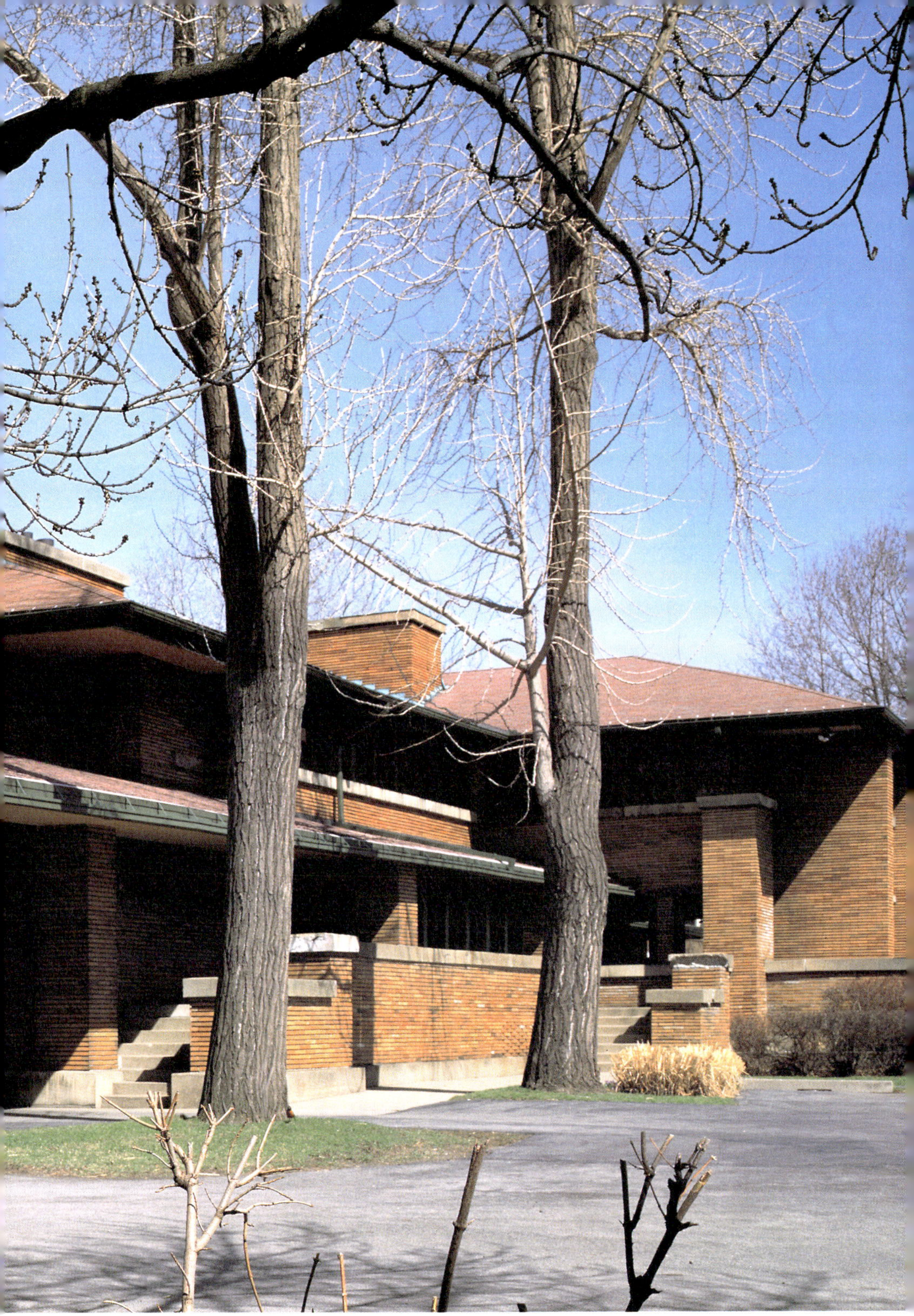

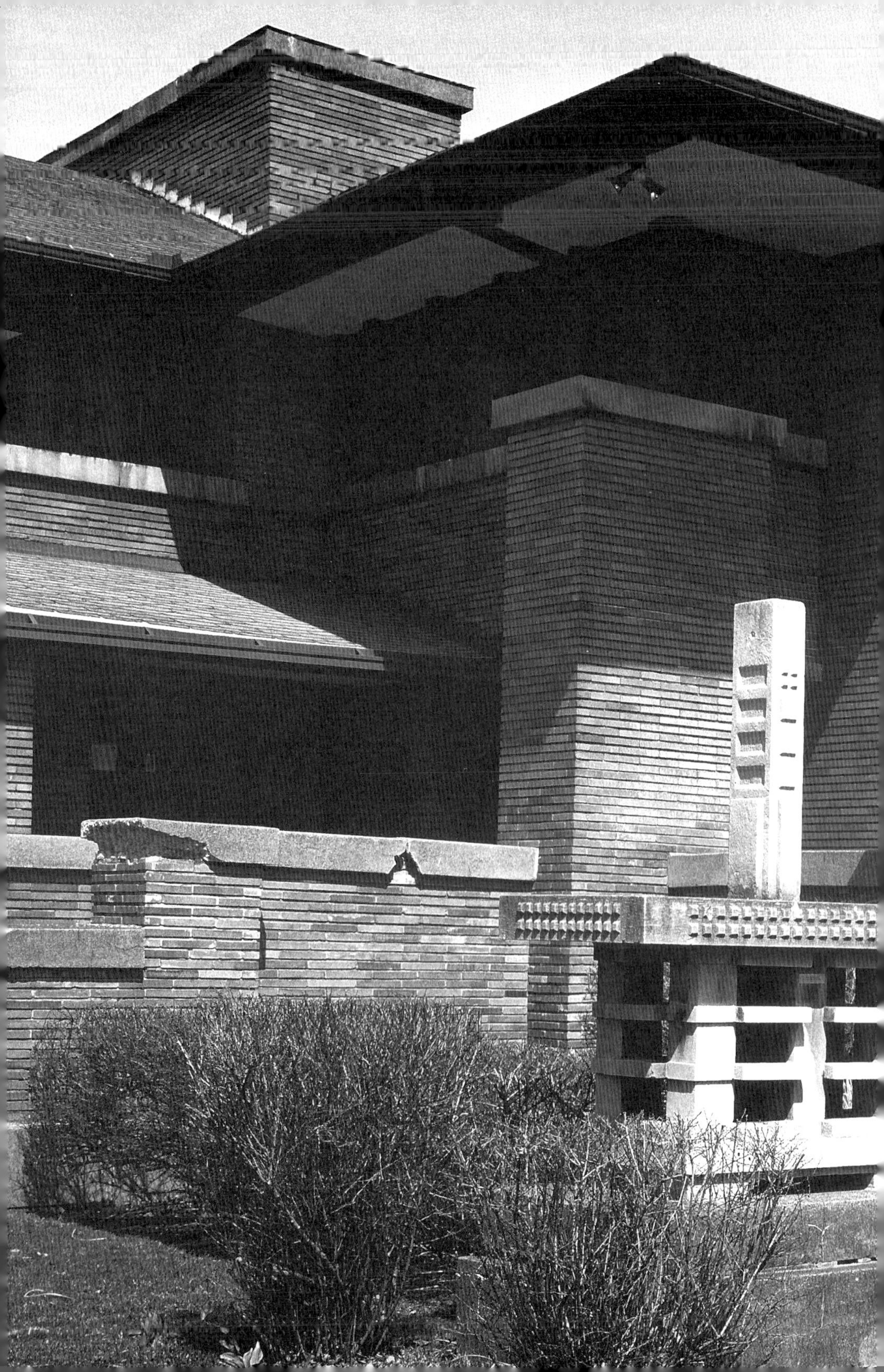

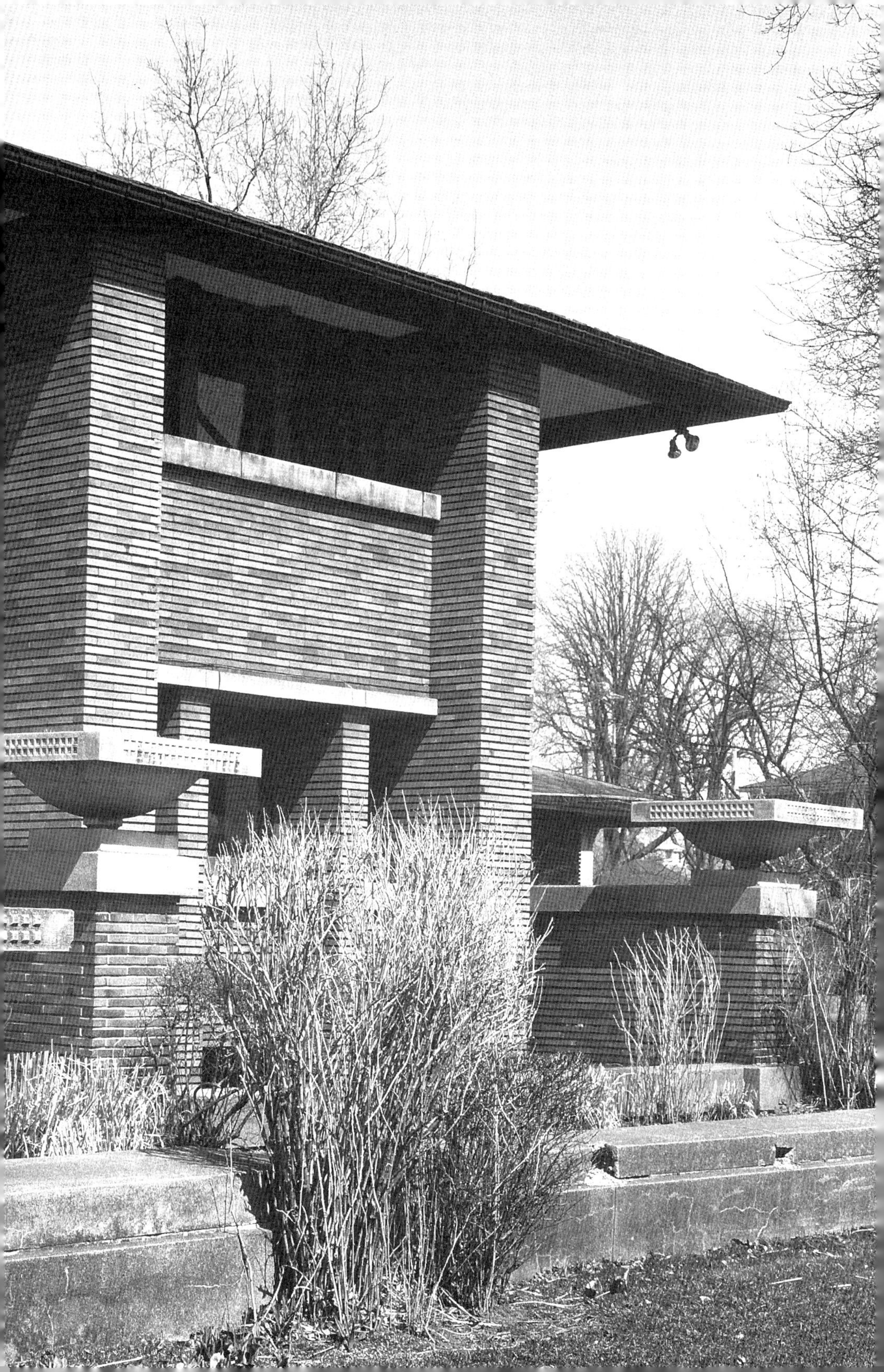

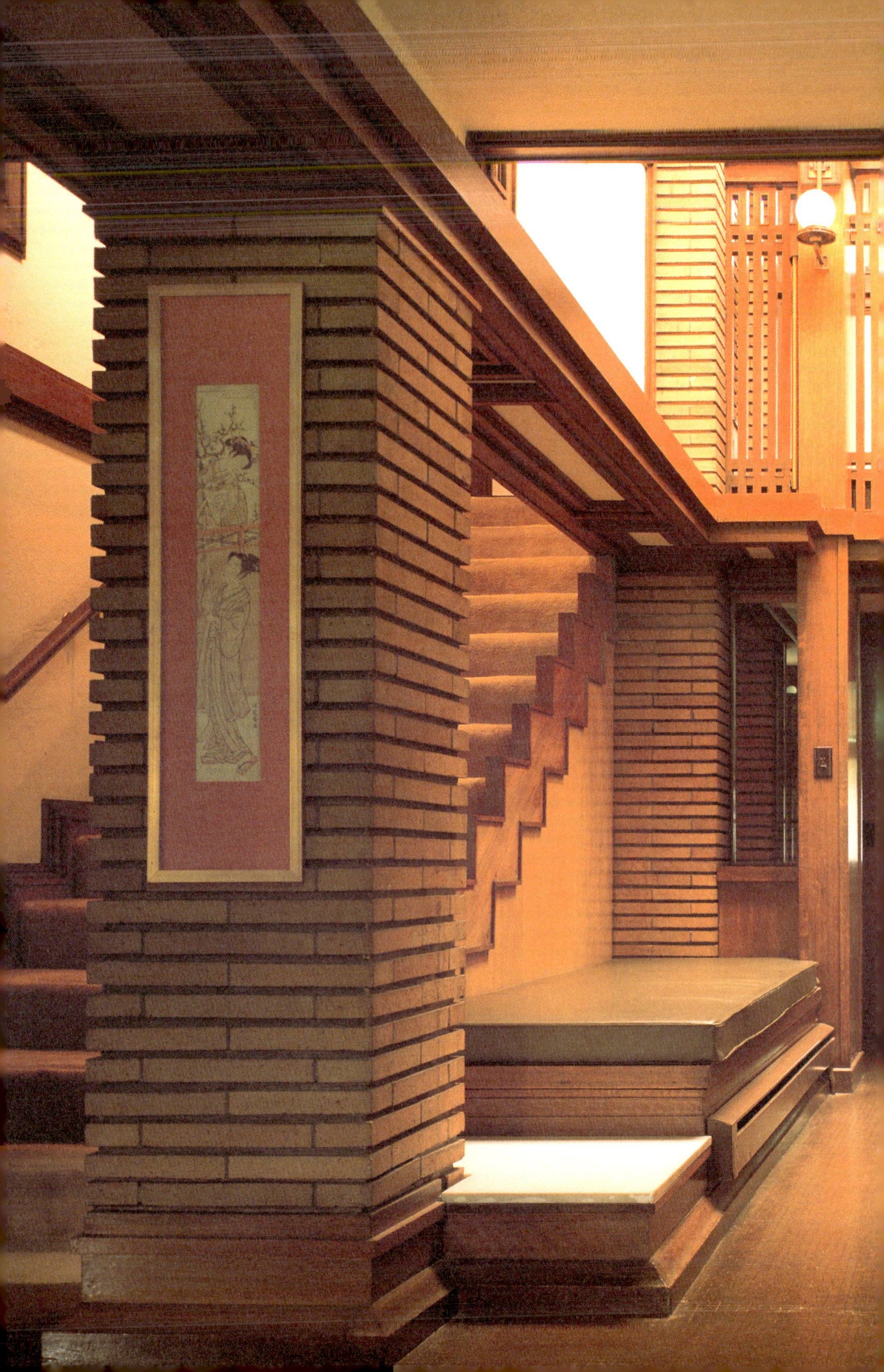

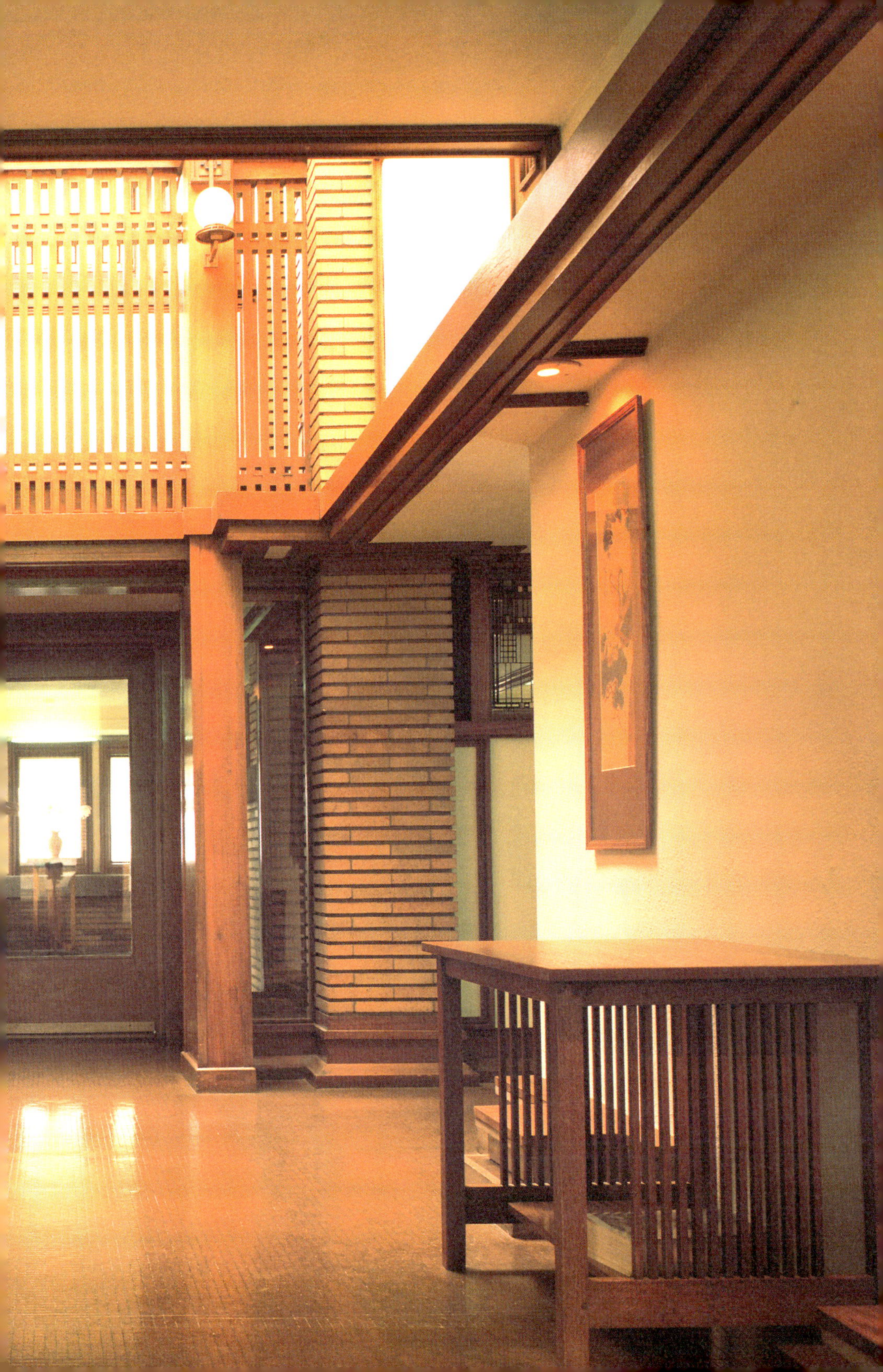

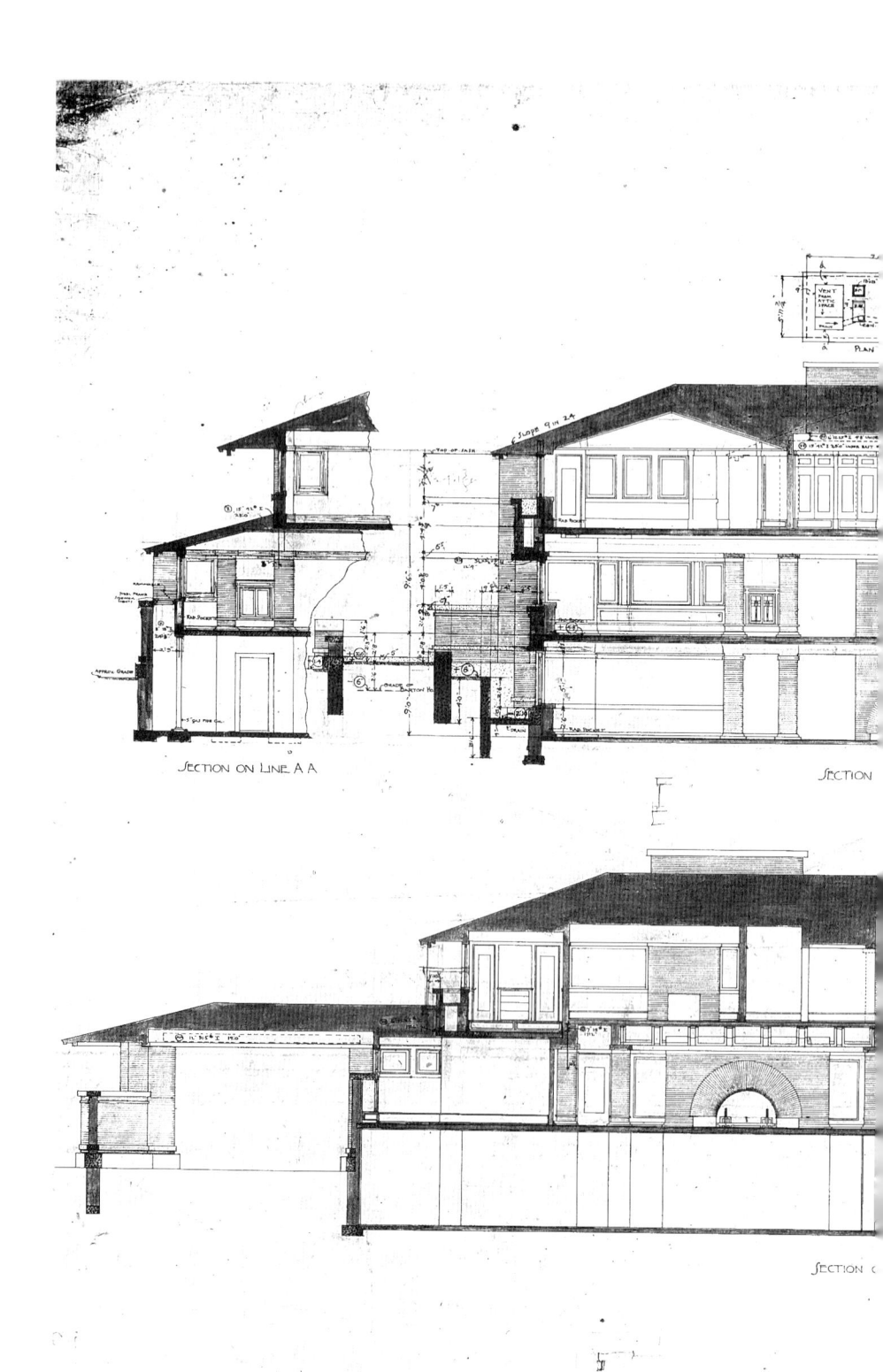

SECTION ON LINE A A

SECTION

■■ SECTIONS
■■ SCALE ONE INCH INDICATES FOUR FEET

SECTION ON LINE BB

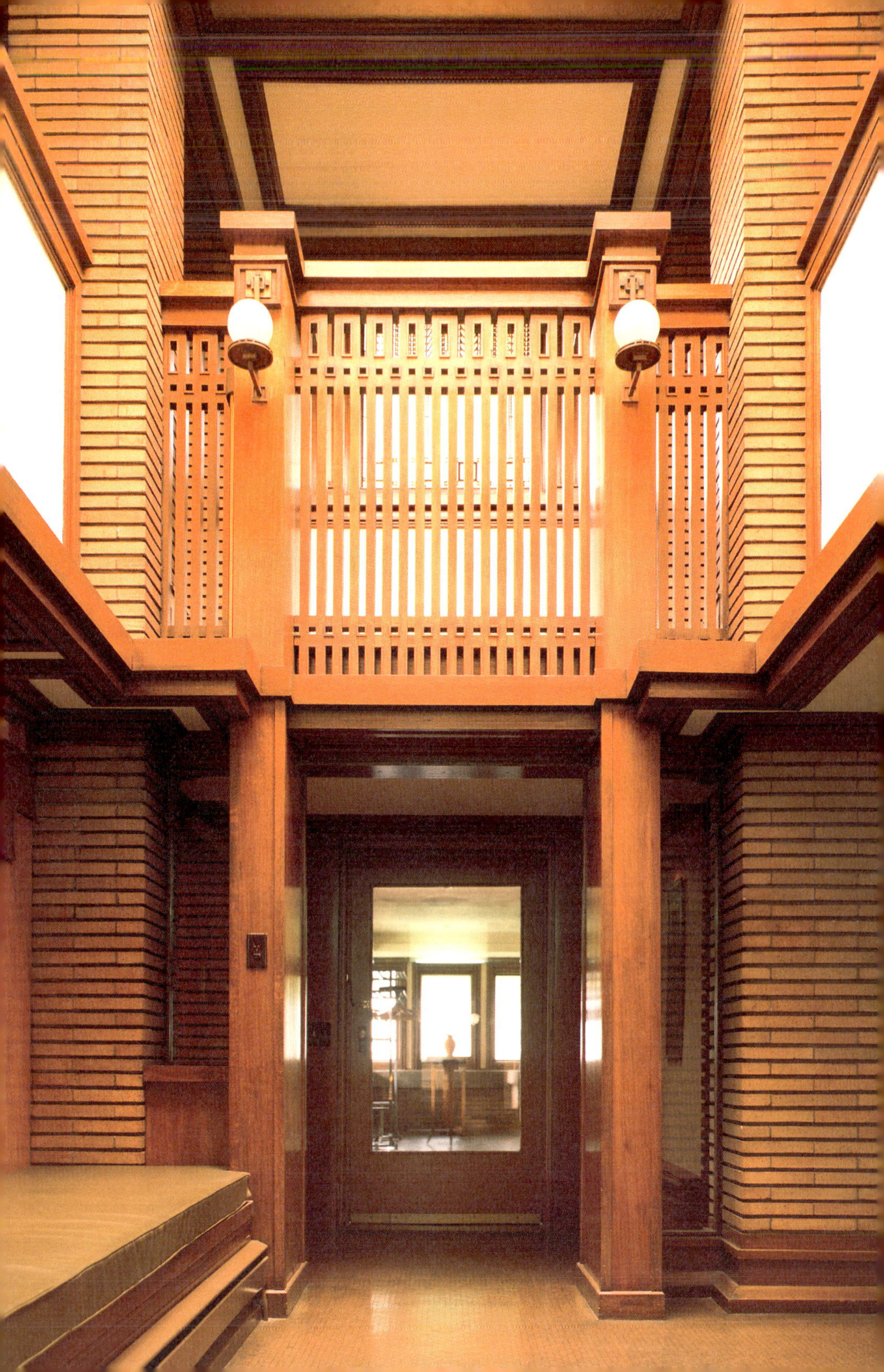

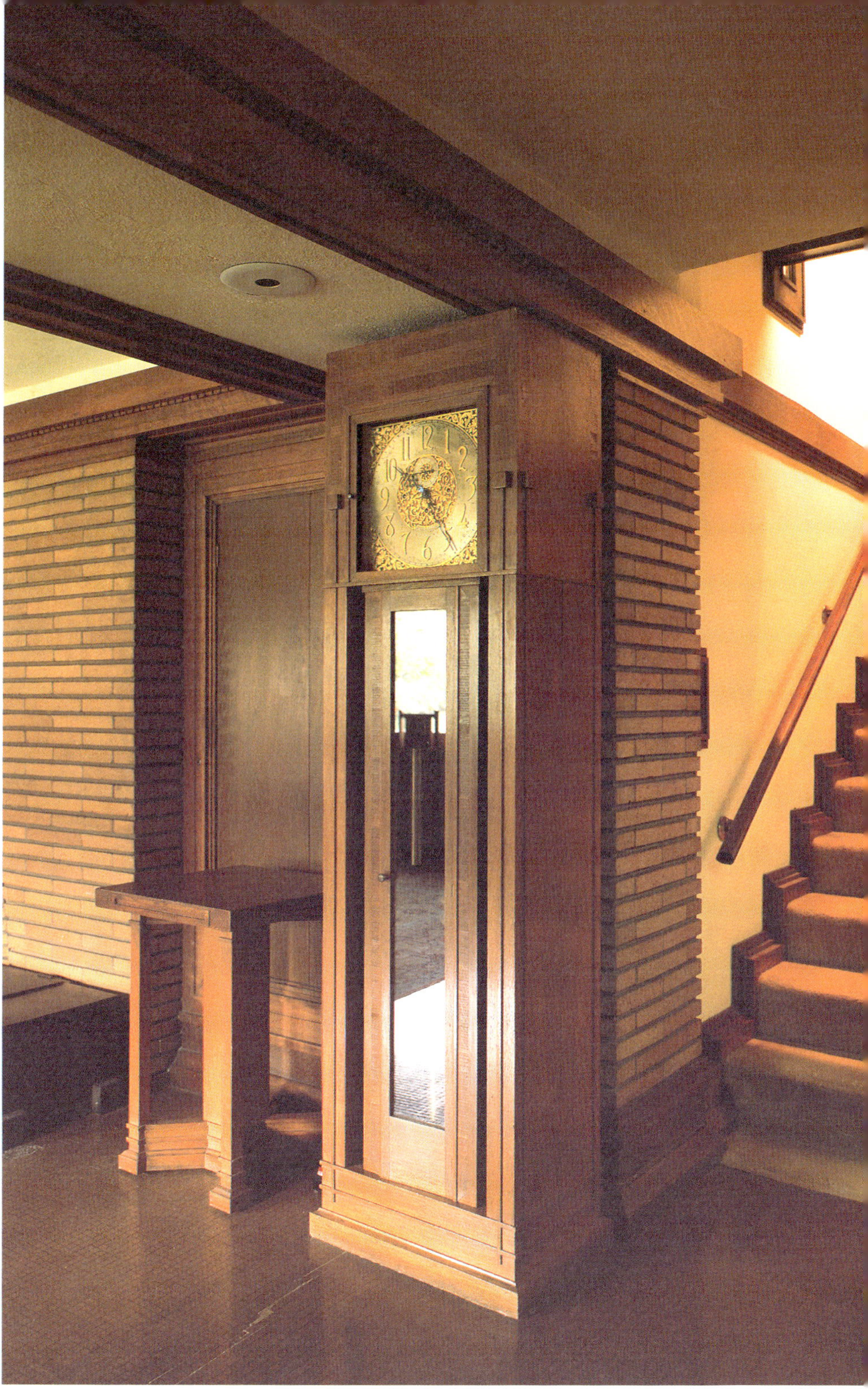

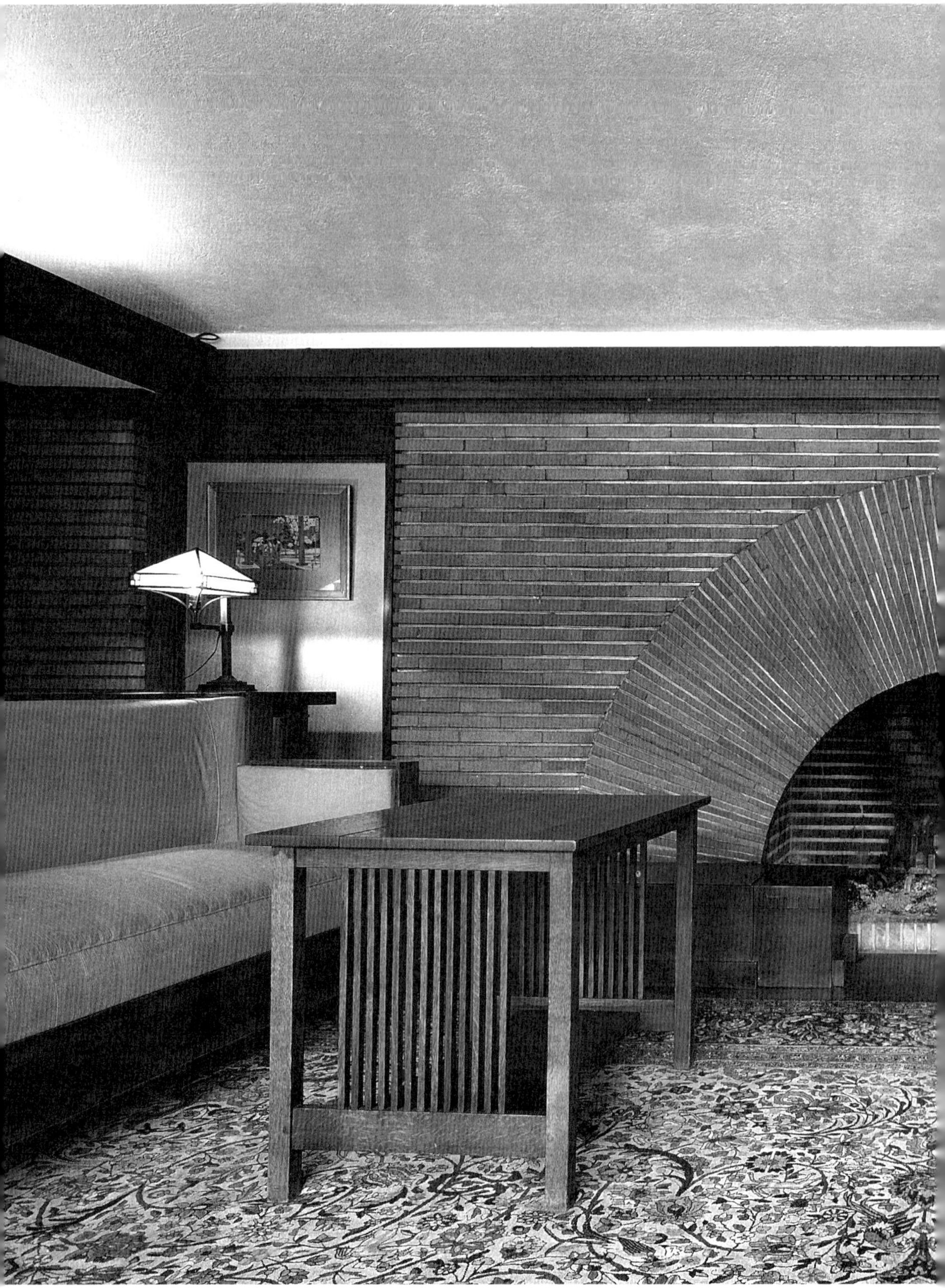

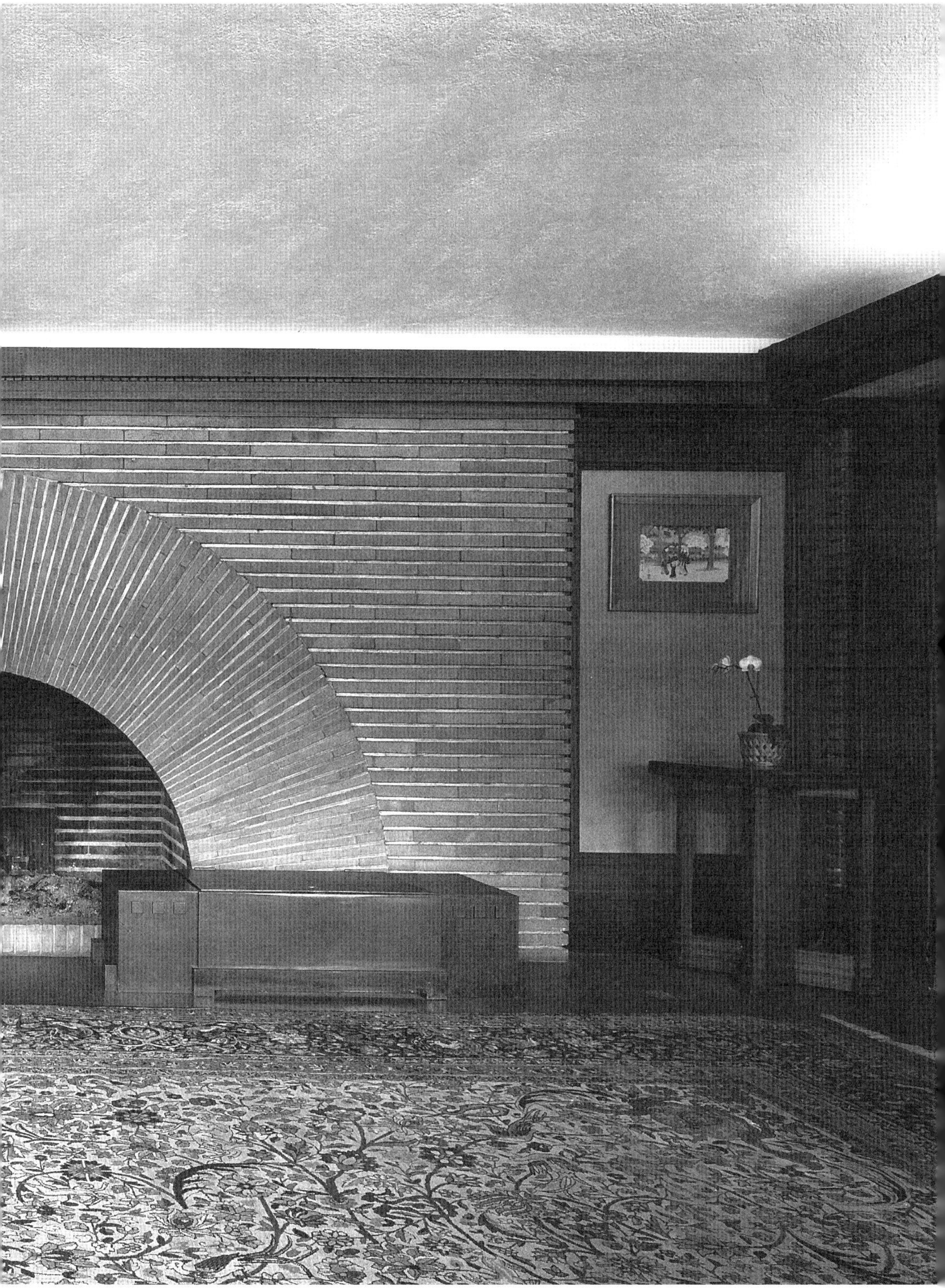

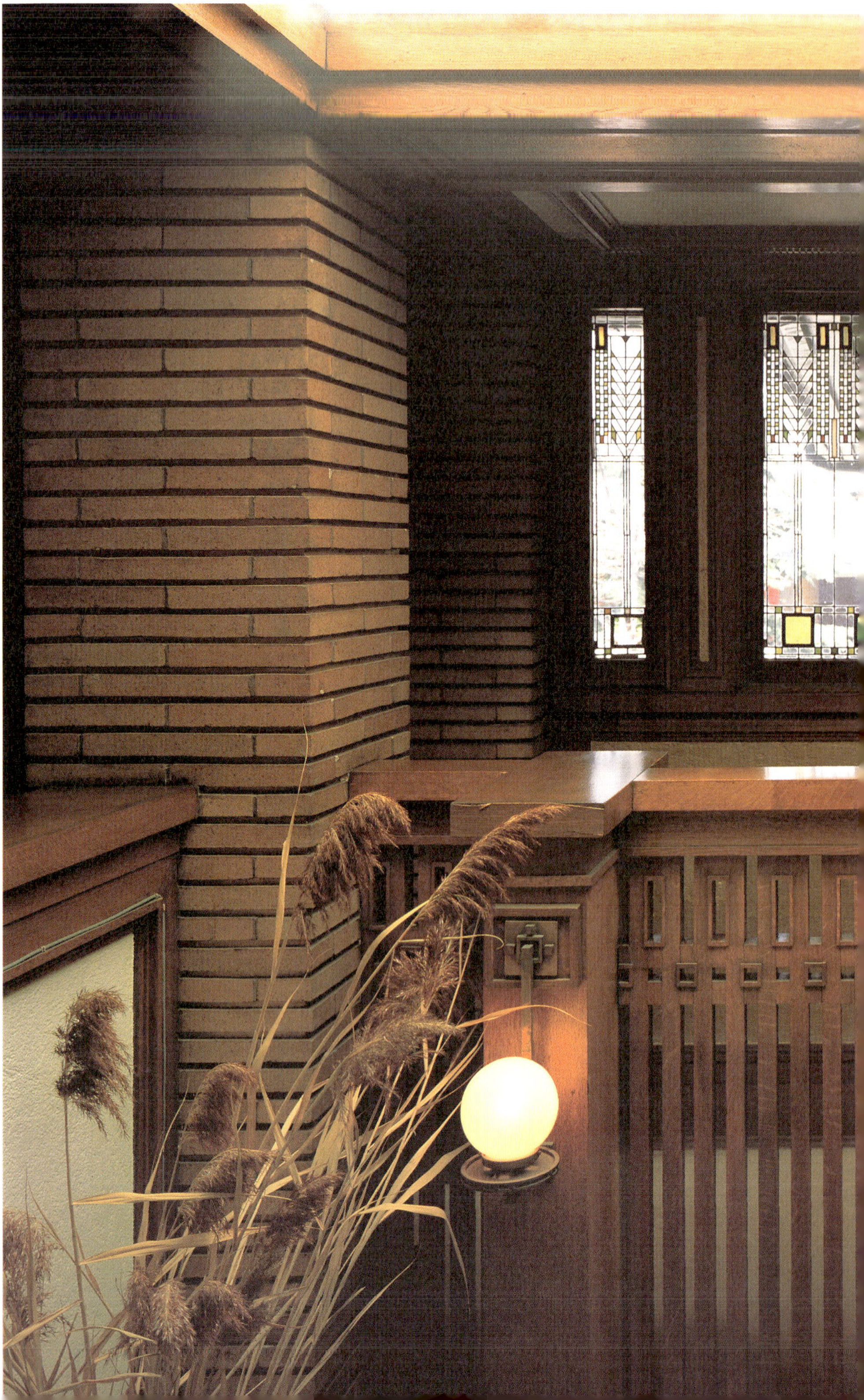

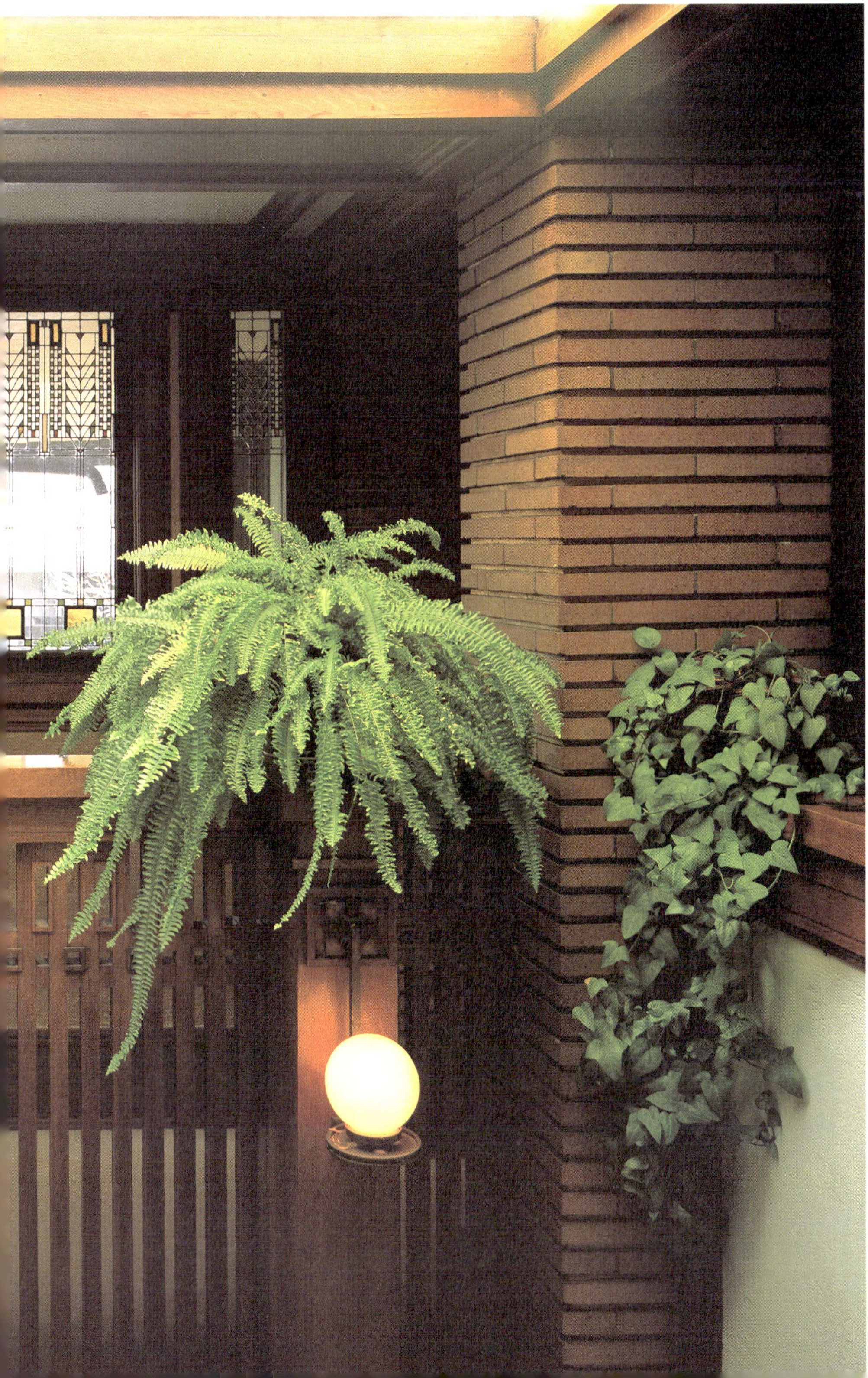

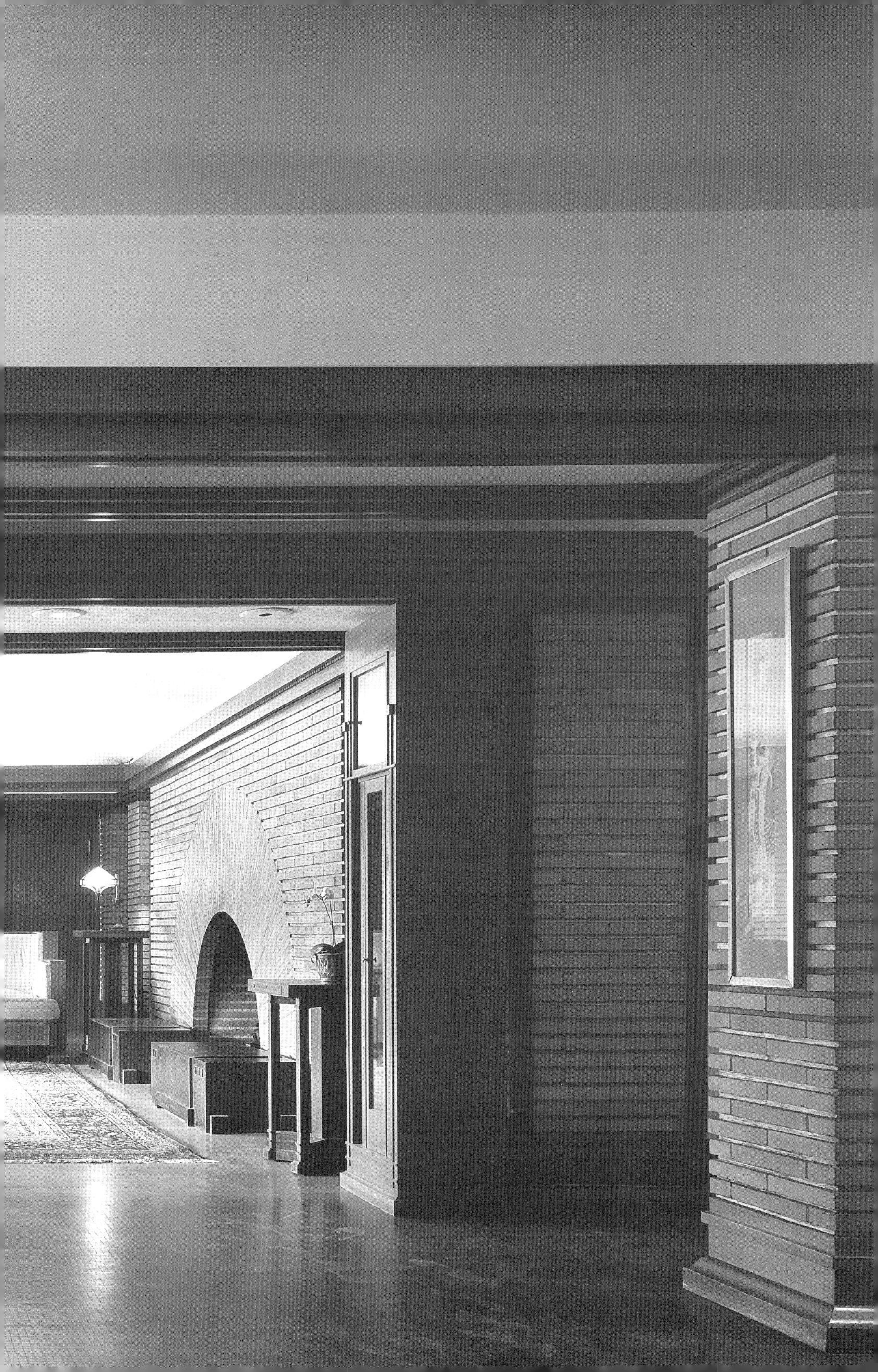

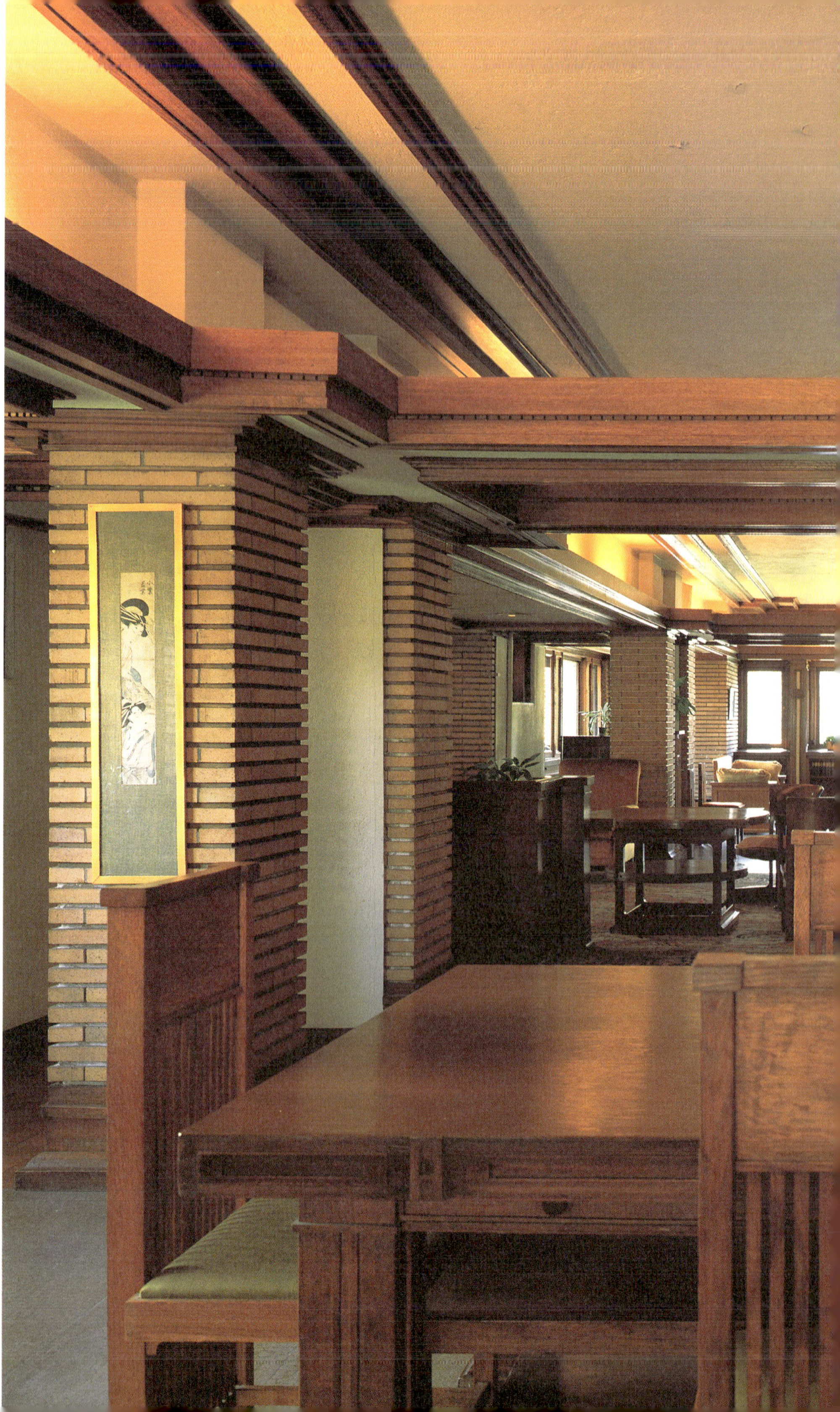

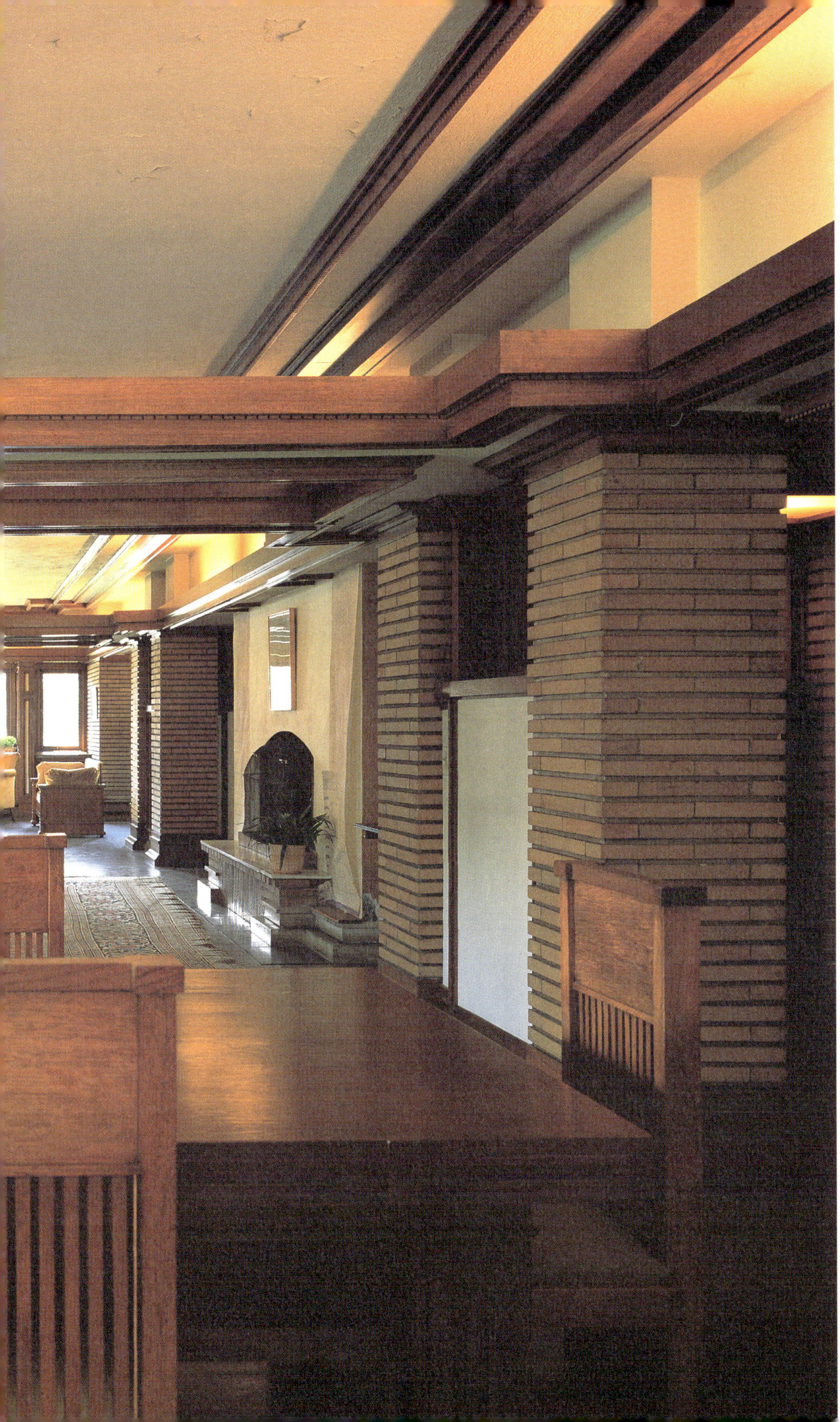

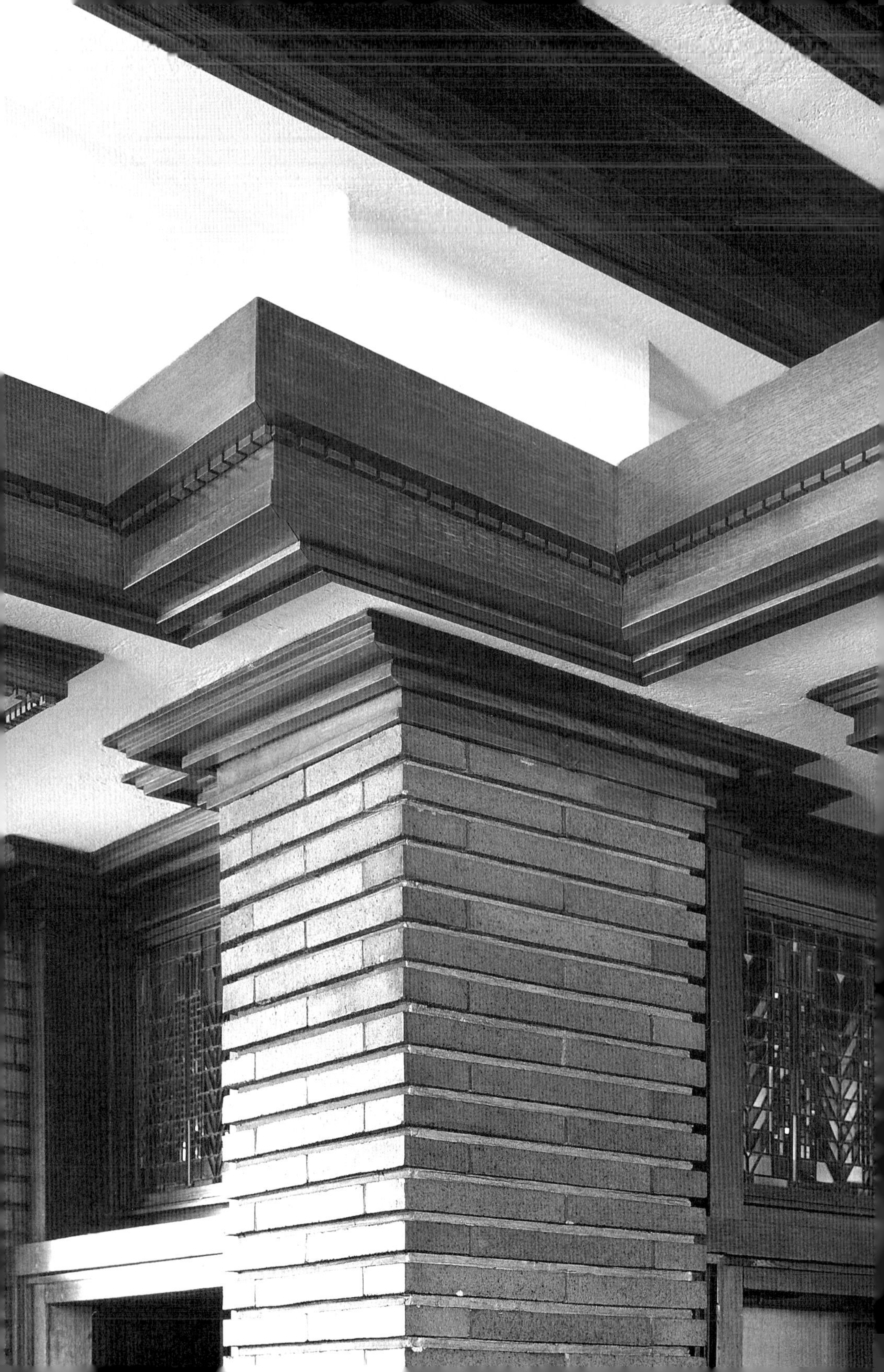

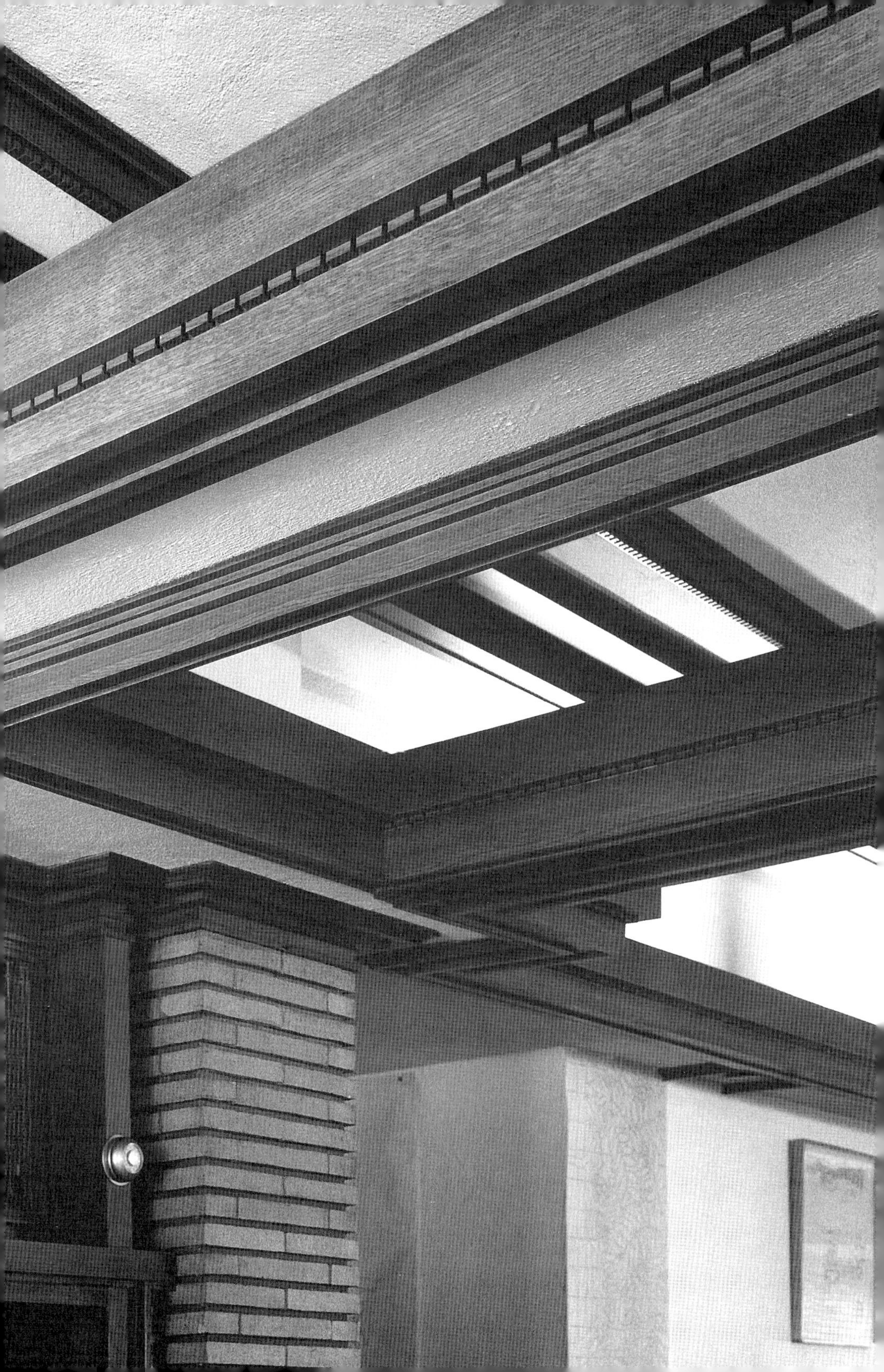

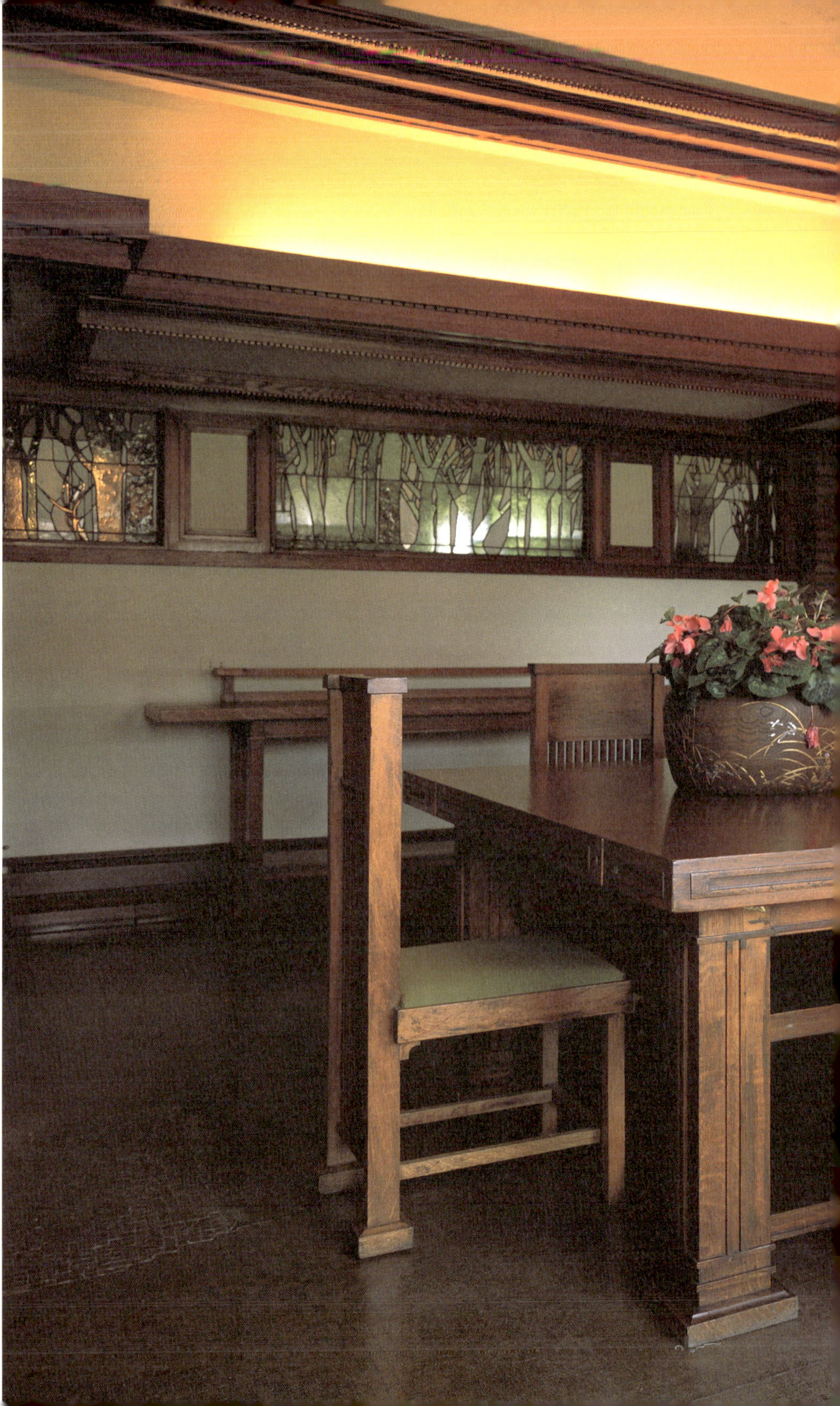

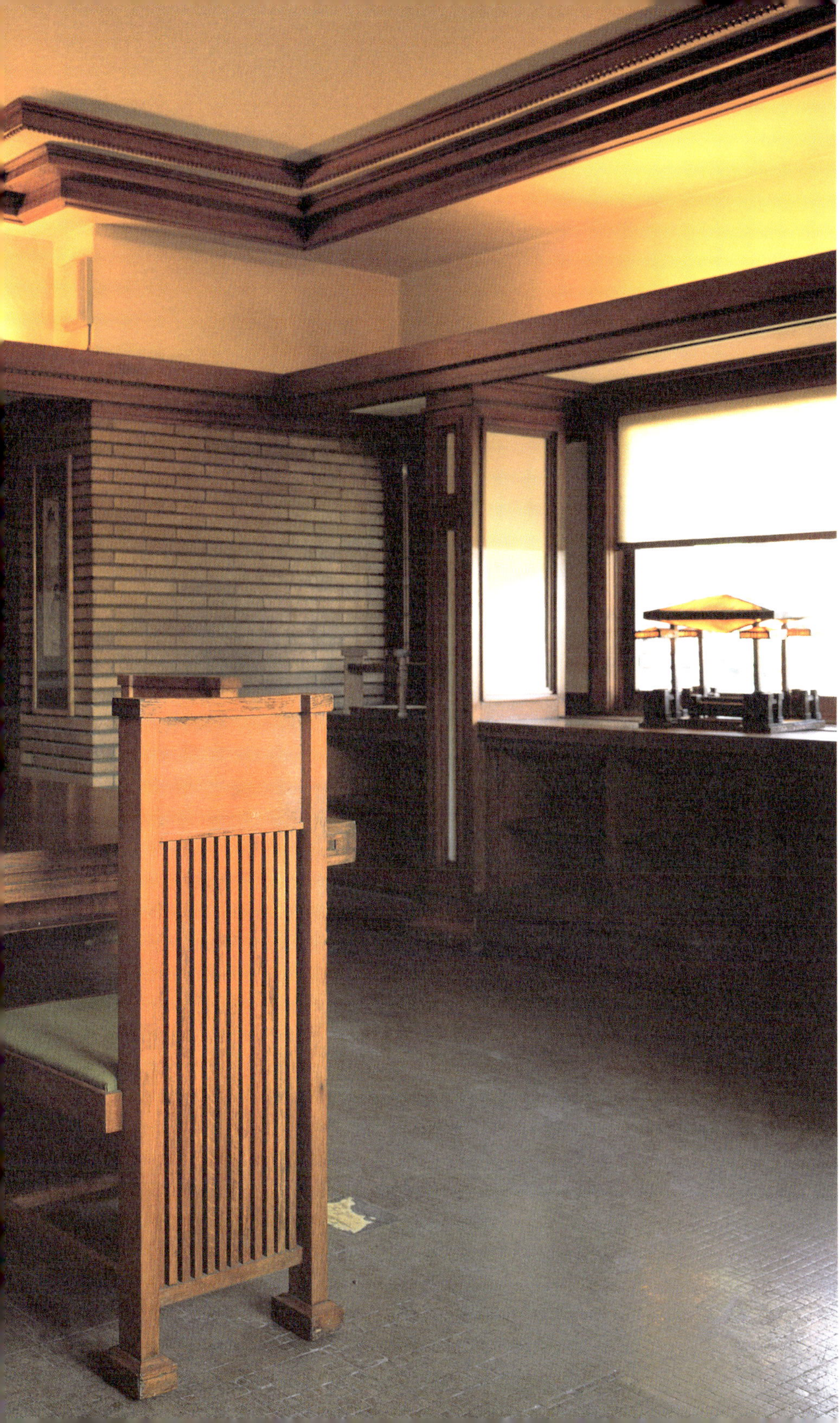

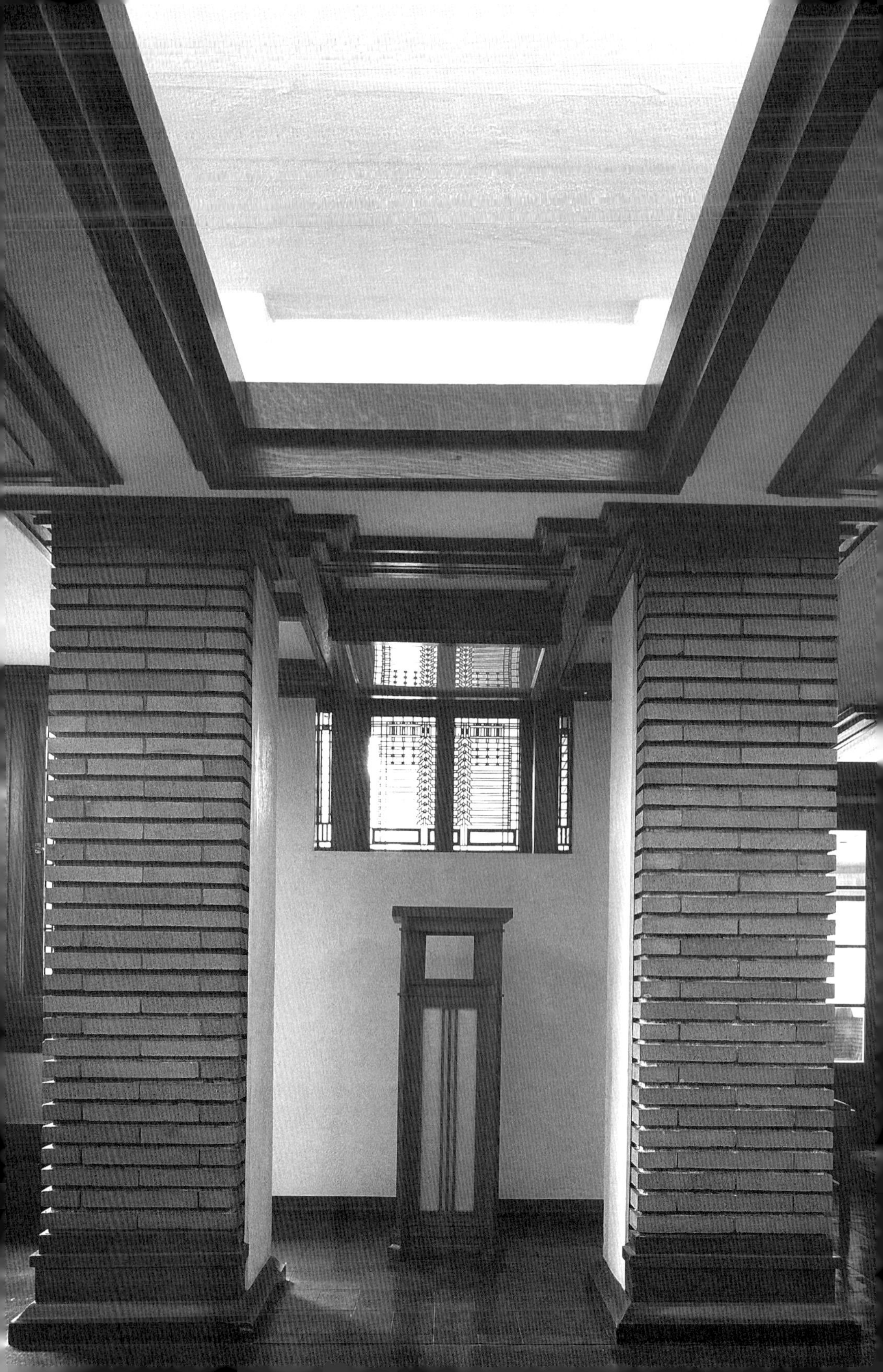

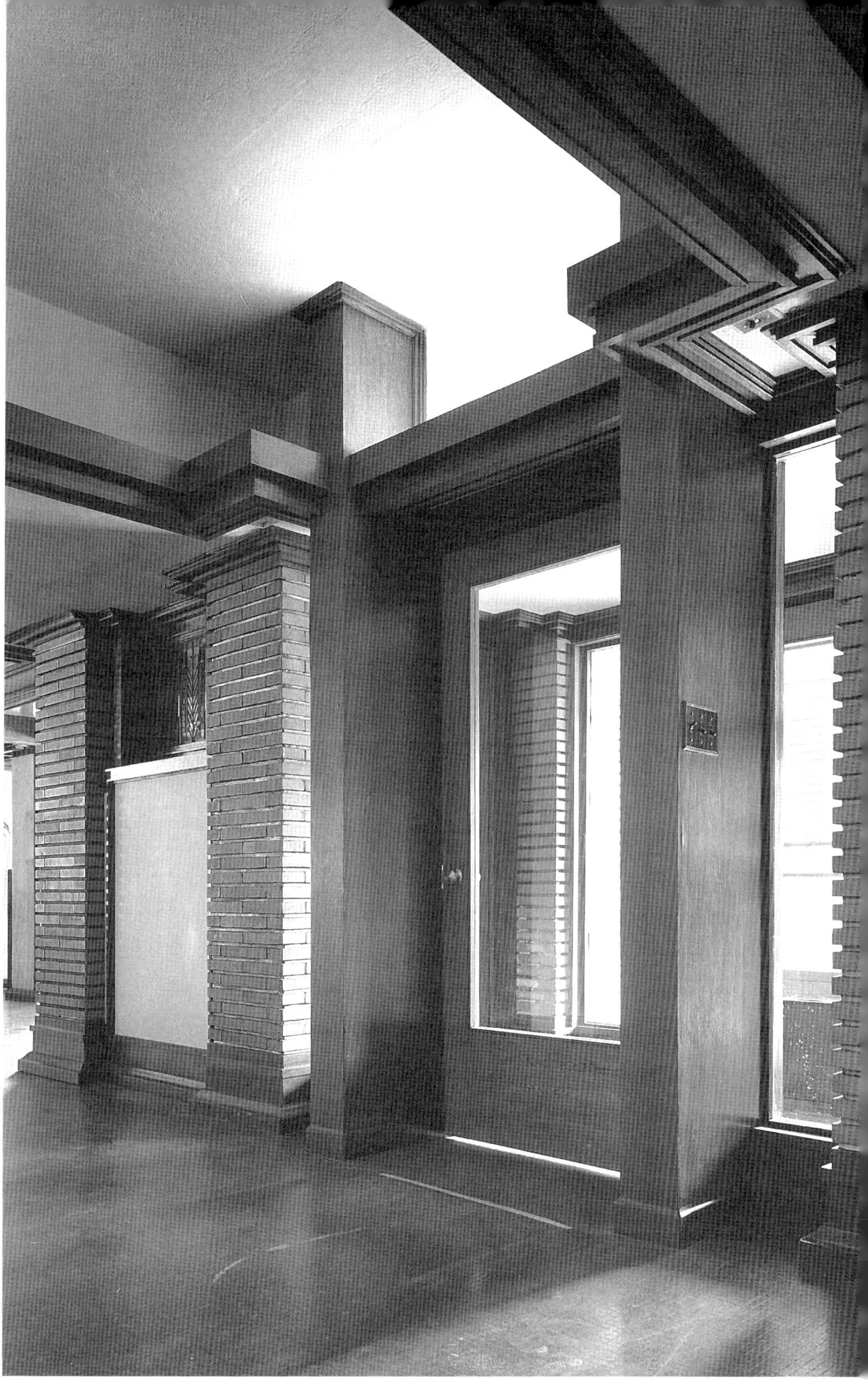

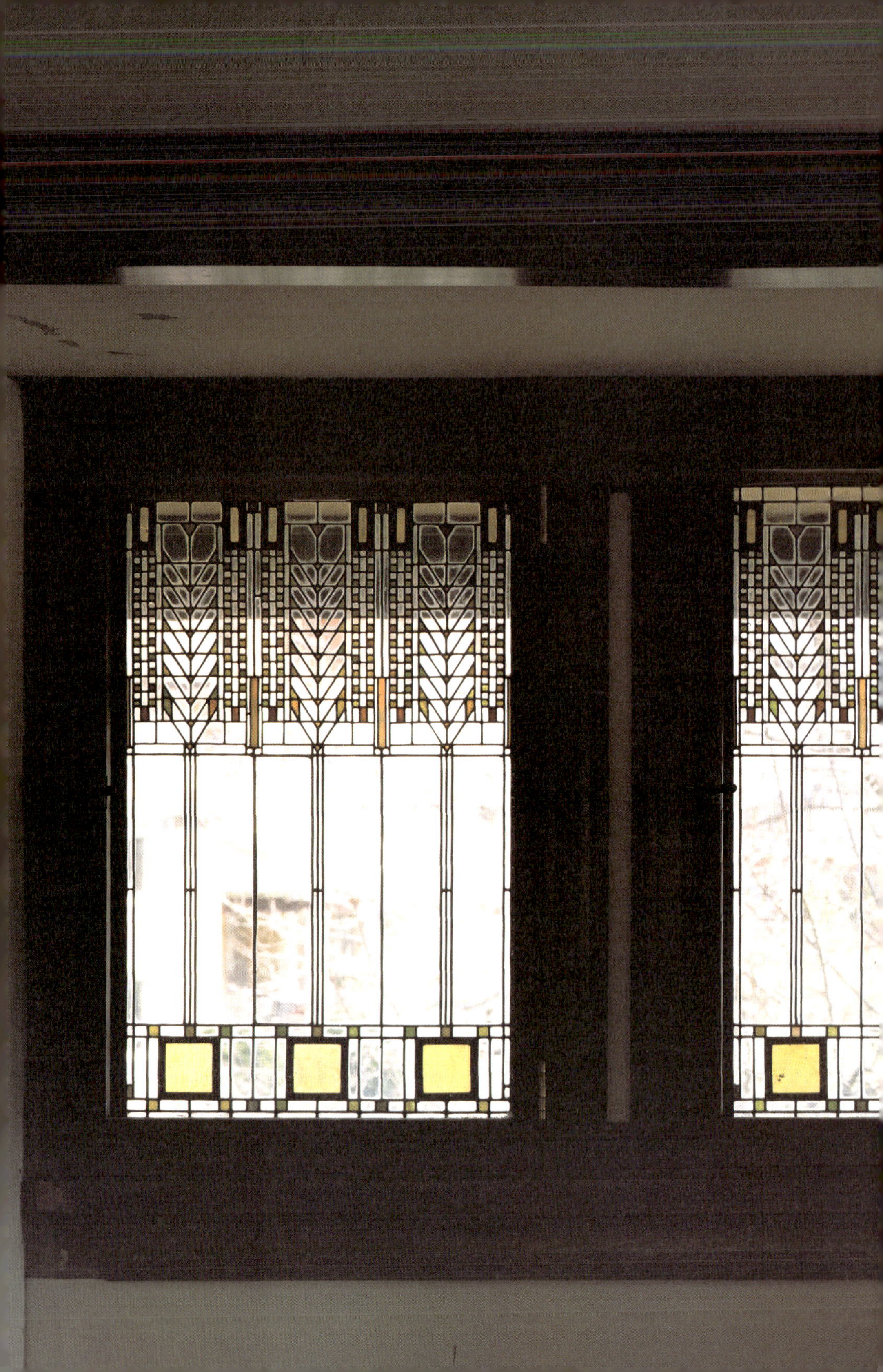

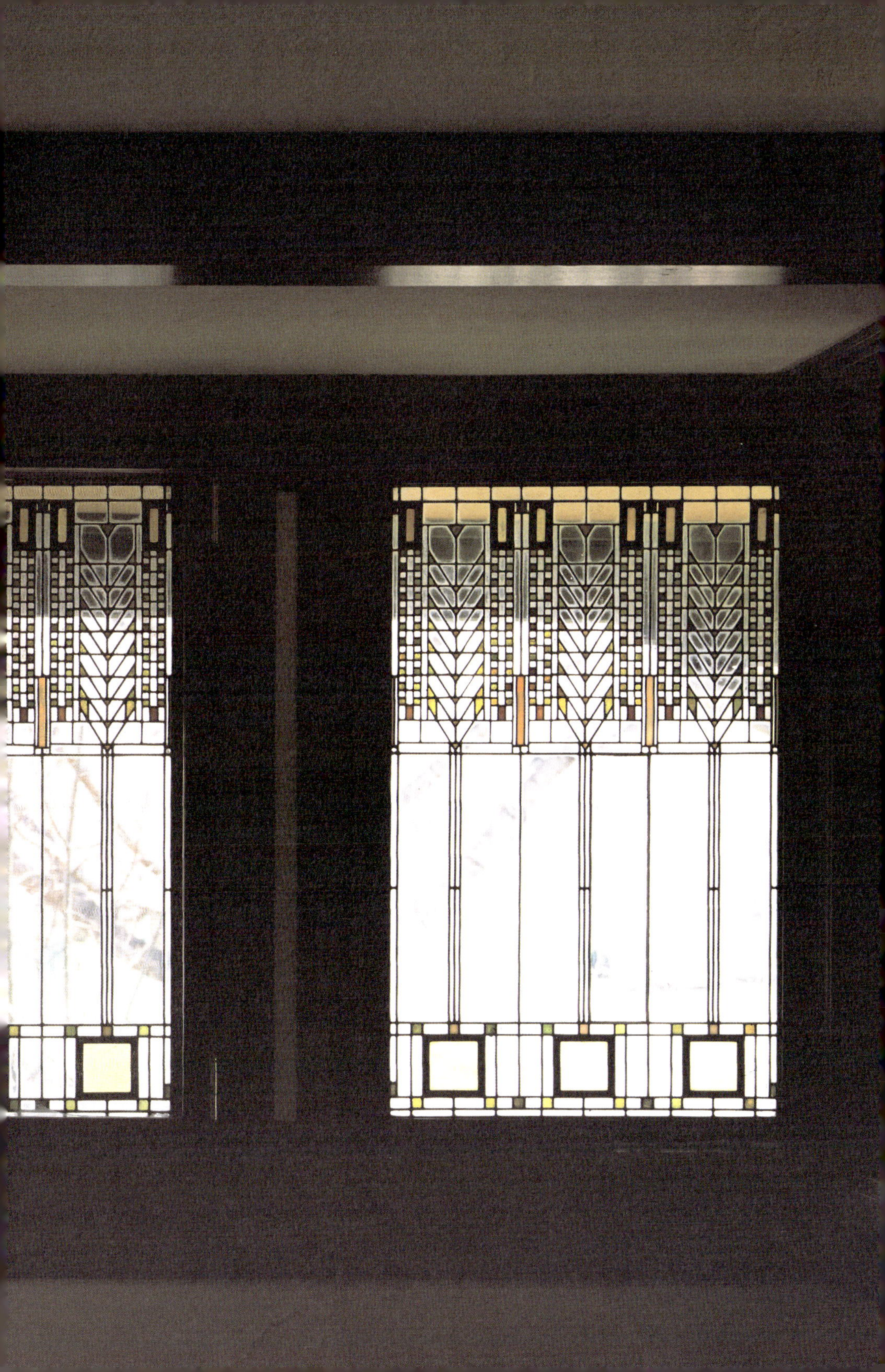

Frederick C. Robie House
Chicago, Illinois, 1908

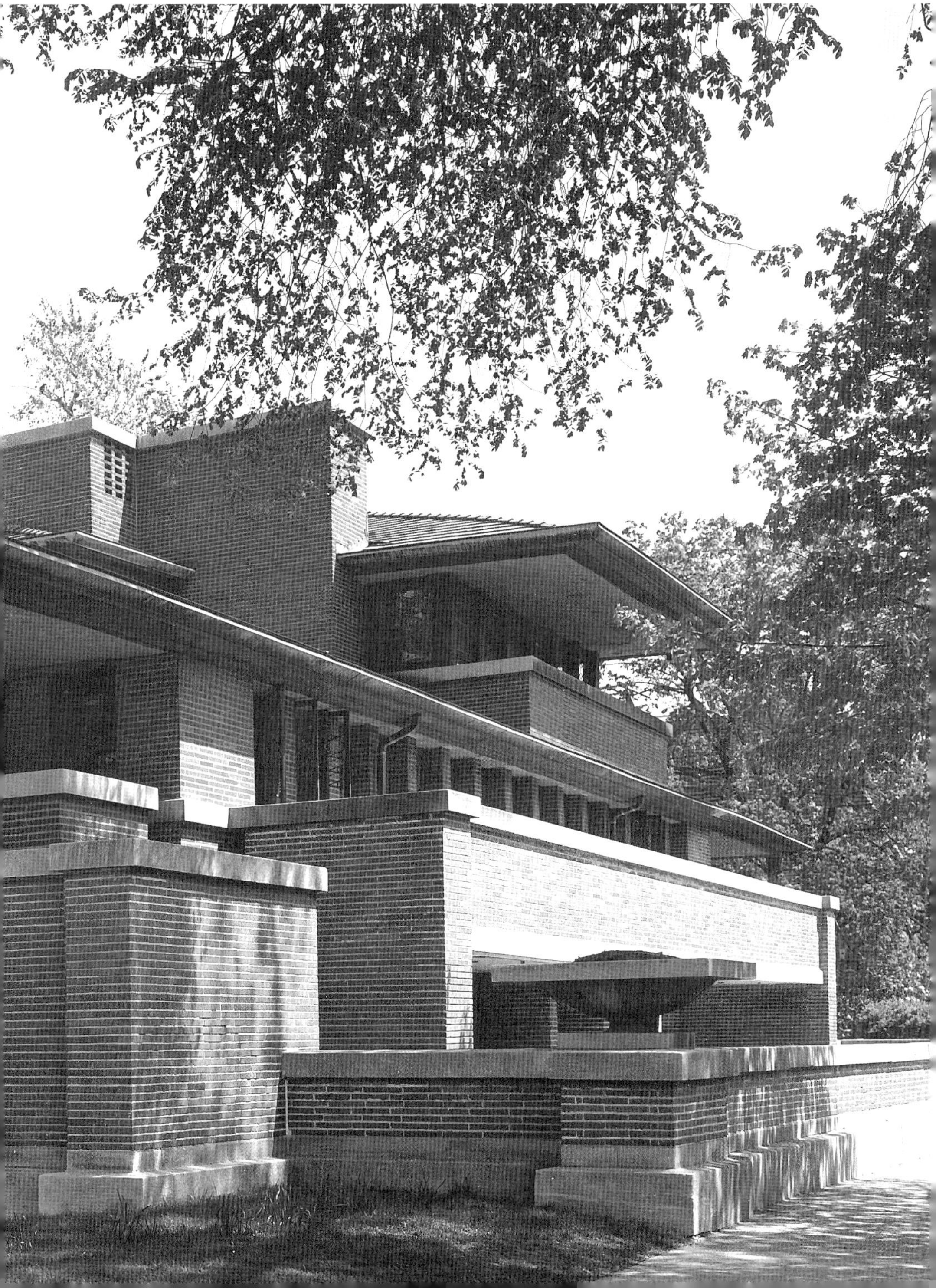

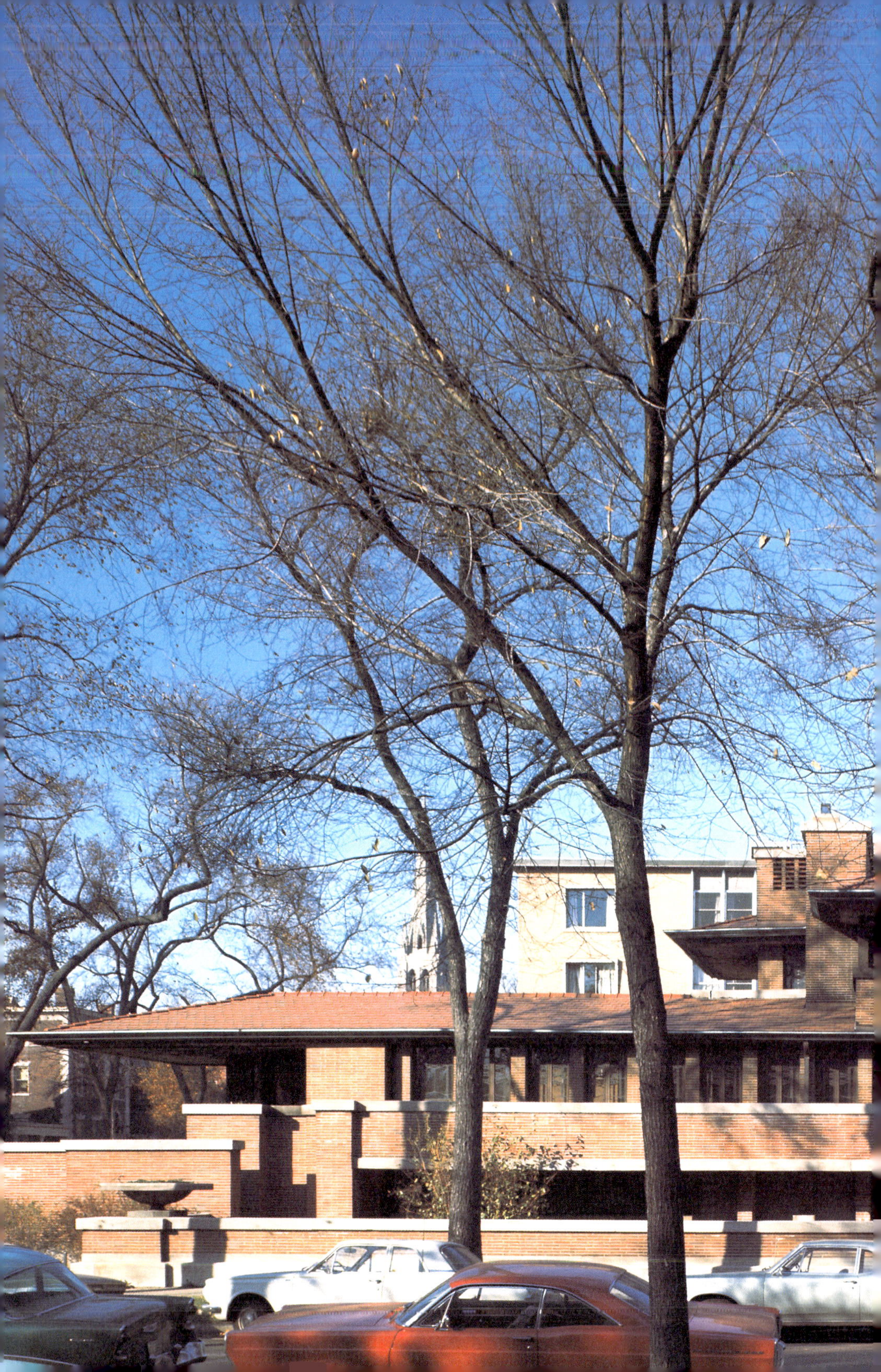

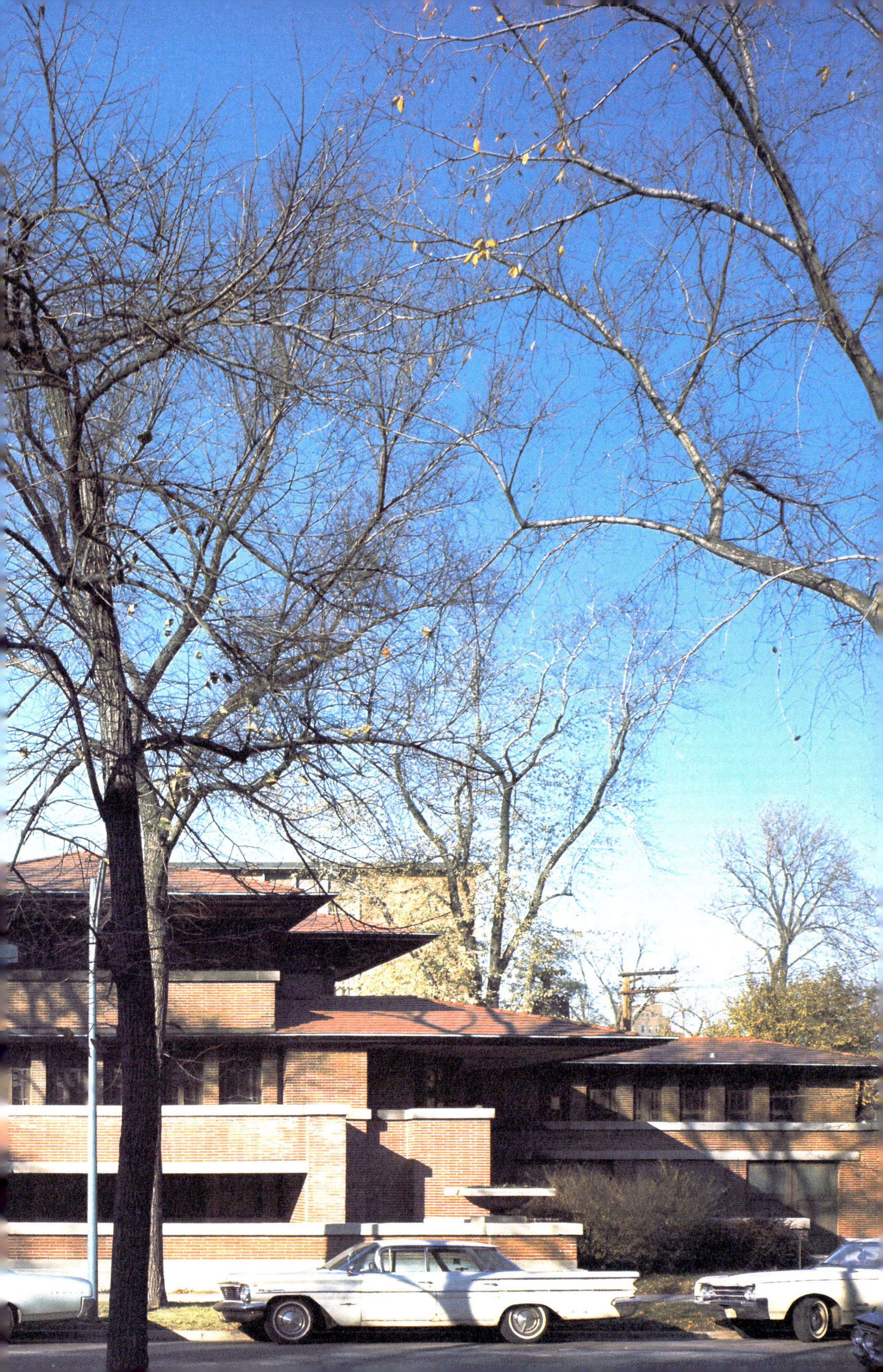

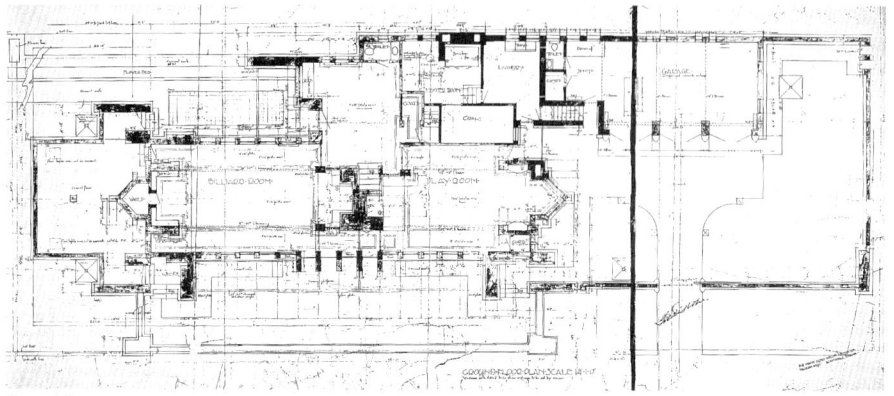

Ground floor

Second floor

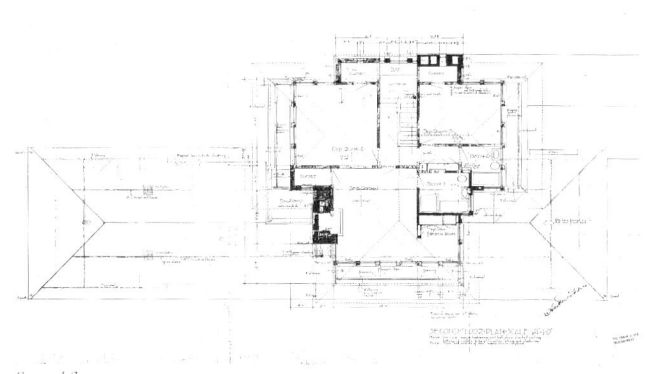

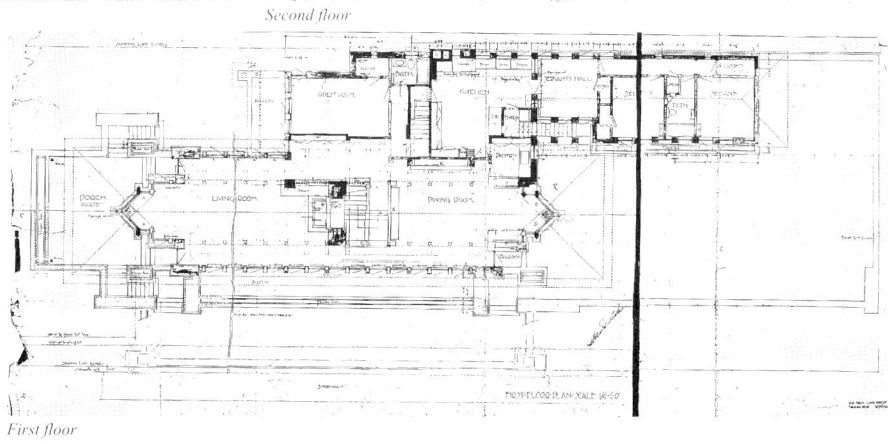

First floor

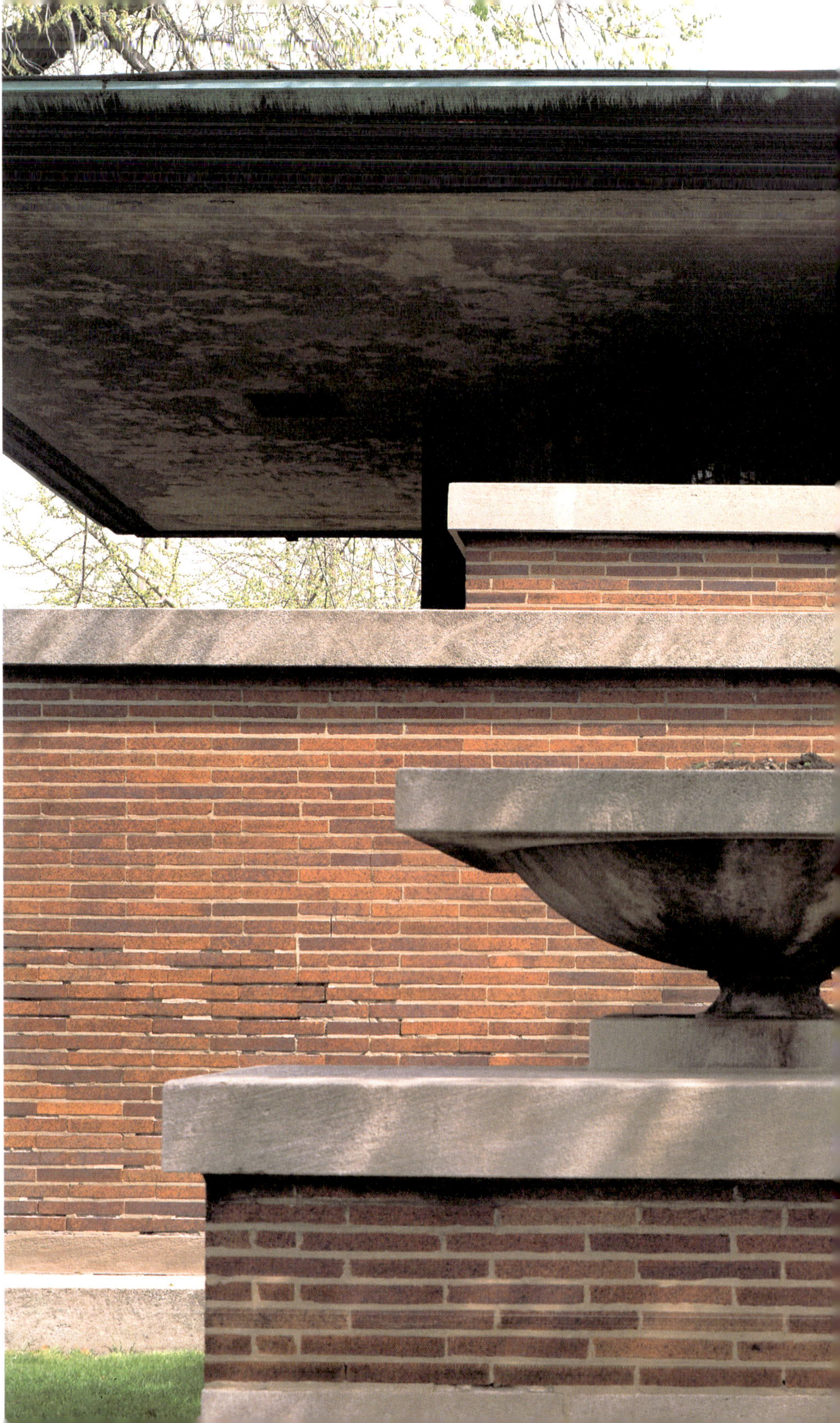

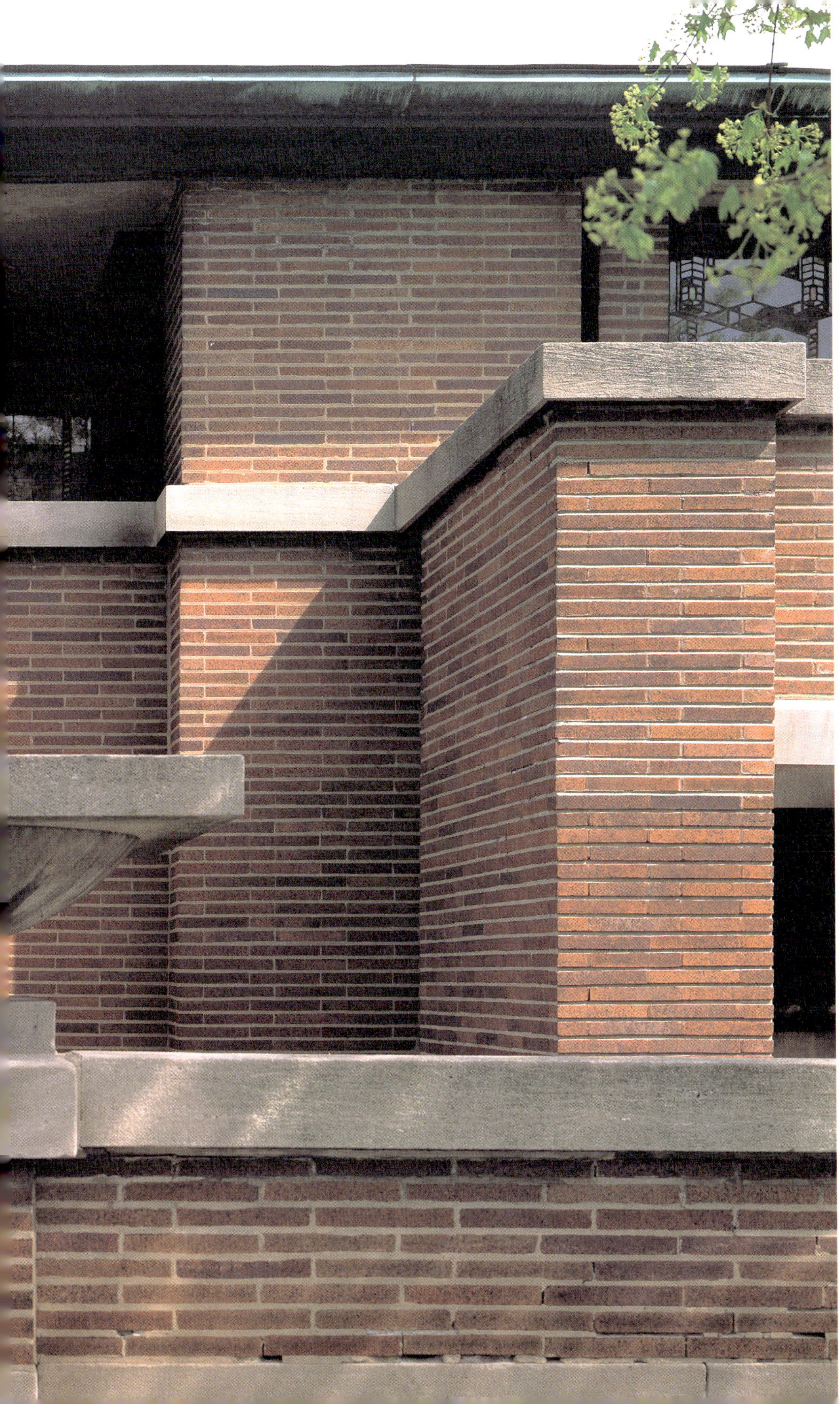

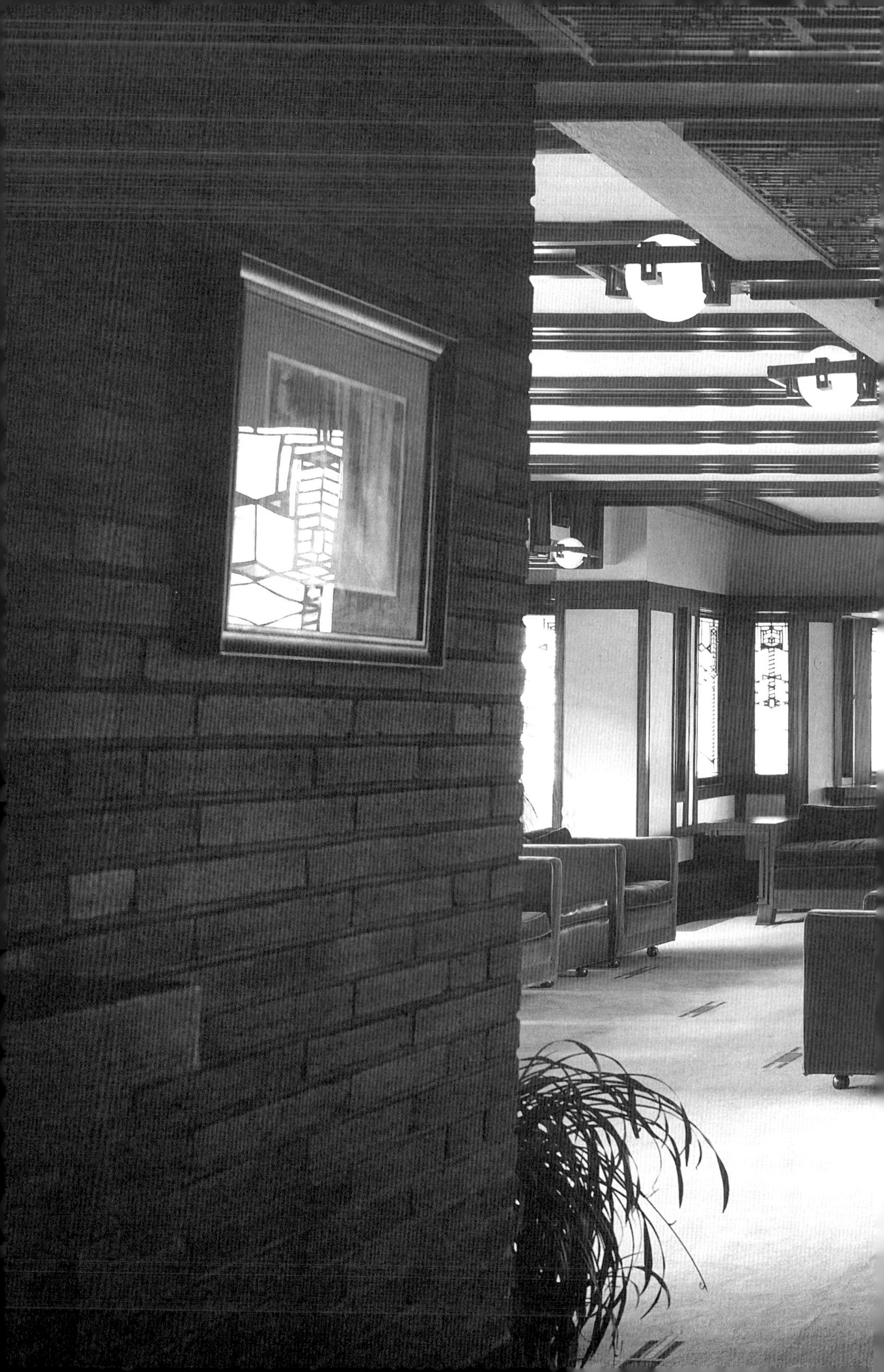

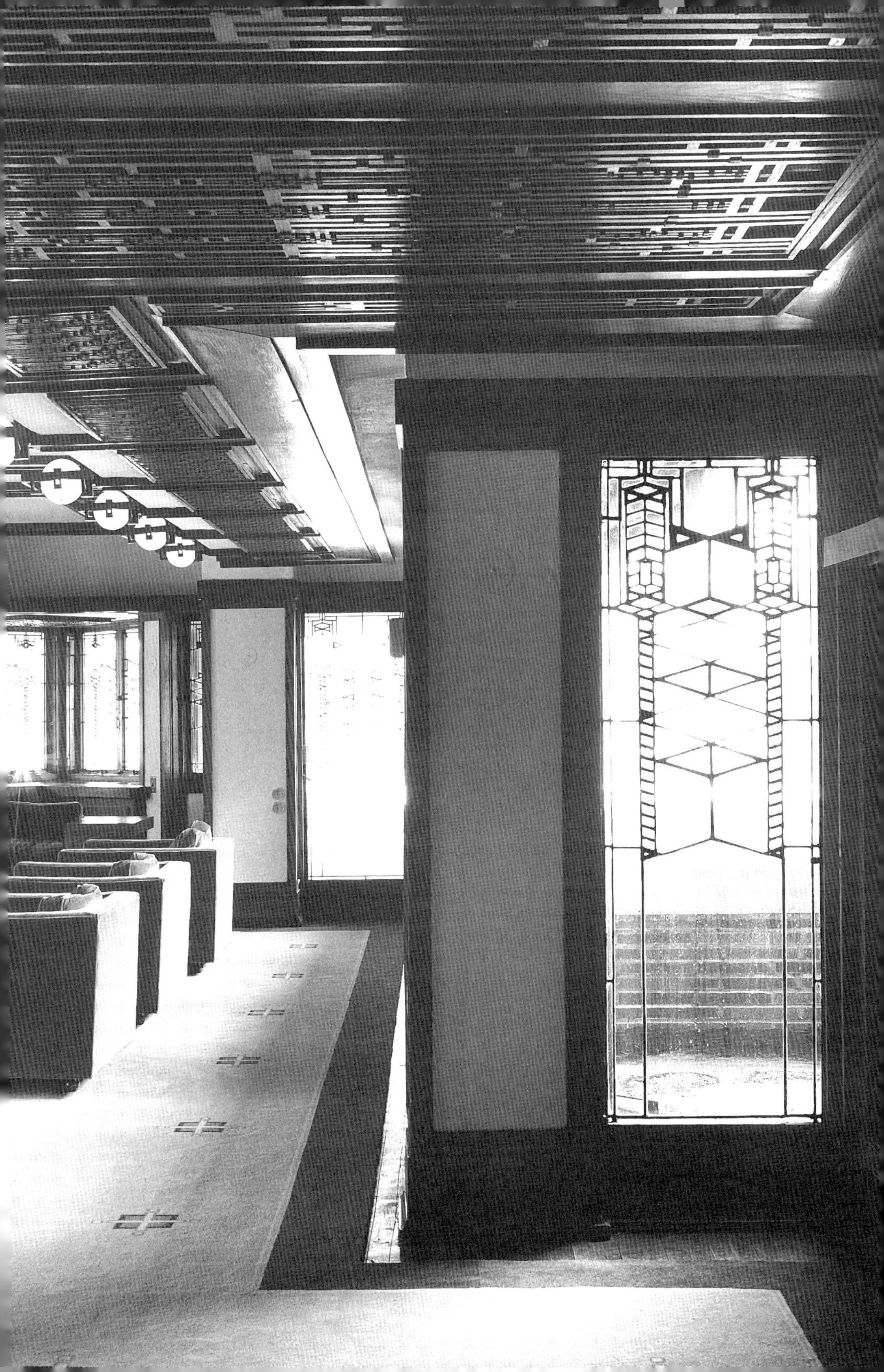

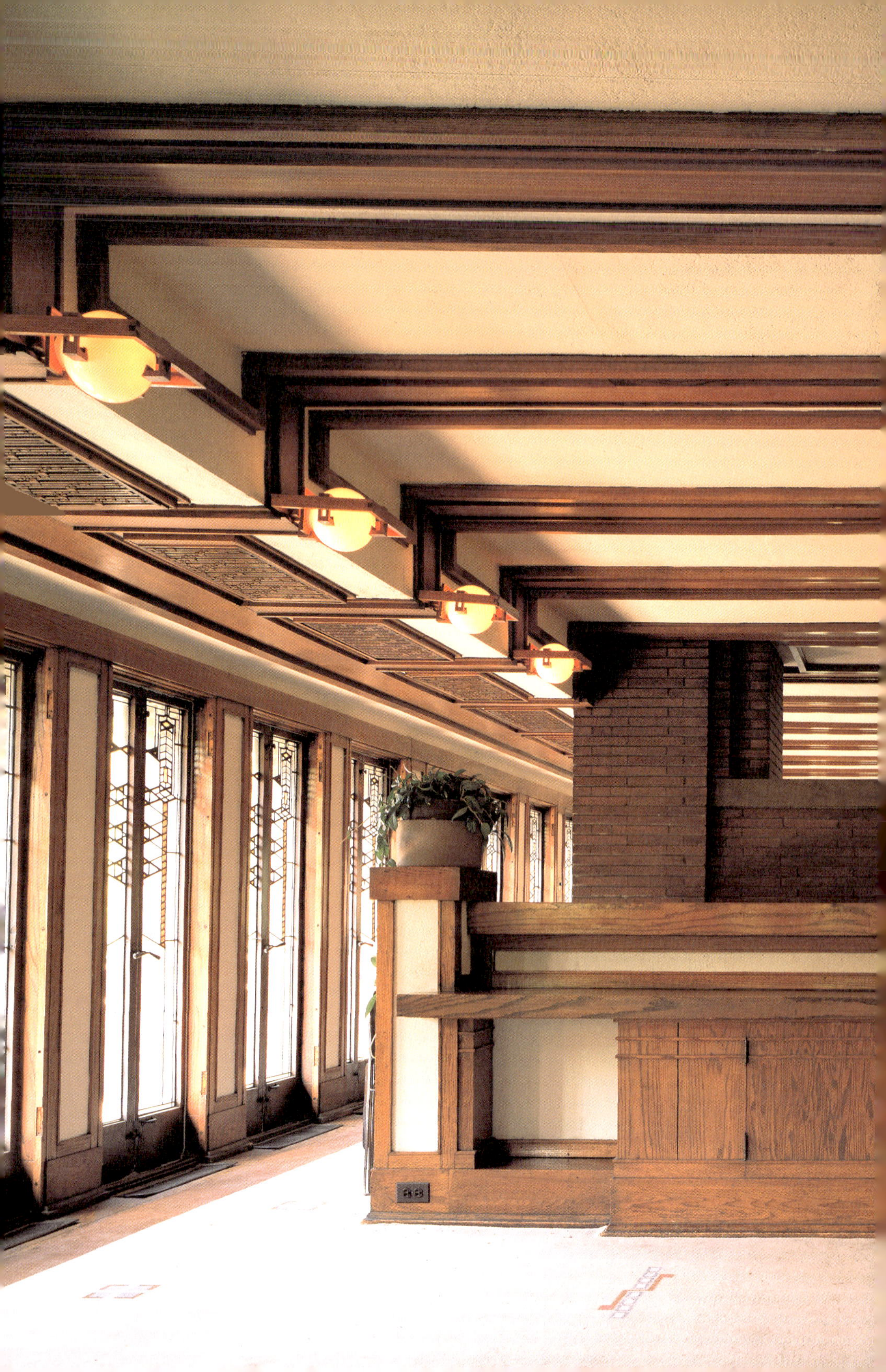

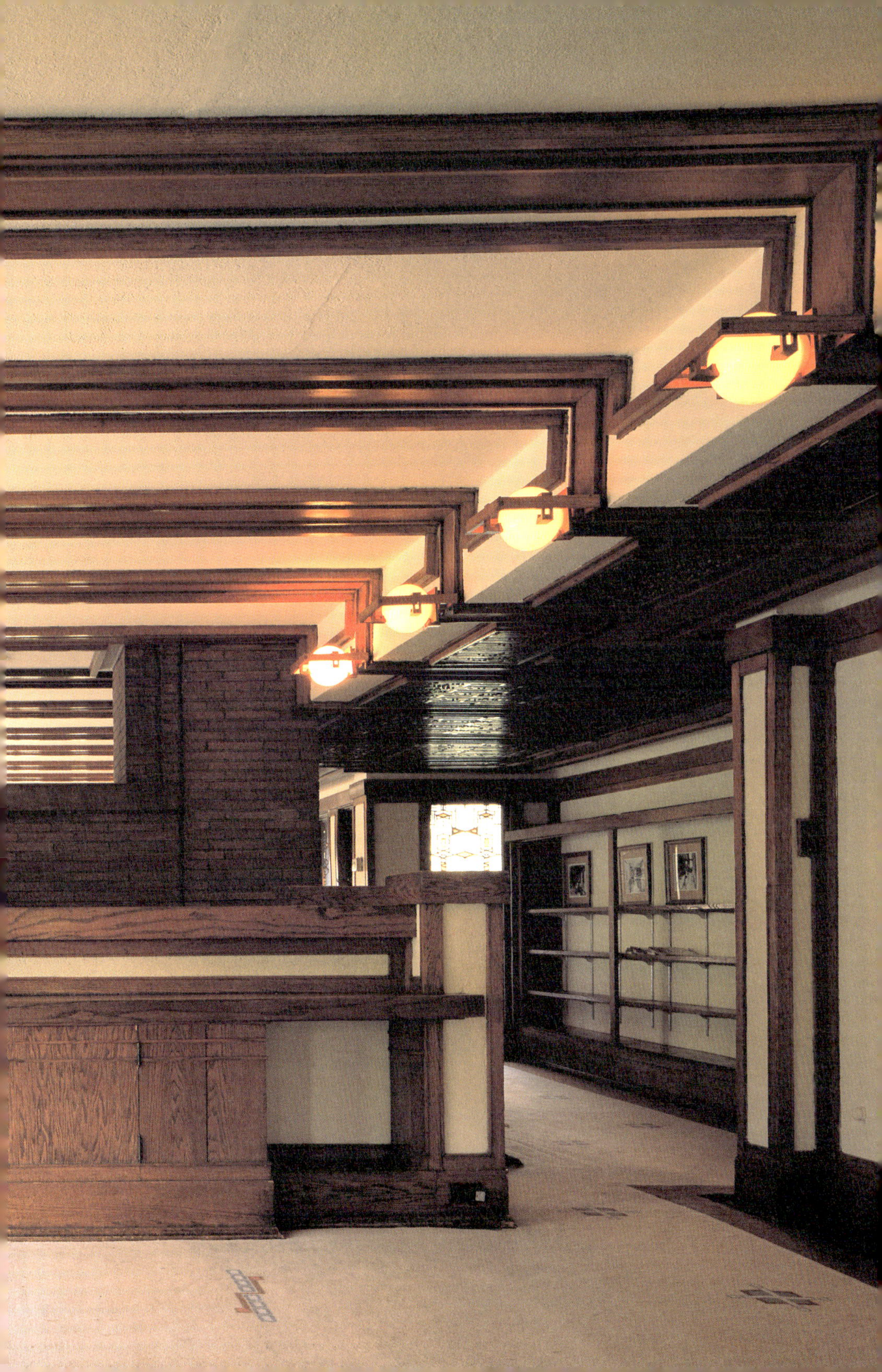

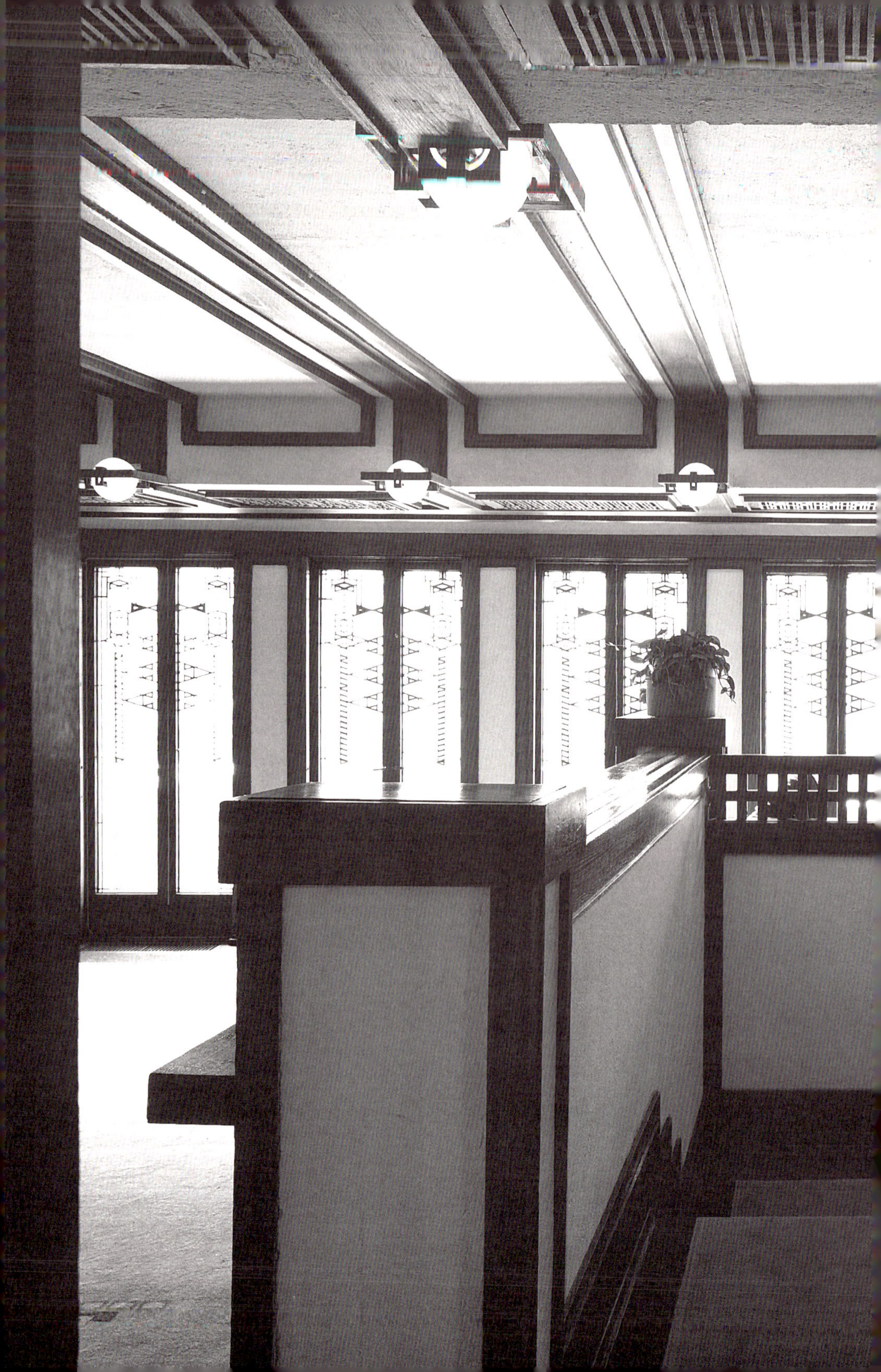

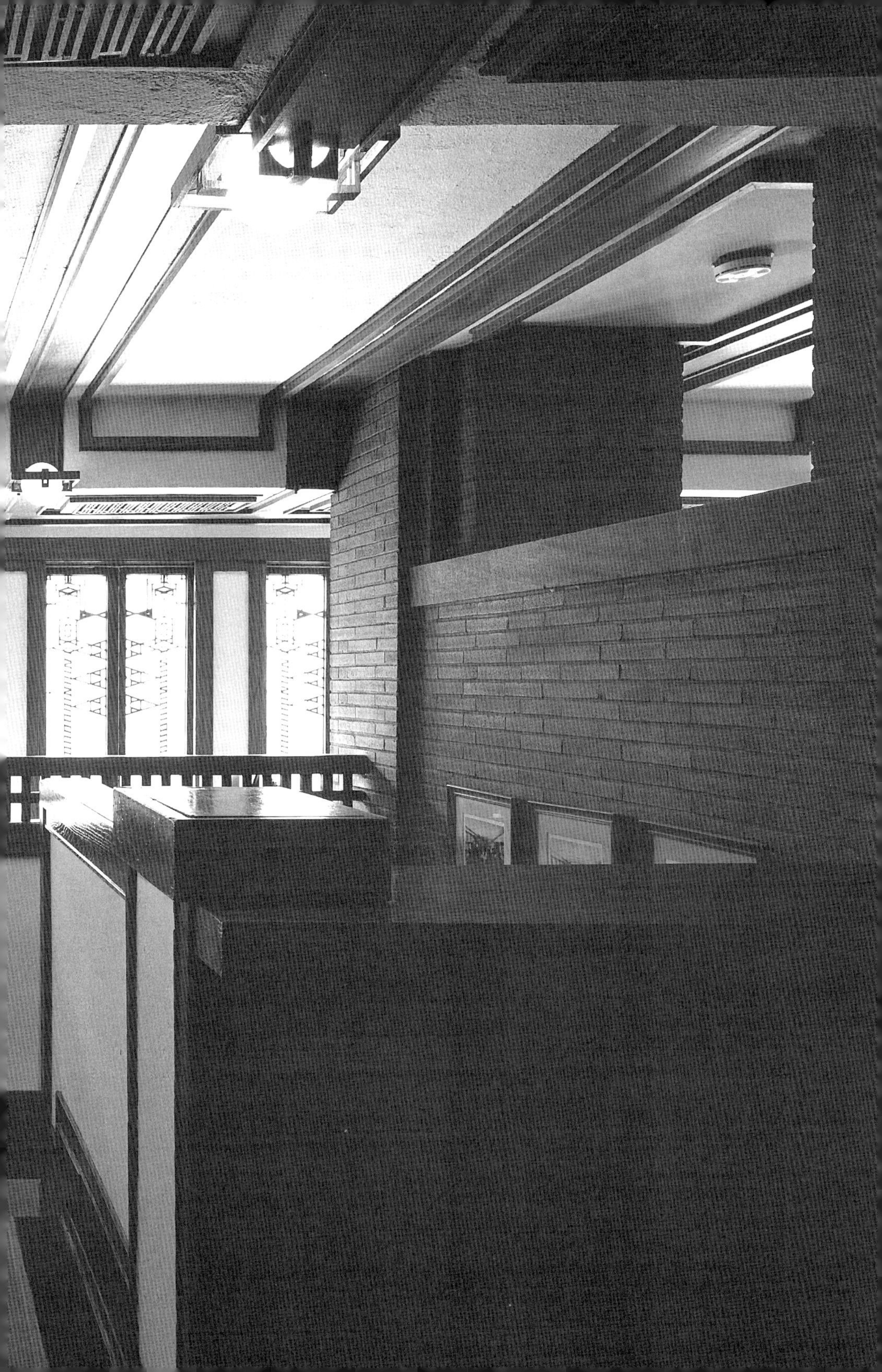

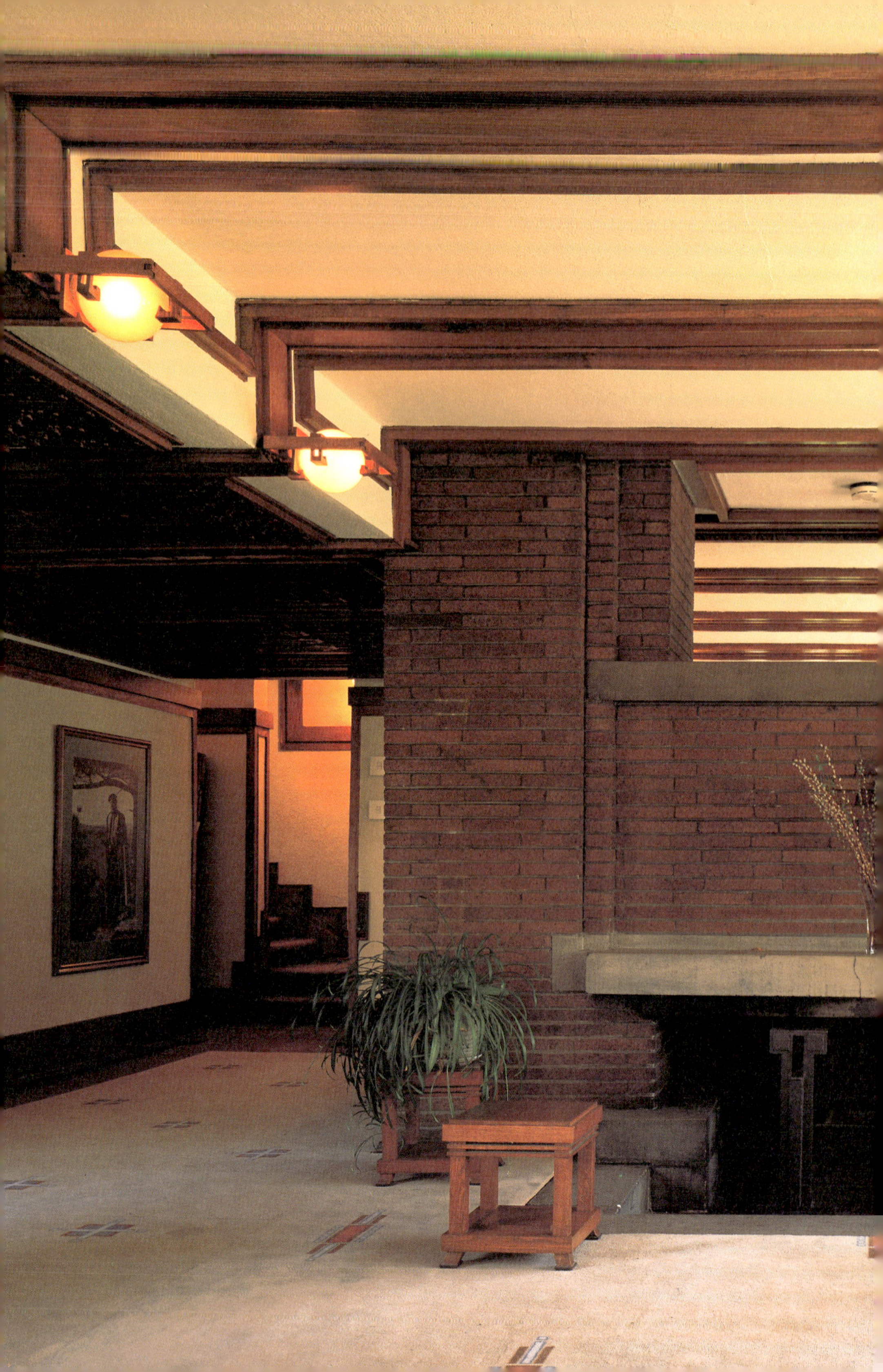

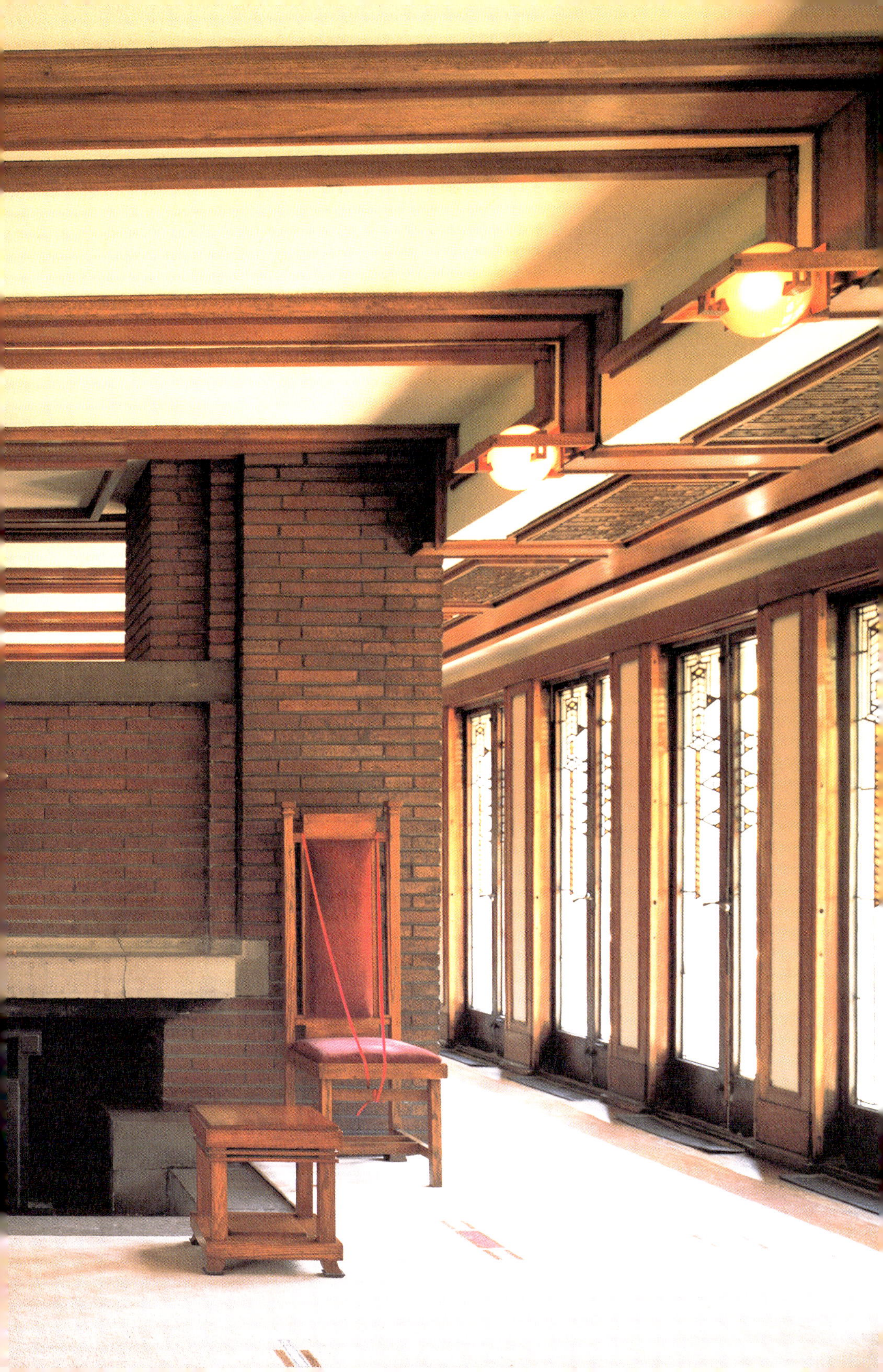

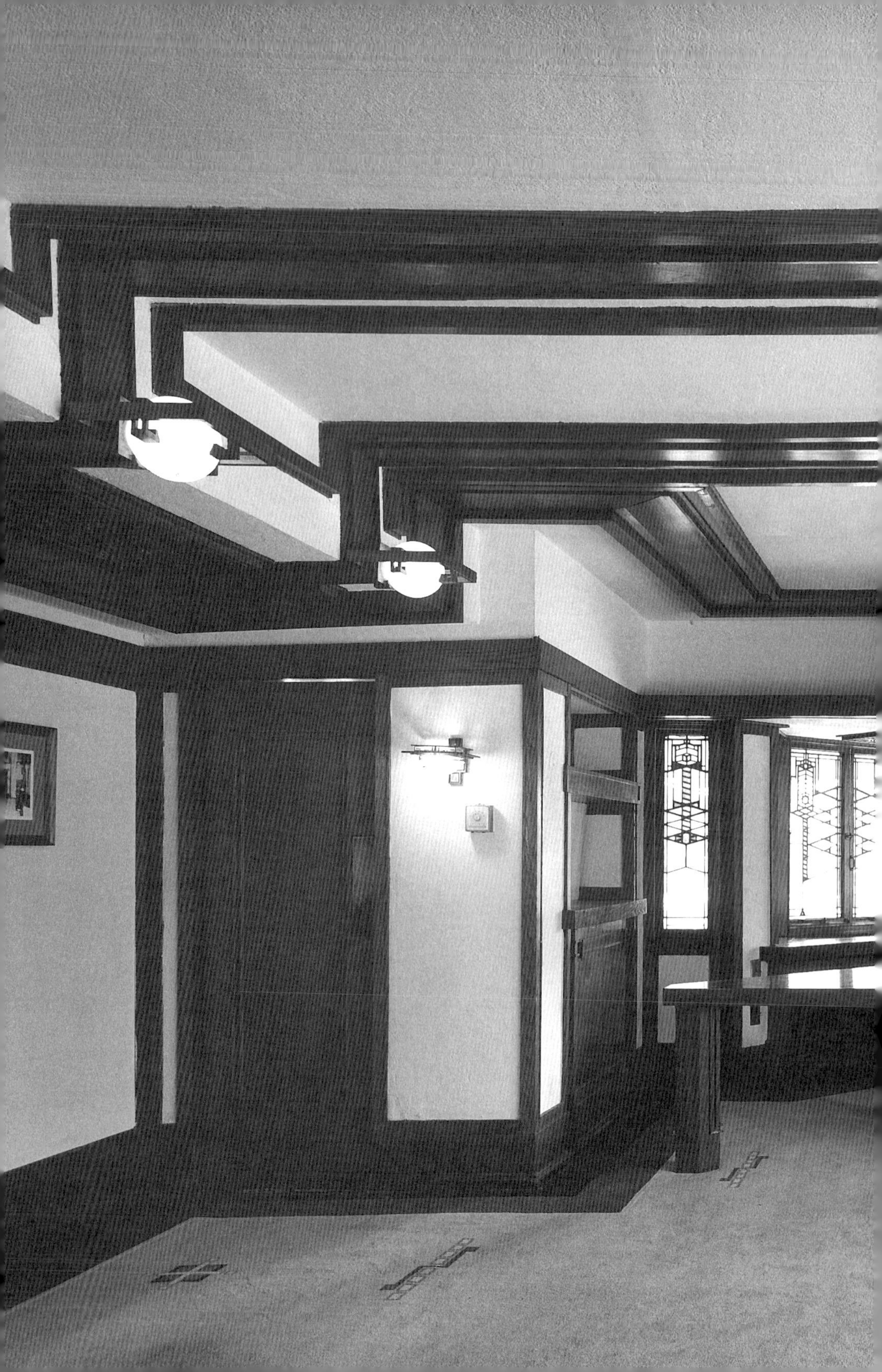

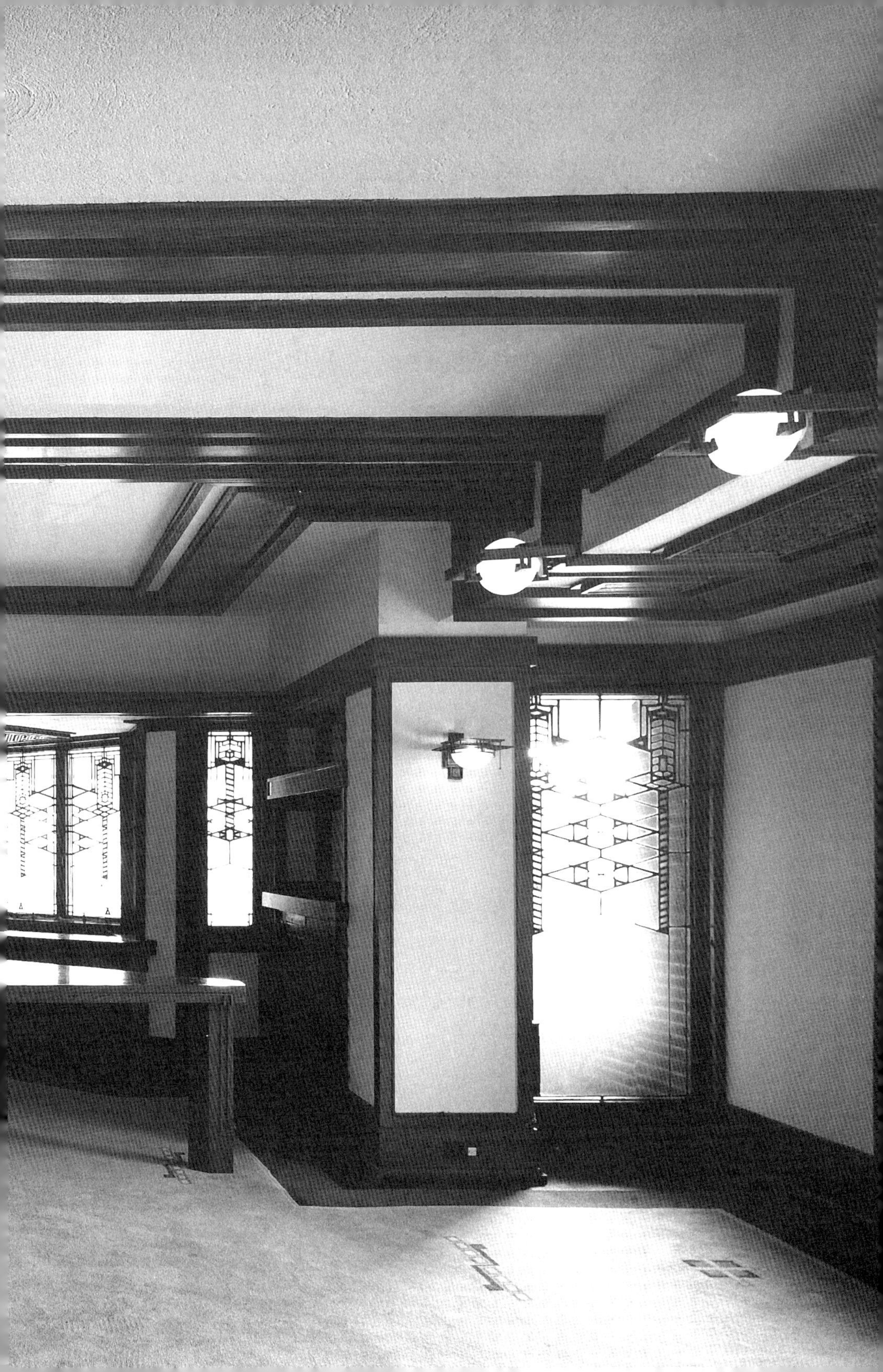

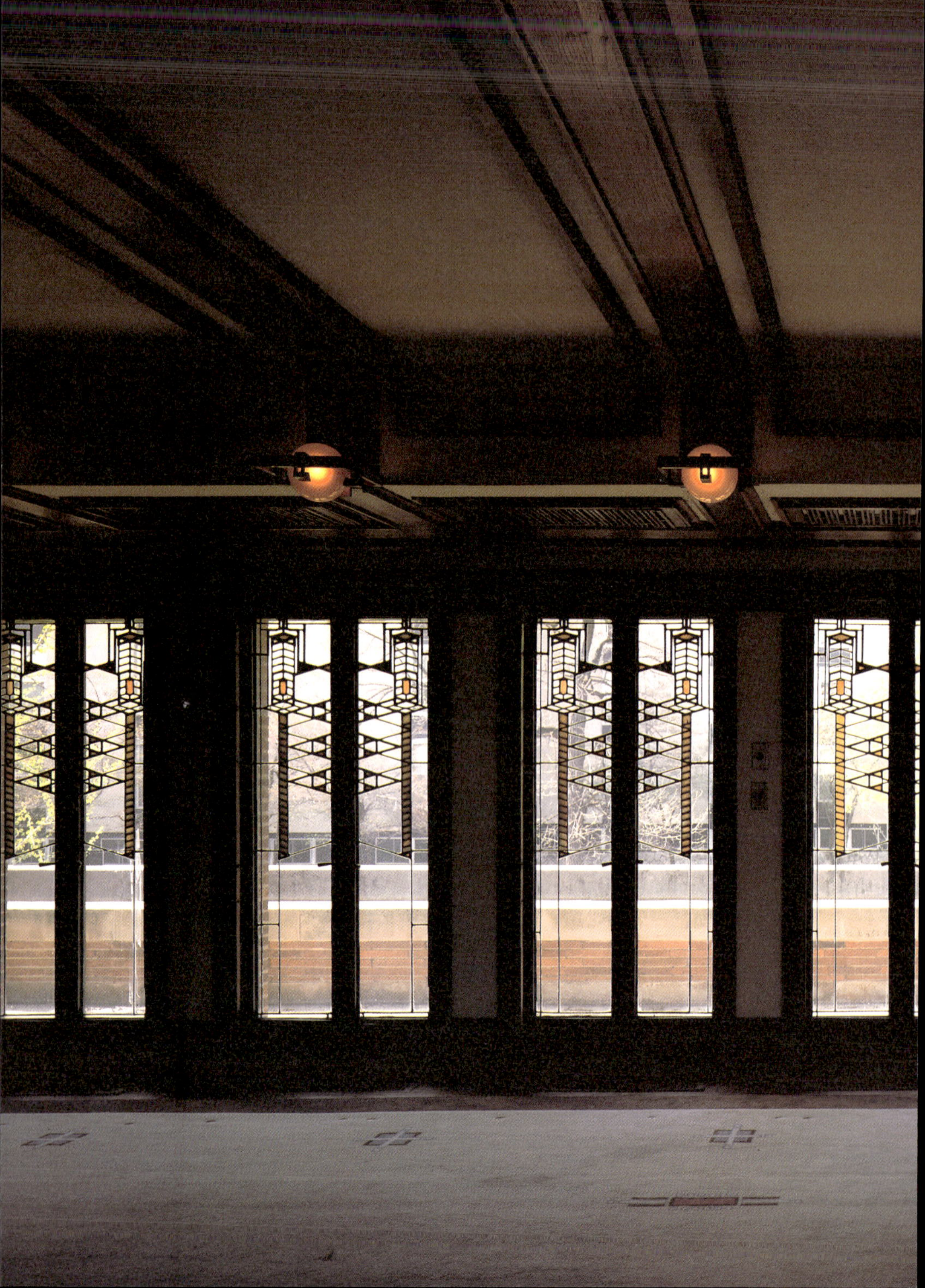

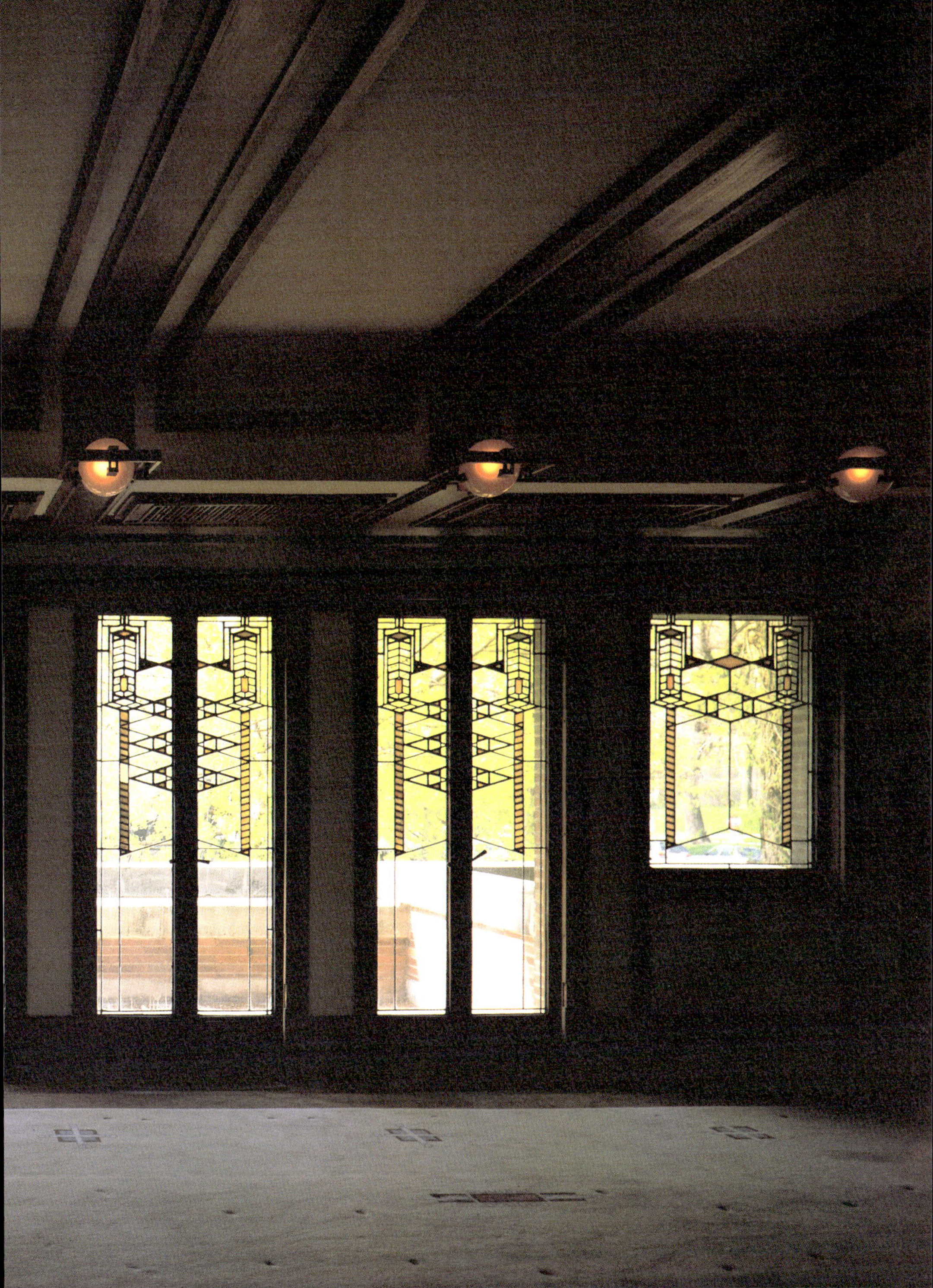

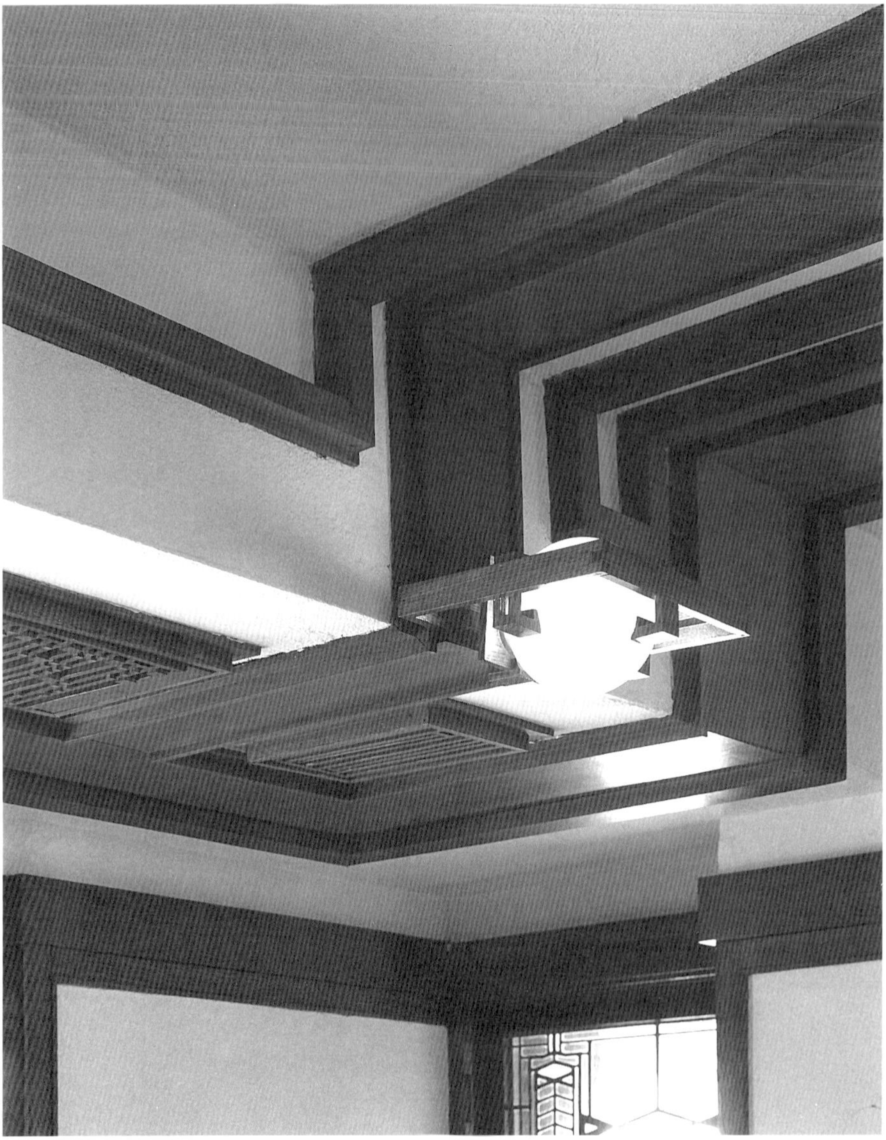

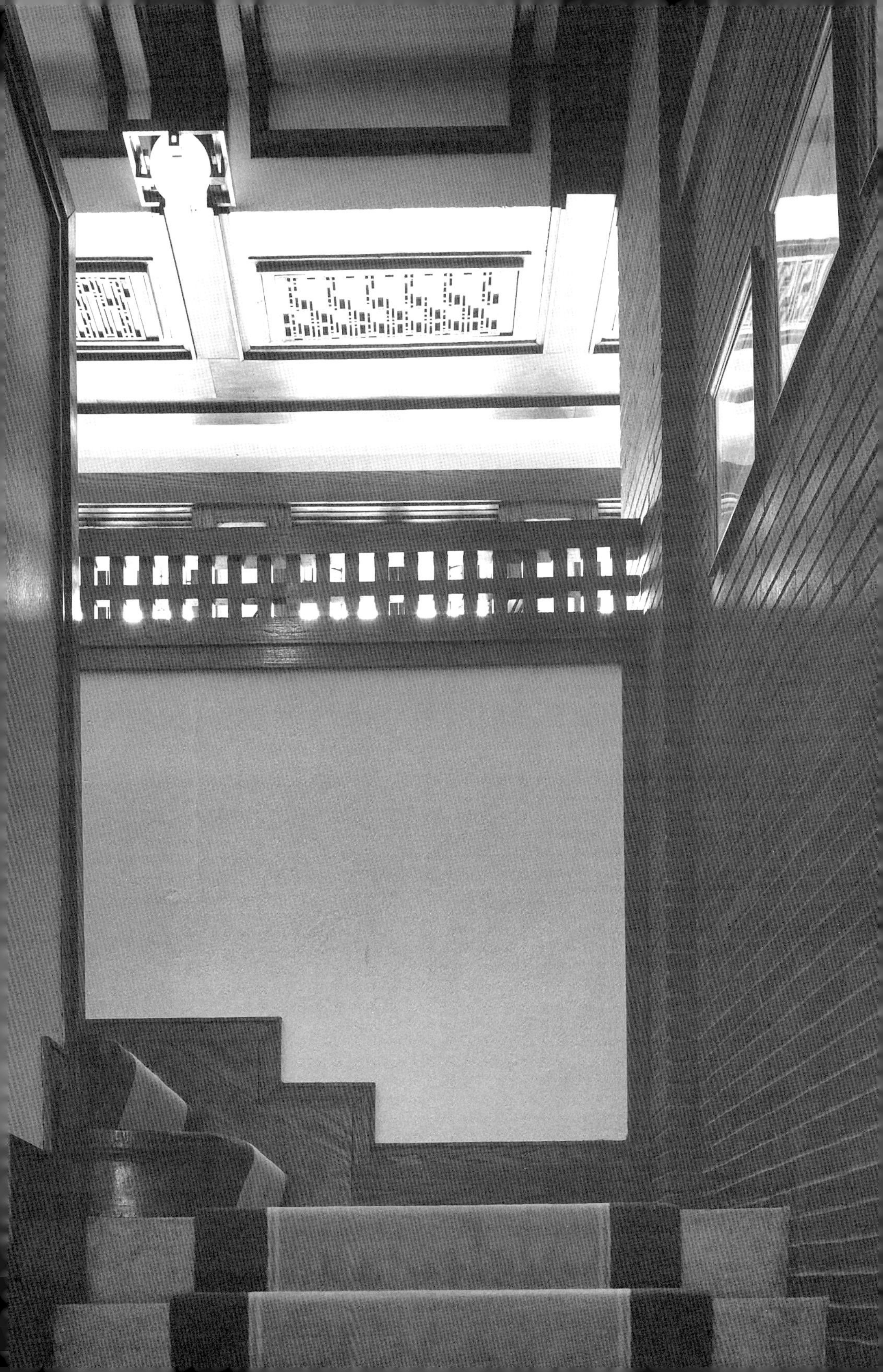

F. F. Tomek House
Riverside, Illinois, 1907

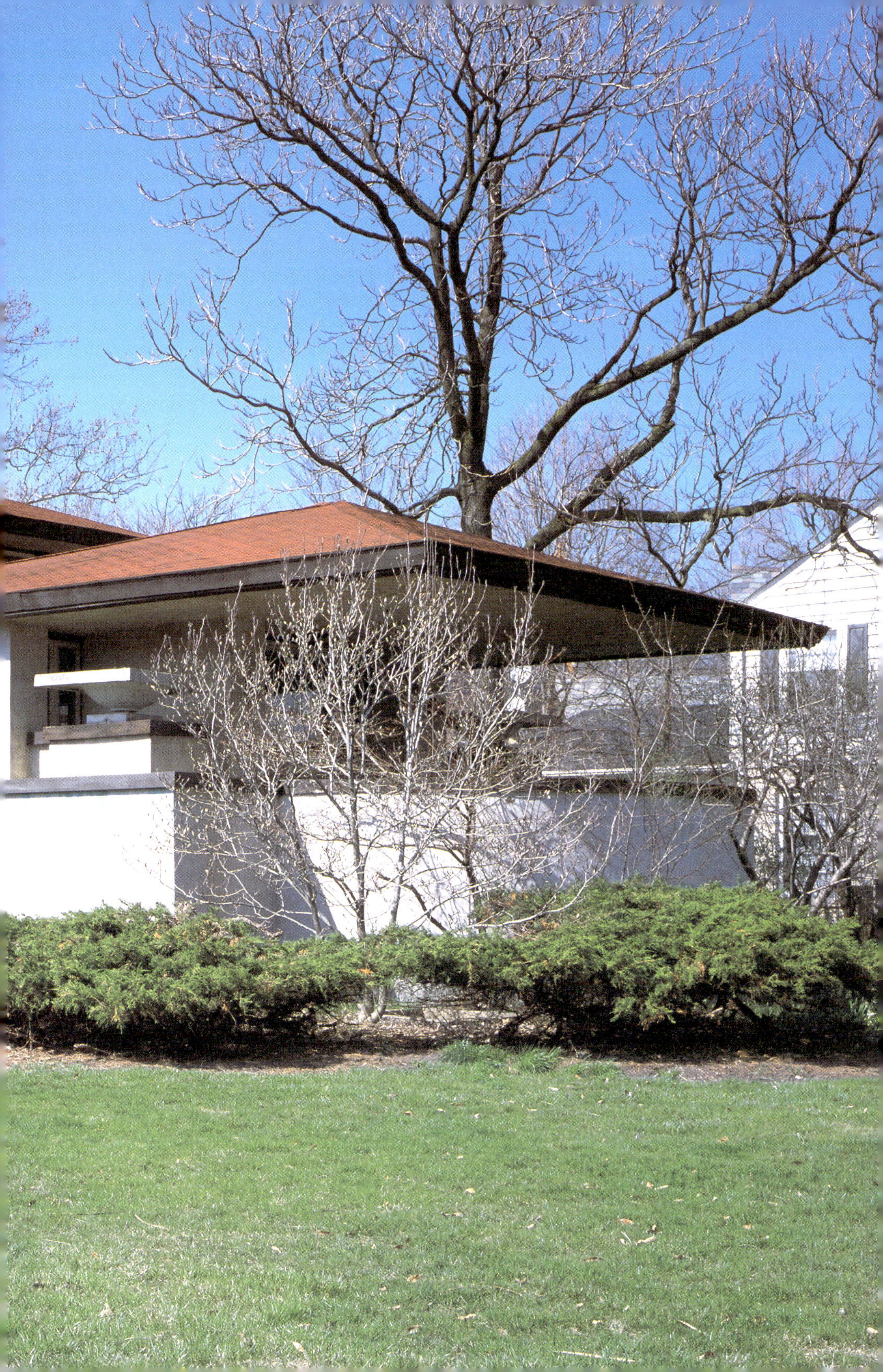

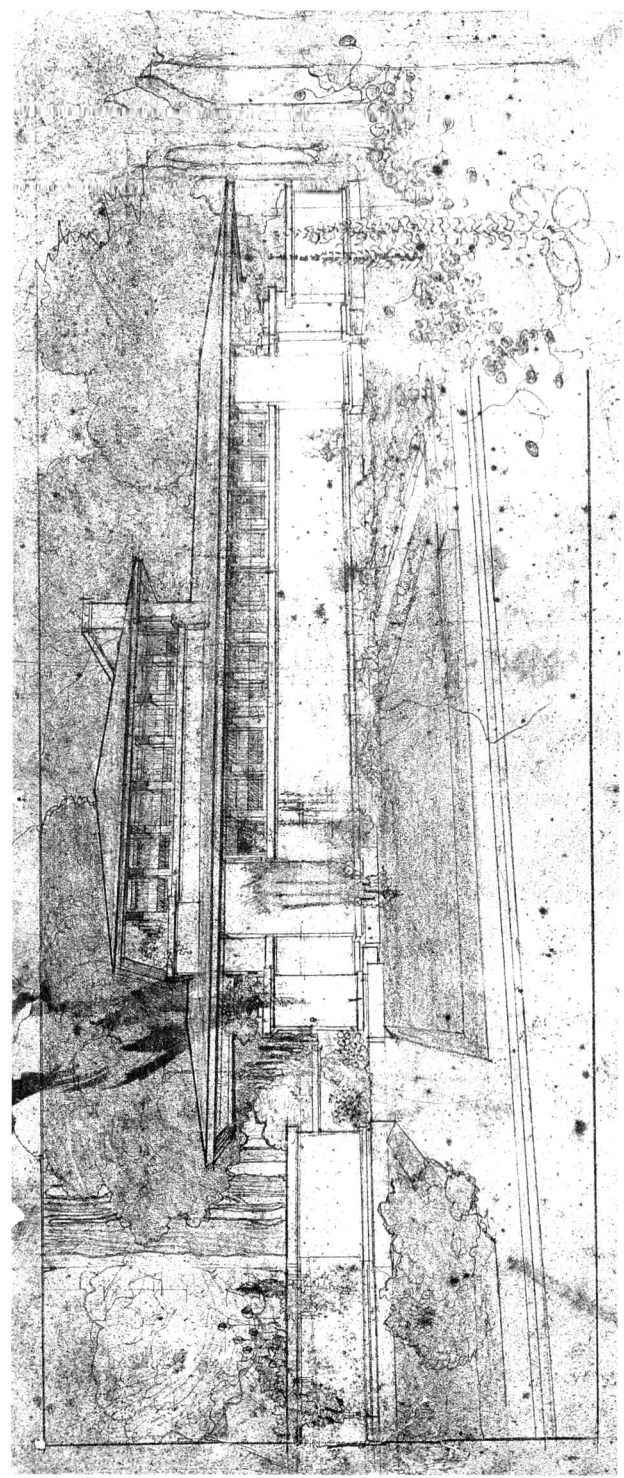

Perspective

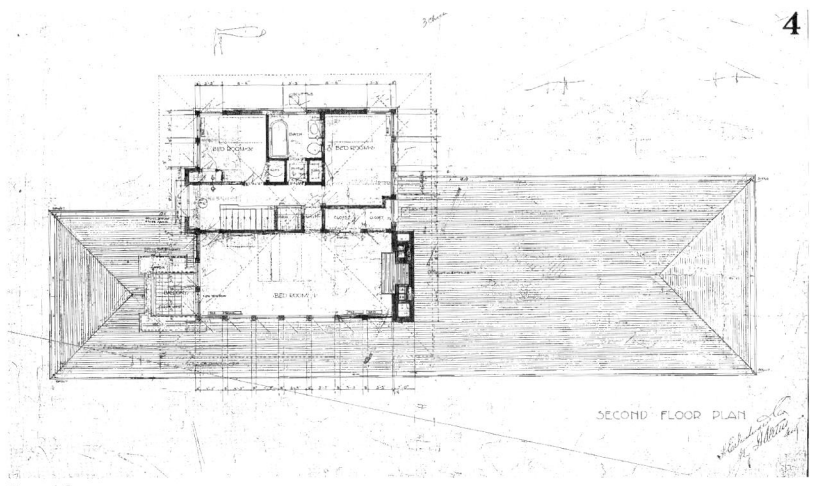

Second floor

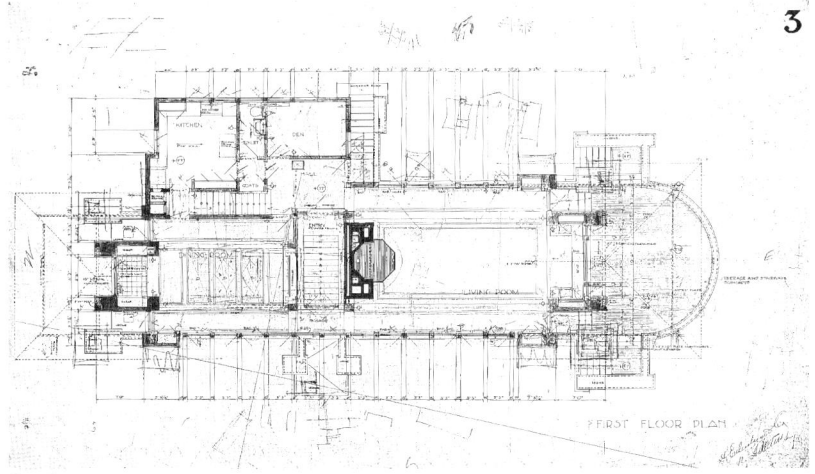

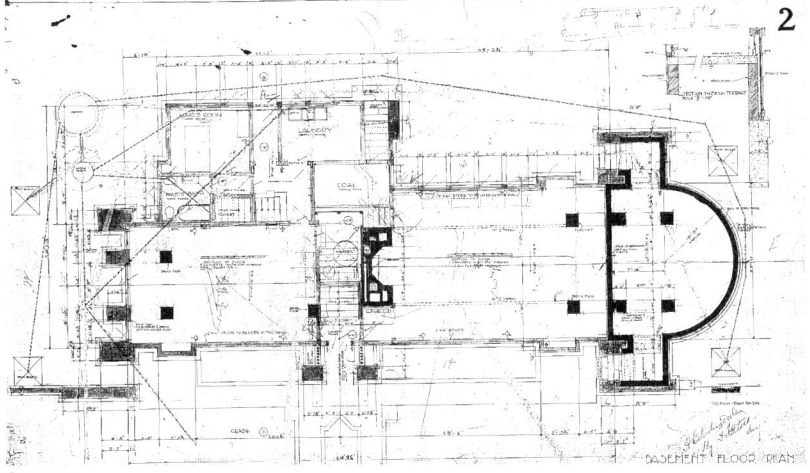

First floor

Basement

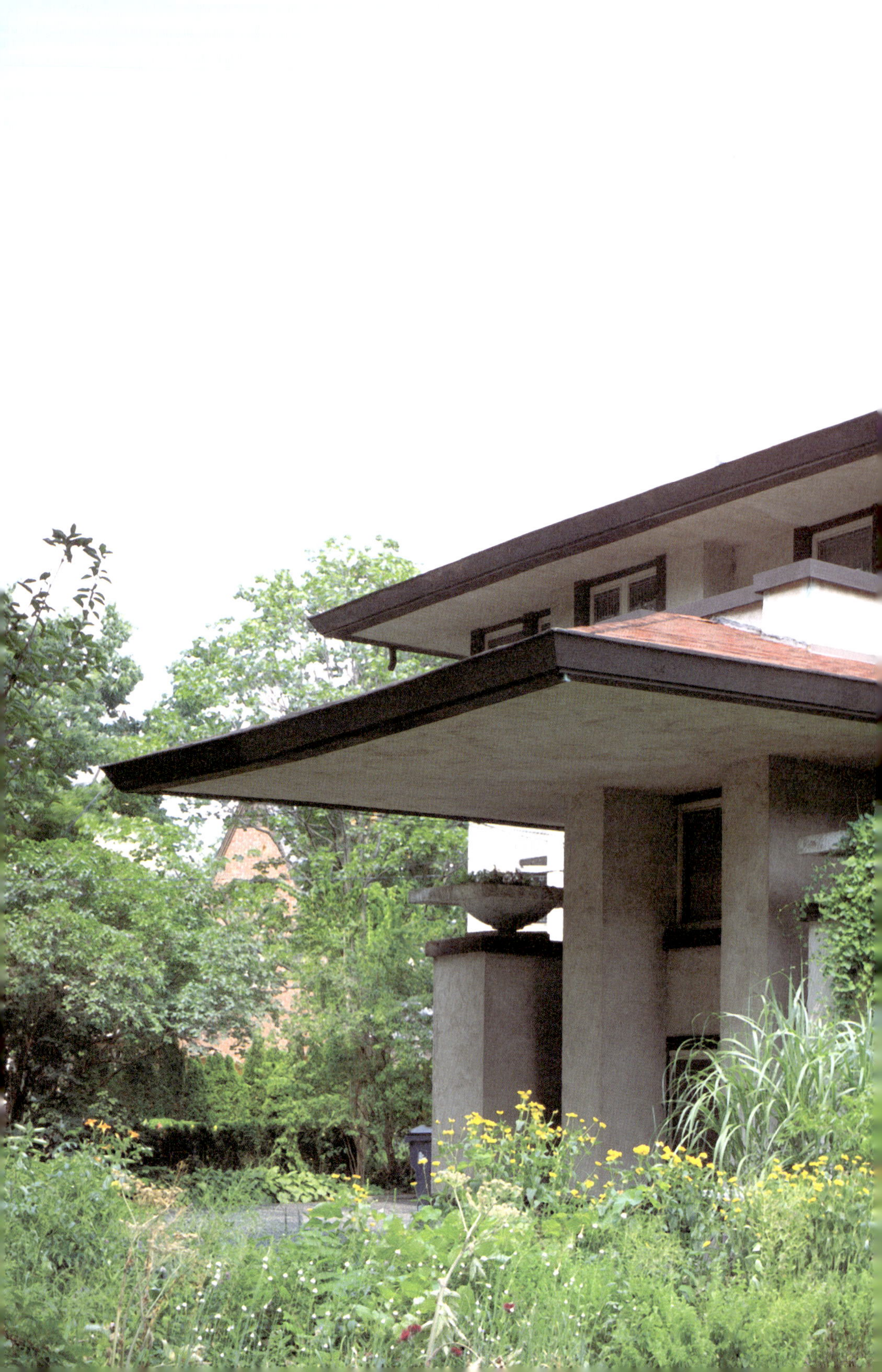

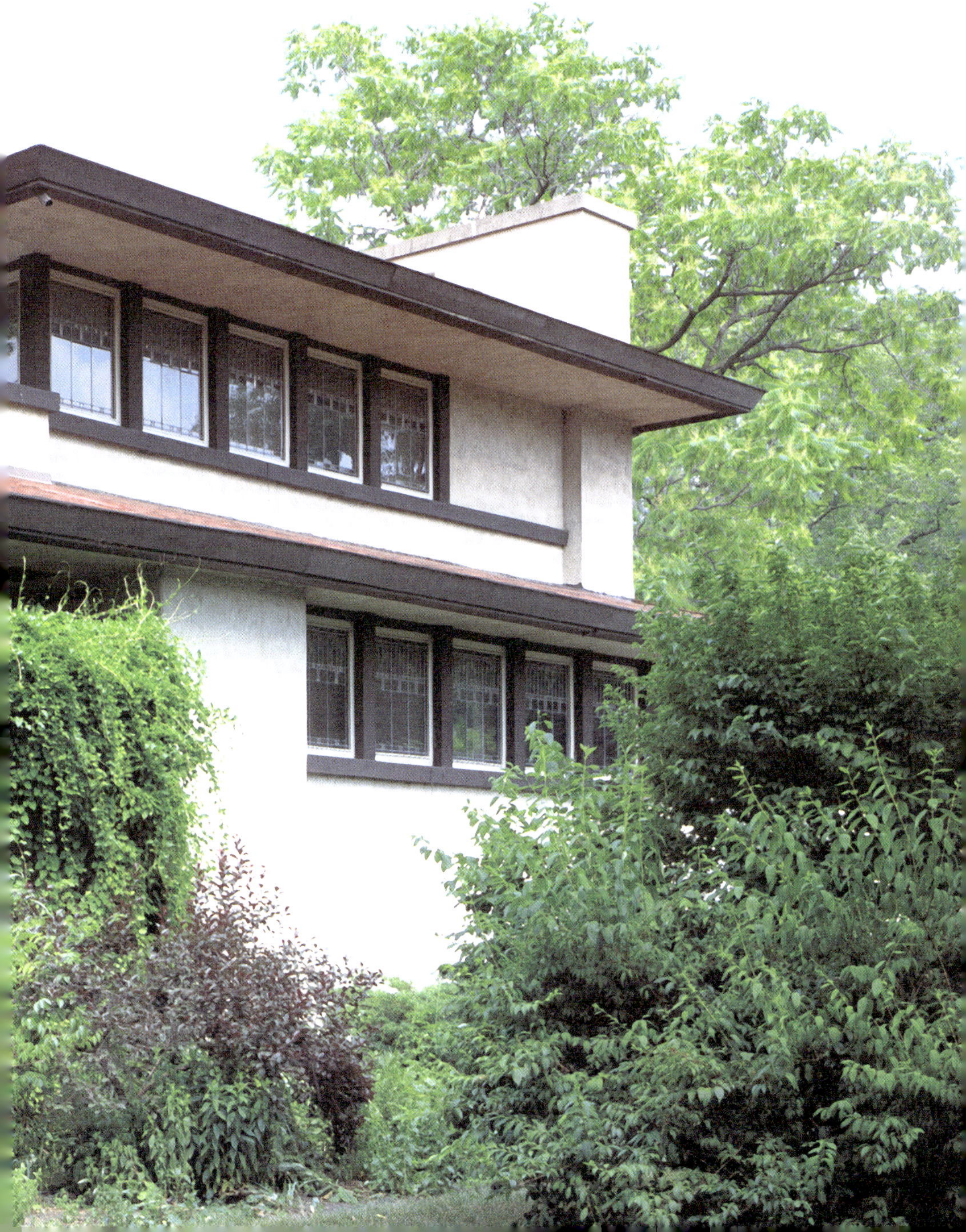

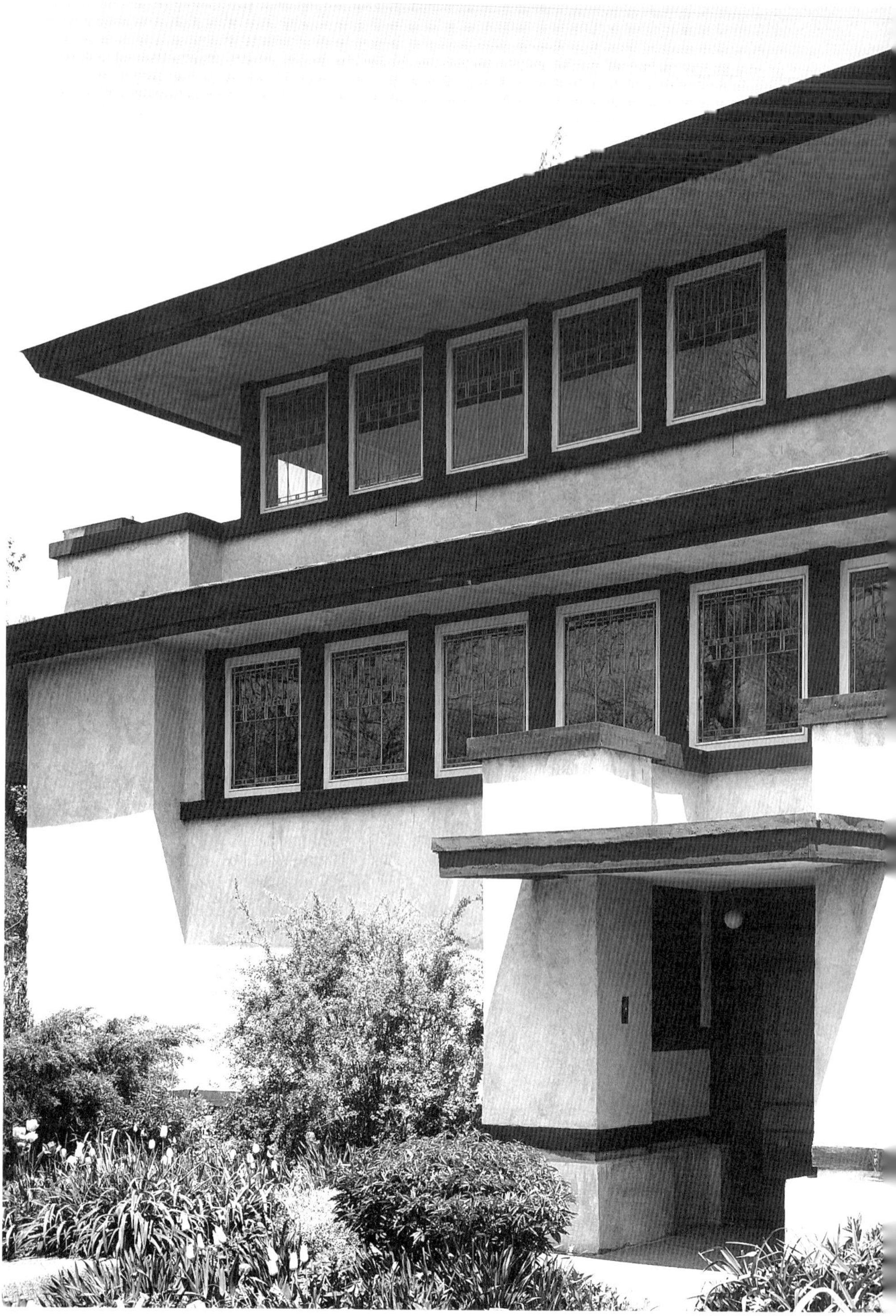

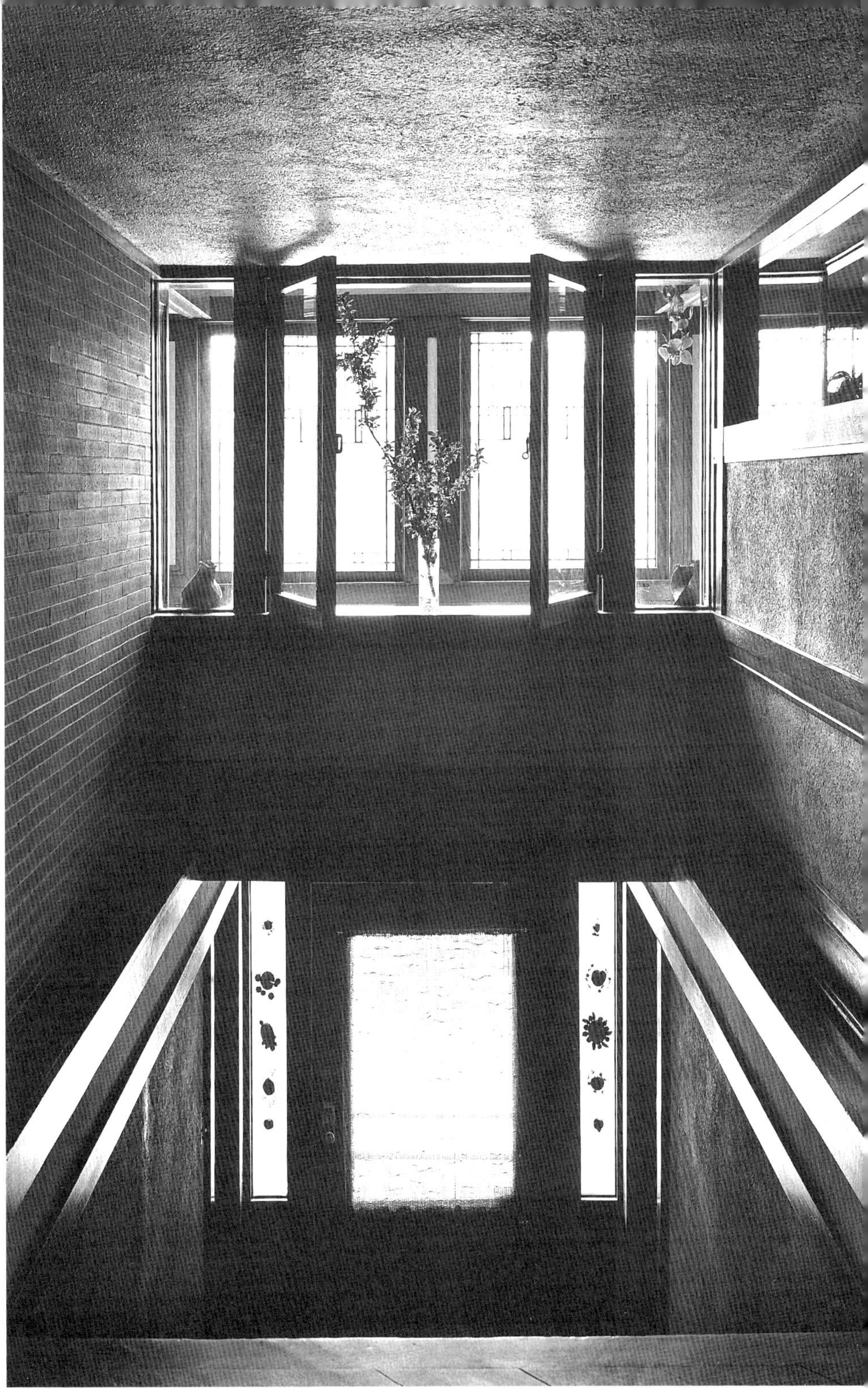

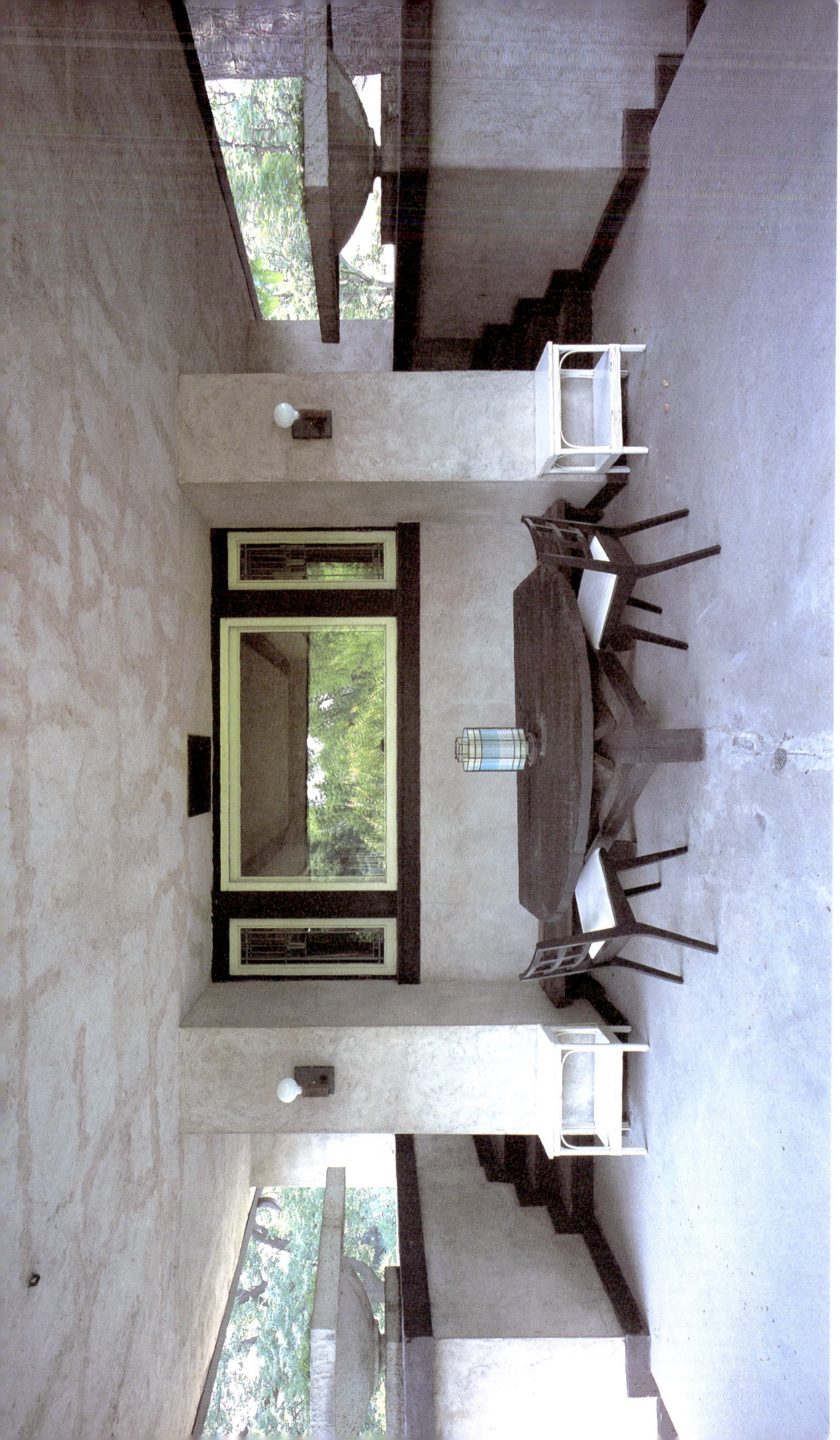

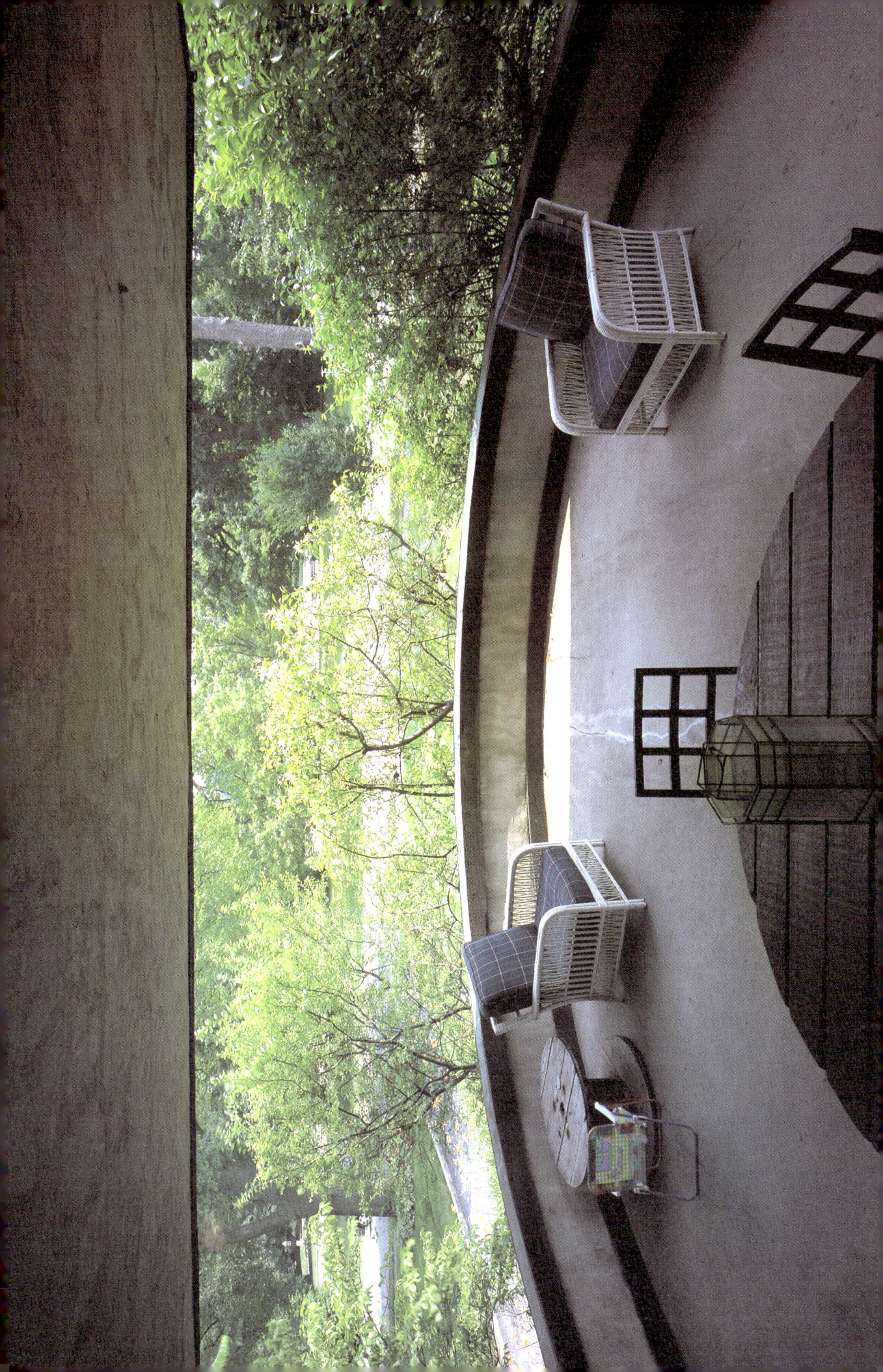

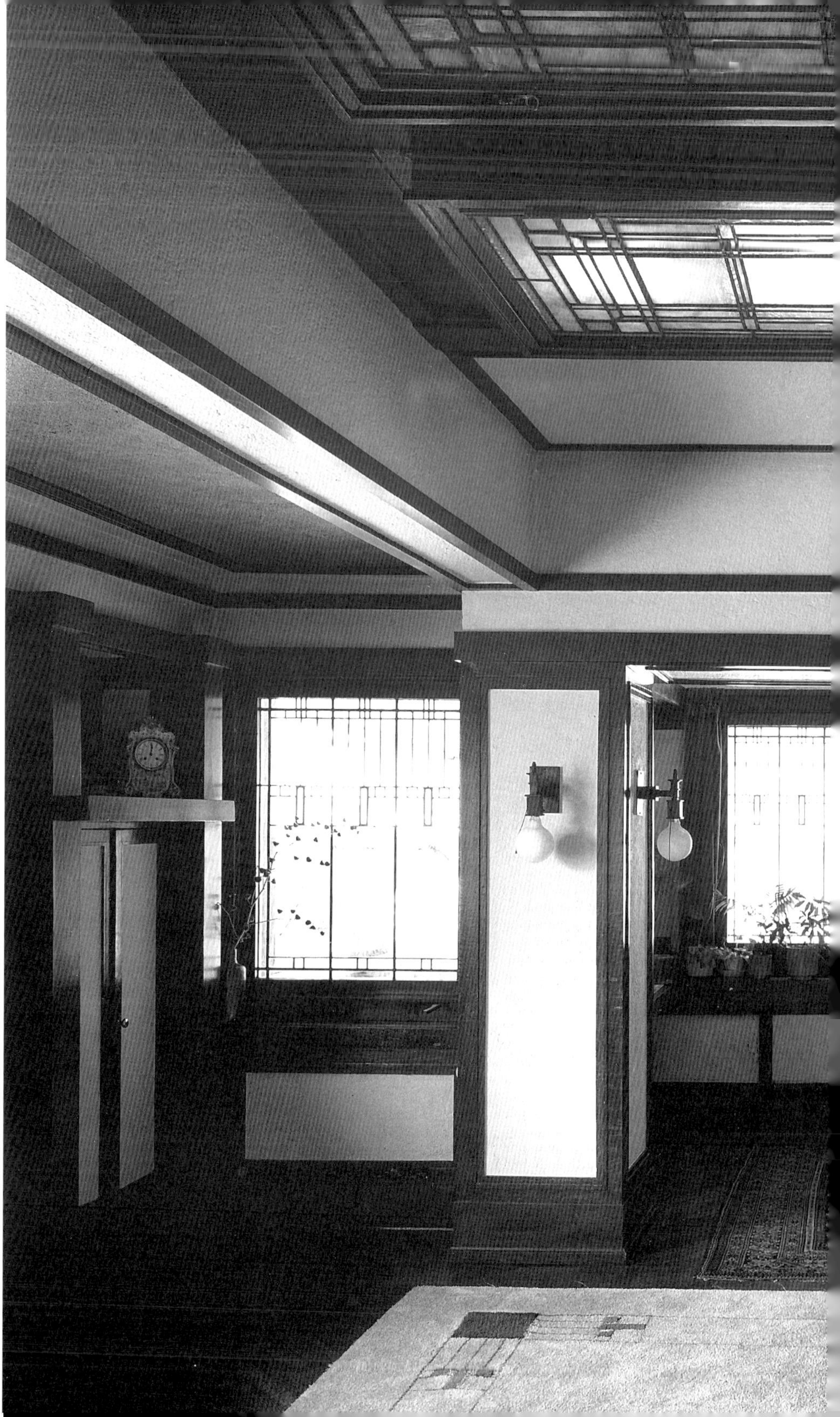

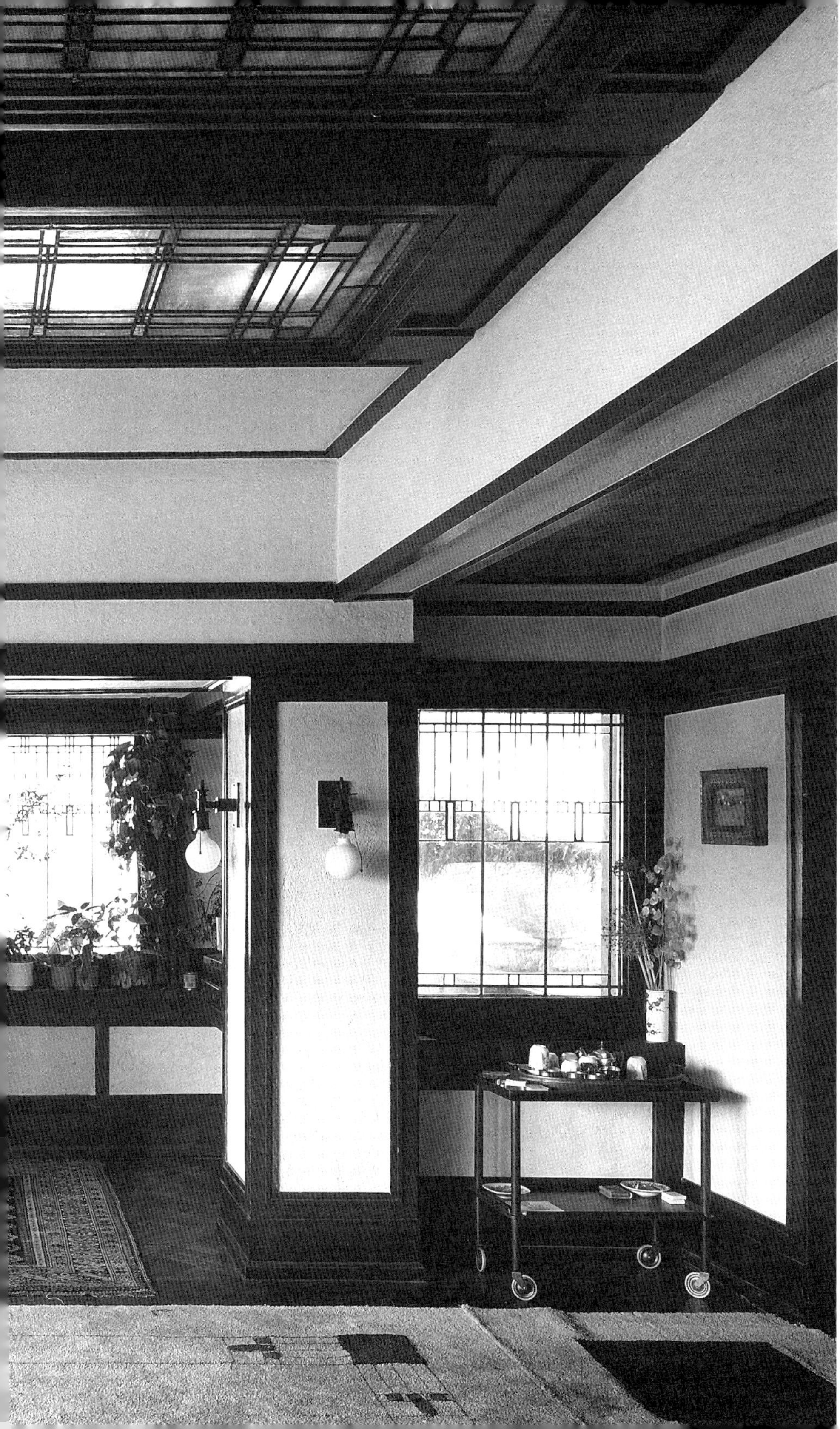

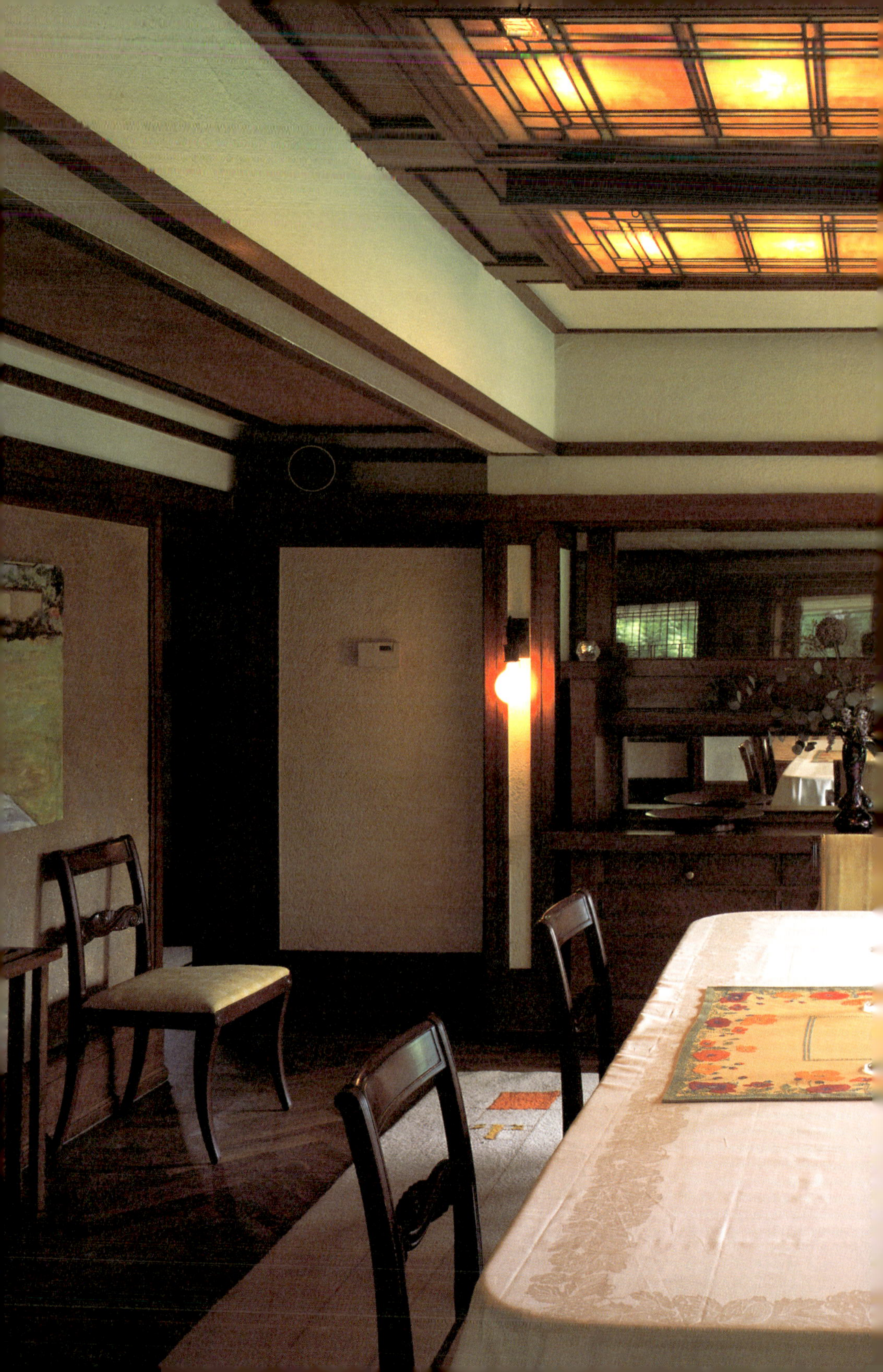

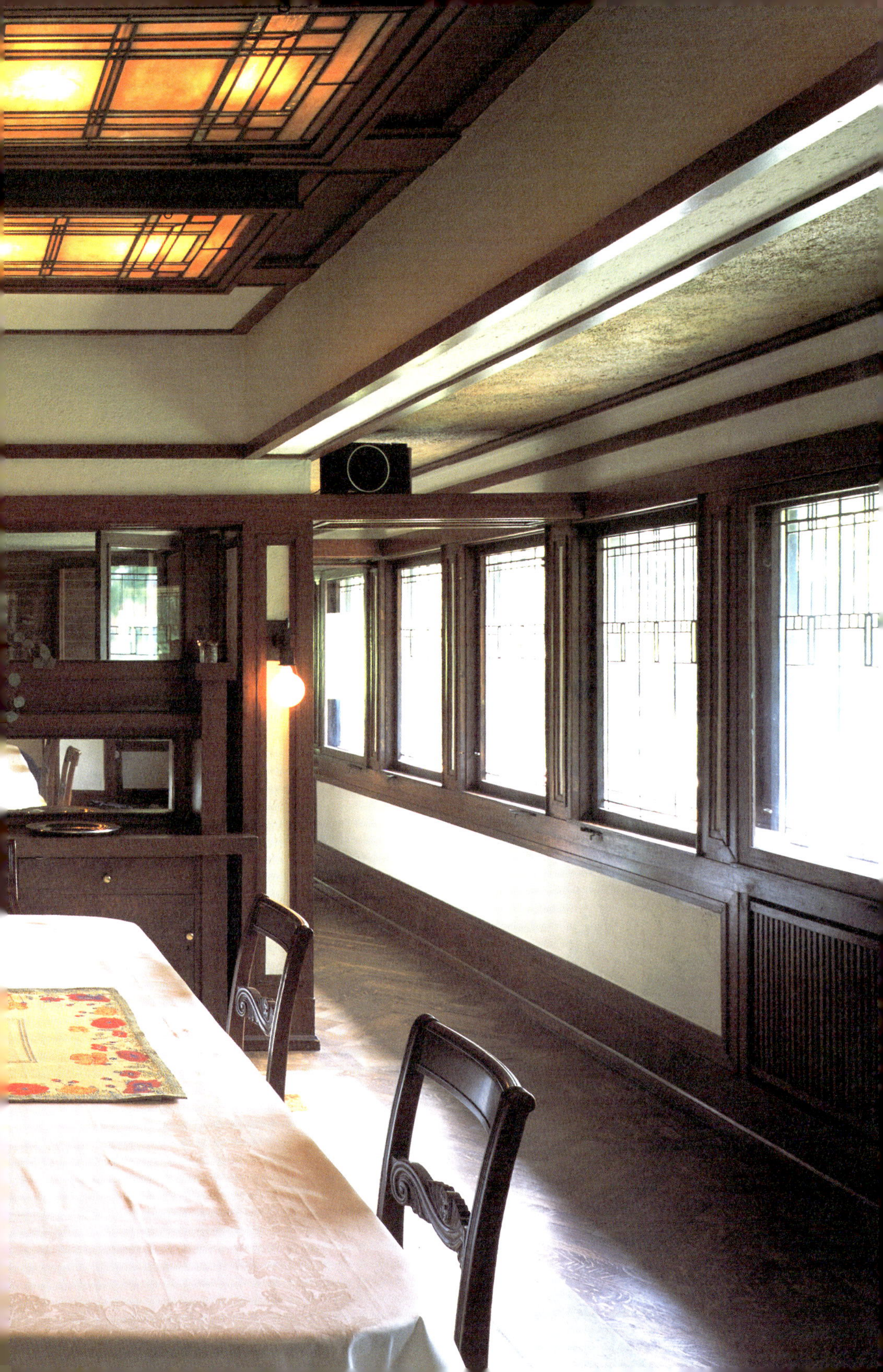

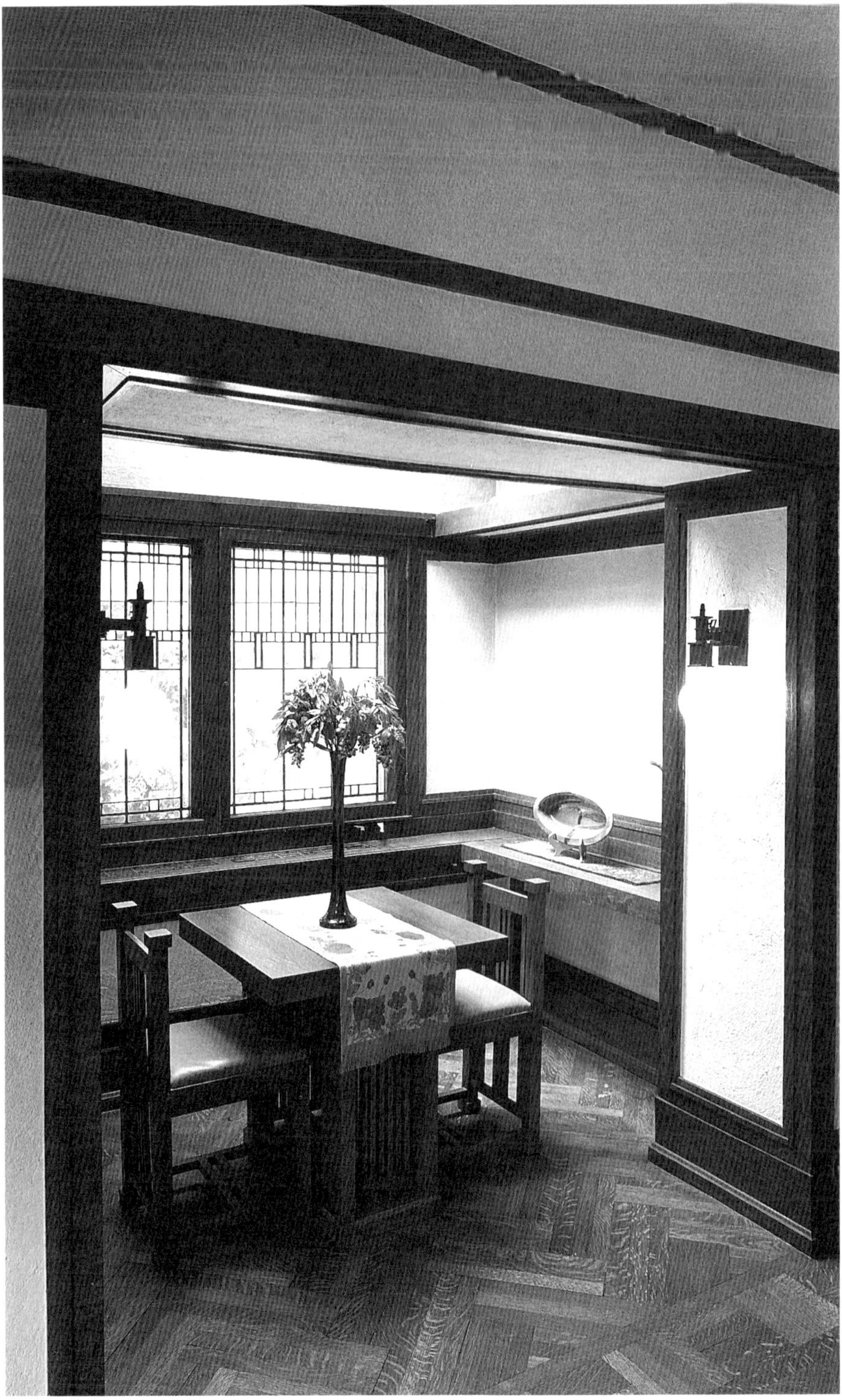

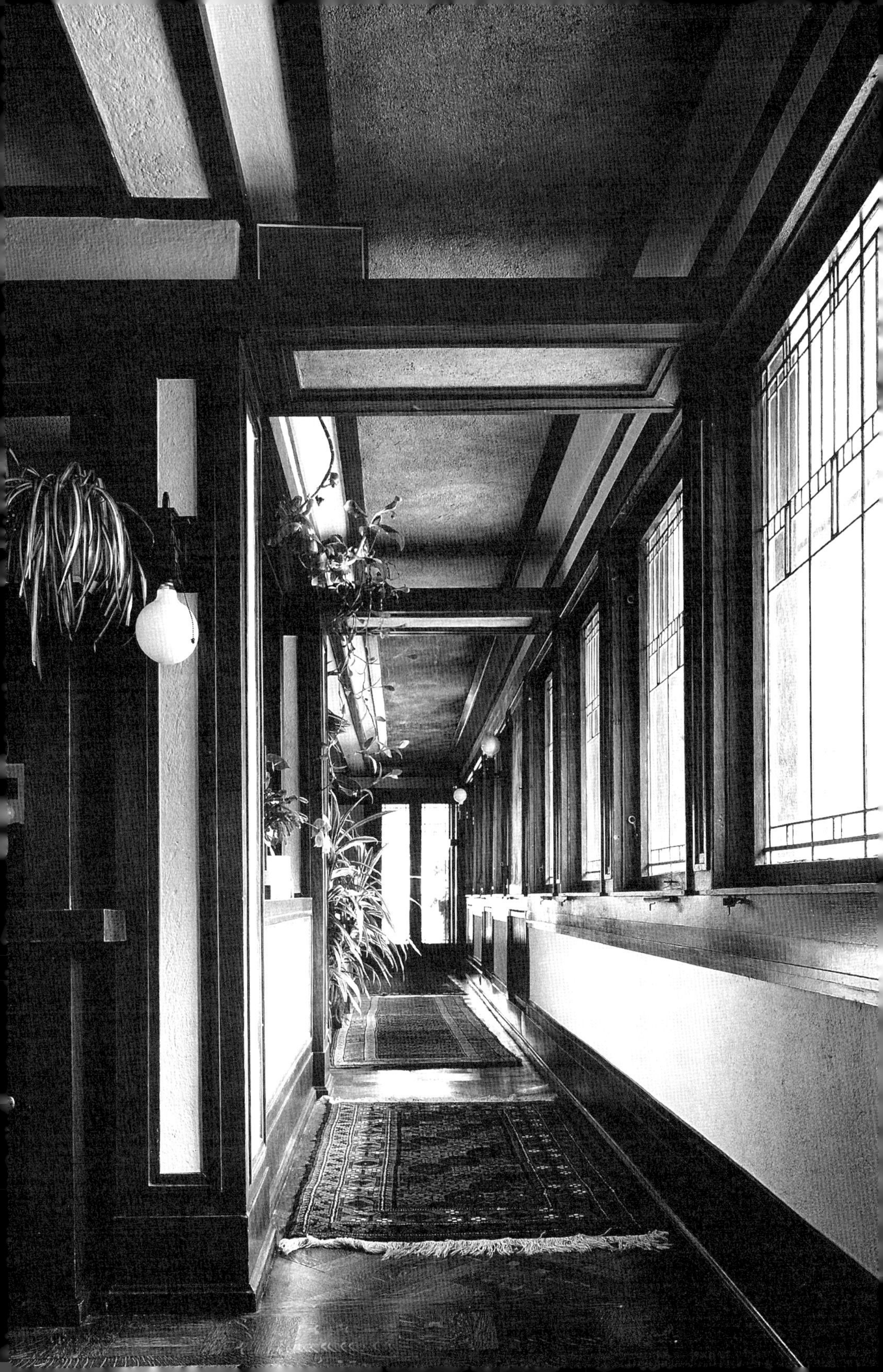

Avery Coonley House
Riverside, Illinois, 1907

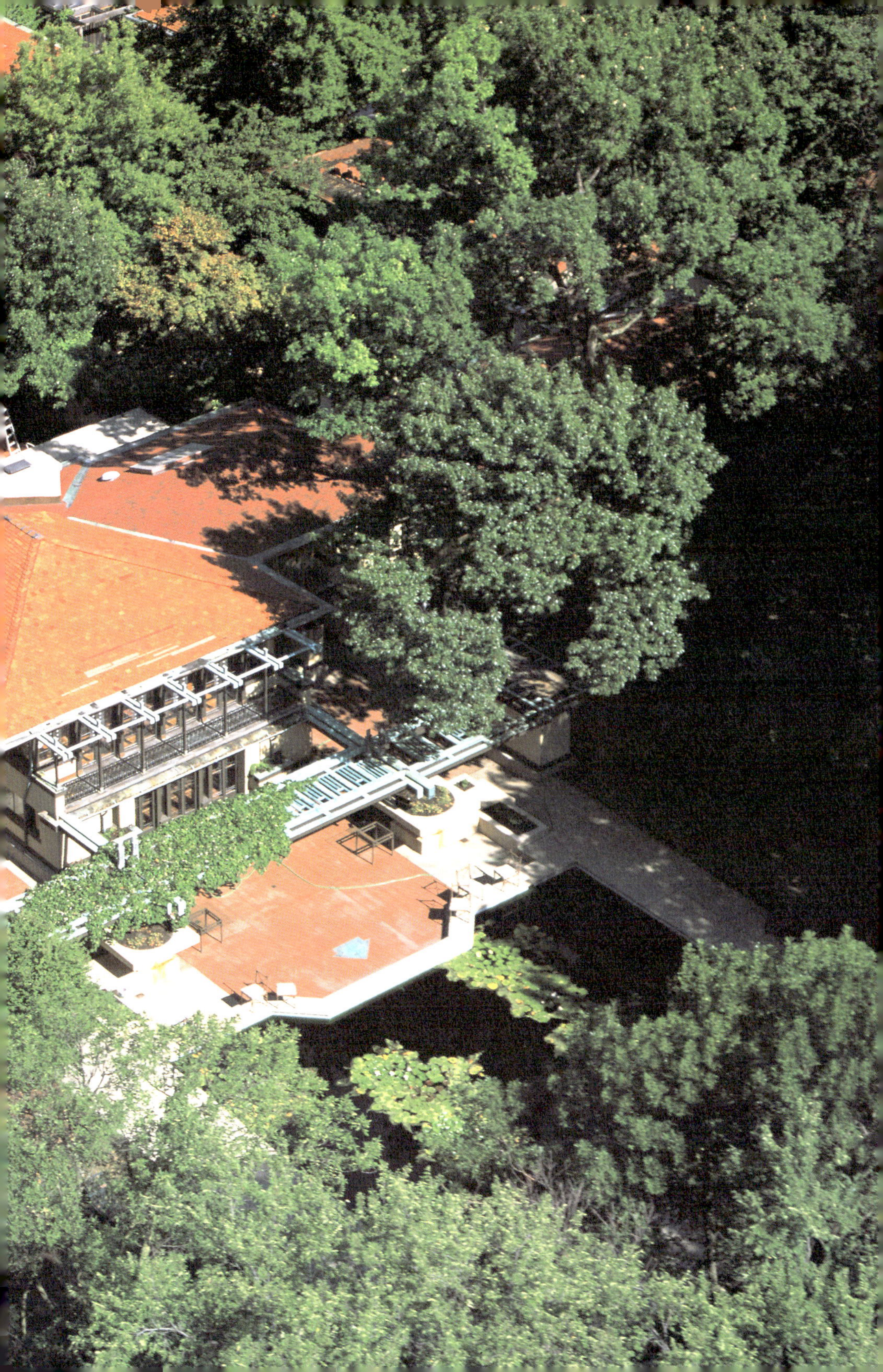

First floor

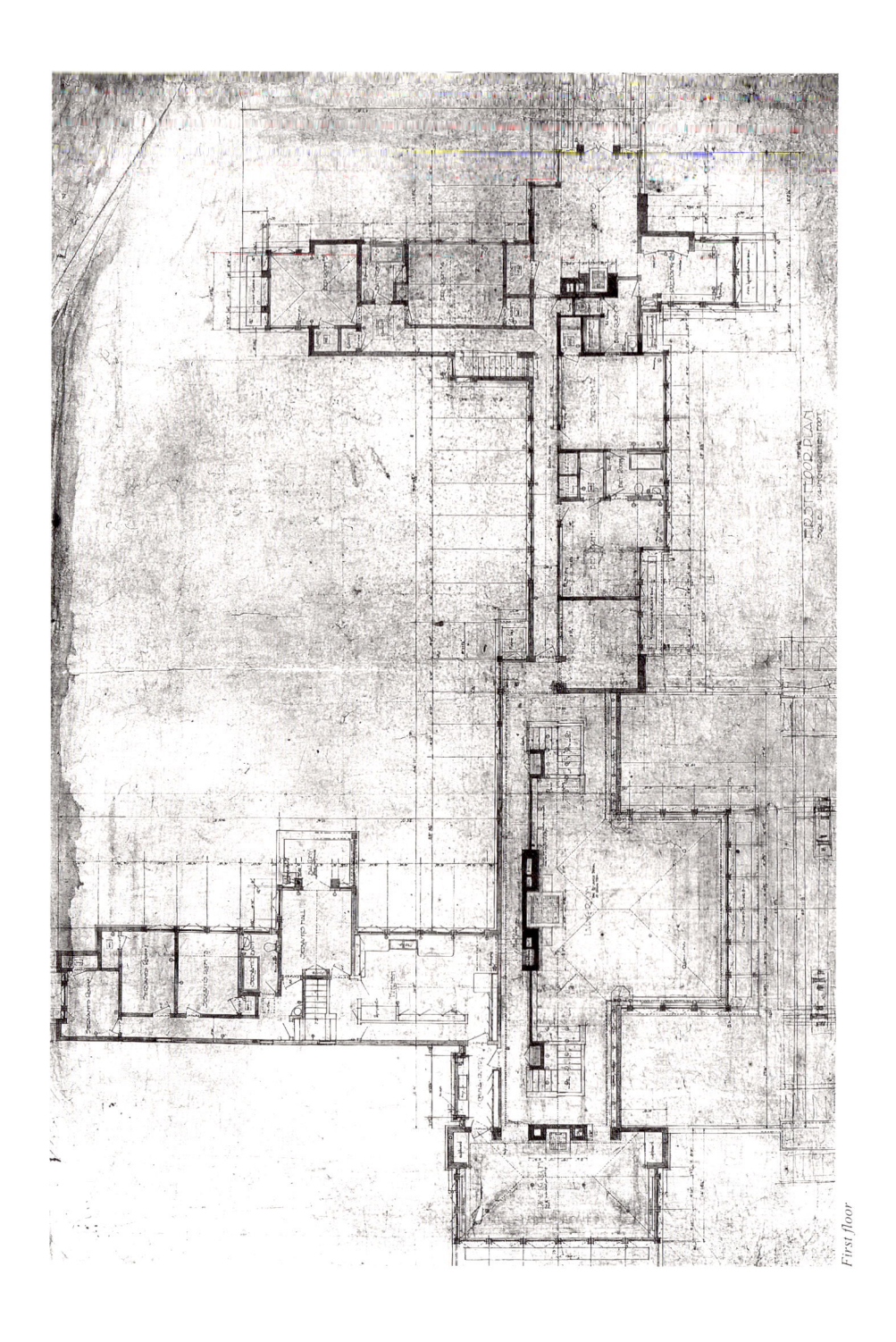

Basement

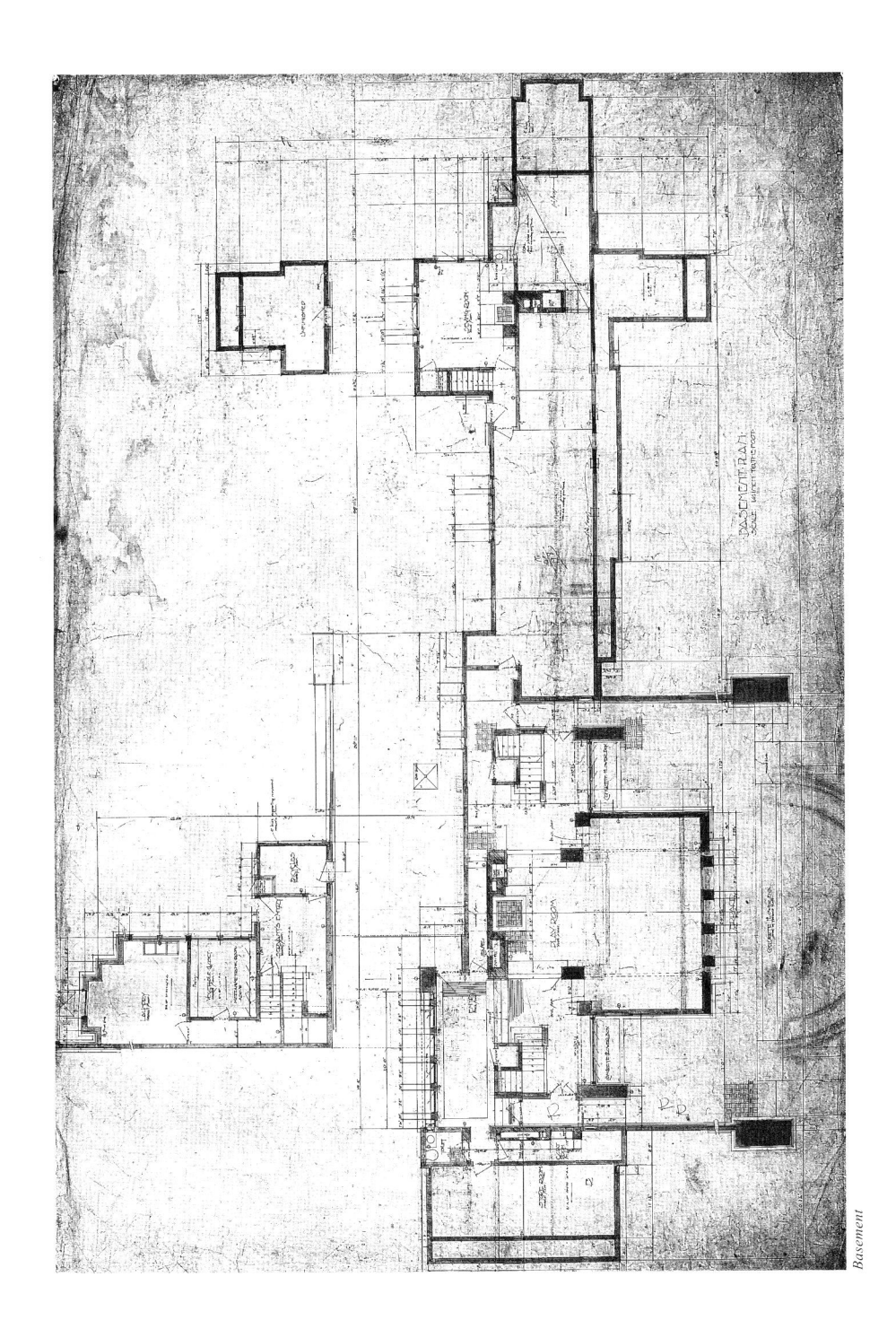

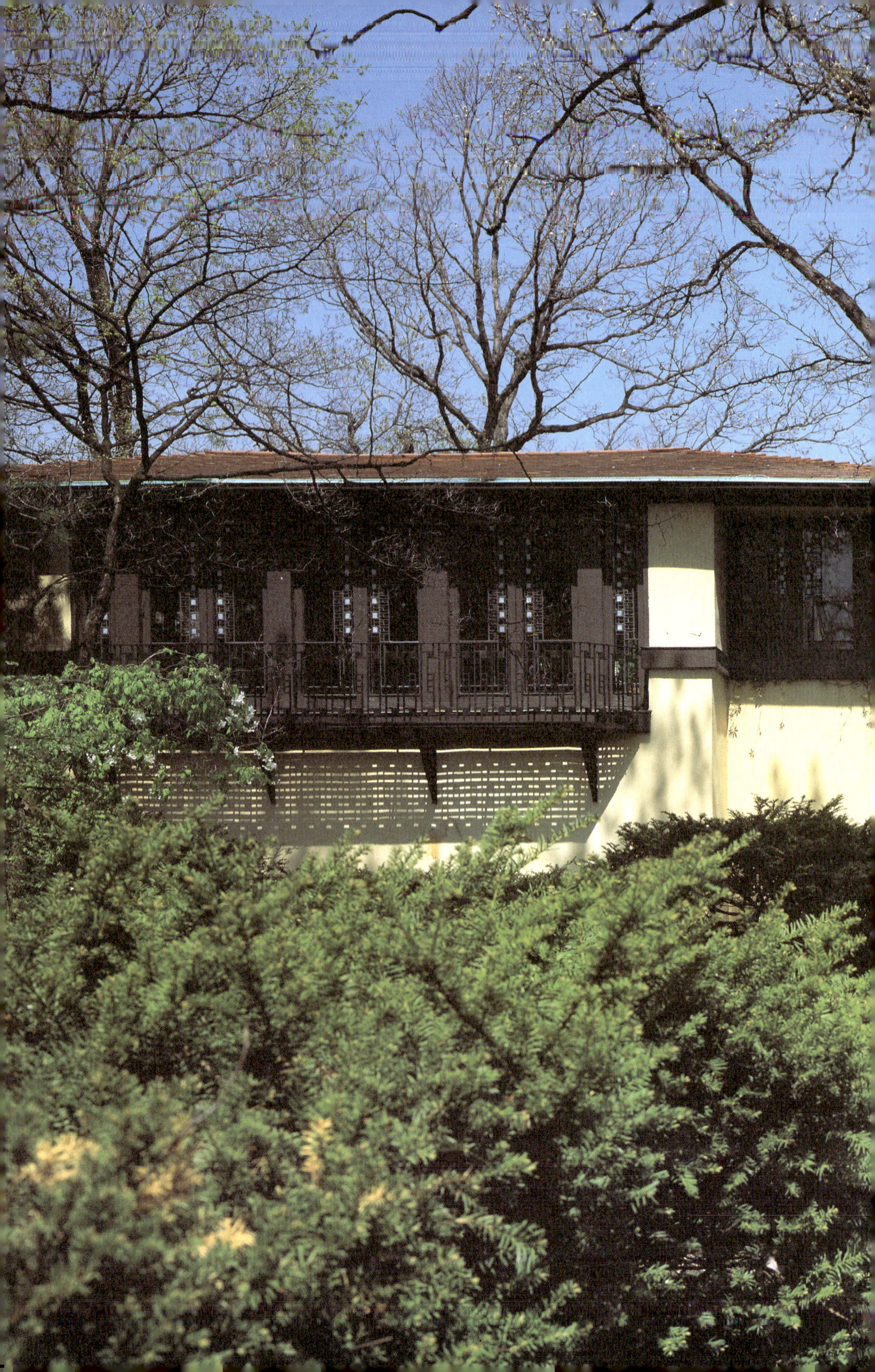

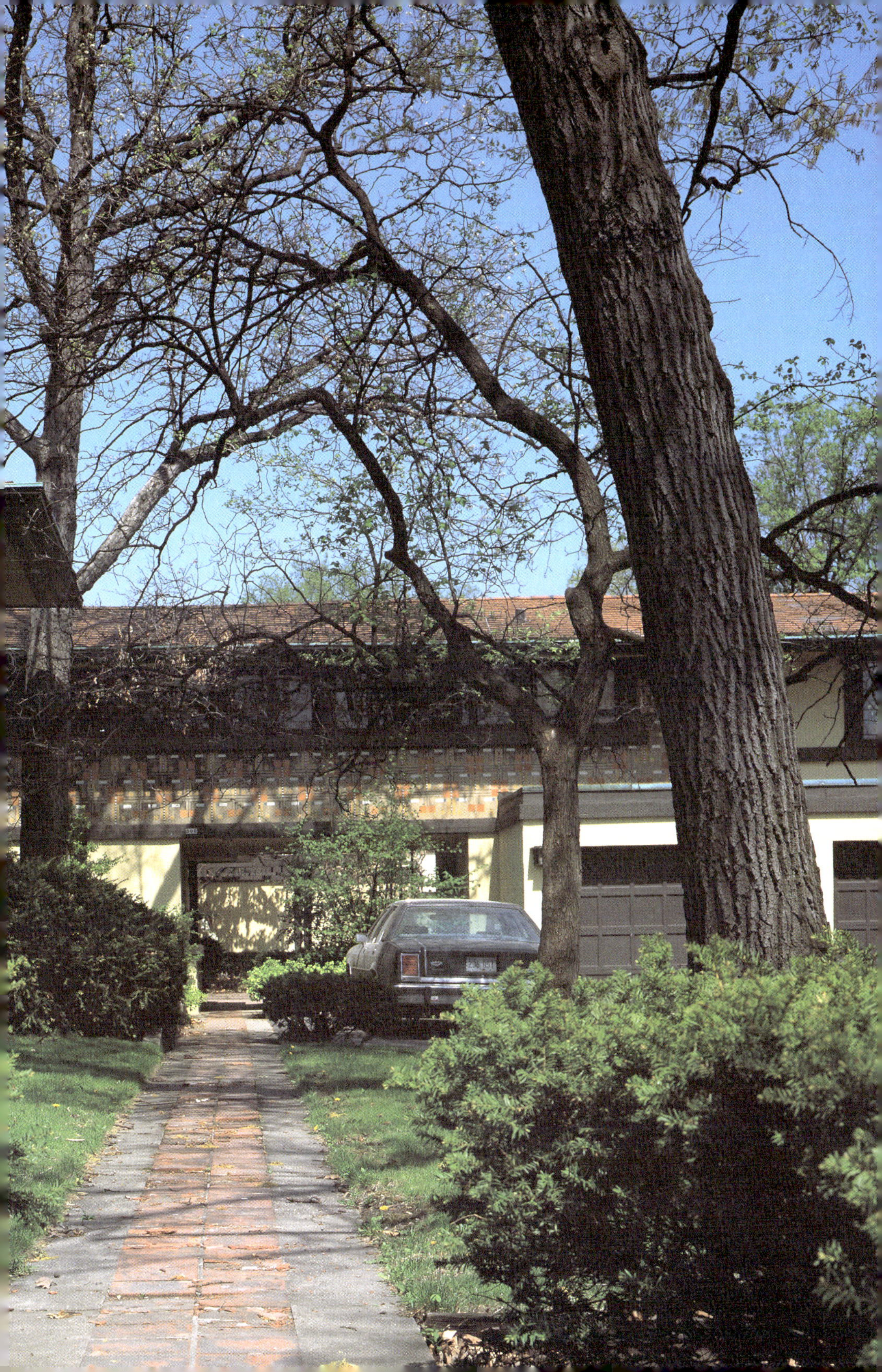

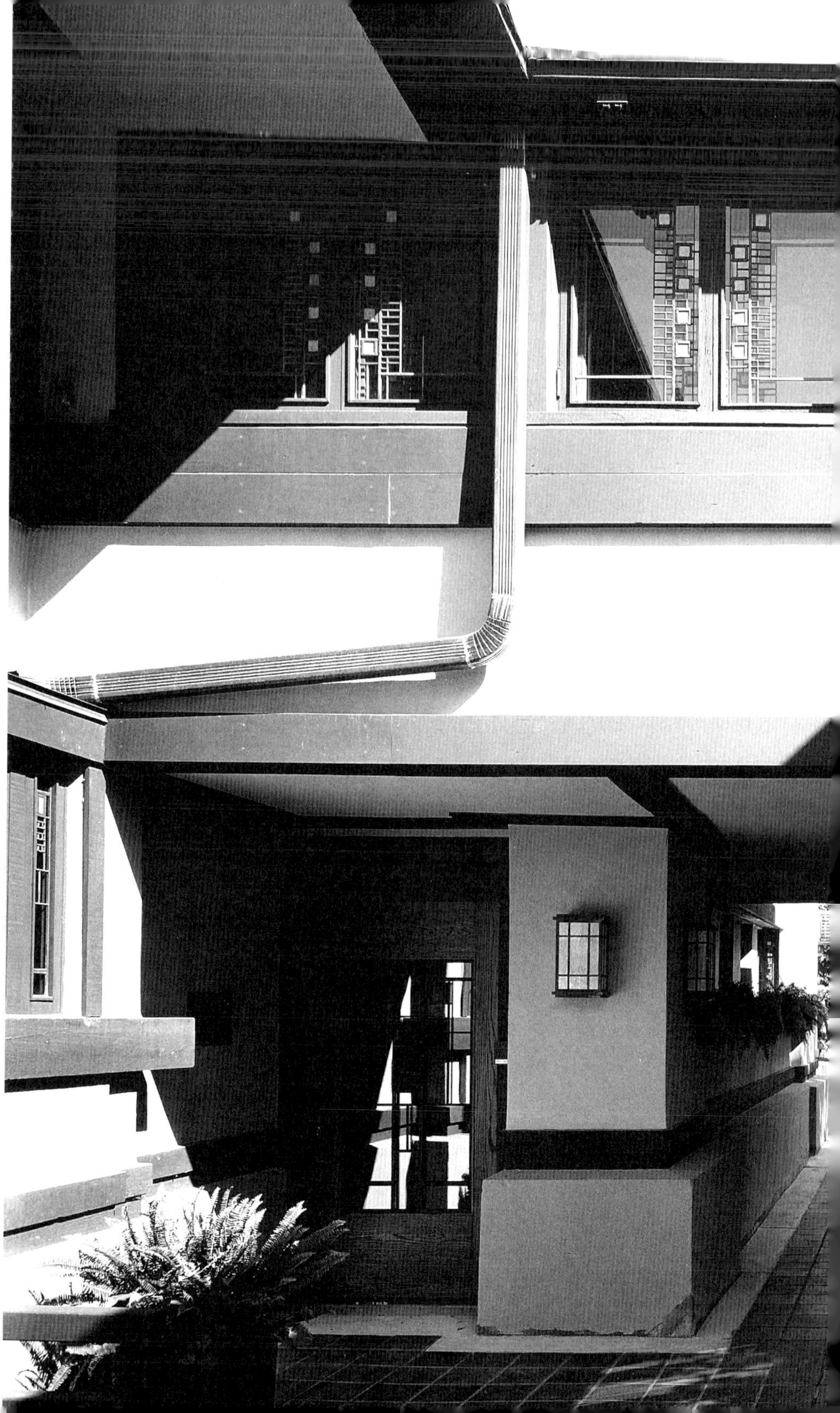

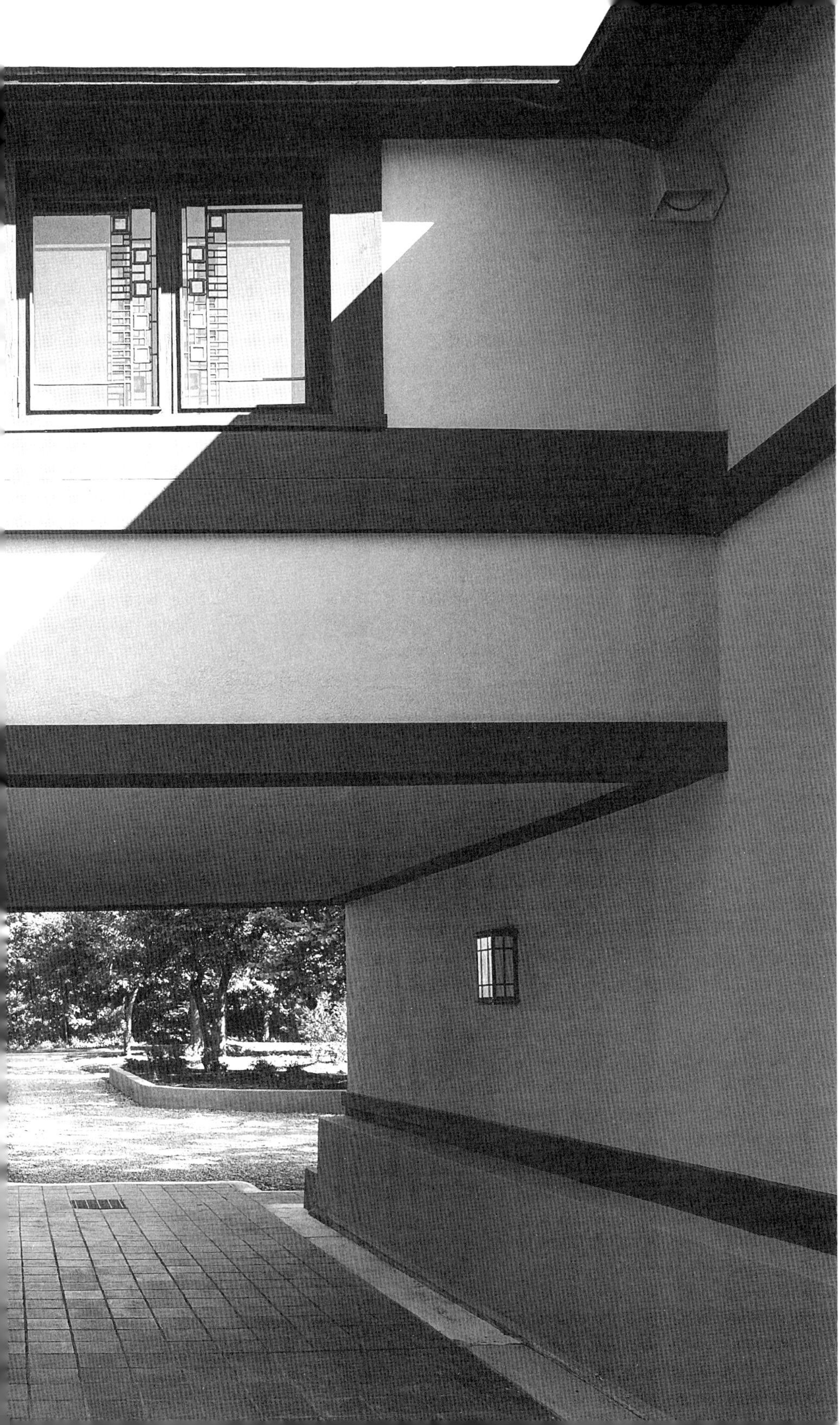

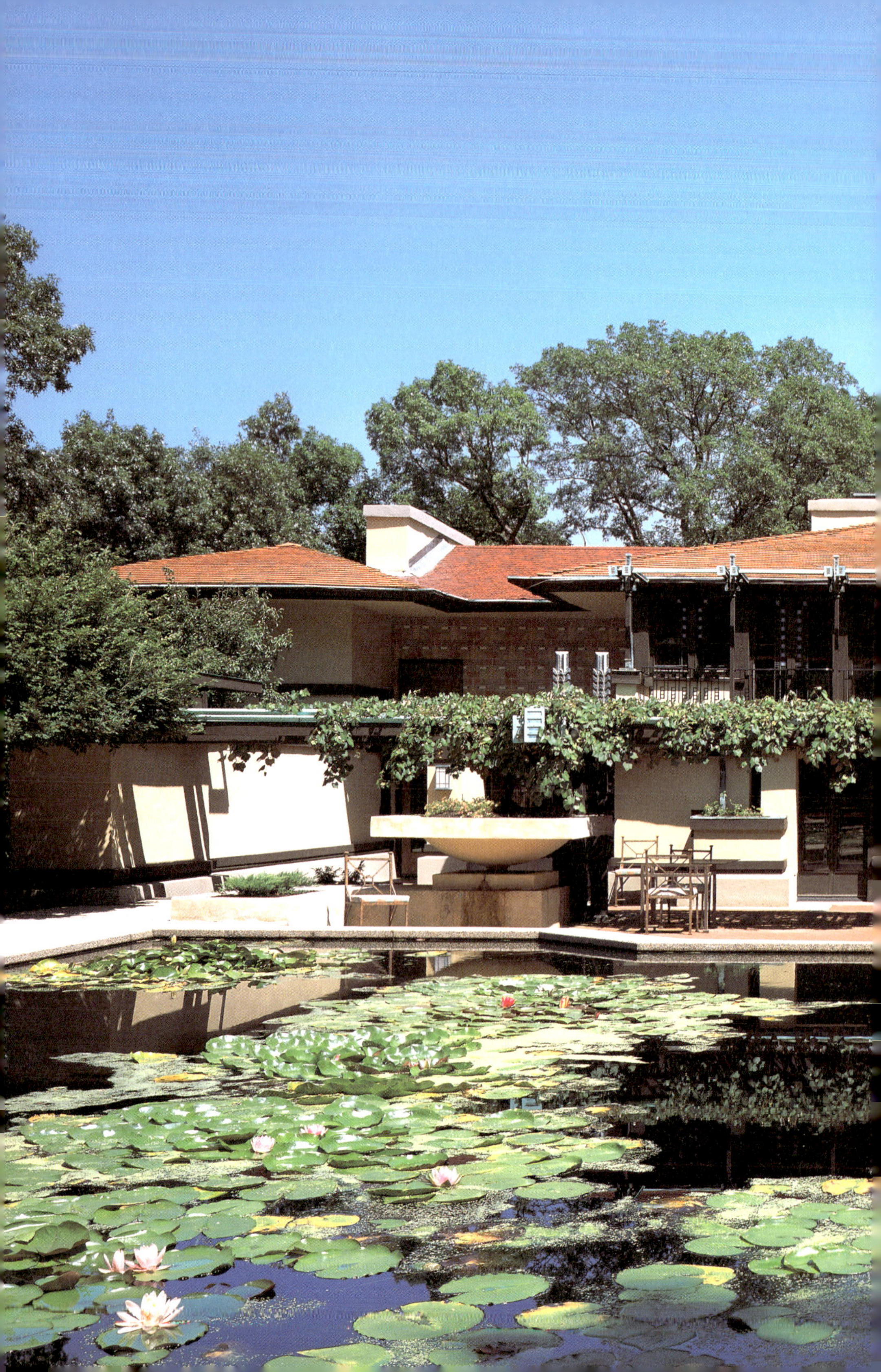

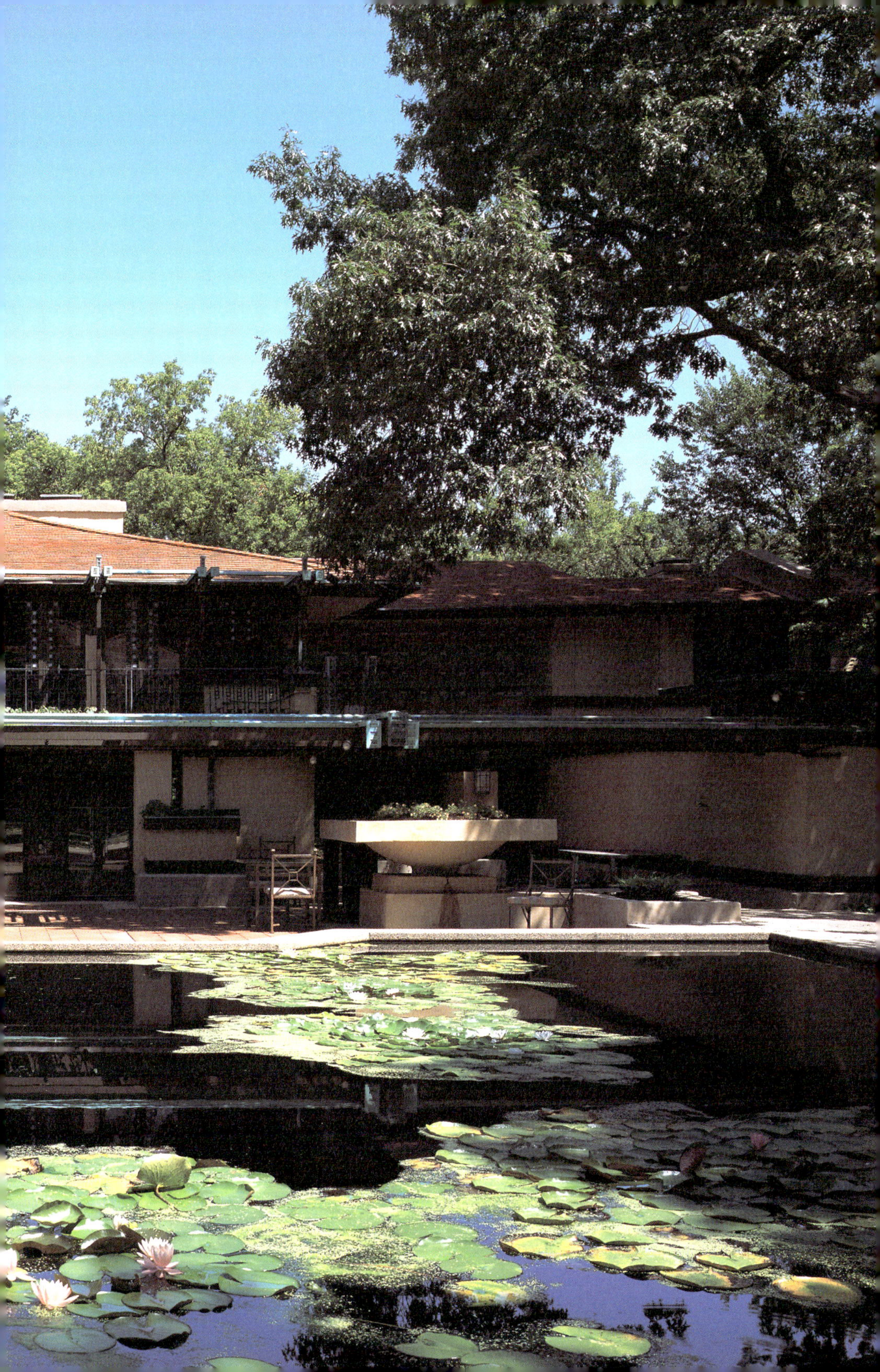

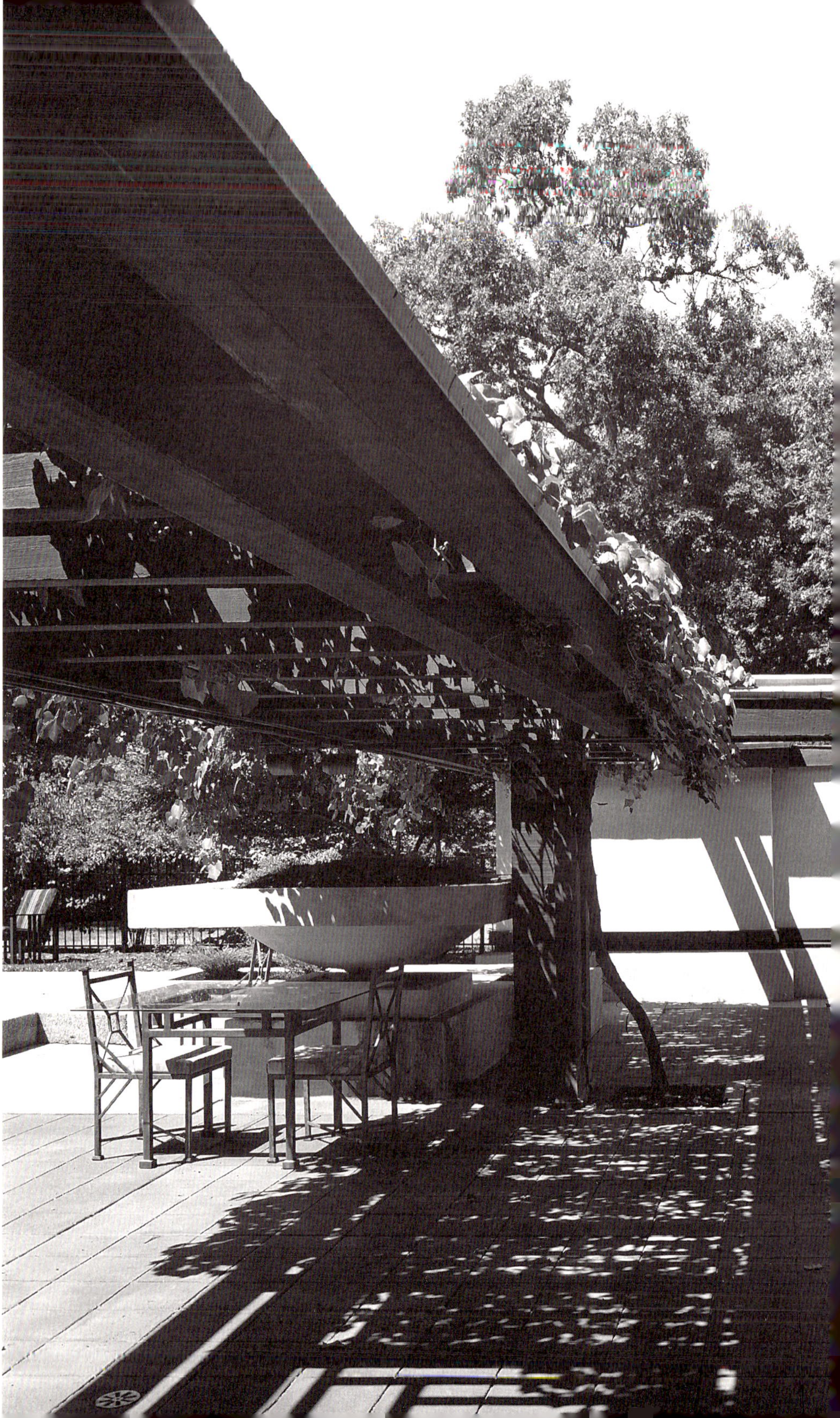

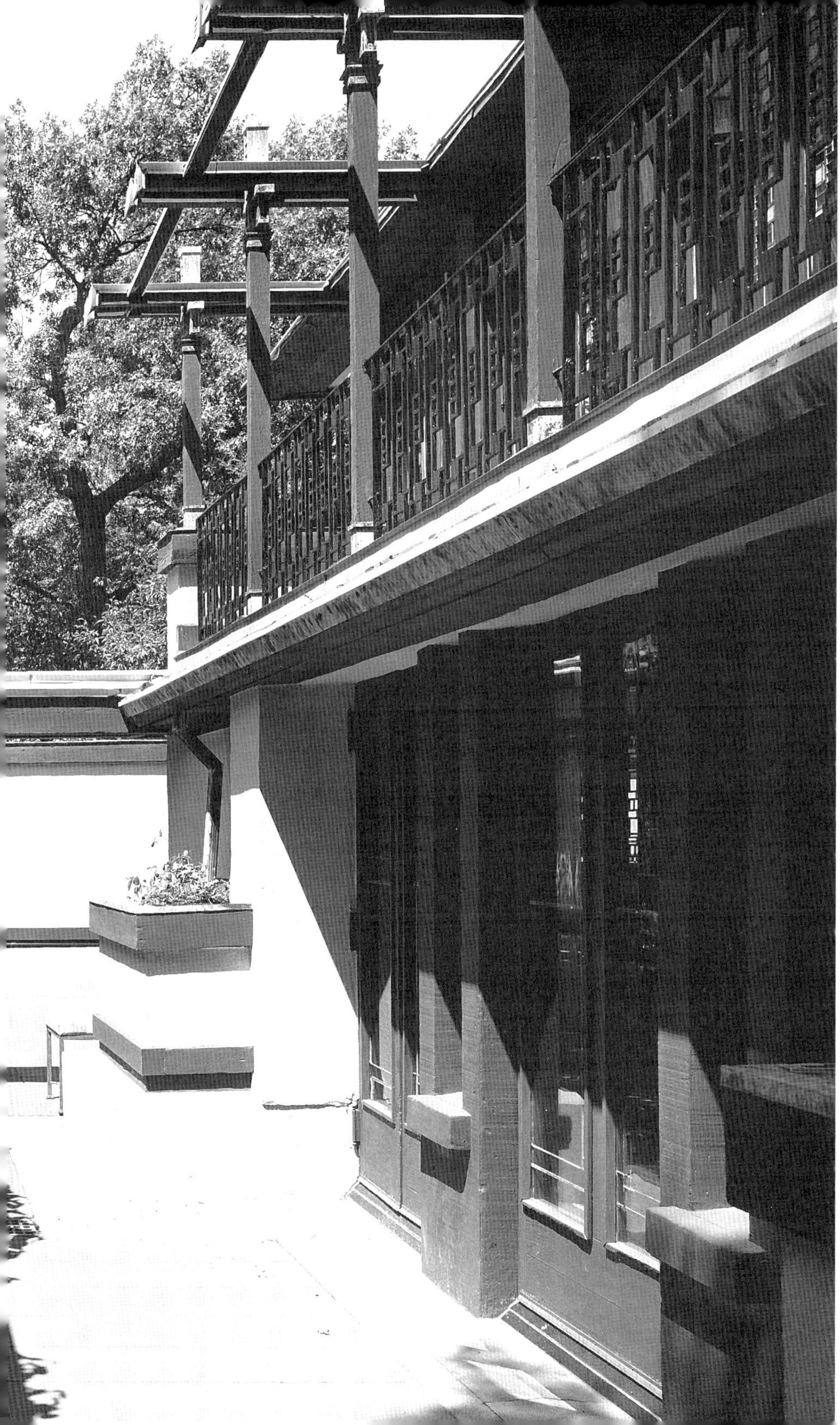

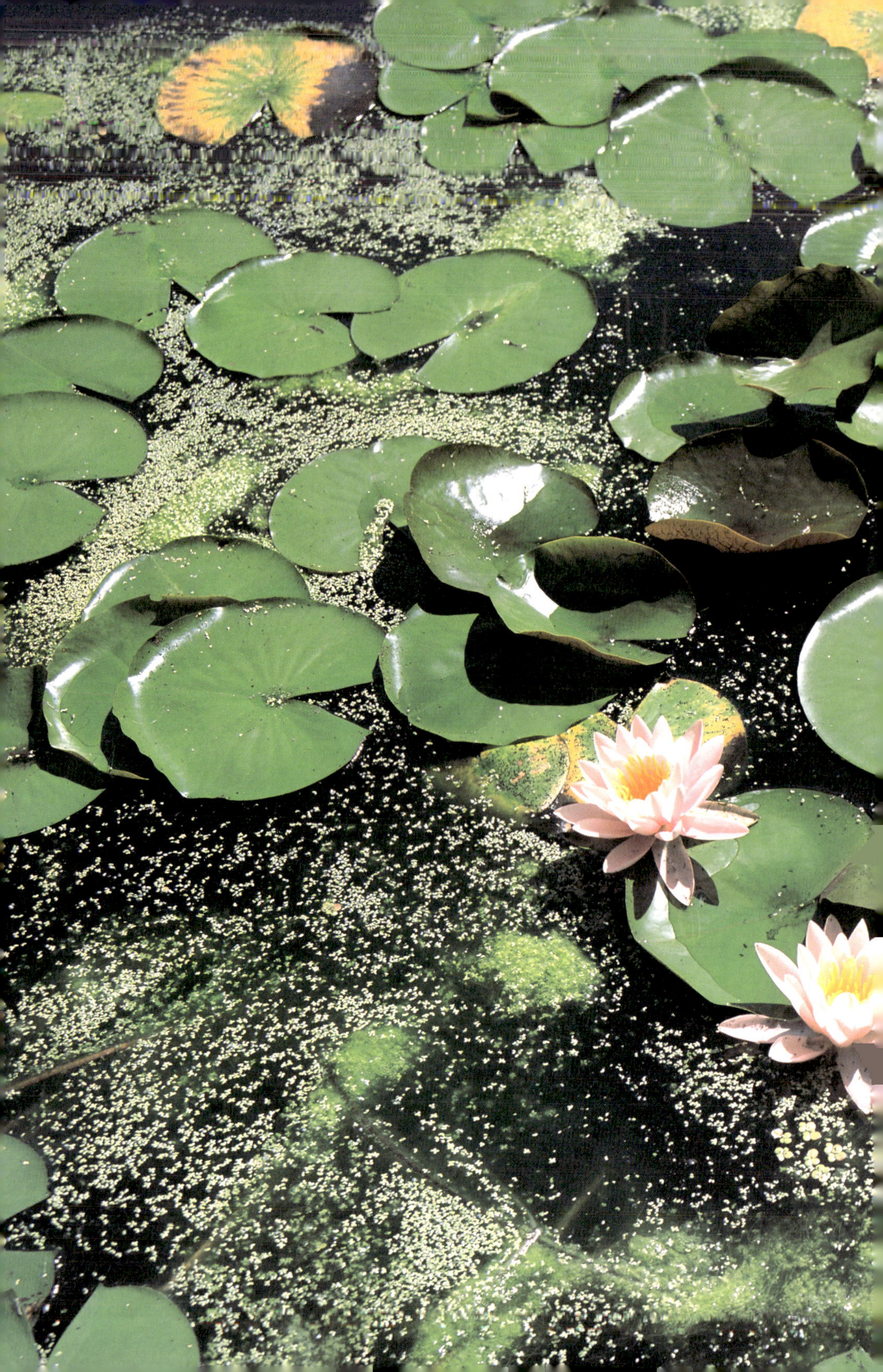

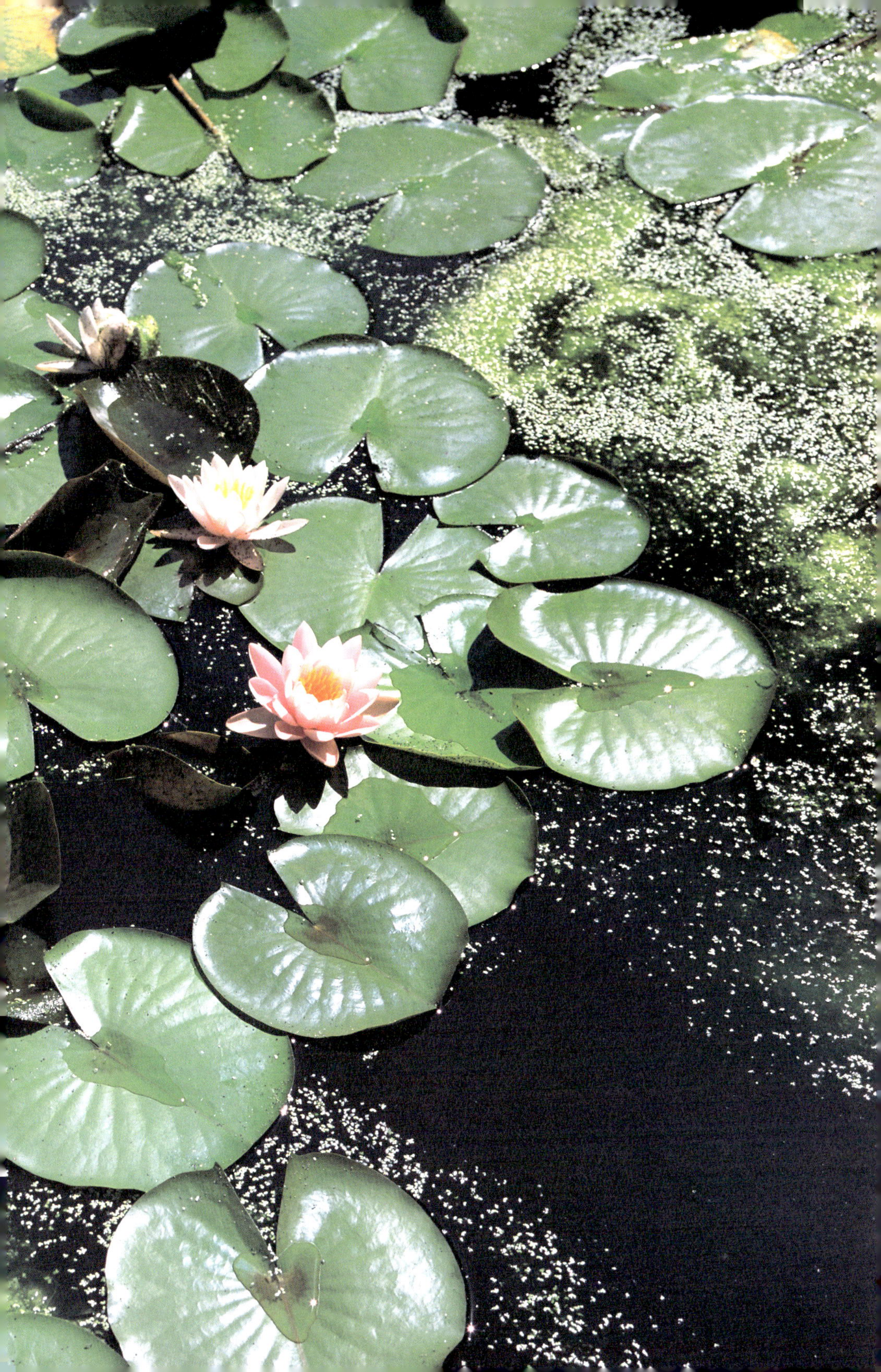

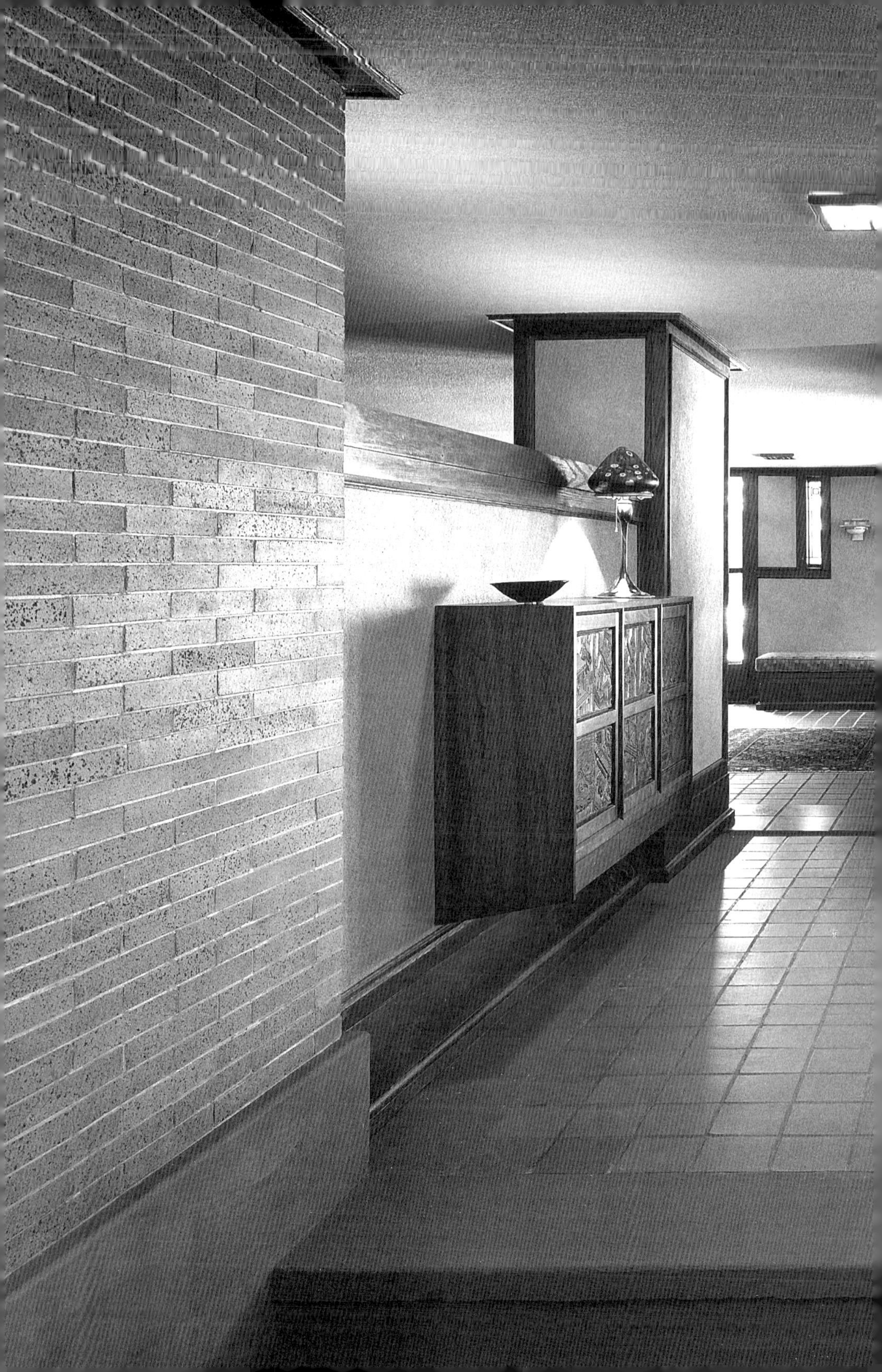

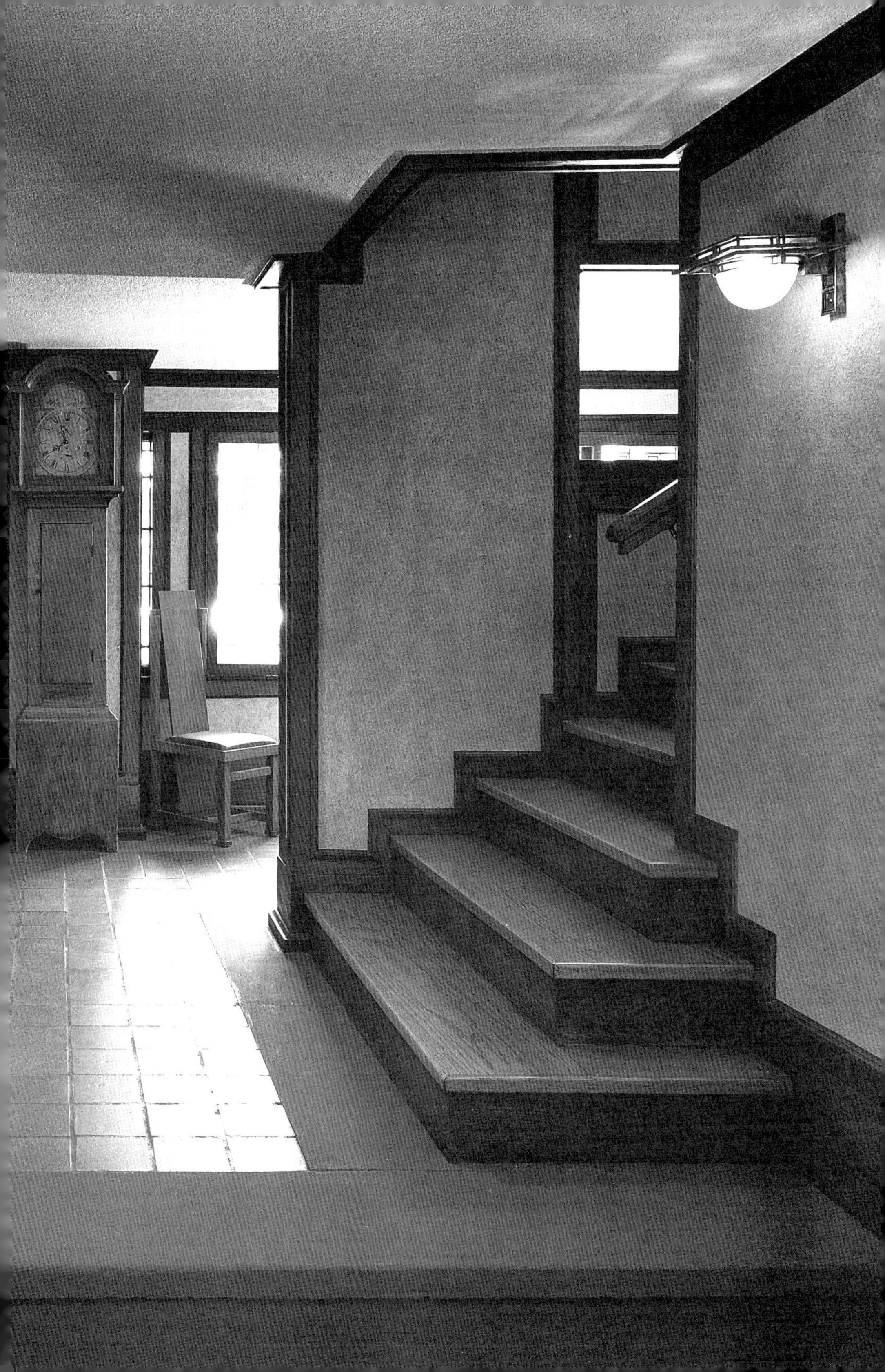

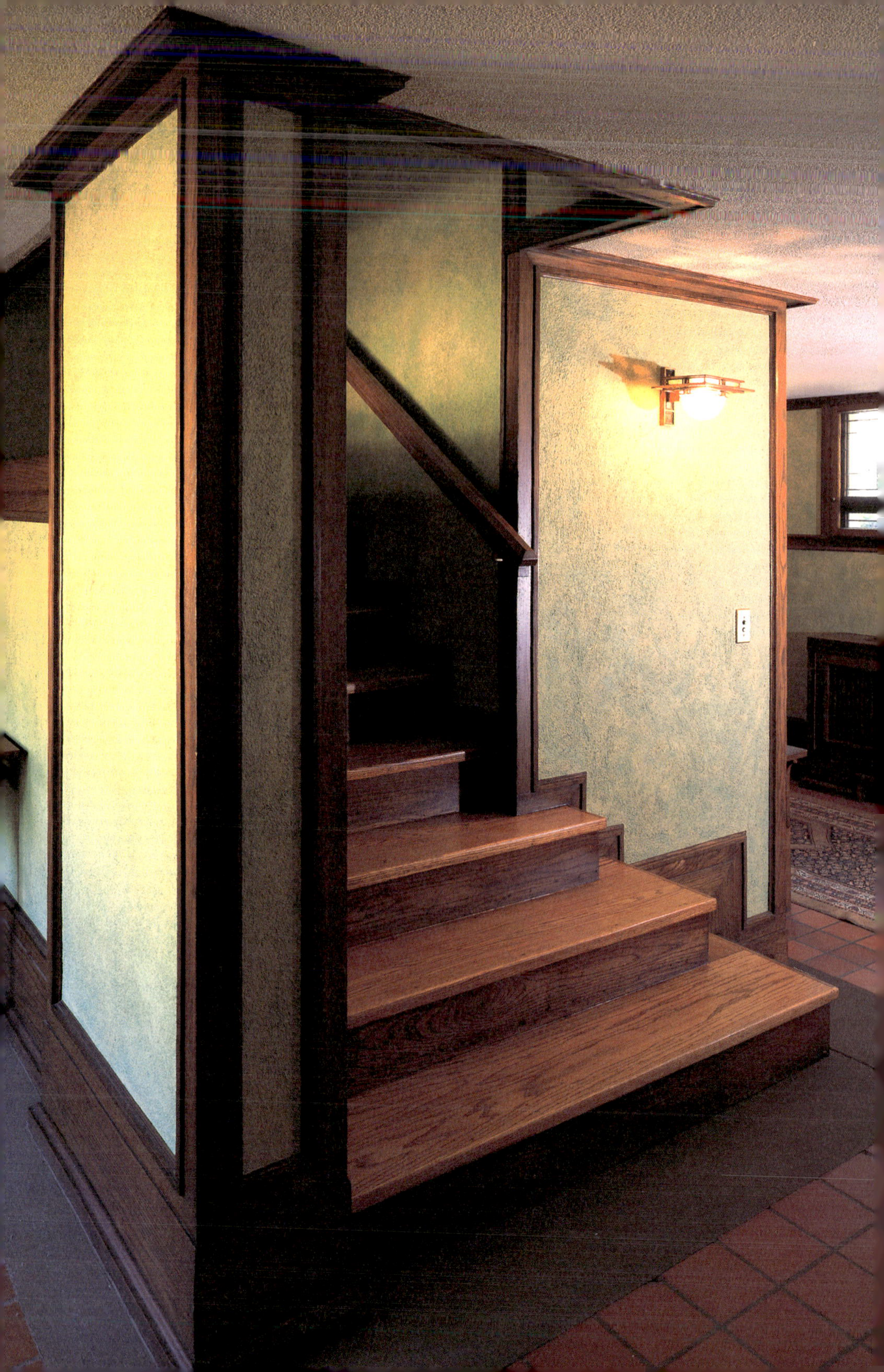

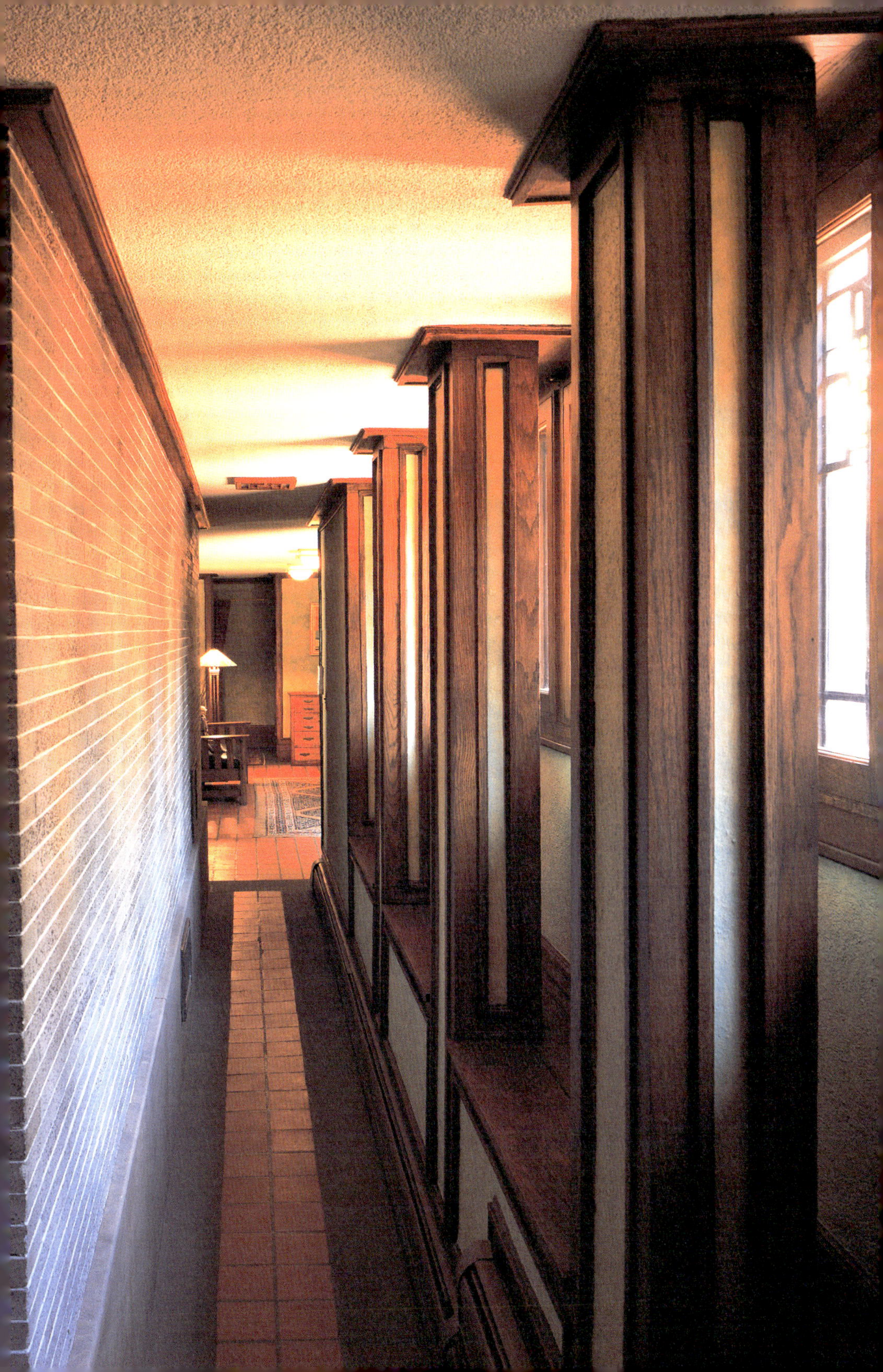

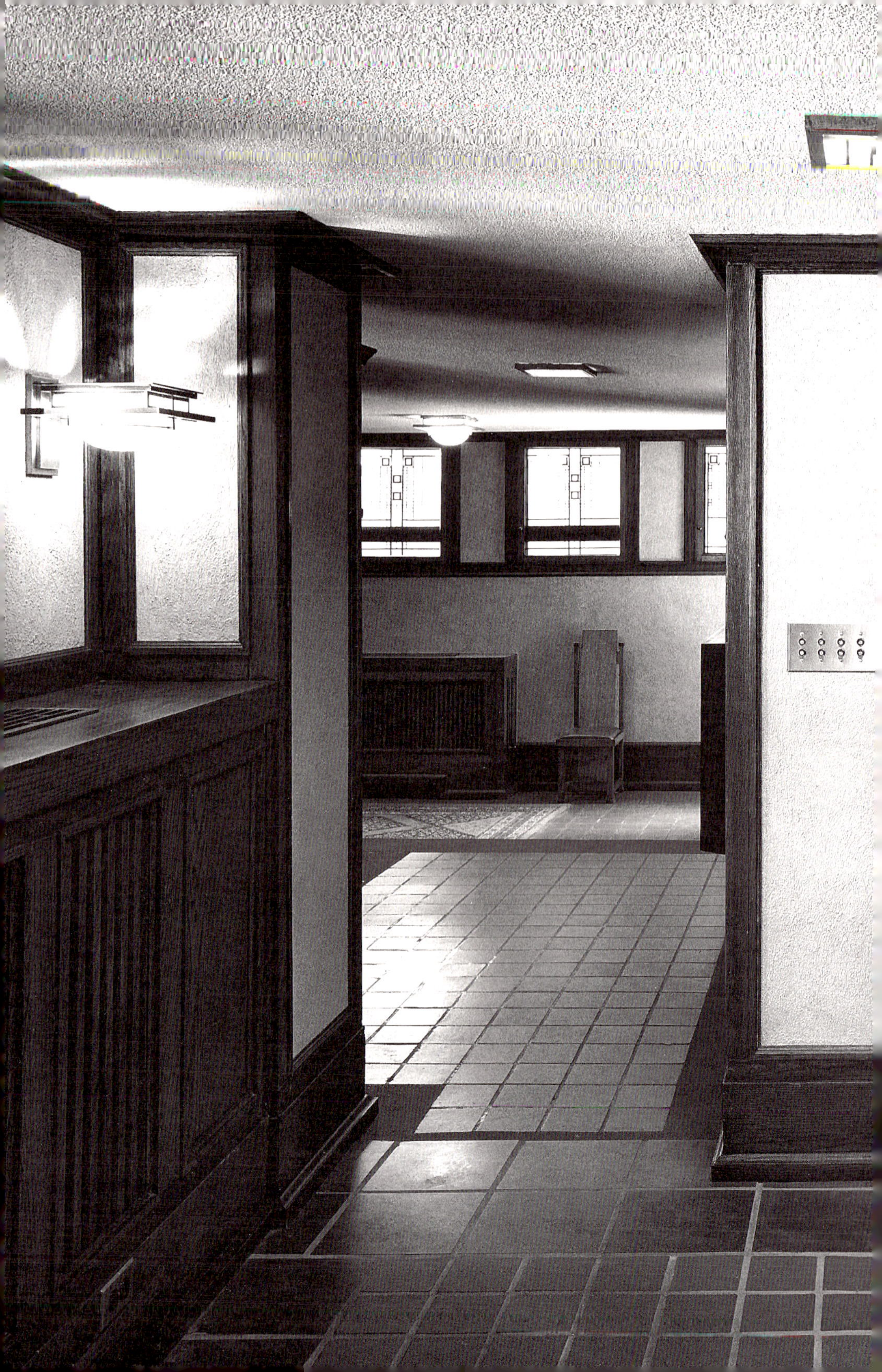

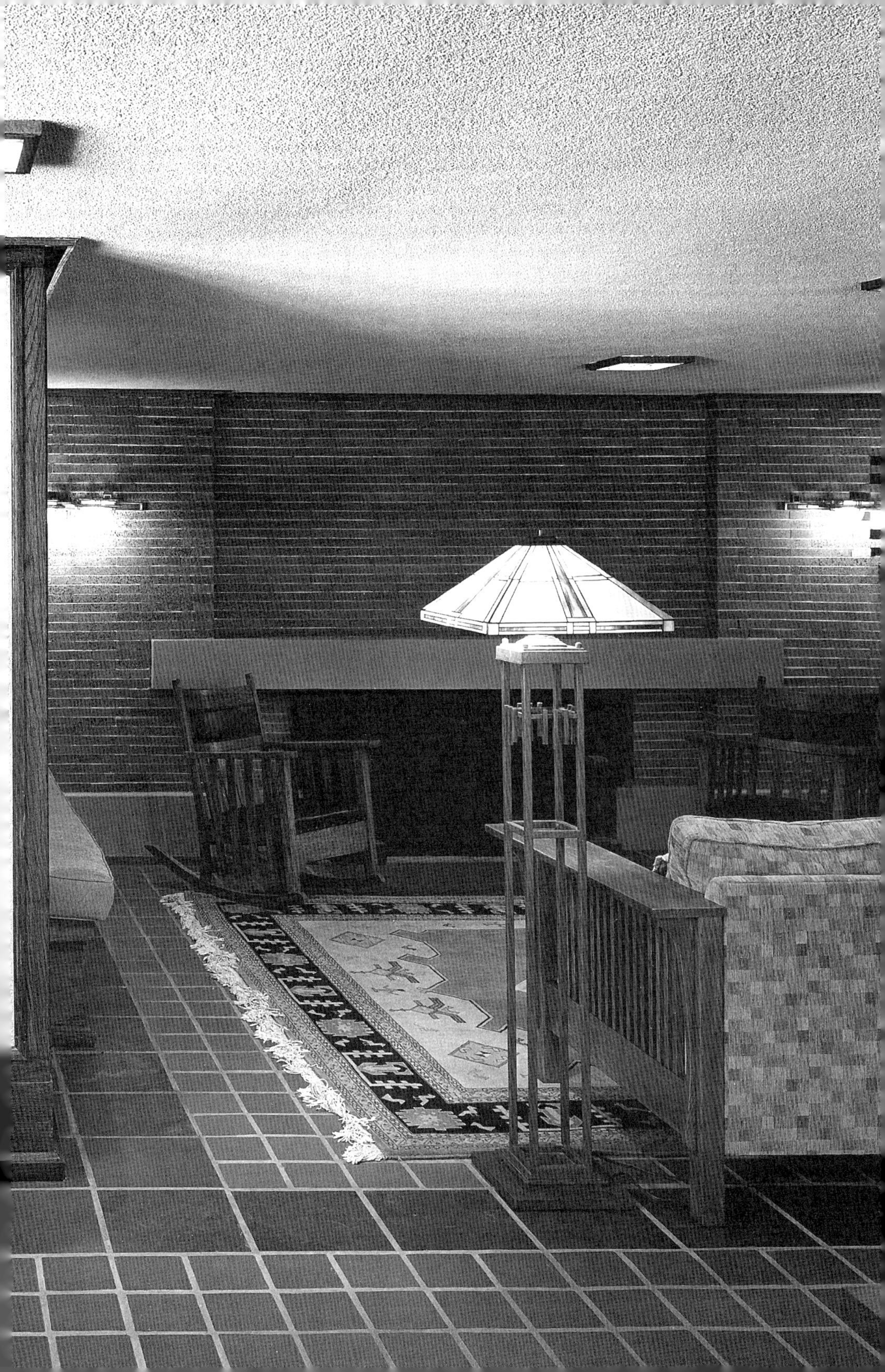

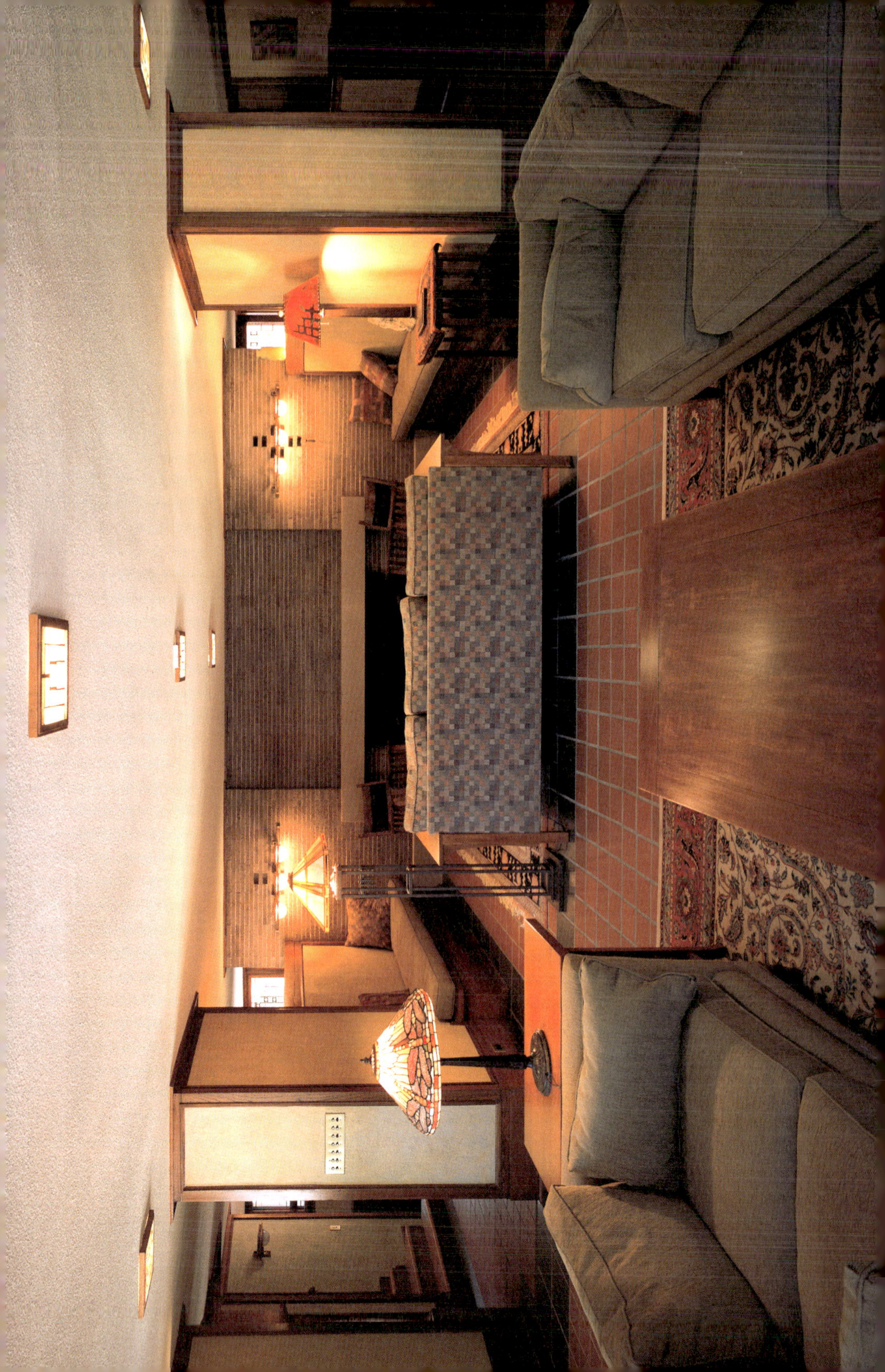

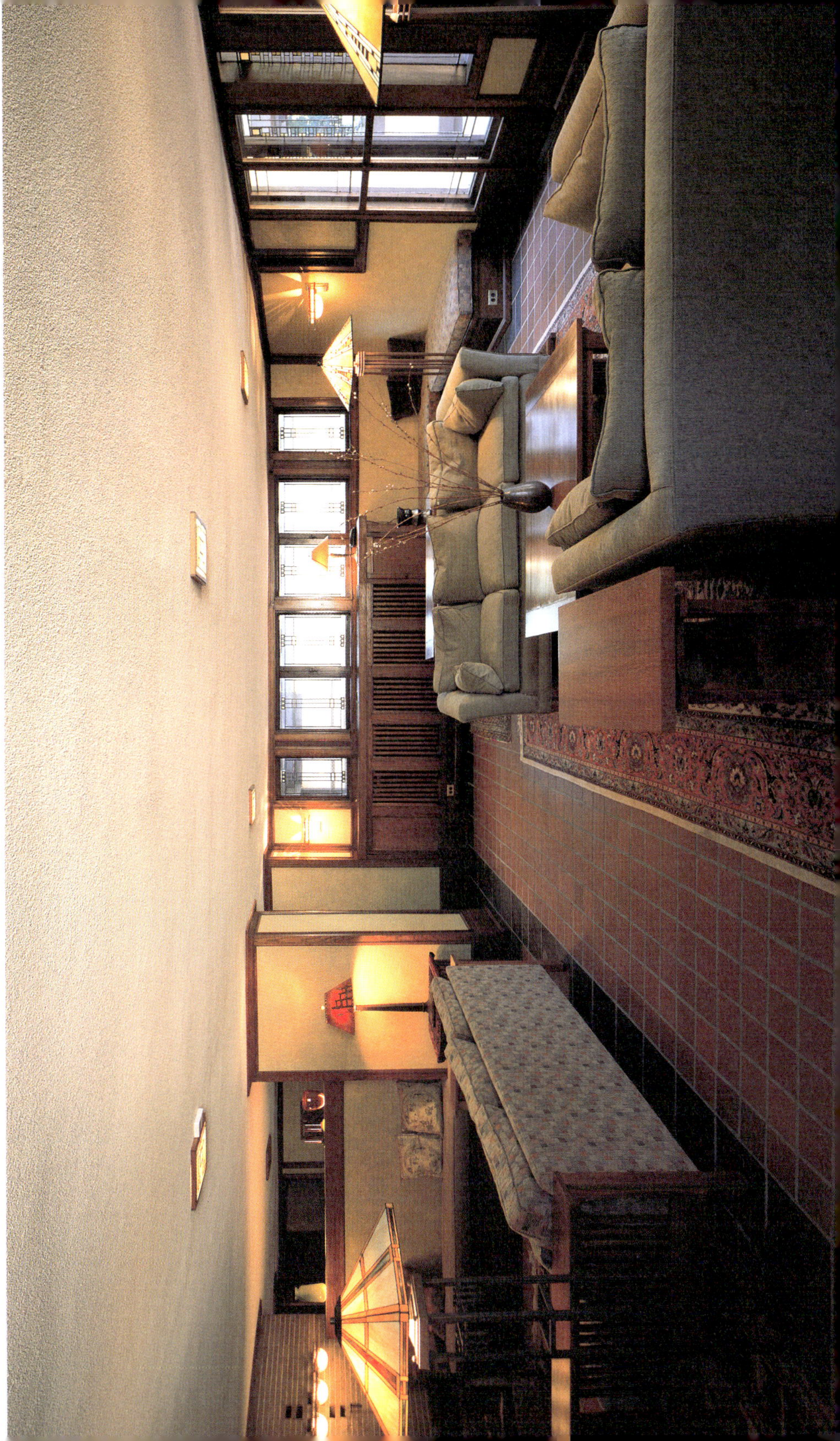

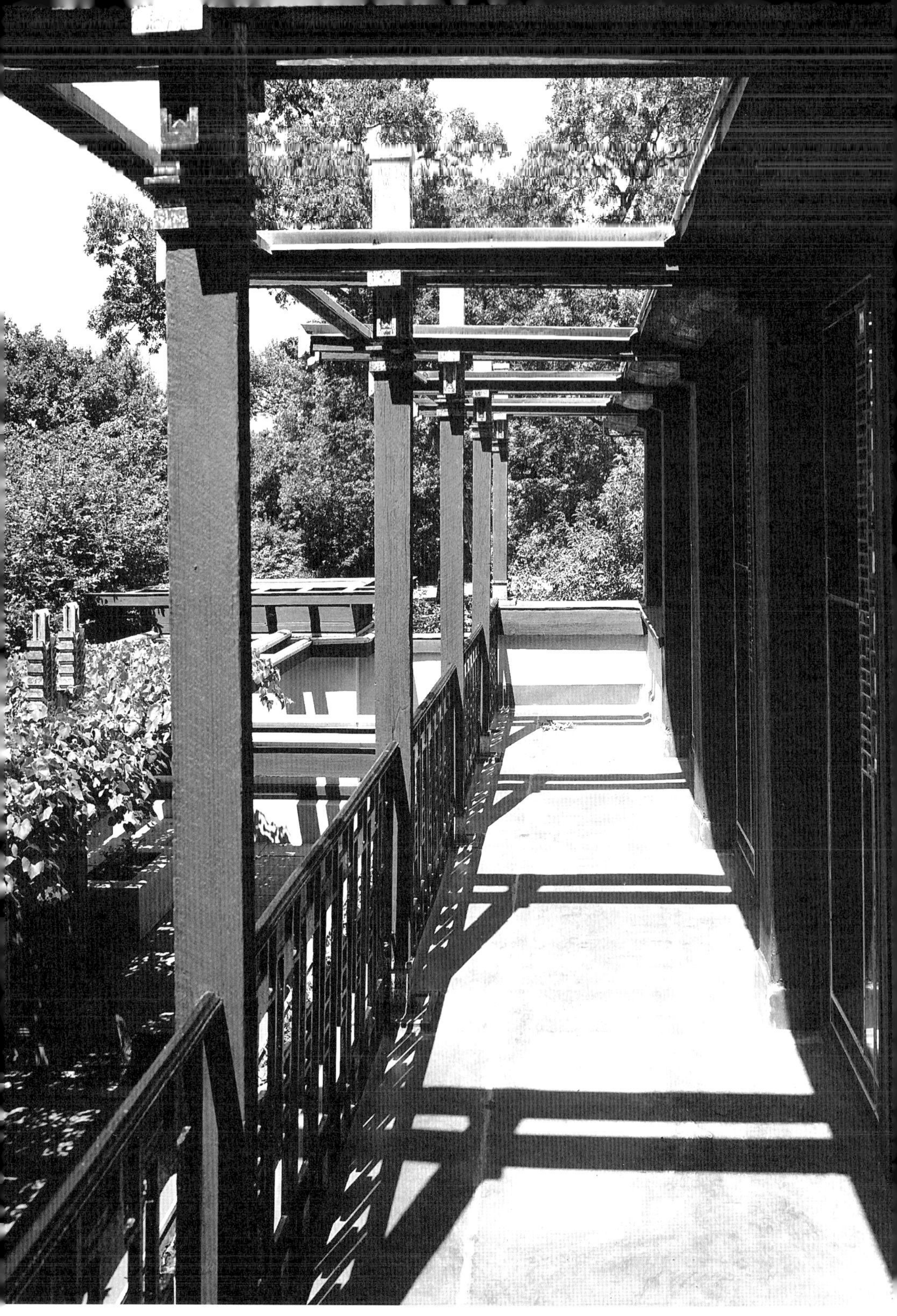

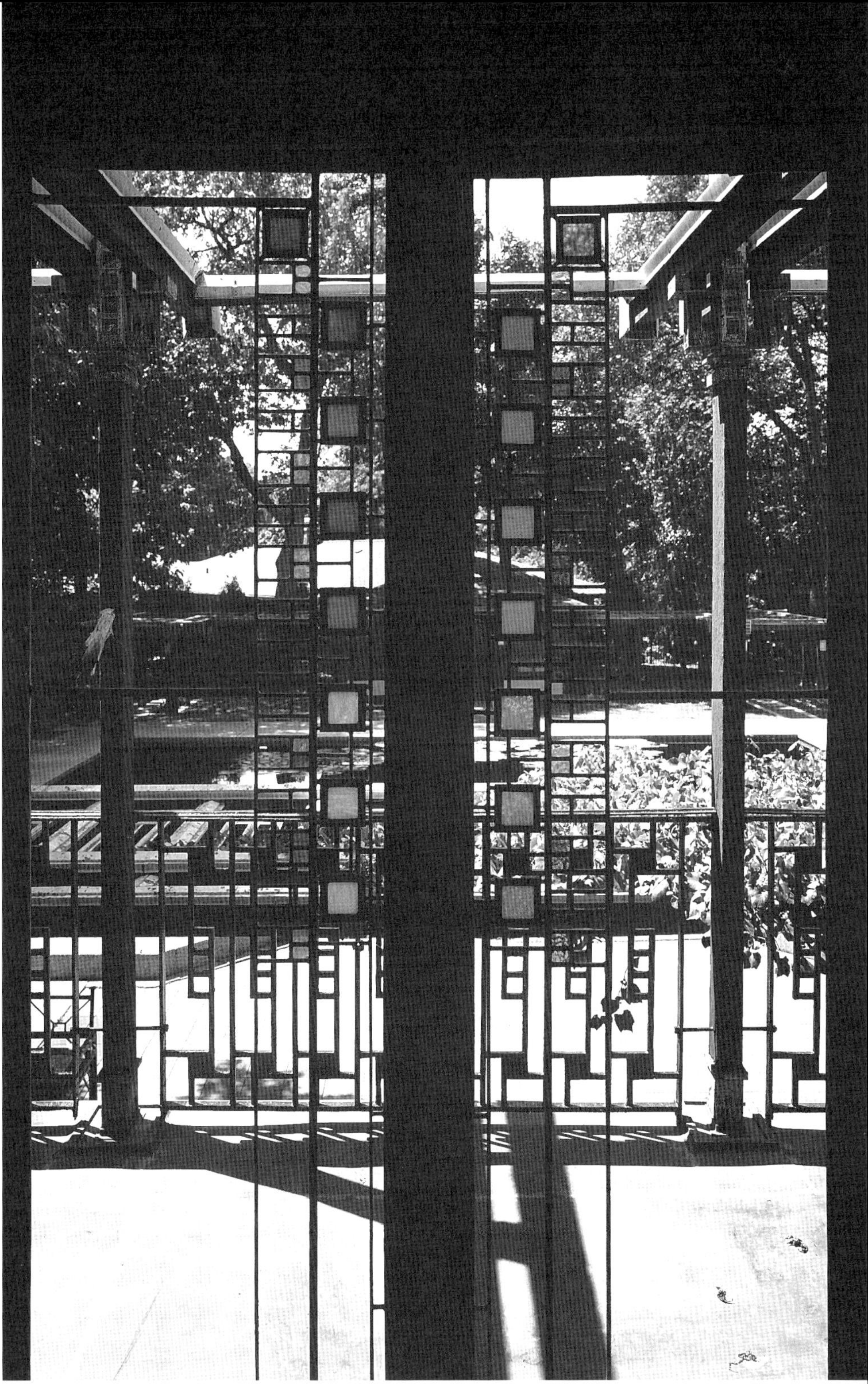

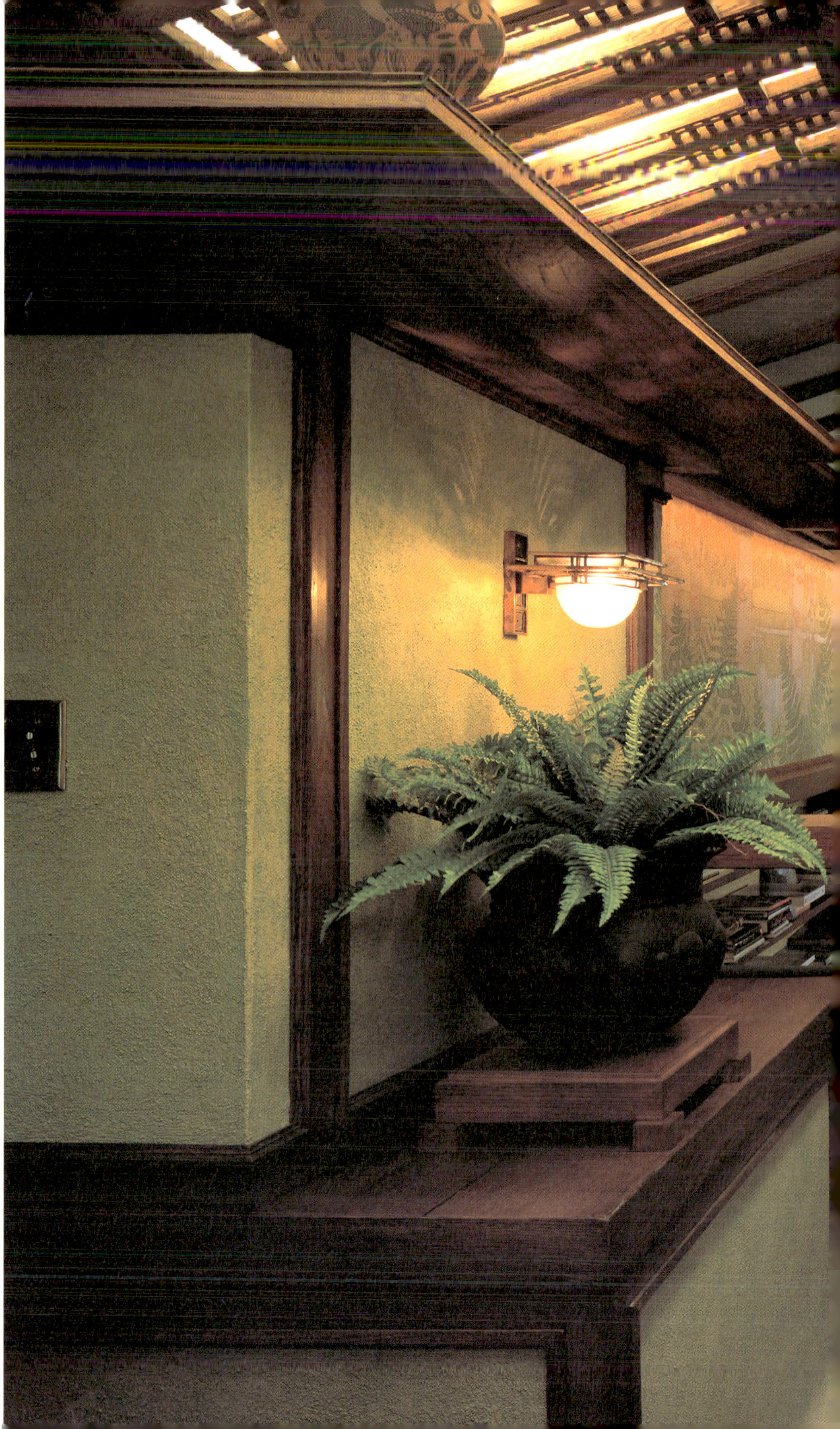

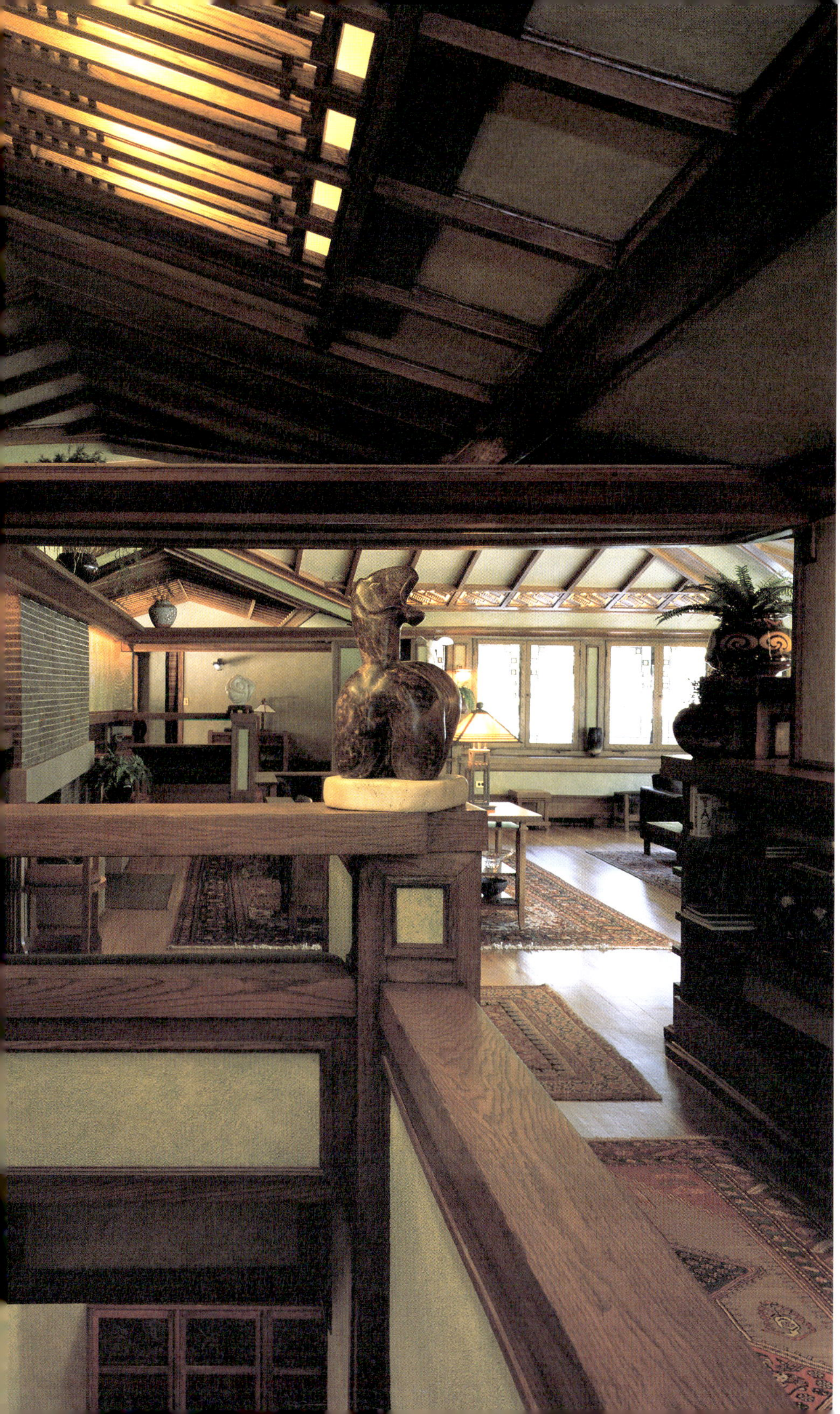

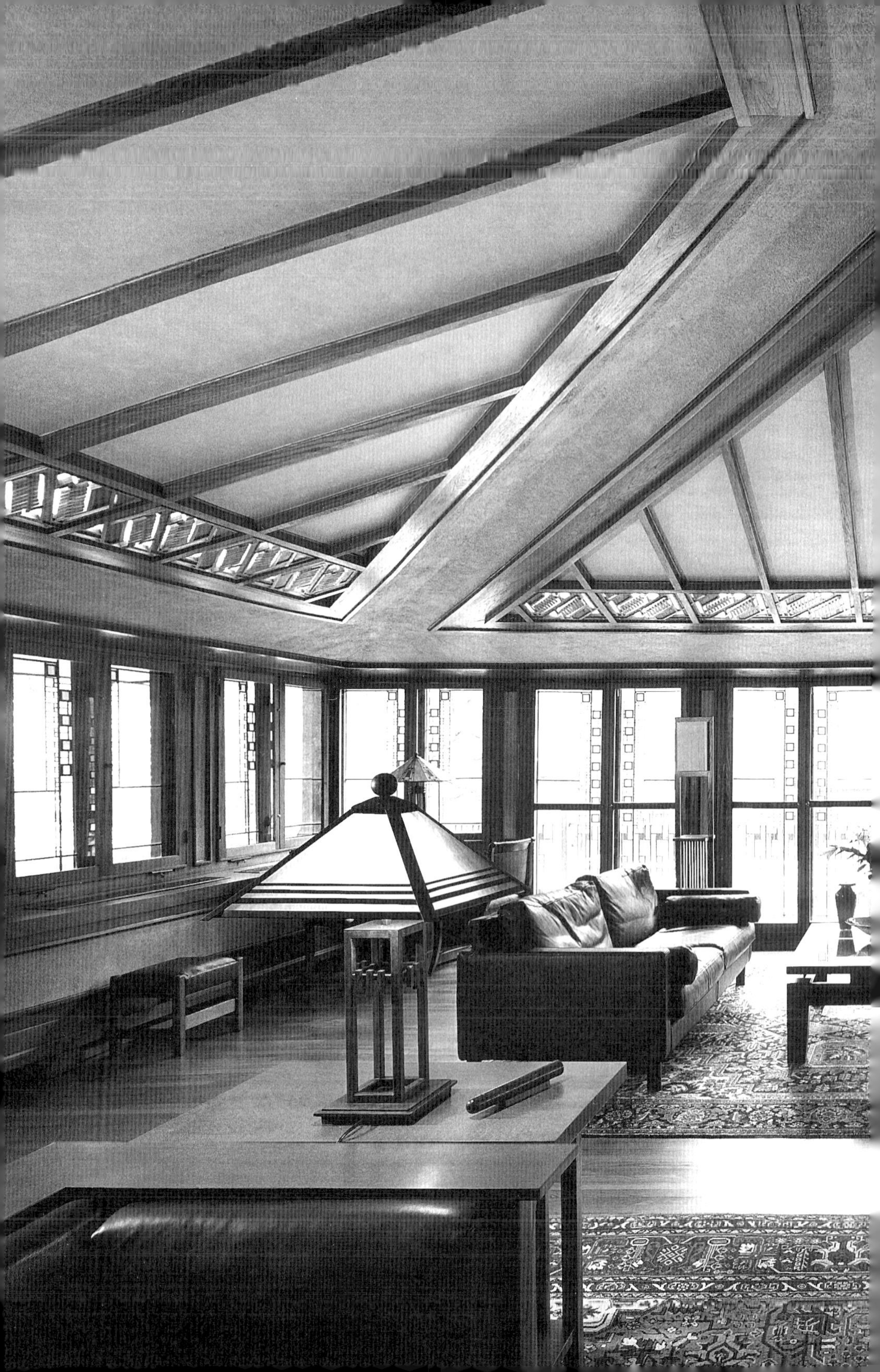

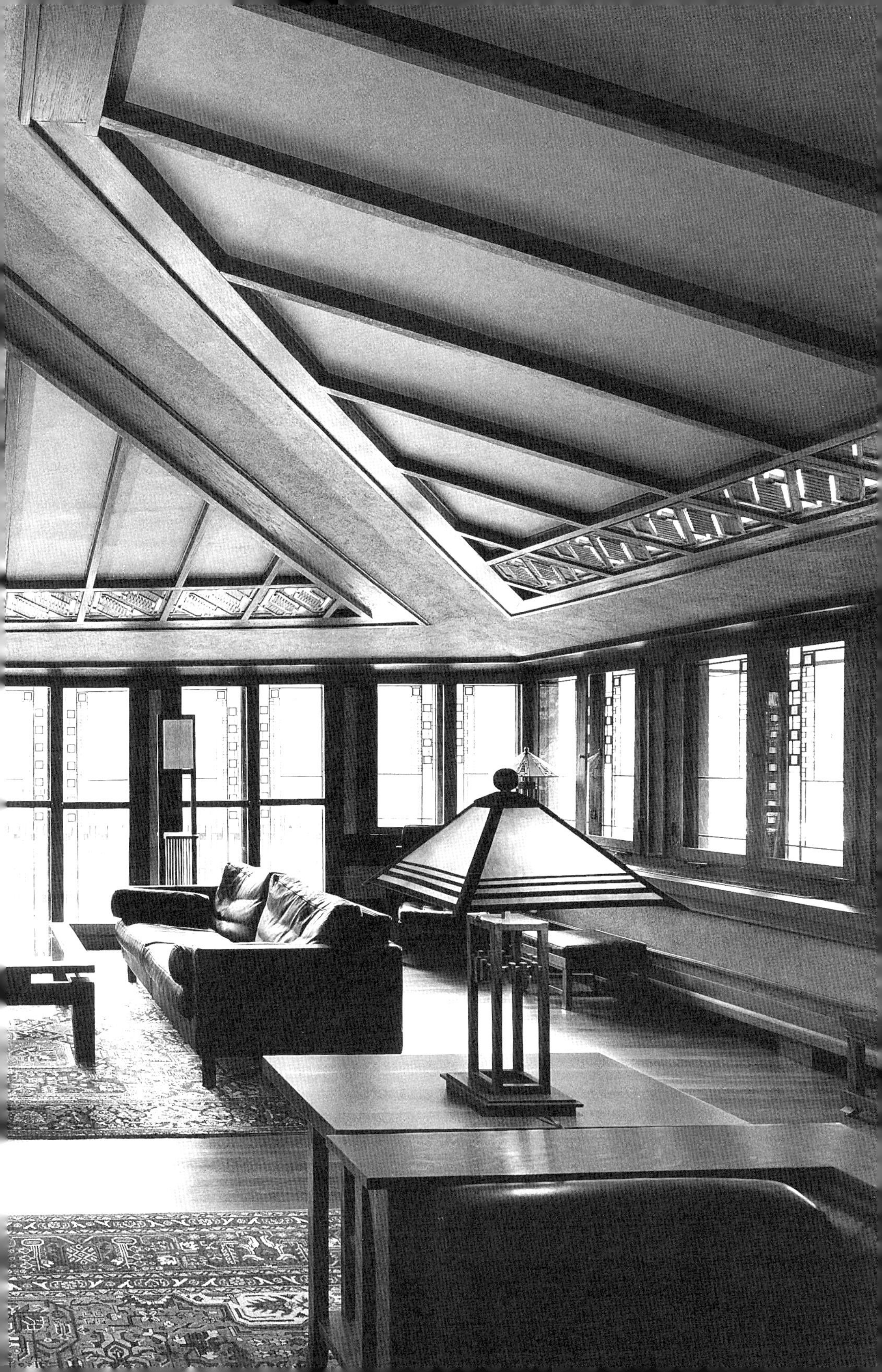

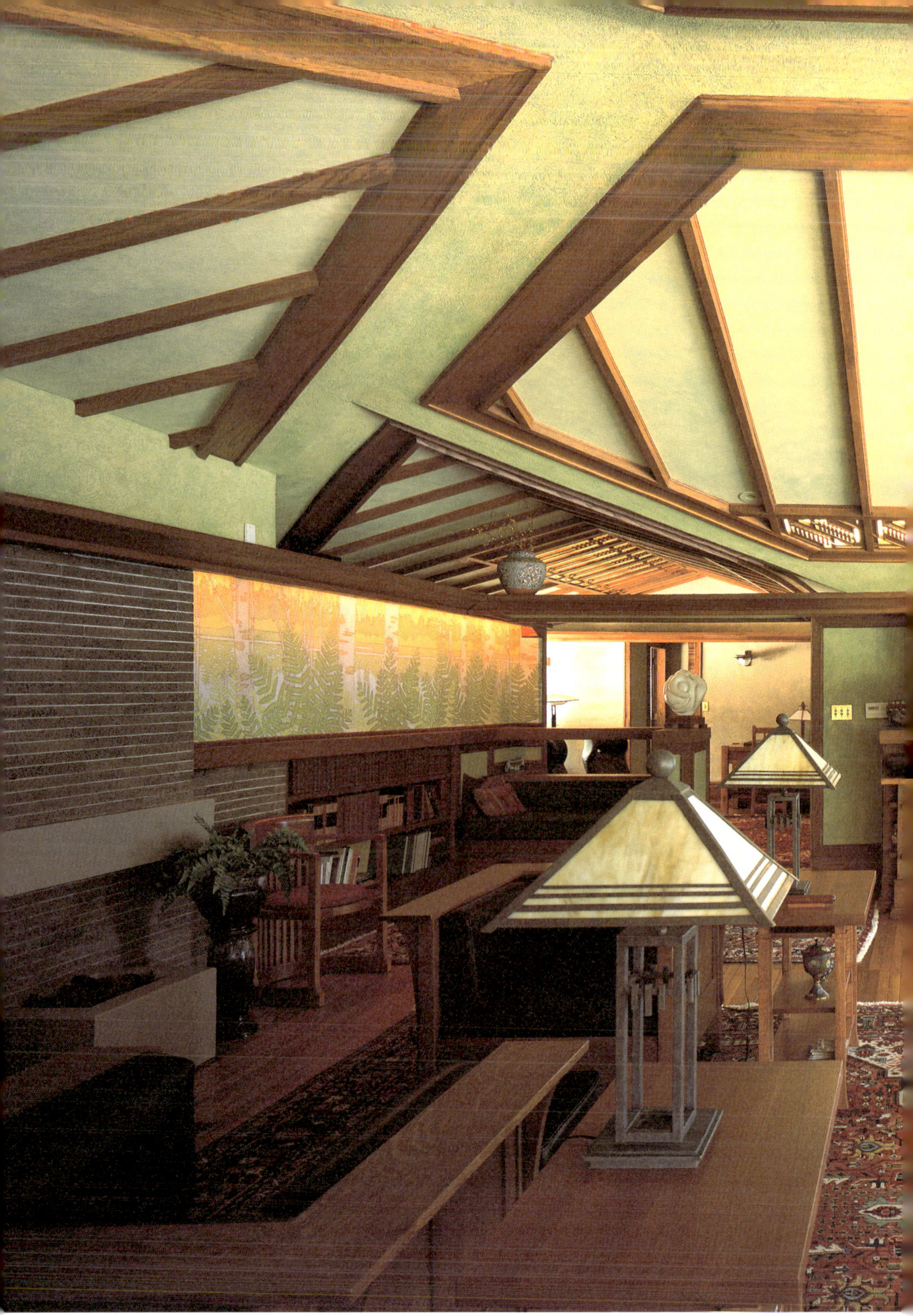

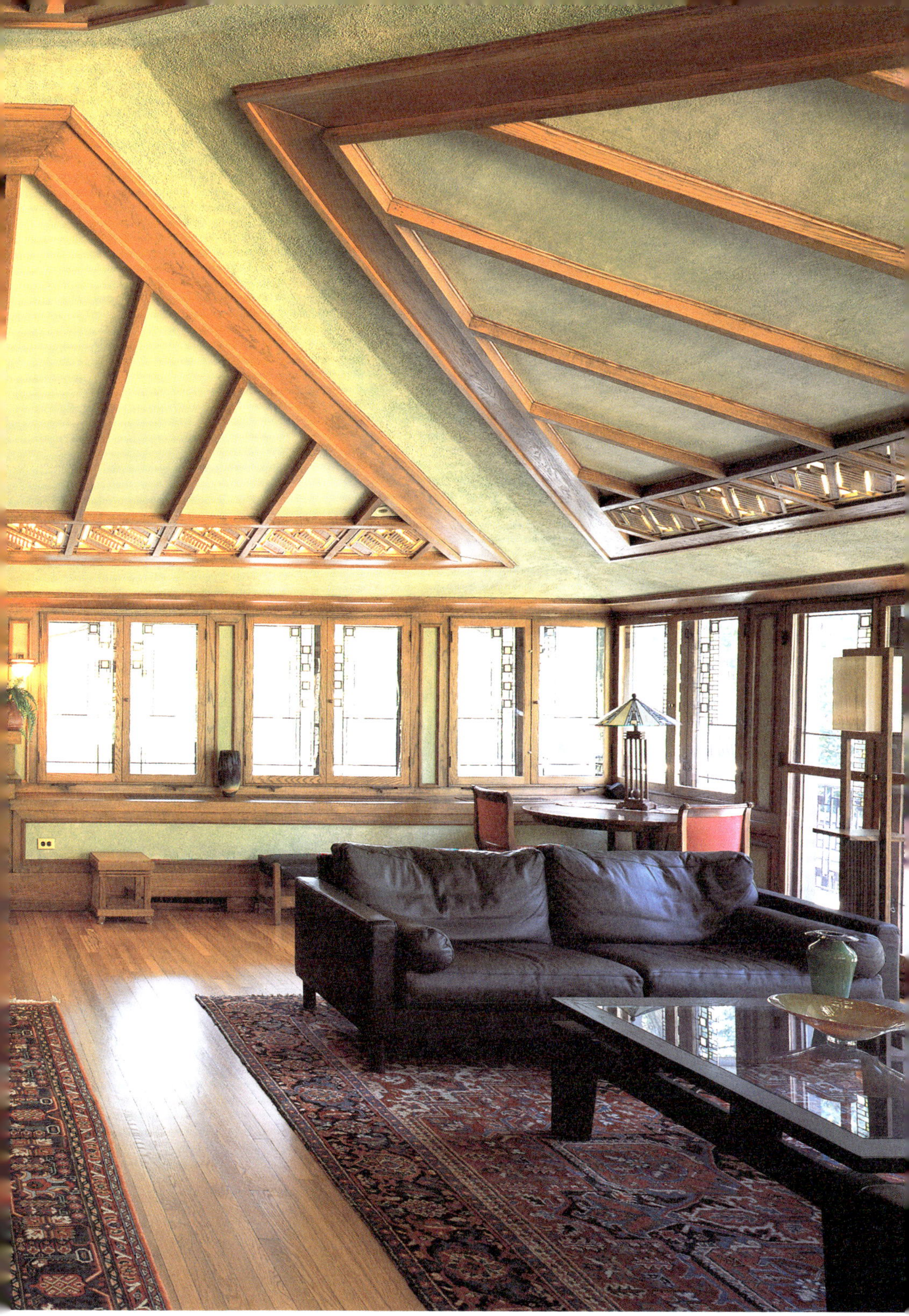

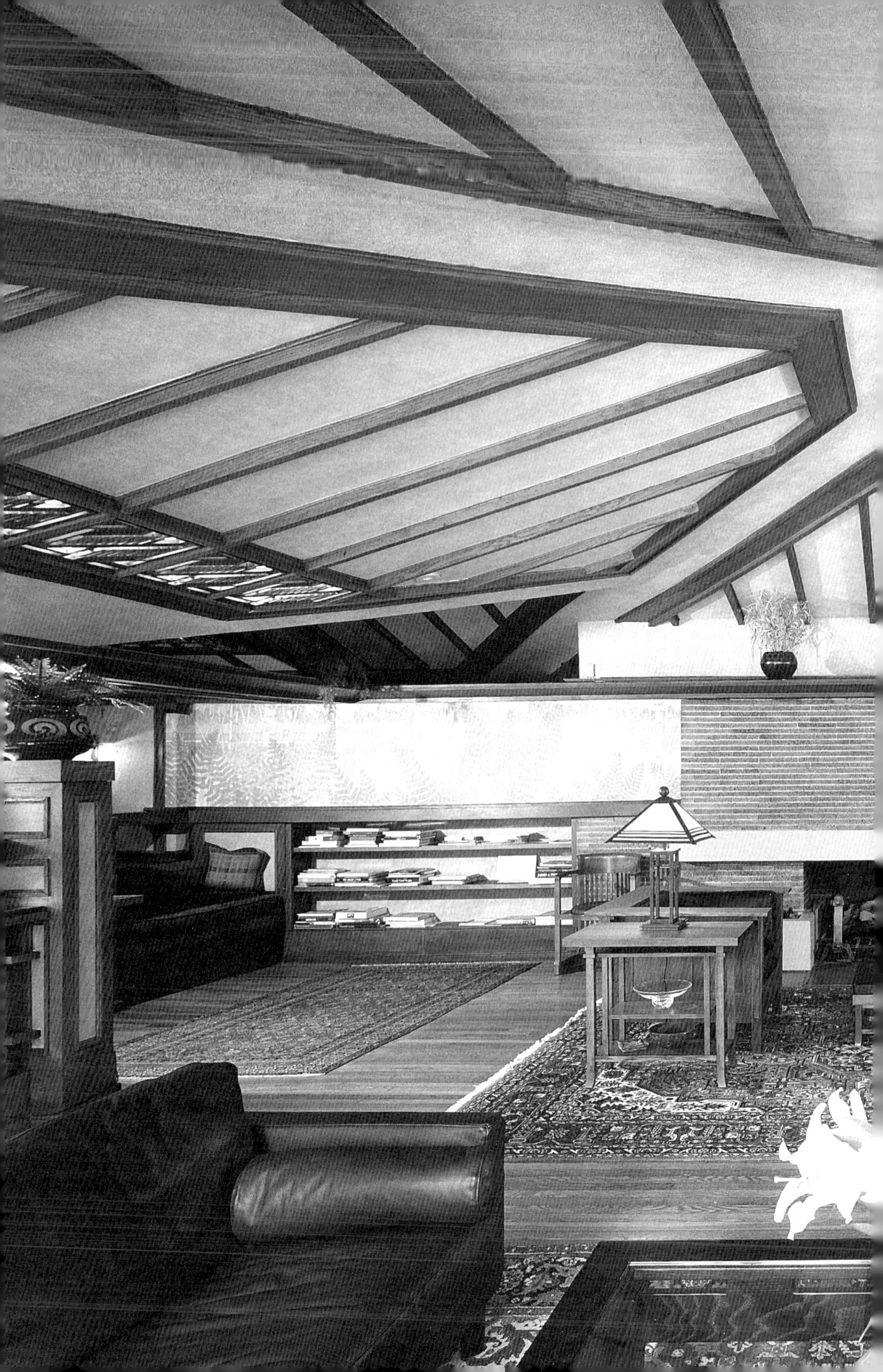

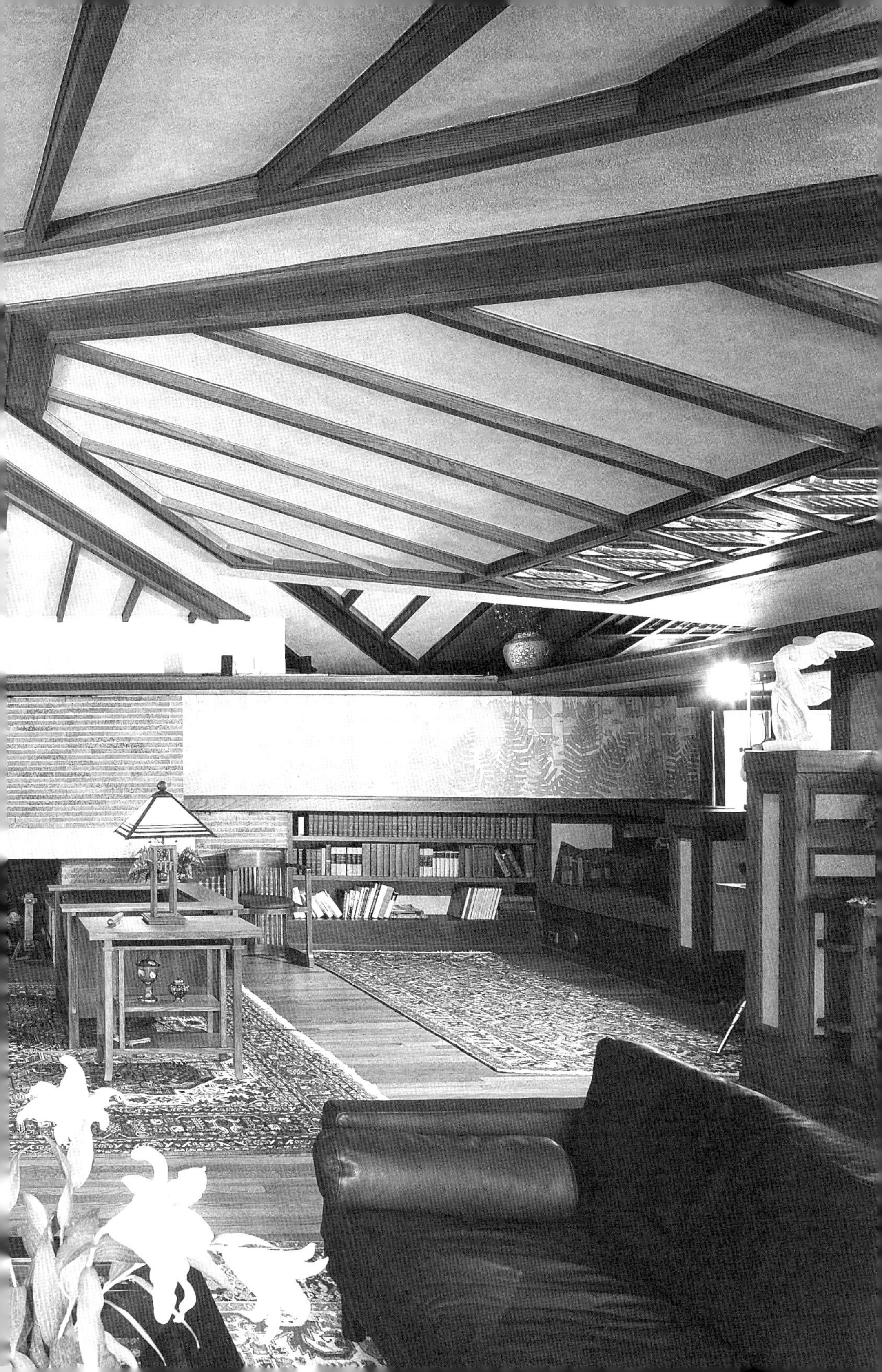

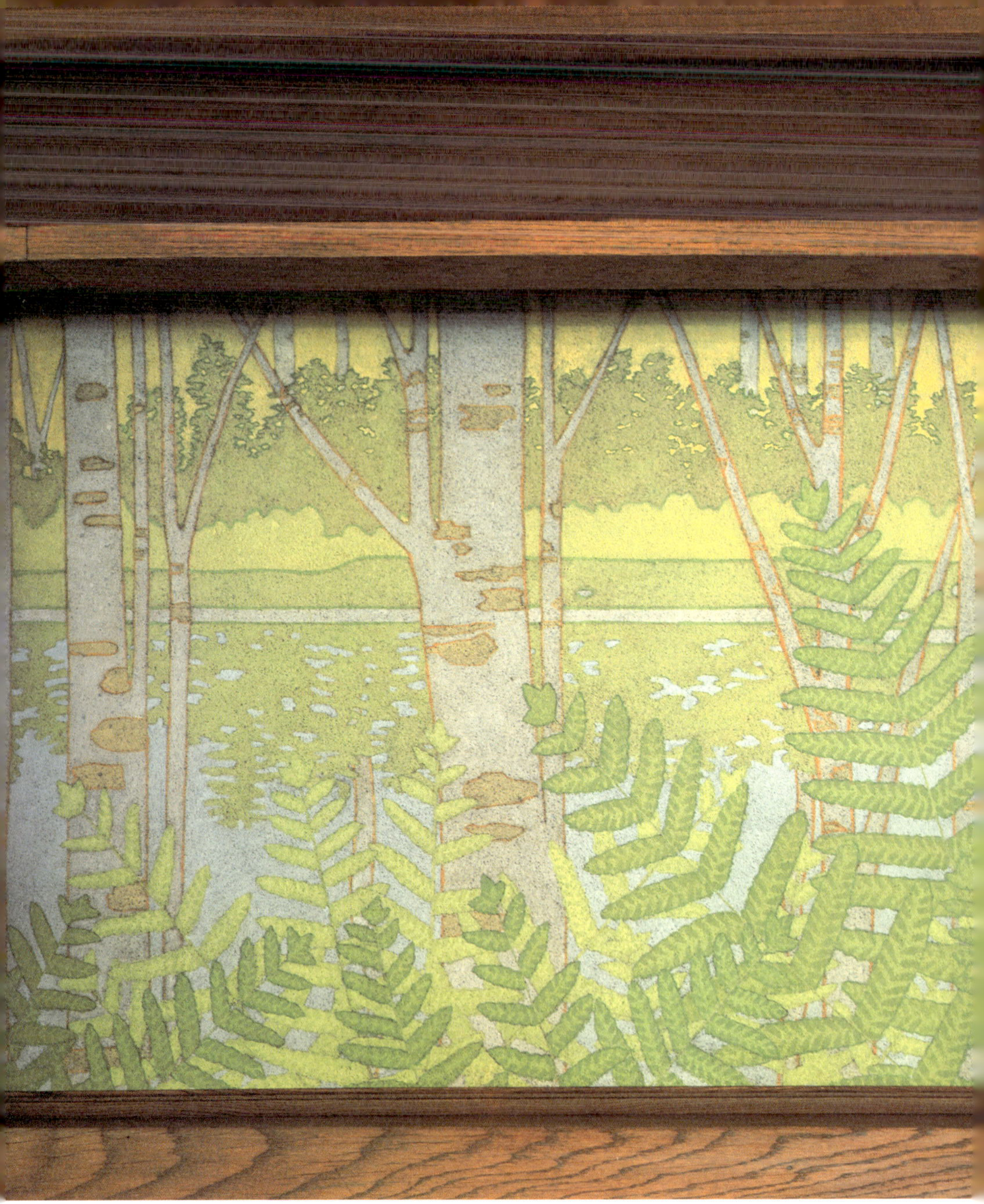

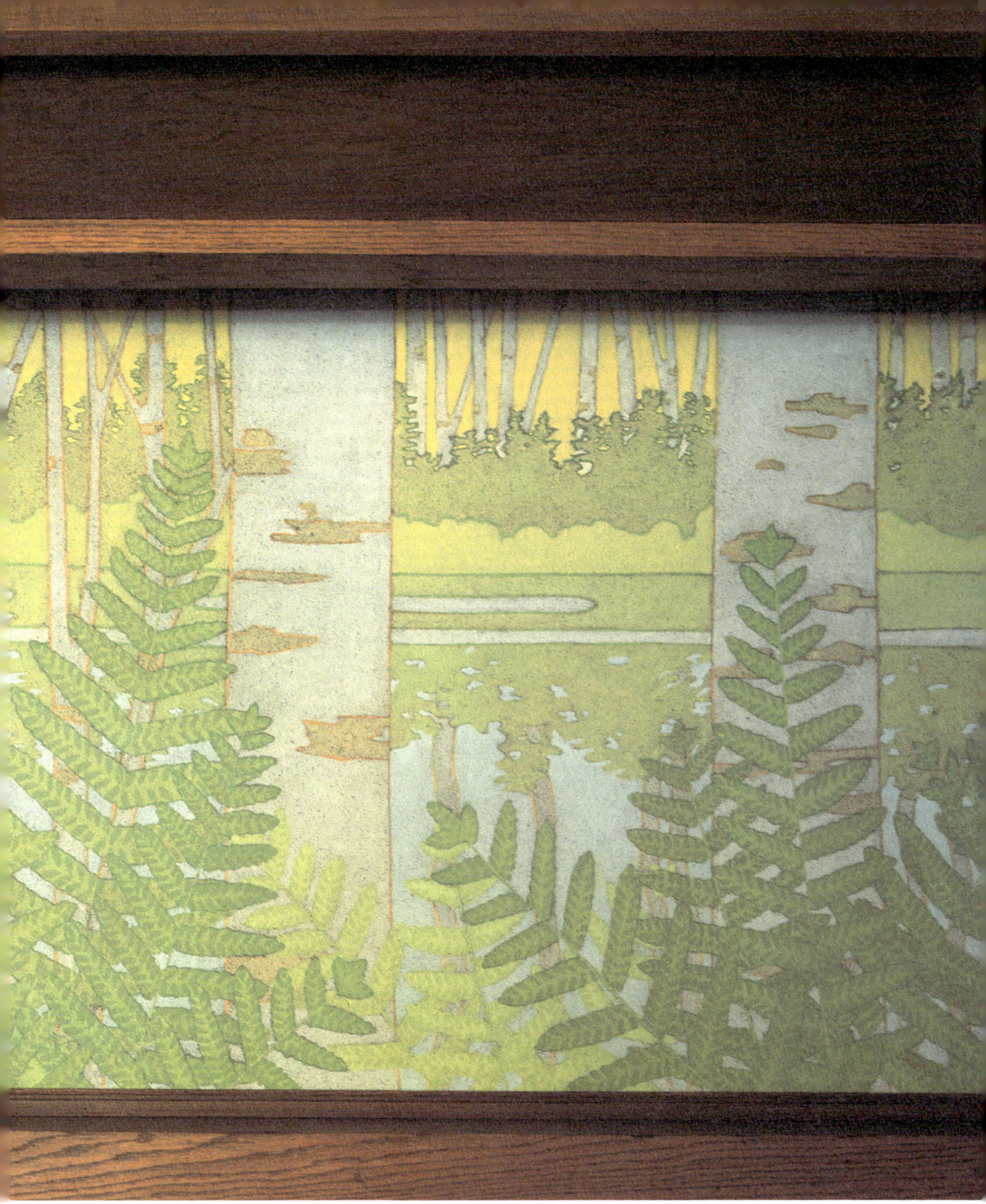

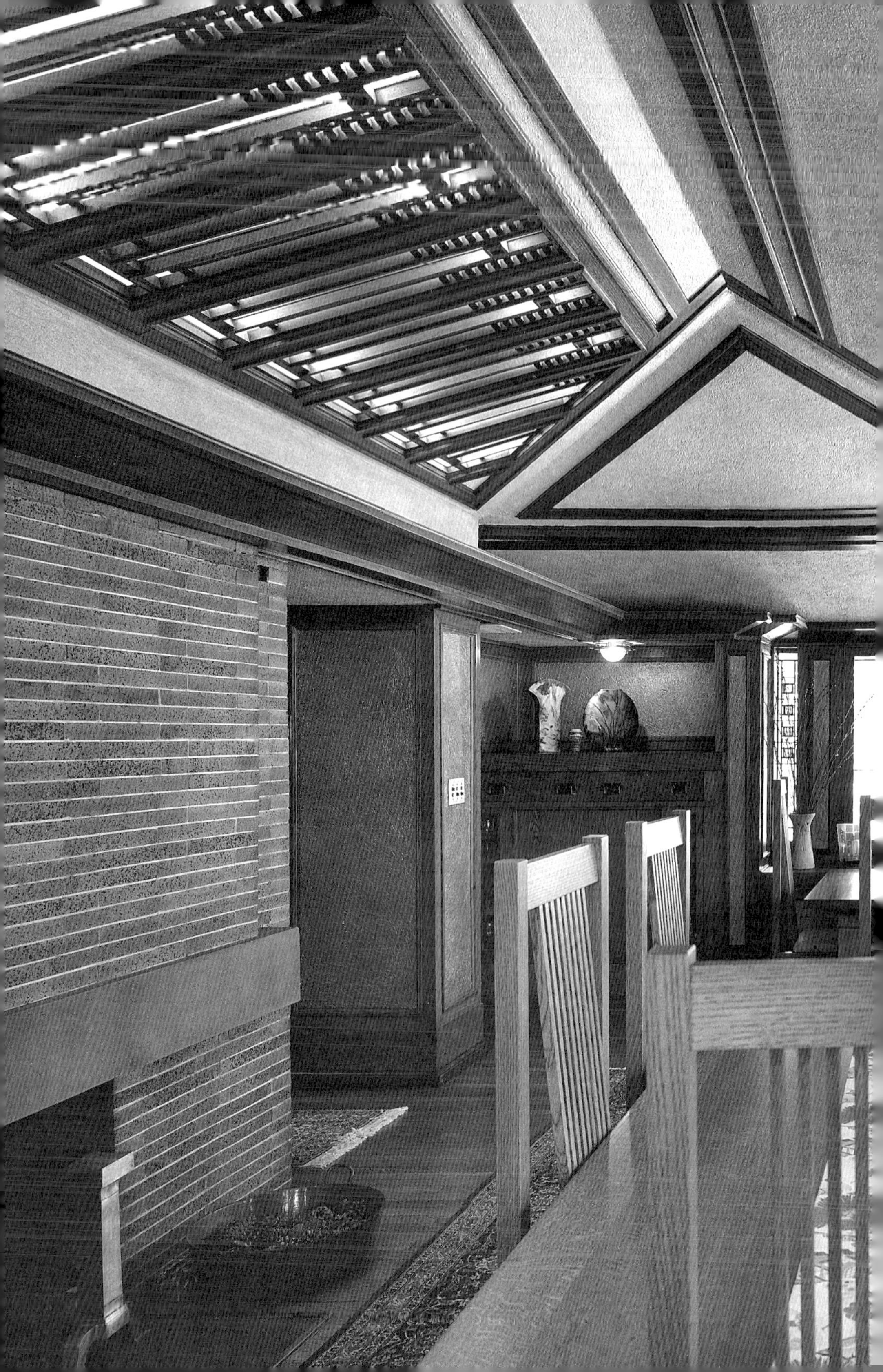

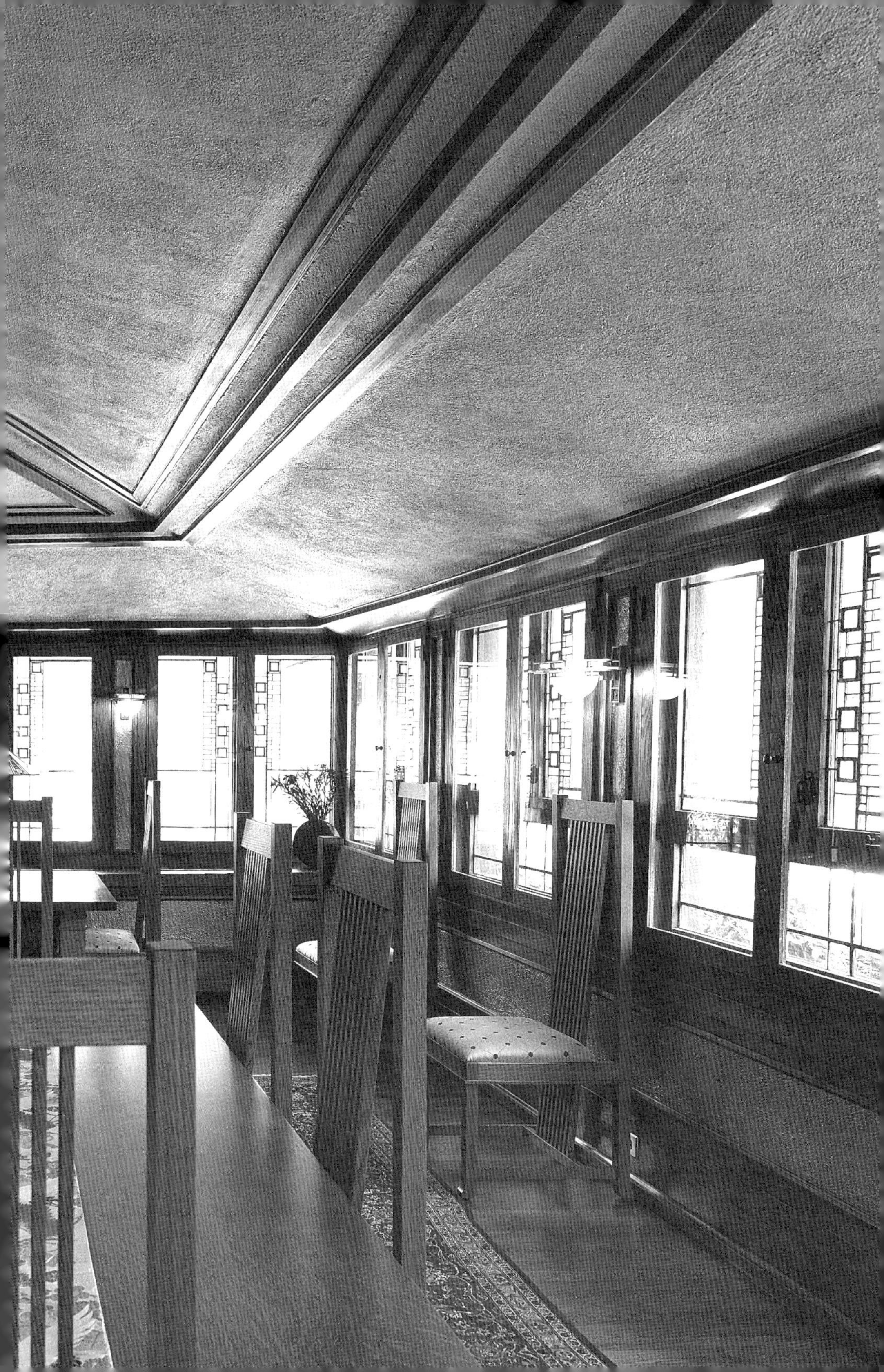

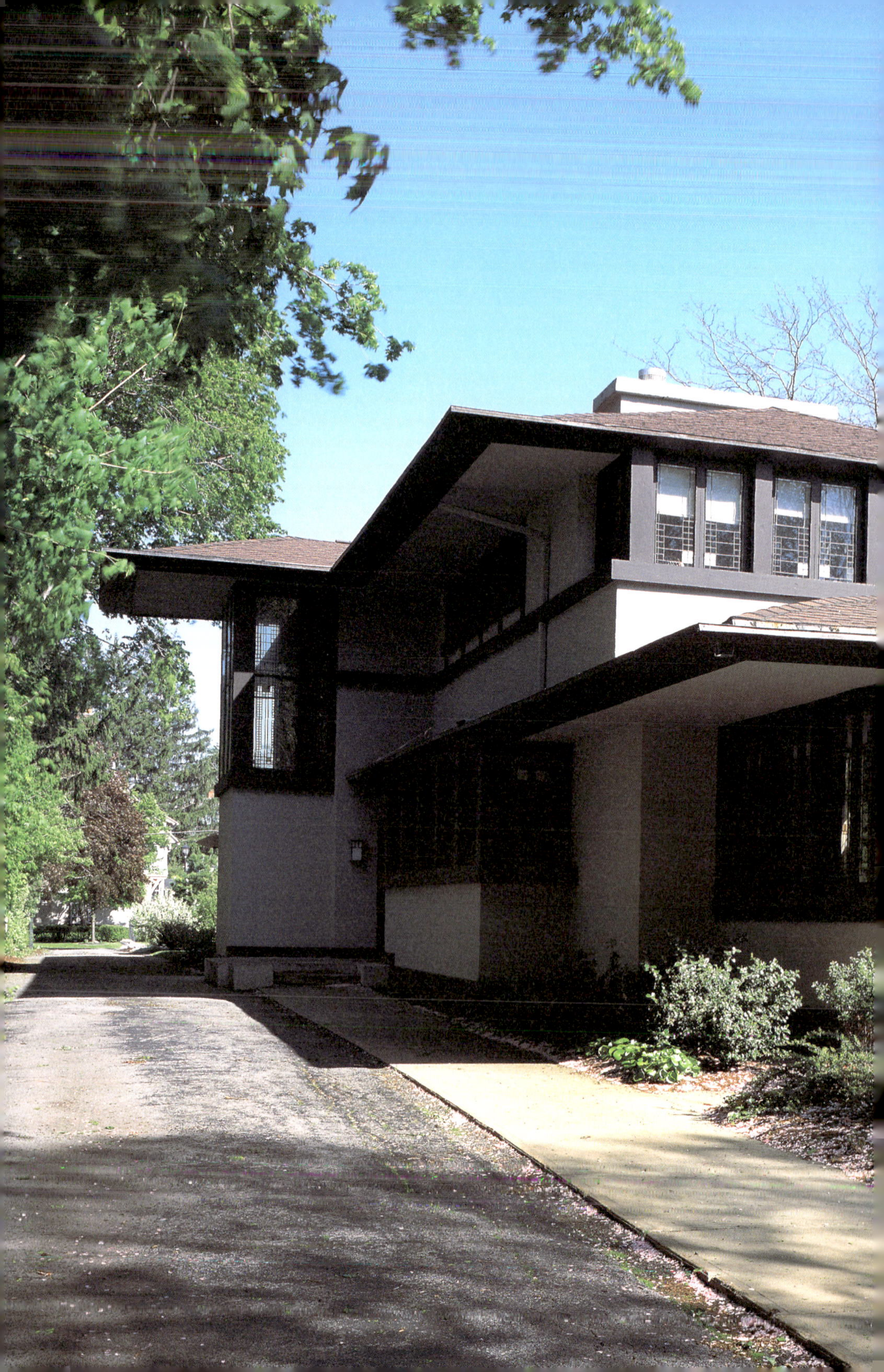

E. E. Boynton House
Rochester, New York, 1907

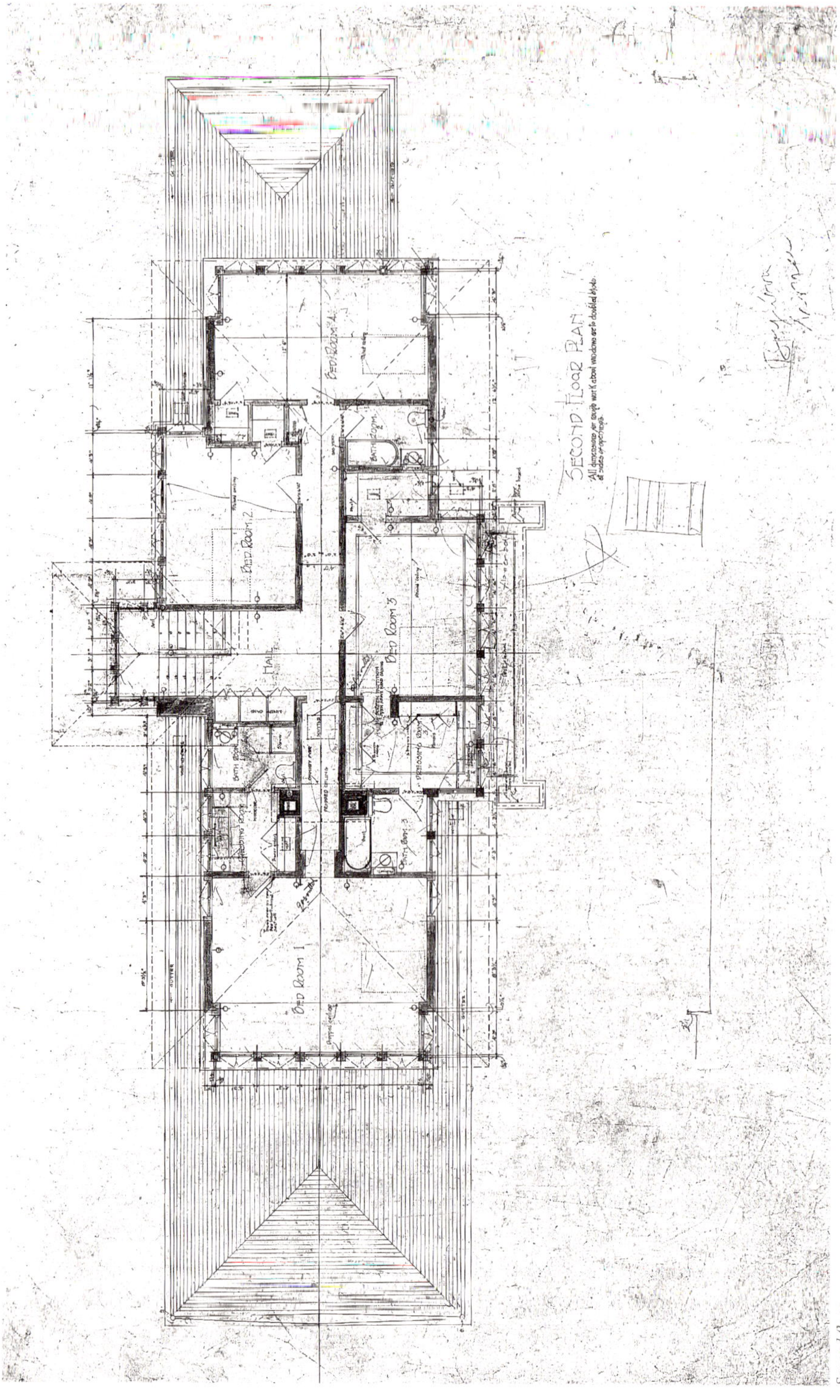

Second floor

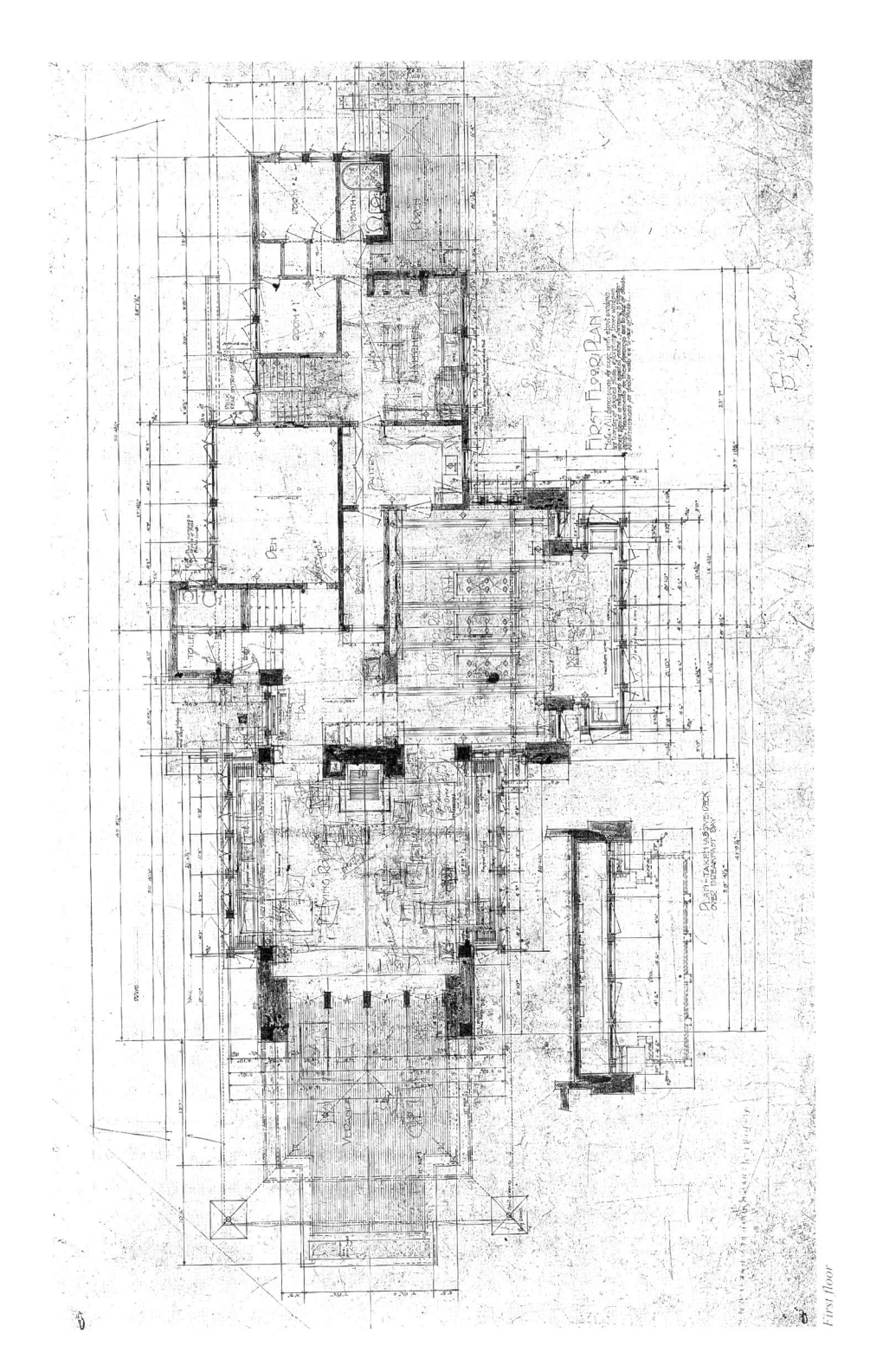

First floor

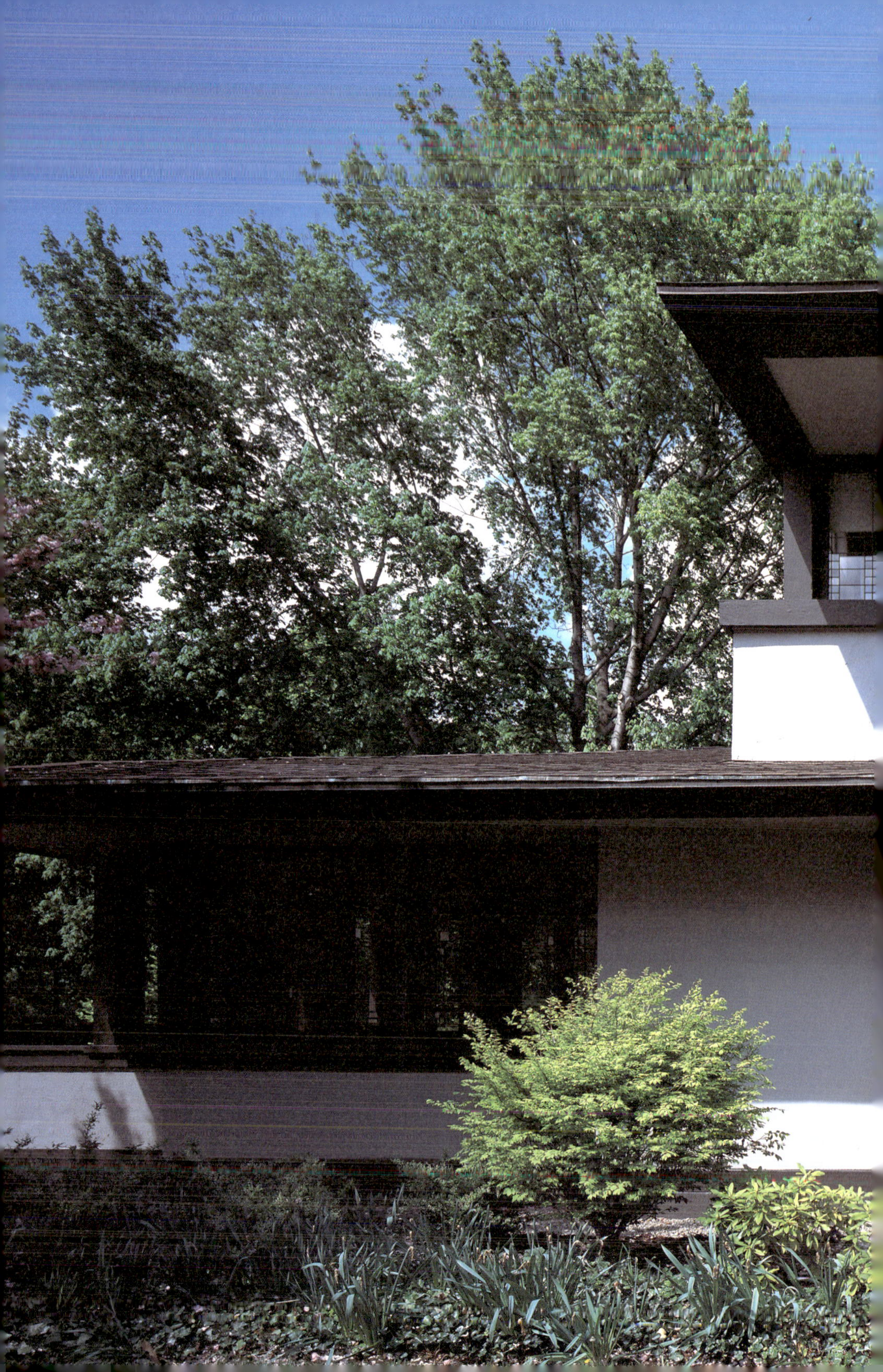

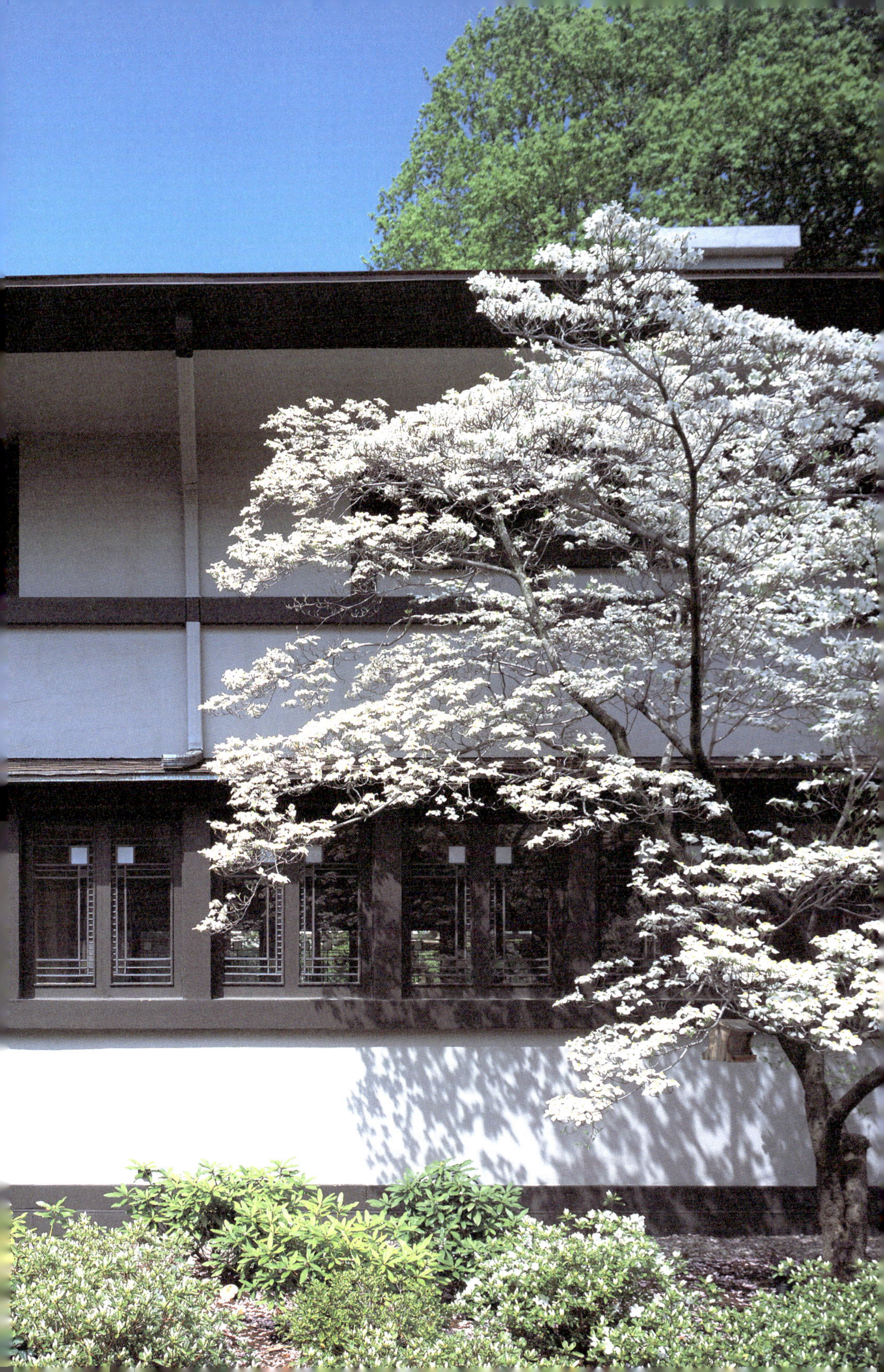

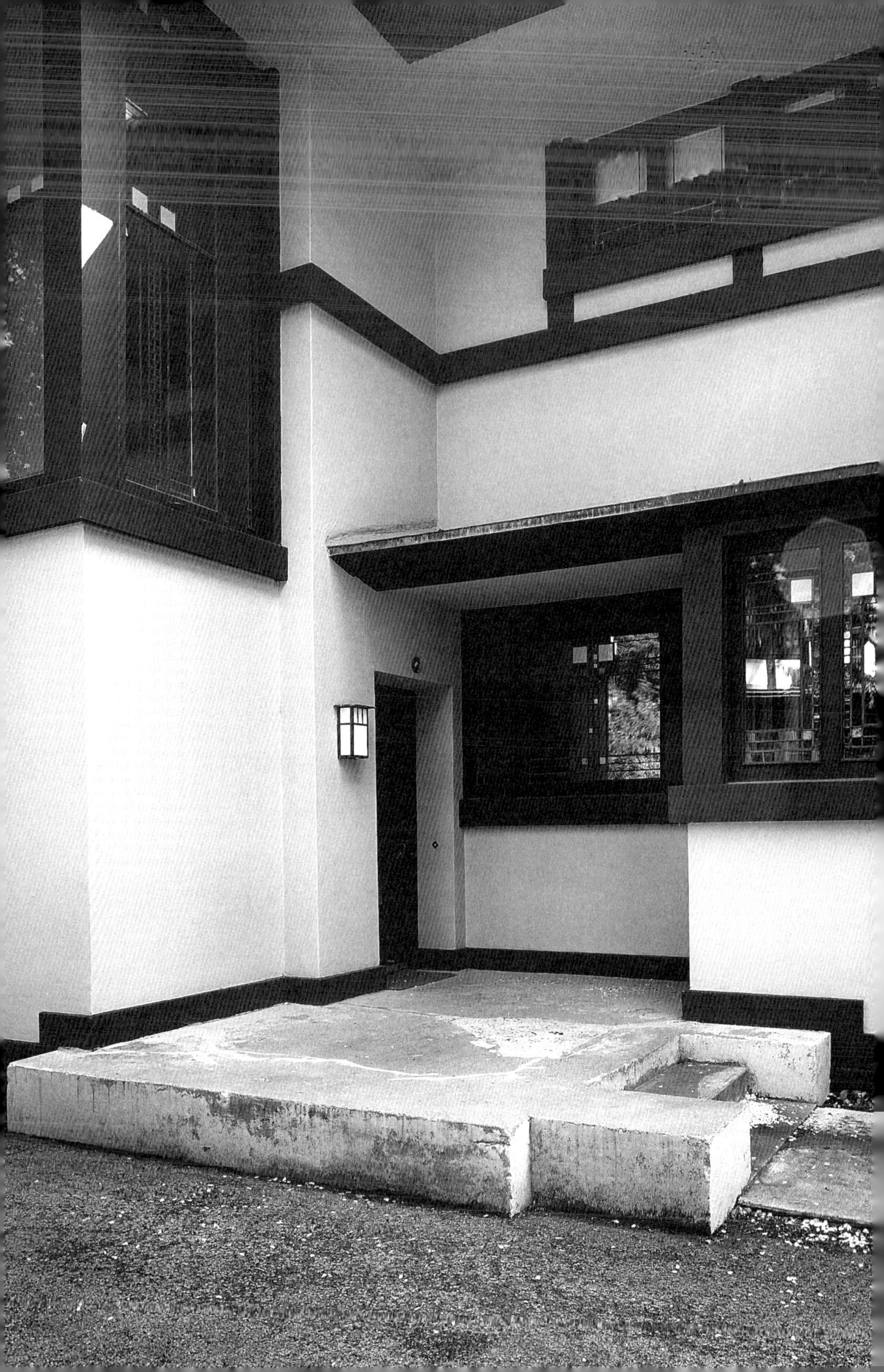

Elevations

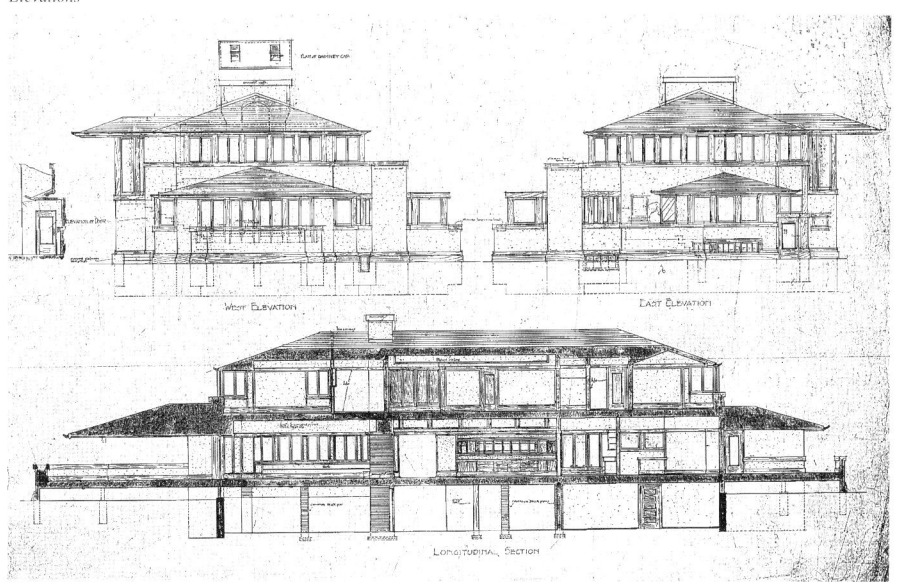

Elevations

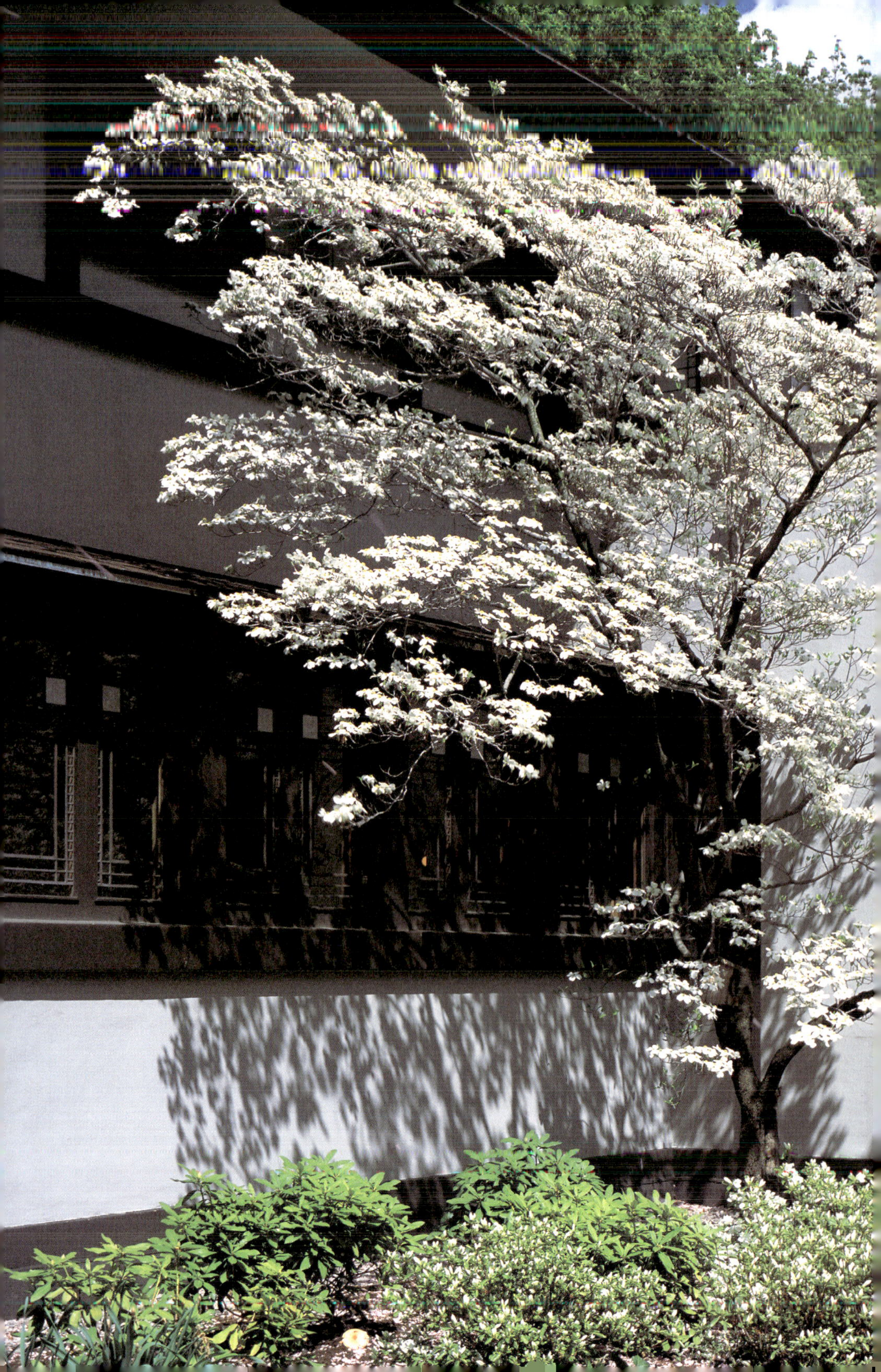

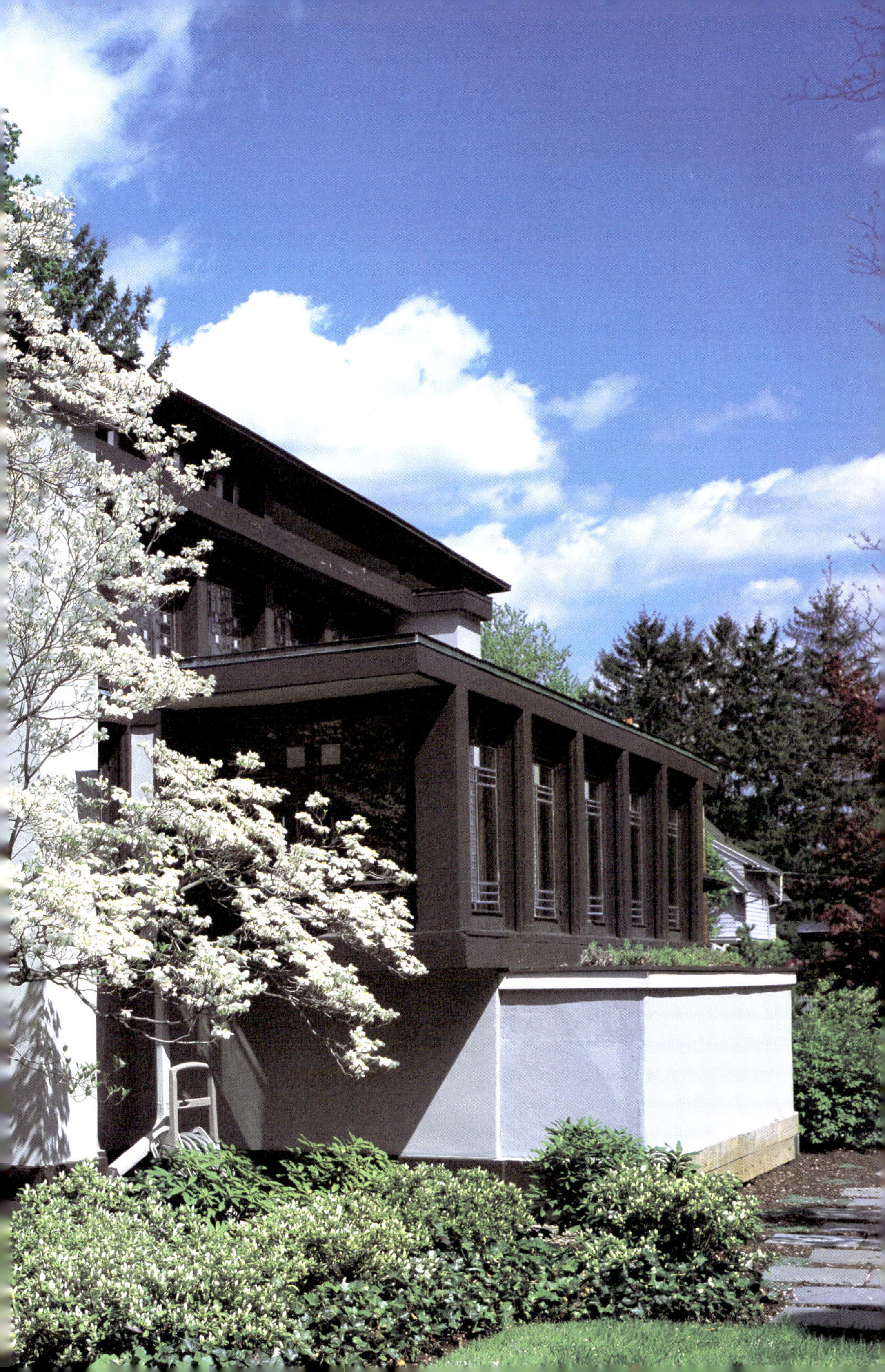

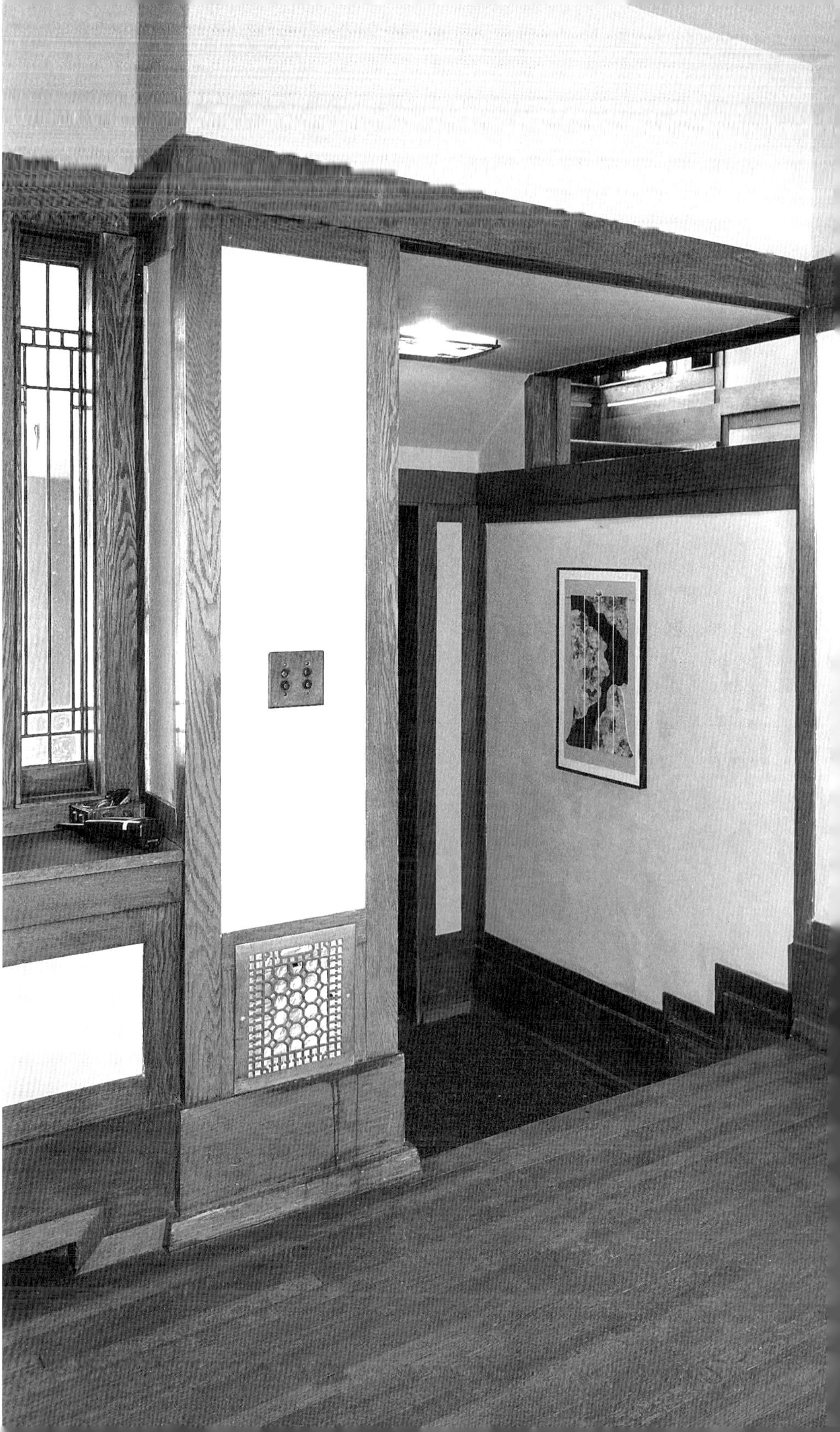

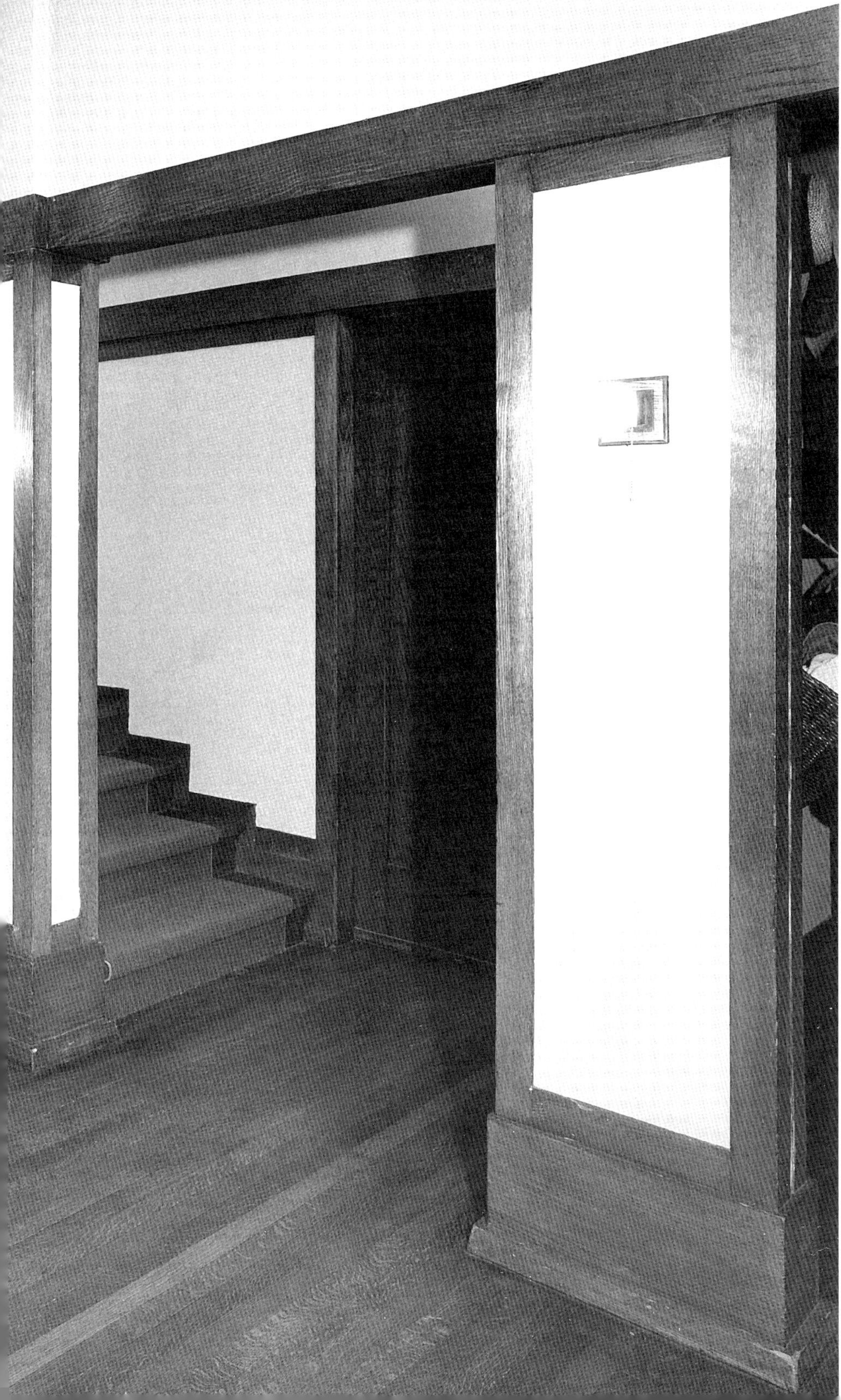

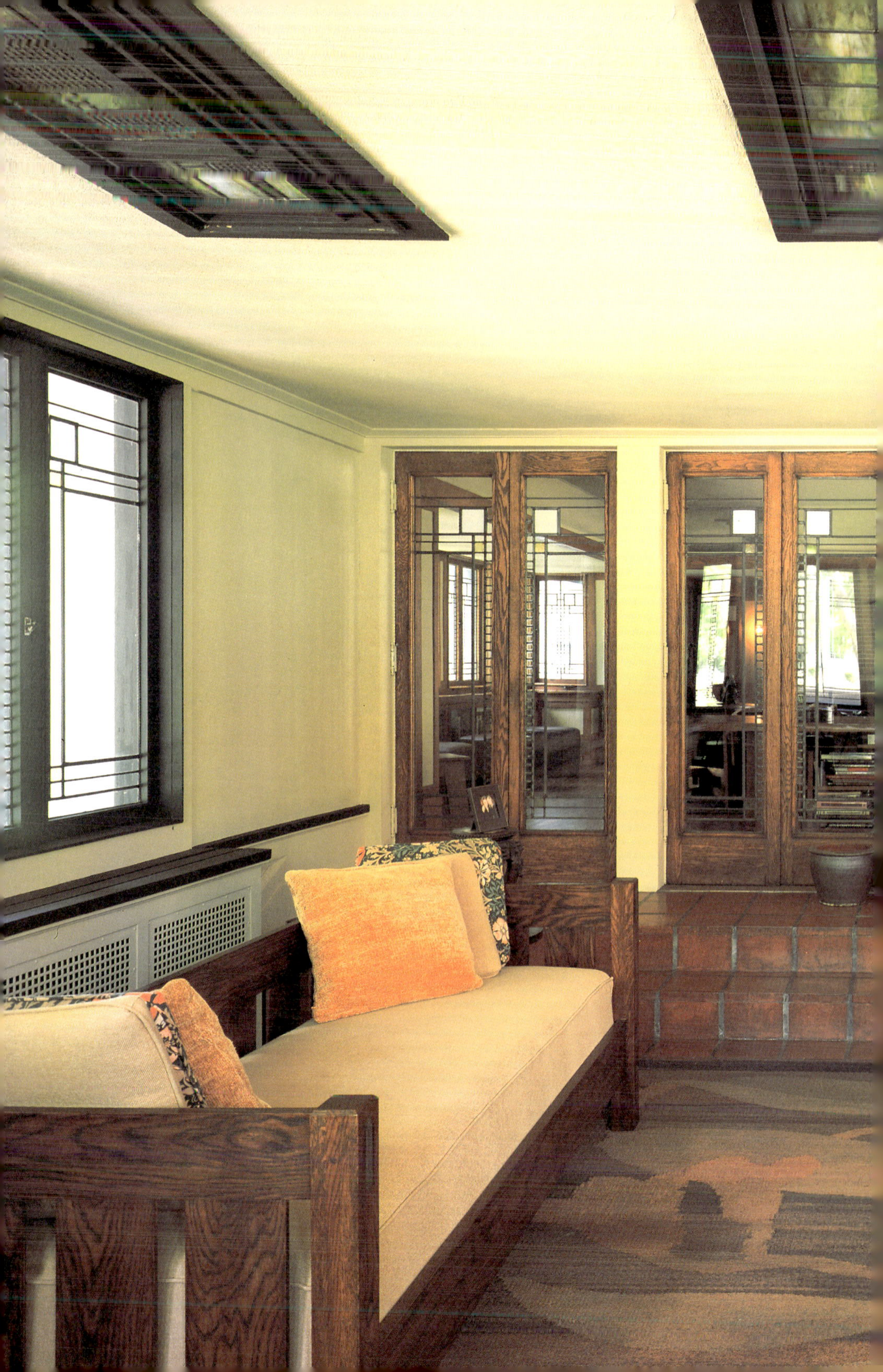

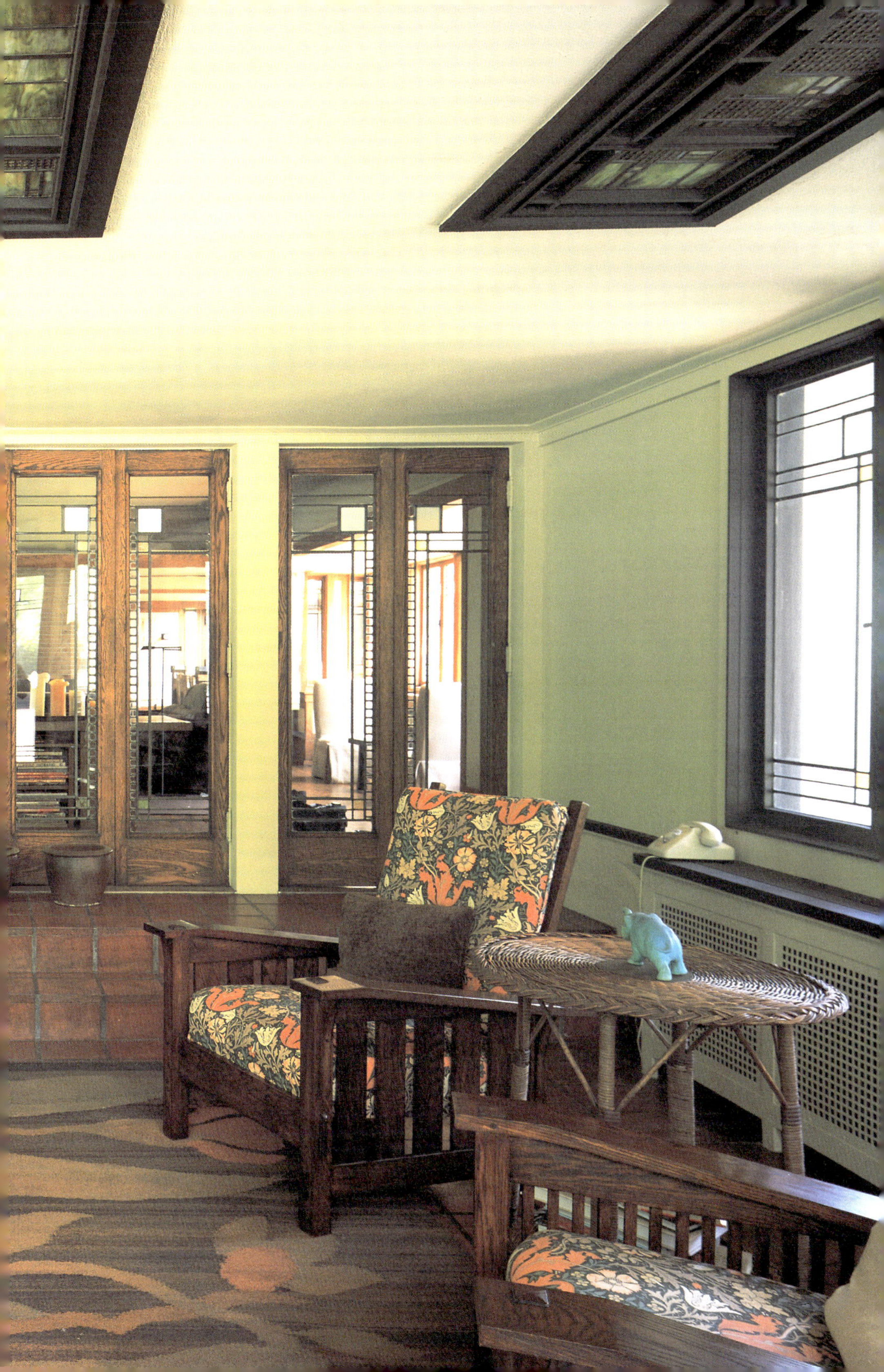

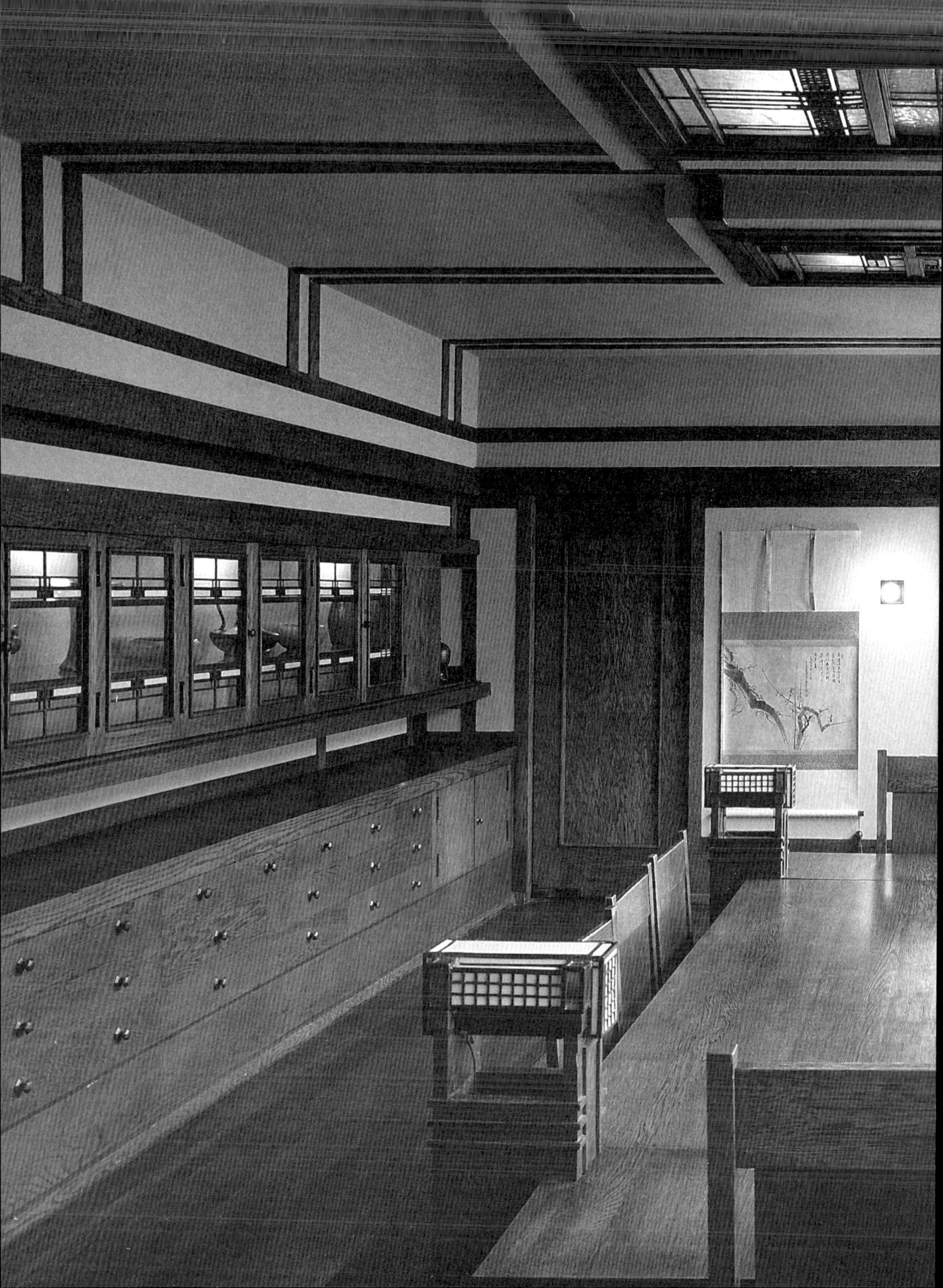

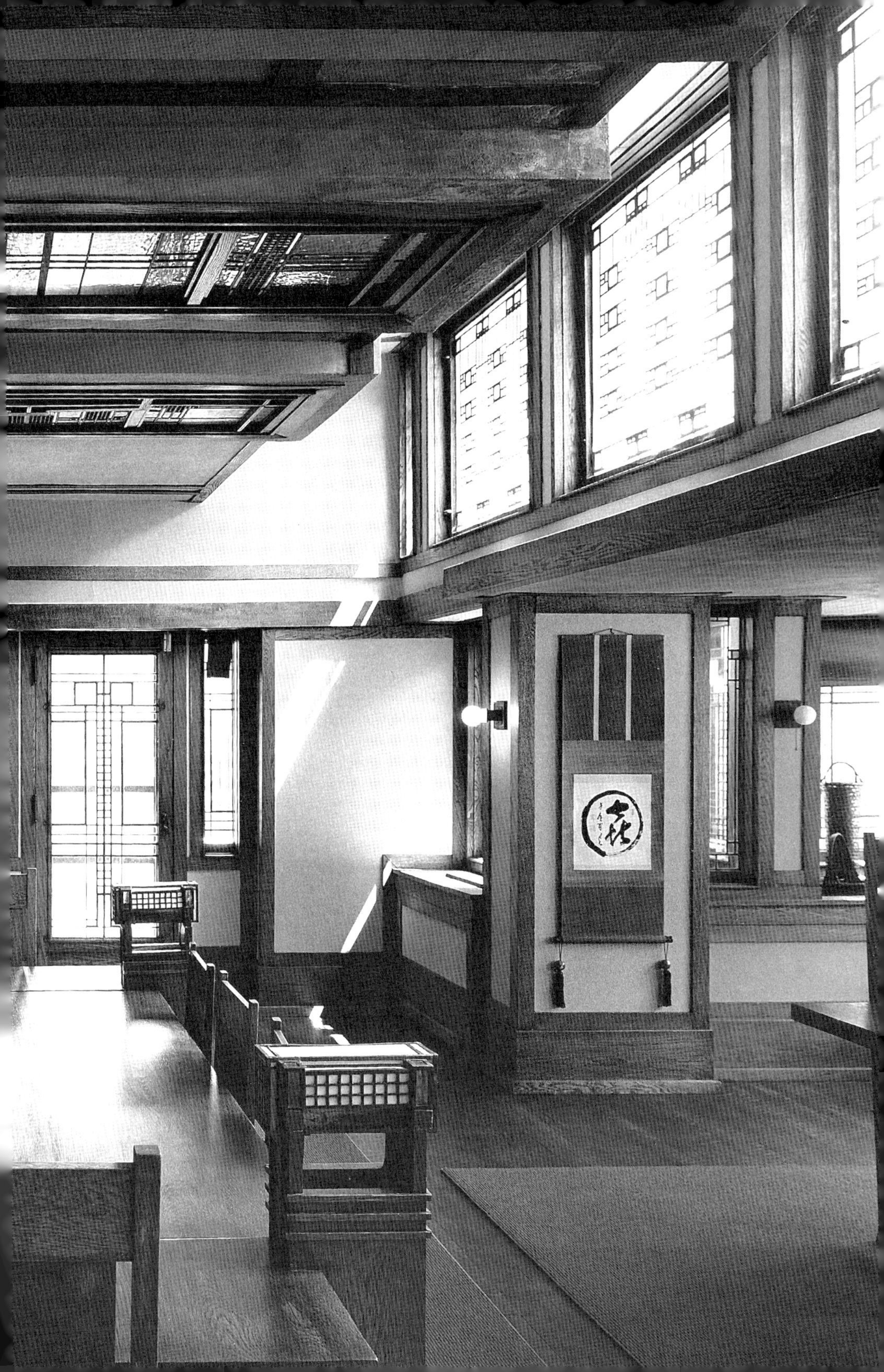

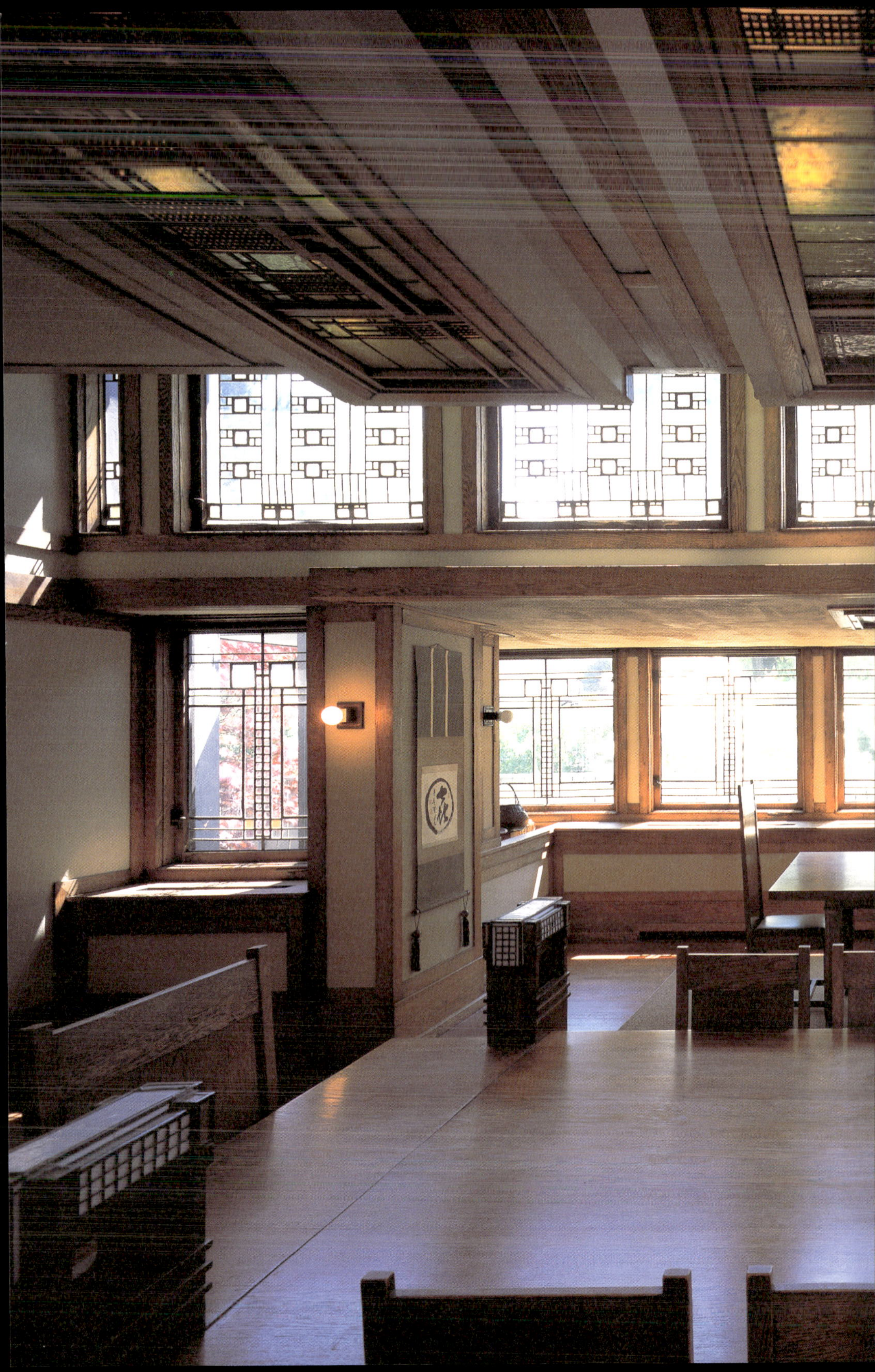

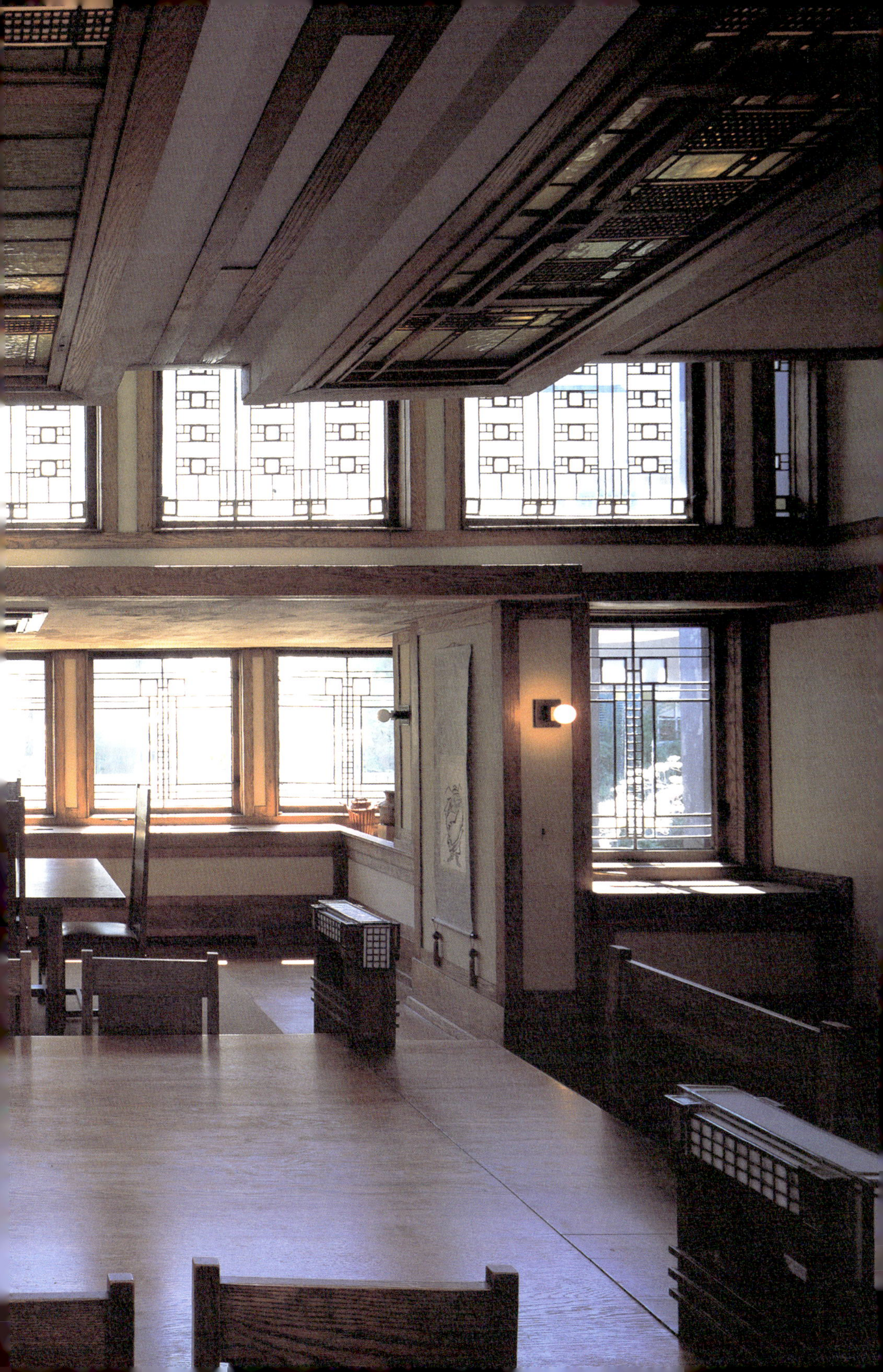

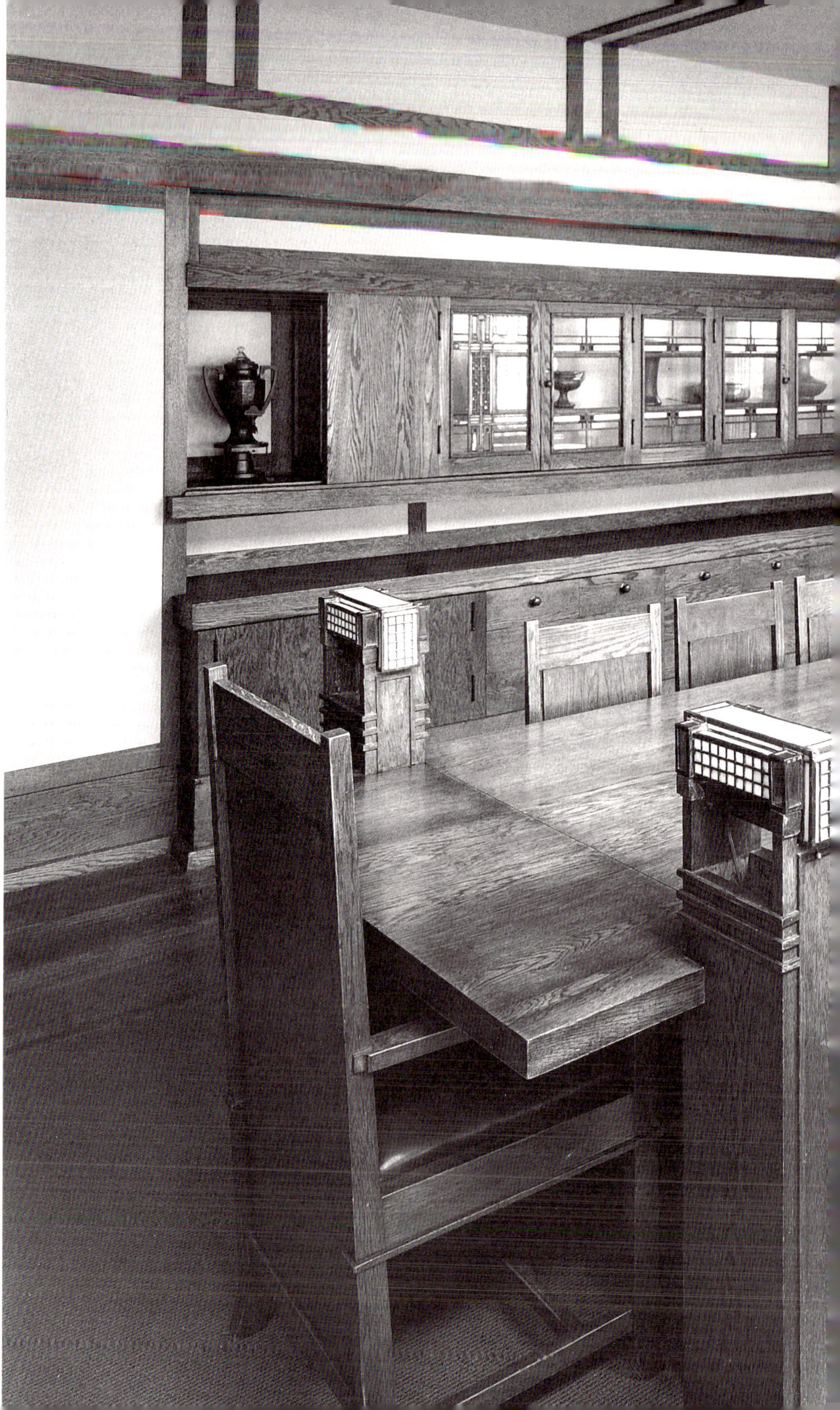

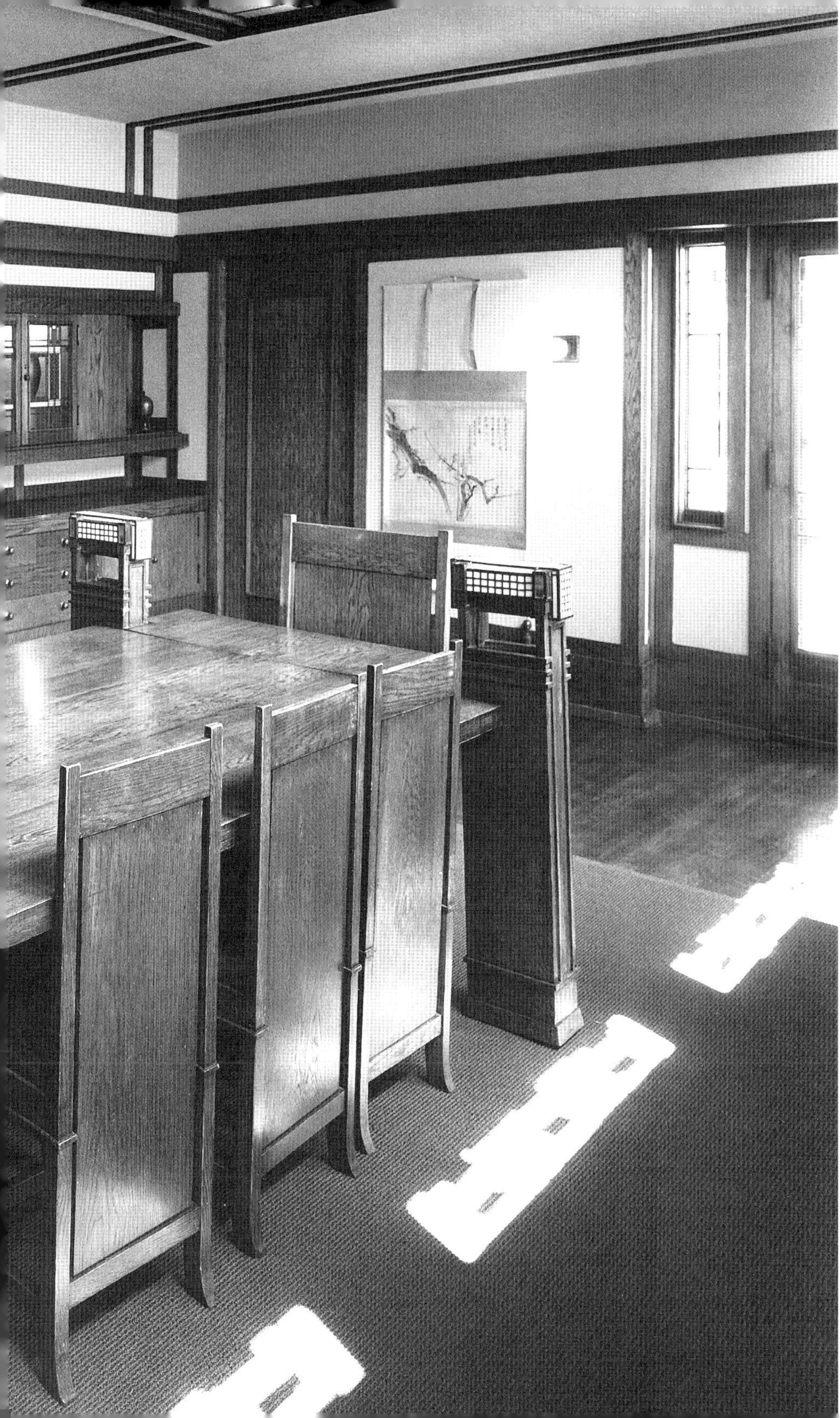

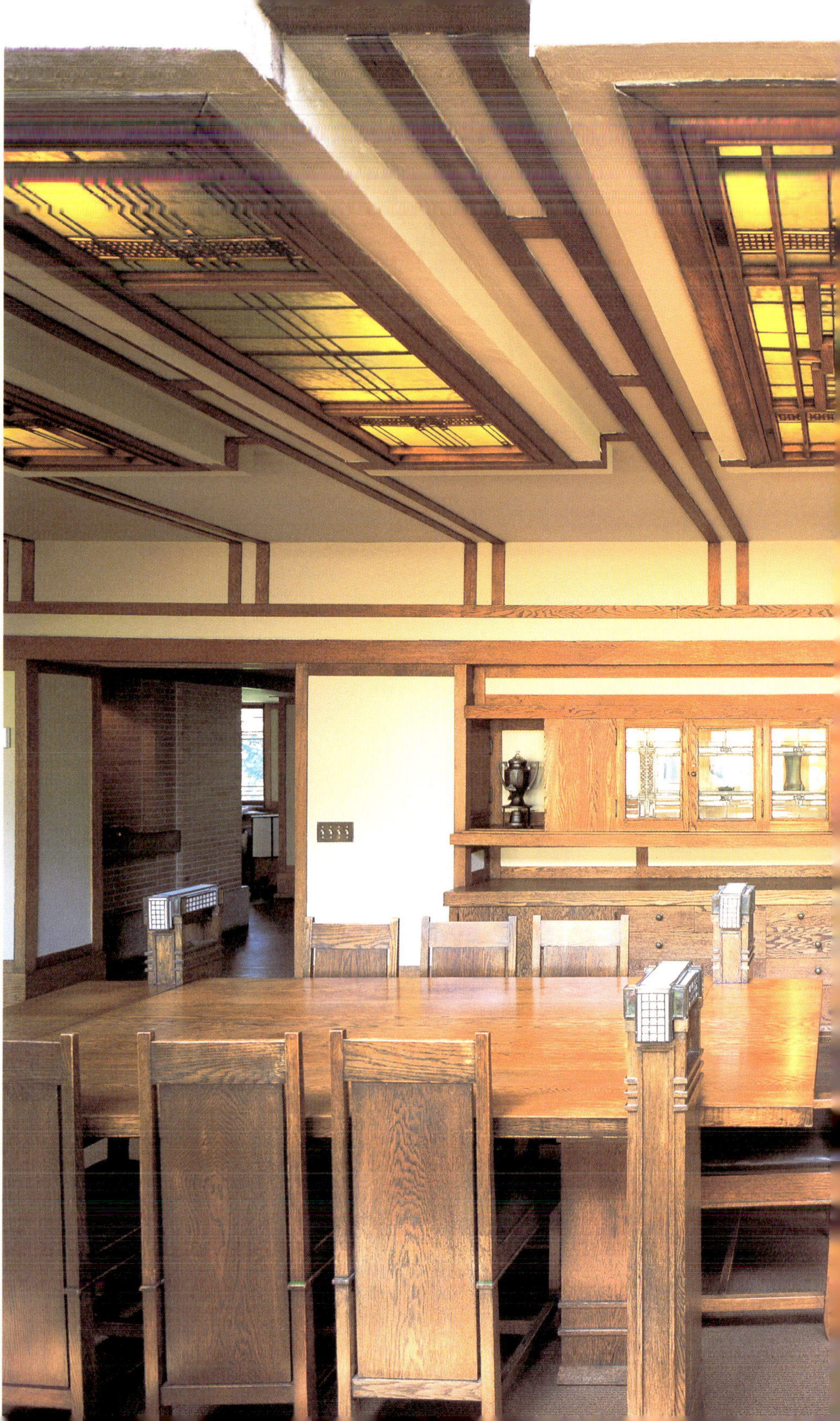

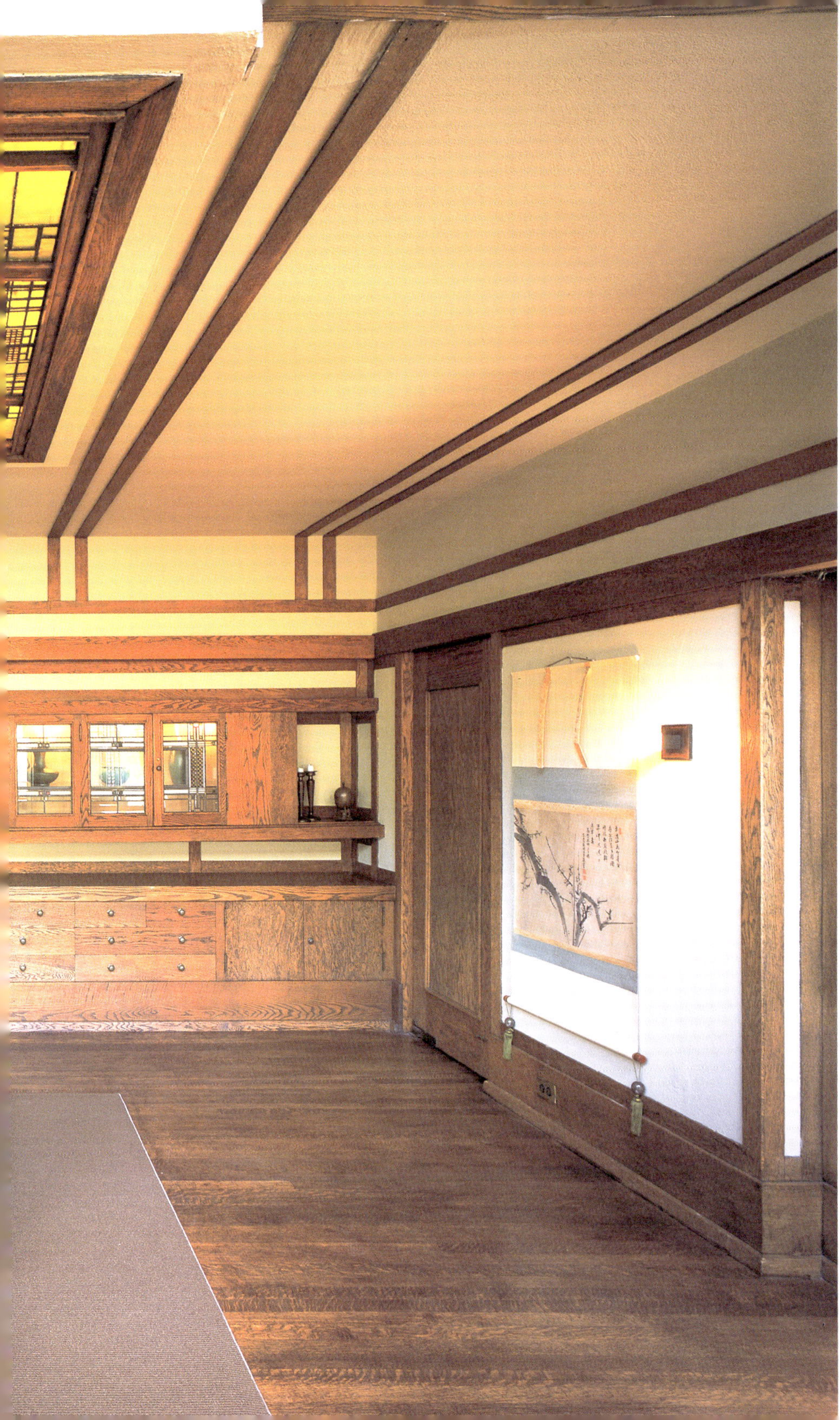

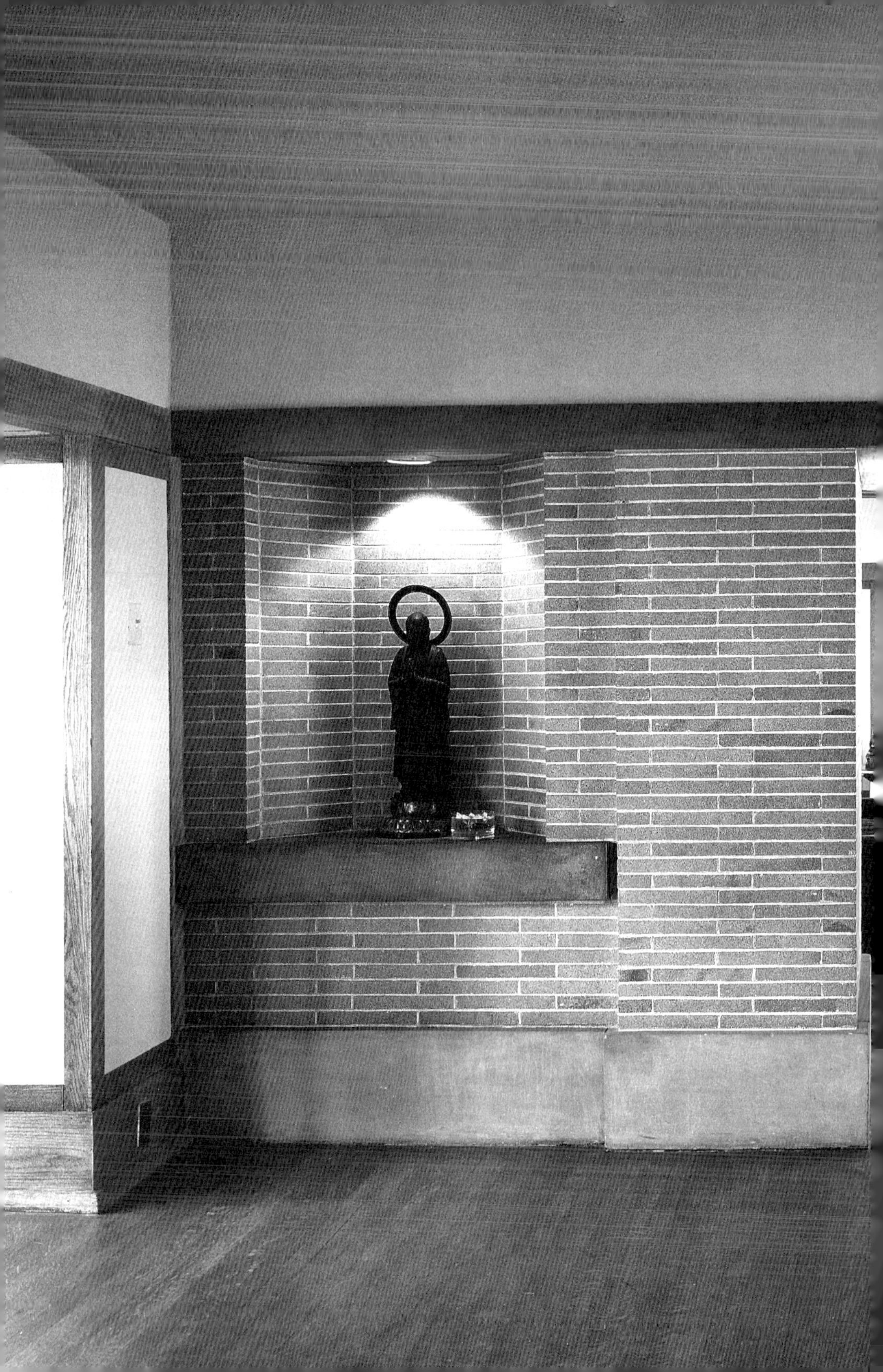

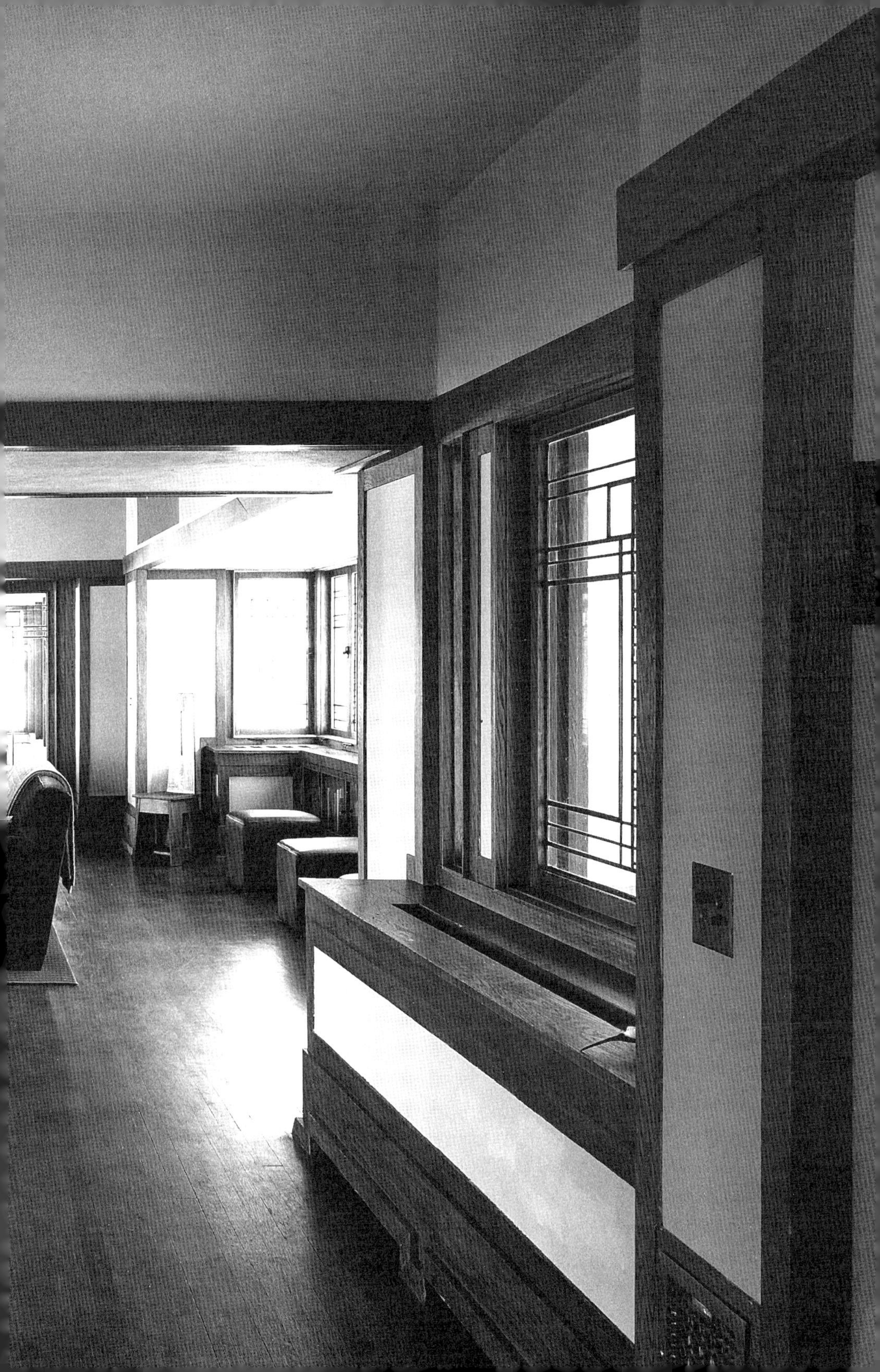

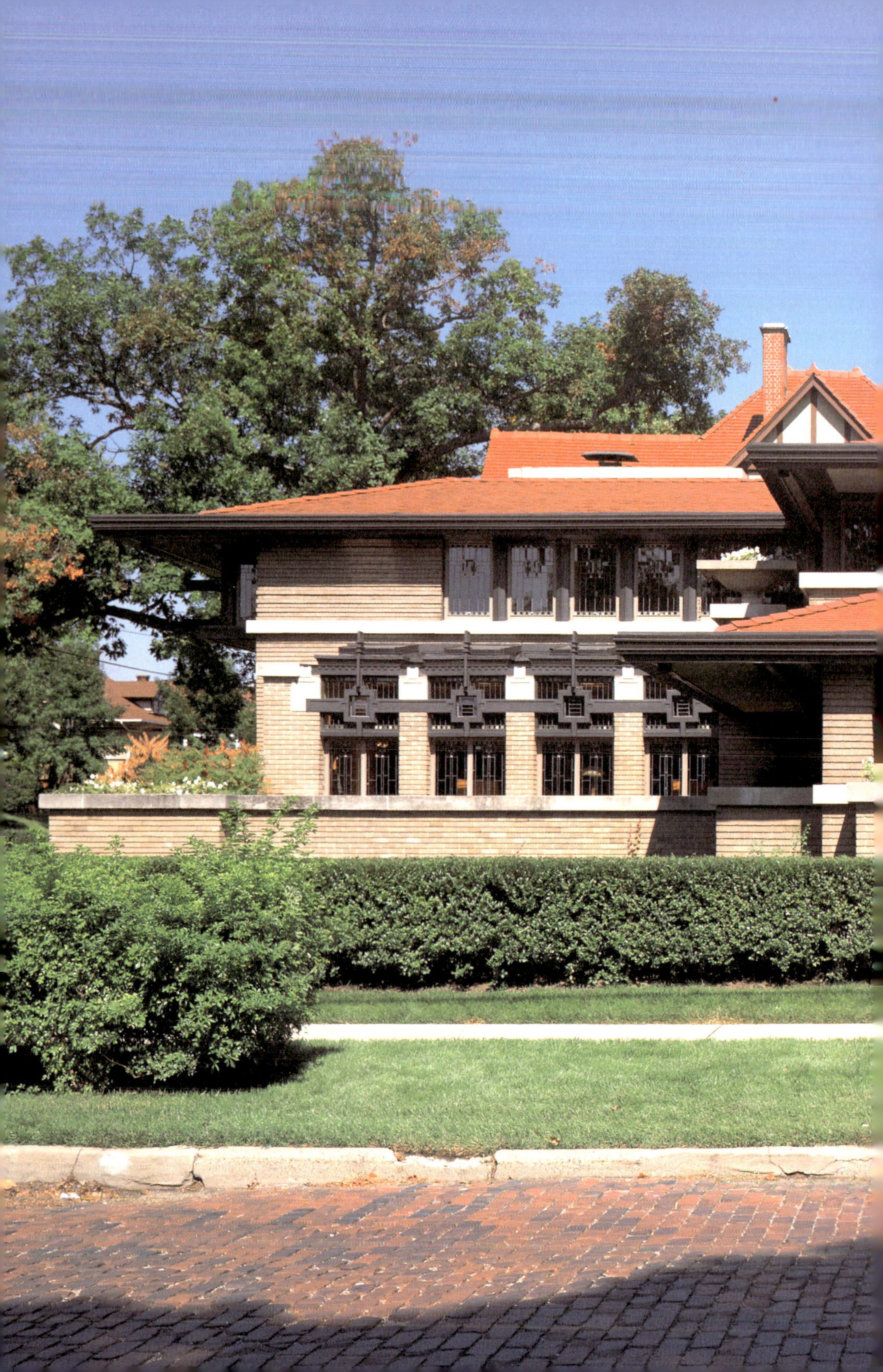

Meyer May House
Grand Rapids, Michigan, 1909

Second floor

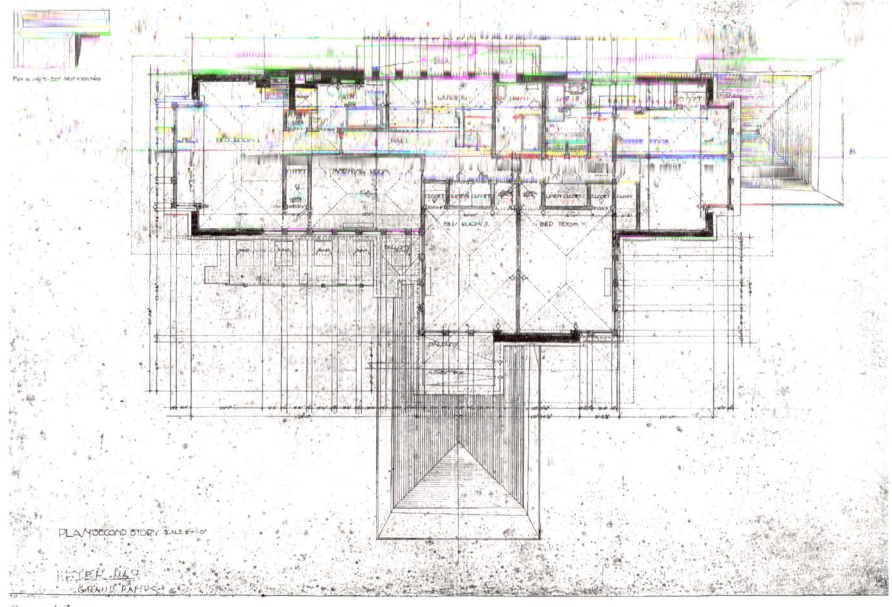

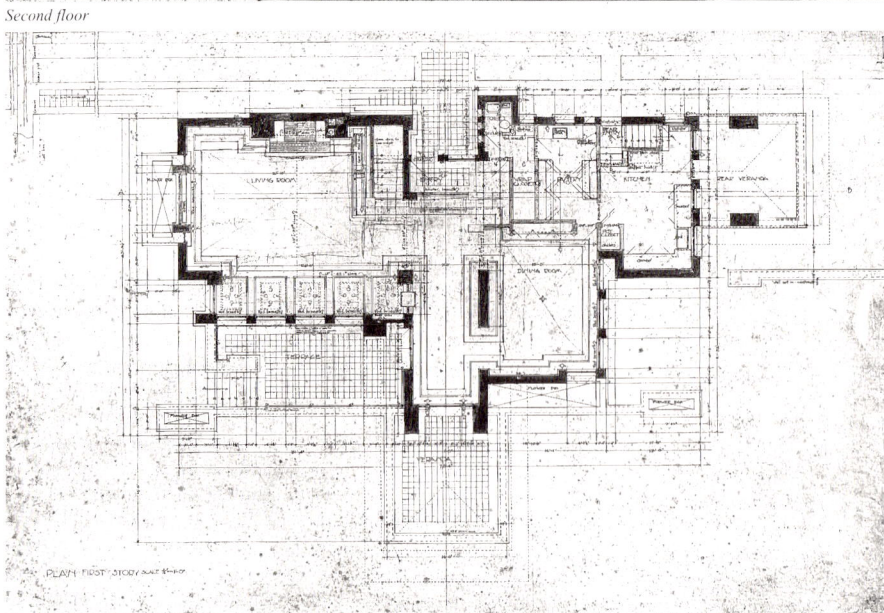

First floor

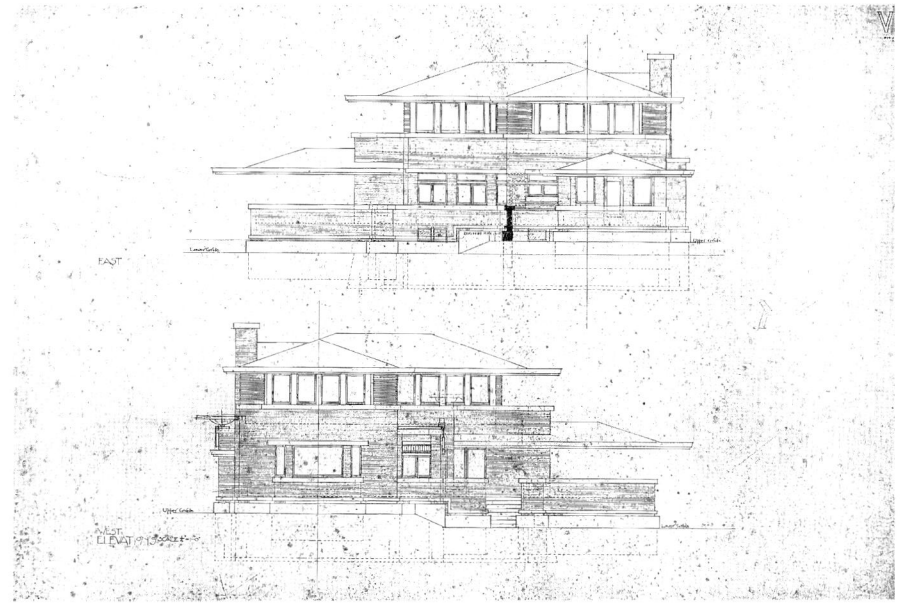

Elevations

Elevations

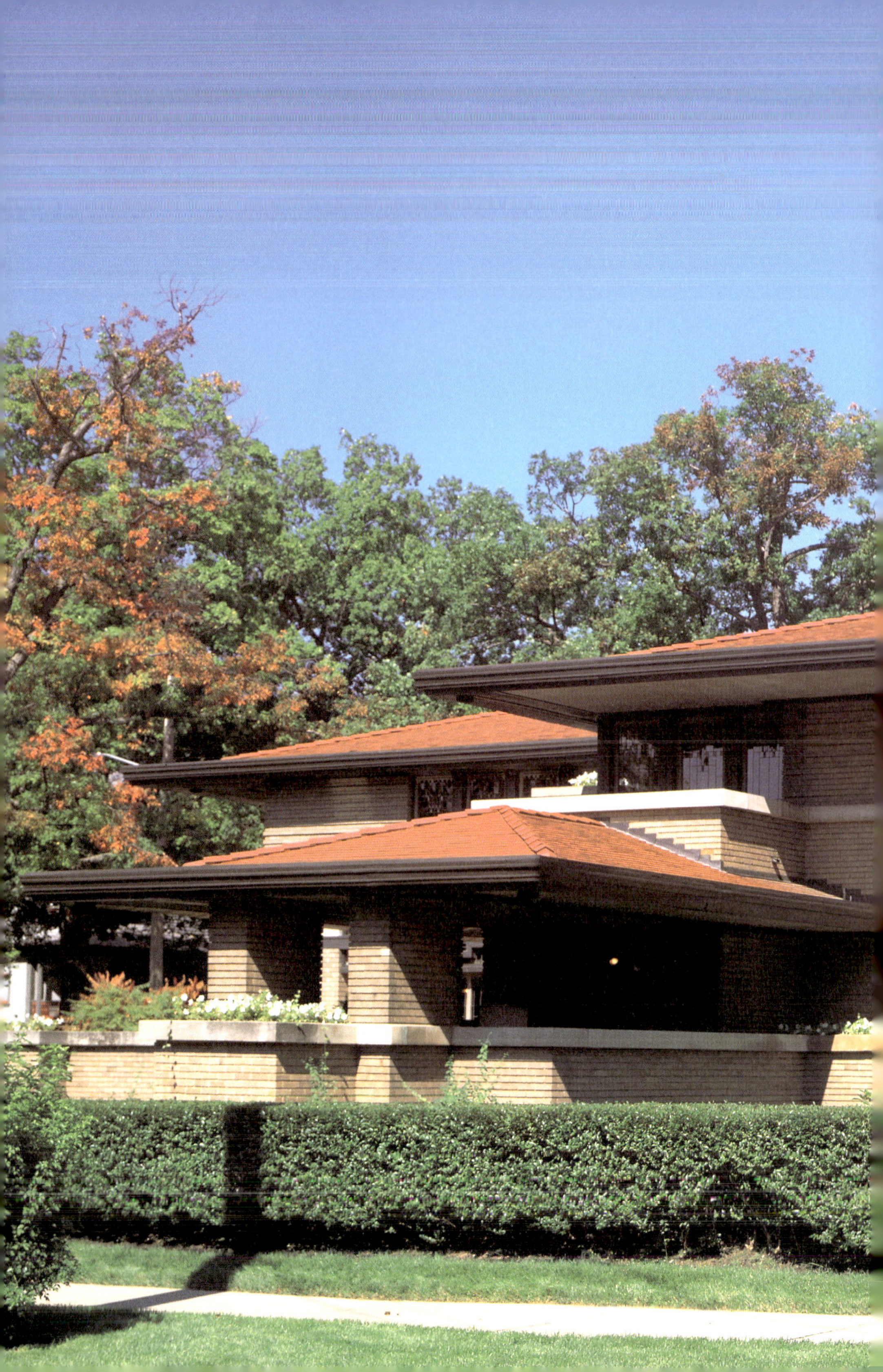

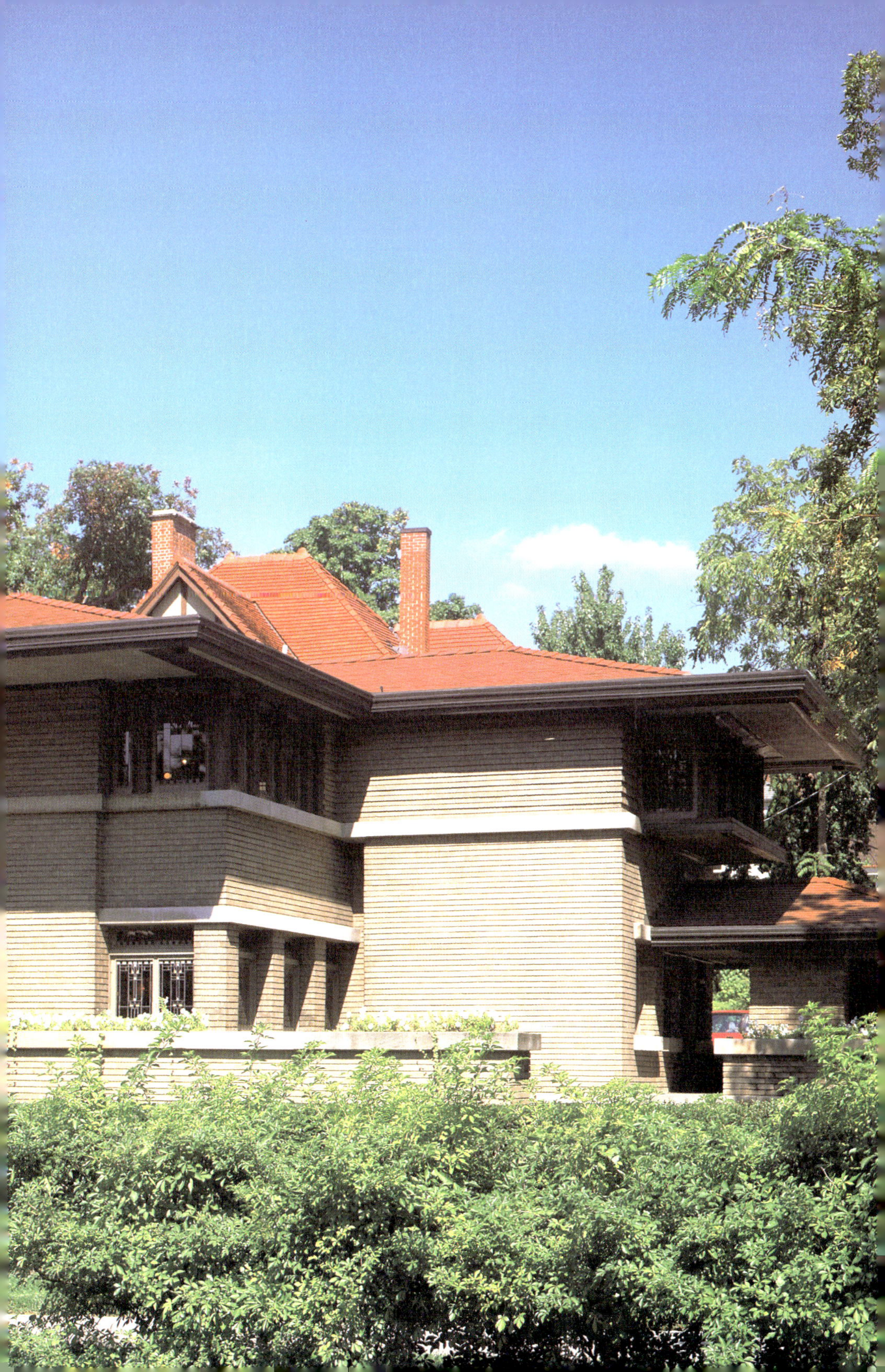

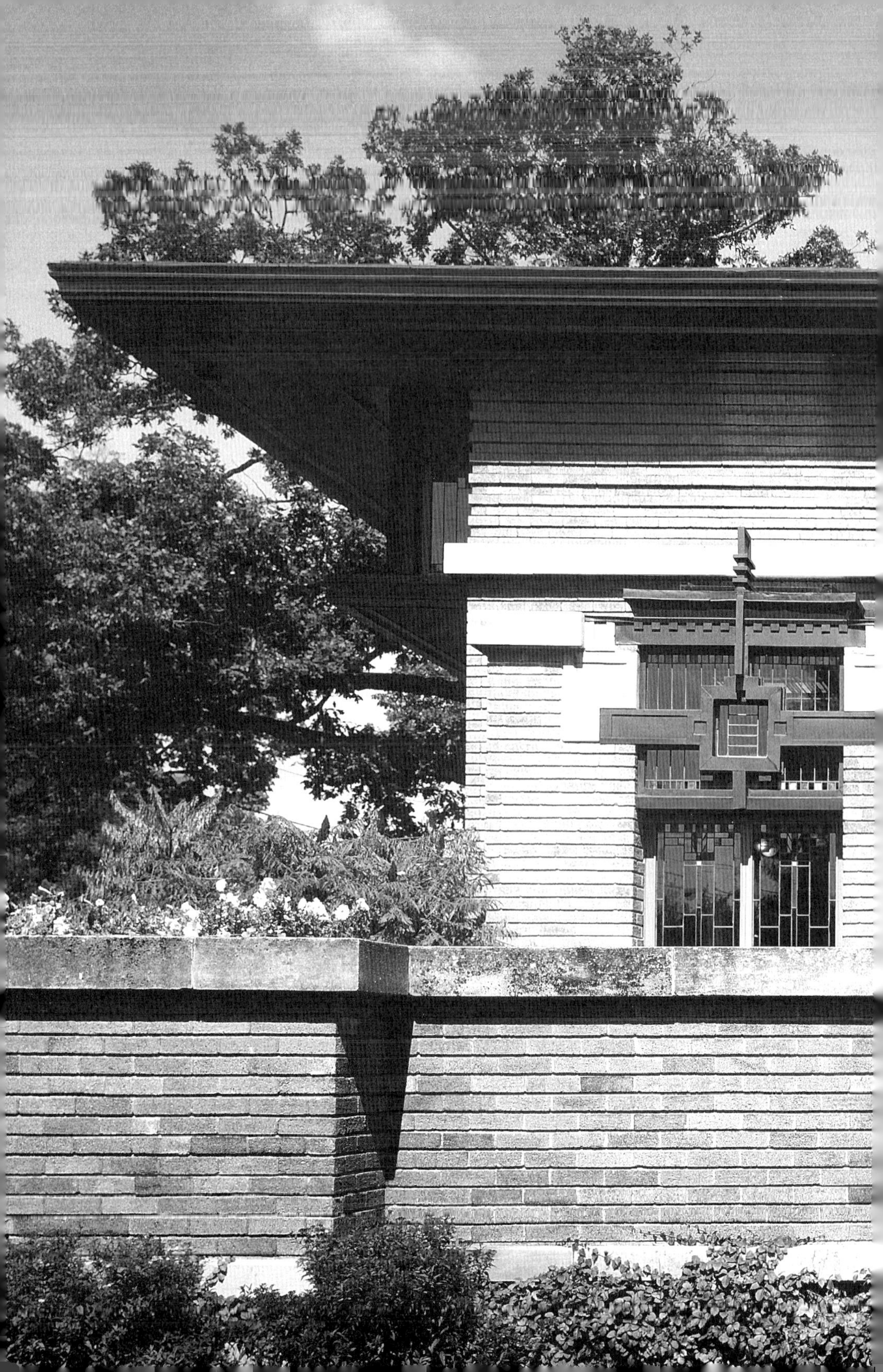

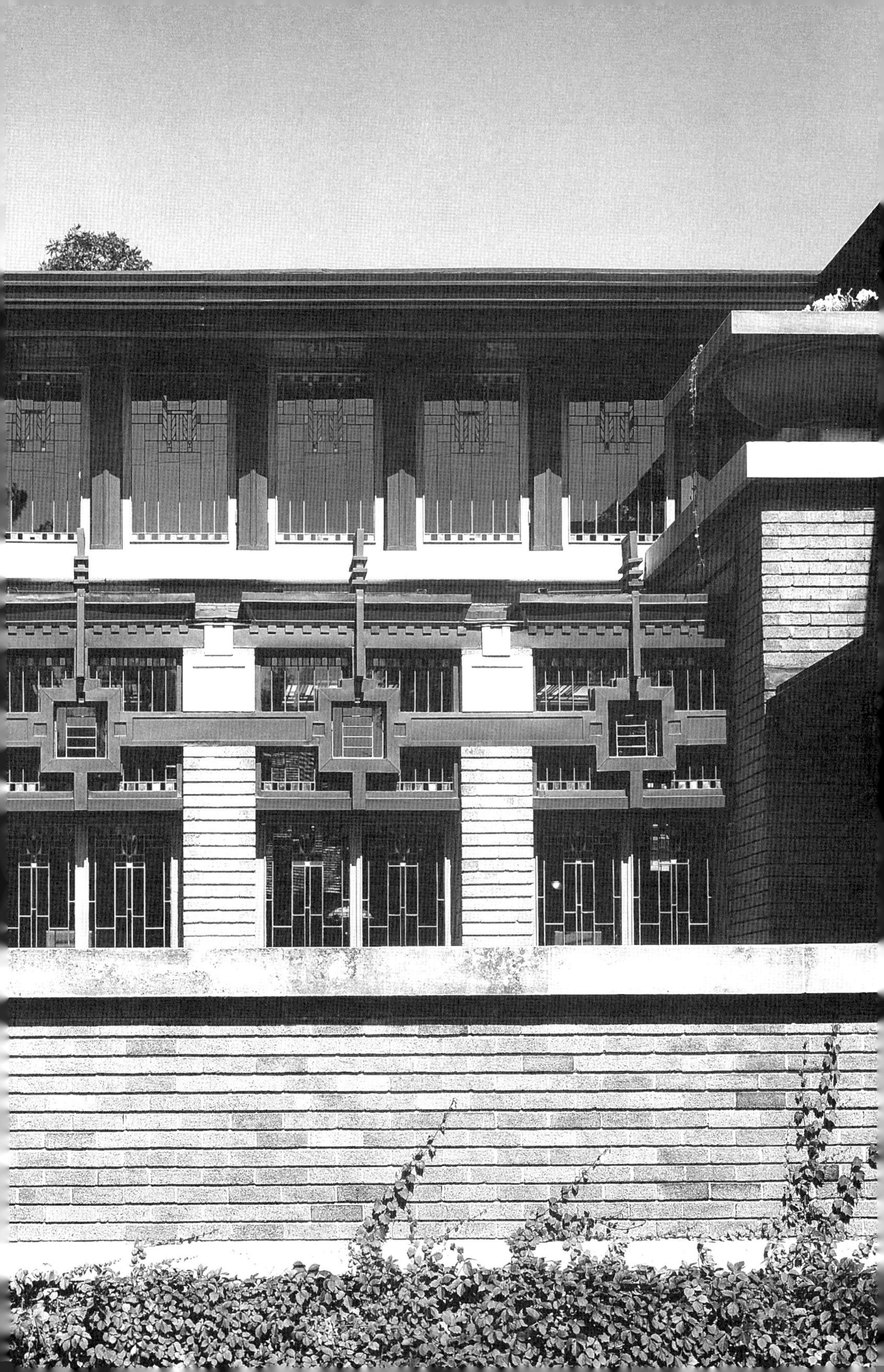

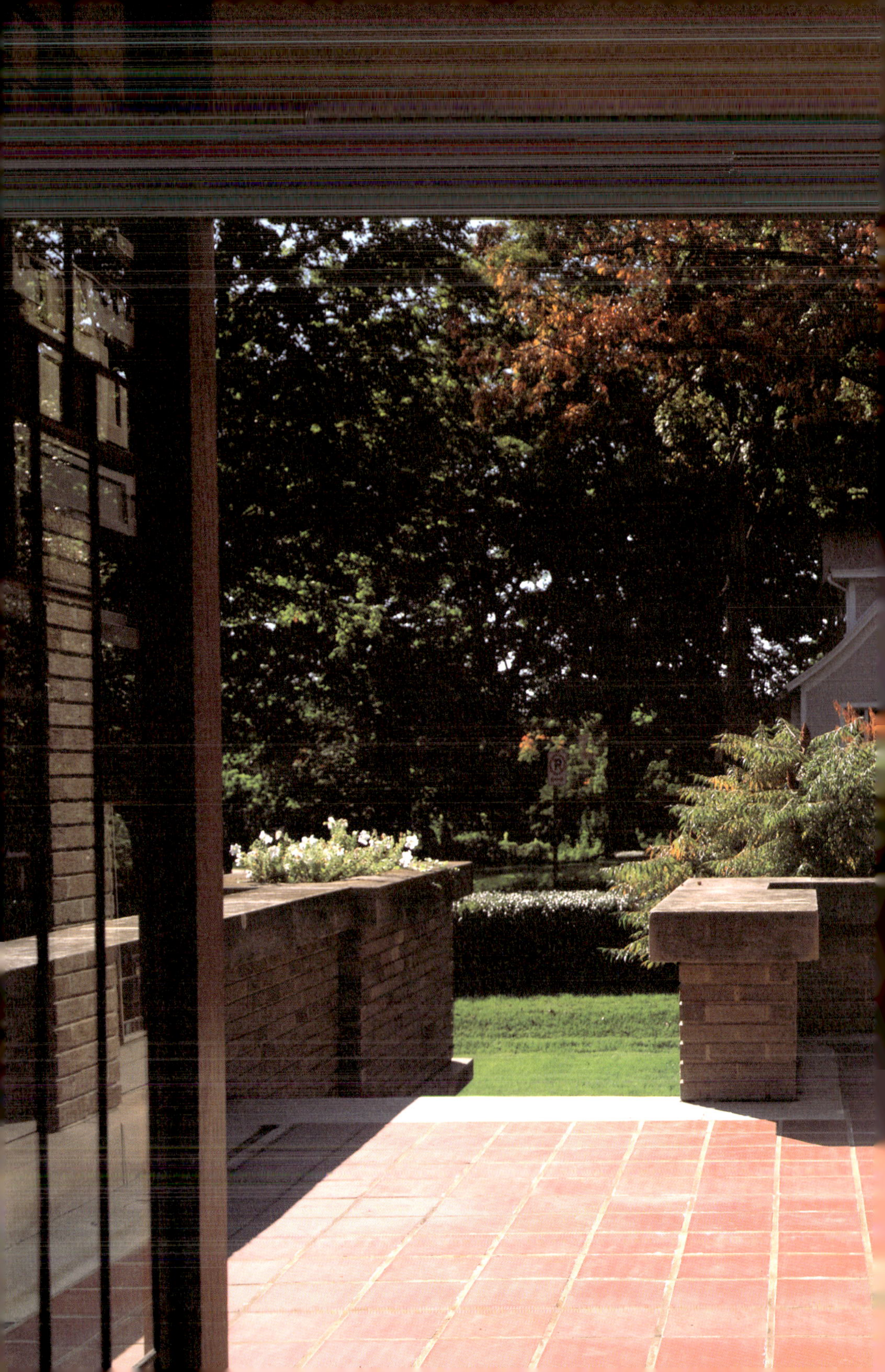

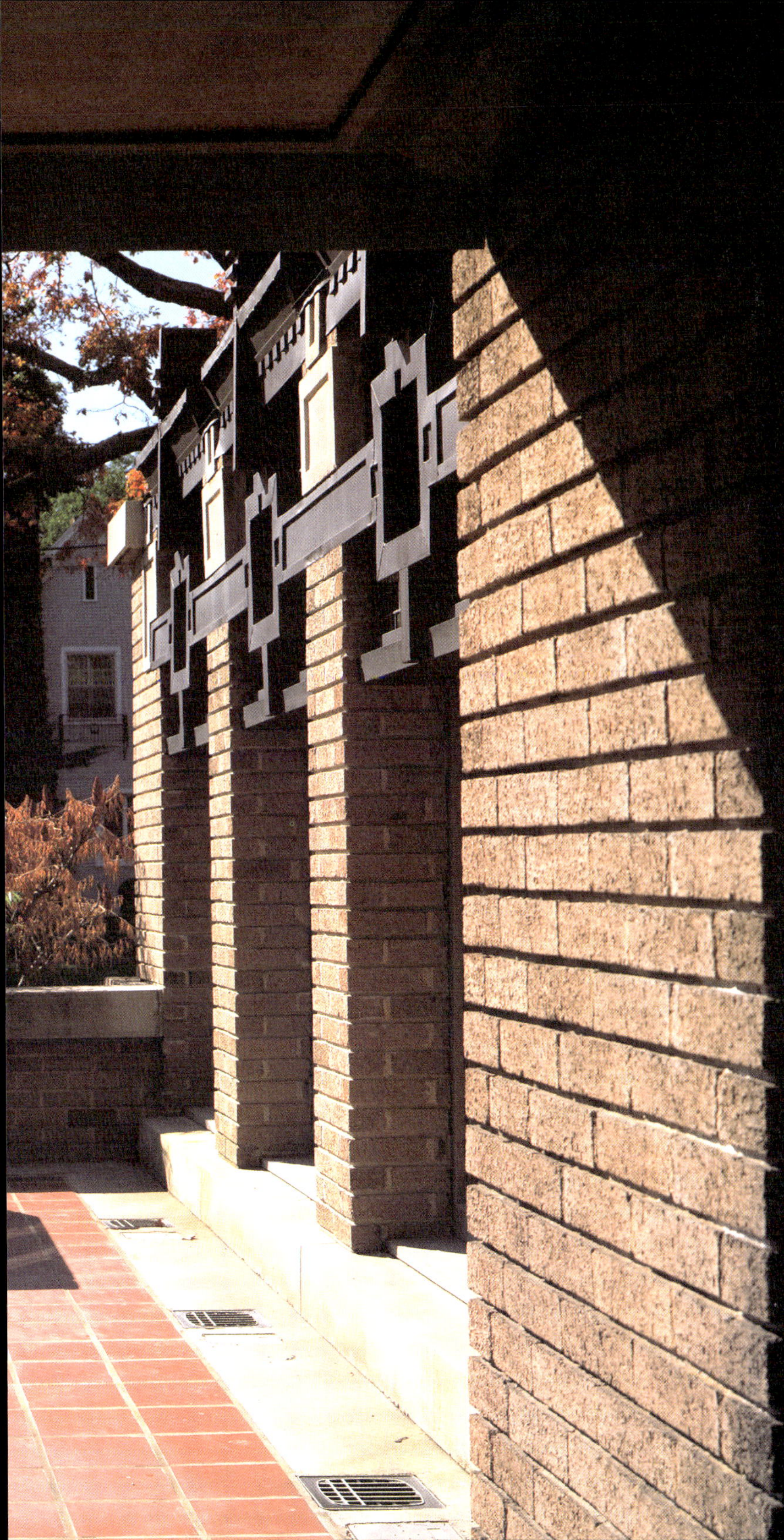

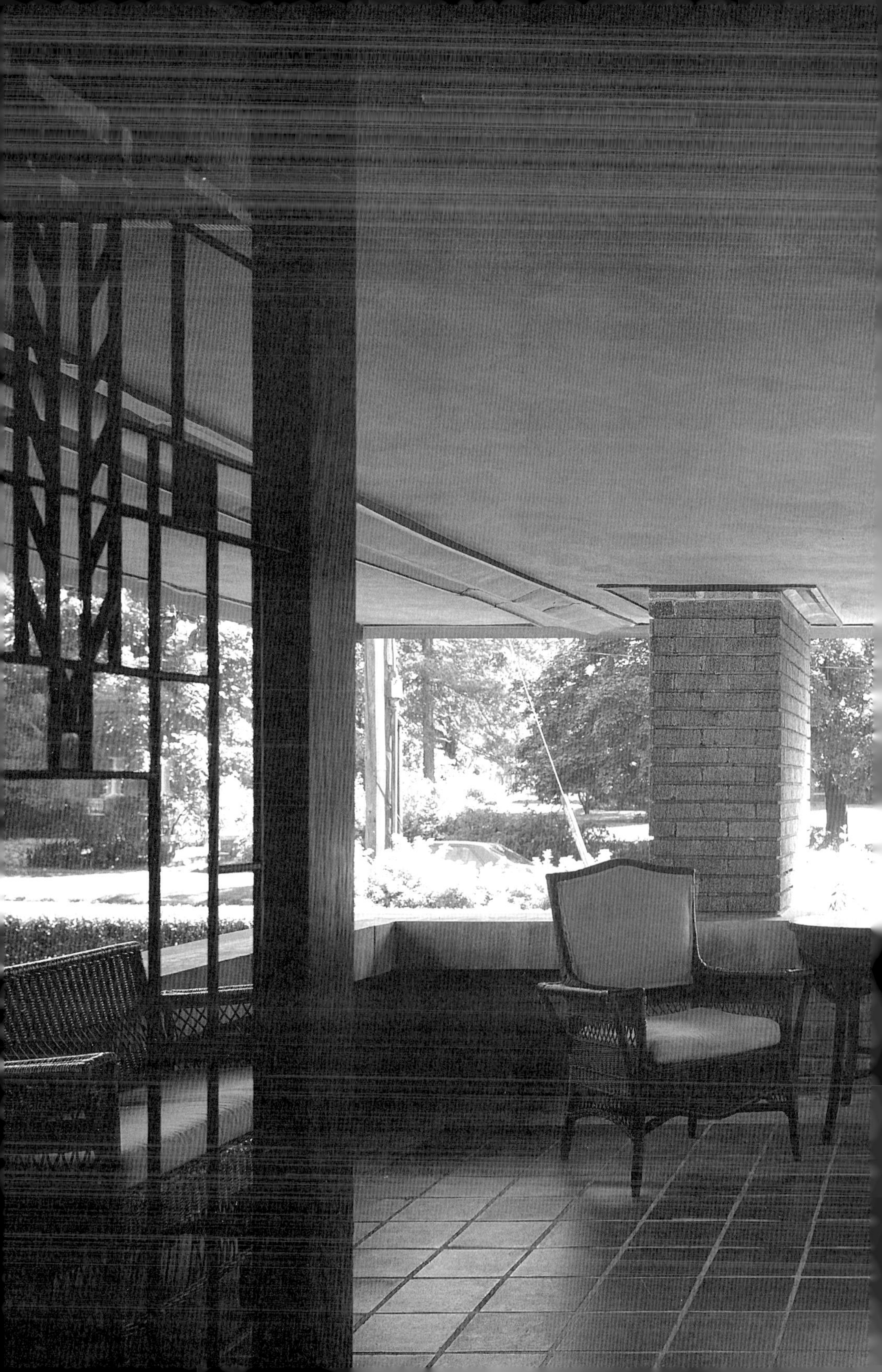

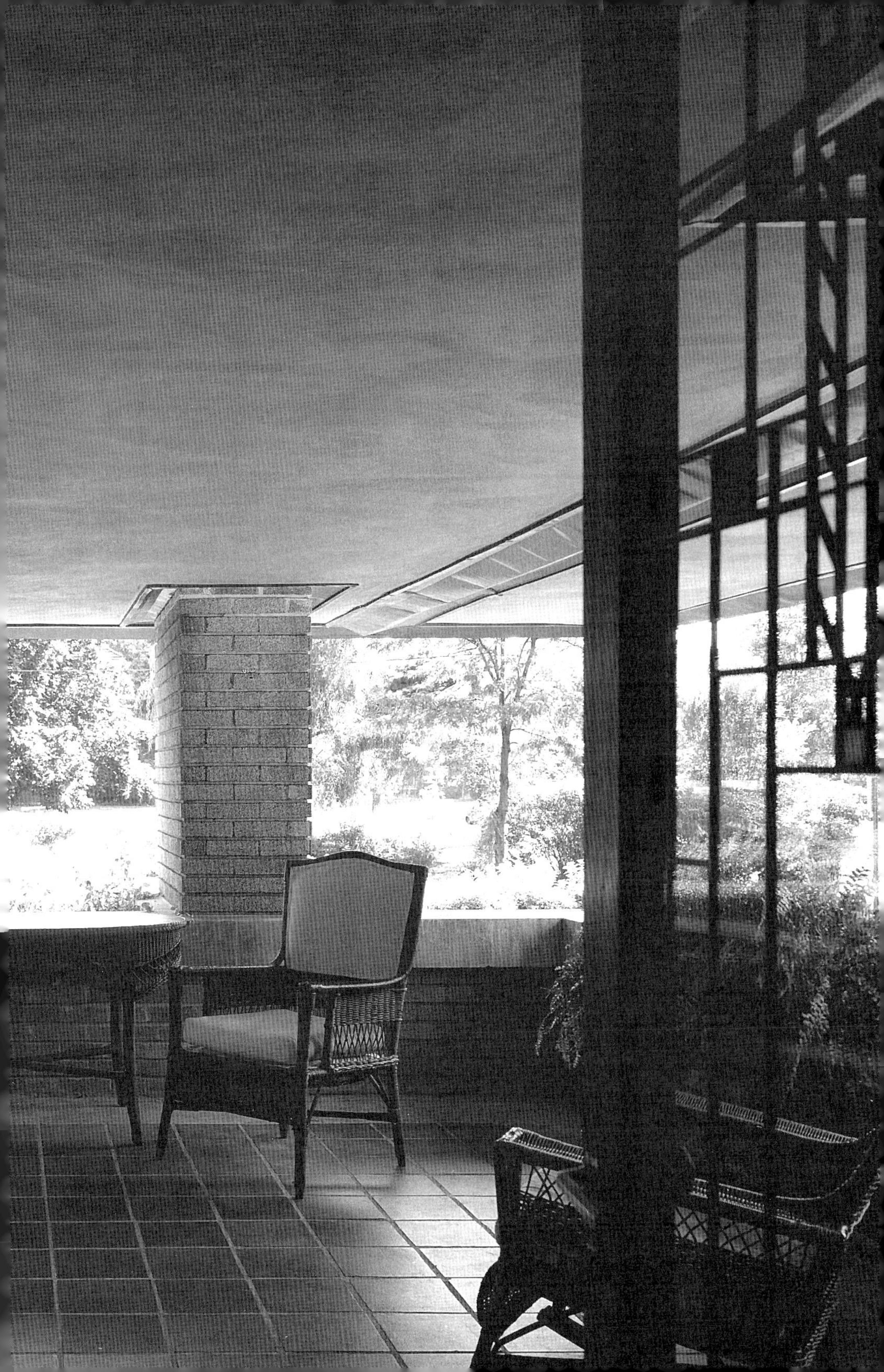

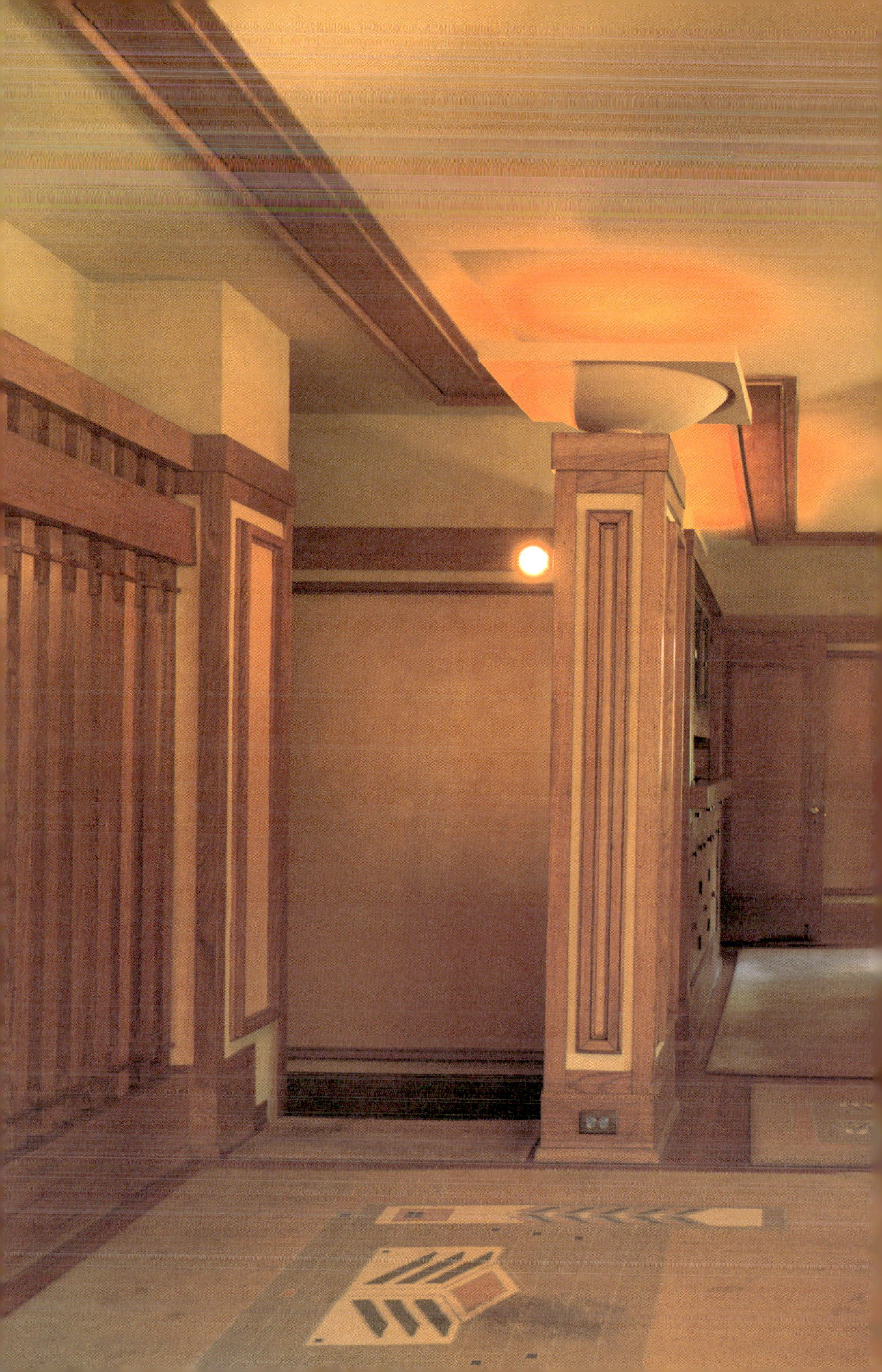

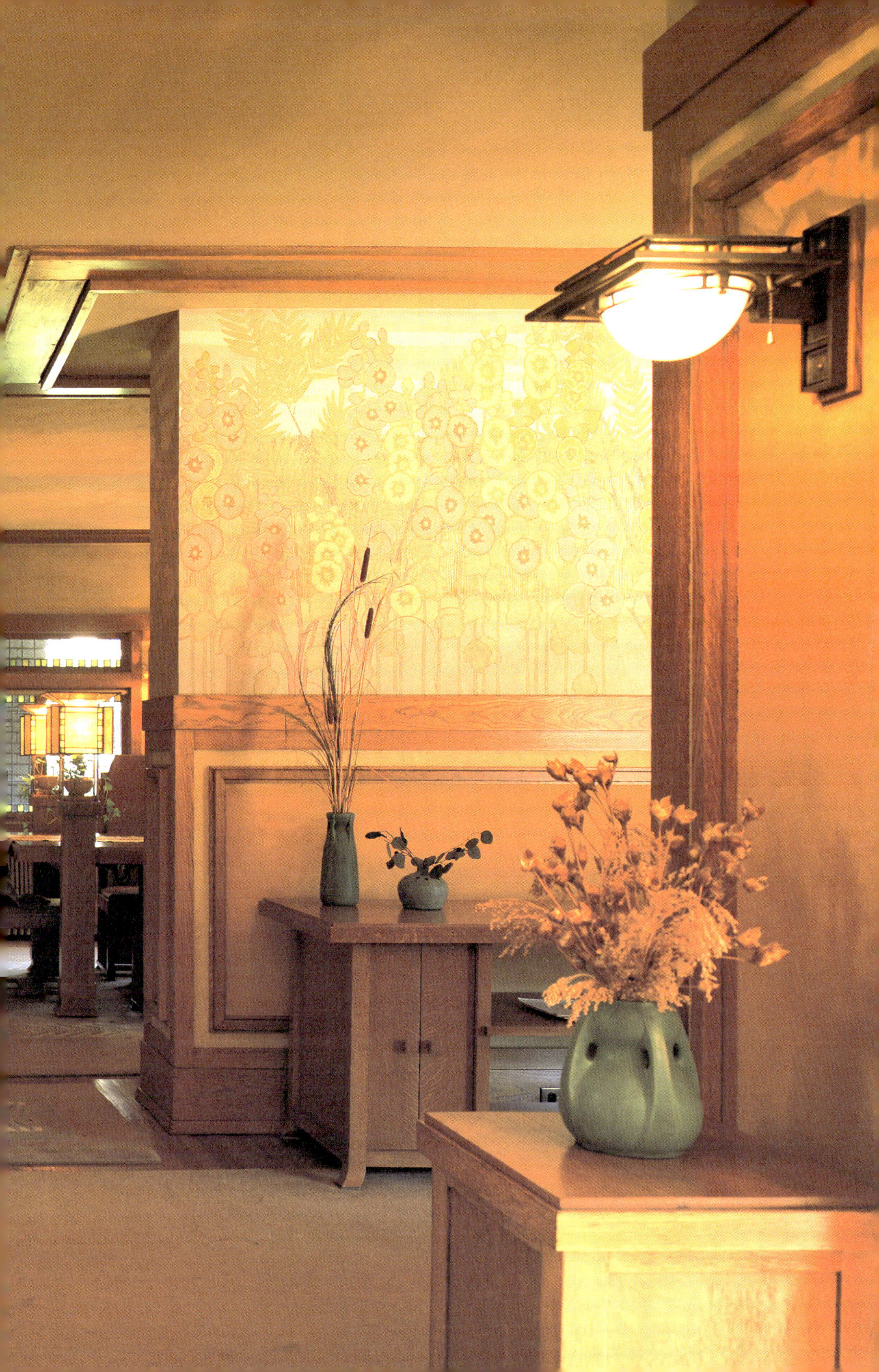

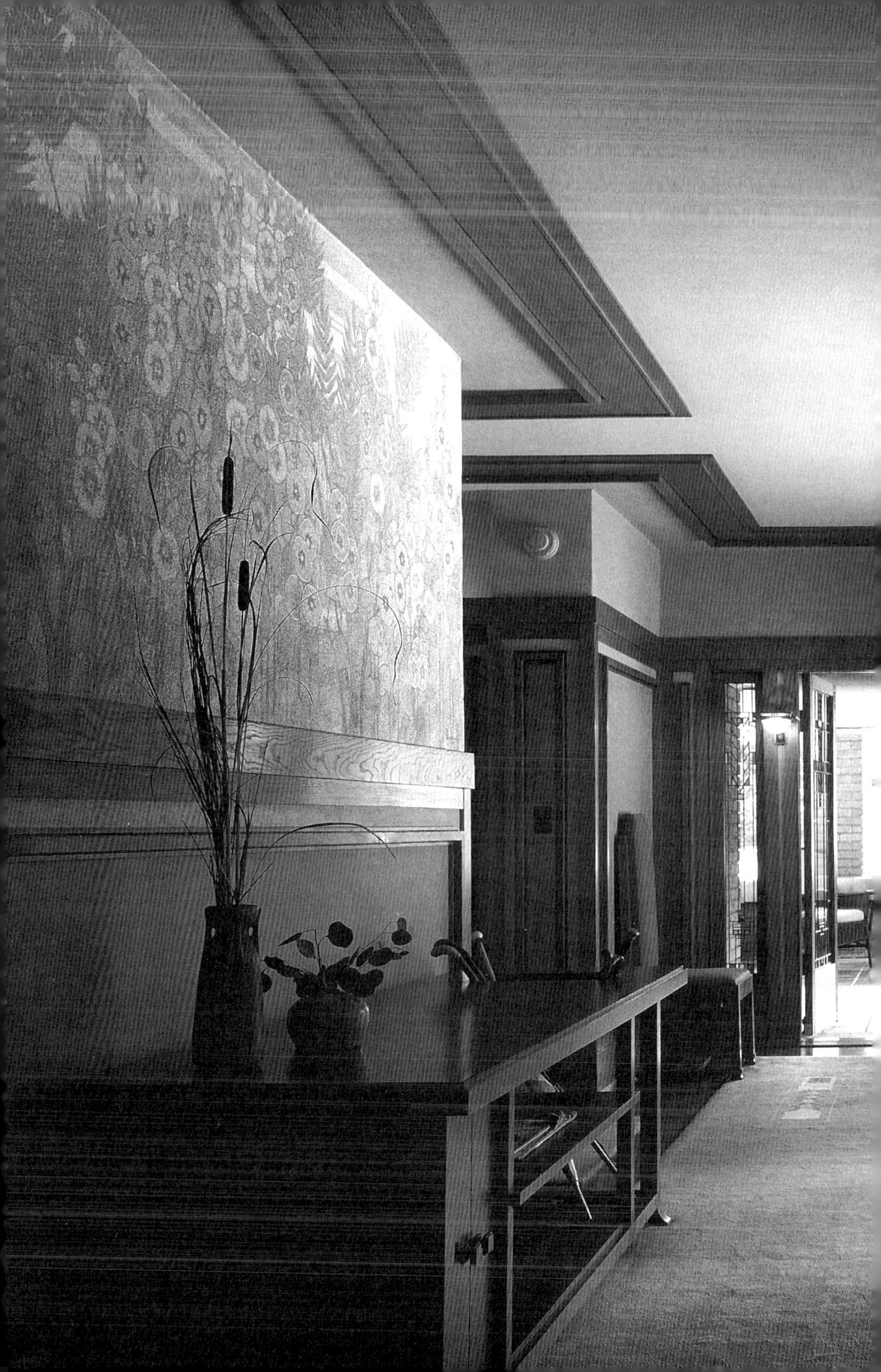

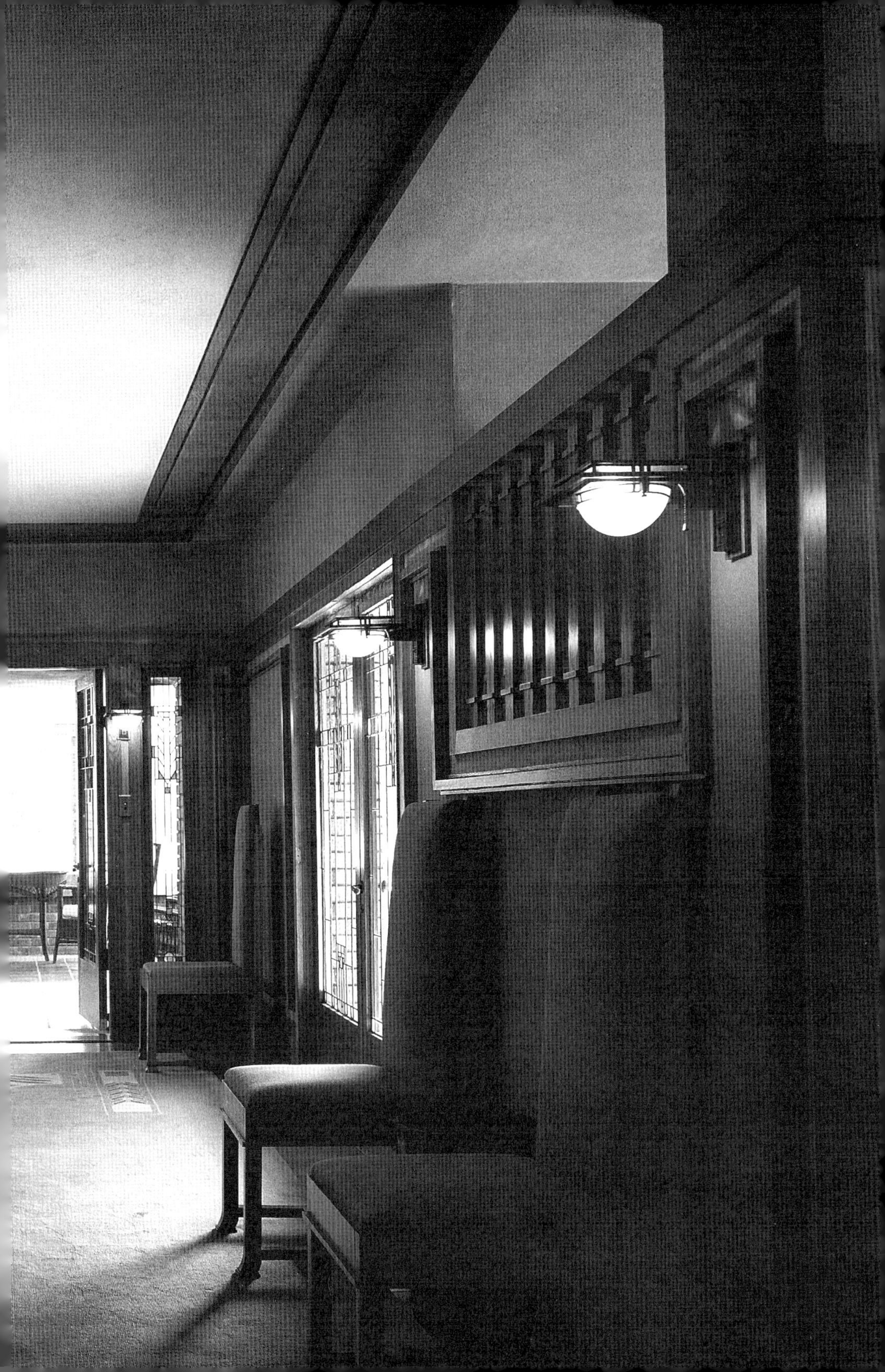

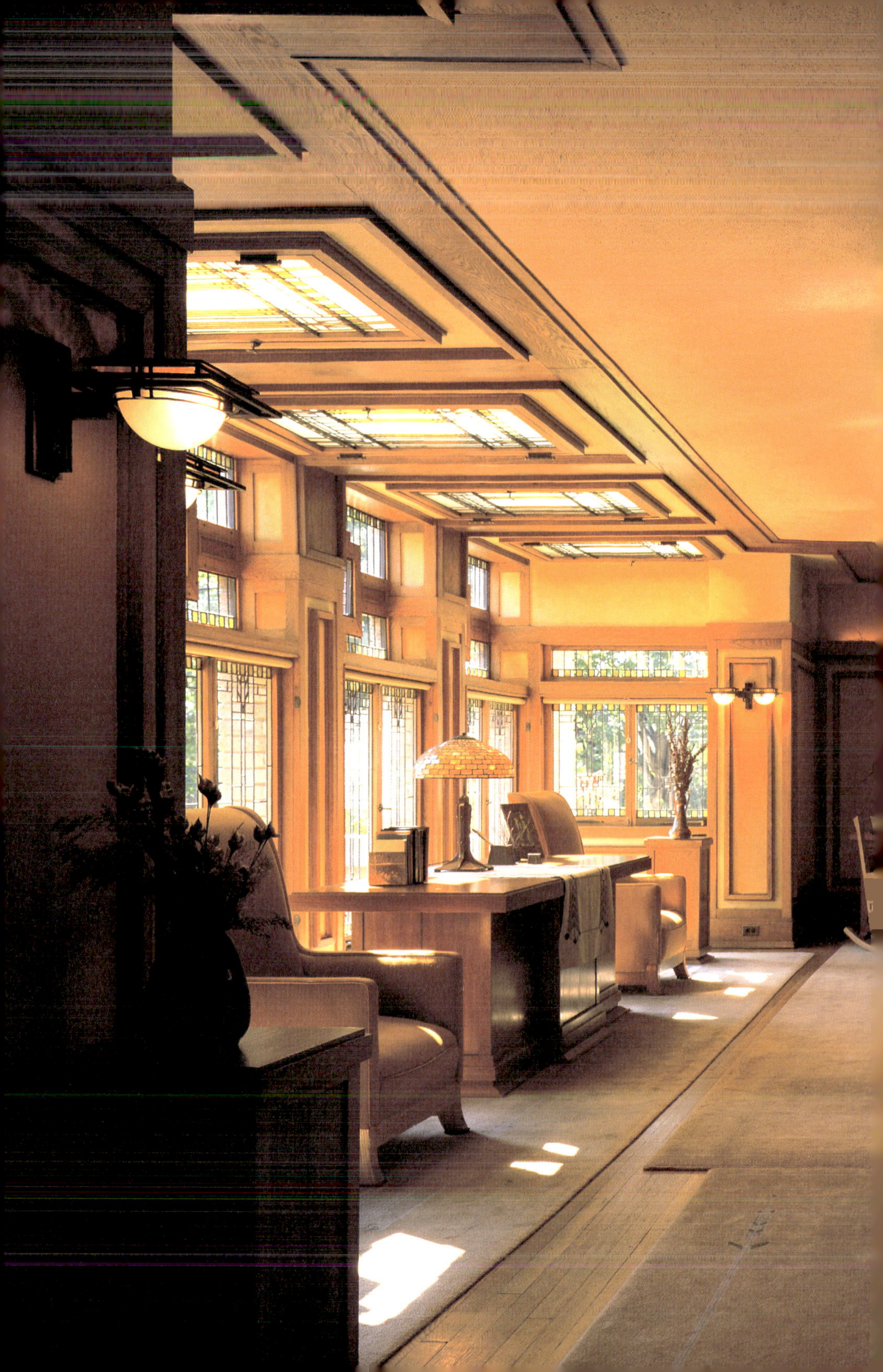

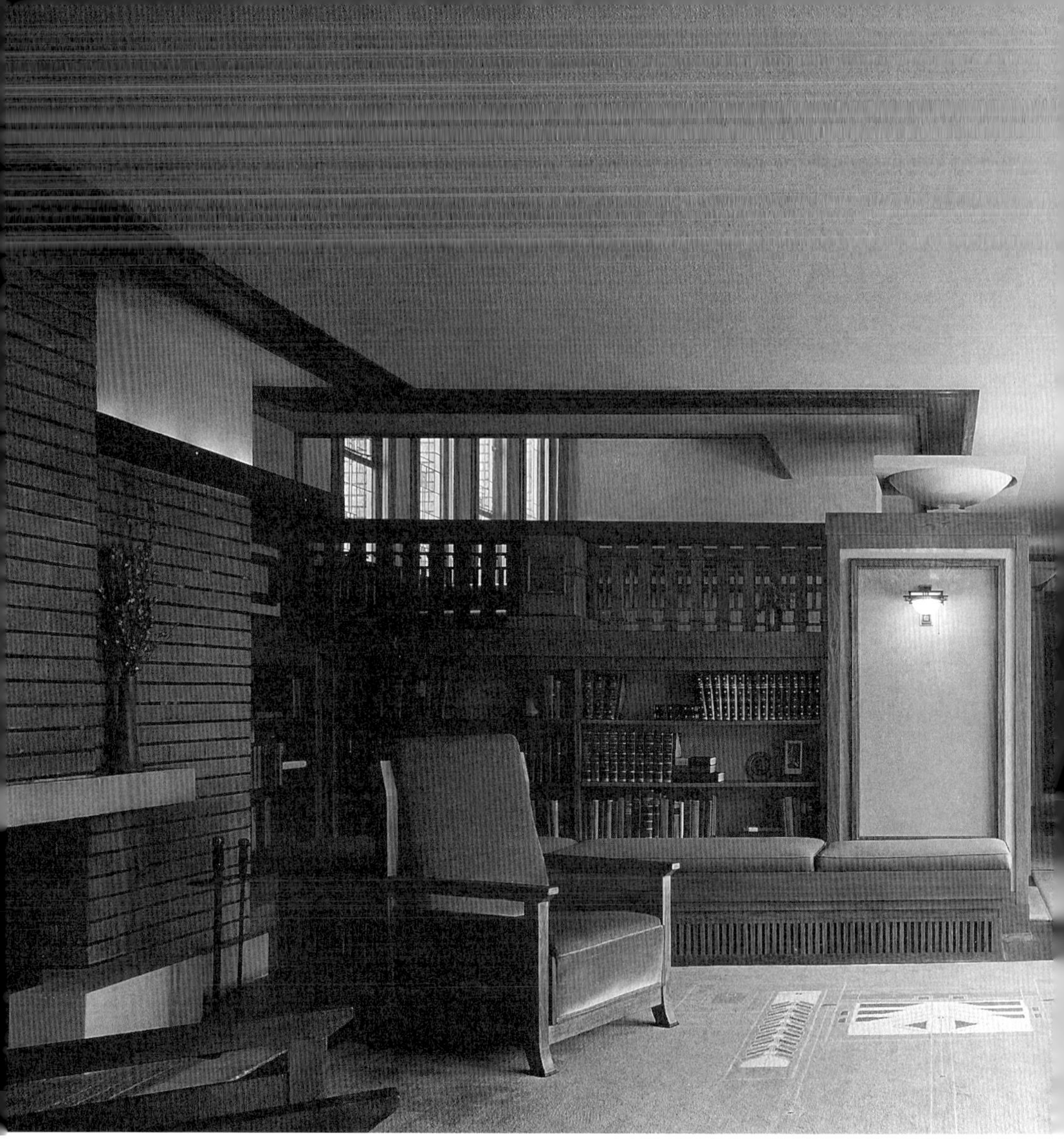

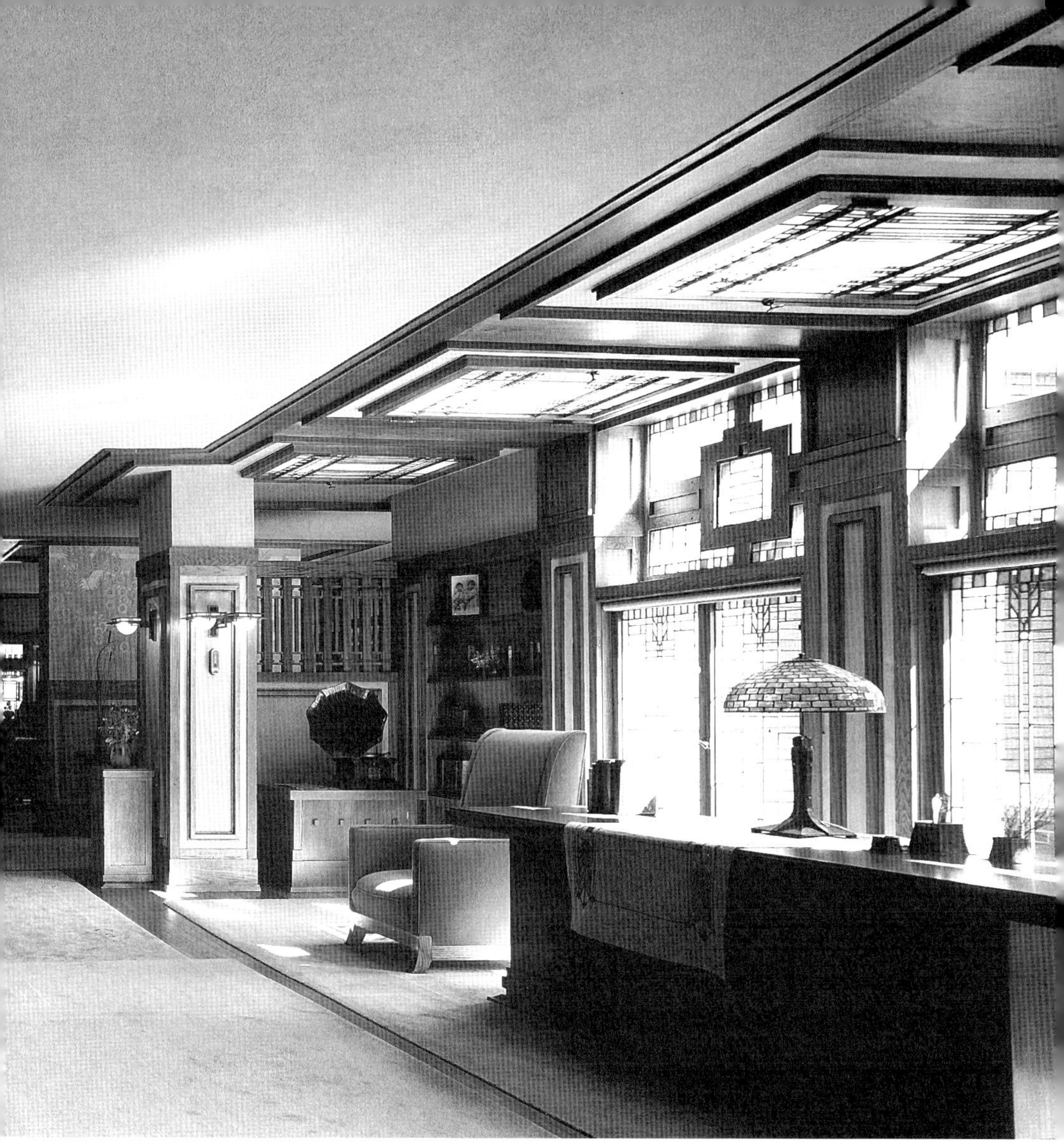

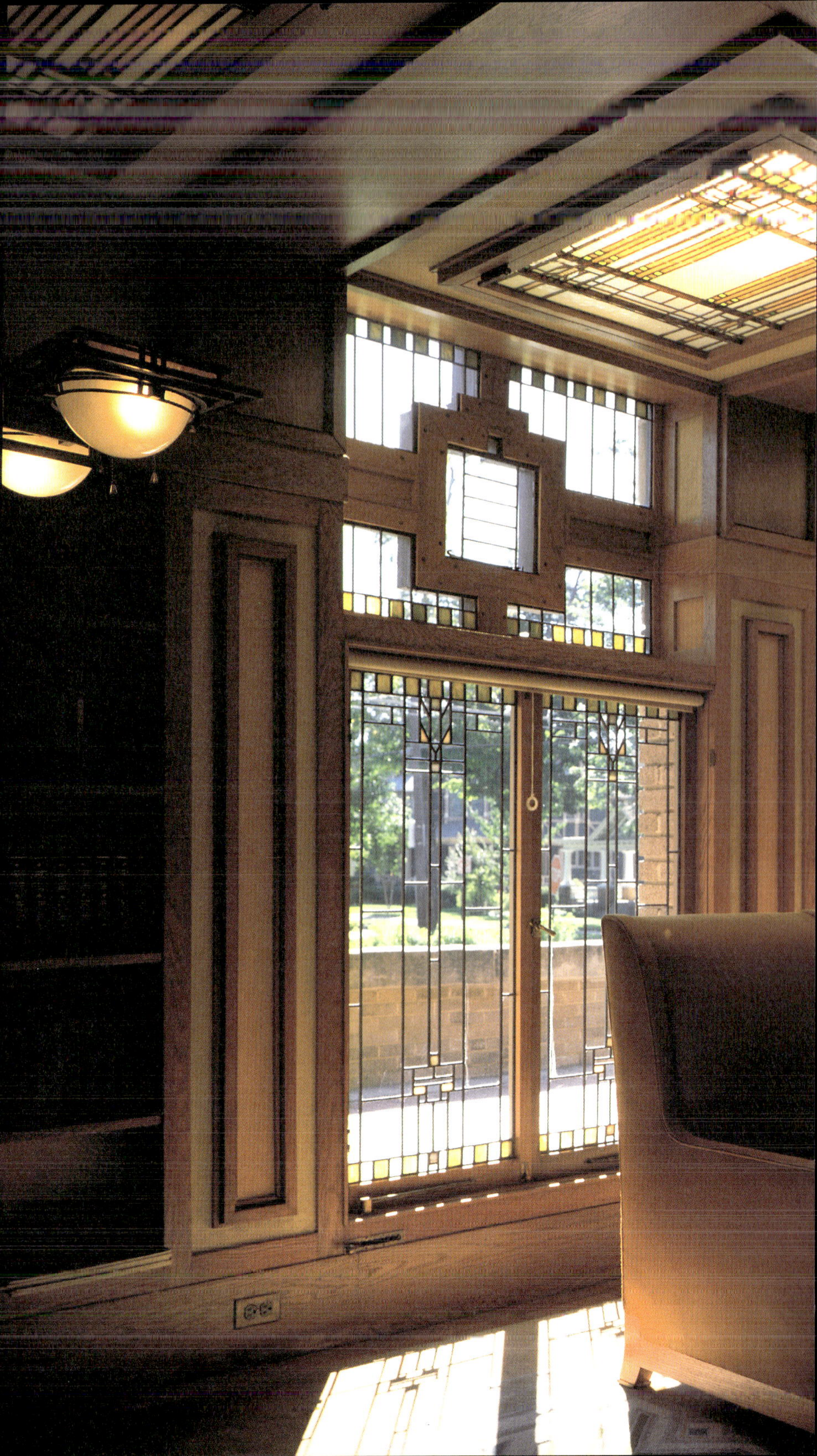

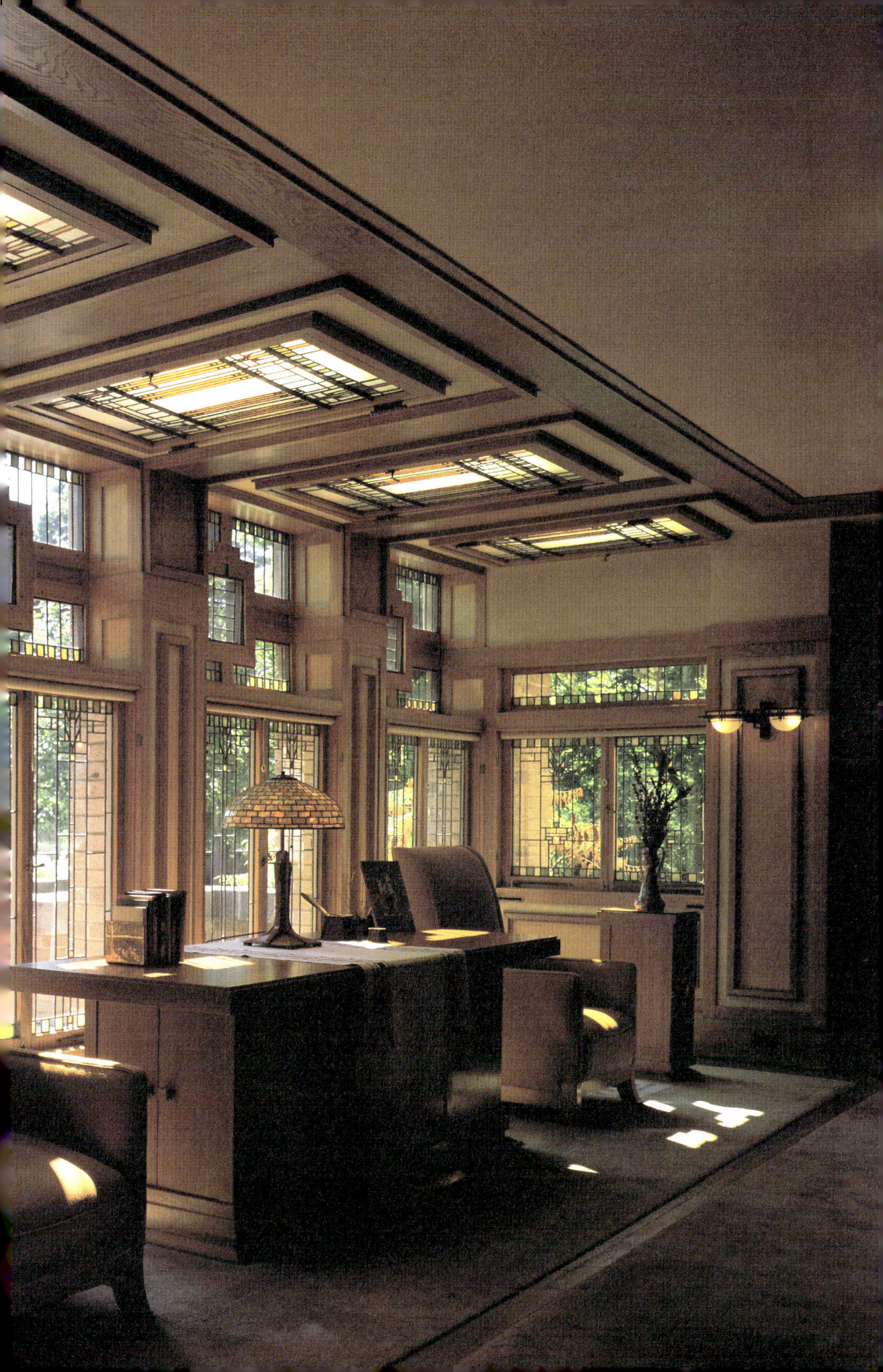

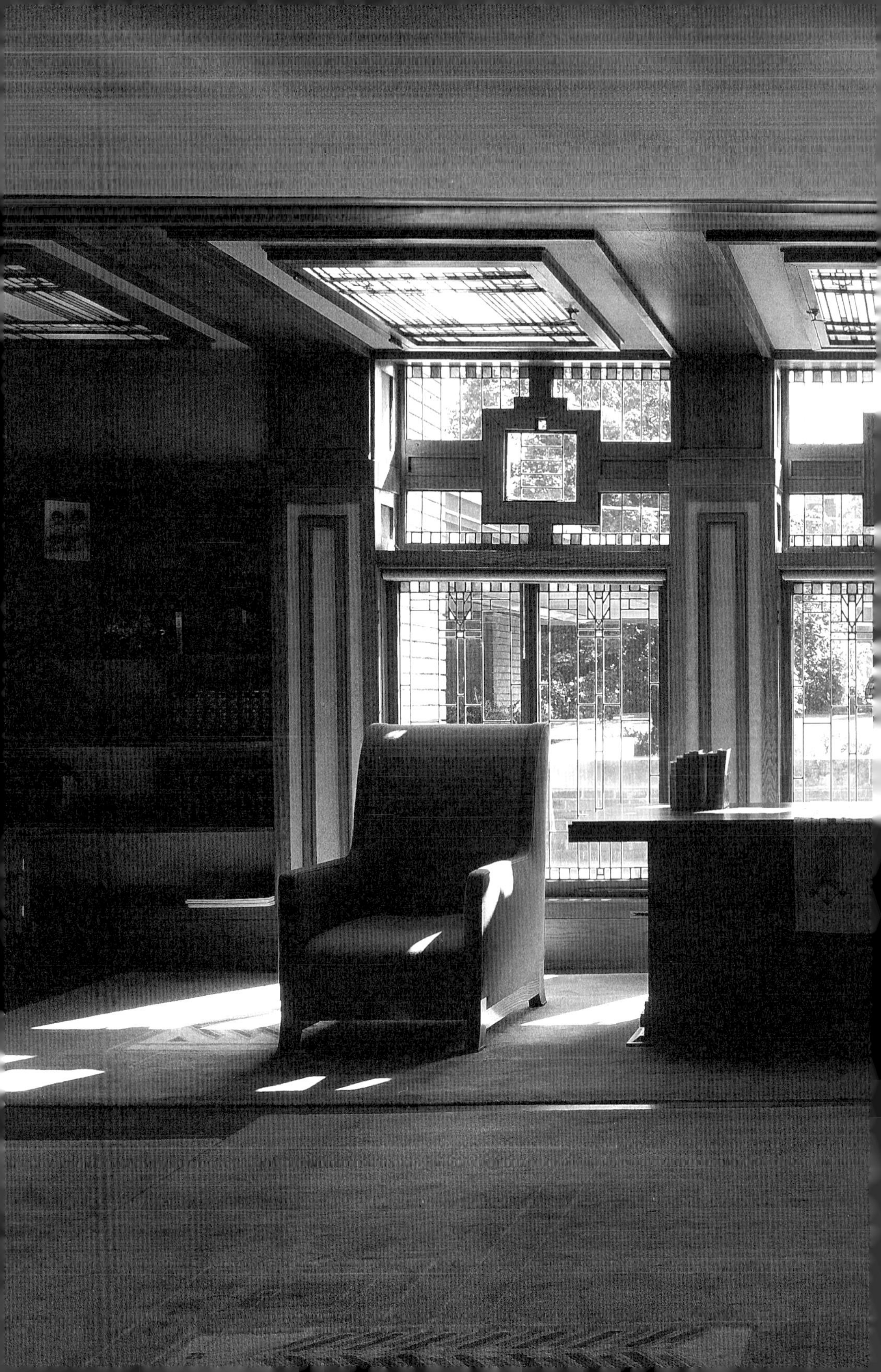

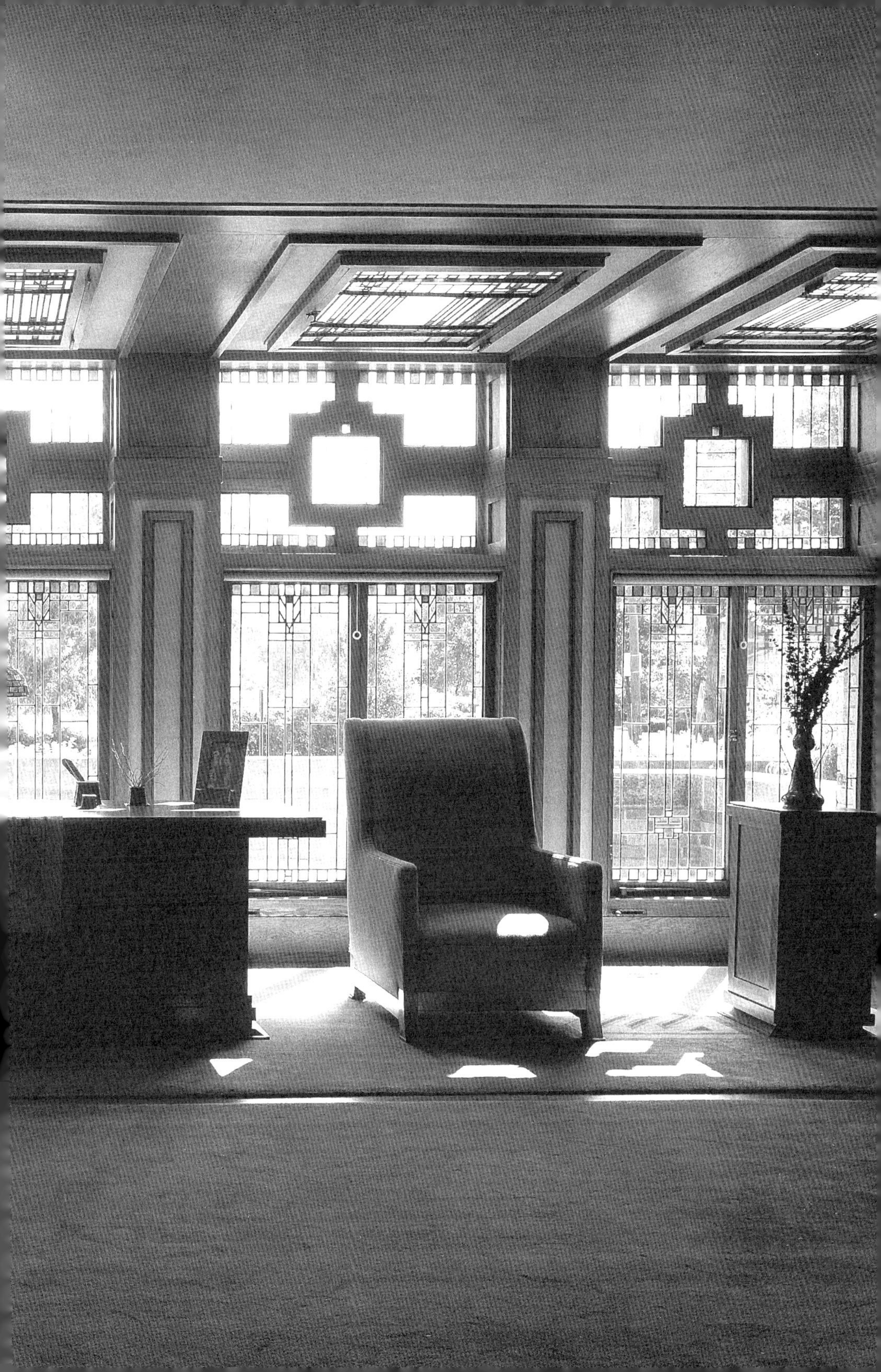

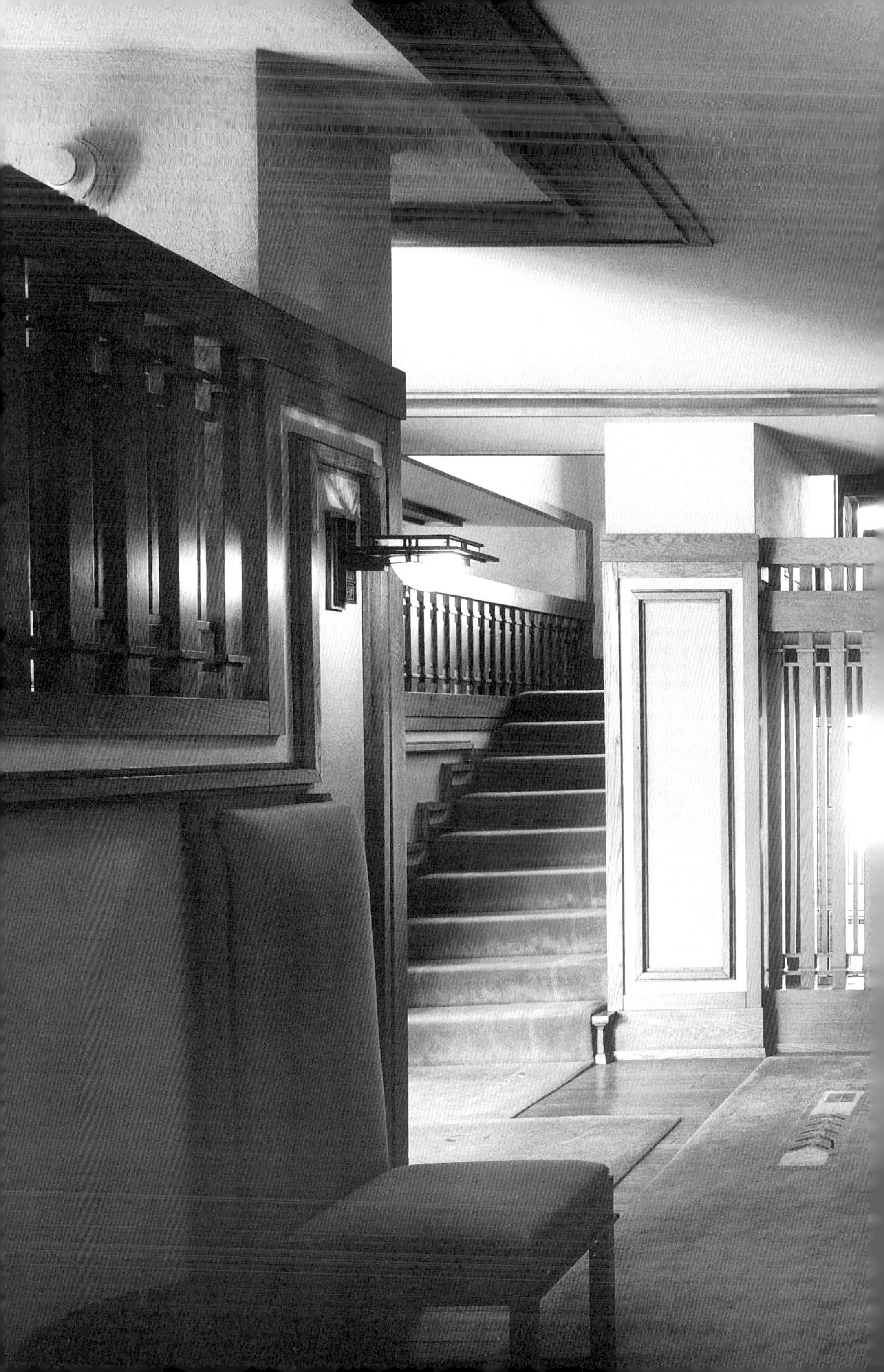

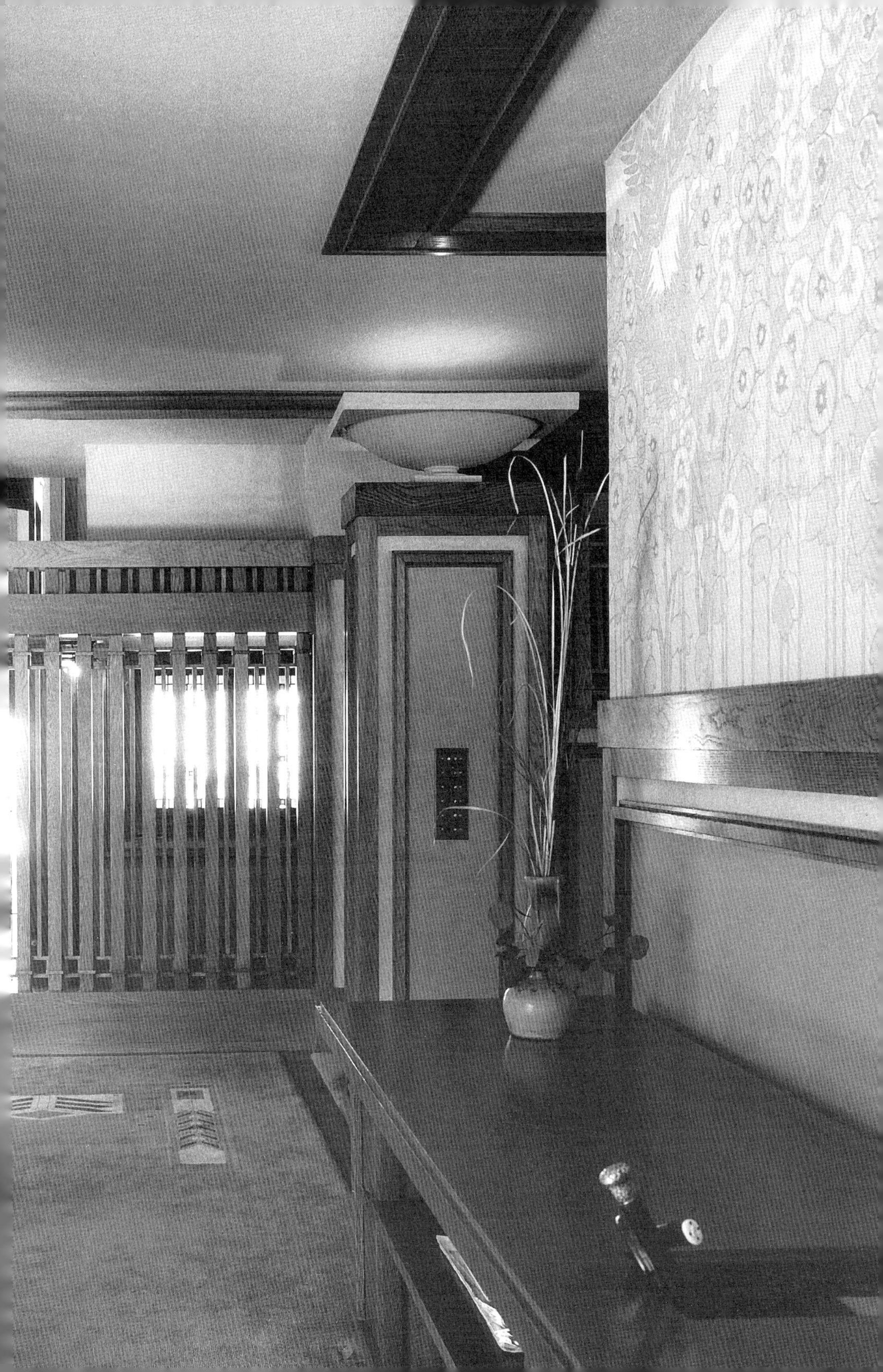

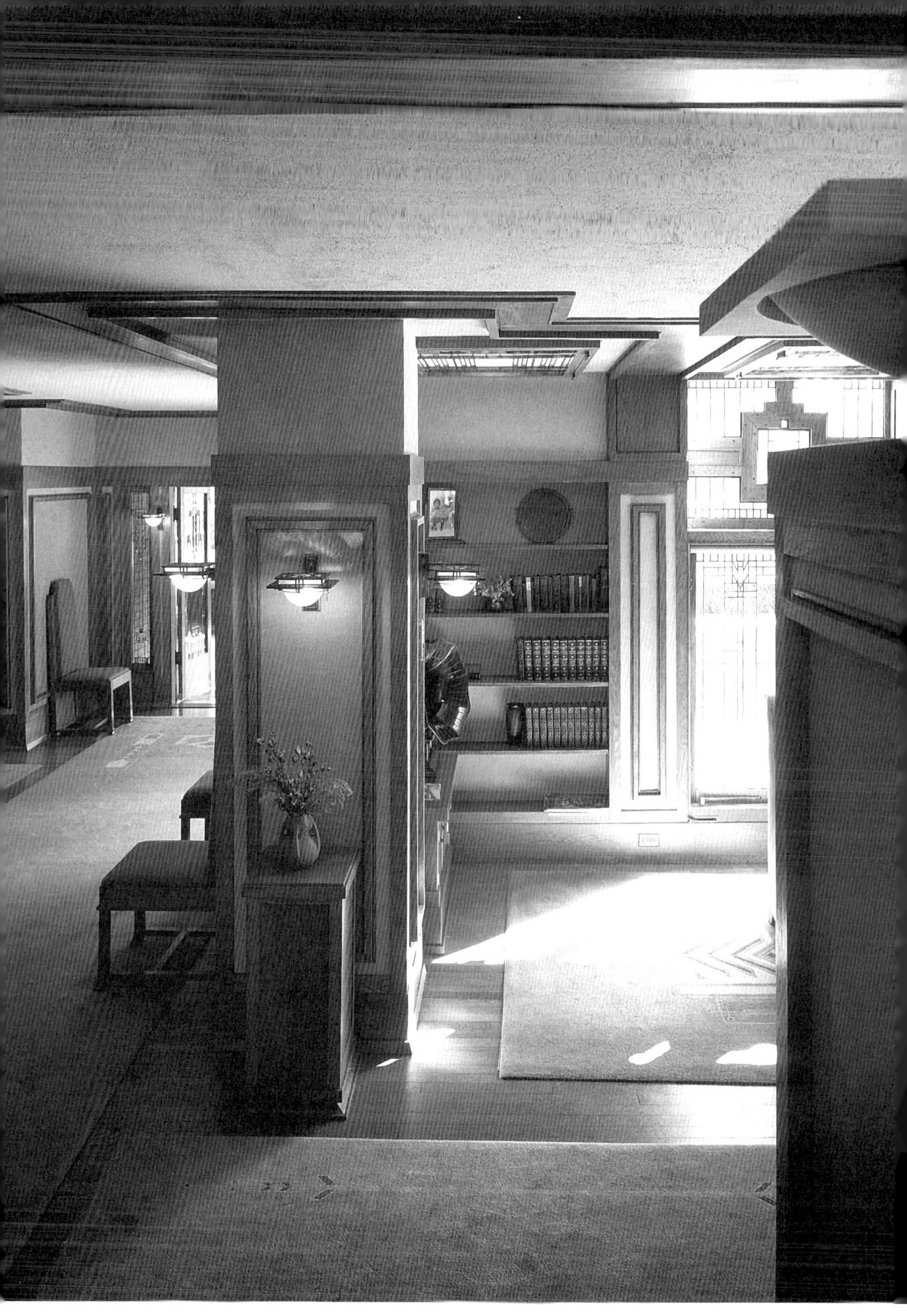

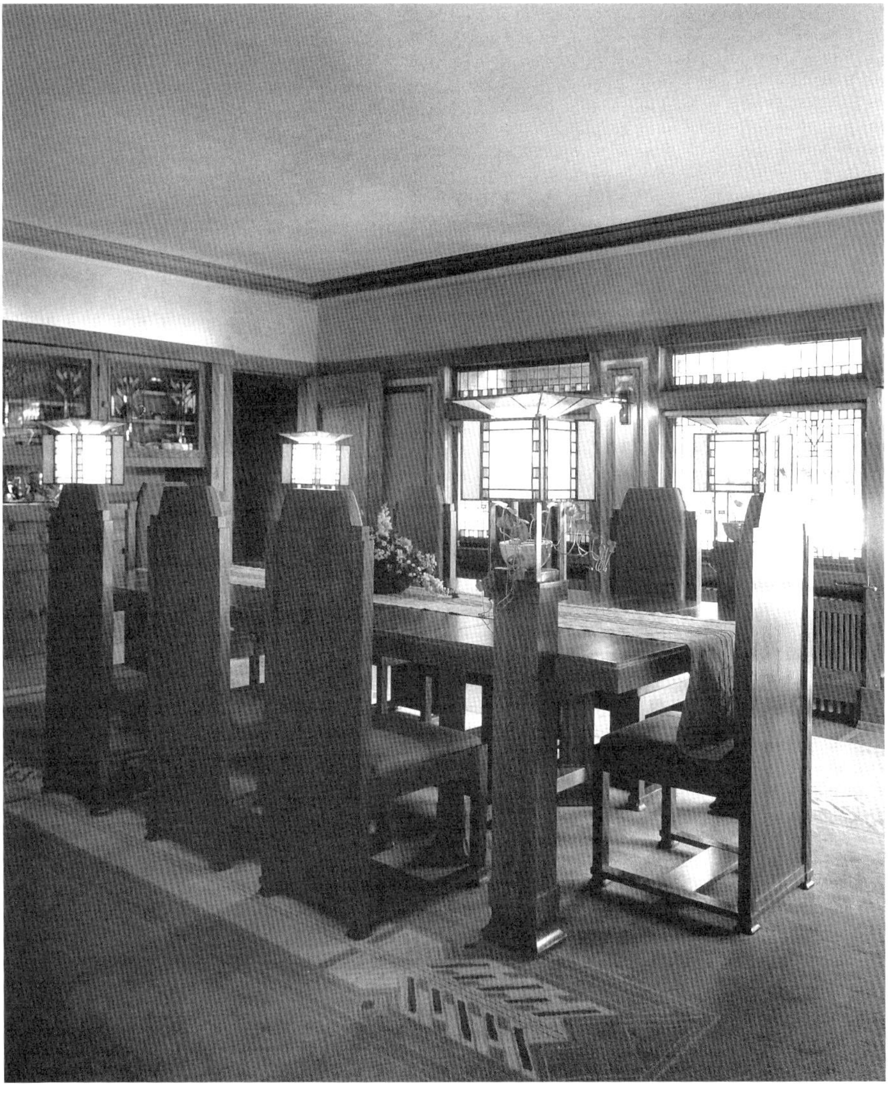

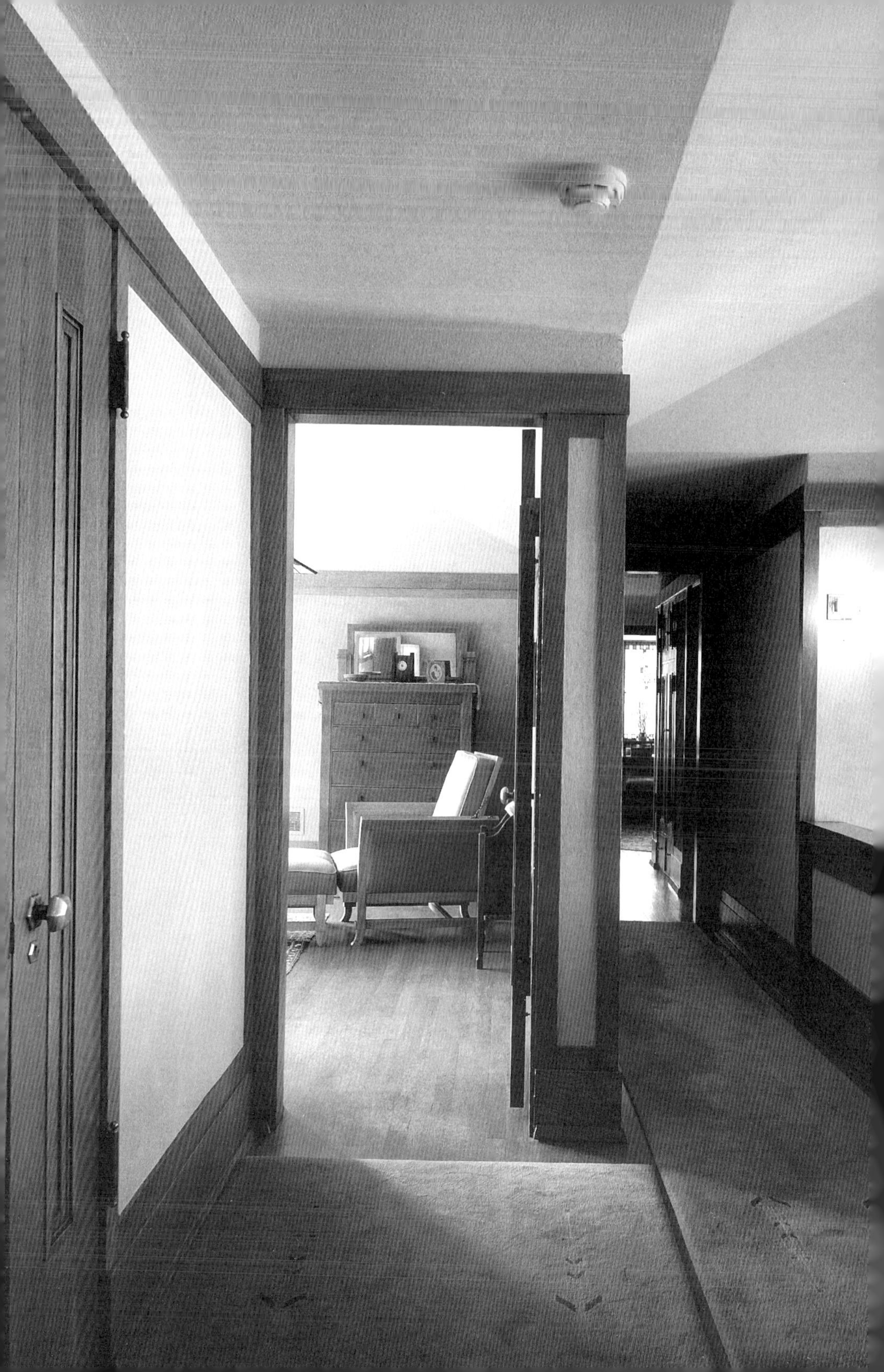

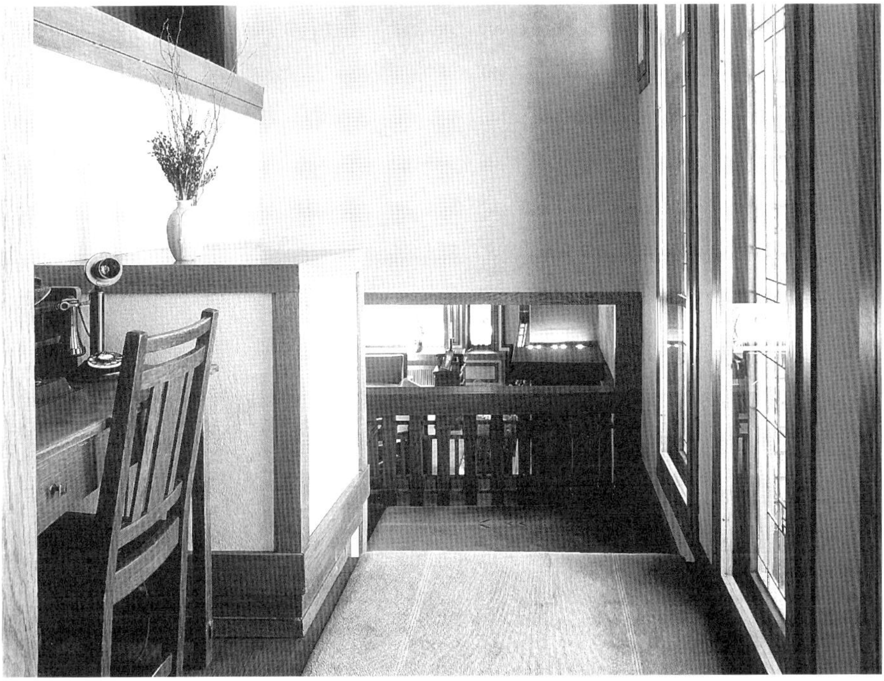

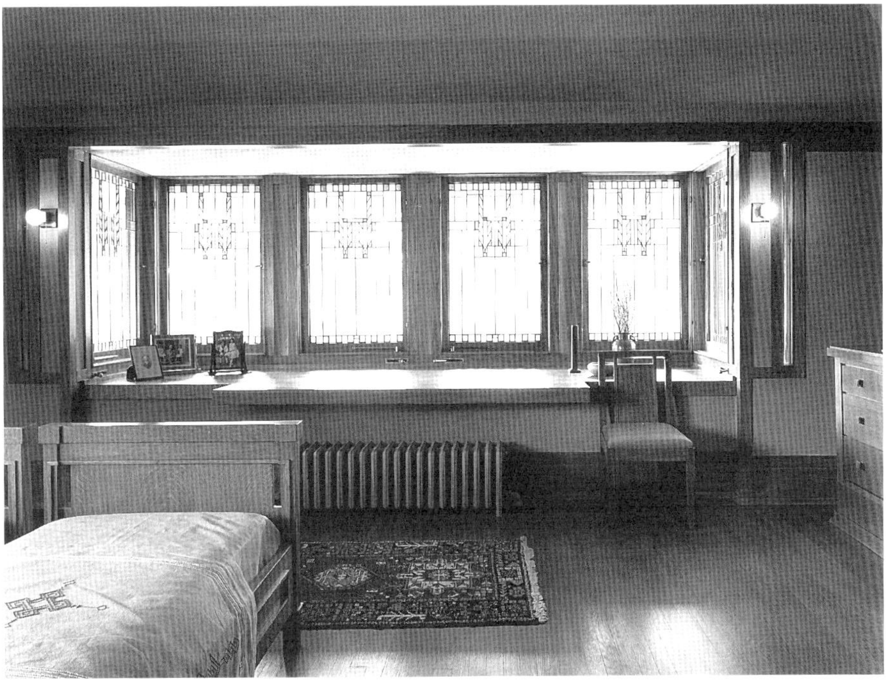

p.34-35

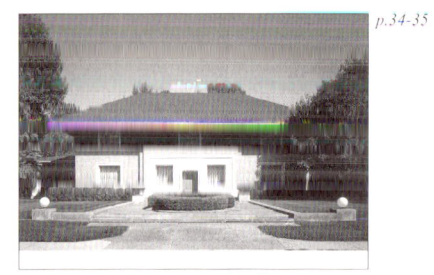

William H. Winslow House and Stables: Street facade

p.38-39

Entrance

p.40-41

Forecourt: entrance on left

p.42-43

View from garden

p.44-45

Breakfast room on right and living room on left

p.46-47

Stables

p.48-49

Entrance hall of main house

p.50-51

Entrance hall

p.52-53

Entrance hall: view toward living room

p.54 p.55

Arcade detail   *Woodwork detail*

p.56-57

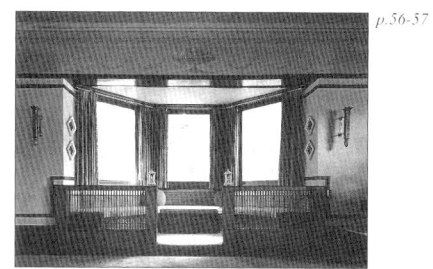

Bench in living room

p.58-59

Dining room

p.60
p.61

View toward dining room from living room   *Woodwork of breakfast room*

p.62-63

Breakfast room

p.66-67

Ward W. Willits House: overall view

p.70-71

Exterior view of living room

p.72-73

Living room

p.74-75

Dining room

p.76-77

View toward entrance foyer from dining room

p.78-79

Toplight and leaded glass windows of dining room

353

p.80-81

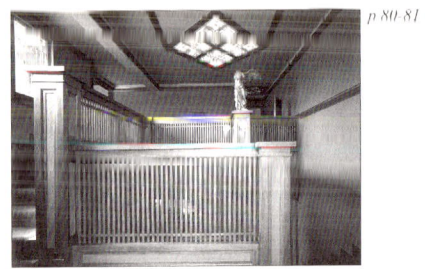

Staircase

p.92-93

Wall detail of dining room

p.82-83

View toward den from staircase

p.94-95

Terrace

p.84-85

Open well

p.96-97

Terrace

p.86-87

Frank Thomas House: street facade

p.98-99

View toward living room from hall

p.90-91

Entrance

p.100-101

Living room

p.102-103   *p.114-115*

Leaded glass windows of hall   *Gallery wing*

p.104-105   *p.116-117*

Alcove   *Exterior view of living room*

p.106-107   *p.118*
              p.119

Leaded glass windows of dining room   *Entrance*   *Entrance detail*

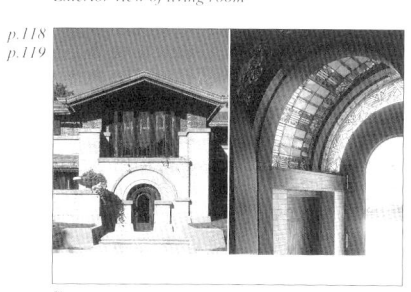

p.108-109   *p.120-121*

Dining room   *Gallery wing: exterior view of staircase*

p.110-111   *p.122-123*

Susan Lawrence Dana House: overall view from street   *Back entrance to kitchen*

355

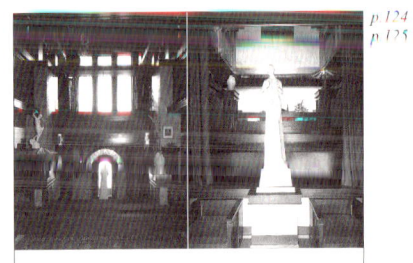

p.124
p.125

Entrance hall   Statue by Richard Bock
                 in entrance hall

p.126-127

Hall

p.128-129

Hall: view toward dining room on left

p.130-131

Fireplace of hall

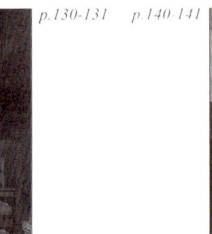

p.132-133

Living room

p.134-135

Living room

p.136-137

View toward fireplace of hall from entrance hall

p.138-139

Dining room

p.140-141

Dining room

p.142
p.143

Dining room from upper   Lamp of dining room
level

p.144-145   *p.154-155*

Breakfast alcove

Gallery

p.146
p.147

p.156-157

Telephone on wall    *Lamp*

Gallery

p.148
p.149

p.158-159

Windows of corridor 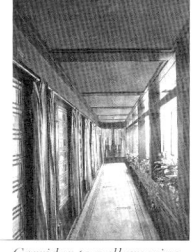   *Corridor to gallery wing*

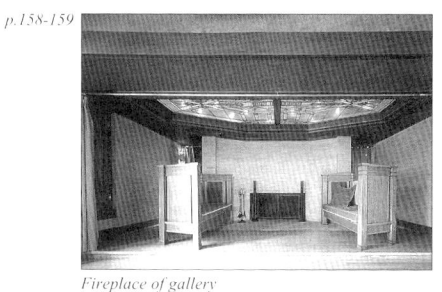

Fireplace of gallery

p.150-151   *p.160-161*

Conservatory beside corridor

Gallery

p.152
p.153

p.162
p.163

Studio   *Studio*

View from main house   *Gallery wing: landing of*
toward gallery wing   *staircase*

357

p.161-165

Leaded glass windows of bedroom

p.166-167

Bedroom

p.168
p.169

Billiard room    *Bowling lane*

p.170-171

Arthur Heurtley House: street façade

p.174-175

Entrance

p.178
p.179

Entrance hall: staircase   Entrance and bench

p.180-181

View toward dining room

p.182-183

Dining room

p.184-185

View toward living room

p.186-187

Living room

Ceiling detail

Darwin D. Martin House: overall view from street

Street facade in winter

View toward entrance

Exterior view of library

p.188-189

p.194-195

p.196-197

p.198-199

p.200-201

p.202-203

p.206
p.207

p.208-209

p.210-211

p.212-213

Entrance hall

Entrance hall    *Wall clock: reception hall on left*

Reception hall

Upper part of entrance hall: leaded glass windows

View toward reception hall from entrance hall

p.214-215

Dining room: view toward living room and library

p.216-217

Interior detail

p.218-219

Dining room

p.220
p.221

Columns between living room and library Entrance

p.222-223

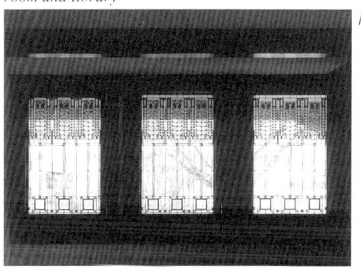

Leaded glass windows

p.224-225

Frederick C. Robie House: street facade

p.226-227

Overall view

p.228-229

Porch: stairs to living room

p.230-231

Exterior detail

p.232-233

View toward living room

p.234-235

Dining room

p.236-237

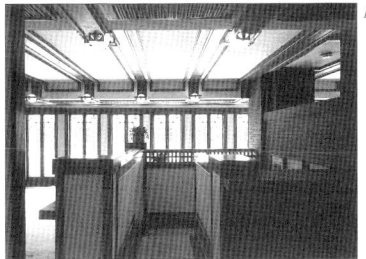

Staircase: dining room on left

p.238-239

Fireplace of living room

p.240-241

Dining room

p.242-243

Leaded glass windows of living room

p.244
p.245

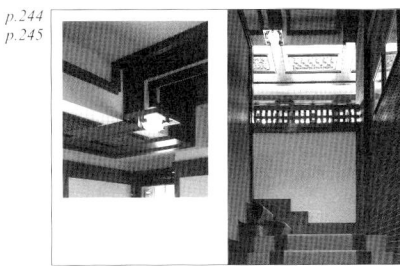

Lighting fixture   *Staircase and ceiling pattern*

p.246-247

F. F. Tomek House: overall view from southeast

p.250-251

View from southwest

p.252
p.253

Entrance   *Entrance hall*

p.254
p.255

Terrace: stairs to living room    *Terrace*

361

p.256-257 
Leaded glass windows of dining room

p.268-269 
Entrance on left

p.258-259 
Dining room

p.270-271 
View from garden

p.260
p.261
Alcove of dining room    *Corridor between dining room and living room*

p.272-273 
Terrace: playroom on right

p.262-263 
Avey Coonley House: aerial view

p.274-275 
Lotus of pool

p.266-267 
View from approach

p.276-277 
Entrance hall

Staircase in entrance hall   Corridor

p.278
p.279

p.288-289

Living room

Playroom: entrance hall on left

p.280-281

p.290-291

Living room

Playroom   *Playroom*

p.282
p.283

p.292-293

Living room

Balcony: living room on right    *View toward pool from living room*

p.284
p.285

p.294-295

Restored mural in living room by George Mann Niedecken

View toward living room from staircase

p.286-287

p.296-297

Dining room

363

p.298-299

p.310-311

E. E. Boynton House: overall view from approach

Conservatory: view toward living room

p.302-303

p.312-313

South view: terrace on left and living room on right

Dining room

p.304

p.314-315

Entrance

Dining room and breakfast bay

p.306-307

p.316-317

View toward breakfast bay on right and living room on left

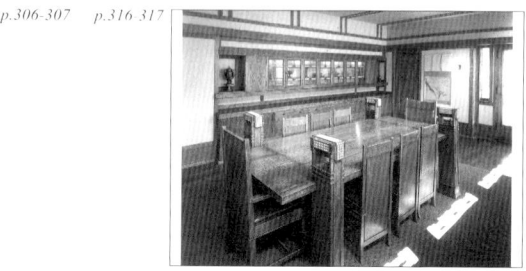

Dining table

p.308-309

p.318-319

Hall

Dining room

364

Hall: view toward living room   *p.320-321*

Mayer May House: south facade   *p.322-323*

View from southwest   *p.326-327*

Detail of south elevation   *p.328-329*

Terrace of living room   *p.330-331*

Terrace   *p.332-333*

Entrance hall: view toward dining room   *p.334-335*

Entrance hall: view toward terrace   *p.336-337*

Living room   *p.338-339*

Living room   *p.340-341*

p.342-343

Corner of living room

p.344-345

Leaded glass windows and toplights

p.346-347

Entrance hall

p.348
p.349

Entrance hall on left and   Dining room
living room on right

p.350
p.351

View toward morning   Above: landing
room from hall   Below: master bedroom

GA トラベラー 004
フランク・ロイド・ライト
〈プレイリー・ハウス〉

2002年9月24日発行

企画・編集・撮影	二川幸夫
文	ブルース・ブルックス・ファイファー
翻訳	菊池泰子
ロゴタイプ・デザイン	細谷巌
発行者	二川幸夫
印刷・製本	図書印刷株式会社
発行	エーディーエー・エディタ・トーキョー
	東京都渋谷区千駄ヶ谷3-12-14
	TEL.（03）3403-1581（代）

禁無断転載

ISBN4-87140-614-8 C1352